A Dictionary of
Gastronomy

A Dictionary of Gastronomy

ANDRÉ L. SIMON AND ROBIN HOWE

NELSON

This book was designed and produced by
Rainbird Reference Books Limited,
Marble Arch House, 44 Edgware Road, London W2
for Thomas Nelson and Sons Limited,
36 Park Street, London W1
P.O. Box 336, Apapa, Lagos
P.O. Box 25012, Nairobi
P.O. Box 21149, Dar es Salaam
P.O. Box 2187, Accra
77 Coffee Street, San Fernando, Trinidad
Thomas Nelson (Australia) Limited
597 Little Collins Street, Melbourne 3000
Thomas Nelson and Sons (South Africa)
(Proprietary) Limited
51 Commissioner Street, Johannesburg
Thomas Nelson and Sons (Canada) Limited
81 Curlew Drive, Don Mills, Ontario

Filmset by Jolly & Barber Limited, Rugby, England.
Printed and bound in Yugoslavia

General Editor: Robin Howe
House Editor: Mimi Franks
Designer: Judith Allan
Line drawings by Stewart Black and Ian Garrard

ISBN 0 17 147 0923

Foreword

A DICTIONARY OF GASTRONOMY was originally written by André Simon, somewhat nostalgically, no doubt, during the total eclipse of gastronomy of the last war years, and published rather too soon after the war, when there were still many shortages and restrictions as regards both food and wine in the British Isles. Obviously, many changes, some of them important, have taken place during the past twenty years in the domain of gastronomy. The cost of living is higher now than it has ever been, but the standard of living is also higher. There is now not only a greater quantity and variety of foodstuffs and wines available than there was twenty years ago, but there is also a far greater number of people who take an intelligent interest in what they eat and drink.

The DICTIONARY OF GASTRONOMY published now has kept the original basic gastronomic truths laid down by André Simon as the foundations upon which Robin Howe has built up a new edifice, a book which is right up-to-date, more complete and of much greater practical value than the original DICTIONARY attempted to be.

A dictionary of this kind cannot be written without a great deal of assistance from a number of people, many experts in their particular subjects. This help, both in advice and in writing individual entries, we have received most willingly, so we would like to give our sincere and grateful thanks to Mr Keith Fenwick Bean, Mr Gabor Denes, Mr L. H. Elston, Mr S. F. Hallgarten, Mr Edward Howe, Mr R. LePelley, Mr R. A. Lewis, Mr and Mrs Hitindra Malik, Mr C. P. Norbury, Mr Edmund Penning-Rowsell, Mrs Helena Radecka, Mr G. M. Rainbird, Dr Bruno Roncarati, Mr Trevor Russell-Cobb, Mr and Mrs James Carlton Shy, Mrs Joan Shoup-Erskine, Mr H. W. Yoxall and Mr L. Elston, Librarian in charge of the Special Collection of the Camden Public Library, London.

André L. Simon and Robin Howe.

Colour Plates

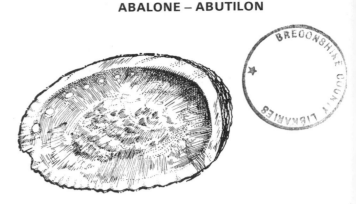

ABALONE (shell)

ABERDEEN HADDOCK. See HADDOCK, SMOKED.

A

ABALONE. An edible gastropod mollusk of the genus *Haliotis*, belonging to the same class as the snail and the sea-slug, sometimes known as sea-ear. It has a thin elongated oval shell and its outer surface is of a uniform dull brownish colour, faintly ridged with spiral undulations, crossed by smaller and close-set, rounded ridges. The central muscle, a broad foot by which the abalone clings to the rocks is the edible portion. When taken from its shell it resembles a very large scallop. Its shell is a source of high-grade mother-of-pearl. It can be bought fresh, dried, salted and canned and is an important item of diet for both the Chinese and the Japanese. The Chinese usually prefer to use abalone in its dried form: the Japanese, who are inordinately fond of it, buy the finest possible quality. Canned abalone is extremely simple to use for it is cured and prepared for quick cooking before being canned. It may even be eaten straight from the can, for example, in a salad, without any further treatment. When it is cooked it must be cooked briefly, otherwise it will become tough. Abalone can be served in a salad or fried with mushrooms or can flavour a soup. There are about six abalones in a can, enough to serve four to five people. Many Westerners might not be attracted by its appearance, but correctly cooked, it gains favour.

Abalone is known as *awabi* in Japan, muttonfish in Australia, ormer in the Channel Islands and paua in New Zealand.

ABBAYE DE CÎTEAUX. One of the cheeses associated with the great religious orders of medieval France. It might be termed a monks' cheese as, in order to eat well on fast days, the monks evolved a number of rich, creamy soft cheeses. The stone-built monasteries afforded excellent cellars for the curing and storage of this type of cheese.

ABERNETHY BISCUITS. Small, hard biscuits, flavoured usually, but not essentially, with caraway seeds and reputed to be 'digestive' biscuits. They probably take their name from a brilliant surgeon of the 18th century, John Abernethy, who published important surgical works which greatly influenced subsequent surgical practice. One of his claims was that local diseases had a constitutional origin and that this origin could be traced to the disorders of the digestive system. That he actually invented the biscuits is not recorded. They could be named after a small Scottish town where they were first made.

ABRICOTINE. A French liqueur made and marketed in Enghien-les-Bains. Its basis is brandy, the pulp of fresh apricots and the pounded centre of their kernels.

ABSINTHE. A potent elixir, the basis of which is wormwood *(Artemisia absitium)* and spirit of high alcoholic strength. It is also flavoured with a number of aromatic plants and possesses a particularly stupefying effect (the worst form of intoxication) unless taken in the strictest moderation. This is why its sale has been prohibited in France, Switzerland and the United States.

It was invented by a Frenchman, a Dr Ordinaire, who lived at Couvet, in Switzerland. He sold his recipe, in 1797, to a Mr Pernod, whose name eventually became synonymous with absinthe all the world over.

An ancient form of absinthe was wormwood wine (bitter wine – *absinthiatum*), called *pesintiton* in the Holy Land. It is perhaps one of the oldest compounded drinks in the world.

ABUTILON. A plant of which there are more than 60 known varieties throughout the world. It is well known as a vegetable in South America and India. The species *Abutilon esculentum* is known in Brazil as *Bencus de deos* and its flowers are eaten

9

cooked with meat. In other countries, especially Asia and the West Indies, its leaves are cooked and eaten in the same way as vegetables, such as spinach. In India the species *Abutilon indicum* is popular as a vegetable. In Europe, however, it is rarely eaten but cultivated as a garden plant for the beauty of its flowers.

ACACIA. The acacia is a small shrub which grows in dry desert country. It is used to make emulsions and also produces a nutritious gum which is used to relieve coughs. The nuts of a species of acacia are used in India as a hair shampoo.

It is one of the plants introduced into southern Europe by John Tradescant in 1656, although the acacia was cultivated in Rome before this date. It has globose heads of highly scented yellow flowers and is found both wild and cultivated in Italy and the south of France. It also grows in abundance in the Dead Sea valley where it is covered by a parasite a vivid scarlet in colour so that at a distance, the trees look as though they are on fire.

In France the young flowers are used by chefs for making fritters, also for a home-made liqueur.

ACCOUB. *(Gundelia tournefortii).* An edible member of the large thistle family. Its roots, shoots and flower buds are all good to eat. Its original home is Syria, but it grows freely in all lands and islands of the Mediterranean. The roots are eaten like salsify; the shoots, when about six inches long, like asparagus; the buds parboiled and tossed in butter, like small new potatoes. The flavour is excellent, somewhat like that of the Jerusalem artichoke with an aftertaste of asparagus.

ACCRA or **ACCRATS.** These are yeast batter fritters enclosing all kinds of titbits, such as fish, vegetables, meats or even fruits. Resembling the Italian *fritto-misto*, they are sold in the Caribbean markets by the 'higglers' or street vendors and are especially popular in those islands which have something of a French atmosphere.

ACEROLA. A small cherry-like fruit, a native of tropical and sub-tropical America, borne on a shrub-like tree, which grows to approximately 12 feet in height. It has a thin skin which varies in colour from a light reddish-yellow to a deep red when fully ripe. The flesh is also of the same reddish-yellow hue, although those acerola with a dark skin have an equally dark flesh. In size they vary from one-half to about one inch in diameter. They have three winged seeds which are large in comparison to the size of the fruit. The flavour is sweet to acid depending upon the genetic type, but their flavour is neither distinct nor pronounced, although there are those who consider it to have

something of the flavour of tart strawberries.

Although called cherry, the flavour of the acerola when cooked is more that of the crab apple. It is rich in vitamin C.

Because the fruit is small and the seeds large in comparison, the use of the fruit in its raw state is limited. Small pieces can be cut from the fruit and added to salads, or it can be made into a purée but its more general use is as a juice. Acerola juice is used to flavour salads, in syrups, to make jellies (preserves), in gelatine desserts and in milk shakes.

ACETIC ACID. Acetic acid is historically the first acid produced deliberately and used by man. It is the substance that causes vinegar to be sour. In crude or unrefined states it is produced in strength of approximately 10 per cent by the action of common bacteria present in the air on the alcohol present in solutions of fermented grains or fruit. The bacteria multiply rapidly in the beverage and, by means of an enzyme contained in their structure, cause the oxygen present in the atmosphere to react with the alcohol creating acetic acid. The most common kitchen use is in diluted solutions of either wine or malt vinegars.

Glacial acetic acid is the refined version, and has many commercial uses. It is produced by the rectification (distillation) of vinegar, or by a commercial process utilising acetylene gas. In this form it is highly corrosive and is only of use in chemical or manufacturing plants.

ACHAR or **ACHARD.** This word is used in nearly all the vernaculars of India to mean acid pickles and salt relishes. The word is of Persian origin, *achār,* although it has been suggested that it came originally from the Latin *acetaria.*

ACHIRA. A species of canna. Its large roots yield a rich starchy meal which is used like arrowroot. There are several species of edible canna and these are eaten largely in South America.

ACID DROP. A boiled sweet which has tartaric or citric acid added.

ACIDIFIERS. Foods which supply the body with an excess of acid tending to acidify the body tissues are termed acidifiers. In general all meat, fish, cereals and grains and their products are thus classed.

The term should not be confused with foods having what is described as an acid taste as there is no correlation. One of the best examples is that of the lemon, which has a very pronounced acid taste, and whose juice contains highly concentrated citric acid, but is not an acidifier.

Ham, eggs, butter, chocolate, fats, artichoke,

ACACIA (branch and flower)

onions, and nuts in general are acidifiers to a lesser degree.

ACID RINSE. The surface of many fruits, when peeled and cut and exposed to the air, turns brown. Although this does not affect their flavour, their appearance is usually spoilt. To prevent this, peeled and cut fruits should be immersed immediately in a bowl of salted water or better still lemon-flavoured water until required.

ACIDS. The word acid comes from the Latin *acidus* meaning sour, and it would be almost true to say that not only are all acids sour, but that all sour substances are acid.

Acids and alkalis neutralize each other and form a salt. In theory one could remove the acidity from sour fruit by adding soda; the result would be horrible because the salts formed would taste bitter and medicinal. From the point of view of taste – though not of chemistry – we usually regard sweetness as neutralizing sourness. In fact, adding sugar does not remove the acid, but produces a sweet-sour combination acceptable to us probably because such a combination spelled 'ripe fruit' to our monkey-like ancestors. The ripening of fruit is always characterized by a change in the proportions of sugar to acid (see SWEET-SOUR). The sensation of sourness, like sweetness, is greater when a dish is hot than when it is cold. Sourness also tends to increase saltiness, though sugar diminishes it.

Acids vary in their basic strength. Of our usual kitchen acids, citric acid (in lemon juice) is stronger than tartaric acid (in wine), and acetic acid (in vinegar) is stronger than both. Mineral acids, such as hydrochloric acid, are much stronger than any organic kitchen acids. Of interest to the cook, small quantities of strong acids quickly disperse but large quantities of weak acids, producing the same degree of sourness, persist. Lemon juice gives a longer lasting sourness than vinegar.

Acids are high reactive substances and tend to break down to simpler substances whatever is cooked in them. Thus they are tenderizers. They break down connective tissue, cell walls and fibres, as when meat is marinated or cooked in wine, lemon juice or vinegar.

Some important acids in food and flavouring are as follows: acetic acid (vinegar); citric acid (lemon and citrus fruits); malic acid (apples and other fruits); tartaric acid (wine); succinic acid (wine); lactic acid (in car batteries and very diluted in some cheap lemonades); hydrochloric acid (very diluted in our stomachs); hydrocyanic acid (formed when bitter almonds or peach stones are mixed with water – exceedingly poisonous); oxalic acid (rhubarb leaves – toxic).

ACIDULATED WATER. Cold water with vinegar, lemon or lime juice added. Used to prevent fruit and vegetables from discolouring.

ACKEE. The ackee is the fruit of a medium-sized tree which, while not indigenous to Jamaica, has remarkable historical associations with the island. It was originally imported from West Africa, probably in a slave ship, and now grows abundantly.

The tree was unknown to science until plants were taken from Jamaica to England by none other than Captain William Bligh of 'Mutiny on the Bounty' fame, hence its botanical name *(Blighia sapida)* in his honour. One of the earliest local propagators of the tree was Dr Thomas Clarke who introduced it to the eastern parishes of Jamaica in 1778.

Jamaica is the only place where the fruit is generally recognized as an edible crop, although the plant has been introduced into most other Caribbean islands (Trinidad, Grenada, Antigua and Barbados) as well as Central America and even Florida. In Florida it is known by different names but does not grow in economic quantities.

Just before the ackee is ripe for plucking it is a vivid and lovely red and if picked and eaten at this stage can be positively dangerous – some say poisonous. When the fruit is ready for eating it cracks open neatly and exposes the fleshy, creamy-white aurillus in which its ebony-black seeds are set. This creamy flesh is cooked and eaten with salt cod, and is one of Jamaica's national dishes. It is also lightly fried and served on toast. Ackee is now exported in cans.

ACORN. Acorns are primarily considered as food for swine but they have been eaten by man from prehistoric times and are still used for food in many parts of the world. There are some 300 species of the oak and the acorns of a large number of these are edible. The sweet acorn *(Quercus esculus)* is still widely eaten in southern Europe and is prepared in much the same manner as chestnuts.

When man depended for food on the spoils of the hunt and had not yet discovered the art of cultivation, there is little doubt that acorns were of considerable importance to his diet. The acorn as a form of food has been referred to by such early writers as the Greek Theophrastus, and the Latins, Pliny, Ovid and Virgil. The Arcadians ate acorns while the Greeks ate figs. However, with the advance of gastronomic knowledge the acorn's value as a food has diminished, although in times of famine or war there are millions who turn once more to the acorn, in particular to make a form of coffee.

The best-known edible acorns are the sweet acorns from the different species of the holm oak. In Britain this oak is chiefly grown as an ornamental tree, but in Spain and in Portugal, where the tree is very common, some varieties of this species are grown for their acorns, which are eaten like chestnuts; in fact, their taste is similar and their food value and price are much the same.

These acorns, called *bellotas* in Spain, are long and rather cylindrical in shape and have a sweet nutty flavour. This type of oak is also common in some of the mountainous districts of Morocco and Algeria and the acorns they produce are often cooked by being roasted in ashes.

ACORN-BARNACLE, ACORN-FISH, ACORN-SHELL. A small shell-fish, conical in shape and with an uneven surface, which lives on rocks in all sea areas. It is sometimes called the turban-shell. The flesh is delicate and usually prepared like crab meat.

ACORN COFFEE. This is a recipe from a Victorian recipe book and we are told that acorn coffee, much liked in Germany, is a substitute for ordinary coffee and considered very strengthening for consumptive people and delicate children.

The acorns are gathered in the autumn when they are ripe, shelled and cut into pieces the size of a coffee berry. They are dried in front of the fire or in a warm oven, and then roasted as ordinary coffee beans until they become a golden colour. Immediately after roasting, the acorns are ground to prevent their becoming tough. While the acorns are being ground, a morsel of butter is added. The ground acorns are then put into airtight bottles.

To use: for adults $\frac{1}{2}$ ounce to 1 pint ($1\frac{1}{4}$) of water is suggested. Acorn coffee is made in the same manner as ordinary coffee.

Also recommended is a mixture of ground acorn and coffee.

ACORN SQUASH. See SQUASH.

ACQUETTE. Both a silver and gold acquette are made. These aromatic liqueurs are distilled without rectifying from alcohol flavoured with cinnamon, cloves, nutmeg and sugar for the silver acquette, and cinnamon, cloves, angelica roots, daucus of Crete, lemon peel and sugar for the gold acquette. Silver and gold leaf is added. This is popular in Italy and the South of France.

ACTINIA. A sea anemone of the stinging variety but which is eaten in certain localities. On the south coast of France a species called *rastegne* is much prized for its crab-like flavour. Round the marshes of Rochefort the *actinia coriacea*, locally known as mule's backside, is eaten in the winter, and the *actinia edulis* is found along the coast of Provence.

ACTON, MRS. ELIZA. Precursor to Mrs Beeton, the first edition of her comprehensive *Modern Cookery for Private Families*, was published in 1825. The *English Bread Book* was published in 1857, but the date of *The People's Book of Modern Cookery* is uncertain.

ADE. A drink made of pure fruit juice and sweetened water or of fruit boiled and steeped in sugar and water.

ADIRONDACK BREAD. This is from the Adirondack Mountains in New York State. It is a baked bread from rough or coarsely ground flour, predominantly high gluten content wheat or rye. It is eaten hot, straight from the oven for breakfast or supper.

ADMIRAL. A hot punch of claret, sugar, vanilla and cinnamon, thickened with egg yolk.

ADOBO. This could be called one of the national dishes of the Philippines. A type of braised stew, usually it is prepared with pork, but there is a chicken adobo and a fish adobo.

ADVOCAAT. A popular Dutch liqueur, based on

AGAR-AGAR

ACORN SQUASH

ACORN

brandy and egg yolks; a sort of bottled egg-nog.

ADZUKI. A small red bean important in Japanese cooking. They are used in several ways. When cooked, mashed and sweetened they are used as a filling for cakes. Adzuki beans are much used in special festival dishes and are an important ingredient in foods cooked in honour of the birthday of the Emperor of Japan. Cooked with rice the red beans make a dish called red rice.

The Japanese also have a sweet concoction, called bean-jam, which is simply a cream made of red beans mixed with sugar. One of the most popular Japanese sweets, *yokan*, not unlike Turkish delight, is made from refined bean jam and agar-agar (which see). It is usually served on black lacquer plates in order that the sweet should appeal to the eye as well as the palate, in true Japanese style.

AEMONO. Salads are popular in Japan and they can be, roughly speaking, divided into two classes. One of these classes is called *aemono* or salads served with various kinds of dressings. The word is also used for salad dressing.

AERATED BREAD. In 1856 a Dr Dauglish invented a process whereby a more digestible form of bread could be made by mixing flour, water and salt without any form of leavening, and instead introducing carbon dioxide by a mechanical method into the dough.

AEREATED WATERS. See MINERAL WATERS.

AFRICA PEPPER. See CAYENNE.

AGAMI. A large game bird of the wader family of which the *Guiana agami* is a prototype. It is better known in Britain as the trumpeter. Its flesh is pleasant but eaten only when young when it is braised like a duck or, if older, stewed to make a consommé. There is a classical South American recipe for this bird, in which it is braised, served with boiled rice and fried pimientos.

The agami has a curious screeching cry and in some districts of Brazil it is caught and kept in a barnyard with the other poultry to act as a guard.

AGAR-AGAR. A name given to a number of seaweeds from Far Eastern waters from which gelatinous substances are obtained. This substance is variously known as Ceylon moss, Chinese isinglass, Japanese agar-agar. It is, in fact, a vegetable isinglass prepared principally in Japan but also in other parts of the Far East. In the main it is the red or gelidium seaweed that is used to make agar-agar and it is much used in the preparation of gelatine-like puddings. It grows on the Atlantic and Pacific coasts of the United States.

Agar-agar is marketed in several ways. In sticks or blocks, like a mass of fine hair, and powdered. Completely tasteless, agar-agar has the property of absorbing and retaining liquid and can be used whenever a recipe calls for gelatine or isinglass. Some varieties take some time to dissolve.

Agar-agar is considerably more effective than gelatine, and it produces a dish which will never flop, for it is capable of taking up to 200 times its volume of water to make a jelly.

AGARIC. A family of fungi of various types of edible and poisonous mushrooms.

AGAVE. The name of a family of succulents or cactus found generally in the desert or dry areas in the southeastern United States. The more common name is the century plant as it is popularly supposed to bloom every 100 years, but actually blooms on an average every seven to nine years. Its thick fleshy leaves are used for a multitude of purposes, from making pulque, the 'drink of the rabbit god', to the feeding of horses in the desert (when the spiny thorns are seared), by the old Apache Indians. Another by-product is the peyote button, a hallucinatory drug used by the Mescale and Yaqui Indians in some of their religious rites.

AGNOLOTTI. A variety of stuffed envelopes of pasta of which ravioli is the best known. Traditionally, stuffed pasta should only be called ravioli when it is stuffed with eggs, ricotta and other cheeses. When the small squares of pasta are stuffed with any of the meat fillings, such as chopped chicken, brains, salami, chicken or with spinach, they should be called agnolotti.

AGON. The name of a small fresh-water fish, plentiful in the Swiss-Italian lakes, particularly Como and Garda. In Italy it is called *sardina*. It has the same taste as the real sardine and is of a similar size. Any recipes calling for sardines may be applied to it, and it can also be salted in the same manner as sardines.

AGRAFA. A cheese of high quality made in Greece and similar in texture and flavour to Gruyère.

AGRAS. One of the sweetest of soft drinks: it is made in Algeria with unfermented grape juice, water, sugar, and crushed almonds.

AGUARDIENTE. The Spanish and Italian form of *aqua vitae* (which see), a raw and strong distillation from wine or sometimes molasses.

AGUNGATE. A South American fruit not unlike the avocado pear in general appearance and texture but with little flavour. It is known in Lima, Peru, as *palta* and is eaten with salt as a vegetable.

AIGUEBELLE. An aromatic liqueur of the char-treuse type, made in green and yellow, the latter being the sweeter of the two. The distillery is in the Rhône Valley, on the site of a Cistercian monastery built in 1137, where three mountain streams meet, hence its name *'les belles eaux'*.

AIGUILLETTES. In culinary French this means thin strips of meat, fowl or game, lifted lengthwise from the body of the bird. Strictly speaking the term should only be used to describe thin slices of fowl, but it is often used also to describe thin slices of meat and even fish.

AÏOLI. A very popular garlic and olive oil sauce, and the most typical dish of Provence. It is a golden mayonnaise in which garlic is used without discretion. In Provence this sauce is made traditionally every Friday and on this day nothing else is eaten except *aïoli sauce* perhaps with poached snails or cod, tiny cold boiled potatoes, baby artichokes, runner beans, pale green beans similar to the American Lima beans, boiled carrots and hard-cooked eggs. Each or any of these items is served separately with a liberal portion of the *aïoli*.

The following recipe will serve 12 people.

12 cloves garlic
3 large egg yolks
salt to taste
approximately 2 cups (2½) olive oil

Crush the garlic cloves in a mortar until reduced to a smooth pulp. Add the egg yolks and salt and mix well with a wooden spoon until these two ingredients are completely amalgamated. Add the olive oil, drop by drop, exactly as for making mayonnaise, and stir, slowly at first, until the *aïoli* thickens. This procedure takes somewhat longer than making the regular mayonnaise as the pulped garlic has already thinned out the eggs. When about half the oil has been used, and the *aïoli* is a thick smooth mass, the oil can be added rather more quickly. The *aïoli* should get thicker and thicker, an almost solid mass. A little lemon juice may be added just before the end. Serve the *aïoli* either in the mortar in which it has been prepared or piled in the salad bowl.

AITCHBONE. An economical joint of beef usually boiled, braised or pot-roasted. It has been called the 'poor man's sirloin'. In Britain it is cut between the rump and the buttocks of beef. It is also found in the United States and there the cut is made across the pelvis bone and includes parts of the rump as well as parts of the top and bottom round. The ancient name for the aitchbone was edge-bone as the joint lies immediately under the rump, which in dressed beef offers itself in view edgewise.

AJI or **AGI.** This is simply capsicum. *Aji* is a name of Indian origin. When the Spaniards arrived in the New World, they did not find the pepper of the Orient, but they found instead an equally pungent plant, bearing pods of all shapes and sizes. These had been cultivated for centuries by the indigenous peoples and some of the names of these plants have survived; *aji* is one of them. On Columbus' second visit to South America the ship's doctor wrote in his diary that the Indians eat a curious root called *name* (yam) which they flavour with a spice called aji (capsicum).

AJI-NO-MOTO. The Japanese name for mono-sodium glutamate, meaning 'essence of taste'; it is often referred to as taste powder.

AKVAVIT or **AQUAVIT.** The Scandinavian form of *aquavitae,* a highly rectified, practically neutral – and brutal – spirit, distilled from grain or pota-toes and flavoured with caraway seeds. Neither sweetened nor aged, it is colourless and is usually tossed down at a gulp, before or at the beginning of a meal.

À LA MODE. Following the fashion; after the style

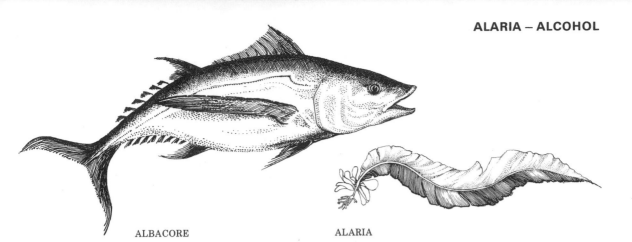

ALBACORE   ALARIA

of: In the culinary sense this applies mainly to beef (which see), braised with vegetables, and to certain desserts, such as pie in the United States, when accompanied with ice-cream.

ALARIA. There are five known species of this sea-weed, which are found in the northern European seas. *Alaria esculenta* grows widely along the Atlantic coastlines and is known as badderlocks in Scotland and murlins in Ireland. Only the central vein, which is sweetish, is eaten.

ALBACORE. One of the tunny or tuna species. The great albacores are distinguished from other tunas by the excessive length of the pectoral fin, otherwise they are the same as the bluefish. It is also called the chicken of the Pacific Coast.

ALBARIZA. See SPANISH WINES.

ALBIGEOISE. Large or small cuts of meat garnished with chopped ham, potato croquettes and small tomatoes stuffed with mushrooms, onions, breadcrumbs, garlic and parsley.

ALBONDIGAS. The name of a popular Mexican dish of spiced meat balls. Its origin is probably Spanish – there are Spanish recipes almost identical – but it is also prepared in Brazil. A similar recipe is known in Scotland as almundigoes.

1 lb. beef
½ lb. pork
1 slice white bread
1 egg, well beaten
1–2 cloves garlic, finely chopped
pinch each of ground black sage, mint and pepper
1 teaspoon (1¼) salt
good pinch ground coriander
2 tablespoons (2½) cooking fat
1 small onion, finely chopped
1 tomato, peeled and chopped

Soak the bread in water and then squeeze dry. Grind the beef and pork together. Mix the meat with the bread, add the egg and the flavourings, salt and pepper. Knead thoroughly, break off pieces of the meat and shape into balls the size of a walnut.

Heat the fat, add the onion and brown it well. Take the onion from the pan, add the meat balls and brown these. Return the onion, add the tomato and 4–6 cups (5–7½) of water. Cook very slowly for 1½ hours.

ALBUMEN. This is the archaic name for egg white, and should not be confused with albumin.

ALBUMIN. This is the protein part of egg white, about 70 per cent of the whole, and occurs in many other foods, such as milk and any plants and seeds; it is also contained in the blood of all animals.

ALCOHOL. Alcohol (potable), which is a liquid whose chemical name is ethyl hydrate, is derived from the reaction of the double decomposition of glucose (sugar) by yeast. This process is termed fermentation. There are other forms of alcohol and chemically there are other means of accomplishing this change. Ethyl alcohol is, however, the only alcohol produced in any quantity that is reasonably safe to drink.

Alcohol is made by fermenting naturally sweet fruit juices (musts), such as grapes, apples, pears, plums; or grains such as corn, rye, barley (worts), in which the natural process of converting starch to sugar has begun. The distillation of these fermented worts and musts into a purer or more concentrated form produces the high proof beverage, or industrial alcohols.

The strength of alcohol produced by natural fermentation normally cannot exceed 14 per cent. Above this strength the alcohol renders the yeast impotent. Wine, or any other beverage requiring greater strength than this, must have alcohol added. This is called 'fortifying'. Wines of less than approximately 14 per cent alcohol content tend to have shorter storage life than those of higher proof. Fortified wines, such as port or madeira, with proofs ranging upward of 23 per cent, have lives of over a century.

AL DENTE. An Italian cooking expression. Literally translated it means 'to the tooth' and it is used to describe food, in particular pasta and rice that is cooked until it is firm to the bite but not soft. It is also often used in reference to vegetables.

ALE. A beer or, as Dr Johnson put it in his dicionary, 'A liquor brewed from malt, to be drunk fresh'. Curiously it is only in England that both beer and ale as names are retained; in Scandinavia only ale *(ol)* is used, and in the other Germanic languages only beer *(bier)*. In history, ale came before beer.

In 15th-century England, ale was commonly used, mixed with water, to boil fish, and was also used as a substitute for sherry in sauces. Queen Elizabeth I's breakfast generally consisted of salt meat, bread and strong ale, and ale was drunk again during the morning.

ALE BERRY. A famous drink from the North Country of England to be drunk as hot as possible before going to bed to ward off colds.

Boil a handful of crushed oats in 2 pints (2½) of water till thick, grating a lump of root ginger into it; strain it off, boiling hot, into an equal quantity of just-boiling ale, adding a generous scrape of nutmeg or cinnamon, and a spoonful of rough sugar.

ALECOST. See COSTMARY.

ALE FLIP. This is a stirrup cup that was drunk before driving home in a gig after leaving a dance. Also known as 'one yard of flannel' or 'bonalay', for a farewell drink, the latter name being perhaps a corruption from a French word or phrase.

To make an ale flip, put into a saucepan 3 pints (3¾) of ale, 1 tablespoon (1¼) sugar, a blade of mace, a clove and a small piece of butter, and bring the liquid to a boil. Beat the white of 1 egg and the yolks of 2 thoroughly, mixing them with 1 tablespoon (1¼) of cold ale. Mix all together, then pour the whole rapidly from one large jug to another from a good height for some minutes, to froth it thoroughly, but do not allow it to get cool before serving.

ALE POSSET. Hot ale and hot milk mixed and sweetened, then flavoured with grated nutmeg or ginger.

ALE-WIFE. An edible North American fish of the shad family, closely resembling the herring. It is caught along the coast of America from the Gulf of St Lawrence to Chesapeake Bay and in some lakes and streams. It exists in such abundance in Lake Ontario, that it is not uncommon to see immense schools of dead ale-wife floating on the surface of the water.

The methods of cooking this fish are the same as for either the shad or herring. It is an inexpensive fish and in the St Lawrence Bay area is called 'gaspereu' and 'sawbelly' and in some localities 'ellwife'. In Bermuda it is called the 'round pompano'.

Ale-wife generally is salt-packed, usually in wooden buckets of 25 lb. weight, but they are also sometimes smoked.

ALEXANDERS (Allisanders Black Lovage). In the United States this name is sometimes given to the indigenous wild angelica.

This is a heavily built umbelliferous herb or vegetable, growing up to four or five feet high in good conditions. It has yellow-green flowers, black fruits, and some resemblance to celery in both general appearance and flavour. It was formerly cultivated for its fleshy stalks and used in much the same way as celery, but celery has now displaced it. It was also one of what were called potherbs in Britain and is probably one of the oldest-known vegetables.

The original home of the alexanders was the Mediterranean, but it has become naturalized British and grows on wasteland and cliffs near the sea.

ALGERIAN WINES. A name which, in the British Isles, stands for a red wine that is deep in colour, full-bodied, rather tart and lacking in bouquet and breed. This is due to the fact that most, if not all, the Algerian wine sold in England during World War II (when there was no other available) and immediately after the war, was of very poor quality. But the vineyards of Algeria, some of the most extensive in the world, with an average annual production before the war of nearly 500 million gallons of wine (now rapidly declining), are responsible for a great variety of different wines, red, white and *rosé*, still and sparkling, sweet and dry. Most of them, unfortunately, are of no distinctive merit, because quantity rather than quality was the rule, but the vineyards of Algeria can give, and have given, some extremely nice wines.

Algerian wines, when produced under French management, were extensively used in France as blending wines. Now that French expertise has, on the whole, left Algeria, and the government has sold off to the highest bidder the 32,000 wineries built and maintained by the French, the future of Algerian wine is uncertain.

ALGÉRIENNE. The French culinary name of a

ALLSPICE (branch, berry and flower)   ALE-WIFE

garnish for meat. It consists of small tomatoes, braised in oil and sweet potato croquettes or sweet potatoes cooked in butter.

ALIGOTÉ. See BURGUNDY WINES.

ALKALI. A chemical substance having the power to neutralize acids. The chief kitchen uses are in ammonia, lye, scouring powders and baking soda. Further, all soaps are made by the reaction of an alkali with a glyceroid (fat).

In foods, all vegetables are basically alkaline, as are acid-tasting fruit, such as lemons, redcurrants, etc. Milk and blood are the only animal-derived foodstuffs that are not.

Very strong alkaline foods are celery, artichokes, turnips, carrots, spinach, lettuce and tomatoes.

ALKERMÈS. A French cordial, crimson red and rather sweet, which used to be very popular in France and Italy. It was coloured with kermès berries, which were not berries at all but small scarlet grain insects of the *Cochineal* genus, full of red dye.

ALLEMANDE SAUCE. See SAUCES.

ALLIARIA. A common member of the cabbage family native to Europe and Asia and naturalized in the United States and eastern Canada. The most common nicknames are 'Jack-by-the-Hedge', 'garlic mustard', 'donkey's foot', and 'sauce alone'. Although once used as a flavouring and salad herb, its use has now declined.

ALLIGATOR APPLE. See CUSTARD APPLE.

ALLIGATOR PEAR. See AVOCADO PEAR.

ALLSPICE. Also called Jamaica pepper. This spice comes from a pimento tree native to the West Indies, Central and South America. It grows in many tropical countries but so profusely in Jamaica that the island produces most of the

world's supply. The pimento tree is striking, with a green, smooth and shining bark and dark glossy leaves. These when crushed emit a strong, spicy aroma. The berries are picked while still green, then dried in the sun until they turn brown. When the berries are allowed to ripen they become a dark purple colour and are filled with a sweet pulp. This is the familiar allspice of our kitchens, looking like large, brown peppercorns.

Allspice is not, as many who buy it ground imagine, a compound of several spices. It is one spice with the flavour of cloves, cinnamon and nutmeg combined. It is a useful spice and is best bought whole and ground when required. The allspice corns are easily ground and when a light spice is required are very useful.

Allspice is used in dishes both savoury and sweet, and in most countries. Ground allspice goes into rich fruit cakes; in Scandinavia it is an ingredient used in marinating fish, and it is a popular ingredient used in several of the Near East dishes.

ALLUMETTES. In culinary French the name applies to a kind of hors d'oeuvre or small entrée. They are matchsticks of puff pastry, baked in the oven and spread with different flavouring garnishes; for example, grated cheese, anchovy sauce or shrimp butter.

Also little cakes made of puff pastry and spread with icing sugar are called allumettes.

ALMOND. The almond is believed to have originated in the eastern Mediterranean countries or even further east, and has been cultivated all round that area for centuries. It has always been in the front rank among edible nuts and its popularity never wanes.

It was cultivated in England before the end of the 16th century but, although its blossom is a familiar and attractive sight in English gardens in the early spring, the trees seldom reach fruition.

There are frequent mentions of almonds in the scriptures for it grows freely in the Holy Land in a more or less wild state. Almonds were among the presents taken to Egypt by the sons of Jacob. The

Romans knew them and called them 'the Greek nuts' suggesting that almonds reached Italy via Greece. In the south of France they have been cultivated since the 14th century. They were introduced to California about the middle of the last century and almond-growing is now an important industry, almost making the United States self-sufficient in this field. The main producing countries are Italy, Spain, France, Portugal, Morocco and Persia. But the almond tree is now grown in many parts of the world, including Australia and South Africa, where the climate is suitably sunny, dry and never humid.

The tree is one of the first of the flowering trees to bloom in the spring. The fruit of the almond which surrounds the nut is tough, fibrous and inedible. But when the almonds are picked green, before they are ripe, and the kernel is still soft and tender, they are considered – and are – a delicacy in almond-producing countries. They are also popular as a dessert. Sometimes the young almonds are preserved in a sugar or in spirit, such as *eau-de-vie*.

There are two main classes of almonds, the sweet and the bitter. For confectionery purposes, sweet almonds are used. The kernel of the bitter almond, as might be expected, is bitter to the taste and can be harmful if taken in large quantities.

Among the edible or sweet almonds there are many different varieties. Some of these will only grow in certain countries. The Jordan almond of Spain, for example, cannot be grown profitably in California, although this state boasts over a 100 different varieties. The name Jordan has nothing to do with the country of that name. It is probably a corruption of the French word *jardin* signifying that they were cultivated or garden-grown almonds.

Although most people know Valencia or Jordan almonds, these are but two types. Italy, possibly the largest almond-producing country in the world, has a large number of varieties, all with different names. Spain also has other varieties than these two best-known types.

Almond as a flavouring, if correctly used, is a flavouring of a delicate kind. Usually only a small quantity is required, but if this is omitted for any reason, the character of the dish calling for it is changed. In early medieval cooking, almond was an everyday flavouring. In the Middle East and in certain Balkan countries many of the sweet dishes are highly flavoured with almond, as are a number of Far Eastern sweets.

However, sweet almonds do not only appear in sweet dishes. They are served whole, roasted or fried. In any of these three forms they are used as appetizers with drinks. Roasted or fried they appear as garnishes to pilaus, and are used in many fish dishes. Trout with almonds is one of the classic examples of this. Chicken stuffed with almonds and rice is a recipe from the Arab countries.

The flavour of bitter almonds has no connection with that of the sweet almond. It is a powerful flavour obtained from the kernels of plums, peaches, cherries and related fruits.

The following are some of the classic methods in which almonds are prepared:

Almonds, to Blanch: Put the almonds into a bowl, in hot water, not more than $\frac{1}{4}$ lb. at a time as they will become soggy if left too long. Leave until the skins wrinkle and loosen. Drain off the water, cool the almonds and then slip off the skins. Place the almonds on a sheet of absorbent paper and leave them to dry for several hours or overnight.

BURNT ALMONDS
1 lb. almonds
$1\frac{3}{4}$ lb. sugar
cold water

Blanch the almonds and dry them in an oven. Put 1 lb. of sugar and 1 cup ($1\frac{1}{4}$) of water into a saucepan and dissolve the sugar over a low heat. Bring to the boil, add the almonds and continue to boil gently until the almonds begin to make cracking noises. Take the pan from the heat and stir until the sugar granulates. Turn it all out into a sieve, shake the nuts and let the sugar drain off into a saucepan. Add $\frac{3}{4}$ cup (1) of water and the remaining sugar and boil to the soft boil stage (237°F). Add the almonds, stir until they are well-coated and remove them as soon as the almonds show signs of sticking. Strain in a sieve and leave until they are cold.

Almonds, Devilled: Fry the almonds in butter (see below). Mix together some salt and cayenne pepper. Take the almonds from the pan and roll them in the salt mixture. Shake them until they are cold.

Almond Essence or Extract: A solution of oil and bitter almonds, about 1 per cent of alcohol of fair strength, used for flavouring puddings, cakes, sweet, ice-creams, pastries, etc.

Almonds, to Fry: Heat some butter in a thick frying pan, add the almonds, whole, chopped or slivered, and fry them for a few seconds until they change colour. Watch them all the time they are cooking as they burn easily. In South Africa almonds treated in this manner are called 'cobbled'.

Almonds, Salted: Fry the almonds, drain them on absorbent paper, then sprinkle generously with salt.

Almonds, to Toast: Put the almonds on to a baking sheet and bake in a moderate oven, stirring frequently, until they brown.

There are 'almond' essences made from the bitter almonds or kernels of the fruits mentioned above as well as ratafias. These are known as *noyeau*

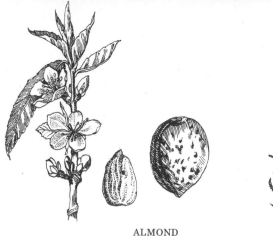

ALMOND

ALOE

with some variations in spellings in many parts of the world.

There is an oil of bitter almonds and an oil of sweet almonds, and the latter is a fatty oil. Both are used, mostly in confectionery, but the bitter more in cosmetic and pharmaceutical preparations because it is cheaper. This oil can be pressed from either sweet or bitter almonds.

ALOE. Aloes, with their rosettes of fleshy, sword-shaped leaves (looking a bit like an aspidistra) are familiar as greenhouse or ornamental plants. They come mainly from Africa. The juice of many species is intensely bitter. They are medicinal plants but also used in some *fernets* and bitters.

When the leathery leaves of aloes are cut a honey-like liquid exudes, which has an intensely bitter taste. Commercially this juice is boiled down to a black treacly substance or a solid residue, and this is what one buys at the chemist (druggist).

By tradition this substance is used to discourage children from biting their nails, but *in very small amounts* it can be of value to those who make wines and cordials at home. It is best to buy supplies from the druggist who will advise on suitable dosage rather than to experiment from the garden, as some species are frankly poisonous.

ALOXE-CORTON. See BURGUNDY WINES.

ALPINA LIQUEUR. A fiery, pale golden-yellow, Italian liqueur made of spirit and distilled with a fruit essence. It is served as a sweet cordial, usually after dinner, and is sometimes used to flavour cocktails.

ALSACE WINES. The white wines of Alsace are made from the grapes grown in the vineyards at the foothills of the Vosges Mountains, facing the Rhine and in the plains towards the Rhine. They are dry wines, with fair bouquet and body, which are sold under the name of the particular species of grape used for each. Thus *Sylvaner* is light and should be also a cheaper wine than *Riesling* or *Traminer*, the Sylvaner grape being a commoner

sort than the other two. *Elbing* and *Burger* are two other common grapes; whilst *Riesling*, the *White Pinot* or *Grey Pinot*, (*Tokay*), the *Gentil*, *Traminer* and *Gewurztraminer* are better sorts from which better and dearer wines are made. Unless of an exceptionally fine vintage, the white wines of Alsace are best drunk when still young, from one to three years old.

Alsace is now divided into two departments: Haut-Rhin (Colmar), and Bas-Rhin (Strasbourg).

ALSACIENNE, À L'. Definition applying to a very great number of culinary preparations, particularly large cuts of meat, goose or duck. The predominating ingredients featured in dishes thus described are braised sauerkraut, boiled potatoes, ham and Strasbourg sausage. Certain preparations based on *foie gras* are also described by this name.

ALUMINIUM (ALUMINUM). A metal used for making a wide range of household utensils. It is a good conductor of heat, resists corrosion and is easily kept clean.

Aluminium is a soft metal which scratches easily but it is capable of taking a variety of finishes. It comes polished, matt and coloured. Milk sauces or milk pudding will sometimes cause discoloration, and even boiling water can turn an aluminium pan black, but neither causes any harm. The pan can be washed by ordinary washing methods, with a nylon scraper or impregnated steel wool. Anything harsh causes pitting. Caustic sodas are all bad as they dissolve the protective coating on the surface of the aluminium and attack the metal underneath. Aluminium pots must always be completely dried before being stored away as dampness is another cause of pitting.

The price of aluminium pots is also an indication of their quality. The heavier the pan, the more expensive it is but the better for cooking. Cast aluminium is the heaviest quality and is used in some cooking utensils but the majority of household pans are made with wrought aluminium. This comes in different gauges or thicknesses. The cheaper the pan the thinner the gauge.

ALUMINIUM (ALUMINUM) FOIL. One of the most important labour-saving aids of today. It is used for wrapping, storing and cooking, and has taken the place of greaseproof paper.

AMANDES, CRÈME D'. Sweet almond liqueur.

AMBER FISH. The great amber fish or amberjack is a food fish found in the Gulf of Mexico and the West Indies. It is also known as the 'yellow tail' but is specifically the California Rockfish. It is a member of the most prolific finny families. It is fun to catch, easy to attract, nice to look at and delicious to eat. Its average weight is six to ten pounds, although some species have been known to attain a weight of 100 pounds. Smaller species are known as common amber, madregala, lemon fish, coronado, but the most highly priced is the yellow tail. It does not keep well and is best when cooked shortly after catching unless preserved. It is best prepared by cutting into fillets or steaks coated with breadcrumbs and fried in deep fat.

AMBROSIA. In Greek mythology, ambrosia was the food of the gods on Olympus, their drink being nectar. According to Hesiod and the poets who followed him, the immortals inhabiting the Olympian mansions fed on the pure and bloodless food of ambrosia, and drank only of nectar, a distillation of refined dew. The word signifies 'immortal' and the drink was a balsamic one designed to preserve immortality. It could bestow immortality to humans who were permitted to partake of it. Mortals who drank of the nectar also gained in beauty and strength, becoming in some measure akin to the gods.

The word has also been applied to various exceptionally delicious and often sweet drinks, which are supposed to have something of the glory of the fabled celestial drink of the gods, also to certain sweet fruit salads and puddings.

AMER PICON. French aperitif produced by redistilling brandy in the presence of Spanish orange peel and infusing it with a formula of barks, roots and herbs.

AMÉRICAINE, À L'. French culinary term for a sauce, chiefly prepared for lobster and other shellfish, with olive oil and tomatoes as the basis, with onions, shallots, garlic, chervil, and tarragon for flavour, and also white wine and cognac brandy.

AMERICAN CHEESE. Cheesemakers in the United States have more or less followed the lead of the Europeans in making cheese. The basic difference is that the locale where the cheese is made is added to the generic title. Thus, you will find a Wisconsin cheddar, a New York brie or an Ohio State munster. The majority of the cheeses made in the States are cheddars, although there are several other important varieties.

Of the latter, the Brick cheese is a brick-shaped, firm cheese, half-way between mild and sharp and yellow in colour. A natural Brick cheese is heavily salted and is cured for at least two months.

Another, Monterey Jack, originated in California and is a cheddar-like cheese, although softer and more delicate. As it ages, it becomes firmer and sharper and may crumble a bit.

Poona cheese is a fat, soft cheese, the colour of a ripe pear and with countless tiny holes throughout the body.

The Tennessee red rind cheese varies from a mild, light yellow, all-purpose cheese to a dark, blue-veined ancient that demands the respect due to worthwhile old age.

Liederkranz began as the American version of Belgian limberger, but it is not so smelly and has a full, fine flavour.

Of the many American cheddars, here are some of the best-known varieties:

Colby and Corn Husker. Midwestern cheddars, they are soft in body and have a higher than usual moisture content.

Coon. A dark-bodied, crumbly cheese, the colour of sweet butter. It is a fine, well-cured cheese of good quality.

Herkimer. This is a New York State cheese, dry and crumbly and with a full, sharp flavour.

Longhorn. This is a yellow-orange cheese, very solid and with a waxy sheen. It has a bite and tang to it and is so-named as it resembles the horn of the Old Texas Longhorn cattle.

Tillamook. A Pacific coast favourite, ranging in taste from mild to sharp. It is to the West coast what Wisconsin cheddar is the the East coast. The basic difference between the two is that Tillamook is made from raw milk.

Wisconsin. This cheddar's flavour ranges from the very mild to a greeny-veined sharp that is almost, but not quite, bitter. It is a firm, solid cheese, from a pale straw to orange in colour.

Vermont. A favourite with New Englanders, this is off-white, tangy and sharp in taste and is a well-cured and aged cheese.

AMERICAN WINES. When wine was first made in the United States is a matter of pure conjecture. It is, however, a matter of historical fact that there is no record, song, legend, or tradition of any of the American Indian tribes concerning the making of wine. Corn (maize) beer, yes, but no wine. To say this is peculiar is to put it mildly. The wild grape is widely distributed over the entire United States, a type of fermentation was known, and the Indians

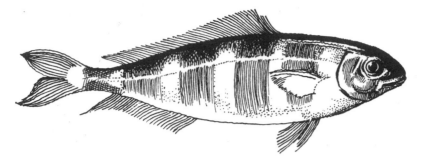

AMBER FISH

did use the grape as fresh fruit, in cooking, and in the preparation of dried foods, of which pemmican is the best known. Even in the extreme northern United States, and on the Canadian coast, wild grape was so prolific that the early Viking explorers, who preceded Colombus, named the country 'Vineland'.

The early Spanish settlements in the New World really took root in the beginning of the 16th century. By the end of the first quarter-century comparatively large towns had sprung up, complex fortifications built, trade established with the aboriginals in the interior and Europe. Saint Augustine, in Florida, was an important port and bastion of the Spanish, and Fort Marion, which exists today, rivalled in size and complexity those of the Old World. History records the dons took wine with their meals, and brandy was stored in the cellars of Fort Marion. But again, who furnished the wine? Was it all imported? Again, no record, yet Florida did and does abound in the native grape. Not the *Vinis Vinifera*, but native grape with names such as Scuppernong, Bullis, and Muscadine.

By the time of the American Revolution in 1776 one finds records of vine crossbreeding and improvement, and the production of wine in marketable quantities. Both George Washington and Thomas Jefferson produced wine in fair-sized quantities on their farms. It is more than likely, though, that these wines were either sweet or fortified wines, as the native grape, the *Vita Lambrusca* is low in sugar. Viticulture and wine-making was fairly limited for many reasons. Among them were shortage of both skilled and unskilled labour, and the reward was less than that of tobacco, cotton, indigo, and rice. All these brought good profit on the European market while the rough American wines were not acceptable in Europe.

In the West, what is now California, the ubiquitous Spanish had imposed a fair degree of order if not of law. Forts, roads and missions were built, and the friars in the missions were making wine of the transplanted Spanish grape for use in holy communion. The Spanish purple grape, which for many years was the standard American wine grape

in the west, was imported by one Father Junipero Serra. This visionary eventually built 17 missions, most of which had vineyards, and his wine production was great enough to ship some wine to Mexico.

Here then is the turning point in American wine history – wine improvement and crossbreeding in the east in 1830, and commercial wine in the west in 1783. The major wine-producing areas of the United States as they stand today are; New York State, Ohio, and California, producing 95 per cent of our wines. While some wines are produced in nearly every state, the quantities are negligible.

Viticulture was a thriving industry in New York State in 1830. Established in the Finger Lakes district, it today ranks second in wine production. Some hybrids grown here are familiar to Europeans, but the majority are unknown beyond the shores of North America. All are basically rootstock of the Lambrusca, the native American grape. Among the most familiar names are the Concord, Elvira, Catawba, Duchess, and Delaware.

To the wine drinker unfamiliar with New York State wines the taste of the Lambrusca grape comes as a shock. Some complain of a 'foxy' taste, which they deem unpleasant, to others it is merely a different taste than the one usually associated with accustomed drink. Experiments with wine made from non-Lambrusca vines grown in the same area reveal the taste is still prevalent, so the conclusion must be reached it is the geography, not the vine. However, to be fair, this characteristic taste is not prevalent in a majority of the better wines.

The United States courts have ruled that champagne is the name of a process used in producing a certain type of wine, although the French disagree, and New York produces genuine sparkling wine that is of the highest quality and can compete with the world's best.

An outstanding sherry is also produced that is exposed to the sun in summer and to the bitter cold in winter for a full four years.

Ohio State really started wine production commerically when Nicholas Longworth, a lawyer, began in the wine growing business near Cincinnati. Longworth's vineyard has long been covered by housing developments, but his start was the beginning of a thriving wine trade in Ohio. The Catawba grape first used by him is still the mainstay. It is curious phenomena of the American public but, in order to market the product, bottles must be labelled 'sauternes'.

There are approximately 30 wineries in Ohio. They make a full range of red, white, sparkling and fortified wines. Drinkers accustomed to the classic taste of *vinifera* are often taken aback by the taste of the Catawba. It does not have the foxy taste ascribed to the New York wines, but has a big, rich, simple taste, and deserves the praise and attention of all who discover its qualities. Alas, wine snobs are wine snobs, and generic names are used to describe what should rightly stand by itself. The sparkling wines are charming, delightful wines that compare favourably with spumantes, sekts, vouvray's, or sparkling hocks. *Rosé* wines from this area bow their heads to none.

Until quite recently Californian producers marketed their wines under the European generic terms and names for ease of identification. More recently there has been a move afoot to label the wine of their better vintage under the name of the grape from which it was produced. State laws have been passed similar in purpose to the French *appellation contrôlée* laws, and these assure the consumer that if he buys a bottle labelled 'zinfandel', he is guaranteed that at least 51 per cent of the grape is zinfandel, and the remainder is of a grape compatible with it. Further, if the label says 'Sonoma Valley', all the grape must be produced in the delimited area. This will have more effect in the future when the true quality which is capable of being produced is reached.

California wines can be broadly placed into three categories; dessert, dry table, and flavoured wines. The flavoured wines are true wines with real fruit flavouring added, and, in some cases, slightly carbonated. They are not meant to be taken seriously but in general are light, refreshing summer-time drinks. The dessert wines include the fortified wines, ports, sherries, and vermouths.

Red wines in California are made from a variety of European grapes. Among them are the cabernet sauvignon, the pinot noir, the barbera and charbono from Italy, and of course the zinfandel.

All parts of the California wine-world produce sparkling wines, ranging in taste from the sweet asti to the dry crisp *blancs*.

AMIRAL, À L'. See SAUCES.

AMMONIA, CARBONATE OF. See BAKING POWDER.

AMOMUM. This is the formal name of a plant of the ginger family native to Asia and Africa, commonly called Grains of Paradise. The species known under the scientific name of *Amomum cardamomum* produces globular pods often called cardamom and even used as a substitute for the true cardamom. Its other familiar names are malagueta pepper and even alligator pepper, and very old cookery books refer to it as grains of paradise. The seeds are extremely pungent and much used in Africa. In the reign of George III of England an act was passed forbidding brewers to add grains of paradise to their beers under penalty of a £200 fine.

AMONTILLADO. See SPANISH WINES.

AMOROSO. See SPANISH WINES.

AMPHICLES. A celebrated cook of ancient Greece, who attempted to simplify the cooking of his day. He was perhaps the first to use vine leaves which he wrapped round birds when cooking, the origin of the dolma we know today. He was against the over-use of spices, seeking the full flavour of the meat being cooked. He also was sparing in the use of spices when making sauces, confining himself to two or three only. His contemporaries sometimes used as many as 20 ingredients.

AMPHITRYON. Succinctly this word means, a host; a dinner-giver. But through the centuries it has come to mean something more. A French author of the early 19th century, Grimod de la Reynière, one of the first writers to attempt to invest gastronomy with an intellectual quality, wrote *Le Manuel des Amphitryons,* a dissertation upon the art of carving, a compendium of menus, together with some informative notes on the polite art of dining.

AMPHORA. A large, slender two-handled terracotta vessel of elongated form, often with a blunt point at the base for insertion into soft ground to keep the vessel upright. It is of Greek origin, the Romans having taken it from Greece. Amphorae were used for the transport and storage of wine, oil, fish-pastes, hazelnuts, etc., and afterwards were sometimes used as cinerary urns. They were frequently ornamented with a design, and sometimes with remarkable sculptures. Many of these vessels had a pointed lid of the same material.

Amphora is also a Greek liquid measure of about two gallons and also a Roman measure of six gallons.

ANADAMA BREAD. A cornmeal and white-flour bread made with molasses and yeast leavening.

½ cup (⅔) cornmeal
2 cups (2½) hot water
2 tablespoons (2½) cooking fat (shortening)

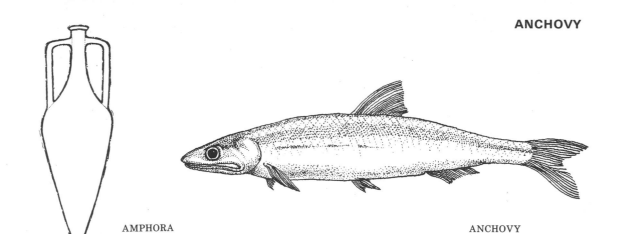

AMPHORA

ANCHOVY

½ cup (⅔) molasses
1 teaspoon (1¼) salt
5 cups (6¼) all-purpose flour
1 cake yeast

Have the hot water in a pan and stir the corn-meal into it just before it boils. Let it boil for five minutes, stirring all the while. Add the fat, stir this well into the cornmeal mixture, then add the molasses and salt. Cool. In the meantime dissolve the yeast in a little warm water. Stir this into the cornmeal mixture then add enough flour to make a stiff dough – whether all five cups will be needed depends on the cornmeal and the flour. Knead the dough well, then cover and leave in a warm place to double its size. Shape into loaves, and place in greased loaf pans. Again leave to rise until light, then bake in a hot oven (400° F.) for 1 hour.

ANCHOVY. The anchovy is a dark blue and silver fish found in the Mediterranean off the coasts of France, Italy and Spain, and on the Atlantic coasts of Europe, but not in the north. Quite often sprats, pilchards, ale-wifes and other lesser members of the herring family, are called anchovies and, although well spiced, pickled or salted, are not the real thing at all.

Although the anchovy can and sometimes does grow as much as eight inches long, the usual size is 2½ to 3 inches, and fresh anchovies are often on sale in Mediterranean fish markets and the Atlantic coast markets of Spain and Portugal. The fresh fish is excellent, with white flesh and a good flavour, but it is nothing like the flavour of the anchovy when cured. This especial flavour and colour develops only after the anchovy has been pickled for some months in salt and is the result of fermentative changes. The salting and pickling of fish is an art known to the peoples of the Mediterranean for thousands of years. Where anchovies are landed, curing is exceedingly simple.

Salted anchovies are much used in Mediterranean cooking, but in northern Europe and America only those anchovies preserved in oil are available and, as a result, few people realize that the anchovy starts life as a small, lively, fresh fish.

One of the reasons for the quick salting of anchovies is that they deteriorate quickly when exposed to the air and need to be highly salted to be preserved. Plain salted anchovies should be soaked a short while in water before being used to remove some of their salt. With the canned anchovy in oil, this is more difficult; so they should always be used with care unless their flavour is intended to play a dominant part in the dish. In Victorian England it was usual to lard meat with anchovies, using them instead of salt. The anchovies blended well into the savoury background without being obvious.

There are literally dozens of ways in which anchovies can be used in cooking. Regarded basically more as a flavouring than a major ingredient, they are excellent in sauces for cold meats, game and poultry. They marry with eggs, make a delicious dressing for broccoli, and in Italy are cooked with spinach. Fillets of anchovy are used in the Italian *antipasti* and in the French hors d'oeuvre, as well as the Scandinavian *smörgåsbord*. They are used as a garnish for the German *Holsteinschnitzel*. In the Mediterranean countries they are served as an appetizer with bread and butter. In Belgium and Holland anchovies are marinated in wine vinegar with thinly sliced onions and slivers of lemon rind, and are eaten with pre-luncheon drinks.

Italy has a dish of fried anchovies which are smothered with a delicious tomato sauce and garnished with truffles, and in Piedmont, one of the centres of Italian culinary genius, one of its most famous dishes is a sauce *bagna cauda*, which consists of anchovies melted in a mixture of oil and butter. This is eaten with vegetables as a dip. Pizzas are garnished with anchovies. Provence has its *anchoiada,* in which anchovies are pounded in a mortar with olive oil and a few drops of vinegar, spread on slices of home-made bread and sprinkled with finely chopped hard-boiled eggs.

A jar of salted anchovies will keep almost indefinitely provided they remain covered by liquid and they are always taken out with a clean spoon. The canned, oiled anchovies also last well, again if kept covered in oil and not exposed to the air.

The value of anchovy as a flavour is that it sharpens the appetite for meat and drink. When used in conjunction with its brother fish and certain fowl, it heightens their flavours.

ANCIENNE, À L'. French culinary term for garnishings and sauces prepared in the 'old style'. Such garnishings are always mixed and dishes cooked in this manner include ragoût of chicken simmered in a white sauce to which such delicacies as truffles, cocks' combs and button mushrooms have been added. There is also a favourite dish *beef rump à l'ancienne* as well as a *poulade à l'ancienne*. The term is also applied to blanquette and fricassée of chicken and veal, treated in a rather special manner.

ANDALOUSE, À L'. This is the French name given to dishes served with tomatoes, sweet peppers, aubergines (egg-plants) often chipolata sausages and a rice pilau.

ANDOUILLE. A large black-skinned tripe sausage, cooked and served cold, sliced, as an hors d'oeuvre. Such sausages are usually sold cooked in France, their country of origin.

ANDOUILLETTES. These are small tripe sausages of mild and bland flavour, useful for picnics. They are usually contained in knobbly lengths of gut, but this does not detract from their flavour. Sometimes they are wrapped in stiff white paper, or pressed into four-sided shapes and glazed with a mixture of veal and pork lard. They can be fried.

ANESONE. A white liqueur with licorice-like flavour, higher in proof and drier than anisette and produced by distillation of anise seed.

ANGEL CAKE. A light, frothy cake made without shortening, leavened with air. Its lightness depends on how the egg whites are beaten, the lightness with which the sugar and flour mixture is folded in, and the temperature at which the cake is baked.

Like all such well-known cakes, recipes for this favourite cake vary from cook to cook. However, certain things are basic. The egg whites should be beaten until they are stiff enough to hold up in peaks, but are still glossy, and the flour gently and gradually folded in.

¾ cup (1 scant cup) sifted cake flour
1 cup (1¼) sifted icing (confectioners') sugar
12 egg whites
1 teaspoon (1¼) cream of tartar
a good pinch salt
1 teaspoon (1¼) vanilla extract
½ teaspoon (⅔) almond extract
¾ cup (1) granulated sugar.

Sift the flour with the icing sugar three times. Beat the egg whites with the cream of tartar, salt, vanilla and almond extract until stiff enough to hold up in snowy-white peaks. Beat in the granulated sugar, 2 tablespoonfuls (2½) at a time, continuing to beat the whites until the peaks are again stiff. Sift about a quarter of the flour over the egg whites and fold in gently. Fold in the remaining flour by fourths. Bake in an ungreased 10-inch angel cake pan in a moderate oven for 30 minutes or until the top is a golden brown. Invert the pan, cool thoroughly and turn out. Serve with strawberries and cream.

ANGELICA (1). Several drinks, all different, are named after this plant. One is a Spanish liqueur that is aromatic, pale yellow and very sweet. Another is a sweet white wine made in California, originally by the Mission Fathers. A third, also hailing from California, is a highly fortified white dessert wine; and fourthly, a must where fermentation has been stopped, used as a base for some aperitifs and cordials (also a product of California).

(2). This is a beautiful plant of which there are over 50 varieties. Here we shall deal only with the *Herba angelica* or *archangelica,* 'root of the Holy Ghost' or 'herb of the angels' because it was supposed to have finally dispelled the plague and protected all those who used it. It is indigenous in such diverse countries as Lapland, Iceland, Spain and France, and grows extensively in Britain, America and New Zealand.

ANGELS ON HORSEBACK.
butter for frying
8 round slices of bread, ½ inch thick
8 large oysters
cayenne pepper to taste
lemon juice
8 slices of streaky bacon

Heat a fair quantity of butter and fry the pieces of bread until a golden brown on both sides. Beard the oysters and sprinkle them with cayenne pepper and lemon juice. Roll each oyster in a slice of bacon. Secure with a toothpick. Lay each roll on a slice of fried bread, place on a baking sheet and bake in a moderate oven long enough to cook the bacon. Serve very hot, garnished with parsley or watercress.

Can be served as an hors d'oeuvre or as a savoury at the end of a meal.

ANGLAISE, À L'. This does not signify any particular garnish. It implies that a dish bearing such a nomenclature is either plain roast or boiled, or

ANGELICA

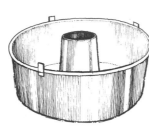

ANGEL CAKE TIN

ANGLER FISH

cooked according to typical English methods. It can mean ingredients coated in a mixture composed of eggs, salt, pepper and breadcrumbs, and fried in deep fat, or fish grilled and served with melted butter, but all too often it means mutton and chicken or vegetables very simply boiled in water or in a white stock.

ANGLER FISH. A large ugly fish of the grouper family that swims in European and American waters. It can reach a length of three to five feet. In the market it appears minus its enormous head with its large mouth, and its curious tapering body skinned. Its flavour is somewhat muddy, but this can be eradicated.

It has been given its name of angler on account of its habit of lying partly buried on the sea floor where it lures its prey. This it does by using a filament which grows from its head. It then hides in rocks and holes in the reef with only its voracious mouth and the tentacle showing. Its camouflage is so perfect that the smaller fish sees only the 'worm' which is the tentacle twitching as it approaches. The smaller fish dashes to it to catch its dinner and finishes up by becoming one.

The flesh of the angler is similar to that of its related groupers, white and flaky, and in the Caribbean is prepared in a chowder or stew of small fish and forms a truly delicious meal. Grilled and sprinkled with lime or lemon juice with a plantain salad, it provides an excellent reason for returning to the tropics.

ANGLUDET. See BORDEAUX WINES.

ANGOSTURA BITTERS. The most renowned brand of bitters. It is compounded in the West Indian island of Trinidad from the bitter and aromatic bark of the Cusparia tree and a number of aromatic herbs and roots, according to the original formula of the late Dr Siegert. The recipe is still a somewhat closely guarded secret. It was originally prepared as a cure for malaria and other tropical diseases, and it was known medicinally for centuries to the people of the West Indies and South

America. Local fishermen stupefy fish with the bark as do the Peruvians with the cinchona bark.

It is chiefly used today, a few drops at a time, in gin cocktails and other similar drinks, including cups. It also peps up soft drinks, whether hot or cold.

Although this is not popularly known, angostura bitters can also be used to flavour soups and sweet dishes. Vanilla ice-cream faintly flavoured with angostura bitters is very good, as is fresh grapefruit.

To flavour 3 pints ($3\frac{3}{4}$) of soup, roughly 2 teaspoons ($2\frac{1}{2}$) of angostura is enough, but it depends on personal taste.

ANIMELLE. In France this is the culinary term for the testicles of male animals, in particular those of rams. In the past testicles were much eaten in France, Spain and Italy, but rather less so today. In the Middle East they are still used extensively and baskets of them are to be seen in every meat market. They are very tender, and many people eat them, often perhaps without knowing what they are eating. In Italian, animelle covers sweetbreads of young animals, usually lambs, which are fried with slices of ham.

ANISE. This is a herb, a beautiful plant, one of the oldest annuals among herbs. Almost everyone must have tasted it at some time, often without knowing it, since the taste of licorice and the word anise are not usually associated by most people. Several famous drinks are flavoured with aniseed or anise.

Anise is native to southwest Asia, northern Africa, and southeast Europe, and has been introduced also in temperate zones. It grows well in India, as well as South America and certain parts of the United States.

Most parts of the plant are used. The leaves for garnishing and flavouring fruit and vegetable salads – they add a slightly sweet flavour. They can also be used as potherbs. The seeds are very widely used. Their flavour is powerful and should be used with discretion to avoid killing all other flavours

29

present. They are used in some curries, in cakes and confectionery, and in certain cheeses and breads, such as the German *Anisbrod*.

ANISETTE. One of the sweetest of French liqueurs made with aniseed, the best of which is from Bordeaux. It is produced as a flavour blend of aniseeds and aromatic herbs, and is always sold colourless. A similar liqueur, sold under the same name, is made in Holland and other places.

ANJOU, VINS D'. The generic name of all the still white wines of the *département* of Maine-et-Loire, within the borders of the former province of Anjou. The white sparkling wines of the same district are mostly sold under the name of *vins de Saumur*. The still white Anjou wines are never sharply dry, and the best of them are distinctly rich, much more suitable as dessert wines than as beverage or table wines. The finest Anjou wine comes from the vineyards of two valleys, both south of Angers – the Loire and its tributary, the Layon.

The best white wines of the Coteaux de la Loire, are those from La Coulée de Sarrant, La Roche aux Moins and Château de Savennières; and the best of the Coteaux du Layon are Le Quart de Chaume, Faye, Beaulieu and Bonnezeaux. Two other famous white wines of Anjou are those of Château de Parnay and Château de l'Aiglerie.

ANNA POTATOES. This is an attractive method of preparing potatoes, neither complicated nor especially difficult. They should be cooked in a special utensil, which is like a two-handled casserole with a tightly fitting lid. However, anna potatoes can be prepared in a pan with a lid which exactly fits.

There are no exact quantities for this recipe – it depends on the size of the pan and the family. The best kind of potatoes for it are the yellow soapy kind, or what the French call Dutch potatoes.

About 4–5 lb. potatoes, preferably all of similar
  size
butter
salt, pepper

Wash the potatoes, cut into thin slices and drop them into cold water. Leave for 30 minutes then drain and dry on a cloth. Sprinkle with salt and pepper. Generously butter the pan all over, sides and bottom. Add a layer of potatoes, flat and in a circle so that each slice of potato slightly overlaps. Sprinkle with slivers of butter, then add another layer of potatoes, arranging them in the same manner.

Continue in this manner until all the potatoes are used up – there should be 5 or 6 layers at least. Cover with the lid and put the pan into a hot oven and bake for 30 minutes.

Turn out to serve, for the finished article is like a cake, well browned on the outside and soft inside. If using the special Anna pan, the cake is turned out on to the lid and this put back into the oven again for one minute. Cut the potato cake into quarters and serve at once.

ANNATTO. A South American evergreen tree, known as *urucu* in the Argentine. It is also a main crop in Jamaica, and produces an edible but tasteless fruit salmon-red in colour. The seeds are used for colouring in confectionery, and both Leicester and Red Cheshire cheeses are coloured with this. Sometimes butter is similarly coloured.

ANNONA or **ANONA.** See CUSTARD APPLE.

ANOLINI. Small envelopes of pasta made of two pieces of pasta placed together with a filling consisting of breadcrumbs, eggs, Parmesan cheese, seasoning and concentrated beef stew. They are served in broth or dry with sauce.

ANTELOPE. This is a collective name applied to a number of deer-like mammals found in Europe, Asia and Africa. Properly speaking the name should be used in connection with the Indian black-buck. The group is divided into four main families; the true, the bush, the capriform and the bovine. What is called antelope in the United States is not the true antelope but the prongbuck or pronghorn antelope, or Rocky Mountain goat, considered by hunters in the United States as good hunting meat.

The South African antelope, known as the eland, is sometimes the size of a bull although there are smaller gazelle-type animals. The swift izard of Europe, and the Pyrenees in particular, is a capriform allied to the chamois.

Older animals in this group are highly prized for their meat, having more flavour than their young. As they can be rather dry eating they need a lot of fat when cooked and they are best roasted.

ANTHOLYTI. This is a round, pale yellow Greek cheese which comes in two or three sizes. It has a mottled, thick rind as wrinkled as a relief map.

ANTICO LIQUOR VINO AMARASCATO or **A.L.A.** The initials A.L.A. stand for Antico Liquor Vino Amarascato, a curiosity of Sicily which, like so much else Sicilian, dates from Graeco-Roman times, and is made by allowing sweet, semi-dried black grapes to ferment in casks made of cherry-wood. The scent and flavour of the wood are imparted to the resultant heavy sweet wine, which is drunk in these parts both as an aperitif and as a liqueur.

ANISE

ANNA POTATO POT

ANTIPASTI. This is the Italian name for hors d'oeuvre or appetizers. They are regional and vary tremendously from the elegant and rather formal approach of the Bolognese to the simple vegetables, olives, sweet peppers, etc., of the Sicilians.

Most midday meals in Italy start with *antipasti*, especially if the meal is going to be without a pasta dish. The most usual form of *antipasti* consists of olives, ham and small artichokes cooked and served cold in oil, various types of salami and other famous Italian sausages thinly sliced, raw fennel, raw broad beans and the many types of fungi in oil. Very popular are paper-thin slices of Italian cured ham combined with fresh figs or melon, which is one of the culinary triumphs of Italian cooking. Fish are also included in *antipasti* dishes, especially squids, cuttlefish, octopus, sardines or anchovy, tunny fish and sea urchins, to name but a few, for the Italians would appear to catch every variety of edible fish the sea offers them. To the enterprising there is no limit to the number of dishes which can appear on the table as *antipasti*.

There are also some hot *antipasti,* usually consisting of fried bread served with chicken livers, or cheese and black olives fried together, Parmesan cheese fingers or fried courgettes (zucchini). Stuffed cucumbers, devilled eggs and spinach dumplings all come under the classic name of *antipasti*.

ANYA or **PERUVIAN POTATO.** This vegetable is a native of the Peruvian Andes, but has been grown in France and in one or two isolated cases in Britain. It looks more like a sweet potato in shape than an ordinary potato. Its tubers are washed and peeled, and cooked like a potato. They are also used in salads.

A OVELHEIRA. A soft, closely textured Portuguese cheese made from ewes' milk, with a salty flavour and a thick rind. It is exported in the main to California for the Portuguese colony there.

APERITIF. An aperitif, designed to sharpen the appetite, is an alcoholic drink taken before a meal. It differs from cocktails in being 'long' and comparatively 'mild' instead of 'short' and 'strong'. In France the oldest and most popular aperitif is dry Vermouth with or without cassis to sweeten it.

APFELSTRUDEL. The best known of the strudels (which see), with an apple filling.

APICIUS. The name of three celebrated Roman gluttons. The first lived *circa* 92 B.C., the second *circa* A.D. 14, and the third about the middle of the 1st century. All three were famous, not for their virtues, genius or any great qualities, but for gluttony and one must also add for their achievements in the gastronomical arts.

The second M. Gavius Apicius is said to have written two cooking books, one on fairly general cooking, the other on sauces. Having squandered a fortune on eating and faced with the prospect of starvation, he commited suicide.

There is a translation of an Apicius book in English; this is probably the work of an editor who called himself Apicius and who tried to combine in one book recipes from both rich and simple tables.

The word apician means one pertaining to epicures or to a luxurious diet.

APIO. See ARRACACHA.

APPELLATION D'ORIGINE CONTRÔLÉE. *AC,* as it is abbreviated, is a hallmark of quality, and the production of *Vins à Appellation d'Origine Contrôlée* (Wines of Controlled Place Names) is carefully determined by law. *AC* wines cover about 10 to 15 per cent of the total wine output in France, the best in the country. The words *Appellation Contrôlée* must be printed on the label, immediately below the name of the wine.

APPENZELL. A full-fat cheese which derives its name from the eastern Swiss canton of Appenzell, but today is also manufactured in increasing amounts in the cantons of St Gall, Thurgovia and

Zurich. It is a cheese of the Gruyère and Emmental type, with the same brown wrinkled skin of the former and smaller holes than the latter. The rind is a golden-yellow and the curd as it meets the skin is a deep yellow, while the eyes or holes are sparsely distributed and no larger than a pea. Its flavour is very delicate.

APPENZEL RAES. A very pungent cheese – the word *raes* means sharp. It is a variant of the Appenzell full-fat but is made with skimmed milk. This cheese is steeped in wine for several weeks, even months. Its curd is grey and contains numerous eyes about the size of a pin head.

APPETITOST CHEESE. A Danish-American cheese which is made from sour buttermilk. It is popular among Danes in America and is made in the United States.

APPETIZER. Something to soothe and at the same time to excite the palate. Like the curtain-raiser at the play, it should prepare one for further and even greater joys to come.

APPLE BRANDY. See CALVADOS.

APPLE BUTTER. An American recipe. Fill a preserving pan with apples peeled, cored and quartered. Add a slight flavouring of cloves, allspice and cinnamon. Cover with good cider and boil slowly, stirring from time to time with a wooden spoon, until the whole becomes a dark brown jam, with only juice sufficient to keep it soft and buttery. Remove it from the heat and place in well-covered jars, and in a few weeks it will be ready for use. It makes an excellent substitute for butter.

APPLE CHARLOTTE. A claimant for the origin of this lavish dish is Carême who created and named Apple Charlotte in honour of Princess Charlotte, the daughter of George IV of England; but there are other claimants including Goethe's Charlotte.

    2 lb. tart apples
    butter
    brown sugar to taste
    lemon juice
    buttered bread

Peel, core and slice the apples. Butter a deep pie-dish and line the bottom with apples, sprinkle with sugar and lemon juice and cover with a layer of bread and butter. Repeat until all the ingredients are used up, the bread and butter forming the top layer. Cover with greased paper, bake for 1 hour, remove the paper, let the crust brown, and serve very hot with plenty of thick cream.

APPLE JACK. See CALVADOS.

APPLES, AMERICAN. The early European settlers of the New World brought the apple to America with them. The English to New England and Virginia; the Dutch to New York and to Pennsylvania; and the French to Canada. After this importation, the apple actually preceded explorers and settlers west. The Indians became acquainted with the fruit, recognized its merit, gathered seeds, planted them and had apple orchards near their villages by the time the settlers moved into the area.

There are over 200 varieties of apple regularly grown and marketed in the United States, with 18 varieties leading all others in popularity. They are the Delicious, Golden Delicious, McIntosh, Stayman, Winesap, Jonathan, Grimes Golden, Wealthy, Gravenstein, Rome Beauty, Yellow Newton, Summer Rambo, Lodi, Yellow Transparent, Esopus Spitzenberg, York Imperial, Courtland, and Baldwin.

The United States produces approximately one-quarter of the world's total apple crop, almost one bushel per head of population. Much of this goes into making cider, vinegar, and canned apple juice – one of the very few pure fruit juices whose flavour is not materially impaired by canning.

APPLES, AUSTRALIAN. Australia on an average produces 15 million bushels of apples a year, of which about seven million bushels are exported. Harvesting season lasts from January to the end of May. Apples are grown in all Australian States.

Perhaps Australia's most famous apple is the Granny Smith. 'Granny' Smith was an old widow who lived on a small farm in Queensland who discovered a self-planted apple tree on her land. She carefully nurtured it and it finally bore the beautiful green apples that since that day have carried her name. Today there must be millions of Granny Smith apple trees scattered around the world, all directly descended from that one tree.

APPLES, ENGLISH. Of all the fruits the apple is the national fruit of the British Isles. Apples are available from August until April; in the case of the cooking apple all the year round.

Could there be a better apple than Cox's Orange Pippin from the end of September until Christmas? This apple raised by Mr Cox, a retired brewer, in 1825 at Colnbrook by London Airport, was possibly a seedling of Ribston Pippin, yet another excellent apple, particularly if linked with port and nuts at the same time. Golden Delicious, too, is another first-class quality apple, as is Tydeman's Late Orange, a cross between Laxton's Superb and Cox's Orange Pippin. Of rather dull appearance this

APRICOT

apple has an excellent flavour; possibly it will be superseded by the Crispin, an apple from Japan.

For an early apple Laxton's Epicure is probably unrivalled, coming at the beginning of September, just before the better-known and highly-coloured Worcester Pearmain which is not to be despised. Following this is Laxton's Fortune raised by the late Mr R. A. Laxton, whose father, Thomas, was a friend of Charles Darwin who used to visit him on his journeys from Cambridge to Bedford where he had a nursery. Not only do we owe much to Mr Edward Laxton for producing Laxton's Epicure and Fortune, but also because he introduced the Lord Lambourne, a cross between Worcester Pearmain and James Grieve, and Laxton's Superb apple.

Among the newer early apples which should certainly be noted is Discovery, a chance seedling found in an Essex garden, now being widely planted. This is probably the best-flavoured early red variety so far to make its appearance, coming in August a little later than Beauty of Bath. It is an excellent apple but so far has proved to be rather a shy bearer. Another newcomer of excellent flavour and appearance is Merton Worcester raised by Mr M. B. Crane, F.R.S. at the John Innes Horticultural Institute; it is a cross between Cox's Orange Pippin and Worcester Pearmain.

As for cooking apples there is very little to beat Reverend Wilks as an early cooker. The other notable cooking apple is Bramley Seedling, most widely grown of all and of excellent cooking qualities.

For those who like Russets there is Egremont Russet, but possibly the finest flavoured apple of all is Ashmead's Kernel, a very shy bearer of exquisite taste, raised by a Dr Ashmead of Gloucester in 1720. An imported apple which does not grow well in England is Granny Smith. When they come from Western Australia they are particularly good. Like most apples their quality depends very much from where they come. This is one of the reasons one cannot generalize too much about apples. They not only vary from country to country, but even from field to field. Very much depends on the soil

and climate. There is an old saying from Normandy: 'The finest cheese, the finest cider, and the finest racehorses come from the same parish.' To interpret this in the modern way means that the soil has to possess not only every major but every minor nutrient for the perfect result.

APPLES, NEW ZEALAND. Taken to New Zealand by the early settlers from Britain. Many areas in New Zealand enjoy ideal conditions for apple orchards and New Zealand apples rate high for quality throughout the world. Four million cases of apples are produced every year, in a period of about 12 weeks, from late January to early May.

APRICOT. A fruit of ancient lineage said to be a native of North China but extensively cultivated in Armenia for centuries. It is now grown in most temperate climates. The best apricots are claimed to come from France, from the Loire valley, while the greatest quantity of dried apricots comes from California and Australia.

Apricots for the markets are usually picked when slightly under-ripe so that they reach their destination in sound condition. This, however, does take away something of their delicious flavour, for the apricot freshly plucked and perfectly ripe from the tree is one of the most ambrosial of fruits, thought by many to be superior to the peach.

Apricots do not contain as much sugar as apples and many other fruits, and in their ripe state are even allowed in moderate quantities to diabetics.

Canned apricots are either whole or halved and not skinned but the skin is so tender no peeling is necessary.

A considerable quantity of the apricot crop of the world is taken for drying. Dried apricots are rich in iron. They are usually dried halved and unpeeled, and have a flavour which has considerable character, stronger than that of the fresh apricot, and drying gives them a dark brown colour. They can be cooked without previous soaking, but a little soaking in the liquid in which they are to be cooked swells them and adds to their appearance.

Cook them slowly until soft. They can be served in salads or alone, and are excellent cold, served with cream.

In the East there is a small, sweet apricot which is also dried, but this is dried whole, complete with kernel. It is a pleasant fruit, somewhat sweeter than the apricot known in the West, and not of such good colour. When dried it looks like a round stone. It needs quite a lot of soaking before being cooked.

Apricots are used a great deal in Middle Eastern cooking. For example, in Persia apricots are cooked together with lamb, with which, say Persian cooks, they have a great affinity. Another apricot speciality of the Arab world is *kamraddin*. In all the candy stores in the Levant one sees long strips of a bright yellow-looking *something* which resembles leather. This is oddly enough dried apricots. Fresh apricots are stoned, fumigated with sulphur and rubbed through a sieve until a thin purée is formed. This is spread in trays and left to dry in the sun until it can be peeled off. In this state it is chewed, as we might chew a handful of raisins, or it is distilled with water and made into sherbets.

Considerable quantities of *kamraddin* are eaten during Ramadan, the Muslim period of fasting. The first drink after the gun has boomed announcing the setting of the sun, is of diluted *kamraddin*. Its main virtue is that it is refreshing and sweet. Also, which is important, it soothes the digestion of the true fasters, those who are a little frazzled after a day with neither food nor water.

APRICOT BRANDY. A cordial, the basis of which is (or should be) brandy flavoured with fresh or dried apricots and sweetened with sugar. It is compounded in England, France, Holland and, better than anywhere else, in Hungary, where apricots are plentiful and inexpensive. Strictly speaking, most apricot brandies sold as such are apricot liqueurs, whereas the Hungarian *barack palinka* is a true apricot brandy, distilled from the juice, pulp and kernel of fresh apricots and unsweetened. Kecskemet in southern Hungary is the centre for *barack* production.

APRICOT GLAZE. This glaze is used either over fruit cakes to hold the garnish of fruit and nuts on the lower portion of sponge cakes before a filling is added, or over uncooked pastry cases which are to be filled with a fruit or even custard filling.

¼ lb. dried apricots
1 cup (1¼) water
¾ cup (1) corn syrup

Put the apricots into a bowl, cover with the water and soak overnight. Cook them in the same liquid until very soft. Drain the liquid through a fine sieve, rubbing through with it half the apricots. Measure the purée. There should be about ½ cup (⅔). Return this to the pan and stir in the corn syrup. Bring to a rapid boil and boil rapidly for 2–3 minutes, or until the mixture is clear.

Take the pan from the heat and use the glaze immediately, quickly applying it on the cake or pastry with a brush. If liked, the decoration may be applied after the first coating of glaze and then another swiftly applied over the decoration. If any glaze is left over, if it is dried, it can be stored. Before using again the glaze must be brought once more to boiling point. This quantity should be sufficient to double coat some 12 to 14 pounds of fruit cake.

The left-over apricots can be used in some other dish.

AQUA VITAE. Literally this means water of life. It is a Latin phrase applied to liqueurs especially the brandies. In the 14th century *aqua vitae* could mean a distillation of wine which had been four times rectified but more often referred to as just spiritous drink. As so nicely expressed by William Younger in *Gods, Men and Wine,* it was the alchemists of a superstitious past from whose 'preoccupation with medieval spirits was the discovery of modern spirits' for it was they who first made brandy. Drinks like the French *eau-de-vie*, Swedish akavit and Scottish whisky have earned this appellation but among the many names given to such drinks some are contradictory. The German expression Schnapsteufel, brandy devil, hardly conforms with the water of life.

AQUAVIT. See AKAVIT.

ARAB BREAD. Arab bread is made both leavened and unleavened and there are several varieties. One of the nicest is the flat, round and non-porous type, which is used rather like a plate, and filled with hot mutton kebabs. It is a meal in itself.

Another slightly larger bread, not quite so thick, is used as a spoon: bits of it are broken off and used for scooping up meat and vegetables. Very popular is the almost paper-thin bread, which keeps fresh for quite a long time. Although at first glance it looks as tempting as parchment paper, it proves on further acquaintance to make good eating. The Arabs often sprinkle their bread with water to make it soft, for they prefer it that way.

Two other main types of bread, both with yeast, are: a plain round or oval shape which when freshly made is soft and pliable, and a flattened whetstone-shaped roll about a foot in length.

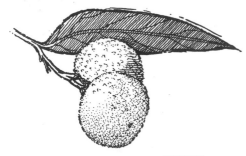

ARBUTE

ARAB COFFEE. True Arab coffee is taken without sugar and milk 'as black as night, as bitter as death and as hot as love'. Coffee as a beverage was first used in Arabia as early as the 15th and 16th century and its stimulating and sleep-dispelling qualities were early appreciated by the Mufti of Aden. According to one writer, the dervishes of the Yemen took it to help them remain awake during long hours of prayer.

In the Arab countries the preparation and the drinking of coffee is a ceremonial ritual, old in tradition and practised today as it was several centuries ago. In the towns, the drinking of coffee is still a sign of true Arab hospitality, both giving and accepting, and the preparation is rather more on the Turkish lines than the desert Arab fashion. Even so, the coffee beans are usually ground at home, in a shining brass grinder which reduces the over-roasted beans to a fine black powder.

Generally Arabs flavour their coffee with a spice. Often it is cardamom, and the whole pod is used, first washed and slightly bruised, not crushed, but rubbed between the palms of the hands until the flavour begins to come out. Other families simply use cloves, lightly crushed but still whole, while a rich family will add a small amount of saffron to the coffee or even ambergris in Egypt.

ARAB TEA. The making of tea in the Arab countries is still considered an important branch of the culinary art. A gleaming samovar with its lighted charcoal is brought into the room and set on the table. With patience you wait until the water boils and pour it from the tap at the side of the samovar over tea leaves in a china pot, in the usual manner. The teapot is then put on top of the samovar or on top of the flue through which the charcoal fumes escape, and left to stew. When it is required it is poured out into thin, narrow-waisted glasses, *istikhans*, which stand on small saucers. It is usually served far sweeter than many of us like, with at least $\frac{1}{2}$ inch of sugar in the bottom of the glass.

ARACHIS. See PEANUT.

ARBUTE. The anglicized name of the *arbutus* or strawberry tree. This is a shrub which grows freely in the southern part of the United States, Mexico, southern Europe, the Canary Islands and Killarney, Ireland. It owes its name to its fruit which is similar in size, shape and colour to the true strawberry. Its flavour is reminiscent of the strawberry but it has neither its aroma nor its melting flesh. It is, however, a pleasant enough fruit and used in Italy and in the south of France to make a spirit. The French also produce a sweet liqueur from the fruit called *crème d'arbouse*.

ARCA. A bivalve mollusk commonly known as *arch*. It is a sort of whelk or small shellfish. Its shell is dark and it is found on all the coasts of France. It is eaten raw or cooked, in much the same manner as mussels.

ARCHBISHOP'S PUNCH. See PUNCH.

ARCHESTRATUS. A Greek philosopher whose book *Gastrology* was a culinary masterpiece. He wrote for 'immortal Greece' and stated his precepts with the zeal of a sublime legislator. He travelled widely in his search for new recipes and new luxuries to delight his table. One of the sadnesses of his life was that he could not eat the things he liked all the year round (would he have liked our frozen and canned foods?), but he brightened when he remembered there was nothing to prevent him talking of all the dishes he liked all the year round. Many of his recipes, which must be some of the oldest in the world – he was writing round 350 B.C. – are said to be still in use in Greece today.

ARCHIDUC, À L'. French culinary name applied to a great number of preparations all of which are seasoned with paprika and blended with cream.

ARCHIMAGEROS. This was the ancient Greek name for what is called today *chef de cuisine*. We in the Western world owe a great deal to Greek cooking, and it is not often realized that many world-famous dishes, thought to be of either

French or Italian origin, are really Greek.

Cooking in ancient Greece was elevated to an art. We owe to them aristology, or the art of dining. To the Greeks also belongs the honour of producing the sages of the kitchen, Orion, who invented white sauce; Lampriadas, who discovered brown sauce. It was a Greek from Rhodes, Agres, who first thought of filleting fish, or so we are told.

ARECA NUT. Nut of the tall areca palm (betel-nut palm) which looks like a slim coconut palm, probably originating in Malaysia but now cultivated over all the hot, damp coastal regions of Asia, with a wide distribution in India. Betel-nut is the fruit of the areca palm, universally chewed by the people of Asia. Mastication is considered to sweeten the breath, strengthen the gum, and tone the digestion. It has a vaguely narcotic effect and produces a copious flow of brick-red saliva which stains the teeth and gums.

The nuts hang in clusters below the leaves. Their outer skins are orange and red in colour and about $1\frac{1}{2}$ inches long. The nut looks rather like a large fawn nutmeg with white flesh. It is used principally wrapped in betel leaf and chewed to aid digestion. Also used as a dentifrice, first being burnt to charcoal and then pounded. See also BETEL-LEAF.

ARGENTEUIL. As a culinary term in French, the word *argenteuil* means a garnishing of asparagus. In French opinion the asparagus cultivated in the Argenteuil region, in the Seine-et-Oise, is the best in the world, enjoying a world-wide reputation with no rivals. See ASPARAGUS.

ARGENTINE SQUASH. *(Zapallito de Tronco).* A squash or marrow, also known as the *avocadella*, and considered to be a good substitute for the avocado pear. It is pinkish-orange in colour and about the size of a grapefruit. Its flesh is firm and smooth and of a buttery texture.

ARGENTINE WINES. The Argentine Republic is one of the most important of the wine-producing nations of the world as far as output is concerned. Wines were first produced there in 1556 from European vines brought via Chile, but a large Italian immigration in the 1880s brought a fillip to wine production. The great majority of the Argentine wines are red table wines, but there are also many other wines made, still and sparkling, beverage and dessert wines, vermouths and brandies. Wine making in the Argentine is an important and up-to-date industry, not an art.

ARISTAEUS. The son of Apollo and the nymph Cyrene. He was worshipped in ancient Boeotia, Thessaly, Arcadia and Thrace. He was the protector of herdsmen, a teacher of bee-keeping and olive-tree cultivation and was also considered to have been the giver of cheese.

ARISTOLOGY. A Greek word meaning the science or art of dining.

ARLÉSIENNE, À L'. The French culinary term for three different sorts of garnitures, all having in common, tomatoes.
1. Small tomatoes stuffed with rice pilau, large stuffed olives, anchovy butter and new potatoes.
2. Sautéed tomatoes, fried onion rings, and fried aubergines.
3. Whole peeled, stewed tomatoes with fried chicory hearts.

ARMADILLO. Not one of the world's most beautiful beasts – the body and head are encased in armour of bony plates – but one which in recent years has become the target of the gourmets. Its flesh is slightly musky and it needs to be cooked with plenty of spices and in good strong wine. Both a clear and thick soup is made from its meat.

ARMAGNAC. The name of the brandy distilled from wine made in the Gers département, in southwest France, chiefly in the district of Condom. There are three main qualities of armagnac, the *grands, fins,* and *petits Armagnacs.* The distinctive flavour of armagnacs is highly prized by some people, who prefer a good armagnac to an equally good cognac, but it is generally acknowledged that the best armagnacs cannot compete with the best cognacs for finesse and breed.

ARMORICAINE. This is not to be confused, as it so often is, with *à l'américaine.* Amorica was the name of the part of Gaul now called Bretagne or Brittany. It is the Roman name, derived from two Celtic words meaning 'seaside', for the land of the Armorici. The culinary term à l'Armoricaine is applied to many French dishes originating from Armorici. As a confusing example, fillet of sole armoricaine is poached sole fillets garnished with poached oysters, soft roes and coated with a *sauce américaine.*

ARMORICAINES. This is the French name for a particularly choice variety of Brittany oyster.

AROMA. In culinary terms this word describes the fragrance of various dishes and wines. It is a word with greater strength than smell or odour, which do not necessarily imply something that also tastes good as does aroma. Nor can one talk glibly of the 'perfume' of food – although we talk of the

AUSTRALIAN WINES: grapes being harvested in New South Wales.

ARECA NUT

ARMADILLO

'bouquet' of wine. Aroma is the right word and it is right and proper that the culinary art should have its own word to describe itself. We talk of the aroma of coffee, the aroma of a stew, of meat roasting in an oven – no, curiously roast meat has a smell, it never is an aroma.

AROMATIC BITTERS. These are alcoholic drinks, sometimes with as high as 40 per cent alcoholic strength, possessing a quite distinctive aroma and taste, as well as less obvious medicinal properties supposed to whet the appetite and help the digestion, hence suitable before and/or after meals. Such are Abbott's aged bitters (U.S.A.), Amer Picon (France), Angostura (Trinidad), Boonekamp (Holland), Campari (Italy), and Underberg (Germany).

ARRACACHA or APIO. A South American plant more commonly called *apio*. It grows in the Andes and also in North America. Its roots are very farinaceous and valued as a food. Arracacha is cooked in most of the ways suitable for potatoes, yams and sweet potatoes; fried, boiled and baked. The roots are also dried and ground to produce a flour which is similar to arrowroot.

ARRACK, ARACK, RAKI. A name widely used in Asia for a fiery spirit generally of local or village manufacture. The word is derived from the Arabic *araq* meaning sweat and juice; also *araq at-tamr,* the (fermented) juice of the date. In Mongolia and Manchuria the spirit is distilled from grain. In Indonesia it is distilled from rice and molasses; called toddy in India, it is the fermented sap of sundry palms. The Turkish type is *raki*, where, as elsewhere in the Middle East, it is distilled from must, except in Iraq where dates are used.

In the Middle East and the Balkans it is known under different names, *raki* in Turkey, *ouzo* in Greece, *zibib* in Egypt, *arrack* in the Lebanon, Syria, Iraq and Jordan, and *mastika* in Bulgaria. In all these regions it is flavoured with aniseed, and when water or ice is added the liquid turns milky-white in colour, and is greatly superior to

the rougher brews known under this name in the Far East.

ARROWROOT. The product of a tropical plant of which the root is used. This is ground and dried in the sun and then powdered to make a highly nutritive form of starch or fine flour. When this is combined with water or other liquid it swells and is more easily digested than other farinaceous forms of food. Formerly it was used a great deal for young children and invalids. It is also used as a thickening for soups, gravies, sauces and puddings, but only half as much arrowroot is needed to produce the same result as with flour. For making milk puddings it is used in the same manner as cornflour (cornstarch) and in the same proportions. It is particularly good for thickening clear liquids as it does not cause clouding in the same way as flour and cornflour do. In this respect it is rather like potato flour. There are arrowroot wine biscuits and plain arrowroot biscuits, both extremely light, digestible and palatable.

The name arrowroot is curious and there are several explanations for it. Some say it was so named by Central American Indians who used the root as a cure to absorb poison from wounds made by poison arrows. Another explanation is the use of the root as an arrow poison. The third and more likely explanation is that it is an approximation of its American Indian name *araruta,* meaning 'flour-root'.

The best arrowroot comes from Bermuda but it is scarce and expensive. Most of the arrowroot we see today comes from the West Indian island of St Vincent where there is a thriving arrowroot industry.

Brazilian arrowroot is better known as tapioca (which see) and there is the Oswega arrowroot of the United States which is generally prepared from maize.

ARROZ CON POLLO. A dish of rice and chicken, very popular in Spain, but one of many similar Spanish dishes. It is cooked with tomatoes, red and green sweet peppers, and garnished with peas

BARBEQUE.

and either young artichokes or asparagus tips.

ARSAC. See BORDEAUX WINES.

ARTICHOKE. A thistle, a native of Europe and North Africa, which has been cultivated for so many centuries that it has improved beyond recognition. It thrives in every part of the world other than the tropics and the Arctic, and, in the opinion of some experts, nowhere better than in California. In the United States artichokes are in season most of the year, in Europe only from June to September.

However, the artichoke had its critics. Pliny asked, with some disgust, why people paid good money for thistles. Much, much later, in the 17th century, they had acquired a reputation for being an aphrodisiac and any wandering basker around the Pont Neuf had only to mention the name artichoke to arouse a dirty snigger.

Nevertheless, the artichoke survived its critics and came to Britain, curiously in the 17th century, where, it must be admitted, it has had a slow passage – and no snigger – and even today cannot be described as either well known or generally liked in this country.

There are three distinct types of plant bearing the name artichoke, and it is curious how this happened, for they are not related. The real artichoke is the globe artichoke, sometimes called the leafy artichoke from the pointed scaly covering of the floweret, a sort of petal which is part of the edible portion of the plant. Then there is the Jerusalem artichoke (which see) and finally the Japanese or Chinese artichoke (which see).

The cardoon (which see), which is regarded by some authorities as a variety of the globe artichoke, and by others as a distinct species, is also of ancient origin. It grew at Carthage and was described by Pliny, also by Dioscorides.

The choke in a globe artichoke needs some explanation. By this is meant the fine growth, almost hair-like in appearance, in the middle of the artichoke, which would develop into a flower if allowed to grow. This portion is not edible. In plain boiled artichoke, which is served whole, it is easy, after you have pulled off all the leaves one by one and dipped them into a butter sauce to eat, to cut out the choke before coming to the *fond*, or bottom, which is the most delicate part of the whole artichoke. It is this part which is so often taken from the artichoke and sold in cans or bottles ready for eating.

ARTICHOKE, Boiled.

Give the artichoke a good – but very good – rinsing under the tap to make sure that all grit is out. Rub a little lemon on the stalk to stop it from going black. Put into a pan with plenty of water,

certainly enough to cover the artichokes completely. Add salt and cook for 45 minutes if the artichokes are large, and 30 minutes if they are small.

Take from the pan with a perforated spoon. Turn them upside down to ensure that they are not filled with water, and serve very hot with plenty of melted butter sauce. As there is always a pile of leaves from eating artichokes, it is a good idea to place a large bowl on the table to collect them.

When the leaves are finished, take a fork or a pointed small knife and, holding the tuft or choke between the thumb and fingers, drive the fork into the bottom and lift up the choke. It should come away neatly in your fingers. The bottom, which you will now meet, is the most delicious part of all, meaty and tender. Eat this with the fork.

ARTICHOKES, Japanese or Chinese

These are small tubers which one writer described as looking like 'petrified worms'. In France, where they are popular, they are called *crosnes du Japon* (and *du Chine*). They are easily cooked and, although most recipe books suggest they should be peeled before cooking, this is not necessary as their skins are so thin.

Wash and gently scrub the artichokes and drop them into boiling, salted water. Cook until tender, about 20 minutes. Drain, peel if liked, although the skin is so thin it can be eaten, return the artichokes to the pan and reheat in butter or add béchamel or lemon sauce. Also, they may be served with lemon juice and a sprinkling of paprika pepper. Serve hot.

ARTICHOKE, Jerusalem.

These are not artichokes at all but the tubers of a species of sunflower and came by their name in an odd roundabout manner. The Italian name for sunflower is girasole which was corrupted by the British into Jerusalem. It was not known in Europe until after the discovery of the New World for it is a native of Canada and the upper valleys of the Mississippi, where it was cultivated by the indigenous peoples for the sweet flavour of its farinaceous tubers. It was brought to Europe by travellers, and has since become a popular vegetable on the Continent, although in Britain it has lost favour in the last 50 years. It was called Canadian potato.

ARTILLERY PUNCH. See PUNCH.

ARVA. See KAVA.

ASADO. The Argentine form of barbecue, but usually a side of sheep or the ribs of an ox, skewered and slowly roasted in the open. In the restaurants of urban districts, *asado* merely means a 'roast'.

ASCIUTTO. The name used in Italy, more particu-

ASPARAGUS   ARTICHOKES (globe, Japanese, Jerusalem)

larly in Sicily, to describe a dry or sharp wine.

ASHBERRY. See ROWANBERRY.

ASHBERRY JELLY. See ROWAN JELLY.

ASPARAGUS. This almost universal favourite vegetable has a long although intermittently recorded history. How it developed from a wild vegetable to the luxury item of today is not known, except that asparagus was already an established and cultivated plant in the 2nd century B.C.

It was the ancient Greeks who first used asparagus as a vegetable and gave it its present name. Theirs was the variety which grew, and still grows, wild on the Mediterranean coast. Later the Romans took it and cultivated it in their gardens, priding themselves on the thick white stems. Even so, the plant was not really cultivated to any great extent until the 16th and 17th centuries. Charles Lamb said of asparagus, 'it still seems to inspire gentle thoughts', although this was not always so, for the controversy that has raged between the two schools of thought, white or green asparagus, has not always been gentle.

France was the home and champion of the famous white asparagus of Argenteuil, where the plant is brought to maturity underground and kept from becoming green. It is the white asparagus which reigns supreme; it is, say French experts, more tender and delicate than the green.

On the other hand, the exponents of the green asparagus ask with scorn, how can anyone prefer white asparagus to the green which has gained its delicate flavour from the sun?

Asparagus did not arrive in England until the early 17th century. Pepys, among others, testified his love of this delicious vegetable. In 1815 asparagus tongs were invented. The early forms of its name in England were sperage, sparage, sparagras, then a corruption into sparrowgrass, and, in fact, to use the correct word asparagus had, recorded a writer in 1791, 'an air of stiffness and pedantry'.

All asparagus must be washed carefully for much of it grows in sandy soil and the tips are often filled with grit. The stalks can be washed in warm water and the tips gently brushed with a soft brush. If the stalks are large, they should be thinly peeled. This can be done with the peeling knife used for potatoes. Any tough ends should be snapped off – they can be put aside used later as a flavouring in a soup.

To cook asparagus:

There are special asparagus saucepans on the market, deep and narrow, but failing this use a double boiler. Gently tie the asparagus in a bundle. Bring the water in the lower portion of the double boiler to the boil, add salt, and place the asparagus in it, upright. Cover the pan with the top half of the boiler inverted so that this encloses the stems. In this way the stalks of the asparagus boil in the water, and the tips merely steam.

Asparagus cooks quick, in 15–20 minutes. The ancient Romans had a saying, attributed to Augustus, 'do it quicker than you can cook asparagus'.

Serve with melted butter, and be generous with it. Asparagus is eaten with the fingers. With the green asparagus, very little of it is wasted; but with the white asparagus, a good deal of the thick white stalk is too tough and fibrous to be eaten.

ASPARAGUS PEA. This is neither a pea nor has it any connection with asparagus. However, the flavour of the pods, which are eaten whole, has something which is suggestive of both the pea and asparagus combined. The plant grows rather like dwarf peas, on twiggy branches, and reaches in a good summer about 18 inches in height. The pods are ready for eating when about an inch long, although many people prefer to wait until they are as much as three inches long. At this stage, however, they are a bit stringy and should be eaten with the fingers like asparagus.

This vegetable is considered an epicure's choice and nothing should detract from its flavour. Boil the still tender young pods in salted water; they will take 10–15 minutes to cook. Drain and serve with melted butter poured over them.

ASPIC. This is the name given to the transparent, light-coloured jelly in which fish, meat, poultry and vegetables are often served. The jelly has a savoury flavour as it is prepared from stock flavoured with vegetables, herbs etc. The stock is strained two or three times and cleared with the whites of eggs before it is allowed to set.

Aspic has many uses. It can be used as a garnish, mixed with mayonnaise to thicken it, to mask varying meats, fish and vegetable dishes, and to set into savoury moulds.

Aspic is sold in powdered form and instructions to use it are given on the packet. While this cannot be as good as home-made aspic, it can be improved if a good clear stock is used in its preparation instead of water.

ASSAM. A province in northeast India, Assam is one of the most important tea producing areas in India. Teas made in this area are generally referred to as 'Assams'. The tea is generally hard and flinty, made from a well-made leaf of greyish-black colour with a handsome gold tip in the higher grades. They are rich heavy teas sought after for their strength, grip, pungency and roughness to produce a strong flavourful brew. They are used for blending with less pungent teas for a milder flavour.

ASSIETTE ANGLAISE. The French culinary name of a selection of cold meats served on the same plate; it should always include a slice of York ham, one of ox tongue, one of underdone sirloin; sometimes a slice of brawn and sometimes, also a slice of galantine.

ASTI SPUMANTI. See ITALIAN WINES.

ATHENAEUS. A Greek writer born in Naucratis, Egypt, in the reign of Marcus Aurelius and he was still living towards the year A.D. 228 when Alexander Severus reigned. Although a native of Naucratis he lived in Rome and in his famous book *Deipmosophistai* (*Specialists in Dining* or the Banquet of the Learned) he described many methods of cooking and serving food as used in Greece today. He wrote of sprinkling herbs over fish or grilled meats and of sauceboats full of oil and vinegar. Even the *keftedes* were mentioned by him. The book is a fund of erudition giving us a glimpse into the foods and even the flowers of his day.

ATHÉNIENNE, À L'.
1. French culinary name for various garnishings or preparations which include onions, egg-plants, tomatoes and pimientos cooked in olive oil.
2. Larded and braised meat garnished with fried eggplants, served with *sauce Madère*.

ATHOL BROSE. This drink of whisky, oatmeal, honey and cream would appear to be the national drink of Scotland.

ATTELET. This word has been often incorrectly used to describe small skewers on which various bits of meat are threaded and then grilled. To be precise, attelets are small utensils shaped like a pin or skewer with ornamental tops.

ATTEREAU, EN. An *attereau* is a skewer but the word is also used to describe a particular dish. Usually *attereaux* is served as hors d'oeuvre, but accompanied by a garnish it can be served as a small entree or main dish. The dish is similar to *brochette* cooking, except that the items cooked are first dipped into a sauce, rolled in breadcrumbs and then cooked in deep fat. The *attereaux* can be cooked on wooden skewers and then transferred to silver ones for elegance or they can be pushed off their skewers before sewing.

Sweet dishes can also be prepared *en attereau* the method being the same as for the savoury variety.

AUBERGINE. Aubergine, egg-plant, egg apple, garden egg, *patliçan, brinjal*, it is all the same, the fruit of a plant which is native to southern Asia. Its exact history is not known but it has been on record for centuries. It is one of the great vegetables of the world and it is probable that India was its natural habitat, although it was known to the ancient Egyptians.

The aubergine can be long and thin, like a sausage, pear-shaped or completely round. It varies in size from very small to something resembling a football. Its colour ranges from white to yellow, from almost black purple to the palest mauve. The more usual are the purple varieties. There are even small ivory-white aubergines which look exceedingly like eggs. They are rather dull in flavour but a heap of them piled pyramid-fashion on a silver dish makes a most unusual and attractive centre-piece for the dining table.

The aubergine must surely be one of the most popular vegetables in the world, for it is eaten throughout the Far East, the Near East, Europe and the Latin countries and the Americas. Considered at one time by the ancients as poisonous, wits dubbed it '*mala insana*' the 'raging apple' because they believed it to cause insanity as well as being poisonous. It was from this erroneous notion of its unpleasant qualities came the custom of soaking the aubergine in cold, salted water for hours before cooking it. This modern cooks have discovered is not necessary, although still many cooks prefer to sprinkle sliced or chopped aubergine generously with salt for some hours and leave it in

AUBERGINES

a colander with a plate and a weight on top. This helps to rid the aubergine of some of its bitterness, also some of its excess liquid, therefore needing less fat to fry it with.

Aubergine can be cooked whole in its skin, peeled, sliced or chopped. In Turkey and the Balkans aubergines are served *en brochette*. Turkey has one of the most famous aubergine recipes in the world *Imam Bayildi* or the fainting Imam. Aubergine can be sliced, fried in deep fat, drained and then served with a dressing of ice-cold yoghourt – another recipe from Turkey. It is cooked with mutton, in the manner of the Near East, and it combines well with left-overs.

Whatever the shape or size or colour, aubergines must be firm and of uniform colour. Those which are soft, flabby and shrivelled should be avoided as they have been kept overlong.

POOR MAN'S CAVIAR.

This so-called caviar is popular in almost all those countries where the aubergine flourishes. Throughout the Balkans there are versions of it, some more highly flavoured than others. The most important thing is that the aubergines are burned over charcoal or thrown directly on to the hot coals of a charcoal grill and allowed to cook until the skin is black, literally burnt and will peel off easily This procedure can be done over a gas flame if neither ashes nor charcoal is available. The flesh is then diced and mashed or it can be put through a blender.

2 fairly large aubergines, treated as above
oil
1 medium-sized onion, grated
1 peeled and seeded tomato, finely chopped
a little green pepper, finely chopped
salt, pepper

Heat a small quantity of oil and lightly fry the onion until it becomes pinky-brown. Add the tomato, the pepper, salt and pepper. Rub through a sieve. Pound or mash the aubergine, mix with the remaining ingredients, blend thoroughly, pour into a glass dish and thoroughly chill. Serve as a salad with thick chunks of dark brown bread. One tablespoonful (1¼) of lemon juice can be added with

advantage. The consistency is that of a thick mayonnaise.

AU BEURRE. With butter or cooked in butter, tossed or sautéed.

AU BEURRE NOIR. With black or nut-brown butter.

AU BLANC. To keep white in cooking by using a *blanc*, which is acidulated water with white flour and seasoning.

AU BRUN. Cooked in brown sauce.

AU FOUR. To bake in the oven.

AUFSCHNITT. This variety of cold, thinly sliced meats of all kinds, including many kinds of sausages, is extremely popular in Germany where they are bought from the delicatessen shops.

AU GRAS. French term for meat cooked and dressed with a very rich gravy or sauce.

AU GRATIN. To brown in the oven or under a salamander (which see). Also applies to those dishes prepared with a sauce and breadcrumbs and baked in the oven.

AU JUS. A term for dishes of meat dressed with their own juices or gravy.

AU LAIT. With milk or cooked in milk.

AU MAIGRE. An expression used for dishes prepared without meat. Lenten fast-days dishes.

AU NATUREL. Applied to food cooked plainly and in a very simple fashion.

AURORE. See SAUCES.

AU ROUGE. Served with or finished in a red sauce.

AUSLESE. A German word professionally used in the wine trade to mean specially selected grapes picked at vintage time. The best and ripest bunches that are picked. When not merely the bunches of grapes but the ripest berries from each bunch are selected, the names used are *Beerenauslese* or *Trockenbeerenauslese.* (*Spätlese* refers to those grapes picked late.) If the wine qualifies, *Auslese* is sometimes indicated on the label.

AUSONE. See BORDEAUX WINES.

AUSTRALIAN WINES. The birth of Australian wine goes back to a spring day in 1788 when Captain Arthur Phillip, the first governor of New South Wales, thrust a spade into earth just cleared of eucalyptus trees and dense growth to plant grapevines brought in his flagship *Sirius* from Rio de Janeiro and the Cape of Good Hope. Until then the whole continent had not nourished a single grape.

The soil and atmosphere at this virgin spot was good for vines but not for wines and locations were changed as more knowledge of wine-making was obtained, by pioneers who studied in Europe, and it was in 1822 that Gregory Blaxland, the explorer, shipped a quarter pipe (about 31 gallons) of his red wine to London.

Queensland, the youngest of the States, is also the youngest of the wine producers.

The first commercial shipment of Australian wine to Britain arrived in England in 1854. Naturally enough this was small but had reached 703,000 gallons by 1896. From 1925, when Imperial Preference gave Australia an opportunity to compete with fortified wines, until 1939 the average shipment to Britain was about three million gallons a year. World War II caused a drop but by 1962 an average of 1,300,000 gallons of wine was sent to the British market from a total export of 1,678,000 gallons.

An interesting feature of Australian wine is the vast increase in home consumption. In 1962 Australia's population, then 11 million, consumed 12½ million gallons in that year.

AUXEY-DURESSES. See BURGUNDY WINES.

AUSTRIAN WINES. Although Austria does not produce any wine in the class of the great wines of the world, there are many pleasing and distinctive red and white beverage wines from the grapes of the vineyards of Lower Austria, Burgenland, and Styria, the three principal wine-producing districts of Austria. Also just outside Vienna there are some old vineyards where the Viennese (and tourists) go to drink the young wine (*Heurige*).

AU VERT. Served with or in a green sauce.

AVENSAN. See BORDEAUX WINES.

AVGOLEMONO, SOUPA (EGG AND LEMON SOUP). This soup is probably one of the best-known of the Greek soups and is a favourite throughout the Balkans.

4 pints (5) strained chicken stock
salt
3 oz. (½ cup) rice
3 eggs
juice 1 large lemon

Bring the stock to the boil, add salt if required. Throw in the rice and cook until this is tender, about 15 minutes.

Whilst the soup is cooking, prepare an egg and lemon sauce. Beat the eggs well, then gradually beat in the lemon juice and very slowly add 2 cups (2½) of the hot broth. Just before serving the soup, add the sauce, stirring all the while. Simmer until the soup is again hot, cover and let it stand for 5 minutes on the side of the stove.

AVOCADO. This is a tropical fruit at best on its home ground. There are three families of avocado: the West Indian, the Guatamalan, and the Mexican. The fruit is pear-shaped, round or obovate, and some varieties weigh more than three pounds per piece. The skin is a brilliant green which changes in some varieties to red, purple or purplish-black as the fruit matures, and varies from smooth to warty in texture.

The flesh is yellow or a pale green and surrounds a single large seed. The flesh is butter-smooth and this has earned it the name of 'midshipman's butter' or 'subaltern's butter'. It has a fairly bland, almost 'no-taste' flavour although some people feel it is nutty.

The best varieties have very little fibre embedded in the flesh.

All varieties of the avocado are native to tropical America, where they have been grown for centuries. With the exception of the olive, no other fruit has such a large percentage of fat as the avocado.

The name avocado is a corruption. It is derived from the Spanish *ahuacate* or *agucate,* which was in turn derived from the Aztec word *ahucatl.* There have been other spellings as well: *albecata, arragoat, avocato* and alligator pear. The form avocado was first used by Sir Henry Sloane in 1669 who spoke of the avocado or the alligator pear. Both names have continued, although efforts are being made to keep but one, avocado. There are many ways to use avocado; in a salad, as a soup, a sandwich filling, or simply halved and served with a dressing.

AVOCADO

BABA

AY. One of the more important wine-producing communes of the Marne *département*, on the right bank of the river Marne about a mile from Epernay. Its vineyards have produced some of the finest still red wines of Champagne during the past five hundred years, and some of the best sparkling champagne wines during the past hundred years. Most of the Ay grapes are black.

AZAROLE. The Neapolitan medlar, the fruit of a kind of hawthorn which grows freely in all lands of the Mediterranean Basin and in the wild state; it is also cultivated in the Paris region for the sake of its berries, which are used for making preserves and liqueurs.

B

BABA. A popular light, moulded cake made with yeast, flour, sugar, butter, eggs, currants and raisins. According to culinary history, its origin is romantic and is a development of *Kugelhupf* (which see). Babas are made in cylindrical moulds, baked and then soaked in syrup, which is poured over them little by little to make them swell. Lastly, they are steeped in rum or kirsch.

They are supposed to have been invented by Stanislaus Leszczyński, King of Poland, in 1609, when he sprinkled rum on his rather dry *Kugelhupf*. This became his favourite cake and history claims that he christened it Ali Baba, the name of the hero in his favourite story from 'The Thousand and One Nights'. It became the rage in Paris at the beginning of the 19th century, but the Ali was dropped. About 1840 a Parisian pastrycook used the same paste minus the currants changed the shape and called the cake *brillat-savarin*. This too in the course of time lost half its name and became *savarin* (which see). In Turkey it is called 'father's cake'.

BABA GHANOUSH. A well-known Arab dish, roughly translated *La Coquette*, and said to be the invention of a lovely Arab girl in an Ottoman harem. It is a purée of aubergine flavoured with garlic, lemon juice, *tahina* paste (which see), and garnished with pomegranate seeds, chopped mint and paprika.

BACALAO. Spanish name for salted cod.

BACARDI. See RUM.

BACON. Bacon is made by curing the whole sides of specially bred pigs in dry salt or salt dissolved in water. After preserving, the bacon is matured for about three weeks, and it is then ready for sale in a pale state usually referred to as 'green' bacon. This is much milder than the kinds generally eaten in England and America. For a smoky flavour, the bacon is simply hung for a couple of days, after curing, above smouldering sawdust.

The quality of bacon varies according to the breed, age and feeding of the pig and the way in which it has been cured. It also varies according to the cut which is being used. When bought it should be an appetizing pink colour with the fat a clear white. Bacon should be stored in a cool place, and it should keep for 10–12 days in winter. In summer it will not last more than 4–5 days in the larder but will, of course, last longer in a refrigerator if kept well-wrapped. Vacuum packed bacon will keep up to about 10 days. It is always marked with the latest dates by which it is wise to use the packet. It should on no account be kept in a deep freeze as the drying action of freezing is intensified by salt and the meat becomes dehydrated and hard.

BADGER. An inoffensive greyish-brown quadruped with a black and white head, of nocturnal habits which hibernates in cold climates in winter. It is not recognized generally as edible although its flesh is supposed to be rather rich and porky. It is fairly common in England, and has become a favourite character in children's books – Mr Badger is one of the main characters in Kenneth Grahame's *Wind in the Willows*.

Edible or not, there are recipes for the cooking of the badger and from time to time it is said Badger Feasts took place in the bar of an inn in Ilchester, Somerset. Following an old custom, the badger was roasted whole in front of an open fire, while the guests, each with a slice of meat on a slice of bread, sat round drinking ale from old-fashioned horn cups.

A big badger can weigh up to about 30 to 40 lb. A fat autumn badger will provide two hams, which, if properly cured, provide a real and unusual delicacy, say the connoisseurs. The hams must be smoke-dried as well as cured. However, the hind legs are the only portions suitable for those who want to try roasting a badger.

BADIAN. The carminative fruit of the Chinese anise tree. It is known as star anise and Chinese anise (see ANISE).

BAGNA CAUDA. A garlic and anchovy sauce, one of the specialities of Piedmontese cooking.

Heat 4 oz. ($\frac{1}{2}$ cup) butter in an earthenware saucepan and very slightly brown 4 finely chopped cloves of garlic. Add 8 pounded fillets of anchovy and stir these ingredients together with a wooden spoon. Finely-chopped truffles are added. *Bagna cauda* is usually served hot in the pan in which it is cooked, at the table over a spirit lamp. Pieces of uncooked vegetables, such as globe artichokes, crisp celery or chicory, are dipped in it.

BAGNES. A cheese from the Bagnes valley, which is used in the preparation of *raclette* (which see).

BAGOZZO. An Italian cheese, made in and near Brescia. It is one of the numerous varieties of Caciotta, a hard yellow-bodied sharp-flavoured cheese, with the outside often coloured red.

BAGUETTE. In France there is more variety in bread than is often realized. Everyday bread for the household is long and cylindrical, flattened and slashed on top. These loaves are usually called *baguettes* of which there are three main types. *Baguette anglaise, baguette gruau,* which is somewhat darker and thinner than the *anglaise,* and *baguette ficelle* which is like a thin stick. (See BREAD.)

BAILLY, HAUT. See BORDEAUX WINES.

BAIN-MARIE. A large, shallow vessel, round or rectangular in shape containing hot water in which a number of smaller and taller pans can be placed so that the water comes not more than half way up. It is designed to keep delicate dishes, such as custards, sauces etc., hot without spoiling. In French kitchens the bain-marie is usually kept on the side of the large stove, but with gas and electricity it must be placed over the lowest possible heat. A bain-marie also fits in the oven.

Cooking in a bain-marie corresponds to cooking in a double boiler. Practical though the American and British double boiler is, the bain-marie has one advantage in that the water surrounds the pots and therefore gives a gentle heat all over, while with the double boiler there is heat only from the bottom of the pan. Both the bain-marie and the double boiler (which see) are essential utensils in any well-equipped kitchen.

BAKE. To bake is to cook food in an oven, that is, with the hot air all around it. To bake successfully it is imperative to know the heat of the oven. A housewife with long experience is often able to judge the heat of the oven by putting her hand in it, but modern ovens with thermometers are foolproof.

Bread, cakes, pies, tarts, cookies or biscuits are all baked. Nowadays we actually bake our meat, poultry and game, although we still talk of roasting. This is simply a hangover from the days of roasting on a spit in front of the fire. Hams, however, were always said to be baked.

BAKE BLIND. This is to bake a pie shell or other crust shell without its final filling. The pastry shell should be pricked all over with a fork, covered with greaseproof paper and then filled with dried beans, rice or crusts of bread (these last ingredients are kept for this purpose). Bake the pastry shell as the recipe directs, remove the greaseproof paper and the beans towards the end of baking and then complete baking.

BAKING POWDER. The name of a number of mixtures such as carbonate of ammonia used as leavening agents when making bread and all forms of light-textured pastry. They can be made at home or bought commercially as a finished product. Commercial baking powders are composed of sodium bicarbonate plus acids of various kinds. Too much of any raising agent spoils both the texture and the flavour of a cake and it is important to follow the advice given in a recipe. In general 2 teaspoonfuls ($2\frac{1}{2}$) of baking powder to 1 lb. of flour is allowed.

When water is added to baking powder or similar mixture there is a chemical reaction and carbon dioxide is given off aerating the mixture; it is therefore essential that any mixture containing baking powder is cooked as soon as possible after it has been made as in many cases the action of the

BAMBOO SHOOTS

BAGUETTE

baking powder will wear off before the mixture is in the oven. When baking powder is added to flour it must always be thoroughly sifted to get even mixing.

BAKLAVA. This is sweet from Turkey and the Middle East generally. It is a crisp, light and delicate pastry of the *mille-feuille* type and consists of wafer-thin layers of rolled-out pastry so thin that you could read a newspaper through it. Each layer of pastry is spread with melted butter, and the eighteenth layer is then covered with chopped, mixed nuts – pistachio, walnuts and almonds. Another 18 layers are added and each is brushed with butter. The baklava is then cut into diamonds, triangles or any shape the cook prefers, baked in a fairly hot oven and, finally, when taken from the oven drenched in a cold sugar syrup and left to cool completely.

The pastry for this sweet, usually bought ready-made, is called *yufka* in Turkey, *phylo* in Greece, and *fila* in the Middle East.

BALACHAN, BLACHAN, BALACHONG. A characteristic condiment of the Burmese and Malaysian cuisines and sometimes called 'the caviar of the Far East'. It is composed usually of prawns, fresh sardines, chillies and other small fish, allowed to ferment in the sun in a heap and then mashed heavily with salt. Although at first smell it may not meet with the approval of those unaccustomed to it, there are many Europeans who have learned to like it. It has been described thus: 'It is much relished by lovers of decomposed cheese.'

BALDERDASH. This word today means nonsense, trash, etc. but its etymology is amusing for the original meaning was a mixture of posset and curds, for example, or even wine and beer.

BALLOTINE. To be correct, the term ballotine should apply only to meat which has been boned, stuffed and rolled, but it is also frequently applied to dishes which are really galantines. It is a kind

of galantine, normally served as a hot dish but can also be served cold.

BALM. See LEMON BALM.

BALTHASAR. The name for a show or presentation bottle holding 2·80 imperial gallons of wine or the equivalent of 16 ordinary bottles.

BALUT. This is a favourite item of food among Filipinos, consisting of the contents of a fertilized duck egg. It is eaten in one gulp just at the point when the baby duck has begun to form inside the egg. It is reckoned a great delicacy and although non-Filipinos, however adventurous, are loath to try it, once they have done so, they are often converted to its rare flavour.

BAMBOO SHOOTS. The bamboo is a most useful tree for it provides both food and furniture. Bamboo shoots are a favourite food in the Far East and are cooked in a number of different ways. They are sold fresh in Eastern markets, sometimes as a whole root, sometimes shredded, or thinly sliced in rounds. There are two types of shoots, the winter and the spring shoots. Winter shoots are considered tastier than the spring shoots and are also more expensive. When the winter shoots are taken from their hard sheath-like coverings they are a soft creamy colour. They are then boiled in salted water until tender – and the time for cooking varies considerably, depending on the age of the shoots. Spring shoots are darker, harder and woody looking and take much longer to cook. The flavour of the young shoots has been likened to artichokes.

Fresh bamboo shoots are seldom seen outside their native soil but the canned shoots are a fair substitute and do not require much cooking since they have already been cooked before being preserved. They retain their crunchiness. Bamboo shoots are canned with and without salt and, unless a recipe specifies salted bamboo shoots, it is usual to use the unsalted ones as salt can always be added later.

BAMMIES. These are cassava cakes and are extremely popular throughout the Caribbean, where they are bought from the market women or higglers. They are considered very nutritious and cheap. Split into halves, soaked in milk, fried in a little butter and served hot, they are indeed good.

BAMYA. See OKRA.

BANANA. 'The banana may be nutritious but it is prosaic. It is among fruits what the cod is among fish.' So wrote Robert Lynd, the gentle essayist.

An unkind remark, for the banana is one of nature's finest gifts to man. It is one of the best-known fruits in the world and was once classed as a luxury. It is a splendid fruit with a prophylactic skin which encloses a sweet and delicious pulp. In those countries where it grows, it is regarded as a staple food and it is well known that a diet of banana will sustain the human body for a long time. There are over 300 varieties, all growing in hot, damp atmospheres.

The early history of the banana is closely woven with mythology. We are told that the serpent who tempted Eve in the Garden of Eden (Paradise) hid in a bunch of bananas, and therefore early classifiers of the fruit call it *Musa paradisiaca* or fruit of Paradise, as well as *Musa sapientum,* fruit of knowledge. The name banana has been taken from an African tribal name. Formerly it was called 'Apple of Paradise' or oddly 'Adam's fig'. Again, originally the name banana was used only for those varieties which are eaten raw, and plantain for the cooking varieties. Nowadays there is less clear differentiation and in India all bananas and plantains are called by the latter name.

BANANA FIGS

Peel two dozen or more bananas and remove the threads. Arrange in neat rows on a wooden platter or tray and leave them covered with a piece of cheese-cloth for 14 days in the hot sun, turning from time to time. Bring in at night. At the end of 14 days they will be a rich dark brown and shrunken to at least a third of their normal size. They can be served as they are or cut into small pieces and put into cakes and puddings.

BAKED BANANAS

Peel slightly green-tipped bananas, sprinkle with lemon juice, and place in a buttered dish and brush lightly with melted butter. Bake in a moderate oven until tender or when they can be easily pierced with a fork.

BANANA FLOUR. A flour made from dried, specially selected bananas. It is a pale greyish colour with a pleasing aroma. It is highly nutritious, easily digested and suitable as a food for both children and invalids. Banana flour can be made into a palatable thin gruel by the addition of milk or water and eaten with cream.

BANANE, CRÈME DE. A distinctly sweet, yellow liqueur made from macerated ripe bananas and either brandy or some neutral spirit. It is made in various countries, including Australia.

BANBURY CAKES. A speciality of the market town of Banbury in Oxfordshire. At its best this pastry cake is an oval piece of exquisite flaky pastry with a mixed fruit filling 'unrivalled', say its protagonists, 'in England to this day'. To get a genuine Banbury cake is not as simple as it was and there are many imitations. In the old days they used to be carried through the town wrapped in a clean white cloth in round wicker baskets.

BANG. An old English beverage made primarily of cider and ale, and not to be confused with *bhang*, sometimes spelt *bang*, which is hemp or hashish. Mix 1 pint (1¼) of warm ale with 1 pint (1¼) of cider, add powdered sugar with grated nutmeg and ginger to taste and finally mix in two large jiggers of gin or whisky. Serve warm.

BANGERS. Affectionate slang name for fried sausages in Britain.

BANNOCK. The Scottish name for a variety of fairly large round cakes. Some are made with barley, others with oatmeal, wheat or pease, according to different localities and tastes.

There are also some superstitions associated with them. Beltane bannocks belong by lore to the shepherds and are eaten on the first day of May, Lammas bannocks on the first day of autumn, Hallowmas bannocks during the first days of winter and St Bride's bannocks on the first day of spring. Different bannocks are baked for different occasions, especially for Hallowe'en and the four quarter days.

However, although custom has led us to believe that bannocks are of Scottish origin (and it would appear that custom is right) history relates that as far back as King Alfred (who is supposed to have burned some cakes) bannocks were eaten throughout the British Isles.

The variety in bannocks is quite pronounced. For example, the Selkirk bannock is a fruit cake, while the Pitcaithly bannock is a kind of festive shortbread. The Aran Isenach, made in the Scottish Outer Isles, is a mixture of flour and fine Indian corn, shortened with butter, while Sauty bannocks have oatmeal, milk, eggs and golden syrup. In many Scottish rural areas bannocks often take the place of bread.

BANON. A strongly flavoured goats' milk cheese

BANANA   BAOBAB TREE   BARBEL

made by peasants in Provence. The cheeses are wrapped in herbs (often rosemary), which gives them their flavour, dipped in *eau-de-vie-de-marc* and then placed in stone jars. They ripen in two months.

BANYULS. One of the most popular of French sweet or dessert wines. The vineyards of Banyuls cover the lower slopes of the eastern Pyrenees, on the French side, and produce both black and white grapes from which there are three grades of wine made: a red wine, which is made from black grapes, fermented with the husks and fortified before being wholly fermented; the *rosé*, also made from black grapes, but fermented away from the husks before being fortified; the white, made from white grapes and fortified before being wholly fermented. Locally, the white wine is called Banyuls, the other two being known as Grenache, and, when old in bottle, Rancio.

BAOBAB. A remarkable tree, indigenous to Central Africa, of medium height but of enormous girth. It grows quickly, yet is one of the longest living trees. It has white kidney-shaped fruit with a spongy acid pulp which is mealy and edible and from it is made a cooling drink which promotes perspiration and alleviates fever. This is a popular beverage wherever the baobab grows.

BAPS. Small round loaves of very soft white bread, the breakfast roll of Scotland. They belong, like the bannock, to Scottish cooking but are usually found in other parts of the British Isles as well. Aberdeenshire claims to make the best. There are two kinds, the floury and the buttery bap.

BARA BRITH. Bara Brith is a traditional Welsh cake, which, literally translated, means, 'speckled bread'. There are two kinds of Bara Brith, both being popular; the rich fruit cake variety, which is eaten at Christmas time, and the bread or bun variety made with yeast and eaten with butter.

BARBADES, CRÈME DES. An old favourite among French liqueurs; it has brandy as a basis and

various citrus fruits and spices for its bouquet and flavour.

BARBADOS CHERRY. See ACEROLA.

BARBADOS WATERS. An early English name for rum.

BARBEL. A river fish of Britain and other parts of Europe. It closely resembles the carp and is recognized by the barbels some of which are at the end of the snout, others at the corner. It does not have a good culinary reputation as its flesh is generally reckoned insipid, although if carefully treated or served with an elaborate sauce it can be improved.

BARBEQUE (American **BARBECUE**). Dryly described in various dictionaries as 'social gatherings where animal carcasses are roasted whole', the institution of the barbecue has become a way of life in America. On fine days, and especially in the hot summer months, the smoke from barbecue fires has become a familiar sight throughout the country. Everthing from fish to the ubiquitous hamburger is cooked out of doors over charcoal. Restaurants throughout the land proudly advertise 'Charcoal-grilled Steak and Lobster', which is just another form of the barbecue. A string of industries has sprung up to cater for the home cook who, proud of his culinary skill, trades his secret marinades and sauces with other neighbourhood chefs.

Basically, however, barbecueing is a simple method of preparing food, requiring only heat generated from hard wood, or hardwood products, without flames, good ingredients and careful attention. The basic implement in America is the brazier, which can range from a plain firebowl with a grill above, to the elaborate stove on wheels, with an electrically driven rotisserie and an oven with heat control mechanism. Fuel is generally pulverized hardwood charcoal in the form of briquettes.

BARBEREY. One of the many French cheeses

which resembles Camembert. It is commonly known in France as *fromage de Troyes*, although it derives its name from Barberey near Troyes. It is made from cows' milk while it is still fresh and warm and is coagulated with rennet.

BARBERRY. This is a shrub the red berries of which are made into preserves, relishes, jams and jellies with a pleasantly acid flavour. The common barberry, which is native to Britain, also grows in every part of continental Europe from where it was taken to the United States.

BARCELONA NUT. A Spanish type hazel-nut.

BARDING. When roasting meat, poultry or game a piece of fat bacon is sometimes tied around the meat or bird. This is known as barding: it gives the meat extra succulence and it also means that continuous basting is unnecessary. The bacon is removed a few minutes before the meat is served so that the meat will brown. Barding is necessary only where the absence of natural fat is pronounced, usually in game birds.

BÄRENFANG. A German liqueur the basis of which is neutral spirit and honey; it is flavoured with lime and mullein flowers.

BARFI. A popular candy from northern India, rather like a fudge which is varied by such flavouring as almond and pistachio nuts. A favourite is called 'national flag' barfi as it is made in three colours, green, white and saffron.

BAR-LE-DUC. A town in France which for several centuries has been famed for its red currant preserve. The preserve itself was famous for being made from whole white currants with their seeds removed by hand. Bar-le-Duc preserves are now made from red and white currants as well as other berry fruits and seeds are no longer so painstakingly removed.

BARLEY. One of the first cultivated cereals and known to have been grown in Switzerland during the Stone Age, it is less nutritious than wheat as it has a lower protein content. As it has less gluten it does not mix so easily with water to form a paste or dough and has, therefore, over the past two or three hundred years, gradually been replaced by wheat as the chief grain for bread-making in Europe. It was taken to North America by the early settlers and is now grown extensively throughout that continent and Europe, and in parts of Asia and North Africa.

It is used chiefly for malt production for the brewing industry and for animal foodstuffs.

BARLEY SUGAR. Originally a brittle, stick-shaped sweetmeat made from water in which hulled barley had been boiled for several hours and to which sugar and lemon were added. The modern method omits the barley and uses tartaric acid to achieve a similar flavour and consistency. Another variety contains glucose instead of sugar as an aid to digestion and as a remedy for mild travel sickness.

BARLEY WATER. An easily digestible and nutritious beverage for young children or invalids which is made by boiling ground barley in lightly salted water. When strained and chilled it may be taken by itself or flavoured with fruit juices, such as lemon.

BARLEY WINE. The name given by brewers, when in a poetical mood, to their best brew of beer, known as malt liquor in the United States.

BARM BRACK. A traditional Scottish and Northern Ireland cake or loaf sometimes flavoured with caraway seeds, currants or black treacle but not necessarily with yeast despite the name ('barm' being the froth on fermenting yeast).

BARM YEAST. This is the scum formed on top of malt liquor when fermenting. It is used to set up fermentation and also to leaven bread.

BARNACLE. A marine crustacean which has been defined as 'a type of shrimp with its head glued to some object and which obtains food by kicking passers-by into its mouth'. It is usually thought of as a nuisance to boat owners but, though not easy to prepare, it makes the basis of a clear, shrimp-flavoured soup when boiled in the shell and strained.

BARNACLE GOOSE. See GOOSE.

BAROLO. See ITALIAN WINES.

BARON. See BORDEAUX WINES.

BARON OF BEEF. A noble joint of beef consisting of both sides of the back or a double sirloin, and weighing from about 50 to 100 lbs., according to the size of the animal. It is always roasted but is now rarely prepared except on particularly festive or traditional occasions. It used to be accompanied by a boar's head and other substantial dishes. As a joint, it is one of ancient origin.

BARQUETTES. A French culinary term to describe small oval or boat-shaped tartlets baked in patty-tins. The tartlets are usually but not always baked 'blind', and can be filled with either sweet or savoury fillings as required.

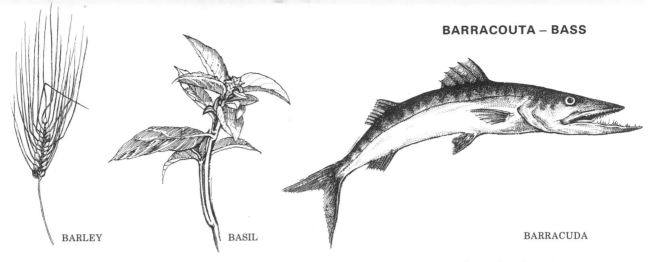

BARLEY BASIL BARRACUDA

BARRACOUTA. A large, rough-scaled, maritime fish, resembling the mackerel, of the family *Thyrsites atun*, and common to the coast of Australia, New Zealand, and South Africa. Commonly called snoek (snook), from the Dutch word for pike. It is valued as a food source and is caught, canned, and sold on a commercial basis in these countries. The flesh of this fish is white, flaky and oily, resembling a tunny (tuna) fish.

BARRACUDA. A pike-shaped, carnivorous fish of the *sphyraenidae* family found in the warm seas of the world. The adults have a tendency to be solitary hunters, while the young fish travel in schools and hunt in packs. The great barracuda of the South Pacific is known to exceed six feet in length and 100 lb. in weight. The barracuda is classified as a game fish, but four species are fished for commercially, the Pacific, the Mediterranean, the Australian and the Great Tropical, found below the Equator in the South Pacific. They are sold as fresh fish or, in many cases, canned and sold under various local names.

BARSAC. See BORDEAUX WINES.

BARSZCZ. This is the Polish spelling of *borsch* (which see).

BAR SPOON. A 'mixing' spoon for drinks, mainly cocktails and fizzy drinks, with a particularly long handle. Shakespeare could never have seen, but surely anticipated one when he wrote: 'He should have a long spoon that sups with the Devil.'

BARTON. See BORDEAUX WINES.

BASELLA. An edible climbing, trailing plant of tropical countries, which is cultivated in certain parts of France. It has been introduced into the United States as a substitute for spinach, which it succeeds in season. It is prepared as spinach and is very mucilaginous when cooked.

BASIL. There are 50 to 60 varieties of basil differing in height, shape and colour. Sweet basil is a bushy plant which grows to a height of 18 inches. Its stems are few, and its leaves are unusual in that each pair of opposite leaves is covered with a bloom yet they glisten on both sides with specks of oil from the reservoirs present. The under surface is slightly downy. When freshly picked the leaves have a flavour similar to cloves but the flavour of dried basil is completely different, being almost curry-like.

Although basil, both in Britain and in the United States, is a neglected herb (it was once an essential flavouring in traditional turtle soup and some sausages), it comes into its own in the warmth of the Mediterranean where it is used to make a delicious sauce, called *pesto* in Genoa and *pistou* in Provence. Its main components are finely chopped basil and crushed garlic and plenty of both (see PESTO).

Sweet basil has its poor relations. Bush or dwarf basil is mainly used for ornamental purposes, but can be used as a flavouring. Lemon basil and curly basil are used both ornamentally and as a flavouring There is also a wild basil which is not a basil at all but a relative of calamint and is sometimes called basil thyme. This too can be used in cooking but it does not have the same flavour as sweet basil.

BASMATI RICE. See RICE.

BASS. A salt-water fish also known as the sea perch and the *bar* (in France), with a liking for fresh water at certain seasons. It is a voracious predatory fish which roams temperate and tropical seas. Gourmets in ancient Rome used to say they could distinguish between a bass caught in the sea at the mouth of the Tiber or between the bridges of the city. They also called it *lupus* meaning wolf because of voracity. It is a fine fish which is not too often seen in British shops. It has a superficial likeness in shape and colouring to the salmon, and in the pink tint of its flesh, but it is not in the least related in the fish family sense. However, in those seaside places where the fishermen sell their wares freshly caught on the beach or in the local fish market bass is given such names as salmon-dace, sea-salmon or white salmon.

The flesh of a bass is firm, lean and delicately flavoured and it retains its texture during cooking. Its skin breaks easily and it is rather bony. Large bass are poached and served with melted butter, *maitre d'hôtel* butter or *sauce hollandaise*. Smaller fish can be grilled, baked or braised or served *à la meunière*. Nearly all ways of cooking salmon can be applied to bass. Heavily spiced sauces should not be used for they will spoil the delicate flavour of the fish. Poached bass is excellent with a *mousseline* sauce and if served cold it can be matched with a green sauce *(sauce vert)* or a nut sauce *(sauce aux noix)*.

BASTE or **BASTING.** To pour or spoon melted fat, butter or liquid over roasting or baking foods.

BATAILLEY. See BORDEAUX WINES.

BÂTARD-MONTRACHET. See BURGUNDY WINES.

BATH BUN. This is a yeast cake or bun of irregular shape containing candied peel, and has a sugar-coated top. When freshly made it is exceedingly good.

BATH CHAPS. The lower cheek pieces of the pig are cured somewhat like bacon as chaps. Although inclined perhaps to be too fat for some tastes, they make an excellent luncheon dish, served cold like ham. Bath chaps were originally the cured cheeks of the local fruit-fed, long-jawed pigs, and the curing was done by experts. Although chaps are made in other parts of Britain the reputation of the Bath chaps has been sustained. The type of pig used for chaps is important, some of the flat-headed pigs being quite unsuitable.

BATH OLIVERS. Large thin, crisp water biscuits popular in England and served with cheese or a glass of wine. They were the invention of Dr William Oliver in the 18th century and were made for him when he was a medical practitioner in Bath. They are still being made in Bath as Fortt's Original Bath Olivers, and sold in long cylindrical tins.

BÂTONS or **BÂTONNETS.** The culinary name of various preparations shaped in the form of sticks. They can be either sweet or savoury, baked or deep-fried.

BATTENBERG CAKE. A cake of two colours, chocolate and pale yellow, almond-flavoured and coated with almond icing.

BATTER. This is a semi-liquid mixture of flour, water and milk or been mixed to such a consistency that it can be beaten or 'battered' or stirred.

Batters may be thick or thin, but even when thick they must be fluid enough to drop easily from the spoon. When they are thin, they should pour like cream from a jug.

When yeast is added to the batter mixture, it becomes a sponge batter, and when a batter is too thick to be spooned or poured, it is called a dough.

Batters are used to coat food for frying, to make pancakes, Yorkshire pudding, etc.

BATTERIE DE CUISINE. The French term for all the cooking utensils required to equip a kitchen, i.e. pots, pans, knives, spoons etc.

BATTUTO. This is the initial preparation in the making of soups and stews in Italian cooking, but more particularly so in Rome. It consists of a mixture of finely chopped onion, garlic, celery leaves and parsley, fried and browned in oil and butter mixed, flavoured with diced fat bacon or ham. The meat, vegetables or broth used in the soup or stew is placed on top of this aromatic foundation.

BAUDEN. A Bohemian sour-milk cheese.

BAUDROIE. One of the French names for the angler (which see) or frog-fish. It is also called *lotte de mer, crapaud de mer* and *diable de mer*.

BAUMKUCHEN. A German tree-shaped cake, on almost every German table at Christmas time. It is extremely decorative but, because of its curious shape, is not a cake which can be baked by the amateur cook. It is covered with a coating of chocolate frosting or of thin fondant and when it is cut it has the effect of layered cake. This layer effect is from the baking.

BAVARIAN CREAM. This was one of the well-known sweet dishes of the past, a soft custard of eggs cooled, mixed with gelatine and whipped cream and flavoured to the cook's taste. It was in the flavouring that cooks, such as Carême, liked to give the pudding special attention. Some cooks used wines or liqueurs, sherries and madeira, port or rum. Others favoured fresh fruit, such as strawberries, raspberries or peaches, and even rose petals. There were Bavarian creams flavoured with nuts, chocolate or simply vanilla.

History does not relate how the Bavarian cream, originally called *bavarois* or *fromage bavarois*, came by its name. One would have thought it might have been simply a Bavarian sweet dish, but this does not seem to be the case.

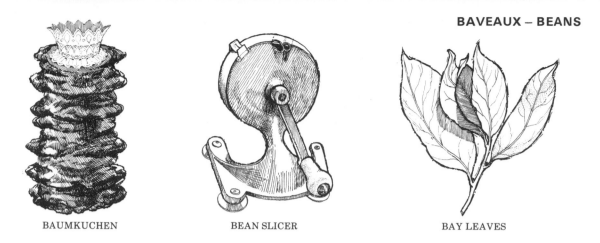

BAUMKUCHEN   BEAN SLICER   BAY LEAVES

BAVEUX. This means 'runny' in French and particularly applies to scrambled eggs or omelettes not completely cooked.

BAY. The bay tree or laurel goes so far back in history it is hard to say where it began. Ovid tells the story of Daphne's transformation into a laurel tree to save her from Apollo, who then adopted the tree as his own. The leaves of the laurel were considered suitable to make into wreaths to crown men of wisdom or conquerors, because of their dedication to the gods of poetry and music.

The bay leaf is among the best known of the kitchen herbs. It is one of the traditional herbs of the bouquet garni (which see), also essential in marinades and court bouillon. It is used to flavour fish, milk custards and puddings.

The bay leaf is similar to the laurel but it should never be confused with a tree called the cherry laurel, the leaf of which has a bitter almond flavour.

Dried bay leaves, unless they are fairly fresh, are useless.

BAYBERRY. This is the popular name of several small shrubs of the species *Myrica*, native to North America and to Britain and known also as candleberry and wax myrtle. The small leaf of California's Sierra sweet bay is used as a flavouring for fish, meats, sauces etc. The flavour is similar to but more subtle than that of the bay leaf.

BAYONNE HAM. See HAM.

BAY SALT. See SEA SALT.

BEANS. Beans have been cultivated by man since the dawn of civilization. For centuries they have been common food in most countries.

One of the oldest beans is the broad bean, also called the Windsor bean and the Longpod. Archaeologists tell us they were cultivated by pre-historic men, which shows their good taste, for the broad bean is considered by many to be among the aristocrats of the bean family.

In Roman times, in the days of the gods, beans were held to be unlucky, connected with death and consecrated to the souls of the departed. The little black spot on their pale skins was considered a sure sign of death. They were nevertheless offered as a sacrifice to the god Apollo but the priests of Jupiter were forbidden to touch them or even mention them.

Beans were used in voting in Roman elections, the white bean being 'for' and the black bean 'against'. When Pythagoras told men to 'abstain from beans' he meant quite simply, keep out of politics or you will get into trouble.

More recently beans were used to figure in Twelfth Night celebrations, for a bean was inserted into the traditional cake and the one who got the bean was made King (or Queen) of the Bean, and master of ceremonies for the evening.

Among the different kinds of bean are:

BROAD BEAN or WINDSOR BEAN. These beans are always (or almost always, for some people maintain that the young pods can be eaten) taken from their pod, which is tough with a thick flannel lining. Cook the beans in salted, boiling water for 15 minutes or until tender. Older beans need blanching for a few minutes in boiling water before being cooked.

DRIED BEANS. Formerly in Britain only the large butter bean or the smaller haricot seemed much in evidence. With the increasing interest in foreign foods, more varieties are in the markets. In the United States the list is longer.

FAVA BEAN. These in America are the broad or Windsor bean of Britain.

FRENCH BEAN. Smaller and more delicate than runner beans, also called snap beans, they need only be topped and tailed before cooking. If not too long, they can be left whole, otherwise snapped into halves.

HARICOT or 'SOISSONS' BEAN. Although most people know haricot beans as dried beans, they are eaten fresh in France and Italy. Cook them in boiling, salted water or stock until tender. Dried haricot beans require overnight soaking.

There are also the pale green haricot or *flageolet* which are a choice variety.

KIDNEY BEAN. Large dark red kidney-shaped beans which are often used for baked beans. It is a matter of regional discussion whether kidney or navy beans make the best baked beans.

LIMA BEAN (Dried). These are shelled Lima beans which have been dried. They are very popular and make some good and inexpensive dishes.

LIMA BEAN (Fresh). There are two classes of Lima beans, the large bean and the baby Lima or butter bean. They are different varieties and their size has no bearing on their tenderness. Many people feel the smaller beans have a more delicate flavour and are usually more expensive. They should be steamed to keep their flavour, although older beans must be blanched in boiling water before being steamed.

Lima beans are of a delicate green colour; if they are moist or shiny, they have already started to spoil.

NAVY BEAN. Small white beans, usually used to make baked beans but many dried beans of varying shapes and sizes come under this name.

OEA BEAN. Black-eyed peas or cow beans, small whitish peas with a black spot are used in the United States, rather more in southern cooking than in the north. Black-eyed peas are an important ingredient in 'Hoppin John' (which see) and some Creole dishes.

PINTO BEAN. A dappled pink bean called by the exploring Spaniards *pinto*, meaning painted, and important in the West. They are the *frijoles* of Mexico.

RUNNER BEAN. Also called scarlet runner and string beans, they are by nature much larger, longer and wider than the French bean and, although even over a foot long, they can still be tender and young. Snip off the 'top and tail' and slice the beans diagonally into thin strips (there are bean slicers to help with this chore). Cook in boiling, salted water until tender.

SOY BEAN. This has been called 'the food of the angels' and it has been known and used in the Orient, where it is indigenous, since 3000 B.C. In spite of its long history, it was unknown in Europe until the end of the 17th century and then was not well known until 200 years later. There are hundred of varieties and millions of acres of soy bean grown throughout the world, for the bean has a high nutritional value and is a rich and cheap source of vegetable protein, with a fairly high fat but low starch content.

BEAR. The family *Ursidae*, a large, heavy, omnivorous animal found throughout the northern hemisphere and some parts of the tropics, but found neither in the African continent (except in the Atlas mountains) nor in Australasia.

All bears are much alike in general outline, with a broad head, extended jaws and massive frame. The heavy paws are equipped with powerful claws and the coat is harsh and shaggy, ranging from palest brown to black. While the bear is not a commercial source of food, it is hunted for sport and the meat is generally considered most palatable, except during the period immediately following winter. In texture it resembles pork but has the darker colouring of beef, with as much fat as well-fed pork. It is prepared in the same way as pork, and one of the outstanding dishes is corned bear.

BÉARN. One of the smallest of the former provinces of France, now mostly the *département* of Basses Pyrenées, from Pau to the Spanish frontier. Its many vineyards produce much ordinary to fair table wines and one quality white wine, known as Jurançon, which has a puzzling bouquet with a truffle-like quality which is unique.

BERNAISE SAUCE. See SAUCES.

BEAT. This means to mix or force air into food by vigorous motion. This can be done by hand with a wooden spoon, fork, beater or even a knife or with an electric beater. After a mixture has been beaten it must never be stirred as this breaks the air bubbles.

Meat is often beaten with a mallet or cutlet bat to tenderize it.

BEATER. This is a device to beat or whip or whisk eggs, and thick and thin mixtures. In most kitchens more than one beater is required. Usually a wooden spoon is best for thick mixtures, and an egg beater or fork, depending on the end result, for eggs and often a knife (for the patient) for beating egg whites. However, an electric beater will accomplish almost everything a fork, spoon or knife does – but is not for an omelette or scrambled eggs as a minimum of beating is required for both.

The most usual beater is the egg beater or rotary beater and these can be bought in different sizes and even more than one of these is advisable. In this beater two interlocking open wire cages are made which revolve rapidly by means of a crank shaft. It is essential that it is sturdy and made of a metal which will not corrode.

BEAUJOLAIS, BEAUJOLAIS DE L'ANNÉE, BEAUJOLAIS VILLAGES, BEAUJOLAIS SUPERIEUR. See BURGUNDY WINES.

BEAULIEU-SUR-LAYON. One of the best wine-producing *communes* of Anjou, in the Maine-et-

BEEF: boiled silverside of beef

BEATER (electric)   BEATER (hand)   BEECH NUTS

Loire *département*; its wines are white, rather sweet and usually sold under the name of Coteaux du Layon. They are noted for their great delicacy and elegance.

BEAUMES-LES-VENISES. See RHÔNE WINES.

BEAUMONT. A good mountain cheese from the Haute Savoie. Its rind is bright yellow, the paste rather light, but softening to a pale beige as the cheese ages. A large cheese, it is usually sold by the piece. While still young the flavour is mild, but as it ripens it develops a strong rustic aroma.

BEAUNE. See BURGUNDY WINES.

BEAUNE, HOSPICES DE. See BURGUNDY WINES.

BÉCHAMEL SAUCE. See SAUCES.

BÊCHE DE MER. The *bêche de mer* is not likely to come the way of the average diner – out in the West, although it can sometimes be obtained in certain oriental restaurants. It is, however, an approved delicacy of every cultured palate in the East and from it is made one of the most delicious soups of the turtle or Toheroa class (which see).

Bêche de mer, also called sea cucumber, sea slug and trepang, are related to the starfish. They inhabit Southeast Asian waters and range from gorgeous jazzy-coloured creatures half a foot long to brown monsters measuring nearly four feet.

There is a species of *bêche de mer* in British waters known by the name of cotton spinner from its habit when attacked of ejecting quantities of sticky threads, which swell in water and form an entanglement from which a fish, lobster or crab has great difficulty in escaping.

There are other species of the sea slug sold under the name of *bêche de mer* in the West Indies, Zanzibar and the West Coast of Africa, but these are vastly inferior. The best *bêche de mer* is found in the Pacific and particularly in the north and northwest waters, in the Timor Sea and inside the Great Barrier Reef. It is highly prized by rich Chinese who buy up huge supplies.

BEECH NUT. Although a familiar feature in the woodlands of many parts of Europe and North America, it is curious that so few people realize the value of beech nuts as food. Their flavour, when husked, is similar to that of the hazel-nut. For centuries beech nuts have been fed to animals. Probably their size and the fact they are bothersome to gather has prevented their more general use as a food for humans. However, in time of famine they have been proved valuable and not infrequently they have been made into a form of coffee, somewhat like acorn coffee.

Beech nut oil is sweetish and does not turn rancid, nor if burnt does it emit a bad odour, as do some oils. It fries a good brown and is particularly good for frying fish. In France, where it is used for cooking, it is regarded as only a little less inferior to olive oil.

BEEF. Beef is the best meat that the butcher has to offer. It is full of flavour, and food value and offers the greatest nutriment of all the *viandes de boucherie*. At its best it comes from oxen, steers or bullocks which have been castrated when young, or from uncalved heifers, and the finest flavour is found in animals between five and six years old. It must be hung by the butcher to ensure tenderness. Beef from cows, which is used mostly for making pot-roasts and stews, is lean and somewhat tough.

Beef can be classified in three categories according to its market value, which in turn depends on its qualities and uses for various forms of cooking, the best cuts obviously being the most expensive. These categories are (1) fillet, sirloin, top rump, rump steak, silverside and the inner parts of the flank and round; (2) top of sirloin, top ribs, fore ribs, shoulder, chuck end of the clod and clod itself; (3) flank, brisket, leg, neck, cheek, shin and knuckle.

Prime beef, when freshly cut, should be of a

57

BORSCH

brilliant red colour, firm and elastic to the touch. The tender cuts should be surrounded and flecked or lightly marbled with fat, which should be white or slightly yellowish according to the breed of the particular animal and the manner in which it has been fed. The flesh should have a fresh, light smell, but the meat will become darker with hanging and the meaty odour will be more pronounced.

FILLET OF BEEF. The fillet of beef, which is rightly considered to be the finest part of the animal, is often cooked whole and not divided into steaks. It is the undercut of sirloin.

CHIPPED BEEF. Lean, top-round beef, corned, smoked, air dried, sliced paper-thin, and packed generally into 2-ounce containers for marketing. Although seldom prepared in the home it is the basis of many home-cooked dishes. It is also called 'dried beef' and is best prepared for use with starchy foods. It has a unique smoky, salty taste, and when lightly sautéed in butter adds zest to bland foods such as potatoes, eggs, or macaroni. One of the more popular recipes is 'creamed chipped beef on toast', a staple breakfast for the American GI of World War II. This is made by preparing a thick white cream sauce, adding the desired amount of chipped beef, and serving hot on buttered toast.

CUTS OF BEEF STEAK. Entrecôte steak. Taken from between the ribs, but sometimes from the sirloin, it should be about one inch thick and at least 8 oz. should be allowed for two.

Double entrecôte: between ¾ lb. and 1 lb.

Minute steak: very thin, about 4 oz. in weight.

Fillet steak: cut from the best part of the fillet and weighing 6-7 oz. at the most; cooked like entrecôtes and tournedos. Filet mignon: cut from the centre of the fillet and then in half lengthways and then cut again into flat triangles.

Tournedos: small round fatless slices of fillet of beef, weighing about 3½-4 oz. and about 1-1½ inches thick.

Rump steak. Cut from the end of the rump it is never less than ¾ inch thick.

Chateaubriand: from the centre of the fillet, a good thickness weighing from 12 oz. to 1 lb.

T-bone steak: a 1 inch-thick strip cut through the sirloin, including the bone and fillet, for two or more people. It is carved by cutting alternate slices from each side of the bone towards the skin side.

Porterhouse steak: about 1½ inches thick and cut from the wing ribs (cf entrecôtes which are cut from between the ribs and are half as thick).

Portmanteau steak: a thickish steak in which a deep pocket has been cut in the side.

Club steak. A steak cut from the fore rib, similar to a porterhouse but cheaper.

Point steak. Cut from the separate muscle to one side of the rump, this cut is held by many to have much more flavour than any other steak, though both the fillet and sirloin are more tender.

BEEF OLIVES. These have nothing to do with olives nor do they look like olives when the dish is served. Thin slices of rump steak are flattened and trimmed, stuffed with a suet, breadcrumbs, lemon and sweet herb filling, rolled and tied with thread and gently cooked in a rich brown sauce.

BEEFSTEAK. The beefsteak is a thoroughly British institution and one which inspired the establishment of The Beefsteak, a club dedicated to beef. The club was established in the reign of Queen Anne, at the beginning of the 18th century.

Today there is still a Beefsteak in London, a descendant of earlier clubs. But a break of 11 years separated the club from the previous one. However, today's Beefsteak has many relics of earlier clubs.

BEEF TEA. A relic of the past. It is a beef broth or essence and was given to invalids to strengthen them, which it no doubt did. The habit of making beef tea lasted well into the 20th century and possibly began to die out between the wars when bottled or cubed meat extracts began to appear.

BEER. Beer is an infusion of malted barley boiled with hops and then fermented.

The earliest written reference to the brewing process appears on a Mesopotamian clay tablet of *circa* 4000 B.C. A wooden model of a brewery dating back to 2000 B.C. was found at Meket-Re in Thebes. Shortly before this time, the Babylonians were brewing some 18 different varieties of beer and even designated two goddesses, Ninkasi and Siris, to watch over its fortunes. More recently, in Western Europe, brewing was carried out in the family, usually by the women, and did not become commercially important until probably the 16th century. Most monasteries had their own brew house which became an important source of revenue.

In the malting process, barley is germinated by being first soaked thoroughly in water and then spread out on a malting floor. The grain (known at this stage as green malt) is dried on a kiln consisting of a fire underneath a wire-mesh floor.

At the brewery the malt is milled and it is then minced with liquor (the brewers' name for water) and run into mash tuns at a temperature which converts the starch contained in the malt into readily fermentable sugars. The resultant extract, called wort, is then boiled in a copper to which hops have been added; after boiling, the hops are strained out of the wort, it is cooled to approximately room temperature and pumped to the

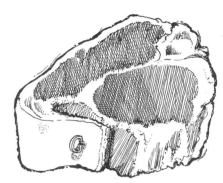

BEEF: PORTERHOUSE STEAK   TOURNEDOS   RUMP STEAK

fermenting vessels, at which stage yeast is added. It is then that the Customs and Excise Officer calculates the duty payable and this amounts to approximately half its total cost.

During fermentation, yeast converts the fermentable sugars into alcohol and carbon dioxide gas, the latter being collected for use at a subsequent stage of the process.

Analysis of an 8 oz. glass of beer taken from an average of leading brands showed that it contained:

Protein	1.4 gm.
Carbohydrates	10.6 gm.
Fat	none at all
Vitamins	a number, including B^1, B^2, B^6
Minerals	notably calcium and phosphorus

Today, in the United Kingdom, the two main types of beer are bitter and mild, the former being made from lightly cured malt and therefore pale in colour and, being highly hopped, it has a bitter, dry flavour, and the latter being made from more highly cured malt (i.e. malt which has been raised to a higher temperature on the kiln) and having a lower hop rate the flavour is more malty and less bitter. It also has a sweet flavour which is derived from the addition of priming – a solution of sugar.

Keg beers (such as Watneys Red Barrel, a pioneer of this type of beer in the 1930s) are in the same tradition as English draught beers but are specially conditioned and racked (filled into kegs) so that they retain their brilliance and palate for a very long time.

Bottled and canned beers generally can be said to be carbonated to a higher level than draught beers and fall into three main categories – pale ales, brown ales and stouts.

All the beers which have been so far mentioned are top fermented as opposed to lager beer which is bottom fermented (the position of the yeast in the vessel at the end of fermentation is what is being described).

BEER CHEESE. This is the German *Bierkäse*, a white, rather strong cheese also known as Weisslacker. There is an American version made in Wisconsin, somewhat firmer and milder than the original.

BEER COOKERY. We are apt to neglect the subtle versatility of cooking with beer. It can be used in a marinade, for basting and flavouring. There are recipes dating back to the Middle Ages which include beer.

Which of the three great beer drinking and producing countries – Britain, Belgium and Germany – originally pioneered beer in cooking is no longer certain, but all three countries have some internationally known recipes in which beer is an important ingredient. Britain has her Welsh Rarebit (which see) and both the Christmas pudding and cake are strongly flavoured and coloured with beer. The Germans have beer soups and cook their sausages in beer, and the Belgians can point to their *carbonnades flamandes*. Outside the 'big three', the Danes spike their soups with beer, and the Swedes blend it with molasses to make a mouth-watering bread.

Cooking with beer in beer-drinking countries was a natural evolution as wine-cooking was in most of France and cider-cooking in Normandy. Cooks are for ever seeking new flavours and those cooks of old not having wine on their doorsteps turned to what came nearest and thought in terms of beer to liven up their stocks, sauces or stews. Fish cooked in beer has as good a flavour as when cooked in wine or cider.

Beer as a marinade will penetrate and tenderize meats, and when used in basting adds not only flavour but also an attractive glaze and colour. Beer mingles or blends into other flavours neatly and well, and once in the cooking pot all traces of alcohol disappear.

BEER FLIP. An old English drink for bell-ringers after a long peal. Beat 8 yolks of egg with sugar, orange juice and spices to taste. Then beat the whites until stiff. Heat 2 pints ($2\frac{1}{2}$) of beer and pour this over the yolks and then pour back and forth from a height so that it froths high. Fold in the egg whites and serve the whole swiftly while hot – while the echo of the bells still rings.

CARBONNADES FLAMANDES

2 lb. lean beef
salt, pepper
2 oz. (4 tablespoons) butter
1–2 slices lean bacon, sliced
1 tablespoon (1¼) flour
mild beer
1 oz. (2 tablespoons) lard
1-2 onions, finely chopped
1 clove garlic, chopped
bouquet garni
1 knob sugar

Cut the beef into 2-inch lengths and sprinkle lightly with salt and pepper. Heat the butter, add the pieces of meat and brown them all over. Take from the pan and put aside until required.

Add the bacon to the pan and let this brown. Take from the pan and put aside. Add the flour to the fat, stir this to a roux and add enough beer to make a thin sauce.

Heat the lard in another pan and fry the onions until brown. Drain and put aside.

Pour the beer sauce into a casserole, add a layer of chopped onions, then one of meat and of bacon. Repeat this until these ingredients are used up, adding the garlic, bouquet garni and sugar. Sprinkle with salt and pepper. If the contents of the casserole are not covered with the sauce, add a little more beer as it is important the meat should be covered. Close the casserole tightly, bring the liquid to the boil on top of the stove, transfer to the oven and cook very gently for 2½ hours. A little vinegar may be stirred into the *carbonnade* just before serving. Serve with plain boiled potatoes.

BEERENAUSLESE. German for 'selected berries' referring to fine quality wines made from specially selected grapes at the vintage time. The wines made from these grapes are not easily obtainable, and the greatest wines of this category are amongst the highest priced in the world. Honey-sweet richness, with a clean, sharp bite make them a wine-bibber's delight.

BEESTINGS. This is the name given to the first milkings after a calf is born.

BEESWING. A light sediment, mostly the mucilage of grapes, sometimes found in old bottled ports; it does not settle upon the glass of the bottle, like crust, but it does not foul the wine when it passes from the bottle into the decanter. It is quite tasteless, whilst the crust is bitter.

BEETON, MRS. Author of *The Book of Household Management* and probably still the best-known writer on food in the world today. Her name is a household one and her book, first published in 1861, has gone into countless editions.

When she embarked upon her *magnum opus* she wrote to her friend Mrs English for advice and received this reply. 'Cookery is a science that is only learned by Long Experience and years of Study which, of course, you have not had . . .'

BEETROOT. In the United States this vegetable is called beet. It was well known to the ancients and there is considerable mention of it both in the writings of the ancient Greeks and the Romans.

Beetroot is the root of a plant of the genus *Beta* of which there are many varieties, including the mangel-wurzel (an unpopular vegetable for human consumption), the white beet used more in the making of sugar, and yet another variety, the sea-beet, the leaves of which are eaten as a green vegetable.

Beets require careful treatment and they should not be cut before cooking or they will bleed while cooking and become pale and anaemic. They can be eaten hot or cold.

BÉGORCE, LA. See BORDEAUX WINES.

BEIGNETS. A French name for any item of food which is dipped in batter and fried in deep fat. There is no real English equivalent. Often *beignets* are referred to as 'puff-paste fritters' but there are many *beignets* which do not answer to such a description. All *beignets* should be light, whereas not all fritters are.

BEL PAESE. The name means 'beautiful country' and the cheese is one of the best known and most popular of the Italian table cheeses. It is the trade name of one of a group of uncooked soft, mild, fast-ripened Italian cheeses.

The first Bel Paese was made in Melzo, near Milan, and it has put this small town literally on the map for on the lid of each box of Bel Paese there is a map of Italy with Melzo marked larger than Rome.

Although intended as a table cheese, Bel Paese serves for cooking. Its softness makes it an excellent melting cheese. It can be thickly spread on toast and grilled until brown. It can, in an emergency, be used in a pizza when Mozzarella is not available.

A version of Bel Paese is now made in the United States, in Wisconsin.

BELAIR. See BORDEAUX WINES.

BELARNO. A hard, rich Italian goat cheese.

BELEGTE BROTE. German open sandwiches, usually prepared with rye bread.

BEETROOT

BELGIAN COOKING. Belgian cooking is a fascinating amalgam. Two languages, French (Walloon) and Flemish, and two cultures make up Belgium, and in the kitchen one finds all the finesse of France, plus the more solid qualities and regional specialities of Flanders. Considered one of the last outposts (along with France) of really fine cooking the quality and abundance of fresh meat and vegetables is on the highest level.

This is a country of specialists, where one specifies precisely the type of potato required (at least twenty varieties are readily available), just as French beans run the gamut from very fine up by half-a-dozen stages to thick. One chooses from an embarrassment of riches in a butcher's shop, for in Belgium, butchery is an art. Practised by as many women as men, husband/wife teams preside over mouth-watering displays of meat and charcuterie, and can as readily give a recipe as sell a joint.

In the excellent street markets, the vendors invite customers to pick their own fruit or vegetables from the stall.

Belgium has given the world one fine vegetable – the chicory (sometimes misnamed endive). A classic Belgian dish is boiled chicory, drained and wrapped in slices of ham, covered with a cheese sauce, and baked golden-brown in the oven.

Mussels are the truly great speciality of the country. They are baked, grilled, cooked in cream, simmered in wine, prepared *à l'escargot* (soaked in garlic butter and parsley) or Provençale (garlic, tomato, pimiento) or simply boiled in white wine with onions and celery, and are eaten by all. French fried (*patates frites*), crisp and golden, are served literally with everything. Stalls sell them on every street corner, too, as well as along country roads. Other roadside specialities are the famous waffles (*gaufres*) of Liège. Sometimes filled with apple, or served with thick cream, the *gaufres (wafels* in Flemish) are part and parcel of Belgium's eating life.

Liège produces its splendid *boudin blanc*, a white sausage tasting of savoury herbs, while the Ardennes region in the south, rich in rivers, produces fresh trout, venison, wild boar and game of every kind. Another Ardennes speciality is ham –

similar to Parma ham, with a smoky salty tang.

Deep-freezing is virtually unknown and universally distrusted. Supermarkets hardly exist, and Belgium remains a country of small supremely good specialist shops. The poulterer cleans and prepares his customer's bird on the spot, just as the fishmonger will deliver him a live lobster if he so requires. The average Belgian is quite ready to wait a while for his food, spends as high a proportion of his income on it as he can possibly spare, regards eating out as an evening's entertainment, and is stoical about rising prices.

Bakers not only bake their own bread (one gets it sliced on the spot), remain open all day on Sunday, and are expert *pâtissiers*, but frequently make their own chocolates too. Belgian pralines are world-famous, as are their gâteaux. Guests frequently bring a cake as a gift to their hostess in much the same way as guests in other countries bring flowers.

The wines drunk in Belgium are French, but the true drink of the country is beer. Now and again the Belgians top the polls as the world's greatest imbibers and some cafés produce a beer list as long as a normal wine list. Curiously, spirits are not allowed on public sale for consumption.

BELGRAVE. See BORDEAUX WINES.

BELLE-ISLE CRESS. See CRESS AMERICAN.

BELLELAY. A Swiss cheese invented by monks in the 15th century in the Abbey of Bellelay near Moutiers in the Bernese Jura. It is also known as *Tête de Moine* (Monk's Head). This is decidedly milder than most monastery cheeses and the reason might be that it is now manufactured in dairies in the district.

BELL PEPPER. See CAPSICUM.

BELLY. The edible part of any mammal's stomach. The belly of the ox makes what is called tripe in England, and in France *gras-double*. Belly of pork is chiefly used in soups and is served cold, as boiled pork.

BELUGA STURGEON. The largest member of the sturgeon family (which see) and chiefly known because of the excellence of its roe, from which is produced the finest form of caviar (which see).

BENEDICTINE. Possibly the oldest and one of the most widely renowned liqueurs in the world. It is distilled in Fécamp in Normandy. Its origin has been traced to the Benedictine monks of Fécamp as far back as 1510, when it is said it was discovered by Don Bernardo Vincelli, a learned monk of the Order. Considered to be an elixir it was given to revive the tired monks and was also administered as a medicine to combat malaria, prevalent at that time.

The Fécamp Abbey was destroyed during the French Revolution and the Order dispersed, but the recipe was entrusted to the *Procureur Fiscal* of the Abbey and eventually came into the hands of a wine merchant, a descendant of the *Procureur*.

The recipe was successfully reconstructed and developed to make the original liqueur which is now shipped far and wide, each bottle of very distinctive shape bearing the Benedictine Order's D.O.M. device – *Deo optimo maximo*, 'To God most good, most great.'

BENEDICTINE, À LA. One of the classical garnitures for fish and egg dishes; it consists of *brandade de morue* and truffles.

BENEDICTINE AND BRANDY (B & B). A drier version of Benedictine, often preferred in the United States.

BENICARLO. See SPANISH WINES.

BERCY. See SAUCES.

BERGAMONT. The bergamonts are North American aromatic herbs of the mint family. They are not much used in cooking, except the red bergamont, also known as fragrant balm, bee balm and Indian's plume. A tea is made from the pungent tender leaves of the red bergamont and it was used on a large scale when the colonists boycotted English tea. They learned of this tea from the Oswega Indians and named it Oswega tea after them. The bergamont leaves can also be used to flavour iced drinks, and this is now their most popular use.

BERNADINE. See RHÔNE WINES.

BERRY. Berries are legion and odes have been written on them. Walt Whitman wrote that the blackberry 'would adorn the portals of heaven'. But perhaps it is fitting to offer C. S. Calverley's small effort on the berry in his *Berries From the Tree of Knowledge*.

'You may swear yourself black, Berry; but you have made a mull, Berry. I paid your bill, Berry, as the young lady in the bar, Berry, and your father, the elder, Berry, know. I don't care a straw, Berry, for a goose, Berry, like you, Berry; but I'll let folks know, Berry, that you've made yourself a regular ass, Berry, and what'll Berry senior say.' See FRUIT.

BESAN. A flour used in cooking in northern India. It is made from *chana dal*, a type of lentil. Ground yellow split peas make an excellent substitute.

BETEL LEAF. The leaf of the betel vine and chewed as an aid to digestion.

BETEL NUT. See ARECA NUT.

BETTY. A simple pudding made with fruit, thinly sliced, and breadcrumbs, arranged in alternate layers in a deep buttered baking dish.

BEURRE MANIÉ. French culinary term for a mixture of flour and butter worked together to a paste until smooth and used to thicken sauces, gravies and soups.

BEURRE NOIR. See BUTTER, BLACK.

BEVERAGE. A term covering a wide variety of artificially made liquid refreshments ranging from simple home-made infusions of herbs, to stimulate or soothe, to fermented beverages which include wines, beers and fruit liqueurs. Thus tea, coffee and chocolate, drunk widely throughout the world as a mildly stimulating refreshment, are perhaps the best known in the ordinary domestic scene, along with bottled beverages such as fruit squashes and other soft drinks.

For stronger stimulation, as tonics and aids to digestion, the lighter fermented beverages such as ales, beers and wine are drunk widely throughout the world.

BEYCHEVELLE. See BORDEAUX WINES.

BICARBONATE OF SODA. Also called sodium bicarbonate and baking soda, this is a kitchen chemical used in preparing bread and any other flour-based confections requiring leavening. It is also useful for removing sour smells from cooking pots, refrigerators, etc.

BIENVENUS-BÂTARD-MONTRACHET. See BURGUNDY WINES.

BILBERRY   BERGAMOT

BIGARADE. See SAUCES.

BIGHORN SHEEP. The wild sheep of the mountainous areas of western North America, so named because of the ram's massive, spiral horns, which resemble those of the Asian argali. Strongly built and standing about 40 inches in height, its coat is tawny yellow in summer and greyish-brown in winter. Both the underbelly and a conspicuous spot on the buttocks are whitish. It is now found mainly near Yellowstone National Park and northward and is stalked as a big game trophy or as a delicacy resembling mutton.

BIGOS. This could be called a national dish of Poland. It is a winter dish of meat (a variety of sausages, ham, fat bacon or game – not lamb or mutton) and its base is sauerkraut. It is rich, well-peppered and served hot.

BILBERRY (BLUEBERRY). The berries of a deciduous dwarf bush, growing wild in Europe, Asia and North America. Although this berry is a native of Britain it does not enjoy the popularity it does elsewhere. It is known by different names in different parts of the country. It is blaeberry in Scotland and in the north of England – also in the north we find the name whinberries. In Surrey they are hurts and in other parts of the country whortleberries.

In the United States bilberries are more usually known as blueberries (although here too we come across other names) and enjoy immense popularity. Cultivated in vast quantities in North America, they are produced from Carolina to Nova Scotia, which gives them a five-month season. The peak of the bilberry season in the States is in June when the berries pour into the markets. There are few seeds in cultivated bilberries, which are sweet-fleshed and tender-skinned with just enough tartness to give distinction to the fruit.

Generally the lighter blueberries are known by this name. The darker berries, some of which are almost black, are known as 'huckleberries' and in some parts of the country all varieties of blueberries are given the common name of huckleberry. One also finds the names whortleberry and bilberry in the States.

Bilberries, huckleberries, blueberries and whortleberries are all marketed by these names in the States in canned and frozen forms as well as fresh.

When these berries are ripe, they are plump, fresh-looking and of a deep colour throughout.

BILTONG. A South African form of dried meat capable of retaining its nutrition value and flavour for many years. Properly cured, biltong is not sun-dried but is hung in long, thin strips from the rafters of some high and draughty shed or loft and left long enough to become like leather in appearance yet excellent to eat, uncooked, grated or cut in thin pieces, as a filling for sandwiches.

BIN. A storage compartment for filled wine bottles, generally of one wine which has been bottled and laid down at the same time, thus ensuring uniformity of quality.

BIND, TO. To moisten a mixture with egg, cream or a sauce to hold it together.

BIRDS' NEST. Birds' nests have been known to the Chinese as a delicacy longer than they have known their other favourite, sharks' fin.

These birds' nests, so much enjoyed throughout Southeast Asia and elsewhere in the world where there is a sizable Chinese community, are the nests of a particular kind of swift or swallow which makes its home around the crags or cliffs of the China coast, in Malaysia and even in Australia.

The nests vary somewhat. In shape they have one flat side where the nests are attached to the wall of the cave, while the outside is the shape and size of a tablespoon or serving spoon. Some are made almost entirely from the dried glutinous saliva of the birds, and these are known as white nests and sell for the most money. Other nests are full of feathers and sea debris and are known as black. These are cheaper. But either type is considered by the Chinese to have a high protein value since the birds feed on small fish as well as an assortment of seaweed and other extraneous matter floating in the sea.

Birds' nests are divided into grades. For example, one ounce of first grade equals 8 oz. after it has been soaked. Second grade equals only 5 oz. after soaking. Fourth grade even less, and so on. But these distinctions apply only to those areas where the birds' nests are a matter of everday cooking, and methods of cooking vary according to the quality of the birds' nests. The best birds' nests are sold ready for use in a pre-prepared form.

Manila Yellow is considered by gourmets as the best; the white nests of Borneo and what was once Indo-China are used for the preparing of savoury dishes, while Thai birds' nests are used for sweet dishes.

BIRYANI. In Indian and Pakistani cooking, a biryani, very much like a pilau, is a meal in itself and does not require any accompaniment. There are no hard and fast rules for its preparation, some are rich, others are not. The difference basically between a biryani and a pilau is that in the first mentioned the rice is first partially cooked on its own and then with spiced meat.

BISCUIT. Originally a French term to describe small, flat, floury cakes which were double baked, it now covers a wider variety of confectionery. In English-speaking countries other than North America the home-cooked biscuit is generally made from a stiff dough of flour, fat, sugar and various flavourings which is rolled into small portions, flattened and pricked or marked with a decorative pattern and baked until crisp. Sometimes the dough is lightly rolled and the biscuits cut into individual shapes, or a slightly softer dough may be put through a forcing tube. The same principle applies to the factory-made biscuit in which Great Britain has specialized.

In North America the biscuit is a small, soft, unsweetened cake, very like a scone, made from leavened dough and used as a hot bread, especially in the southern States.

BISHOP. A hot or cold mulled wine, usually made with a basis of port and flavoured with orange, cloves, star anise and cinnamon.

BISMARCK HERRING. These are herrings in vinegar and served as hors d'oeuvre.

BISQUE. It is not easy to decide whence this name is derived. In earlier times it was applied to a

purée of wood pigeons, other poultry and game, but not to shellfish; other authorities declare it to be a word of Provençal origin. Today the name is always confined to a thick shellfish soup, usually lobster or crayfish.

BITKI. These are simply Russian style rissoles or hamburgers, made with raw ground beef and variously flavoured. Some are round like balls, others flat discs. Some are dipped in egg and breadcrumbs, others not. They are often served with sour cream or a thick tomato sauce, even a madeira sauce, or garnished with fried onions and sautéed potatoes and parsley.

BITTERS. The generic name of various highly scented and flavoured mixtures of more or less alcoholic strength; they may be divided into two main categories, aromatic bitters and flavouring bitters. The first are used as short (aperitifs and digestifs) drinks; the second to add flavour to various drinks.

BITTO. An Italian cheese made from cows' milk, ewes' milk or goat and cow milk mixed. It is a hard cheese of the Emmentaler group with small eyes. It is sometimes eaten fresh but more frequently allowed to ripen for two years before eating. When fully cured it is grated and used for cooking.

BLAAND. This is a refreshing drink which hails from the Shetland Isles, made by pouring hot water on to buttermilk to make it separate. The resulting curd is drained, pressed and eaten as 'kirnmilk'. ('Kirn' means churn.) The whey is allowed to stand until it ferments and begins to sparkle.

BLACKBERRY. A particularly favourite fruit for making jams, jellies, pies and puddings. It is the common name of the fruit of a large number of semi-bushes with long rambling growth, growing wild in woods and along hedges all over the temperate zone of the northern hemisphere. The fruit is like the raspberry. Also called bramble.

Blackberries deteriorate quicker than most fruit after being picked and should be eaten or cooked the day they are gathered. When they are ripe they are a shiny black, but are not necessarily ripe because they are black. They must be soft as well and easily detached from the stem. Ripe, sweet and juicy they are among the finest of the berry fruits.

In the United States blackberries have been cultivated since the second half of the 19th century but not so long in Britain.

BLACKBERRY PIE. Use a deep earthenware pie dish and pack it full with blackberries, sprinkling sugar in between the layers. Fill up with the moist pulp of over-cooked apples. Cover with a

(Opposite) BOTTLES: bordeaux and burgundy bottles; the former have high shoulders; the latter, sloping ones
(Overleaf) BOUILLABAISSE

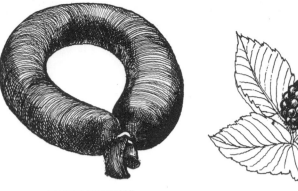

BLACK PUDDING

BLACKBERRY

layer of short pastry, and bake in a hot oven until the top is brown and crisp.

BLACKBERRY BOUNCE. A refreshing and delicious drink that depends for its special flavour on both the blackberries and the brandy. The preparation of the drink calls for 1 pound of sugar for each quart of cooked and strained blackberry juice. The sugar and blackberry juice (which is thick) is boiled together for 5 minutes, skimmed and cooled. To each gallon of juice is added a quart of brandy and the finished drink is spiced to taste.

BLACKBERRY BRANDY. A spirit distilled from fresh blackberries in France, Germany and Switzerland. It is called *Brombeergeist* in German.

BLACKBERRY CORDIAL AND LIQUEUR. Spirits which have been sweetened as well as flavoured with blackberries, cordials and liqueurs, produced mostly in Germany and Switzerland; also in Poland, where *Jerzynowka* is a popular blackberry liqueur. But the German *Kroatzbeere* is reputed the best of all of them, not too sweet and with a bouquet of the wild blackberry.

BLACKCURRANT. The fruit of a European bush which has received considerable attention from horticulturists during the past two hundred years and so greatly improved. There is a related species which grows wild in many parts of North America, from Nova Scotia to Virginia. Its fruit is edible although not greatly prized.

Blackcurrants are more appreciated in Britain than in the United States. They are made into jams and jellies, pies and puddings, as well as ice-creams. Fresh ripe blackcurrants are a rich source of Vitamin C.

Like most fresh fruit, blackcurrants are only worth buying when they are very fresh. They should look firm, clean and glossy. If they are withered or dusty looking they are stale and should be avoided.

BLACKCURRANT ICE-CREAM

Boil 1 lb. of blackcurrants with ½ lb. (1 cup) sugar until the fruit is quite soft. Pass through a fine sieve, add a squeeze of lemon and beat in as much fresh cream as desired. Pour into an ice cube container and freeze in the usual manner.

BLACKCURRANT GIN. A Dutch gin flavoured with blackcurrants.

BLACKCURRANT LIQUEUR. A sweet, dark red liqueur and one of the most wholesome. It has been known for centuries. As far back as the 16th century monks in the Dijon area were producing a blackcurrant ratafia to which many medicinal properties were attributed. This kind of liqueur is made in various countries, but chiefly in France where it is called *crème de cassis.*

BLACKFISH. A colloquial name given to many species of fish, ranging from the American tautog (Black sea bass) to a small fresh-water fish similar to the blenny found in the Australian streams.

BLACK DIAMOND. A Canadian cheddar-type cheese.

BLACK HAW. Also called stag-bush and sheep-berry. It is wild shrub of the honeysuckle family that bears edible fruits of a bluish-black colour. They are sweet, contain single black pips and are about half an inch in length.

Jams and jellies are made from the haw shrub, also a cordial.

BLACK PUDDING or **BLOOD SAUSAGE.** Black puddings, 'small otemeale mixed with blood, and the liver of either sheep, calf or swine, maketh that pudden . . .' This is taken from the *English Housewife's Booke,* published in 1600.

This was one of the first so-called puddings and traditionally interesting because many illuminated manuscripts show the winter pig-killing and the preparation of blood puddings. Nowadays it is the butcher who makes blood sausages, except on some farms where the pig is killed on the premises.

There are various methods of making black puddings, but in the main the ingredients are the

(Previous page) CHAMPAGNE: the *vendeur* at the Champagne harvest.
(Opposite) CHARLOTTE: apple charlotte.

finely ground trimmings of pork fat, onions, herbs and pigs' blood. This mixture is filled into the gut, tied up and brushed over with blood (this makes them black, hence their name) and boiled. Often the pudding ends are tied together to form a circle. Once cooked, the puddings will keep for several days.

Black puddings are also popular in France where they are sheathed in a black skin, and easy to recognize in the charcuterie where they hang in long strings of sausage shapes.

Although black pudding recipes are basically the same, blood and fat with seasoning and onion, other ingredients vary considerably. Some French recipes include chestnuts, others apples, cream or spinach and spices. On the whole, black puddings are more popular in France than they are today in Britain except probably in the North.

This type of sausage, however, is not confined to Britain and France. Germany, the Scandinavian countries and the United States also have their versions of blood sausages.

BLACK RASPBERRY. See RASPBERRY.

BLACKSTRAP. The American nickname given to very heavy molasses originally made in the West Indies, now applied locally to any dark cane syrup. It was the basic source of the famous 'Medford Rum' made in New England in the early 17th century and a staple of trade at that time. It is now used as a source of sugar, and for refining into the various grades and types of syrup and molasses.

BLANC DE BLANCS. The name for a wine made exclusively from white grapes of Champagne vineyards and supposedly lighter than the traditional kind, made from both black and white grapes.

BLANCH. To blanch meat or vegetables is to plunge them into boiling water for a given length of time, usually two or three minutes, after which they are thrown into a bowl of cold water and left until cold. With meat this is done for the purpose of giving firmness to the flesh and thus facilitate the operation of larding, also to preserve the whiteness of certain meats, such as rabbit, chicken, sweetbreads etc. Calves' head and feet are blanched to soften them and thus make them easier to trim.

Ox tongues, almonds and fruit kernels are said to be blanched when, through the action of hot water, the skin can be easily peeled off.

BLANCHOTS. See BURGUNDY WINES.

BLANCMANGE. This is a sweet pudding which in Britain has sunk very low indeed. A French invention, it is said to have originated in Languedoc; according to Grimod de la Reynière, the dish was difficult to make and, in fact, he doubted whether anyone could make the true recipe correctly as the secret of its preparation had been lost in the French Revolution. What he would have said of the modern British blancmange would probably beggar description.

BLANQUETTE. This is a white ragoût, fricassee or stew based on lamb, chicken or veal, with the sauce made from the liquid in which the meat has been cooked. It is bound with a liaison of egg yolks and cream, garnished with mushrooms and small onions and served with parsley and croûtons.

BLARNEY. A well-named Irish cheese of so-called Swiss type. It is butter-yellow in colour, accentuated by its vivid red rind. It has many large, glistening eyes but there the resemblance to Swiss cheese ends.

BLAYE. See BORDEAUX WINES.

BLEND. To combine two or more ingredients rather less vigorously than by beating.

BLENDER. A kitchen machine, either electrically powered or operated by hand, and used to mix and purée a variety of ingredients by the rotary action of the blades. Blenders, called liquidizers in Britain, are used for chopping and grinding all kinds of food.

BLENDING. A perfectly legitimate way of improving the quality of different wines which are not perfect individually; or in order to secure the continuity of supply of wines of an accepted type, irrespective of differences due to varying climatic conditions from year to year. Thus a non-vintage champagne is the wine made in a year when the grapes did not get all the sunshine they needed, but blended with the wine of former good vintage years always kept in reserve for the purpose. A sherry, one which bears a well-known name such as Fino, Amontillado, Oloroso, etc., or a well-advertised brand of sherry, are different wines so well 'matched' or blended together that the colour, bouquet and style of each wine remains the same year after year.

BLEU (to cook au bleu). This is a method of cooking fresh-water fish, especially trout, prevalent in France, Germany, Austria and Switzerland. The fish must be killed immediately it is caught and at once plunged into boiling court bouillon (which see). Sometimes the fish is plunged into the boiling

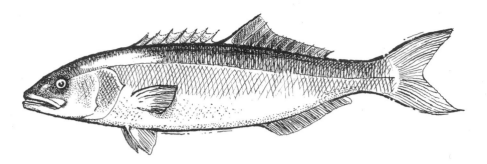

BLUEFISH

liquid alive. Cooked in this fashion the skin of the fish, especially trout, takes on a bluish tinge, and this can be accentuated if the fish is sprinkled with pure vinegar before being plunged into the liquid. It is cooked in five minutes.

BLEU D'AUVERGNE, also known as Bleu de Salers (see below) or Bleu Farmier. See CHEESE, BLUE.

BLEU DE BRESSE. See CHEESE, BLUE.

BLEU DE HAUT-JURA. See CHEESE, BLUE.

BLEU DE LAQUEUILLE. See CHEESE, BLUE.

BLEU DE L'AVEYRON. See CHEESE, BLUE.

BLEU DE SALERS. See CHEESE, BLUE.

BLEU DE SASSENAGE. See CHEESE, BLUE.

BLEU DES CAUSSES, also known as Bleu de Quercy. (See CHEESE, BLUE).

BLINI. Russian pancakes or blinis are often one's first introduction to Russian cooking. They are usually prepared with buckwheat.

The correct method of serving blinis is to stack them in a pile wrapped in a cloth to keep them warm, and offer them with a variety of items for individual spreading. Hard-boiled eggs, mashed sardines, salted or smoked salmon, sour cream, herrings; all can be spread over the warm, inviting blinis, served usually as part of the *zakuski* (which see).

The usual size of the Russian pancake is about 5 inches across

BLOATER. The bloater is a herring that has been caught near enough to the shore to be brought to port and cured while still fresh, known locally as longshore herring. This means it has not been salted in the hold of a drifter. A Yarmouth bloater

is reckoned to be the best because by the time the herrings arrive opposite Yarmouth on their way to the spawning grounds during October and November they are in prime condition. Unfortunately bloaters do not keep well.

At one time bloaters were part of the British breakfast, high tea and even supper but in recent years they have rather lost their popularity – or it may just be that their fishing and distribution is uneconomic. The usual method of cooking bloaters is to split them open, grill them, season with salt and pepper, add a pat of butter and serve hot.

A bloater paste is a relish still popular in Britain as a sandwich spread. It is easy enough to make in these days of electric blenders. Put the cooked bloaters into the blender, adding salt, pepper and butter and mix to a smooth paste. Rub it through a sieve and put into small jars.

BLOOD SAUSAGE. See BLACK PUDDING.

BLUE CHEESE (U.S.A.). See AMERICAN CHEESES.

BLUE CHESHIRE. See CHESHIRE CHEESE.

BLUEFISH. A member of the sea bass family and resembling in outline the mackerel, the bluefish is present in almost every ocean and is variously named, e.g., 'elf' in South Africa, 'tailor' in Australia. It is bright blue in colour with a body shaped like a projectile and large, sharp teeth. The average fish weighs about 6 lb. although some specimens have been caught weighing as much as 50 lb. Bluefish appear intermittently in huge shoals, frequenting both shore line and open sea, but the spawning grounds are unknown. It is greatly esteemed as a game fish, being a tremendous fighter, and is also much sought after as a sea food for its firm, tender and sweet-flavoured flesh.

BLUE DORSET, BLUE VINNEY. See DORSET CHEESE.

BLUE WENSLEYDALE. See WENSLEYDALE CHEESE.

BOAL. See BUAL.

BOAR'S HEAD. The ancient ceremonial dish at Christmas feasts in England was the boar's head and has been so since Norman times, for it was the Normans who introduced it. Today at banquets and special dinners, a boar's head is still served and it is featured on Christmas culinary shopping lists, but it is seldom a genuine boar's head. It is all too often simply a brawn which has been set in a boar's head mould. The moulded head is then glazed and decorated. Where a true boar's head is used it is not often from a fierce wild boar but something considerably tamer.

However, when a boar's head was a boar's head it was splendidly stuffed, boiled or roasted, placed on a large platter, decorated with laurel leaves and borne in procession and triumph to the dining hall to be greeted by the assembled guests with the singing of the carol, 'A Carol bryngyn in the Bore' head', one of a collection of carols written and published in 1521 by Wynkin de Worde.

BOAR, WILD. The wild boar is still abundant on the continent of Europe and in many parts of Asia, but it became extinct in Britain many centuries ago as a result of systematic persecution and the decline of the forests. Attempts were made to reinstate the creature but without success.

Boars are still hunted in many parts of France, where they are abundant. In France, the boar up to the age of six months is called *marcassin*, when a year old *bête de campagnie*, at two years *ragot*, from three to five *sanglier*, and finally *solitaire*. The flesh of the *marcassin* is greatly esteemed for its delicacy.

BOB WHITE. See QUAIL.

BOBOTEE. A South African ground meat dish, baked in the oven and flavoured with curry powder, sugar, lemon juice, chutney, onions and shredded almonds.

BOCK BEER. The name given in the United States to a special brew of beer, usually darker and stronger than the average beer, as well as sweeter. It is brewed in winter for use in spring: Bock Beer Day is supposed to herald the coming of spring.

BODEGA. The Spanish name for a wine store or cellar which has been adopted wherever wine is drunk as a name for wine bars and stores.

BODY. In reference to wine, body is a quality. A wine that lacks body is thin and dumb; a wine with plenty of body is a wine of full alcoholic strength, and its right proportion of both sugars and acids of the grapes from which it was made.

Body is also used in the tea trade in describing the strength of infused tea. Thus a tea with 'full body' would be one that produced a full-flavoured rich drink without bitterness.

BOILING. In cooking, boiling means cooking food in water or other liquids at boiling point, and water is said to be boiling when it reaches 212° F. and bubbles vigorously, with clouds of steam.

In the cooking of meat and other protein food, full boiling point is not always desirable, but for certain culinary processes it is essential. A rolling boil is one where the liquid boils very fast.

BOLA. The most popular Portuguese cheese, semi hard and of the Edam type, made from cows' milk round but flattened at both 'poles'.

BOLETUS. The genus *Boletus*, a fungus, is represented in Britain by many species, some of which may be eaten with safety while others are distinctly poisonous. *Boleti* have no gills but carry the spores within a great number of fine tubes compressed to form cushion-like masses beneath orange caps. These tubes vary in size and colour according to the species to which they belong.

In France there are some seventy species of this fungi and unless one is expert the only boletus mushroom which can safely be gathered is the *Boletus edulis*, known as the *cèpe de Bordeaux*. It has a bronze-coloured cap, white underneath, on a white and swollen stem.

BOLOGNA SAUSAGE. See MORTADELLA.

BOMBAY DUCK. A fascinating sight along the beaches of any of the small fishing villages just outside Bombay are the lines of Bombay duck hung out to dry. Less fascinating is their odour.

Why the Bombay duck is thus called by Westerners no one appears to know. The fish, in its fresh state, is long and thin like a dart, with an almost transparent appearance, and has no resemblance at all to a duck. It weighs some three ounces and grows to a length of 10 to 12 inches. It is not exclusive to Bombay for it is fished for in abundance in the Bay of Bengal, and along the Gujarati coast, north of Bombay.

It is known as bummalo in India and when eaten fresh it is exceedingly pleasant in flavour.

Much of the catch, however, is dried until it becomes hard and stiff and looks like a piece of pale drift wood. Once it is dried it is used as a flavouring for curry dishes and is exported throughout the world.

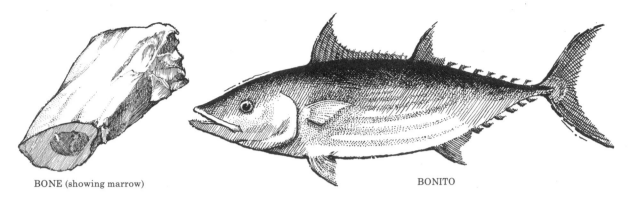

BONE (showing marrow)   BONITO

BOMBAY DUCK SALAD

Take 6 Bombay duck and either toast, fry or roast them and crumble into small pieces. Mix with finely chopped chilli pepper, thinly sliced ginger, minced onion and a little mild vinegar.

BOMBE. See ICE-CREAM.

BOMMES. See BORDEAUX WINES.

BONDE or **BONDON** or **BONDART.** A small, loaf-shaped, whole-milk, soft Neufchâtel-type cheese made in Normandy, in the Bray country.

BONE, TO. The art of boning meat or poultry, although not difficult, cannot be acquired by verbal instruction alone. It is exceedingly useful, because joints are so much more easily carved when boned. Usually the butcher will do all the boning required. The only rules which can be given are to use a sharp-pointed knife, to work with this close to the bone, and to use every possible care to keep the outer skin as whole as possible.

BONE MARROW. Saw the marrow bones (or ask the butcher to do this) into neat pieces, cover the ends with a paste made of flour and water, tie them in a floured cloth, then boil for 2 hours. Remove the cloth and crust and put the bones on a napkin on a dish. Set the bones upright and serve with toast. The marrow should be scooped out with a marrow spoon and spread on the toast with a sprinkling of salt and pepper.

BONES, DEVILLED. Formerly devilled bones were found regularly on menus, but seldom today. Few people seem to bother with this quite pleasing dish, although devilled turkey bones from the Christmas left-over turkey are occasionally served.

Make a mixture of mustard, cayenne pepper and mushroom ketchup. Lay a coating of butter over the bones, then spread the savoury mixture on top and grill or broil the bones under a good heat.

BONITO. The bonito is allied to the tunny fish and is a member of the mackerel family. The name was given it by the Spanish or Portuguese.

Tunny and bonito are very nourishing. Dried and flaked bonito is a popular ingredient in Oriental cooking, especially in Japan. It can be prepared for the table in any of the ways for tunny.

BONNE FEMME, À LA. Cooked in a simple style; in particular, it refers to a soup.

BONNEZEAUX. See LOIRE WINES.

BONNES MARES. See BURGUNDY WINES.

BORAGE. Reputedly a herb from the Middle East, this is one of the most common wild flowers of the Mediterranean.

The plant is small, covered with coarse, irritating hairs, with sky-blue flowers. The flowers are sometimes used for decoration and are candied. But it is the leaves which are important. They have something of the flavour of cucumber. It should always be part of the 'garden' in a Pimms (which see).

The young leaves are sometimes used in salads. The flavour is good but the leaves must be finely chopped first, for their hairy texture can be unpleasant. They mix well, finely chopped, on yoghourt and cream cheese, or the leaves are sometimes boiled and mixed with ravioli stuffings, or they can be dipped in batter and fried in deep fat. Borage is seldom on sale in the market.

BORDEAUX WINES. Bordeaux, situated on the last great curve of the river Garonne before it joins the Dordogne to unite in the Gironde estuary, is one of the most agreeable cities of France and the capital of the largest fine wine area in the world. The population, including the suburbs, is about 450,000. With an average crop of over 3 million hectolitres of *Appellation Contrôlée* red and white wine it produces a third of the *AC* wines of France and about 5 per cent of total French production. The vineyard area, much reduced in the last twenty years, is now 109,000 hectares and there are 9,000 growers.

The great attraction of Bordeaux wines lies not only in the distinction of its famous red and white wines, but in their variety of style, quality and price. This is the result of the variations in situation and soil from vineyard to vineyard as well as from district to district.

GRAPE VARIETIES. The different types of grape and the way they are proportioned in the vineyards is also responsible for the fascinating variety of Bordeaux wines. The chief red wine grapes are *cabernet-sauvignon, cabernet-franc, bouchet* (a type of *cabernet* grown in St-Emilion and Pomerol), *merlot,* and small percentages of *malbec* (known as *pressac* in *St-Emilion and Pomerol*) and *petit verdot. Cabernet-sauvignon* is the leading Médoc grape, giving the wine its 'wiriness' and tannin-astringency in youth and fruity delicacy in maturity; in St-Emilion and Pomerol the dominant grape is the *merlot,* producing softer, more rapidly maturing wines. The white wine grapes are the *sauvignon, sémillon* and, marginally, the *muscadelle.* Also employed occasionally are the *colombard, ugniblanc* and even the *riesling.*

THE AREAS. There are four main red wine areas producing what in English-speaking countries only is known as claret, from *clairet,* meaning clear and indicating a light wine. They are the Médoc, Graves, St-Emilion and Pomerol. There are also four minor areas: Fronsac, Bourge, Blaye, and the Premières Côtes de Bordeaux.

There are two main white wine districts: Graves and Sauternes, and four lesser areas: Entre-deux-Mers, Cérons, Loupiac and Ste Croix-du-Mont. Among the minor areas both red and white wines are produced in Bourg, Blaye, Premières Côtes and Entre-deux-Mers.

Inside the main areas there are further subdivisions, mostly based on *communes* and usually having different *appellations.*

APPELLATIONS CONTROLÉES. Every Bordeaux wine-growing district, *commune* and even each single vineyard has its controlled *appellation,* and all wine-growing and selling is based on this. This *AC* system, finally devised in 1935, specifies the territorial limits, the grape types permitted, the conditions of planting and cultivation, and the maximum production permitted per hectare. The finer the wine district the lower the top limit of permitted quantity. A vineyard may be entitled to several *appellations.* Ch. Latour at its lowest is a Bordeaux Supérieur, but also an Haut-Médoc and a Pauillac. It will use the third and highest *AC,* but surplus production above the allowed limit or insufficiently good wine may be de-classed as Bordeaux Supérieur. There are approximately 40 different *ACs* in the Gironde *département* which contains all Bordeaux wines. The vineyard area is about 75 miles from north to south, with a maximum width across the two rivers of 30 miles.

THE MÉDOC. This is basically divided in two: the Haut-Médoc, running north from Bordeaux to just beyond St-Estèphe, and the Bas-Médoc extending up to the Atlantic. This latter term is not now used, and it is designated as Médoc, which is the *AC* of its wines.

The Haut-Médoc includes the cream of the great red Bordeaux estates. Six of its *communes* are entitled to their own *appellation:* Pauillac, St-Estèphe, St-Julien, Margaux, Moulis and Listrac. Margaux's *AC* now includes the *communes* of Cantenac, Soussans and most of Labarde and Arsac. All other wines in the area which fulfill the *AC* stipulations are labelled Haut-Médoc.

The Haut-Médoc is also dominated by the famous, now controversial 1855 classification, made for the Paris International Exhibition of that year. This selected about 60 leading growths whose reputation and price over many years on the Bordeaux market had given them a special status. These became known as the *crus classés,* with below them the *crus bourgeois,* the *crus artisans* and the *crus paysans* (no longer used). The classed growths were divided into five classes in strict order of preference, and this has caused much subsequent heart-burning. Furthermore, one red Graves, Haut-Brion, was included but no St-Emilions or Pomerols, then of little account. The most vociferous complainant for over 100 years has been Mouton-Rothschild, which disdained its appointed rank as head of the second class, and has consistently proclaimed its parity with the four first growths, Lafite, Latour, Margaux and Haut-Brion. A new classification has been promised, or threatened, according to viewpoint, for the past ten years, but owing to conflicting views has not yet been imposed. A common view is that there should be three classes only, that they should include leading red Graves, St-Emilions and Pomerols and add some prominent *crus bourgeois.* In the following Haut-Médoc *communes* the classed growths are marked with an * and placed in their 1855 order, though this does not necessarily accord with current evaluations, it is the order that is used by everyone connected with the wine trade. Only the best known outside France are listed.

HAUT-MEDOC. *Pauillac.* Includes 18 classed growths, more than any other *commune.* Big, fruity wines, usually deep in colour and flavour, slow-developing. Lafite*, Latour*, Mouton-Rothschild*, Pichon Longueville (Baron* and Lalande*), Pontet Canet*, Batailley*, Grand Puy Lacoste*, Mouton-Baron Philippe* (formerly Mouton d'Armailhacq), La Couronne, Monpelou.

St-Estèphe. Adjoining Pauillac, the wines are

BORAGE

generally tougher, and take time to come round. Many *crus bourgeois* in this heavily vine-planted *commune*. Cos d'Estournel*, Montrose*, Calon Ségur*, de Pez, Meyney, Marbuzet, Phélan-Ségur, Capbern, Le Boscq.

St-Julien. South of Pauillac, and the heart of fine Médoc wines, more delicate than their neighbours to the north, and more body than Margaux to the south. Léoville (Lascases*, Poyferré*, Barton), Gruaud Larose*, Ducru Beaucaillou*, Langoa Barton*, Branaire*, Talbot*, Beychevelle*, Gloria. Wines labelled St-Julien only are suspect in this heavily classed-growth *commune*.

Margaux. Ch. Margaux*, Rausan Ségla*, Rauzan Gassies*, Lascombes*, Malescot*, Boyd Cantenac*, Marquis de Terme*, La Bégorce. Renowned for the bouquet and delicacy in fine years.

Cantenac (with Margaux *AC*). Wines similar to Margaux but rather more substantial. Brane Cantenac*, Issan*, Cantenac Brown*, Palmer*, Le Prieuré*, Angludet, Martinens.

Soussans (with Margaux *AC*). Similar style to Margaux but less delicate. Siran, La Tour de Mons, Paveil de Luze.

Arsac (part with Margaux *AC*). Fruity, less subtle wines. Le Tertre*.

St-Laurent. Lying inland from the estuary, the wines are on the hard side. Le Tour Carnet*, Belgrave*.

Moulis. Another hinterland *commune,* with strong wines which can show quality after long maturation. Chasse Spleen, Poujeaux, Dutruch, Maucaillou.

Listrac. Even tougher wines, full of tannin, but with authentic Médoc quality. Fourcas Dupré, Pierre Bibian, Fonréaud.

Macau. Nearing Graves border, wines are strong with earthy quality. Dominated by Cantemerle*.

Ludon. Similar to those adjoining Macau. La Lagune*. Half a dozen other *communes*, among them Avensan, Cussac, Cissac and St Seurin, produce some excellent *crus bourgeois*.

MÉDOC (BAS-MÉDOC). The wines lack the distinction of most Haut-Médocs, but are often well made and good value. Among the best-known vineyards, spread among various *communes*, are Laujac, Loudenne and Patache d'Aux.

Some white wines are made in the Médoc, notably at Ch. Margaux and Loudenne, but its *AC* is Bordeaux Supérieur.

GRAVES – RED. The best red wines come from six *communes* immediately to the south and south-west of Bordeaux: Pessac, Talence, Léognan, Villenave D'Ornan, Cadaujac and Martillac. The wines tend to have a certain 'strike' or earthy taste, and are often slightly less full-bodied and rounded then Médocs. The leading 13 wines were first classified in 1959. Those that produce classified white as well as red wines are marked with a †. The best known include Haut-Brion†, La Mission Haut-Brion, Pape Clément, Haut-Bailly, La Tour Haut-Brion, Smith-Haut-Lafitte, Domaine de Chevalier† and Bouscaut†. There are few red *crus bourgeois* of importance.

GRAVES – WHITE. This large, elongated district, which runs from the outskirts of Bordeaux to Sauternes and beyond, produces a large number of dry to medium dry wines, mostly with little-known names. The recent Graves classification included nine dry white growths, some listed above in the red Graves list. Others are Laville-Haut-Brion, Carbonnieux, Olivier, Couhins, Malartic Lagravière, and La-Tour-Martillac. These are drier and much more distinguished than the general run of white Graves.

CÉRONS, STE CROIX-DU-MONT, LOUPIAC. Although Cérons is on the left bank and the other two small districts are on the right bank, all wines are sweet, although not so luscious as the Sauternes. Growth names are unimportant, but the value for money is often excellent.

SAUTERNES. This famous area includes Barsac (also entitled to its own *AC*), Bommes, Preignac, Fargues and Sauternes itself. About 24 of these wines were included in the 1855 classification, which here has produced no controversy. The most famous wine is Yquem, followed by Coutet, Climens, Suduiraut, Rieussac, etc. These wines are produced from grapes infected by the 'noble rot' (*pourriture noble*), which dries up the grapes and gives that wonderfully concentrated flavour which makes them among the great dessert wines of the world.

ST-ÉMILION. This district lies about 20 miles east of Bordeaux, across the two rivers. The wines are softer than the Médocs, round and rather rich by claret standards. Classified in 1955, with 12 *premiers grands crus* and over 60 *grands crus*. There are two main parts: the Côtes, near the attractive town of St-Emilion and overlooking the Dordogne Valley, and the Graves-St-Emilion on the plateau which also include Pomerol. The leading Côtes wines includes Ausone, Belair, Canon, La Gaffe-lière, Magdelaine and Trottevieille. The smaller Graves area, so-called owing to the gravelly soil, includes Cheval-Blanc, Figeac, La-Tour-du-Pin-Figeac and La Dominique. In any comprehensive re-classification Cheval-Blanc would certainly be in the top group, and possibly Ausone too. St-Emilion is a large vineyard area, with a group of *sub-appellations* on its perimeter.

POMEROL. The only major Bordeaux area unclassified, although unofficial listings of the top dozen or so exist. The wines are fuller, more fragrant and fruitier than the adjoining St-Emilions, but often lack the final distinction of their neighbours. A small region of modest vineyards, it is headed by Pétrus, another certain candidate for first-growth status; and among many growths with almost equal claims to mention there are Vieux Château Certan, La Conseillante, Petit-Village, Certan, Clos Réné, L'Enclos, La Fleur, Trotanoy and La Croix de Gay. Two sub-districts are Lalande de Pomerol and Néac.

FRONSAC, BOURG AND BLAYE. These three right-bank districts, downstream from Pomerol, provide excellent medium-quality claret. The Fronsac wines are the most distinguished, full-bodied, fruity and rather like the lesser St-Emilions. The best Bourg growths make powerful wines that develop well, while the Blaye wines are lighter. The latter two districts also produce white wines, but not Fronsac.

ENTRE-DEUX-MERS. This tongue of land be-tween the two rivers, narrowing as they approach their confluence, produces a mass of dry white wine of fair quality, and a little red too. One sub-division is the Graves de Vayres, so-called from its soil, but producing a white wine of lesser quality than the real Graves. The Premières Côtes, which

produces red wines and fairly sweet wines is a long thin slice of the 'tongue', overhanging the right bank of the Garonne.

LEADING VINTAGES OF THE LAST 25 YEARS. Red – '45, '47, '48, '49, '52, '53, '55, '59, '61, '62, '64, '66, '67.

White – '45, '47, '49, '50, '52, '53, '55, '59, '61, '67.

As dry white Bordeaux vintages are less variable than the sweet wines, the above list is slanted towards the latter.

SERVING BORDEAUX. Red: Stand up in a reasonable constant temperature of 62–68° F. for the better part of 12 hours, to allow sediment to fall. It pays to decant all clarets, as it aerates and softens the wine that at first opening may be a little hard. The younger the wine the longer the pre-drinking decanting time, but even a sound wine of 20–25 years should benefit from an hour in an unstoppered decanter.

White: The sweeter the wine the cooler it should be served. A dry graves will drink well at about 52° F., a Sauternes at under 50° F. But even luscious Sauternes should not be frozen in the refrigerator, as this kills the wonderful aroma and flavour. There is no point in decanting unless an old wine has some deposit, which is quite harmless. But the

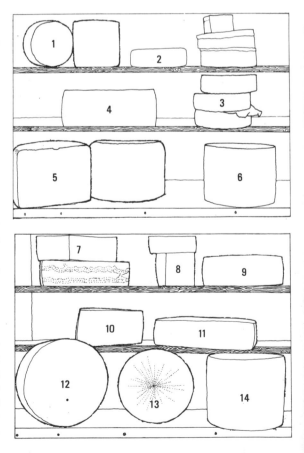

CHEESES, ENGLISH: 1. Stilton; 2. Derby; 3. Caerphilly; 4. Dunlop; 5. Blue Cheshire; 6. White Cheshire; 7. Sage Derby; 8. Wensleydale; 9. Creamy Double Gloucester; 10. Farmhouse Double Gloucester; 11. Leicester; 12. Cheddar; 13. Blue Cheshire; 14. Red Cheshire.

BEAN POT

wine will benefit by having the cork drawn a quarter of an hour before serving. All Bordeaux wines should be served in generous-sized glasses, with a pinched-in top; but only half-filled.

BORDEAUX SUPÉRIEUR. See BORDEAUX WINES.

BORDELAISE, À LA. A French culinary term for different garnitures. One is simply the *sauce bordelaise*, another features *cèpes*, another *mirepoix* (which see), and the fourth a garnish of artichoke bottoms and potatoes.

BORDELAISE SAUCE. See SAUCES.

BÖREK. *Börek* is a savoury-filled pastry, sometimes fried, sometimes baked and a speciality of Turkey and the Balkans. Some are very small, others large. In every case the pastry is rolled to paper-thinness. Among the most popular *böreks* are those which are very small and filled with meat or cheese and then shaped either as cigarettes or tiny cushions. These are usually fried. Larger *böreks*, with similar fillings, are baked and generally prepared with several layers of pastry.

BORSCH. There are almost as many spellings for this aristocrat among soups as there are recipes. It is the national soup of both Russia and Poland and it is impossible here to enter into a discussion about its origin. It is the most internationally famed of the Slav soups and it varies as much as a recipe can do. There are thick and thin borschs as well as hot and cold. One borsch is so clear and light in colour it is almost a white consommé, with beetroot colouring. Not all borschs have beetroot, although many do. Nearly all have a basis of *kvas* (which see). All borschs are served with a sour cream garnish.

BOSCQ, LE. See BORDEAUX WINES.

BOSSON MACÉRÉ. A Provençal goats' milk cheese macerated in wine or brandy.

BOSTON BAKED BEANS. Boston is known as the Bean Town because of its old tradition of the weekend dish of baked beans. In the days of the Puritans the Sabbath lasted from sundown Saturday night to sundown the following evening, and the beans provided the Bostonians with a hearty dish, easy to prepare and leaving time for the strict Sabbath observances. The bean pot could be kept going in the slow heat of the stove to serve as Saturday supper and also breakfast the following day. Furthermore, busy housewives had the services of the local baker, who called every Saturday, collected the family's bean pot and took it off to be baked in the community oven, often situated in the cellar of a nearby tavern. The bean pots were returned either Saturday evening or Sunday morning with a bonus in the shape of a piece of brown bread.

Many people then, and some even today, believe that the brown richness of Boston baked beans is largely due to the earthenware bean pot with its bulging belly and narrow neck in which they are cooked. Failing such a genuine bean pot, any really deep earthenware casserole can take its place, provided that it has a well-fitting cover and is oven-proof.

1 lb. navy beans
1¼ quarts (1½) cold water

CHEESES, GERMAN: 1. Tilsiter; 2. Allgäuer Emmenthaler; 3. Camembert; 4. Romadur; 5. Brie; 6. Harzer-Mainzer; 7. Weinkäse; 8. Butterkäse; 9. Edamer; 10. Frischkäse. A cheese warehouse.

2 teaspoons (2½) salt
¼ cup (⅓) soft brown sugar
1 teaspoon (1¼) dry mustard
¼ cup (⅓) molasses
¼ lb. salt pork
1 onion

Rinse the beans. Put them in a pan with the cold water and bring to the boil. Allow to simmer for 2 minutes, then take from the heat and let stand for several hours or overnight. Add half of the salt, cover and simmer for about 1 hour or until tender. Drain the beans, saving the liquid.

Measure 1½ cups (1¾) of the bean liquid and combine with it the brown sugar, remaining salt, dry mustard and molasses. Put the beans into a bean pot and pour this liquid over them. Cut the salt pork into several chunks and add this and the onion to the beans. Cook for 5–6 hours at 300° F. (Gas Mark 1–2). If the beans show any signs of becoming dry, add more of the bean liquid.

BOSTON BROWN BREAD. A moist, brown American bread cooked by steaming in baking powder tins.

¾ cup (1) rye flour
¾ cup (1) yellow cornmeal
¾ cup (1) Graham flour
½ teaspoon (⅔) baking soda
¾ teaspoon (1) salt
½ cup (⅔) molasses
1½ cups (2) buttermilk
¾ cup (1) raisins (optional)

Sift the dry ingredients together, make a well in the centre, add the molasses, buttermilk and raisins, if used. Stir well. Place rounds of greased paper at the bottom of one pound baking powder tins. Grease the sides of the tins and fill them about three-quarters full. The tins must be tightly covered so that the bread does not force itself out as it rises. Place the tin in a pan filled with enough boiling water to reach half-way up the basins and steam for 3 hours, keeping the water at over the halfway mark all the time. Remove from the tins immediately and serve piping hot with butter – and Boston Baked Beans (which see).

Makes three loaves.

BOSTON BUTT. The unsmoked, square cut from above the shoulder of pork. See HAM.

BOTARGO. Botargo is the roe of the grey mullet and sometimes goes under the grander name of red caviar. It has a unique flavour, is as thick as caramel, extremely rich and adheres somewhat to the teeth and roof of the mouth. It is not now known in Britain, although Samuel Pepys records on 6th June 1661: 'We stayed talking and singing and drinking great draughts of claret, and eating botargo and bread and butter till twelve at night.' Botargo in Pepys's day was called 'a sausage made from the eggs and the blood of mullet'.

BOTTLES. Bottles are containers in which to store and carry liquids. The earliest bottles were made of skins sewn together, but the ancients also used ones made of stone, alabaster, glass, ivory, horn, silver, and earthenware. Modern wine-bottles are made of glass composed chiefly of silica, soda and lime in varying proportions. The shades of green of wine-bottles, other than plain white ones, are imparted by iron oxide. Quart and pint bottles must, by law, contain a fourth and an eighth of a gallon, but the actual liquid contents of bottles, half-bottles or quarter-bottles are not legally defined, a fact taken advantage of by some unscrupulous dealers in wine. According to current commercial usage, wine bottles should never appreciably vary from the accepted standard of contents of 26⅔ fluid ounces per reputed quart, or 6 quarts to the gallon, equal to 4 imperial quarts of 40 fluid ounces each. The more usual names of bottles in Great Britain, besides half-bottles and quarter-bottles, are the magnum (two bottles), double-magnum (four bottles), tappit-hen (three imperial quarts), imperial pint (three-quarters of the reputed quart or ordinary bottle). Outsize bottles, for show purposes more than for practical use are:

Jeroboam or Double Magnum	4 bottles or	3·20 litres or 0·70 gallons
Rehoboam	6 bottles or	4·80 litres or 1·05 gallons
Imperiale (Claret)	8 bottles or	6·40 litres or 1·40 gallons
Methuselah	8 bottles or	6·40 litres or 1·40 gallons
Salmanazar	12 bottles or	9·60 litres or 2·10 gallons
Balthazar	16 bottles or	12·80 litres or 2·80 gallons
Nebuchadnezzar	20 bottles or	16·00 litres or 3·50 gallons

BOTTLE, TO. To preserve food in liquid.

BOUCHÉ. Literally, stoppered with a cork, and often meaning the best wine in the house as opposed to the *ordinaire* from the cask.

BOUCHÉES. Small puff pastry patties. Tiny savouries and hors d'oeuvre titbits which, to be traditional, should be only 'mouthfuls' (*bouche* = mouth). *Bouchées à la reine* are small patties filled with chicken ragoût and an invention, so we are told, of Marie Leszczyński, wife of Louis XV.

BOUCHET. See BORDEAUX WINES.

BOUCHONNÉ, VIN. French for corked wine, a wine made undrinkable by a musty or otherwise defective cork.

BOUQUET GARNI

BOUGROS. See BURGUNDY WINES.

BOUILLABAISSE. Although the bouillabaisse appears in many cooking books as a soup, it is not intended as such. It is a fish stew. To prepare the true Marseilles bouillabaisse away from the shores of the Mediterranean is a fairly useless occupation. The *rascasses*, the *hirondelles de la mer* and other fish are only available along parts of the Mediterranean coast, and they are essential. One might well make an excellent fish stew, but not a true bouillabaisse.

The history and fame of the bouillabaisse go far back through the centuries. Every French gastronomic writer, and others as far back as Pliny, have written about and expounded his or her theory. Each has his only true, only authentic recipe, and each recipe is different. Most of these recipes, we are informed, make a Marseillais wince. However, this 'noble' dish did inspire Thackeray, who liked his food, to write a famous ballad to the bouillabaisse he ate with such relish at Terre Tavern in Paris many years ago.

BOUILLON. The French term for stocks or broths. In plain cookery it describes the liquid of the stockpot, in classical cooking language this liquid is usually called *consommé blanc* to distinguish it from clarified *consommé* which is also referred to as double or rich *consommé*.

Bouillon or stock is used as a basis for soups and sauces.

BOUQUET. The aroma and the greatest charm of all good wines.

BOUQUET GARNI. The French culinary term for a faggot of herbs, an English name which has been so completely ousted by the French expression that few people know any more what a faggot (which see) of herbs is.

In classical cooking the herbs are all tied together and often put into a piece of muslin. This is to facilitate their removal as soon as they have given sufficient flavour to the dish.

The classic bouquet garni consists of three stalks of parsley to one of thyme and one bay leaf, but there are many deviations. In Provence, they include a strip of dried orange peel, which in some dishes is excellent. Some cooks add marjoram, others winter savory or lemon thyme. It is obviously a matter of taste, one cannot be dogmatic about it. The important point is to use a bouquet garni.

BOURG. See BORDEAUX WINES.

BOURGEOISE, À LA. A name given to various dishes, usually of large pieces of braised meat, prepared *à la mode bourgeoise*. Such dishes always include young carrots and turnips cut in neat uniform sizes, button onions, braised and glazed, and small cubes of lean cooked bacon. It implies modest home-style cooking.

BOURGOGNE. See BURGUNDY WINES.

BOURGOGNE GRAND ORDINAIRE. See BURGUNDY WINES.

BOURGOGNE ORDINAIRE. See BURGUNDY WINES.

BOURGOGNE PASSE-TOUT-GRAINS. See BURGUNDY WINES.

BOURGUEIL. Wine from the Côte de Bourgueil in Touraine. The best *commune* is St Nicholas de Bourgueil. The wines have a noticeable taste of raspberry and should be drunk young as they generally mature in five years.

BOURGUIGNONNE, À LA. This description as a rule is applied to dishes in which red wine, more especially Burgundy wine, is used plus small braised onions, mushrooms, and often rolled and grilled bacon as well.

BOURRIDE. A dish of fish from Provence, France, almost as popular as *bouillabaisse* (which see) but which does not require the same variety of fish.

Its success depends on its sauce, another speciality of Provence cooking, *aïoli*.

This is not a soup, for the fish is served on toast which has been soaked in fish stock and thickly spread with *aïoli*. Extra *aïoli* is served separately.

BOURSAULT. A triple-cream cheese from France.

BOURSIN. A well-known French triple-cream cheese now widely distributed.

BOUSCAUT. See BORDEAUX WINES.

BOXTY BREAD - BOXTY ON THE GRIDDLE. An Irish Hallowe'en dish which, like colcannon, has inspired poets to rhyme.

BOYD CANTENAC. See BORDEAUX WINES.

BRA CHEESE. A salty, hard, almost white, compact cheese, sharp and salty in flavour. Named after Bra, a town in Piedmont where the cheese originally was made by nomads.

BRAINS. See OFFAL and VARIETY MEATS.

BRAISING. This is a combination of baking and steaming. In the old days it was carried out with a special type of pan which had a sunken lid for holding live charcoal. This meant heat was applied above and below.

Braising pans are still available, although not with the sunken lid. They are usually rectangular in shape with a deep, tight-fitting lid. However, other pans and casseroles may be used.

When meat is braised it is usually placed on a bed of chopped vegetables, and flavourings such as onion, herbs and often bacon are added. Just enough liquid is added to moisten the contents of the pan; it is then covered and the meat (or whatever is being braised) slowly cooked.

BRAMBLE. See BLACKBERRY.

BRAN. This is the brown outer layer of a cereal such as wheat obtained in the process of making flour. It is mainly used for livestock but some is prepared for human consumption in the form of washed bran or as a breakfast cereal.

BRANAIRE. See BORDEAUX WINES.

BRANDADE. A Provençal dish which consists of salt cod pounded together with milk and oil until the mixture slowly becomes a thick creamy substance in which not one flake of fish is discernible. Pepper, freshly grated nutmeg, lemon juice and crushed garlic is added to taste. The brandade is served on a dish surrounded by fried bread or it can be served in vol-au-vent cases.

BRAND CHEESE (*Brandkäse*). A German hand cheese made from sour milk curd. During the ripening process the rind is either moistened with beer or the cheeses put into disused beer kegs, or both.

BRANDER. See GIRDLE.

BRANDY. The spirit distilled from wine. Brandy as a name has no geographical limitations and it should be qualified as French brandy, Spanish brandy, Californian brandy etc. The best brandies are always known by the name of the district where the wine from which they were distilled was made: Cognac brandy, Armagnac brandy and so on. Although any kind of wine can be distilled it is only certain types which are really suitable for distillation. Brandy has an alcoholic content of 40 per cent or more.

Cognac is the name of a small town on the River Charente in France famous all over the world for the excellence of its brandy. After Cognac, the brandies of Armagnac are the finest distilled in France.

The spirit which is distilled from the husks of grapes, that is to say the skins, stalks and pips left after the wine has been drawn, is not entitled to the name brandy. In France it is called *marc* (the 'c' is not pronounced) and in Italy *grappa*.

Brandy of fine quality and some age is drunk neat, as a liqueur, and should be neither sweetened nor coloured. Plain and young brandies are drunk with tap or soda water as a refreshing drink, or with hot water and sugar to ward off or cure a cold. Brandy is also used in the mixing of such drinks as blazers, cocktails and punches.

BRANDY COCKTAIL. This is brandy poured on to cracked ice, flavoured with a dash or so of angostura bitters and strained into cocktail glasses.

BRANDY SAUCE (HARD SAUCE). See SAUCES.

BRANDY SNAPS. These are crisp wafer-like biscuits rolled as soon as they are baked and while still soft into a cornet or cylinder shape. The biscuits harden almost immediately and glisten a dark chestnut colour. The hollow centre is filled with cream and this is often flavoured with brandy.

BRANE CANTENAC. See BORDEAUX WINES.

BRASENOSE ALE. A bowl containing three quarts of heated ale, sweetened with sifted sugar (although sugar is optional) and with six roasted

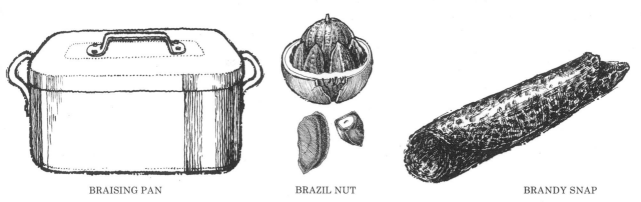

BRAISING PAN   BRAZIL NUT   BRANDY SNAP

apples floating in it. At Brasenose College, Oxford, it used to be brought into the refectory after dinner on Shrove Tuesday and passed round. In other colleges where the same custom prevailed, a similar brew was named Lamb's Wool.

BRASSERIE. Originally this referred to beer-shops where beer or cider was sold and even made. They were popular in Germany and eastern Europe but became established in Paris in the middle of the 19th century. In Paris they soon became the meeting places for literary men. Nowadays they are mostly cafés or restaurants where food and drink are served.

BRATWURST. A sausage of German origin now eaten in various parts of the world where there are communities of German or Scandinavian stock. It is made of lean pork and heavily seasoned with herbs and spices, including sage, nutmeg and ginger and is generally served hot, with vegetables.

BRAWN. This is made from the trimmings of a pig after being killed or from the pig's head, gristle and feet. It is cooked with a bunch of herbs, often sage and marjoram, but it is a matter of taste. The yellow skins of large strong-flavoured onions are added, plus peppercorns, salt and grated nutmeg or cloves. All of this is cooked in water until the meat comes off easily from the bone. The meat and some of the remaining liquid is poured into a mould, usually oblong or square in shape for easy cutting, pressed and allowed to set for 24 hours.

When required for use, boiling water is quickly poured over the bottom of the mould and the whole brawn is slid out and served on a bed of fresh parsley accompanied by a bowl of mustard sauce.

BRAZIL NUT. One of the best known and most appreciated of all edible nuts, also known as the Para or cream nut, and the *castanha* in Brazil. The tree yielding the nut is one of the largest in the Amazon forest.

The nuts are borne in a large spherical fruit (or container) up to 6 inches in diameter, in appearance not unlike a coconut, with a hard, woody outer casing about $\frac{1}{2}$ inch in thickness. A dozen or so nuts are developed in the container. They are closely packed rather in the same way as segments of an orange. When the fruits ripen they fall with a crash to the ground where they are gathered and the nuts extracted. Collecting the heavy fruits – they can weigh from 3 to 4 pounds – can be quite hazardous for they often fall from a height of 100 feet.

When the fruits are collected (and after the casing has been skilfully broken) the nuts are washed, graded and then sent off to the world markets.

Brazil nuts can be used in all manner of ways. They are easy to grind, to slice and to chop. It is called the 'King of Nuts' and its calorific value is high.

BRAZILIAN COOKING. There are many who claim that Brazilian cooking belongs to the great cuisines of the world. It is an interesting, even fascinating cuisine, basically Indian, Portuguese and African, influenced by but never dominated by the larger number and variety of immigrants who have come to the country and remained.

Many of what are today considered national and regional dishes in Brazil were taught to the original settlers by the Indians.

There are dishes of Arab origin, also Sudanese. The African slaves brought with them a love of food highly seasoned and spiced.

Finally there is the traditional dish of *feijoada completa*, which is indeed a complete meal, also a complete ceremony. It consists of a variety of meats – and variety is the operative word – cooked with black beans, onions and garlic and can take from 6 to 26 hours to prepare. When it is served the meat is separated from the beans and traditionally arranged. Sliced oranges and hot sauces and manioc are served with it. Along with the *feijoada completa* rum is served. It is thought of mainly as a luncheon dish as it is extremely heavy, and guests are expected to stay for some time afterwards to exclaim at the splendour of their hostess's efforts.

BREAD. Bread is made of ground grain, the flour of wheat, barley, rye, oats and other cereals, and its history is the story of civilization. The Stone Age woman baked her bread from a type of coarse grain. It was a tough bread, seemingly impervious to decay, for bits of flat, hard and charred bread have been found by archaeologists and declared by experts to be bread.

The first recorded bread was made by the Egyptians, the Jews and the Chinese. Millet and buckwheat are among the first recorded cereals. In ancient Egypt we are told there was a public oven in every village, and every rich family had its own private oven. Everyone had a supply of fresh bread daily, and by the time the Pharoahs were in power both leavened and unleavened bread were used. Bread said to be 3,500 years old has been found in the Asasif Valley in excavations on the site of the Ramassis temples. Some of this had characteristics of modern rye bread, some proved to be a type of honey bread or cake, and some even bore a curious resemblance to plum pudding.

Unleavened bread influenced the lives of the Israelites and Christians alike. There is considerable mention of it in the Old Testament, and this bread might have been made of wheat, barley and lentils, all mentioned in the biblical histories.

The first leavened bread came by accident when an Egyptian baker left some dough out in the warm sun and it fermented. This produced the first sour dough, and, the story continues, the beginning of yeast and beer.

Wheat and rye are the chief cereals for making bread, as no other cereal contains sufficient gluten to make a good loaf.

Much of the bread sold in Britain and America is made in automatic plant bakeries and requires very little baking skill. France, Germany, Austria and the Balkan countries still produce bread of the old-fashioned type popular with those who are connoisseurs of bread.

It is not possible to give here all the varieties in bread. French bread is generally thought of as being a yard of bread, shaped like a baton. But there is variety in the size and thicknesses of these batons, and there are other types of French bread.

The Germans and Austrians specialize in black bread, 'Land' breads and rye breads, or bread flavoured with caraway seeds and poppy seeds.

The Scandinavians also have a large array of dark breads, crispbreads, etc., and the Turks produce a soft brown aromatic bread that must be eaten fresh.

Ireland has its soda bread, among others and the British have a large variety in old-fashioned shapes and sizes, the best known of which is the cottage loaf, which is marked into two sections, both round, looking like one ball of bread, baked a golden brown, sitting comfortably on top of another. There are cob loaves and tin loaves. Boston brown bread, Graham bread, Johnny cake, rye bread and spoon bread are American favourites.

All countries produce decorated breads, such as elaborate plaited breads, and some of the British harvest festival breads look as though they have been sculpted.

BREADCRUMBS. There are four types of breadcrumbs:

BROWN BREADCRUMBS

Collect all scraps of bread, crusts of toast not otherwise required. Leave them on a tray or rack till enough are collected, not in a tin for they will go mouldy. Bake in a moderate oven until they are of a uniform brown. Put through a grinder or a blender or pound in a mortar until fine, then pass through a sieve. Keep in a jar until required. Use for covering pies etc., but not for frying.

BUTTERED OR FRIED BREADCRUMBS

Heat some butter in a frying pan until hot. Stir in as many white breadcrumbs as the fat will absorb. Stir and fry the crumbs until they are brown and crisp. Serve as a garnish.

FRESH BREADCRUMBS

Take a stale white loaf and cut into thick slices. Remove the crusts. Rub the bread on a grater or coarse wire sieve. (This can be done in most blenders.) These are for bread sauce (which see), puddings and for frying. Make fresh breadcrumbs only as required as they will turn mouldy if kept for long. They are the best for egging and crumbing.

WHITE BREADCRUMBS

Prepare as for brown breadcrumbs except only dry the bread in the oven and do not allow it to brown. These may be used for frying but they must be sifted until very fine. Do not use for puddings etc.

BREADFRUIT. The name of both a tree of the mulberry family and its fruit. The tree, which is handsome, grows from 30 to 40 feet in height with fragile branches and large leathery leaves. The fruit is green, large and melon-shaped, about eight inches in length, with a rough surface and is taken from the tree before it is fully ripe.

It is a staple foodstuff in its native habitat, the Indonesian archipelago, where three trees are considered adequate to feed one man for a year. Its chief fame is associated with Captain Bligh's attempt to plant it in Tahiti, and the resultant mutiny on H.M.S. Bounty.

Breadfruit can be prepared in many ways that the potato is cooked. One very pleasant way is to hollow out the centre and fill it with various local fruit bits, wrap the breadfruit in a plantain leaf

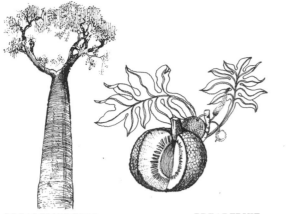

BREADFRUIT TREE ·   BREADFRUIT

BREAM

and bury it in live coals to bake for a few hours. Or it can be cooked in the coals without the filling and served thickly sliced with butter. When the skin splits, and the fruit is soft to the touch, it is ready to eat. The breadfruit has been successfully transplanted to all tropical countries of the world.

There is also the African breadfruit tree, which must not be confused with the true breadfruit tree, although it belongs to the same family, and grows in west tropical Africa. Numerous brown seeds, about one-third inch long are embedded in the pulp of its massive fruit, which weighs from 18 to 30 pounds. After roasting or boiling, these are eaten as dessert nuts. They are also fried in oil or ground to a meal and used to thicken soups etc.

BREAD PUDDING. There are several kinds of bread pudding. Some are cooked with an egg and milk and custard and flavoured with currants, nutmeg etc., and others are savoury and flavoured with onions, salt, pepper, parsley and cheese etc.

BREAD SAUCE. See SAUCES.

BREAKFAST. In England, an institution which rarely fails to intrigue visitors from many of the Continental countries. According to the Oxford Dictionary, the first recorded use of the word breakfast was in 1463, but Elizabeth Woodville, wife of Edward IV, in her diary dated 10th May 1451, wrote: 'Breakfasted. The buttock of beef rather too much boiled, and the ale a little the stalest.' An earl and his countess in the same century leave us another record, for they break-fasted on 'two loaves of bread, a quart of beer, a quart of wine, two pieces of salt fish, six baconed herrings, four white herrings'.

By the time of Elizabeth I, breakfast was still not the meal known in Britain today. Right into the early 19th century breakfast even for the 'gentle folks' was a meal of bread, meat and ale or wine.

Then came a change to gargantuan meals in the wealthier households, with sideboards covered with silver dishes which held such delights as chicken livers, mushrooms, stewed kidneys, chops

and steaks; there might be fresh trout or potted salmon, grilled sole or poached haddock, cold roast beef, rich and rare, pressed beef and galantine of chicken, veal or game pie, home-made scones to be eaten with good country butter, toast and marmalade, baked apples or other cooked fruit, tea and coffee, and of course porridge. It was as if all the housewives and cooks of England had taken to heart Mrs Beeton's warming and warning words: 'The moral and physical welfare of mankind depends largely upon its breakfast'.

Now in the reign of another Elizabeth the English breakfast is a pale ghost of its former self, with its 'sheet anchor', to quote Mrs Beeton again, of eggs and bacon, kippers, kedgeree and poached eggs on toast; in the interests of time or diet, many Britons reduce this still further to a mere boiled egg, or toast.

WEDDING BREAKFAST. This particularly British function has nothing whatever to do with bacon and eggs and takes place after a wedding ceremony. This meal is called a breakfast because the 'haste to the wedding' presupposes the impossibility of a meal until the ceremony is over. Today it consists generally of wedding cake and champagne, plus 'small eats'. The original bride's cake was made from aromatic ingredients, crowned with an icing made from sweet sugar and bitter almonds, emblematic of the sweetness and pain in every marriage.

BREAM. Some fishermen consider the flesh of the freshwater bream to be rather tasteless, but on the Continent there are many who hold it in high esteem.

The bream is a species of carp and all recipes for carp may be applied.

There is also a sea bream which is common in most European waters and in the United States which has a better flavour. In Far Eastern waters there are several species of fish which are called bream.

BREED. The most seductive and rarest quality of wine; also the most difficult to describe. It is the privilege of the finest wine only, of wine that is endowed with an outstanding personality, a discreet yet fragrant bouquet, perfect poise of flavour and strength and a lingering attractive 'farewell'.

BRETONNE, À LA. This French culinary term usually implies the dish is served with a garnish of beans.

BREWIS, FISHERMAN'S. A Newfoundland dish. Skin and bone some fresh fish, put in a pan with boiling, salted water and cook until tender. Soak some hard bread overnight. Next morning put it into cold water and bring slowly to the boil, cooking for 5–10 minutes. Fry some small pieces of pork fat until the fat runs. Add the fish and the brewis. Toss lightly and heat thoroughly.

In the north of England brewis signifies an oatcake soaked in broth, mashed and seasoned with salt and pepper. The word probably comes from the French word *brouet* meaning pottage.

BRÉZÉ. One of the best white wines of Saumur. Light, graceful, and yet vigorous, it is *pétillant* (fizzy) for quite some time and ages slowly.

BRICK CHEESE. A truly American cheese invented in the middle of the 19th century by a Wisconsin dairyman of Swiss descent who used bricks pressed on top of the curd to force out the whey.

It is a firm and elastic cheese quite strong in flavour, cream-coloured and with numerous small eyes.

BRIE. A famous French cheese, farm-made, whole-milk, and mould-innoculated; it is quite round, usually 14 inches across, quite flat, soft when ripe and about six pounds in weight. It is made in the *département* of Seine-et-Marne and three different varieties are named after Melun, Coulommiers and Meaux.

Brie has been known for several centuries. Henry IV of France (1553–1610) was given some by Queen Margot. The Great Condé (1621–86) demanded that Brie should accompany a Victory wine. At the Congress of Vienna (1814) Talleyrand sent a Brie which won a gastronomic competition against 60 cheeses from participating countries. A French historian has even asserted that this victory restored France to the esteem of the other European powers.

BRILL. A European salt-water fish of real gastronomic merit. It is similar to the turbot but more oval-shaped with smooth scales and no tubercles. Its flesh is very delicate and light although generally regarded as slightly inferior to the turbot. It is in season throughout the year but at its best from April to August.

There are similar looking flatfish found throughout the world, especially in Far Eastern waters, which are called brill but they do not have the same quality of flavour. There is also a Mediterranean brill of good flavour but that caught in the Atlantic is considered by many fish-lovers as the best of all.

BRILLAT-SAVARIN, Jean Anthelme. Author of *La Physiologie du Goût*, published shortly before his death (1826). He began life as a lawyer then entered politics, becoming Mayor of Belley, his birthplace. To escape proscription during the reign of terror, he fled first to Switzerland and then to the United States of America, where he spent three years as a refugee. At one time he played in the orchestra of a New York theatre. On the fall of Robespierre he returned to France, in 1797.

His gastronomical book, a witty compendium of the art of living, took him many years to write; it is still reckoned as one of the best in existence.

BRINE. A simple salt-water mixture used to preserve the colour of apples and pears while they are being prepared for cooking, or for preparing vegetables for pickling or for keeping or bottling. Vegetables are sometimes brined by being arranged in layers with salt sprinkled between them without water.

Brine can also be a mixture of salt, saltpetre, sugar and water for salting meat to keep and preserve it. Meat which is put into a brine is usually later smoked.

BRIOCHE. This is a type of cake made from a light yeast dough. The most usual shape resembles the British cottage loaf, that is, a ball surmounted by another ball, and they come in all sizes. But there are also *brioches* baked in a circle, and another, *brioche mousseline*, which is baked in a tall tin and looks like a chef's hat. Whatever the shape, a *brioche* should be a rich brown.

The *brioche* is of French origin and for many brings nostalgic memories of drinking hot chocolate in the morning or afternoon in more leisurely days. *Brioche* has been made in France for several centuries and it has been copied throughout Europe, particularly Austria and Switzerland, where it has become naturalized.

According to some authorities the first *brioches* were made in Brie, hence the name, and Brie cheese was used in the pastry. There are other equally valid claims to the fame of inventing the *brioche*, some of which are more whimsical than accurate.

BRION, HAUT-. See BORDEAUX WINES.

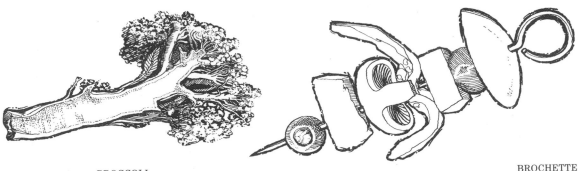

BROCCOLI   BROCHETTE

BRISKET. This is best rib in Europe and shoulder cut in the United States. It is the breast of the animal, the part covering the breast-bone. It can be braised, stewed or boiled fresh but it is frequently salted or pickled in a brine, or pressed for corned beef.

BRISLING. A small Norwegian fish of the herring family, resembling a sardine.

BRISTOL CREAM. The registered name of a sherry, rich and of fine quality.

BRISTOL MILK. The name used by several Bristol wine merchants for a fine sherry of their blending and shipping.

BRITTLE. A form of sweet or candy the basis of which is syrup or molasses. It generally contains nuts and has the characteristic of being easily broken into small pieces, while being solid but easily chewable.

BROCCIO. One of the smallest and best cheeses made in Corsica from goats' milk or sour ewes' milk. It is eaten plain or cooked. *Falulella,* a cheesecake, and *fiadene,* a special cake, are made with *broccio* in Corsica.

BROCCOLI. A *Brassica,* and one of three such vegetables believed to have originated in Italy. Botanically all the broccoli and cauliflowers are varieties of the same species and this causes some confusion of terminology. The popular name is Italian and derives from *brocco,* a shoot, the earliest form of the vegetable being loose spikes.

Broccoli has a long history. It has always been a favourite among gourmets and was highly esteemed by the Romans, from whom we have one of those useless but endearing anecdotes which make history live. Drusas, son of the Emperor Tiberius, one day ate so much broccoli that his father chided him for his greediness which, considering the extraordinary eating habits of wealthy Romans in those times, makes one wonder how much broccoli

the young man did, in fact, consume.

There are many varieties of broccoli, available in autumn, winter and spring. The heads range in colour from pure or creamy white through green to dark purple. They may be branched, as in the Italian Green Sprouting or Calabrese, or single, as in the Christmas Hardy Heading and the many Roscoff varieties.

The stalks, buds and most of the leaves are edible. Broccoli should have firm, dark leaves with compact bud clusters. They should be cooked in very little water until just tender, drained, and served with melted butter. The little heads, although soft, must remain whole after cooking. Frozen broccoli is available the year round and is cooked in the same manner.

BROCHETTES. A small skewer of metal, wood or even silver on which pieces of meat, fish or vegetables are threaded or skewered for grilling.

BROCHON. See BURGUNDY WINES.

BROIL. See GRILL.

BROKEN TEA. See TEA.

BRONTE. A wine-producing district of Sicily from which Lord Nelson took one of his titles. Nelson sent wine to England labelled Bronte, but it was, in fact, marsala. The M.V. Brown Collection of Wine and Sauce Labels in the London Museum includes an 18th-century plated label bearing the name Bronti. The name occurs both in this form and as Bronte on labels in the collection.

BROSE. Originally this seems to have been a simple Scottish dish of oatmeal with boiling water poured over it and occasionally a little salt and butter mixed with it. It was stirred up with the shank of a horn spoon and allowed to form knots. With this was served fresh sweet milk and, accord-to the Scots, is a dish that has been the backbone of many a sturdy Scotsman. *Brose and Butter* is the title of a favourite old Scottish tune.

There are several kinds of brose. Mussel brose with mussels added; kail brose with cabbage; milk brose, made with milk instead of water; Knotty Tams, made with beestings and oatmeal; blind brose, or brose without butter, and fat brose, which the monks ate 'on Fridays when they fasted', a more substantial dish with the addition of an ox or sheep's head. The most famous brose of all is Athol Brose (which see).

BROTH. This is a thin or unclarified soup and is of considerable value in that it is much lighter than consommé or clarified soup, for it contains all the soluble constituents of its ingredients, meat, vegetables and cereals, none of which have been removed by straining. Such broth is both stimulating and nourishing and if made with additional vegetables and cereals, and eaten with bread and potatoes, makes a substantial dish.

BROU DE NOIX. A French liqueur prepared with fresh walnuts crushed and steeped in brandy or some other spirit and sweetened.

BROUILLY. See BURGUNDY WINES.

BROWN, TO. This is a preliminary preparation to the cooking of many stews and casserole dishes, more especially in Italian cooking. The meat can be either fried or grilled. This seals in the juices so that the substance of the meat retains more flavour, which browning improves. Also, it gives a better colour.

To make a brown stock, bones are browned in the oven. In many dishes vegetables are also browned before the liquid is added.

BROWNIES. An American confection, rich and chewy, made from flour, butter, eggs, baking powder and, usually chocolate.

BROWN RICE. See RICE.

BROWN SAUCE. See SAUCES.

BROWN SUGAR. See SUGAR.

BRUNOISE. A French culinary term which has three meanings.

1. A method of shredding vegetables very finely, i.e., cooks talk of shredding carrots, celery, leeks, onions, etc., into a *brunoise* and then cooking them in butter or some other cooking fat or oil.

2. A mixture of vegetables, i.e., carrots, turnips, leeks, onions etc., not necessarily shredded, browned in butter or other fat prior to being made into a soup, stew or a stuffing.

3. A mixture of vegetables diced and used as a flavouring for crayfish and other dishes.

BRUNCH. A meal which is neither breakfast nor lunch but which combines some of the features of both and is served mid-morning.

BRUSSELS SPROUTS. A variety of cabbage introduced into Britain from Belgium in the 19th century. Sprouts are miniature cabbages with neither a heart, like the common cabbage, nor a head like the cauliflower. They grow in clusters along the stalk of a branching cabbage-like plant shaded at the top by a canopy of spreading leaves. Each small sprout has a mass of thin spoon-shaped leaves all very closely and compactly wrapped round one another.

In France, sprouts *(choux de bruxelles)* are tiny and of a quality seldom found in Britain or America where there is a preference for the larger variety, although the smaller and firmer they are the better the flavour. London writing in his *Encyclopaedia of Gardening* (1822), stated that the Belgians despised Brussels sprouts more than one-half inch in diameter.

BRUT. A French word used originally in connection with sparkling champagne to denote a wine that was wholly unsweetened. Other champagne shippers adopted *nature* to denote their driest wines.

BRUXELLES CHEESE. A soft, fermented Belgian cheese, made from skimmed cows' milk, on farms in the Louvain area.

BRUXELLOISE, À LA. A French culinary term for a garnish which includes Brussels sprouts and *pommes château* (which see).

BUAL. The English spelling of the Portuguese boal, one of the finest species of grapes grown in the island of Madeira, and one of the best Madeira wines, originally made exclusively from boal grapes. It is a pale gold wine with a soft, gentle quality. Slightly drier than the average madeira, it is especially good with after-dinner coffee or with a rich, creamy sweet.

The wines of Madeira sold under the name of bual are not so dry as the sercial but not nearly so sweet as the malmsey wines.

BUBBLE AND SQUEAK. True bubble and squeak consists of fried cold boiled meat and greens. They first 'bubble' in water while cooking, and then 'squeak' in the frying pan.

BUCK. The name for the adult male deer, the one

BISON

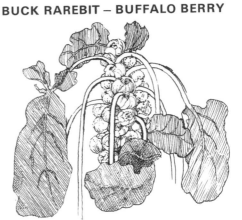

BRUSSELS SPROUTS

exception being the red deer, of which the adult male is called a stag or hart.

BUCK RAREBIT. A Welsh rarebit (which see) topped with a poached egg.

BUCKLING. Herrings which are beheaded and brined or dry-salted before being hot-smoked (as distinct from the cool-smoked kipper and bloater), at a temperature of about 212° F. Thus the fish are smoked and cooked simultaneously. British fish-mongers used to import buckling from Germany but they are now produced in London.

When they are in good condition, with moist flesh, they are very good and can be used in the same way as smoked trout. Skinned and filleted, buckling can be served as they are or tossed in an oil and vinegar dressing, sprinkled with finely chopped fresh dill and served with thin slices of buttered brown bread.

BUCKWHEAT. Botanically, buckwheat is not considered a true cereal but, because its seeds yield a flour from which bread can be made, it comes, gastronomically, into the cereal class. Another form of the name is beechwheat: its seeds were supposed to resemble the beech nut and this idea is reflected in the Latin name given to it by botanists. It is also called Saracen wheat, and is grown extensively in Siberia and parts of Holland, France and Italy. It is hardly used at all in Britain but a fair quantity is produced and used in the United States.

In the United States buckwheat flour is often mixed with wheat 'middlings' in order to modify the flavour and make it more delicate. It makes for a lighter and somewhat sweet batter which is also easier to handle.

BUFFALO. A type of heavy oxen found in tropical areas of the Old World and long domesticated in the Orient. Buffalo are characterized by their long, angular horns and broad, splayed feet which are adapted to wading. These animals mainly feed on aquatic grass and plants. The hide makes good leather, the milk is excellent to drink and as a source of butter; in India it is clarified and called *ghee*, and the meat is prepared as beef although, while resembling beef in most ways, it has a slightly sweet taste and is very tough. The name is often misapplied to the American bison, which is not of the same family.

The American buffalo, or 'Indian cattle', was once the most populous of the mammals on the North American continent. A large bovine of the genus Bison, with a large head, heavy forequarters and relatively light hindquarters, a large hump between the shoulders, 14 ribs while domestic cattle have only 13, dun-brown in colour, a heavy, shaggy fur, and weighing upwards of 3,000 pounds, it once roamed the continent from the Atlantic to the Pacific, and from Canada to Texas. Through senseless slaughter with no pretence of sportsman-ship, over 50 million animals were killed between 1800 and 1900.

The hump and tongue of the buffalo were prize delicacies to both the Indian and the white man, and buffalo ribs cooked over a hickory fire provide a rare treat. The meat of the buffalo resembles that of the normal beef cattle, to which it is kin. It does not, however, have the strong taste usually associated with game.

Once almost extinct, today herds of bison are on the increase in many National Parks in the United States and Canada, with large herds being privately owned both for show and meat. As the population of the herds in the parks must be controlled, this provides a small source of meat that can be procured commercially. The meat is prepared in the same way that any beef product is cooked, but the true, delicate flavour is best brought out by barbecuing.

BUFFALO BERRY or **BUFFALO CURRANT.** An American shrub of the family *Elaeagnaceae*, culti-vated in the western plains area both as an orna-mental bush and for its edible berry. It grows to a height of 18 feet, with thorny stems, and small silvery leaves. The fruit is small, yellow, tart, about the size of a currant and contains one seed.

The fruit is used in making tarts, pies, jellies and preserves. The names buffalo berry and buffalo currant are interchangeable.

BUFFALO FISH. A large, coarse, freshwater fish which is a member of the sucker family. Typical habitats are in bayous, shallow lakes, and large rivers. It is found in one of its three species, the large-mouth, the small-mouth, and the black buffalo fish, in waterways in most states east of the Mississippi river. When of medium-size, two to five pounds, it is widely eaten but the flesh in larger fish is coarse.

BUFFERHEAD DUCK. See DUCK, WILD.

BUFFET. In culinary terminology, the word buffet means a sideboard, a long, low table, a counter, even a cabinet. The origin of the word is unknown.

In the 16th century we read of Italian banquets where all the hot dishes came in from the kitchen but all the cold dishes were arranged on the buffet. In England, during the Middle Ages, the buffet was more literally a sideboard, simply a plank of wood placed in a convenient place for serving and carving.

Buffet also refers to a type of eating house, somewhere in which a fairly quick snack may be obtained, especially at railway stations.

Buffet luncheons and dinners are probably a development of the Russian *zakuski* or hors d'oeuvre and the Scandinavian *smörgasbord*.

BULB BASTER. The bulb baster is particularly good for basting meats, poultry, game vegetables in a casserole or, for that matter, anything which requires basting. They are best when the tube end is made with fireproof glass or metal as some of the plastic models collapse in very hot fat or liquid and are therefore, useless.

BULGARIAN WINES. There are many vineyards in Bulgaria and they produce some of the most acceptable wines made in the Balkans, although none can be claimed as fine wines.

BULLACE. A small tree and its fruit, a member of the plum family, and related to the damson plum. It is native to Europe where it has been semi-domesticated, but is rare in the United States. It is common in England where, though the fruit is inferior to the Continental version, it is used in making jam.

In the southern United States it is also the name given to a variety of the wild purple grape, though the spelling is changed to bullis. The bullis is rich purple, thick-skinned, with four seeds or pips, and much juice. The skin contains a large percentage of tannin. Not commercially cultivated in quantity. though it is a traditional source of jams, jellies and conserves.

BULLY BEEF. A name seldom heard today when the more gentle nomenclature, corned beef, has taken its place. The origin of bully beef is French, when *bouli* (boiled) beef was used on labels on the tinned army rations of the French in the Franco-Prussian War of 1870–71. It became British Army slang, bully beef or just bully, in World Wars I and II.

It is pressed boiled beef cured in a manner that makes it suitable for keeping a long time in a can. Corned is an old English word for cured, and the usual cut of beef corned is brisket. The red colour of bully beef is due to a liberal use of saltpetre in the curing, but the New England custom is to use far less saltpetre in the curing and thus the beef is of a grey-brown colour which is distinctive.

Bully beef may be eaten straight from the tin, sliced as cold meat, with pickles or salad. Or it can be carefully stewed or made into a ragoût. But probably the best manner of cooking it is to fry it in fat with plenty of onion in an open pan, which is probably much like the *miroton* which French soldiers on the march used to prepare for themselves out of their *bouli*.

BUN. In Britain bun is the name given to a round and usually glazed cake of varying size. It is mildly sweet and often spiced or flavoured and contains currants, raisins or peel. Many of these are traditional. Hot Cross buns are heavily spiced and eaten on Good Friday, never at any other time of the year. They were made originally in honour of an Anglo-Saxon goddess Eastre whose name-day fell in the spring. With the coming of Christianity, goddesses went out of favour, but the cakes or buns remained, now marked with a cross to bring them up to date and keep up yet another of the many superstitions of heathen days – for the cakes were marked with a cross to ward off evil. Good Friday was an evil day so it was logical to mark the Easter Bun with the new sign of the cross.

There are other buns, the famous Bath Bun (which see), Chelsea Bun, which is square, Sally Lunns, and a host more. Scotland has a black bun which is a rich fruit cake enclosed in a pastry covering. In the United States, buns are plain and soft, and often used with hamburgers.

BUNDNERFLEISH. This is a speciality of Grison, in Graubunden in Switzerland, and is dried meat – beef, mutton or goat – which is served in wafer-thin slices.

BURDOCK. This is a large plant with leaves over a foot long, common in most parts of Europe

BURDOCK   BULB BASTER

except the extreme north. In Scotland young shoots are peeled and used in cooking, prepared in the same way as salsify. Both leaves and roots were once used in the making of old-fashioned drinks, such as burdock ale, or mixtures such as dandelion and burdock wine. In the Far East, particularly in Japan where it is known as *gobo*, burdock has been so much improved upon as a root vegetable, it is now considered as something distinctly Japanese.

BURGOS. A very soft, popular Spanish cheese named after Burgos province where most of it is made.

BURGUNDY WINES. The vineyards of Burgundy produce some of the finest wines of the world; in fact, no other district attains such quality for both red and white table wines. But the acreage is small (only 64,500 acres of *Appellation Contrôlée* vines), the situation northerly and the climate precarious. Hence the output is modest compared, for instance, with that of Bordeaux. In the five last vintages the average was only 14,624,500 cases of *Appellation Contrôlée* wines.

Further, the ownership of the vineyards is divided between many thousands of proprietors. The average property is only 1½ acres. Nearly all these peasant-proprietors make their own wine, and there is much unevenness of skill and conscientiousness. Few, however, have the resources to ship their product. Most sell to the *négociants* (shippers) who when necessary blend their multifarious purchases, mature, bottle and ship them. Hence the shippers have a crucial importance in the Burgundy trade. Their reputation is as important as that of the vineyard or *commune*.

Even in the case of certain famous wines made from one vineyard, the shipper's name provides the criterion. The *grand cru* vineyard of Clos Vougeot, the largest in Burgundy, consists of 125 acres but is divided between 60 proprietors. So genuine Clos Vougeot of the same year may show markedly different quality and character according to the shipper's style and skill.

There is little *domaine* bottling in Burgundy,

compared with the scale of château bottling in Bordeaux. But *domaine* bottled wines are usually of high quality. The general table of precedence is:
1. single-vineyard *grands crus* (also known as *têtes de cuvée*);
2. single-vineyard *premiers crus* (or *premières cuvées*);
3. other single-vineyard wines;
4. *commune* wines, made all from vineyards of a single *commune*;
5. (a) for the Côte de Nuits, *Vins fins de la Côte de Nuits*, also called *Côte de Nuits Villages* (made from four minor *communes* of the Côte) and (b) for the Côte de Beaune, *Côtes de Beaune* and *Côte de Beaune Villages* (similarly made from minor fields in or adjacent to the commune of Beaune);
6. *bourgogne*;
7. *bourgogne grand ordinaire* or *bourgogne ordinaire,* which are the same thing and which, despite the 'grand', are not so good as *bourgogne*;
8. *Passe-tout-grains* (red) and *aligoté* (white).

For Chablis the table of precedence is:
1. Chablis *grand cru;*
2. Chablis *premier cru;*
3. Chablis; ....
4. petit chablis.

All fine red burgundy on the Côte d'Or and in the Chalonnais is made from the *pinot noir* grape. Ordinary red burgundy can be made from the *gamay*, but if so, in the case of the northern areas, the wine must be sold as *bourgogne passe-tout-grains*. However, the *gamay* is permitted in the Mâconnais and insisted on for named growths in the Beaujolais, where this grape does better, on granitic soil, and the *pinot noir* is only permitted in cheaper bottlings.

Fine white burgundy is made from the *chardonnay* grape, or its related *pinot blanc*. In Chablis the *chardonnay* is known as *beaunois*. Ordinary white burgundy is made from the prolific *aligoté*, but in France, when this is used, it is obligatory to state the fact on the label.

The long, narrow, main Burgundy field begins a

91

little south of Dijon with the no longer important *Côte de Dijon*. At Fixin begins the great Côte d'Or, divided into two sections, the northern Côte de Nuits and the southern Côte de Beaune. The Côte de Nuits provides nearly all the fine red wines and has few, but fine, whites; the Côte de Beaune produces nearly all the fine white wines, but has some excellent reds. Before listing their *communes* it should be stated that many have hyphenated the local village or town name with that of their finest vineyard; e.g., Gevrey-Chambertin, Chambolle-Musigny. A blended wine from vineyards all over the *commune* (e.g., Vosne-Romanée) will be *like* the wine of its greatest vineyard, Romanée-Conti. But of course it will not be so fine.

Following is the list of the Côte de Nuits *communes*, mentioning their *grands crus* wines and giving the numbers of their 1st crus in brackets, as the latter gives some indication of their relative importance. Fixin (6). Gevrey-Chambertin (21), a big wine, slow to mature, with two of the greatest *grands crus*, Chambertin and Clos de Bèze and six others with the vineyard name hyphenated to Chambertin (without Gevrey). Morey-St-Denis (24) produces sturdy wines similar to Gevrey-Chambertin, with 4 *grands crus,* Bonnes Mares, Clos de Tart, Clos de la Roche and Clos-St-Denis. Chambolle-Musigny (19), with softer wines, has for its *grands crus* Musigny and the remainder of Clos de Tart. Clos Vougeot (3) has the *grand cru* of that name. Its ancient château is the headquarters of the famous Confrérie des Chevaliers du Tastevin.

Flagey-Echézeaux wines, for the most part, are sold under the name of its southern neighbour, Vosne-Romanée (10). The *grands crus* of the latter are the tiny Romanée-Conti (usually the finest of all) and La Tâche, and the larger Richebourg and Romanée-St-Vivant. Echézeaux and Grands Echézeaux are accepted as *grands crus* of Vosne-Romanée. Nuits-St-Georges and Premeaux (40) are usually listed together. The Côte de Nuits ends with the minor *communes* of Prissey, Comblanchien and Corgoloin, which with those of Brochon in the north are sold under the comprehensive name of Vins Fins de la Côte de Nuits or Côte de Nuits Villages.

The first *commune* in the Côte de Beaune is Ladoix-Serrigny (6). Then comes Aloxe-Corton (13) with the red *grand cru* of Corton and the superb white of Corton-Charlemagne. Then Pernand-Vergelesses (5), Savigny-les-Beaune (22) and Beaune itself (29) follow. The ancient town of Beaune contains the picturesque Hospices, endowed by its founders and subsequent benefactors with 32 fine vineyards throughout its *côte*, the finest of which rank for quality with the recognized *grands crus*. Pommard (26), Volnay (28), Monthélie

(10) and Auxey-Duresses (8) lead to Meursault (17), the first of the famous white wine *communes*. It produces some red wine, but this is generally sold under the name of Volnay. Puligny-Montrachet (11) and Chassagne-Montrachet (13) are also famous white wine *communes*, though Chassagne also produces excellent reds. The *grands crus* are Montrachet, Batârd-Montrachet, Bienvenues-Bâtard-Montrachet, Chevalier-Montrachet and Criots-Bâtard-Montrachet. Montrachet is generally accepted as the finest dry white table wine. The Côte de Beaune ends with Santenay (3), St-Aubin (8) and the three Cheilly- (3), Dezize- (1) and Sampigny- (2) Maranges *communes*.

Behind each *côte* of the Côte d'Or is a Haute Côte producing unimportant wine, mostly from *gamay* or *aligoté* grapes.

The next area is the small Chalonnais, with 4 named *crus* – Mercurey and Givry, both nearly all red, Rully nearly all white, and Montagny all white. The Mâconnais produces much decent red and white wine, with one famous (and often very good) white wine, Pouilly-Fuissé. The neighbouring *appellations* of Pouilly-Loché and Pouilly-Vinzelles are only slightly inferior.

The Beaujolais has a bigger area of *Appellation Contrôlée* wines than all the rest of Burgundy put together, and since its red grape, the *gamay*, is a big yielder it produces more than half of *A.C.* burgundy. It has nine named growths, listed in the order of the price they usually fetch: Moulin-à-Vent, Côte de Brouilly, Juliénas, Fleurie, Brouilly, Morgon, Chénas, St-Amour and Chiroubles. The first two require a few years to mature; the rest can be drunk young, even as the now fashionable *Beaujolais de l'année*. Wines listed as Beaujolais Villages or Beaujolais-hyphenated with 36 named areas of origin come next in quality; then Beaujolais Supérieur, and finally Beaujolais. Most white Beaujolais (much of which used to be sold as Mâconnais *blanc*) is made of the *chardonnay* grape.

The demand for Beaujolais, which used to be quite cheap, became so great that even its liberal output could not supply this. Hence much stretching of the wine, or even faking, came about. The same unfortunately applies to certain *communes* of the Côte d'Or, notably Nuits-St-Georges and Pommard. The buyer who cannot afford single-vineyard wines from the Côte d'Or or named growths of beaujolais must pay great attention to the reputation of the shippers.

The same caution applies to the detached district of flinty dry white wine, Chablis, about 75 miles north-west of Dijon. Its area is tiny, its climate frost- and hail-ridden, and its average annual output little over 500,000 cases. But its reputation is great. Consequently hundreds of thousands of bottles labelled Chablis are sold

BURNET

which contain little if any genuine Chablis. It is safe to buy the *grands crus*, Blanchots, Bougros, Clos, Grenouilles, Preuses, Valmur and Vaudésir, or if these are too expensive then one of the 24 1st *crus* which are now generally grouped under seven main titles: Côte de Léchet, Fourchaume, Montée de Tonnerre, Monts de Milieu, Montmains, Vaillons and Vaucoupin.

Much of the less good wine of Burgundy is turned into sparkling Burgundy, red, *rosé* and white. The first two are drinks for the unsophisticated. But sparkling white Burgundy, particularly if made by the *méthode champénoise* is, not indeed a substitute for champagne, but an acceptable alternative. A fair amount of still *rosé* is made, of which the best is Rosé de Marsannay. Most of the makers of burgundy keep the skins, pips and stalks and distil this pulp into *marc de bourgogne,* a pungent spirit.

Fine recent vintages have been 1959, 1961, 1964, 1966 and 1969. The 1963, 1965, 1967 and 1968 should be bought with great care.

Grands crus of the Côte d'Or must have a minimum strength of 11.5°, and of 12° for five great whites. *Commune* wine must reach 11° for white and 10.5° for red. The other areas have similar scales, running from 12° for the best whites and 11° for the best reds, down to 9° for Petit Chablis and Beaujolais. To maintain quality, the amount of wine per acre is controlled, from a maximum per acre of 1,609 bottles of *grands crus* of the Côte d'Or up to 2,712 bottles for Mâcon and Beaujolais. These quantities are slightly increased in very favourable years.

There is much debate about changes in the methods of vinifying Burgundy since World War II, but the problems are too technical to be discussed here. Those who like full, slow-maturing and long-lived wines should buy from shippers who use the so-called *méthode ancienne*. Those who like young, fresh, fruity wines, and do not mind about their keeping qualities, should ask for those made by the *méthode nouvelle*.

BURGOO. Traditionally, a sailing ship stew concocted of ships biscuit, salt pork, and any dried or available vegetables, cooked in salt water until thick enough to eat with a fork.

In North Carolina, the name is also given to a rich and savoury stew composed of small bits of chicken, pork, beef, fresh corn (maize), okra, tomatoes, and butter-beans, cooked slowly, and with a variety of spices. It is the traditional accompaniment of barbecued pork.

BURIDDA. An Italian fish stew, a speciality of Genoa, which is cooked and served in the same casserole. The Genoese use a variety of fish for this favourite stew, sometimes all of one kind, sometimes an assortment.

BURNET. A herb with a cucumber flavour, neglected these days in Britain but once an essential in a herb garden. It was taken to America by the early settlers. It is found, however, in French and Italian cooking, where it is a classic ingredient in butters and sauces. The leaves are also used, as borage is, in drinks and salads.

BURNS NIGHT. A commemoration supper held each year on January 21 for Scotland's famous poet, Robert Burns, at which a haggis is piped in. There are over seven hundred Burns societies scattered throughout the world and there are some slight divergences in procedure. Only one aspect is constant, the piper always receives a dram of whisky.

Traditionally the meal should include cock-a-leekie soup, herrin' and tatties (herring in oatmeal or soused, with potatoes), haggis with mashed neeps (turnips) and tatties, and oatmeal cakes and Scottish 'guidbread'.

BUTT. An English wine and beer cask of 108 gallons.

BUTTER. This is a natural product churned from the cream of milk and is one of the most highly concentrated of all dairy foods. It is made from the fat or cream of milk and may be salted or not and coloured or not. It should contain less than 16 per cent of water and not less than 80 per cent of fat.

There is also cultured, or Danish-type butter, which is made from cream to which specially selected bacterial cultures have been added to enhance the natural butter flavour and to develop a mild acidity.

It takes the cream from 18 pints of milk to make 1 pound of butter.

Butter is mentioned a number of times in the Scriptures, frequently along with honey. It has figured in the diet of man ever since he gave up hunting and took to agriculture. Like yoghourt, butter is supposed to have been discovered accidentally by wandering herdsmen carrying milk in goatskin vessels on their camels. The jolting of the beasts acted as a sort of churn, agitated the milk, and butter, or sometimes yoghourt, was formed. The herdsmen tasted the new product, liked it and learned to make it deliberately. First they beat the milk in a bowl, and then they put it into a skin vessel which they pushed to and fro. Finally someone more inventive devised a churn, and thus was butter properly born.

There are abundant records to show that butter has been used in Europe from the Middle Ages right through to modern times. In the 12th century the Germans were exporting butter to Norway; and Normandy butter was marketed in Paris during the 14th century.

As the centuries went by so the processing of butter improved and a wooden churn was developed in Normandy about 1600 and appeared in a modified form in Switzerland shortly afterwards.

Until the beginning of the 20th century butter was always made on individual farms and in small dairies and then marketed through the grocers or jobbers who in turn transported it to the large cities. Now the making of butter is centralized, carried out by large firms who take the milk and cream from the farmers and produce their butter for distribution not only throughout the country of origin, but, as in the case of countries like New Zealand, Australia, Denmark and Ireland, throughout the world. Modern hygienic buildings have replaced the cowsheds, hand milking has been superseded by a pulsating electrical machine. Everything is rigidly examined to see that the milk is pure and of high fat content, which in turn means a butter of high quality. The secret of good butter lies not in the manufacture but in the milk and cream used in production.

For eating, and for much of our cooking, butter has no equal, both for flavour and for its enriching qualities. A simple melted butter sauce makes an ocean of difference to an equally simple dish.

BUTTER, BLACK. 1. This should really be brown butter. Cook as much butter as required in a thick frying pan until brown, not black. Add some finely chopped parsley and capers and just before serving a little vinegar. To 4 oz. ($\frac{1}{2}$ cup) of butter add a scant tablespoonful ($1\frac{1}{4}$) of vinegar.

Serve with skate or other poached fish and eggs. If using bottled capers, the vinegar is better omitted.

2. Black butter can also be butter cooked until it is a dark brown, without any additions.

BUTTER CREAM. This is equal quantities of unsalted butter and caster or icing (powdered) sugar, beaten together until it is as creamy as clotted cream. It is generally used as a filling for cakes.

BUTTER CURLER. A piece of fairly sharp, serrated metal, slightly curved, attached to a small handle. As it is drawn over the surface of a piece of butter it takes the butter away with it in the shape of a curl.

BUTTERFISH. A flat-bodied, silver-blue fish sold in fish markets from Cape Cod, where it is called whiting, to Brazil. There is a related species on the Pacific Coast from British Columbia to Mexico. Both average from 9 to 11 inches in length and from half to 1 pound in weight. Both species are highly prized for their texture and flavour.

BUTTERMILK. (See Milk).

BUTTERNUT. These are the oily nuts from the white walnut tree of North America and the nuts are sometimes called white walnuts. They do not keep long and are usually served or toasted like almonds. In 1863 the term 'Butternut' was used to describe one who wore the uniform of the Confederate Army.

BUTTER PADDLES. Rectangular sticks of wood with a handle, scored on one side and used to make butter balls.

BUTTER PITS. These are the seeds of a gourd found on a spiny shrub on sand dunes in South-West Africa and Angola and locally known as *nara*. Both the pulp of the fruit and the seeds are eaten and for four months of the year often constitute the staple food for the local people. The pits resemble a plump pumpkin seed, and contain about 45 per cent of oil which is similar to almond oil.

BUTTERS, SAVOURY. These are compound butters or, to give the French name, *beurres composés*. They are mainly used for hors d'oeuvre,

EGGS: a casserole of baked eggs.

CABBAGES (curled leaf, smooth leaf)

canapés, with grilled fish and meat, or for flavouring sauces, and consist of various flavourings beaten into butter. This is done by pounding the flavourings in a mortar, adding the butter, passing it all through a sieve, and then allowing it to harden. The process can be simplified by using a blender or liquidizer to pulverize the flavouring before adding it to the butter.

The following are some examples of such butters:

SHRIMP BUTTER. Finely pound as much shrimp flesh as required, mix with an equal amount of butter and rub through a sieve.

LOBSTER BUTTER. Pound raw or cooked coral and the soft part of the head of the lobster, add an equal quantity of butter and when well blended rub through a sieve. This butter is used to flavour hot lobster dishes and is stirred into the hot sauce to thicken it and give it an extra flavour.

ANCHOVY BUTTER. Pound as many anchovies as required in a mortar and add twice as much butter, blend thoroughly and pass through a sieve.

BUTTER SAUCE. See SAUCES.

BUTTERSCOTCH. A rich flavouring made of brown sugar and butter; also the name of a popular hard toffee or candy; possibly of Scottish origin.

BUTTIRI. An Italian cheese made in Calabria, a variety of Cacciocavallo. A large knob of butter is put inside the cheese, which is shaped like a huge elongated fir cone, so that each segment contains both butter and cheese.

BUTTER ONION. See ONION.

C

CABBAGE. The cabbage belongs to one of a hundred varieties of *Brassica oleracea* and is therefore related to Brussels sprouts, cauliflower, kohlrabi, spring greens, and turnips. It is a reliable vegetable and one of the oldest known. It was probably cultivated in Britain in the Middle Ages by monks in their kitchen gardens, and in a 15th-century manuscript there is an entry which reads: 'Take cabaches and cut hom on foure . . . and let hit boyle'. On the other hand, it has also been said that the cabbage was introduced into Britain in 1560.

Apicius has a number of good cabbage recipes in his book. The Emperor Tiberius comes again into cabbage history (see BROCCOLI), this time chiding his unfortunate son Drusas for not eating enough cabbage. Perhaps because Tiberius believed it prevented drunkenness? Cato praised the cabbage and declared it not only prevented drunkenness but also saved his family from the plague.

There are several varieties of cabbage but they fall into two main classes, those with smooth, and those with curled leaves. There are spring, summer and winter types. They can be eaten raw, cooked or pickled, for the cabbage is versatile. A recently imported member of the cabbage family is the Chinese *pets'ai* (which see).

Cabbages should be solid and hard, the head heavy. The outer leaves of shop cabbages usually have been taken off and the stem cut close to the base. Old cabbages will smell when cooked and are not fit for eating. Slight worm injury or some sliminess near to the heart, if not too great, can be cut away. Cabbages must be well washed and preferably left in cold salted water for 30 minutes before being used.

The Dutch have a particularly good white cabbage which is very hard and keeps well. But most cabbages deteriorate quickly. Good red cabbages, round and hard as a ball, are extremely good cooked. See also RED CABBAGE.

CABBAGE PALM. Any member of the palm family whose terminal bud is eaten as a vegetable. Also called the cabbage palmetto, it is found in the West Indies, near the coastline of the southern United States and in Bermuda. The West Indian version is the *Roystonea oleracea* and Bermuda has the *Sabal palmetto*. It can be used as a salad similar to endive or cooked like cabbage.

ÉPLUCHAGE

CABECOU. A small wheel-shaped French goats' milk cheese. It weighs only a few ounces and is in season from April to November, but some three million are sold every year.

CABERNET. See BORDEAUX WINES.

CABERNET FRANC. See BORDEAUX WINES.

CABERNET SAUVIGNON. See BORDEAUX WINES.

CABINET WINES. See GERMAN WINES.

CACAO. A tall tree native to South America, where it grows wild in the rain forests of the Orinoco and Amazon rivers. It was imported into Mexico before Columbus, and there the beans were used as local currency as well as for making a cocoa drink. The seeds, the size of an almond, are enclosed in a fruit the size and shape of a ridge cucumber. The seeds are fermented and treated to make cocoa and chocolate.

CACAO, CRÈME DE. A very sweet liqueur with a strong chocolate taste. The name Chouao, the district in Venezuela where the finest cocoa beans once grew, usually appears on *crème de cacao* labels. Today, however, the Chouao valley is built over.

CACIOCAVALLO. An Italian spindle-shaped cheese with a pointed end and a neck and head at the top. There is no generally accepted explanation for the origin of this curious name, which means 'cheese on horseback' – *cacio a cavallo*. One theory is that the cheeses, which are tied in pairs and hung over poles to cure, look as though they were hung over a saddle.

If the cheese is to be used for eating, it is matured for from two to four months, but if it is to be grated and used in cooking, it needs up to 12 months. The cheese has a smooth, firm texture, keeps and travels well. It has a pleasant sharpish flavour which is distinctive.

CADAUJAC. See BORDEAUX WINES.

CADDY. See TEA-CADDY.

CAERPHILLY. This is a white, crumbly Welsh cheese with a distinct taste of buttermilk and is not unlike a medium-ripened Cheshire. It does not keep long and it lacks the elasticity of Cheddar. It is mildly but definitely salty, and one of the most easily digested of the British cheeses.

The cheeses are made in a flat, circular shape about nine inches in diameter and two and one-half to three and one-half inches high. This size is said to have been chosen to enable pitmen to hold a slice of Caerphilly between their thumb and fingers and eat it while working, without getting too much dust on it.

CAESAR SALAD. A Californian variation on the green salad.

CAFÉ, CRÈME DE. See COFFEE LIQUEURS.

CAFÉ AU LAIT. Coffee and hot milk served in equal proportions and, according to the French custom, both poured into the cup at the same time. See COFFEE.

CAFÉ COMPLET. A Continental breakfast which includes a jug of coffee and boiled milk, rolls or croissants, butter, jam and sometimes a boiled egg.

CAFFEINE. See COFFEE.

CAFFE LATTE. In Italy, half coffee and half milk usually served at breakfast, especially to children. It is made with drip or Neapolitan coffee.

CAHORS. The wines of Cahors in the Périgord region of France were known to the Romans, and Virgil is said to have mentioned them in his writings. They are of a very dark colour, the darkest of all red wines. While they have always been classed as good wines, their appeal is specialized. Cahors wine takes five to six years to mature and, when properly made, does not show sign of age. Cahors wine lovers say that one only tastes Cahors after the second glass. They are perhaps strange wines, certainly invigorating and said to be good for the health. They do not have the subtlety of the great wines, but are in a class by themselves with a straightforward appeal.

CAIRANNE. See RHÔNE WINES.

CAKE PANS (CAKE TINS). These come in great variety and are mostly of thin sheet metal, usually aluminium but also coated iron or steel. Many modern pans are treated with a special non-stick finish, coloured brown, gold and sometimes black and this takes a great deal of the work from cake-making. Cake pans must be thin in order to transmit heat evenly and quickly and thus not retain heat when taken out of the oven and continue cooking the cake.

CAKES. There are large cakes and small cakes, wedding cakes and tea cakes, the number of cakes having positively no limits other than the skill, imagination and available supplies of cooks, amateur and professional.

CALAMANSI   CAKE PANS

Cake-making depends, as many things in this life do, on certain rules. Keep these rules and cakes are likely to turn out perfect each time. Then it is realized the well-baked cake is not a matter of luck, but a matter of doing what does not always come naturally, of doing something correctly and precisely.

CALABRESE. See BROCCOLI.

CALAMANSI. A small acid fruit, peculiar to the Philippines, which looks rather like a small round gherkin. It is used in many ways in which a lime can be used. Mixed with papaw it makes a good sweet drink with a flavour similar to that of orange juice.

CALAMARY. A common name for certain varieties of cephalopods which have elongated bodies with ten arms or tentacles. Like cuttlefish, the calamary has a pouch of black liquid, usually called ink, which is used when it senses it is in danger. It squirts it out to make a 'smoke' screen. This liquid is used commercially as sepia.

Calamary are considered a delicacy in Mediterranean countries. The very young calamary can be delicious when small, dipped first into egg and breadcrumbs and then fried in deep fat. One of the pleasures of simple seashore eating in the Mediterranean is the serving of these little calamary accompanied by a simple wine.

Large calamary are better more firmly treated and preferably stuffed. See also SQUID.

CALAMONDIN. A small spiny citrus tree native to the Philippines and now cultivated in the United States. It bears a loose-skinned fruit of extreme acidity which is used as a source of naturally concentrated vitamin C. The juice is also used in the preparation of various artificial flavourings.

CALF. The young offspring, under 12 months old, of any bovine animal, but in particular of the domestic cow. There is an odd co-existence in the words calf and veal. While the animals were alive they were, in Anglo-Saxon, calf, pig and sheep. When they were killed they became, in Norman French, veal, pork and mutton. Strictly speaking veal is only milk-fed calf; a calf is, according to authorities, an immature animal that has subsisted in part or largely on foods other than milk.

The meat of the latter is drier, coarser in texture and with a more pronounced grain in a deeper red, and the fat has a yellowish tinge. In common parlance, a calf is usually of beef stock and killed when it is from three to ten months old, by which time it has begun to have some qualities of beef without the marbling, which is so important to beef. For veal calf, see VEAL.

CALF FOOT. The feet of calves or any other edible animal are valued by cooks for the jelly which is obtained by cooking them for several hours. This jelly is nourishing and good when correctly prepared.

CALIFORNIA WINES. See AMERICAN WINES.

CALLALOO. A type of spinach popular in the West Indies. It is also the name of a West Indian dish of stewed okras, dasheen or cassava leaves, salt meat and other ingredients, all simmered gently together.

CALON SÉGUR, CH. See BORDEAUX WINES.

CALORIE. A calorie is a unit of heat, not a unit of nutrition. The body requires a certain amount of fuel to provide it with energy. This fuel comes from food and is measured in units of heat or calories. The normal person needs between 2,500 and 3,000 calories per day, although those who are slimming can manage with as little as 1,500. However, the precise number varies according to age, occupation and sex. A hard-working labourer needs up to 5,000 calories per day.

CALVADOS. An apple brandy named after Calvados, a town in Normandy, a region rich in apple orchards. It is matured in oak casks: the best calvados is not bottled until it is six years old. The casks give calvados a golden brown colour. Applejack is an American equivalent, but this is marketed younger than calvados.

It is said that the Vikings, who settled in Normandy over 1,000 years ago, developed the manufacture of alcohol from apples. A Normandy custom, still practised, is to drink calvados not only as an appetizer, but during the meal, whenever there is a pause. This is called a *trou normand*, which can be translated as meaning making a hole for more food.

CAMEL. The camel, children are taught, has two humps and belongs to a family of mammals which includes members with one hump. The one-hump members are called dromedaries. Moses forbade the Jews to eat the flesh of the camel, but no such law restricts the Arabs. Camel meat can be seen in any of the Arab markets where meat is displayed. The hump, feet and stomach are regarded as delicacies by those who appreciate camel meat.

CAMEMBERT. This is the best known of the French cheeses and bears the name of a village in Normandy. Until 1944 there was a statue there of Madame Harel (it was destroyed during World War II) who was supposed to have invented Camembert about 1790. She is said to have left her secret with her daughter, who married a M. Paynel, and their descendants claim they are the only real makers of Camembert. But the fame of this cheese can be traced back much earlier, many years before the good lady was born.

The best thing that happened to Camembert was the invention of the little boxes in which it is packed, making it possible to export it all over the world. But the little white box is no longer protected by law, and there are many imitations. The only protection the genuine Camembert has is that the name of the place where any cheese sold as Camembert has been made must appear on the boxes.

Camembert is a soft-paste, round cheese, made from cows' milk, neither skimmed nor heated nor pressed. It is fermented after it has been sprayed with *Penicillium candidum*, a white mould which was introduced in 1910. A ripe Camembert when at its prime is neither hard in the centre nor so runny that it collapses when cut. When a Camembert is perfect, it is perfect, and one can believe the story that Napoleon kissed the waitress who offered him his first Camembert.

Camembert is good from October to June and the best months are January to April.

CAMOMILE. A common herb found on heaths and wasteland where the ground is dry. Preparations for it are old-fashioned and instinctively one thinks of *Arsenic and Old Lace*. There are two species of it used in the rustic parts of Europe to make a *tisane*, or tea, which was regarded at one time as a universal cure for loss of appetite, also as a relief for headaches.

Camomile is also cultivated and sometimes enters into the composition of some vermouths and aperitifs.

CAMPANIA. See ITALIAN WINES.

CAMPARI. Popular Italian aperitif, highly flavoured and definitely bitter, made in Milan.

CANADIAN WINES. Canada has a small wine industry centred in Ontario, which produces between four and five million gallons of red and white table wine annually. The wines are classified as Sauternes, Rhône wines, white Claret, sparkling Burgundy, Champagne, Port and Sherry. There are also some Concord sweet dessert wines, as well as dry and sweet vermouths. None of them are considered of more than homely but acceptable quality.

CANAPÉS. In the vernacular French a *canapé* is a couch or a restful seat, but in culinary terms it means bite-size pieces of food spread on edible bases, usually bread, then garnished. Almost everything that is tasty and appetizing may be used, fish, flesh or fowl. Canapés may be cut in different shapes and rest on different bases. They may be elaborate (although it is best to avoid over-elaboration) or as simple as liked.

Usually the base is spread with butter before being garnished with the different edibles, which are often masked with aspic and piped with thick mayonnaise or flavoured butters. The simplest base is of toast made from day-old bread, or any of the black or rye breads, especially pumpernickel. Caviar or *paté de foie gras* stand at the top of any list of canapé spreads.

Canapés are served with cocktails and at buffet parties.

CANARY WINES. Wines from the once famous vineyards of Palma and Teneriffe, sometimes called Canary sack. Popular in the 16th century but now a declining industry.

CANDIED PEEL. The best candied peel is made from the citron (which see) but it can be made with the peel of almost any citrus fruit; many cooks prefer to make a mixture of candied peels, to provide an attractive choice.

CANDIES. The American name for what the British call sweets. All types of 'sweets' come

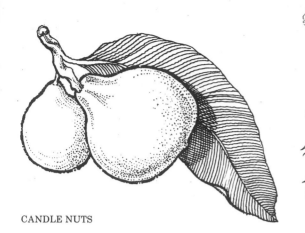

CANDLE NUTS

CAMOMILE (plant and cross-section of flower)

under the name candies in the States. Barley sugar is one of the oldest of candies and, suggests one writer, may have been the original sugar plum which was described in *The Spectator* in the 18th century as looking like 'so many heaps of hail stones'. Nowadays a sugar plum is any favourite candy remembered from school days.

CANDLEFISH. A marine fish of the northern Pacific coast of America, related to the smelt, and highly esteemed as food. The fish is so oily when dried that if the body is equipped with a wick, it may be used as a candle and was so utilized by the American Indians. Various members of this family are spread throughout the world, the South African example being called the halfbeak.

CANDLE NUT. These are the hard-shelled nuts from a handsome tree, native to Malaysia and the Pacific islands, but now cultivated in other hot countries. The nuts are so rich in oil they will actually burn like a candle. They are threaded on to the midrib of a palm leaf or thin stick and then lit, hence the name.

The cultivated nuts are used in cooking in the areas where the candle tree grows.

CANDY or **SWEET THERMOMETER.** A useful instrument in any kitchen for those who make jams, preserves, candies etc., showing at a glance when the different candies are ready to remove from the heat; from the standpoint of economy, it is an essential aid. Also it takes the guess-work out of candy cooking.

CANESTRATO. One of the most popular of the Sicilian cheeses. A strongly flavoured cheese, it is moulded in baskets and hardens sufficiently to be grated.

CANE SUGAR. See SUGAR and SUGAR CANE.

CANETON À L'ORANGE or **À LA BIGARADE.** The French name for braised duck served with an orange sauce.

CANNELONI. These are numbered among the largest of the stuffed pasta of Italy. They are squares of pasta cooked in boiling salted water, then stuffed, rolled up and browned in the oven. Sometimes they are baked with butter and sprinkled generously with Parmesan cheese or else, as in Tuscany, they are covered with a sauce and baked until the top is a golden brown.

CANON, CH. See BORDEAUX WINES.

CANS or **CANNED FOOD.** There was and is a kind of gastronomic snobbery about eating from cans, as well as a vast amount of ignorance. But, whether gastronomes like it or not, cans have come to stay and most people admit they are extremely practical and useful, and at times even essential.

Obviously too much eating out of cans is not good. We should not live a kind of 'open sesame' existence. There are many people who probably believe anchovies have been born and bred in cans, or have never realized a fresh sardine is a delicious lively fish or that a pineapple grows in the ground.

There are some who think canned food has no nutritive value, but this is not so. Canned food loses none of its food value. More food values have been lost by bad cooking than were ever lost by modern canning methods.

CANTAL. See FOURMES DE CANTAL.

CANTALOUPE. See MELON.

CANTEMERLE, CH. See BORDEAUX WINES.

CANTENAC. See BORDEAUX WINES.

CANTENAC BROWN, CH. See BORDEAUX WINES.

CAPE GOOSEBERRY. One of the best of the tropical fruits. It is a small yellow-green fruit resembling the gooseberry in size and shape but enclosed in a paper-thin, pale brown crinkly husk. The skin of the fruit is thin and waxy and surrounds a juicy pulp which contains many small seeds, again like the gooseberry. It has several names, including *tipari* in India and *poha* in Hawaii. It is sometimes called the husk tomato and is related to the ground cherry.

The flavour of the cape gooseberry is distinctive and pleasing. It can be eaten raw as a dessert fruit, cooked as a compôte, made into a sauce or jam, or used as a filling for a pie.

Although it is a native of Brazil, it appears to have gained its name from the Cape, for it grows well in South Africa as well as in many tropical and sub-tropical countries.

CAPERCAILLIE or **CAPERCAILZIE**. The capercaillie or wood grouse is a game bird which is increasing its numbers in Scotland. Unfortunately its eating habits, feeding on the young growths of pine trees, does tend to give its flesh a turpentine flavour. One trick used to disguise or eradicate this flavour is to stuff the bird with raw potatoes before cooking and discard them afterwards. Another is to steep the bird in milk for two to three hours before plucking. The capercaillie should be drawn as soon as it is shot and then hung for at least a week, and much longer to make them really tender. Some connoisseurs state they are at their best when high, one such going further to say epicures keep them until amputation is required and only the breast portion can appear.

CAPERS. The flower buds of a wild, Mediterranean, thorny climbing shrub. Capers have been used as a condiment for thousands of years and are found growing wild on old walls in Cyprus, in Sicily and on the shores of the Dead Sea. They appear on archaeological sites as far east as the Persian steppes. Whether they were wild there or were brought to these remote places in the past is not known, for they are not used in Persian cooking.

Capers also grow wild in North Africa well down into the Sahara and there, to guard themselves against the heat, their leaves are always turned edgeways to the sun. Where they grow wild in the intense heat the plants are always armed with prickles; but the cultivated capers which are grown in France are without spines. The flower of the plant is enchantingly pretty, like a pale edition of a passion flower.

The capers or flower buds are salted and preserved in vinegar. Good capers should be olive green, firm and have a piece of stalk left on them.

CAPON. Not as large as a turkey nor as small as a fowl, the capon is a happy compromise between the two and owes its existence to a curious Roman law called the Fannius Law or *Lex Fannius*.

This law was passed when the city was at its height of glory and extravagance, and the senators viewed with dismay the gluttony of the wealthy. The Consul, C. Fannius, feared that the enormous consumption of hens would lead to their extinction. Therefore came his edict, that the Romans should dispense with the fattening and eating of hens – but he said nothing about the cock. This omission is possibly explained because the cock was honoured among the Romans as a warlike bird and enjoyed no great reputation in culinary circles.

Amidst considerable grumbling at what was reckoned as an infringement of their personal freedom, the Romans gave serious thought to their culinary problem, and it was a skilled surgeon who, remembering how eunuchs were created, performed a neat operation of 'snipping' on some doubtless protesting cocks and transformed these warlike birds into cackling eunuchs of the barnyard. They waxed fat, their flesh became more tender and succulent than that of the forbidden hen and furthermore they increased in size. The fate of the cock was sealed, the extinction of the hen prevented, and when Fannius himself was served some roast capon he pronounced its praises. From then on nearly all male chickens underwent the ingenious transformation which made them so welcome at the epicure's table.

So the capon is a roaster which has been gelded. There is more flesh on him after caponizing than on any other bird, his fat is marbled and worked through the lean tissue, rather than pocketed as with other fowl. He can be cooked and served in all the ways of a chicken as well as a turkey. His minimum weight is about 6 lb. and the maximum 10 lb., and his age for eating is between 7 and 10 months.

A Norfolk capon is not a fowl but a red herring. Capon was formerly used in English as a jocular name for certain fish.

Capons continued in high favour throughout the centuries. Shakespeare wrote: 'And then the Justice, in fair round belly, with good capon lined'. At the beginning of this century capons went out of fashion, possibly because their gelding became too expensive or too troublesome. Again great minds set to work and came up with the pill. Today's capon is injected in the neck with a hormone tablet, a quick and easy gelding. So capons have regained favour. In France, as so much poultry is sold undressed, this method of caponizing is forbidden as occasionally the tablet does not dissolve and there is a risk of it being eaten by humans. In England the necks of the capons are removed before they are sold, thus there is no danger.

Hens are also caponized to increase their size and these are called *poulardes* or simply fat hens.

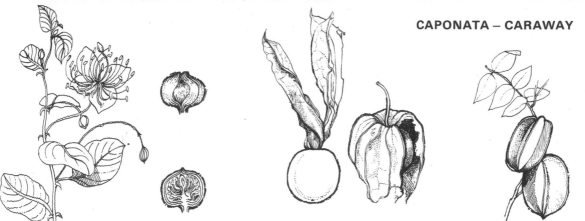

CAPER (flower and bud) CAPE GOOSEBERRY CARAMBOLA

CAPONATA. A type of Italian fish salad which is found in various forms and with slightly varying names round the Italian coast.

CAPPUCINO. In a culinary sense this means in Italy coffee flavoured with milk or cream until its colour is the shade of the robe of a Capuchin monk.

CAPRIAN. A goats' milk cheese from Italy.

CAPRINO. A goats' milk cheese from the Argentine.

CAPSICUM or **SWEET PEPPER.** Under these names come a multitude of peppers, large and small. There are the large bell peppers, which can be red, yellow or green, varying in strength from vaguely sweet to hot and pungent, and used as a vegetable. There are long green and red peppers, the tiny bird peppers, and many others, often indigenous to one country. The capsicum is considered as a South American plant but was brought to Hungary as long ago as 1585 where it has become naturalized, is used in numerous dishes and become synonymous with Hungarian cooking. Hungarian paprika is probably the best of all the powdered capsicums.

CARAFE. Derived from an Arabic word which meant water bottle. Nowadays a carafe is put to better uses in wine-drinking countries, where it is filled with wine for the table. Carafe wine usually means cheap local wine sometimes served free with meals.

CARAMBOLA. A curious fruit which is seldom seen growing wild outside of its native habitat, the Malay archipelago, and is certainly a feature of the markets in this area. However, it is cultivated extensively in Hawaii and was probably brought to the islands by early Chinese immigrants. It is a translucent, yellow-green colour, some four or five in. long and two in. in diameter, with five prominent ribs which means that when it is sliced the slices are star-shaped.

There are two varieties, the sweet and the sour. The flavour of the fruit, which is watery, is cool, refreshing, astringent but pleasant. It is not usually cooked, but in Hawaii juice is made from both the sweet and sour varieties.

CARAMEL. Sugar cooked until it is dark brown and sticky and used to coat moulds for puddings and custards, or to form the base of an egg custard. A favourite French pudding is *crème caramel*. The everyday name for caramelized sugar is 'Black Jack'.

CARAMELIZE. To dissolve sugar slowly in water and boil steadily without stirring to a dark brown colour. This expression also means to give a thin caramel topping by dusting the top of sweets with caster or icing (confectioners') sugar and grilling slowly.

CARAMELS. These are candies or sweets made of cream or condensed milk, butter, sugar and glucose which are variously coloured and flavoured. Some of the cheaper varieties, sold commercially, are made with other fats, including coconut fat. Usual flavours are chocolate, vanilla and coffee, and some caramels have a fresh milk flavour. Caramels generally are soft in texture but if they become dry they are invariably spoilt.

CARAWAY. This is a spice which has been used since ancient times. It grows wild in Europe, including Britain, in temporate Asia (Turkey and Persia) and in North Africa, and has naturalized itself in North America. The seed of the wild plant is stronger than the cultivated one: it is grown commercially in Holland, Russia, the Balkans and other parts of Europe, but not in Britain.

The young leaves of the caraway have a mild flavour, something between dill and parsley, not in the least like that of the dried seed, although as the leaves age, their flavours change.

In Tudor days caraway was important in English cooking, but its use has declined and even the once famed British seed cake has gone almost out of fashion or favour. Both Austrians and Germans use a lot of caraway in their cooking, especially in cheese, bread and pastries. The Hungarians add it to their *gulyas*. It is cooked with sauerkraut, cabbage and potato dishes.

An aromatic oil obtained from the seeds is used by distillers to flavour such drinks as kümmel, anisette and schnapps, and it is also used medicinally.

CARBOHYDRATES. A group of foods essential to a balanced diet, including sugars, starches and cellulose, containing carbon, hydrogen and oxygen. These starchy carbohydrate foods include potatoes and all grain products, biscuits and cakes, and usually supply some two-thirds of the energy needed by the body.

CARBONADO. One of the national dishes of the Argentine, both delicious and unexpected.

2 lb. beef
2 oz. (4 tablespoons) butter
4 onions, sliced
1 large tomato, peeled and sliced
salt, pepper to taste
½ cup (⅔) stock
2 each pears, peaches and apples, peeled and sliced
4–6 potatoes, cut into small cubes
handful of raisins

Grind the beef. Heat the butter and lightly fry the onions and, as these begin to brown, add the tomato. When both these ingredients are fried, add the meat, salt, pepper and stock; cover and cook gently for 1 hour. Add the fruit and the potatoes and continue cooking gently until these are tender. At the last moment drop in the raisins.

CARBONNADES FLAMANDES. See BEER COOKERY.

CARBONNIEUX, CH. See BORDEAUX WINES.

CARDAMOM. In the Orient these exceedingly aromatic seeds are called 'Seeds of Paradise' and were carried to Europe from Asia over the old overland spice routes, even in ancient Greek and Roman days, when it was used mainly as a perfume. It is said to have been grown in the Gardens of Babylon seven hundred years before Christ was born, but if this was so – and the gardens certainly were fabulous by all accounts – the cardamom was well out of its usual habitat. It is a member of the ginger family and grows prolifically on the Malabar coast of India, in Ceylon and, to a certain extent, in Mexico and Central America.

It is the dried pods which are used in our kitchens. The pods vary greatly in length and colour,

from almost white to a dark reddish-brown, known as black cardamom. Inside the pods are the tiny seeds. Many of the darker seeds are bleached to comply with current taste. Cardamom seeds have a reputation for being stimulating as well as being antiseptic. The texture of the seeds is hard, the flavour pungent, almost exotic.

Cardamom seeds are used in many Eastern dishes, particularly in Indian curries; Kashmiris use it to flavour tea, and the Arabs their coffee. They flavour several liqueurs, cakes and pastries in Scandinavia, Germany and Russia.

CARDINAL FISH. Popular name given to fish of the genus *Apogon*, found in warm waters throughout the world. *Apogon imberbis* is common in European waters. The name, sometimes applied mistakenly to the European red mullet, refers to the colour, which resembles the scarlet of a cardinal's robe.

CARDOON. The cardoon is a member of the artichoke or thistle family, growing to a height of three and sometimes four feet. The stalks and the thick ribs are eaten and are full of flavour. The ribs can be treated in the same manner as asparagus and the leaves like spinach. The leaf ribs are called 'beet-chard' and the cardoon is sometimes known as chard in the United States.

CARÊME, ANTONIN. Marie-Antonin Carême, to give him his full name, was a cook who, famous in his day, has been revered ever after by all cooks, especially those who also write about cookery.

Born in Paris in 1784, Carême from an early age was interested not only in the practical side of cooking but made a deep study of the culinary art.

Although he moved from kitchen to kitchen, often seduced by high salaries, he did not accept every financial inducement. An offer by George IV to triple his salary to come to London was turned down, 'for London was too *triste* an abiding place for a man whose soul, out of kitchen hours, was given to study'.

CARIGNAN. See RHÔNE WINES.

CARMINE. Red colouring used in confectionery.

CAROB. Also called locust seed, locust bean and St John's bread. It is the sweet-flavoured, fragrant seed in the coloured pod of an evergreen tree which grows in the eastern Mediterranean, but is probably native to Asia. The entire fruit, excepting a few hard seeds, is edible, both fresh and dried. It is rich in sugar, also in protein. It is also a popular ingredient in Chinese cooking.

The husks mentioned in Luke 15:16 and the

(Opposite) FIASCHI: the straw-covered *fiasco* is perhaps the most familiar of Italian wine bottles. Included here are other well-known Italian wines.
(Overleaf) FISH: trout with almonds and jellied eel.

CARDAMOM

CAROB

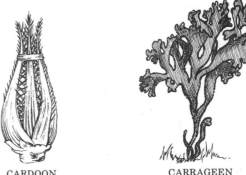

CARDOON

CARRAGEEN

'locusts' eaten by John the Baptist are both said to have been carobs; the latter reference – a wrong translation – explains the name locust bean.

CAROLINA RICE. See RICE.

CARP. The carp belongs to the large family of cyprinoids of strictly freshwater habitation and are found throughout Europe, Africa and North America. They range in size from the gudgeon and the minnow of an average length of 6 inches, to the Indian mahseer of 6 feet or more. Some like clear water, others muddy. Izaak Walton, in 1653, gave some elaborate recipes for cooking carp, and two centuries later Mrs Beeton added her quota with a small brochure.

Carp were brought to Europe from China. They are a favourite Central European, Jewish and North German dish. Both the North Germans and the Poles traditionally eat carp on Christmas Eve and in Germany it is the custom not to scale the fish on that night, whatever method of cooking is used, so that everyone eating the carp can save one scale which he puts into his purse as a charm to bring luck the whole year through.

Some species of edible carp are covered with scales, some have few scales but large ones, others simply a scattering. All carp must be carefully cleaned and washed in several changes of water, and finally washed in acidulated water. The spleen, which lies behind the head, must be removed. If the fish is to be poached, it does not require scaling: the scales can be removed with the skin when the fish is cooked and served. Otherwise it must first be scaled.

The roe of the carp is a delicacy and can be cooked in butter and served separately.

Carp can be cooked *au bleu* (which see), in beer, baked, stuffed, poached or braised, whole or sliced.

CARRAGEEN or **CARRAGHEEN MOSS**. Also known as Irish Moss. This is an edible seaweed used in most parts of Ireland and there are several varieties. It is also common on many other coasts of northern Europe and parts of North America. It is found on the rocks at low tide and is best gathered in April and May. When it is bleached and dried it will keep for years.

As an item of diet its uses are varied. It is used mainly as a vegetable gelatine in the making of aspics, a carrageen moss blancmange, as well as a carrageen milk jelly. In Northern Ireland it is served as a hot drink at night to induce sound sleep. It is also claimed that carrageen moss will cure dyspepsia, coughs and colds.

CARRÉ DE L'EST. A rich, square-shaped cheese of the Camembert type. It is softer than Camembert and has a white crust. It is Alsace-Lorraine's rival to Camembert and it has something of the flavour of a mild *Maroilles*. There are two types, *Carré de l'Est fleurie*, and *Carré de l'Est lavé*.

(Previous page) FRITTERS.
(Opposite) FRUITS AND VEGETABLES: 1. Limes; 2. Sweet Potatoes; 3. Mangoes; 4. Yam; 5. Papaw; 6. Indian Gourd; 7. Persimmon; 8. Custard Apples; 9. Guavas; 10. Aubergine (Egg-plant); 11. Sweet Pepper; 12. Pomegranate; 13. Manioc; 14. Areca Nut; 15. Ginger Root; 16. Okra; 17. Chayote; 18. Passion-fruit; 19. Chilli Peppers.

CARROT. The carrot is of very ancient lineage, originally of Eastern origin, then migrating to Europe, where it flourished. Pliny wrote of the carrot: 'They cultivate a plant in Suri like the wild carrot and of the same properties, which is eaten raw or cooked, and is of great service as a stomachic...' There are references in ancient Chinese and Japanese records, but not in Indian records until 1826. In Europe almost all the writers of cook-books or herbal treatises have mentioned the carrot. Apicius in his Roman cookery book gave recipes for fried carrots as well as carrots prepared with parsnips.

It is now an attractive vegetable with sweet flesh and tender pretty foliage. It is recorded that the ladies of King Charles I of England's court used to wear the foliage as a decoration instead of feathers.

Carrots are usually available all the year round but the finest are the smallest and the freshest.

Carrots are grown for their roots. Some are long and tapering, others short and rounded; some are bright red, others yellow; and some almost translucent. They are rich in vitamins A, B and C, although not more so than other vegetables. They can be prepared in a variety of ways, as a vegetable plain and simple, boiled, baked, fried, mashed, whole or sliced. When young and fresh they are delicious raw. And they can be made into sweet and savoury dishes of very pleasant flavour.

Generally speaking the deeper the red of the carrot, the better it is.

CARTE, À LA. A French phrase used in restaurant menus to indicate dishes which may be specifically ordered as distinct from *table d'hôte*.

CARVING. In Britain by the 17th century etiquette demanded certain niceties of language when talking of carving game or fowl. Correct manners required one to speak of 'rearing a goose', 'lifting a swan', 'saucing a capon', 'unbracing a mullard', 'trussing a chicken', 'disfiguring a peacock', etc.

Today carving is one of the least understood of the arts of the table. Good carving saves food and adds to the enjoyment of it. Bad carving wastes food, time and flavour. The essence of good carving is to allow the knife to do the cutting. The hand that holds the knife must guide it but not drive it.

CASABA MELON. See MELON.

CASHEW. There is not only a cashew nut but a cashew fruit, and both are esteemed in the countries where they grow. The cashew is indigenous to Brazil but has been widely distributed among the warmer countries of the world, having been carried by early explorers, mainly Portuguese.

It is, we are told, the Portuguese who established the tree in Goa, India, and the word cashew is derived from the Portuguese word *caju* which was adopted by them from the original Brazilian Indian name *acaju*. Most of the cashews eaten in the United States today come from India.

Attached to the flower end of the cashew fruit, as if by an afterthought, is the nut, olive in colour and like a kidney bean. This is encased in a leathery double shell, between layers of a membrane containing a powerful oil which can irritate and burn, but protects the nuts from insects – as well as being a wart remover. The oil is driven off when the nut is roasted to make the shells easy to remove.

CASHEW LIQUEUR. Made from the fruit of the cashew tree in Goa, on the west coast of India. It is strong and the better qualities resemble Hungarian *barack palinka*.

CASK. See WINE CONTAINERS.

CASSAREEP. This is the prepared juice of the cassava. It forms the basis of many sauces in the West Indies and is an indispensable ingredient for West Indian Pepper Pot (which see). The cassava or tapioca plant, also called manioc, mandioc, yucca or jucca, is a common food plant in all tropical and sub-tropical areas, particularly in South America and South Africa.

CASSATA ALLA SICILIANA. 1. *Gelato*. Ice-cream made in coloured layers with candied fruits and almonds. 2. *Dolce*. A favourite Sicilian sweet dish.

CASSATA ALLA SICILIANA
1½ lb. ricotta
1 cup (1¼) fine sugar
2 squares bitter cooking chocolate
2 tablespoons (2½) sweet liqueur or rum
¼ lb. mixed glazed or candied fruit
1 spongecake 10–12 inches in diameter

Rub the ricotta through a sieve into a bowl. Add the sugar, blend well, grate in the chocolate and add the liqueur and beat to a custard-like consistency. Add the mixed fruit and put aside. Cut the sponge cake into 3 slices of equal size and cover the bottom of a round mould with one slice. Spread the ricotta cream over the cake, cover with the second slice and spread with the remaining ricotta. Cover with the third slice and put into a refrigerator and keep overnight. Turn out to serve and sprinkle the top with icing (confectioners') sugar.

CASSAVA. See MANIOC.

CASSAVA CAKES. These are a Jamaican speciality served hot, toasted and spread with butter.

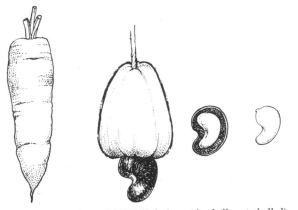

CARROT   CASHEW (fruit, nut in shell, nut shelled)

CATFISH

CASSEROLE. A casserole is a cooking vessel in which meat, fish, poultry, game and vegetables are cooked slowly and usually for a long time. As a method of cooking it is one of the oldest known. The original casseroles were made of clay or brick pottery, and even today some of the best casseroles are made from earthenware or terracotta.

Generally, oval-shaped casseroles are more useful than round ones as these, for example, will take a whole chicken. However, a casserole can be round or oval, squat or tall, large enough to feed an army, or small enough for one serving. They are made from pottery, enamelled cast-iron, terracotta, china, fireproof glass, copper and enamel. Many modern casseroles are highly decorated, some have severe lines, others are fat and comfortable looking. There are even electric casseroles. Extremely useful are long oval casseroles used for cooking fish, complete with a strainer. All casseroles have a tightly fitting lid and two handles.

CASSIA. A near relative to the cinnamon tree. It is often confused with cinnamon but it differs from it in that the cinnamon flavour extends to the leaves, which is not so true in cinnamon. In India cassia leaves are used in curries, and are often mistaken for bay leaves, which they vaguely resemble.

Cassia buds, with an equally vague resemblance to cloves, are sold in the Indian markets and in Western shops. These are especially useful when a quick strong cinnamon flavour is required.

Several species of cassia are used medicinally. The name *cassia fistula* was given to the Pudding Pipe tree, a native of India, which produces pods containing a laxative pulp. The leaflets of other species are the senna leaves of medicine.

CASSIS. 1. This is a Burgundian liqueur made of blackcurrant juice, of 15 per cent to 20 per cent alcohol. It is used as a digestive, but is also mixed with a young *aligoté*, the ratio being one of cassis to three of wine, and makes a good summer aperitif.

Crème de cassis is a sweeter version of cassis, drunk only as a liqueur.

2. Cassis is also the name of red, white and *rosé* wines from the vineyards a few miles to the south-east of Marseilles.

CASSOLETTE. The French name for small individual glass, porcelain or metal dishes of different shapes and capacities used for presenting hors d'oeuvre, hot or cold, or small entrées, or even small dishes of ragoût combined with a white or brown sauce.

CASSOULET. A famous French dish and one of the finest of the French stews, a splendid combination of white, dried beans baked in a casserole with meats, onions, garlic etc. Like so many French recipes, it is a dish of considerable regional dispute, each district claiming it produces the best *cassoulet*. What goes into it is a matter for local traditions. Toulouse, which claims the best of the *cassoulets*, insists that preserved goose (*confit d'oie*) must be an ingredient, easy for Toulouse since it is the home of the fattened goose.

However, the real answer is that a good *cassoulet* can be made by anyone with time and patience, for its preparation, whatever its ingredients, takes a long time – anything up to 3 days, although it can be pushed into one day.

CASTOR or **CASTER SUGAR.** See SUGAR.

CASTILE. See SPANISH WINES.

CATALONIA. See SPANISH WINES.

CATCHUP or **CATSUP.** See KETCHUP.

CATFISH. The name given to a variety of European fish, such as the sea-wolf, the dogfish, and in the United States to the members of the *Ictalarus* family. This is one of the most widely spread food-fish in America, and ranges upwards in size to over 150 lb. The most commonly sought and caught varieties are the bullhead, the blue cat, the channel cat, the flathead and the white cat. The best size for eating is from 1 to 2 lb. Catfish and hush puppies (which see) are as traditional in the southern United States as fish and chips in Britain. The popularity of the catfish is such that there are many fish farms solely devoted to rearing them for both the wholesale and retail markets.

CAUDLE. This was a hot drink, hot and spiced, that was popular both in England and Scotland for centuries. It was a drink which had substance, good for a cold night or for a labourer setting out for the long drive home after a winter's day in the market. It varied in flavour. Most recipes included oatmeal, spiced with nutmeg, mace, cloves etc.

CAUDLE SAUCE. See SAUCES.

CAUL. A membrane in the shape of a net covering the lower portion of the pig's or sheep's bowels, used for wrapping up ground meat, salpicon, sausages etc. It is cleansed and prepared by the butcher and resembles a thick veil, ribbed with white fat. Its function is to protect food from the heat of the oven and to add fat. Sometimes a piece of caul is sold with a leg of mutton to cover it while roasting. Caul is used more in Italian and French cooking than in British or American.

CAULIFLOWER. This favourite vegetable, with broccoli (which see) is a Brassica. Both plants are natives of Asia and Europe and have been cultivated for many years for their flowers or inflorescence. Both cauliflower and broccoli have been much improved over the centuries and the flowers increased in size by careful cultivation.

CAULIFLOWER À LA POLONNAISE

Soak and drain the cauliflower and then put the cauliflower head uppermost in a pan of boiling salted water and milk in equal quantities, enough to cover the cauliflower. Cook until the cauliflower is tender. In the meantime prepare a garnish. Rub the yolks of 2 hard-boiled eggs through a wire sieve and mix with 1 tablespoon (1¼) of finely chopped parsley and 2 tablespoons (2½) of breadcrumbs previously browned in butter. Mix these ingredients together and sprinkle over the cauliflower immediately before serving. Serve very hot.

CAVIAR. Caviar, which is mainly produced in Iran and Russia, comes from the salted roe of the sturgeon; the finest of all from the sterlet. The latter, in the days of the Tsars, was reserved for the royal tables. Strictly speaking, only sturgeon eggs should be called caviar. The so-called 'red' caviar, although delicious in its own way, is prepared from the eggs of salmon, and scorned by true caviar devotees as a feeble substitute for the genuine article. However, this type of 'caviar' does have an excellent and completely distinctive

flavour and, oddly, when used as a flavouring in bland fish dishes, it surpasses the black.

The name 'fresh caviar' applies to the choice firm, but not too ripe eggs of the three main sturgeon species, yielding roes of three sizes. But one learns with experience that all which glistens black and oily is not true caviar. The eggs of the cod, the catfish, the whiting, shad and mullet are also pressed, processed and dyed to give the dark colour, which should, but does not always, denote true caviar. However, the connoisseur can tell by the taste what he is eating and the real expert can tell even in which particular waters the sturgeon was caught.

Caviar at its best is eaten *au naturel*, that is, on brown or white bread – without butter. The caviar itself should be fat and oily enough not to require the addition of any other fat. Neither does it require the addition of such embellishments as lemon juice, chopped hardboiled eggs, chopped onions or onion juice. However, some caviar, being more salted than others, can take a little lemon juice. *Malosso* is a term applied to any caviar which is mildly salted – and for many this is preferred.

Once a jar of caviar has been opened it will quickly lose its freshness. It should not be kept too long. If, however, caviar must be kept for a short time, re-cover the container and lay it on its side to allow the oil to seep through the grains. If keeping for a few days, turn it from time to time. After dipping into a jar, flatten the disturbed grains with the blade of a knife, so there are no holes for the juice to run through. This drains off the moisture from the remaining grains.

Red caviar is also eaten a great deal in Russia and the Balkans, and especially in Turkey, but it is not regarded as caviar – rather as a pleasant or delicate item of eating for hot days.

Sturgeon caviar and caviar from the salmon are often served together; the black or grey sturgeon caviar in small bowls (or large bowls) and the sliced, pressed, salmon caviar in oval-shaped dishes. Chopped spring onions are served separately, also wedges of lemon.

The following are descriptions of the main caviar types:

Beluga. This is a large-grained caviar coming from the sturgeon of the same name. It is for the gourmet and those 'who eat with their eyes'. The grains are black, medium-black and fine grey. There is also a 'golden caviar' which every connoisseur hopes to find one day.

Osetr. A caviar which comes from a smaller sturgeon than the Beluga (which can weigh up to 2,000 lb. and more). The Osetr weighs only 700 lb.

Sevruga. A species of sturgeon yielding the smallest grained caviar, which is much appreciated by caviar fanciers.

CELERY

CELERIAC

CAULIFLOWER

Payasnaya. A coarsely grained, lightly packed black caviar, heavily salted and produced from genuine grains, but from those which have been damaged in the sieving process, or are premature. Cheaper than the whole grain caviar, it is a favourite among experts, especially Russians, many of whom prefer this type of caviar to any other. It is largely prepared in Astrakhan for export and packed in barrels.

CAYENNE PEPPER. See PEPPER.

CELERIAC or **CELERY ROOT** or **TURNIP-ROOTED CELERY.** This is the root of a particular kind of celery seldom seen in Britain although in France, Italy and Germany it is grown and cooked in large quantities. It is a true celery grown for its roots rather than its stalks, although these can be cooked and eaten rather like seakale. The roots can be peeled and thinly grated and used raw in salads and are excellent when cooked. The skin is inclined to be stringy so this must be thinly pared before the celeriac is cooked.

CELERY. This is yet another of the most used vegetables in Western cooking to which we owe much to the adventurous tastes of the Romans. Maecenas, we read, a great noble and bon vivant of the balmy days of Imperial Rome, is reputed to have fed celery to his asses before slaughtering them for consumption. All kinds of poultry were given celery to eat, for it was felt that celery imparted a special and desirable flavour to their flesh. Roman gourmands wore celery wreaths upon their heads during their gargantuan feasts to counteract the effects of alcohol.

Celery is served raw – and when it is fresh, young and crisp this is the finest way of serving it. There was a fashion in Britain to serve celery only with its ends curled, in tall glasses. It can, however, be cooked: braised to make a main vegetable dish; used in a soup; cooked and garnished with a Béchamel sauce; and fried. For salads and cocktail appetizers, thick sticks of celery are often stuffed with plain or flavoured curd cheese.

CELERY SALT. This is salt flavoured with celery.

CELLAR. A cellar can be defined in two ways: as an underground chamber in which is stored wine, or coal, or perishables, or any other kind of material best kept underground; as a collective noun for bottles of wine. If there is no cellar in the house, one can have a cellar of wine in almost any part of it provided the temperature is fairly even and does not get terribly cold in winter or too hot in summer.

The best temperature for a wine cellar is 55° F., but 5 or 6 degrees up or down will not hurt the wine, providing the temperature remains fairly steady. Furniture for a cellar should consist of bins, properly numbered; a table for the essential implements for opening the wine; corkscrews; a candle stuck in a bottle; and a hammer and chisel for opening cases. If possible a sink and a collection of glasses ready to hand for tasting the wine after it is decanted. To complete the equipment of the cellar a cellar book is needed.

CÈPE. An edible fungus, the most delicious of the Boletus.

CEREAL. Cultivated grasses and their seeds or grain. The word is connected with the Cerealia, Roman rituals to honour Ceres, the goddess of the harvest. The seeds are used all over the world, wheat and rice being the major sources of cereal food for man, with barley and oats as the principal cereal food for domestic livestock.

Breakfast cereals were first manufactured in the United States towards the end of the 19th century, as an addition to the earlier oatmeal porridge and mush. By the turn of the century ready-to-eat packaged cereals revolutionized the American breakfast and later spread to northern Europe.

CERO. Either of two large, mackerel-like fish, caught for food and sport and found in the warm parts of the western Atlantic from the Carolinas to Brazil. The king cero, also called the cavalla, pintado, or kingfish, is abundant in the waters of Florida and is renowned for its tremendous, almost vertical, leaps to measured heights of 20 feet. The flesh is flakey white, slightly oily, and delicious when prepared in almost any of the classical methods of cooking.

CÉRONS. See BORDEAUX WINES.

CERTAN, CH. See BORDEAUX WINES.

CERVELAS. A French short and fat sausage interlarded with pork fat which is highly seasoned with garlic.

CEVABÇIÇI. Serbian grilled rissoles or *kofta*. They are small rolls of ground meat always grilled over charcoal. As they are often cooked in open-air restaurants, and sometimes on the pavement outside, together with *razniçi* (which see), the air of Belgrade in the late summer is laden with the appetizing odour of grilled meats. Both types of grill are served with chopped raw onion and to the accompaniment of a bottle of red wine for, as the Yugoslavs say, 'what is *cevabçiçi* without wine?'

CHABICHOU. A French goats' milk cheese and one of the best known of the Poitou cheeses. It is small, cylindrical in shape and in season from April to December.

CHABLIS. See BURGUNDY WINES.

CHABRIS. A French goats' milk cheese made in the Chabris district, a small village in the Indre *département*. It is made with the same technique as Camembert and packed in similar boxes.

CHAFING DISH. A deep metal pan, with or without a water basin underneath, heated by charcoal, electricity or a spirit flame. It can be used without the water basin as a skillet in which to cook quickly prepared dishes at the table for informal entertaining; these may range from scrambled eggs through a wide variety of dishes from stewed kidney to lobster Newburg. The water basin is added for dishes requiring longer cooking, or for keeping food hot.

CHAI. A building in France, and especially in Bordeaux, where wine is stored above ground. *Chais* can be large, low sheds or bigger buildings. Most vineyards have at least two *chais*; the one where older wine is kept is generally a darker place than that for new wine.

CHALONNAIS. See BURGUNDY WINES.

CHAMBERTIN. See BURGUNDY WINES.

CHAMBOLLE-MUSIGNY. See BURGUNDY WINES.

CHAMBRÉ. This should mean a red wine ready to be served at the temperature of the room or *chambré*.

CHAMBRER. French term for bringing a red wine that has been in a cold cellar gradually to the temperature of the room where it is to be served. The time needed depends on how cold the cellar is and how warm the room. Serving red wine too cold, allowing each guest to warm his glass of wine in his hands, is far better than plunging bottles in hot water, placing them near a fire or hot pipe, or rinsing the decanter with hot water. All such time-saving devices are inexcusable; they are bound to kill the bouquet of the wine.

CHAMOIS. A horned, hoofed, ruminant mammal native to the mountains of Central and Southern Europe, Southeast Asia, and from Spain to Asia Minor and the Caucasus. It has become rare in the Alps where it may be taken only in a specified season and manner. The flesh is considered a table delicacy.

CHAMP. A popular potato recipe and favourite Friday dish from Northern Ireland.

Champ is made from peeled potatoes, freshly boiled, drained and pounded with a beetle – a kitchen mallet or masher will do. At the same time another vegetable – previously cooked in milk – is pounded into the potatoes.

CHAMPAGNE. The name of the sparkling wine made from both the black and white grapes, mostly black, grown in the vineyards of the former province of Champagne on both sides of the River Marne, between Reims and Épernay, west of Châlons-sur-Marne. The two chief differences between champagne making and the making of the best still wines are:

1. The wines of different vineyards or growths are blended together to secure a champagne *cuvée* important in quantity and uniform in quality, each *cuvée* being sold under the name or registered trademark of its shipper, instead of under the name of a vineyard – château, *clos*, *domaine* or *cru*.

2. Unlike still wines, champagne is partly fermented within the securely corked bottle in which it is bottled at an early stage. This means that the carbonic acid gas generated by fermentation cannot escape, as happens when young wine ferments in casks, and it remains in solution in the wine until the cork is removed and the wine poured

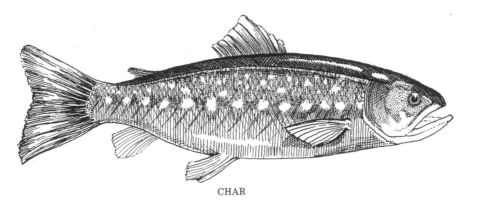

CHAR

out. The gas then rushes out of the wine and in so doing makes it 'sparkling'. When wines not only from different Champagne vineyards but from different vintage years are blended together the wine thus obtained is known as a non-vintage champagne; when the wine made in any one year is good enough not to need the backing of older reserves of better wines, it is known as a vintage champagne. Most champagne is pale gold in colour, but there is some which is made to look like raspberry vinegar by the addition of a little cochineal or red wine, and called *champagne rosé*. There is also some still table wine, both red and white, made from Champagne-grown black and white grapes. It can be very good but it is always expensive. There is also some wine made from Champagne grapes which is slightly effervescent and called *pétillant* or *crémant*.

CHAMPAGNE, FINE (COGNAC BRANDY). According to French law, no brandy may be sold as *fine champagne* unless it has been distilled from wine from the Grande Champagne or Petite Champagne vineyards of the Charentes.

CHAMPAGNE, PETITE (COGNAC BRANDY). The name of the few acres, adjoining the Grande Champagne vineyards of the Charente *département* the vines of which produce the wine from which is distilled some of the finest of the Cognac brandies.

CHAMPIGNON. The French name for the button mushroom.

CHANTE ALOUETTE. See RHÔNE WINES.

CHANTERELLE. One of the common edible fungi which is excellent freshly picked or dried.

CHANTILLY. In culinary French *chantilly* means whipped cream which has been sweetened and flavoured with vanilla.
The name chantilly originally comes from a particularly good thick cream once produced by French royalty at a model dairy in Chantilly.

CHAOURCÉ. Another cheese which resembles Camembert but is much larger. Rich and creamy, it comes from the Champagne district and is good between November and May.

CHAP. The lower jaw or half of cheek, especially of pig. See BATH CHAP.

CHAPATI. A North Indian unleavened bread, flat and round, about eight to ten in. in diameter and eaten hot.

CHAPON À L'AIL. A crust of bread well rubbed with raw garlic and tossed into a mixed salad. This imparts a garlic flavour to the salad.

CHAPTALISATION. The French term for the addition of sugar to fermenting must to build up the alcoholic content of the wine being made. A declared percentage is permitted but the practice is controlled by the authorities. The process is named after the Comte de Chaptel, a chemist and minister of Napoleon who first experimented in sugar addition. This should never be used for the best wines, but alas, it does occur.

CHAR. A member of the salmon family (Salmonidae) found in the deep lakes of the British Isles, Scandinavia and the Alps, and in the colder waters of the lakes and streams of North America. Any statement made about the char must be considered provisional, as it has been the subject of some dispute among ichthyologists. There are many varieties of European char, including some 12 recorded in Britain; one of the best known of these is that netted in the deeper parts of Lake Windermere in spring and summer, and prepared and marketed as potted char. Then there is the *omble chevalier* of the Swiss lakes and the Savoy. Among New World varieties are the American brook trout and the Rangely Lake of Maine. The Arctic char, which is still being studied, lives in the sea and ascends rivers to spawn. Char average one to two lb. in weight, but can range to 35 lb. Char are generally cooked like trout.

CHARANTAIS. See MELON.

CHARCUTERIE. This French word is usually translated pork butchery, but it really means the art of preparing meats, in particular pork.

Pork butchery is a harsh translation and does not in any case convey the true implication of the word when one thinks of the French *charcutier*, who is a master of the art of transforming the pig into delectable morsels for the pleasure of pork lovers. Every small town has its *charcuterie*, and every large town has several, and every good French *charcutier* does his best to keep up the standards demanded of him.

CHARD (SWISS CHARD). A beet, *Beta vulgaris cicla*, with leaves of dark green, yellow or bright red but without the normal large terminal root. The leaves and succulent stalk are cooked in the same way as pot herbs and contain a great deal of food value, including vitamins A, B and C and minerals.

Chard is found in Europe, but is mainly grown commercially in the New England states.

CHARDONNAY GRAPE. See BURGUNDY WINES.

CHARLOTTES. There are two *charlottes* known to the classical cuisine, the *charlotte russe*, which is cold, and the *charlotte aux pommes*, which is served hot. Both have one feature in common: a framework of biscuits or sliced bread which hold a sweet filling.

CHARTREUSE. The name of a famous liqueur made originally by the Carthusian monks at their monastery of La Grande Chartreuse, near Grenoble, from 1607 until 1901 when the monks were expelled from France and took refuge in Tarragona in Spain. There they continued to make their liqueur, urging people to drink *une Tarragone*. Today there are two types of chartreuse on the market, one of them being green and of high alcoholic strength, the other yellow, less potent and much sweeter.

After 1901 the French Government sold the trademarks and an imitation chartreuse was made and sold in France. The bottles were identical to those of the monks except that in the left corner of the genuine bottle one can read *Lith.Alier*, and on the post-1901 imitation bottles *Lith.* without Alier, the name of the printer of the original label. After World War II the monks were allowed to return to France and once more they made their own chartreuse.

CHASSAGNE. See BURGUNDY WINES.

CHASSAGNE-MONTRACHET. See BURGUNDY WINES.

CHASSELAS. See LOIRE WINES.

CHASSE SPLEEN, CH. See BORDEAUX WINES.

CHASSEUR, À LA. The French culinary name for game or poultry cooked in white wine with mushrooms and shallots. Also a sauce (which see).

CHÂTEAU. French for castle, country house, the homestead of a wine-producing estate large or small, ancient or modern.

CHÂTEAU BOTTLED. A wine that has been *mis en bouteilles au château*, or bottled where it was made and by the people who made it. It is a guarantee of authenticity, and it used to be also a guarantee of quality when the owners of the château refused to give the 'château bottling' to any of their wines which they did not consider up to standard. But there are now châteaux where every vintage is bottled at the château, good or not so good; the owners claim never to make bad wine.

CHÂTEAUBRIAND. The French culinary name for a steak of superlative quality, cut from the fillet and particularly thick. It is usually grilled (broiled) and served with *pommes château* and a *sauce béarnaise* (which see).

The châteaubriand naturally has its story. One is that it was invented in the Paris restaurant Champeaux where the chef in a moment of inspiration conceived the idea of cooking a carefully chosen steak between two others of slightly inferior quality. The sandwiched steak not only gained the juices of its two companions but, being padded, cooked at ideal slowness. Then we are told that the name of this steak was given to honour the great French writer and statesman of the Napoleonic era, Vicomte Châteaubriand, and yet another which claims it was invented by Montmireil, chef to Châteaubriand. Probably there is some truth in all the various stories.

CHÂTEAU CHALON. This is not the name of a particular château but the finest white wine of the *communes* of L'Etoile, Voiteur and Ménétrue, in the Jura *département*, France. It possesses great vinosity and a quite distinctive and somewhat austere quality, more like a very dry sherry than an ordinary table wine. Richer, and much rarer, are the *vin de paille* and *vin jaune Château Chalon* made in exceptionally fine vintages.

CHÂTEAUNEUF-DU-PAPE. See RHÔNE WINES.

GERMAN FOOD: Dicke Bohnen mit Rauchfleisch and Eisbein mit Sauerkraut.

CHÂTEAUBRIAND

CHAUDFROID SAUCE. See SAUCES.

CHAVIGNOL. 1. A French goats' cheese, soft and small and a speciality of Sancerre. Also called *Crotin de Chavignol.*
2. See LOIRE WINES.

CHAYOTE. A name given to *Sechium edile*, more commonly known as the custard marrow or, in France, as the *brionne*. This vegetable is the fruit of a climbing plant cultivated in South America, the Antilles, and parts of North Africa, from where it is exported to France. It is a large, green and gourd-shaped fruit, with firm white flesh and a delicate but unmistakable flavour. It is cooked in a great variety of ways as a vegetable and is often used in soups, and in tarts and pies. The flesh, cooked with sugar and fresh lime juice resembles stewed apples.

CHEDDAR CHEESE. Horace Annesley Vachell called this great English cheese 'the everyday, cut-and-come-again cheese'. It is a hard-pressed cheese and the most important of its kind produced in Britain. One of the oldest of the English cheeses, it was originally made exclusively from the milk of cows grazed in the Cheddar district of Somerset. Its true home is the city of Wells, in that county.

In England there are two kinds: farmhouse Cheddar and factory Cheddar. English farmhouse Cheddar is the finest of all Cheddars; it is also the most expensive, possibly because there is so little of it. It is made from May to October and from the milk of a single herd of cows, usually shorthorns. Obviously this limits the number of cheeses which can be made. Farmhouse Cheddar is always made by an expert.

Most of the farmhouse cheese is still made in Somerset but the number of farmers making it is dwindling each year, purely for economic reasons. A farmhouse Cheddar, and even these vary, is usually ripe when 6 months old. The flavour and texture of a truly great farmhouse Cheddar is unforgettable.

Cheddar cheeses come in all sizes, but probably the largest Cheddar Cheese ever made was one which weighed 1,232 lb. It was presented to Queen Victoria.

Factory Cheddar cheese is made from mixed milk, that is milk from different farms and herds. It is produced all the year round.

CHEDDAR CHEESE, CANADIAN. This is a factory-made cheese, produced in Canada since 1864 when the first factory was built in Ontario. It is made from unpasteurized milk. When it is mature it is very good and some say it equals English farmhouse Cheddar.

CHEESE. The history of cheese-making is long and its origins are lost in antiquity. Its discovery undoubtedly was an accident, a simple matter of milk curdling. Archaeologists have established that cheese was known to the Sumerians (4000 B.C.) whose tablets contain references to it, as do the Egyptian and Chaldean artifacts. David was delivering cheese to Saul's camp when he had his famous battle with Goliath. Homer sang of cheese.

The wicker baskets used by the ancient Greeks for the draining of cheese were called by them *formos*, which became *forma* in Latin, from which came the modern Italian *formaggio* and later the French *fromage*. From the Latin *caseus* for cheese we have the German *Käse*, the Dutch *kaas*, the Irish *cáis*, the Welsh *caws*, the Portuguese *queijo* and the Spanish *queso*. In Old English it was *cese* or *cyse* and later became cheese.

Cheese history is fascinating. The Greeks trained their athletes on it, and their wedding cakes were made of it. The Romans knew a number of varieties, and in wealthy households there were special ovens for smoking cheeses. Cheeses travelled with the armies of Caesar. Genghis Khan carried cheeses as a mainstay diet. Marco Polo, the famous traveller, brought back reports of cheeses as made in the East.

Cheese has been prized through the ages, improving and changing all the time. Today there are several thousand types of cheese, and of these France claims over 500 varieties.

GERMAN WINES: Zell, in the Moselle district. Old casks (*Fuder*) in a cellar in the Rheingau.

Today cows' milk is the basis of most cheeses, with goats' milk a close runner-up.

Cheeses differ according to the milk from which they are made, and some, such as Cheddar, Cheshire and Stilton, are subject to endless variations due to the season, the quality of the milk used, and individual treatment.

But cheese not only differs because of the quality of the milk, but also according to mineral salts which have passed from the soil of the pastures through the grass eaten by the cows, goats, ewes or other mammals, whose milk is made into cheese. Then cheese differs according to the manner of its being made and the skill of the cheese-maker.

There are the uncooked and unfermented cheeses of which there are two sorts, the soft and the hard.

Then there are cheeses which are fermented after being 'cooked', such as Cheddar, Parmesan (Italy), and Gruyère and Emmenthal, made by both the French and the Swiss.

Entries for the main cheeses will be found under their own names.

CHEESE, BLUE. The following are the main blue cheeses of the world.

BLEU D'AUVERGNE also called BLEU DE SALERS. A fine French cheese which is made in the Auvergne *département* not far from the home of Roquefort. It is made from cows' milk, and therefore less sharp or piquant than Roquefort. It has neither crust nor rind and is sold in silver paper banded with green. Its size and shape is that of Roquefort and it is in season November to May.

BLEU DE BRESSE. This is an important French cheese, rich and darkly veined with a soft, creamy texture. It is one of the softest and best of the blue-veined cheeses and unlike any other, although some experts call it an imitation Gorgonzola, which it is not. It is available all the year but at its best in the spring.

BLEU DE HAUT-JURA. A semi-hard, delicately blue-veined cheese made from cows' milk in the upland pastures of the Jura. It is shaped like a mill-stone. The paste is floury white with blue veinings and stays this colour even when aged. The rind is yellowish or reddish coloured. This cheese is best from early autumn to late spring.

BLEU DE LAQUEILLE. A French cheese made of cows' milk in the southwest of Puy-de-Dôme, in the Bleu d'Auvergne district. It resembles Roquefort but in order to produce a harder crust it is drained and salted at a much higher temperature.

BLEU DE L'AVEYRON. One of the best of the French blue-veined cheeses made from cows' milk and matured in caves.

BLEU DE SASSENAGE. A French cheese made in the Isère region which resembles the delicately veined Gex cheese in texture and flavour. A semi-hard, blue-veined, cylindrical cheese made from cows' milk and sold in two sizes, one weighing just over 1 lb., the other $4\frac{1}{2}$ lb.

BLEU DES CAUSSES. A French cheese similar to Bleu d'Auvergne made in Central France and matured in caves, as in Roquefort.

BLUE CHEESE (U.S.A.). A domestic American cheese which, although made according to the Roquefort formula, cannot be sold as Roquefort.

BLUE CHESHIRE. See CHESHIRE CHEESE.

BLUE STILTON. See STILTON CHEESE.

BLUE VINNY. This is also known as Dorset Blue and sometimes Blue Vinid and is a hard cheese made from skimmed milk manufactured near Sherborne in Dorset. It is not made in the quantities it was formerly and is therefore often difficult to obtain. In fact, Blue Vinny has never been more than a famous local cheese as there was never enough of it to go round, even as far as the London markets. It was always a farmhouse cheese with a paste as white as chalk and the blue vein a horizontal streak running right through, not irregular, as in most blue-veined cheeses.

The name Vinny is connected with the old West of England word vinew, and derived from an Old English word *fynig*, meaning mouldy.

CHEESE, BLUE-VEINED. There are more than 50 varieties of the fine blue-veined cheeses of which the oldest is Roquefort. According to legend, Roquefort was discovered possibly before the Christian era. Pliny wrote of Roquefort as 'the cheese that bears away the prize at Rome'. Legend has it that a shepherd in the rocky country of the Causses left his lunch of bread and curd cheese in one of the cool caves there intending to return to it later. But it was weeks before he returned. Curious, he opened the package instead of throwing it away, tasted the cheese – and made gastronomic history.

Not all blue-veined cheeses have been developed or invented as a copy of Roquefort, many have their own beginnings and their own legends.

All the great blue-veined cheeses are different in their way and yet perhaps for some obvious reason others are much alike with only a subtle difference between them.

The three best-known, indeed world-known, blue-veined cheeses are Roquefort, Stilton and Gorgonzola, which have become models for most of the others and have their own entries.

CHEESECAKE. What a splendid history this favourite cake has had, a history packed with praise. Ancient Sicily in its day was renowned for its cheesecake: the *Cassata alla Siciliana* variety is still famous.

CHEF'S HAT

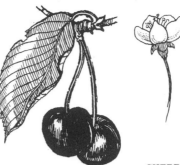

CHERRY (fruit and blossom)

Moderns are left amazed at the many and varied mentions of cheesecake. Demosthenos, Aristophanes and Socrates all left notes on the subject. The Greek historian Athenaeus wrote exhaustively on it, while Cato, the philosopher, and one of the outstanding cooks amongst the ancients, made his contribution to gastronomy with a recipe for cheesecake which delighted his fellow Romans. It was rich in cheese and honey, thick with eggs, and heavily flavoured with poppyseeds.

From these early beginnings we have the cheesecake of today.

Probably today more cheesecake is eaten in the United States than anywhere else in the world, and never has there been so much variety in its preparation and so many different blendings. Britain at one time was fond of small, delicate cheesecakes, in particular the Maids of Honour, which, it is said, Anne Boleyn produced to please her fickle husband King Henry VIII. France has never had much to do with them, although a kind of cheesecake called *talmouse* was made. The Germans have persevered and their cheesecakes are superb.

CHEF'S HAT. A tall white hat which is in fact a copy of the hat worn by Orthodox priests. The chef's hat is said to be of Greek origin. Many famous cooks to escape persecution sought refuge in monasteries, and some of the latter enjoyed a reputation for good food and wine. The cooks, enjoying the sanctuary of the monasteries, carried on their fine art but also sought a distinction from the other monks, which was found in the innovation of a white hat instead of the conventional black. This was authorized and now the white hat is worn by chefs the world over.

CHEILLY. See BURGUNDY WINES.

CHELSEA BUN. A traditional English yeast bun.

CHENAS (BEAUJOLAIS). See BURGUNDY WINES.

CHENIN BLANC. See LOIRE WINES.

CHERIMOYA. A tree of the custard apple family originally found only in Peru and Ecuador, but now cultivated in the southern United States. Growing up to 25 feet high, the tree has a fragrant yellow bloom which produces a delicately flavoured, faintly acidulous fruit weighing as much as 16 lb. It is generally eaten raw as a refreshing summer dessert.

CHERRY. There are many different varieties of cherry which are cultivated in all parts of the temperate zone and belong to one or the other of two main varieties of sour and sweet cherries. The most extensively cultivated of the sour cherries are the amarelles, which grow widely in Sweden, the morellos and damascas. Among the sweet cherries are the geans or *guignes*, the hearts or *bigarreaux*, and the dukes.

The amarelles are pale red cherries with a colourless juice, sharp of taste but not too acid, used as a dessert fruit. In France this variety is known as *la cerise anglaise*. Morellos are either black or dark red and always bitterly acid. They are best used for cooking, jam-making or distilling. Damasca is a very small bitter Dalmatian (Yugoslavian) cherry from which maraschino is made.

The sweet cherry tree is a variety of the wild cherry. It originates from Greece and the East where it has been grown for centuries. Geans or *guignes* are either black or red, the cherries being soft and sweet. The flesh of the black variety is dark-coloured, while that of the red variety is translucent. Bigarreau cherries are distinguished by a firm breaking flesh and the colour of their skin, hence their various names, such as black hearts, white hearts etc. Duke cherries are hybrids between sour and sweet cherries which originated in the Médoc and are known in France as *royale* but have been called May Queen in Britain and the United States.

There are many varieties of the American cherry, all edible and ranging in colour from light yellow to dark purple and in flavour from tart to dead sweet. In addition to their usual uses, they are also a staple in making pemmican by some tribes of the

Plain states. In summer, one sometimes sees a wild cherry tree surrounded by drunken or unconscious birds who are 'with drink taken' from eating cherries whose juice has fermented and become highly alcoholic from the hot summer sun.

One of the best early British cherries is Early Elton, which has a delicious flavour. A good late cherry is Napoleon Bigarreau, called Royal Anne in the United States. There has been a revival of sour cherries in the United States and Germany.

Cherries are refreshing and highly esteemed as fruit and they can be eaten raw or cooked, made into jams and jellies, and used in pies and puddings.

CHERRIES IN BRANDY

3 lb. sweet ripe cherries
½ lb. (1 cup) sugar
brandy

Wipe the cherries with a soft cloth, cut off the stems to ½ inch, and pack the cherries into jars, cover with brandy, seal and store for 6 weeks. Dissolve the sugar in 3 tablespoons (3¾) of water and cook over a low heat, stirring all the while. Drain off the brandy and stir this into the syrup. Strain through muslin (not absolutely necessary), pour the syrup back into the jars, seal and store again for a further 2 weeks.

A few crushed cherry stones, a small piece of cinnamon or a few whole cloves may be added.

CHERRY HEERING. A Danish cherry liqueur with a world-wide reputation, now known as Heering's Cherry Brandy. Peter Heering started selling this liqueur from a small shop a little more than 150 years ago and the company, now much enlarged, is still in the family. The only change has been in the shape of the bottle.

CHERRY PLUM. See MIRABELLE.

CHERRY STRUDEL. See STRUDEL.

CHERVIL. A herb closely related to cow parsley and somewhat resembling true parsley. It has been cultivated since the beginning of the Christian era. Its natural home is southern Russia, the Caucasus and the Middle East.

Chervil is an important herb in French and Italian cooking, although it is not greatly favoured either by British or American cooks. It is a lacy-leafed plant which produces small white flowers. Its flavour is delicate, reminiscent of aniseed. Because of its delicacy, chervil is usually accompanied by other stronger herbs, such as chives. There are curled- and straight-leaf varieties.

Chervil is not used in dishes which require long cooking for it is a herb which demands to be eaten fresh. It can be chopped or served whole. It is one of the classic herbs in *omelette aux fines herbes*, also in a *ravigote* sauce (which see). It is used to season soups, salads and sauces, and it has a peculiar affinity with cheese, eggs and beef. It makes an excellent garnish and is used to flavour white wine vinegar.

CHESHIRE CHEESE. A hard cheese made from cows' milk, rather like Cheddar. Unlike Cheddar, however, it cannot be imitated anywhere in the world. This is because it derives its special qualities from the salt deposits in the soil which impart a high degree of salinity to the milk of the cattle from which Cheshire cheese is made.

Cheshire cheese is made in three varieties, red, white and blue. The most usual form is red, and this colour is obtained by the use of annatto. The best cheese is coloured in this way and it is this cheese, when allowed to mature, which becomes Old Blue Cheshire, so rarely encountered. White Cheshire is really a pale yellow, also slightly dyed.

Cheshire cheese is the oldest British cheese, or at least the earliest to which any reference can be found. It was most certainly famous abroad long before Stilton or any other British cheese. Curiously it is always referred to as Chester cheese on the continent of Europe.

CHESTNUT. Known as the Spanish chestnut in Britain, and as the *marron* in France, this large brown nut has been popular as a nutritious and versatile food since the times of ancient Greece. The kernel when peeled and cooked is sweet and slightly floury and may be prepared in a great variety of ways as a vegetable. It is used in stuffings, soups and sauces and is widely popular as a sweet when puréed or glazed with sugar.

The tree used to grow extensively in the northern United States but was virtually destroyed by blight at the end of the 19th century. The tree in Britain bears only small fruit which are difficult to shell and cook. Thus nearly all edible chestnuts in Britain and the United States are imported from Italy and France, sold both fresh and dried.

CHEVAL BLANC, CH. See BORDEAUX WINES.

CHEVALIER-MONTRACHET. See BURGUNDY WINES.

CHEVEUX D'ANGE. The name of the finest grade of vermicelli. The name used also to be given to a *julienne* of carrots, very finely shredded, sweetened with sugar and flavoured with vanilla, and then cooked and used as a filling for small tarts or a charlotte.

CHIANTI. See ITALIAN WINES.

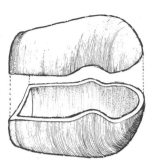

CHICKEN BRICK

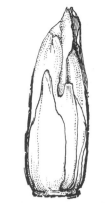

CHICORY (cultivated)

CHESTNUT

CHICKEN. The common domestic or barnyard fowl (if there are still barnyards in this day of battery-fed birds) is descended from the wild jungle fowl of eastern Asia. The earliest mention of the domestic fowl occurs in a passage of a Greek author, *circa* 570 B.C., at about the same time that Aesop was admonishing the foolish milkmaid: 'Don't count your chickens before they are hatched'.

The Romans were scientific fowl breeders with a preference for red and black plumaged hens which, they thought, to be the best egg layers. White hens they considered delicate and these were unpopular.

Poultry culture has developed to a fine art today, and the average fowl, before it reaches the market or the freezer of the supermarket, passes through what can only be described as a metamorphosis. But whether barnyard bird or battery-fed, the chicken, like the potato, bread and rice, is one of those items of diet which most of us can eat almost every day without nausea.

There is a story, told with variations, of King Henry IV of France who coined a slogan: 'I want each of my peasants to have a chicken in his pot on Sunday'. Well, if this story is true, surely the king, if he came back to earth today, would be pleased to see that not only every peasant, but every townsman too can have his chicken in his pot, and not only on Sunday but on every day of the week as well.

The chicken, cooked and served in hundreds of different ways, has become the most popular bird in the world.

CHICKEN BRICK. An inexpensive earthenware container which is made in two halves, almost like two halves of a sarcophagus and originates in Tuscany. It just holds one medium-sized chicken which is cooked peasant-style in the brick.

CHICKOO. See SAPODILLA.

CHICK PEA. One of the dried vegetables of which there are several varieties, called *gram* in India, *garbanzo* in Spain, Mexico and the Philippines. They are considered to be very nourishing and are extensively cultivated in India as well as in southern Europe and the Middle East. Most chick peas require soaking overnight before using and need to be cooked for about 1 hour.

Chick peas are hard, round and corn-coloured, somewhat earthy in flavour and lend themselves to some excellent dishes. They can be cooked until soft, mashed to a smooth purée and served with *tahina* (see SESAME SEED) in the Middle East style. They are made into soups and curries or served cooked until tender as a vegetable.

CHICORY, CULTIVATED. This chicory was developed from the wild chicory, *Cichorium intybus*. There is considerable confusion in Britain about chicory, a vegetable much eaten in France and Italy – and now increasingly in Britain, where it is often known as endive. The French word for endive is *chicorée*. The names *chicorée* and chicory are both derived from the Latin word for a plant, *cichorium*, of which there are two kinds, *Cichorium intybus* and *Cichorium endivia*. The second of these is a vegetable, the leaves of which cluster together closely in the same manner as cos (romaine) lettuce.

Real chicory was at one time called 'succory' and sometimes *witloof* (this is a Dutch word meaning 'white leaf'; the current terms in the Netherlands are *witlof* and *Brussels lof*). It is a clump of crisp white fleshy leaves, yellow-tipped; if they are green the chicory is stale. Most of the chicory sold in Britain comes from Belgium, France and Holland, and it is becoming increasingly popular. It is available almost all the year round and although it seems expensive it is extremely unwasteful, for all there is to do is to take away a few outside leaves and wash it. In the United States it is called French endive or witloof-chicory.

CHICORY, WILD. This is *Cichorium intybus*, a wild perennial plant with clear, bright blue flowers. It is a weed native to Europe, including Britain, and became naturalized in the United

States where it now grows wild in fields and waste lots and along roadsides. The young leaves of wild chicory are used in salads to give a touch of bitterness which many people like.

The root contains a certain amount of starch and sugar which, on roasting, is changed into a caramel-like substance and has, therefore, been used in the manufacture of a coffee substitute since 1722 – although there are other dates given, 1769 in Sicily and *circa* 1800 in Holland. At one period it was used to adulterate coffee rather than flavour it, and in England, in 1832, its use was forbidden by law. But since so many people liked its flavour the law was repealed in 1840. In France, and in some communities in the United States, coffee blended with chicory is overwhelmingly preferred, and each year tons of chicory root are imported into the States.

Cicoria de Treviso is a highly decorative Italian variety of chicory with a pretty pink flower.

CHIFFONADE. The French culinary term which usually refers to all green plants, herbal or otherwise, which are cooked in butter. It does, however, especially mean a mixture of lettuce and sorrel, chopped and simmered in butter. The simmered herbs or vegetables are used as a garnish for soups.

CHILEAN WINES. The best wines of South America are made in Chile and are usually extremely drinkable dry wines without pretensions.

CHILE PINE NUT. The Chile pine or monkey puzzle tree bears massive cones the size of a man's head, each with 100–200 seeds. These are called *pinones* in Chile and eaten when they begin to ripen. Roasted they have a good flavour and in some regions are an important food.

Other related species grown elsewhere have edible seeds, for example the parana pine or candelabra tree of Brazil and the bunya-bunya pine of Queensland. The bunya-bunya has seeds two to three in. long and in years of plenty the Australian aborigines grow fat eating them. Roasted, the nuts resemble chestnuts in taste.

CHILLIPEPPER. This is a member of the capsicum family and an important condiment in the cooking of India and some neighbouring countries. It is native to tropical America and the West Indies.

The Portuguese took chillies to India in the 17th century where black pepper had been used for pungency; but the bright red hot chilli soon ousted it. It is used in its fresh state, either green or red, and dried.

The long period of cultivation has resulted in many varieties of chillies, differing in taste, size, shape, colour and pungency. However, the usual

shape is elongated, conical and somewhat flattened. It is very pungent. The African varieties of chilli are the hottest. Japanese chillies are the least pungent.

CHIMAJA. The dried root of the Mexican wild cherry tree. It is finely ground and used as mildly flavoured spice in Mexican cookery.

CHINESE ARTICHOKE. See ARTICHOKE.

CHINESE CABBAGE. See PETS 'AI.

CHINESE COOKING. Not the least of China's ancient arts is the art of cooking. It is the oldest living nation on earth, so it is not surprising to find that it is the cradle of all culinary arts east of India.

Throughout China's long history, through its periods of bright achievement and of darkest stagnation, the people have continued to cook. Often the sheer necessity for survival has taught the Chinese never to despise anything which might possibly be edible. Curiously they have taken immense risks, but experimenting with new items of food and combinations of flavourings and seasonings has made their cooking one of the most interesting, even fascinating, in the world.

China is a vast country and it would be a rash person indeed who would attempt to describe Chinese food collectively. It is as if one were asked to describe the food of Europe, where there is a wealth of difference between Sicily in the south and Sweden in the north. In a country the size of China regional differences are marked. What is eaten in the Mongolian and Muslim restaurants is vastly different from the wine-cooked delicacies of Nanking. Any Chinese gourmet can tell immediately from which area or school of Chinese cooking a dish originates.

Basically there are five main schools of Chinese cooking, with several minor or lesser schools interwoven. The 'Big Five' are Canton, Szechuan, Honan, Fukien and Shantung.

CHINESE FIVE SPICES MIXTURE. A 'secret' mixture of five essential spices used in Chinese cooking. It is highly perfumed and a little goes a long way. It is a subtle spice mixture and can usually be bought in shops specializing in Chinese or Vietnamese foods. It is said to consist of equal quantities of finely ground anise, star-anise, cinnamon, cloves and fennel seed.

CHINESE GOOSEBERRY. Light brown-skinned, somewhat hairy, oval fruit about the size of a large plum. It has a pale green flesh and the seeds are not unlike a gooseberry. Its flavour is delicious and it

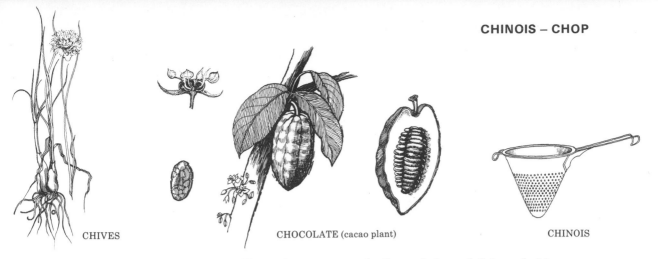

CHIVES CHOCOLATE (cacao plant) CHINOIS

can be eaten raw or cooked with sugar. The main source of supply is New Zealand.

CHINOIS. A fine-mesh, conical strainer.

CHINON. See LOIRE WINES.

CHIPOLATA. In old culinary dictionaries this denotes a garnish of chestnuts, vegetables and small chive-flavoured sausages. It is a corruption of the Italian *cipollata*, a chive. It has now come to mean an especially small sausage.

CHIPS. One of the best examples of the sometimes confusing differences in British and American nomenclature. In either case chips are cooked potato in one form or another. In America chips are what the British call crisps, while the British chips are American French fried.

CHIROUBLES. See BURGUNDY WINES.

CHITTERLINGS. Correctly speaking these are the small intestines of any animal and the small tripe. In butchers' shops these opaque white objects are often hung up for sale prepared for the pot. Sometimes they are plaited. Chitterlings of pigs are often used for sausage skins.

The name also applies to small scraps or trimmings from a freshly-killed pig and to some small sausages. Chitterlings are usually prepared by the butcher and require either grilling or frying. They are served with creamed potatoes and an oil and lemon dressing in France.

CHIVES. These are related to the onion, having just about the same flavour, only more subtly so, the main difference being in the size of the bulbous base. Chives which grow in clumps have virtually no base.

Chives are native to Europe and also grow wild in the northern United States and Canada. They have been used in common with other members of their family as long as there are records.

Chives are used to flavour cheese dishes, sauces, potato and other salads, and fish, and chives are particularly good in scrambled eggs or omelettes and with buttered beetroots and cream cheese.

CHOCOLATE. A general term for the products of the cacao bean, which was first brought to Europe from Mexico in the early part of the 16th century and rapidly became popular. The cacao tree grows up to 25 feet high and bears clusters of flowers which stem directly from the main branches. The flowers produce ridged, oval pods each carrying 30 to 40 seeds, ranging in colour from white to pink and yellow. These are stored in boxes in their own pulp until fermentation takes place, when they are dried in the sun and eventually roasted until the shells fall away. What remains are called 'nibs', and these are ground until the fat in them liquifies; the rich, dark liquid is then cooled in moulds and thus becomes slab chocolate. The production of good quality chocolate requires a high degree of skill; the best contains little added starch or sugar.

Cocoa is obtained by first removing a large part of the fat from the nibs and then powdering the cooled block.

For centuries chocolate has been drunk hot in Europe and North America, and is now popular iced or mixed with coffee and sprinkled with grated orange peel or nutmeg. Cocoa is a cheaper but equally nutritious and fortifying beverage and is well known to sea-faring men the world over as a restorative brew second only to rum.

Slab chocolate is still used not only as a sweetmeat but as an essential part of the hard rations on any arduous expedition. In the kitchen slab chocolate is used extensively in sauces, cakes and many of the richer puddings, in all of which it has a particularly happy affinity with rum.

CHOP. There are several gastronomical meanings to this word:

1. a small piece of beef, pork or mutton cut from the ribs or loin: it is fried, grilled or braised;

2. to cup up meat, vegetables or fruit with a quick, firm movement into small pieces;

3. a Chinese or Indian seal or official stamp used to authenticate goods such as tea, herbs, etc.

CHOPSTICKS. Specially prepared sticks about ten inches long, four-sided at the finger-hold and then round and tapering at the point.

Mention of chopsticks conjures up Chinese food for most people, who forget that the Japanese, Koreans, Thais and many other peoples in the Far East use chopsticks. There is a distinct division in the Orient where chopsticks end and fingers begin and this division is both culinary and religious.

There are many kinds of chopsticks. Those for eating are of one kind while those used in the kitchens are of different types. For picking up cakes and sweets there is yet another variety. Wood is the principal material for making chopsticks, but they are also made of ivory, which corresponds to the Western ideal of real heavy silver; of bamboo and bone, and in some countries, notably Korea, of silver. For silver, although heavy, is a great detector of poison in food. Perhaps the most valued are the real ivory chopsticks which turn a mellow yellow with age.

CHOP SUEY. This, as far as the Chinese are concerned, is an agreeable foreign dish. It is a made-up dish which was especially prepared for American clients by enterprising and pioneering restaurateurs. It consists of several kinds of vegetables, such as bamboo shoots, bean sprouts, celery or water chestnuts, together with chicken or pork.

CHORIZOS. Highly spiced sausages made with lean and fat pork and used a great deal in Spanish cooking, also in the Philippines. The best are reputed to be made in Estremadura in Spain towards the Portuguese border, an area noted for its *charcuterie* (which see).

CHOUCROUTE. See SAUERKRAUT.

CHOUX PASTRY. See CREAM PUFF PASTRY.

CHOW-CHOW. The name given in the United States to any mixed vegetable pickle flavoured with mustard. Originally chow-chow was a Chinese sweetmeat consisting of pieces of orange peel, flavoured with ginger and other condiments preserved in a thick syrup.

CHOWDER. A hearty, tasty, thick soup made from a variety of foodstuffs and often with a milk base. From America come clam, corn and catfish chowders; from France, *bouillabaisse*; and from Italy *zuppa di baccala*. The name chowder is a corruption of the French *chaudière*, a large, heavy pot used by the farmers and fishermen to cook the local soups and stews.

CHOW-MEIN. An everyday Chinese dish. There is dry and wet chow-mein and the basis of both is the same: fine Chinese vermicelli with pork, celery, bean sprouts, eggs, cabbage and seasonings.

CHRISTMAS PORRIDGE. In Scandinavian countries a dish of rice (called *risgrynsgröt*, literally rice-grain porridge, in Sweden) is always served on Christmas Eve, before the traditional dish of carp or goose, to prepare the stomach for the riches to follow. Its preparation varies slightly; thick or thin, with cream or with milk, but always with a knob of butter and two almonds, one blanched, the other not.

CHRISTMAS PUDDING. The richest and best known of British puddings and an essential part of the Christmas ritual, always served at the end of Christmas dinner.

The Christmas pudding, a solid mass of compressed fruit, nuts, eggs, suet and breadcrumbs, flavoured with spices and brandy – surely a culinary achievement – began its career as plum broth or porridge. It was not until well into Queen Anne's reign that the pudding began to change its consistency until it finally developed into the solid concoction we know today.

No pudding should be cooked without its silver coin, a ring, a thimble and a button, kept from year to year. To find the coin foretells future wealth; the ring means marriage; the thimble foretells spinsterhood and the button, bachelorhood.

The decoration of the pudding is important. A sprig of holly, bright with scarlet berries, should grace the top. Finally, the pudding, liberally soused with brandy, is lit and brought to the table encompassed in blue flames.

CHUSCLAN. See RHÔNE WINES.

CHUTNEY. Chutney has come to mean in many minds a kind of sweet pickle, not unlike a chunky jam, which it most certainly is not. Chutneys, which are an important part of Indian cooking, are relishes, side dishes to curry, and made fresh every day often for each meal. They can be hot or cooling, spiced or not.

CIDER. Cider is, with wine and beer, one of the oldest and most universally enjoyed forms of fermented beverage. It is – or should be – obtained by the fermentation of the juice of ripe cider-making apples. These differ from eating or cooking apples, as eating grapes differ from wine-making grapes, chiefly because of their higher proportion

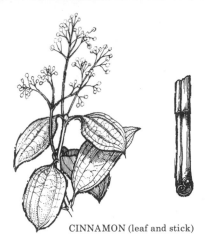

CINNAMON (leaf and stick)

CITRON

of acidity. In cider, the principal acid is malic acid and the alcoholic content varies from 2 per cent to 8 per cent. According to French law cider must not contain less than 3·5 per cent of alcohol by volume. In England there is no limit to the alcoholization of cider. In the United States, slightly alcoholic cider, is known as hard cider in opposition to sweet cider which is chemically treated, sweet and free from all alcohol. In Spain, *sidro* is practically always sparkling. There is some sparkling cider, which is naturally sparkling in the sense that it produces its own carbonic acid gas through finishing its fermentation after it has been bottled and securely corked. But the majority of sparkling ciders are carbonated, the desired quantity of carbonic acid gas being pumped into them.

Cider is used to make a distilled apple brandy called Calvados (which see) in France and Applejack in the United States.

CIDER VINEGAR. Vinegar made from unprocessed cider which has gone beyond the complete stage of fermentation (see VINEGAR).

CINCHONA BARK. The bark of the tree and shrub *Cinchona* belonging to the family *Rubiaceae* and found in tropical and sub-tropical countries. It is the primary source of quinine, which is used as a pharmaceutical and as a flavouring for certain mineral waters.

CINNAMON. Cinnamon and cassia, together with several other plants of the same family, all provide products with more or less the same cinnamon flavour. In many countries these are confused and are treated as one article. In Britain only genuine cinnamon is allowed to be sold as such.

True cinnamon, Ceylon's most important spice, of somewhat recent introduction to the West, is native to Ceylon although that country no longer commands the world's market as it did. The Dutch in the 16th century were the first Westerners to discover it. Any recipe prior to this time calling for cinnamon would refer to cassia.

Good cinnamon has a delicate flavour, while cassia is somewhat pungent. Cinnamon is used in cakes and sweet dishes, in curries and meat dishes. For cakes etc., ground cinnamon is preferable, but it should be bought in small quantities, used quickly and kept in a tightly sealed container. For savoury dishes or to flavour syrups, it should be used in quill form, easily obtainable in most good food shops.

CINNAMON FERN. See FIDDLEHEAD FERN.

CINSAUT. See RHÔNE WINES.

CIRCASSIAN CHICKEN. A Turkish speciality. It is cold, cooked white chicken meat over which is poured a thick, cold sauce made from chicken stock and ground walnuts, garnished with melted butter coloured red with paprika pepper. It has a story of having been brought to Turkey by a beautiful girl slave of Circassian origin. Similar recipes appear elsewhere from Russia to Hyderabad in India.

CIRO. See ITALIAN WINES.

CISCO. Name given to more than 20 species and subspecies of the genus *Leucichthys*. These fish are similar to but rather larger than the chubs. They occur in suitably cold, clear waters in Europe and Asia, but are most prevalent in the Great Lakes region of the United States. Important commercially, they are smoked and salted in large quantities, as well as eaten fresh.

CISSAC. See BORDEAUX WINES.

CITRIC ACID. A crystalline acid commonly found in most fruits. It is used in preserving fish, colouring vegetables and in manufacturing jams, carbonated beverages and pastries. The tart or sour flavour of some citrus fruits comes from this acid.

CITRON. French *cédrat*. This fruit is a variety of the true lemon and originated in the Himalayan region, where it grows prolifically but is largely ignored by the local population which finds no use for it. It was carried to the West in ancient times and was known in Europe from about 300 B.C.

Today it is cultivated in the Mediterranean countries and the West Indies. Citrons are often seen in Italian fruit shops, large and unprepossessing with knobbly skins, like ugly overgrown lemons.

The main use for citron is in the form of candied peel. The oil obtained from the outside skin is used in perfumery and in flavouring some liqueurs. It can also be used as a substitute for Seville oranges to make chunky marmalade.

About half the world's crop of citron is used in the United States.

CITRUS. A family of trees with dense evergreen leaves and white flowers which are sometimes tinged with red. The fruit is round or oval and varies from pale yellow to reddish-orange in colour, the most common being the lemon, the orange, the lime and the grapefruit. All these are juicy and flavoursome, whether sweet or sour, and contain large quantities of vitamin C. They grow in all the warmer countries of the world and are sold in every continent, for the table and for the manufacture of soft drinks and bottled and canned juices.

CIUPPIN. A well-known Genoese fish dish in which a number of curiously named Adriatic fish are included. The sea-hen or the crooner, the sea-scorpion, the praying-fish, the sea-truffle, the sea-date and the sea-strawberry are but a few of these fish.

CIVET. The French word *civet* applies in the main to a ragoût of furred game cooked in red wine and garnished with small onions, cardoons and mushrooms, and then combined with the blood of the animal concerned. This liaison of blood is essential in the preparation of the dish, the name of which comes from the word *cive* (green onion) with which the dish was originally liberally flavoured.

CLABBER. A term used in the United States for milk which has soured and thickened, but has not yet separated into curds and whey. (See CURD.)

CLAFOUTI(S). A favourite and traditional peasant-inspired fruit pudding from the Limousin. It is about as simple a pudding to make as can be imagined. Raw fruit, usually stoned black cherries, are laid in a baking dish and a thick egg batter is poured over them before being baked in a hot oven. It is eaten warm and looks like a tart when finished.

CLAM. There are many different varieties of bivalves called clams, but the two commonest sorts found on the Atlantic coast of North America are the round or hard clam and the long or soft clam. Clams may be fried, pickled and prepared for the table in many other ways, but the most popular use of them in the United States is in clam chowder, or steamed and served with butter.

CLARET. The English name for the red wines of Bordeaux, since the 12th century. There has never been any other red beverage wine to possess so great a variety of styles and types, or a better balance of the qualities wine should have: colour, bouquet, flavour, breed, and charm. Claret has been the standard and pattern of all other table wines sold under the name of claret, which should be qualified by their country of origin, such as Spanish claret, Australian claret, Californian claret, and so on. See BORDEAUX WINES.

CLARETE. The Spanish name for any light red beverage wine not deserving of bearing the name of its vineyard.

CLARIFIED BUTTER. This is one of the best of the frying mediums, but extravagant. From 8 oz. of butter, after it has been clarified, only 6 oz. (¾ cup) remains. However, both the flavour and colour of the food cooked in clarified butter is improved. Also, with the removal of the salt and water, the butter is less apt to burn.

CLARIFY. To clarify is to clear or free fat or liquids from impurities. To clear fat, it must be melted in a pan and about one-third of its volume in water added. This is then boiled for a short time and then strained into a jar. Let it become cold and then carefully take off the cake of pure fat which rests on top, leaving the water and other impurities behind.

Both meat broths and savoury or sweet jellies require egg whites to clear them. The egg whites are added to the pan of liquid while it is still cold. It is then brought to the boil and the egg white is whisked carefully all the time, and then left just below simmering point for 15 minutes. The egg white acts as a magnet as it coagulates, carrying with it to the top of the pan all the scum, leaving a clear liquid below. The liquid is allowed to cool and then strained through muslin.

CLEMENTINE. See ORANGE.

CLERK MULON, CH. See BORDEAUX WINES.

CLIMENS, CH. See BORDEAUX WINES.

CLOS. See BURGUNDY WINES.

CLOVES (branch and bud)

CLAMS (hard- and soft-shelled)

CLOS DE BÈZE. See BURGUNDY WINES.

CLOS DE LA ROCHE. See BURGUNDY WINES.

CLOS DES PAPE. See RHÔNE WINES.

CLOS DE TART. See BURGUNDY WINES.

CLOS DU PAPE. See RHÔNE WINES.

CLOS RENÉ. See BORDEAUX WINES.

CLOS-ST-DENIS. See BURGUNDY WINES.

CLOS VOUGEOT. See BURGUNDY WINES.

CLOTTED CREAM. A speciality of Devon and the West of England. The cream is skimmed from scalded milk and warmed over a slow heat. In Devon this is served with a Devonshire tea with scones and jam, but it can also be served with pies and stewed fruit.

CLOVES. One of the best known and liked of all spices. Their native habitat is Southeast Asia, but they were used in China before Christ and were known to the Romans. For some time the trade in cloves was a monopoly of the Portuguese and the Dutch, but finally it was developed in many other countries outside their sphere of influence, notably Zanzibar and Madagascar.

The clove tree grows to a height of 32 feet, an evergreen with crimson flowers. The cloves are the dried flower buds.

Cloves vary considerably in size and appearance and in their pungency, depending on their origin and age. They should be well-formed and not shrivelled.

The clove is a powerful antiseptic, which makes it doubly useful in pickles, broths and curries. However, cloves should be used with discretion as their flavour can be overpowering.

CLUB SANDWICH. The classic club sandwich consists of three slices of toasted white bread made into a single sandwich containing two layers of filling, the first being sliced breast of roast chicken and lettuce, the second of fried American bacon and sliced tomatoes. Both layers are spread with mayonnaise, the completed sandwich being cut into four triangles and pinned with wooden skewers surmounted by stuffed olives.

CLUB STEAK. An American cut of beef from the end of the short loin.

COALFISH. So called because of its colour, the coalfish (*Pollachius virens*) is an important and highly esteemed food fish akin to the pollack, found on both coastlines of the Atlantic. It is related to and resembles the cod, but is darker, shinier and has a longer jaw.

One of the kindred species of the Pacific is found from Alaska to southern California and is generally sold fresh, although it is also smoked and salted. The liver is particularly rich in vitamins.

COATING. In the kitchen this means to cover an ingredient, usually fish, cutlets, rissoles or croquettes, with a covering or coating. There are three main types of coating:
1. seasoned flour and beaten egg;
2. dry white breadcrumbs with beaten egg;
3. fritter batter.

COBBLER. 1. A long drink, made of whiskey, rum or wine (claret), served in a goblet filled with crushed or shaved ice and garnished with fruit such as a slice of lemon or lime, and an aromatic plant such as mint or fennel.

2. A deep-dish fruit pie, made with a thick crust of unsweetened biscuit dough and with no bottom crust. The top crust is not pierced, but left intact to retain the flavour and aroma.

COBNUT. See FILBERT.

COCA. The dried leaves of a South American shrub found in warm, moist areas of that continent

also much used in the production of cola beverages, but for this the cocaine is removed.
used in medicine, e.g., cocaine. Coca leaves are also much used in the production of cola beverages, but for this the cocaine is removed.

COCHINEAL. A small insect allied to the greenfly. The cochineal crop is a valued one in Central America where it yields the scarlet dye important in the colouring of so many foods. In its rough commercial form the cochineal looks like a shrivelled currant. Indeed, the first specimens brought to Europe in the year 1518 were regarded as being of vegetable origin. Their real nature was only discovered later with a microscope. It is the female insect which provides the dye. When quite young she attaches herself to a plant, sucks the sap vigorously and never moves again, remaining in the same position until, having been fertilized, she lays her eggs and dies. A 'cochinealery' resembles an orchard, but one composed of small cacti which are kept trimmed low, for the easy gathering of the crop. When ready for the market the insects are brushed off into baskets and baked in an oven.

Thousands of pounds of this odd adjunct to cooking is exported annually.

Cochineal is tasteless and odourless and is used as a colouring in confectionery, also to colour wines and liqueurs.

COCIDO. See OLLA PODRIDA.

COCK-A-LEEKIE. One of the best of the Scottish soups, made from chicken broth and leeks, salt and pepper, and usually prunes.

COCKLE. A relation of the oyster, various species of this small but nutritious mollusk are found on seashores in many areas of the world and are eaten extensively in northern Europe, North America and parts of Asia. Its shell is ribbed and varies in colour from white to brown, red and yellow. It can take tremendous leaps and sometimes when thousands leap in unison to meet the incoming tide people on the seashore imagine they are being pelted with stones.

The flesh is pale and delicately flavoured, and is usually eaten boiled with a variety of condiments, or is used in sauces accompanying other seafoods.

COCK'S COMB. The comb of the cock, fleshy and often voluminous, which used to feature in considerable quantities in classical dishes, frequently labelled *à la financière*, or as a garnish.

COCKTAIL. A short, cold drink generally based upon one of the spirits but occasionally made with wine and with flavouring and/or colouring added to increase the eye appeal. It is stirred and shaken, often served with ice and garnished with fruit or vegetables.

The origin of the cocktail is controversial, but the brandy cocktail (dry champagne poured over a brandy-soaked sugar lump) is recorded in publications of the first part of the 18th century. It is possible that it was first concocted in Bordeaux, as the French word *coquetel* is admitted by several writers to have originated there.

COCOA. See CACAO and CHOCOLATE.

COCO DE MER. Coco de mer is an extraordinary double-coconut, indigenous to the Seychelles and said to have been the fruit with which the Devil tempted Eve. Thus the Seychelles strengthens its claim to be the original Garden of Eden.

The fruit takes ten years to ripen and it is important to take it at exactly the right point of maturity. If it is too young it is watery and tasteless, if too old, it has already hardened and lost its flavour. When ready for eating its flesh is like a jelly, firm, but of a soft milky transparency.

COCONUT. The fruit of the coconut palm, one of the most important trees of the tropics. It is a tall and shapely tree, unbranched but topped by a plume of foliage. The fruit is about the size of a man's head and has a green outer covering which becomes brown when ripe. Inside is a thick brown fibre surrounding a hard shell with three basal pores, commonly known as eyes. Within is the flesh, sweet and edible, and the coconut juice which can be extracted by puncturing two of the eyes. A single palm can produce a hundred or more nuts in a year.

Gastronomically, the meat of the ripe coconut is used in a large number of dishes, both in the tropics and elsewhere. To many, coconut is a dried, grated flavouring used principally in sweet dishes. It is possible to buy shredded coconut of various kinds, flaked coconut, ready toasted coconut, and fine grated desiccated coconut. All of these have their own special flavour.

Coconut milk is not the coconut juice, the thin liquid which pours from the coconut, but is made by squeezing the coconut flesh with a little water until a thick liquid is produced. This, if left overnight in a refrigerator, will form into a thick cream.

When the coconut is fully grown but not completely ripe, and still green outside, it is picked from the tree, the top slashed off, and the coconut juice inside drunk. This is refreshing, sweet and cool, and one of the finest natural drinks in the world, and the reason for saying that 'a coconut is like a bottle of milk which grows on ice'.

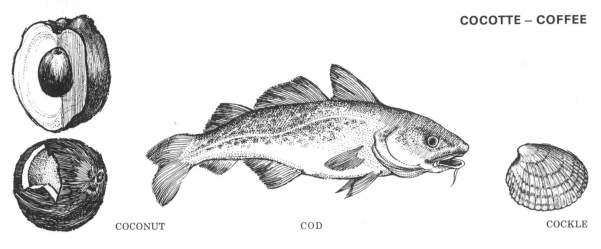

COCONUT   COD   COCKLE

COCOTTE. The French name for a cooking pot which is usually oval but sometimes round with a handle on either side. Ideally it is a heavy copper pan and large enough to hold a chicken (*cocotte* is also the French child's name for a chicken). However, modern *cocottes* are made from fireproof glass or porcelain, as well as metal. The *cocotte* has a close-fitting lid and is an indispensible item in any French kitchen. The foods cooked in such dishes, in which they are also served, are described as *en cocotte* or *en casserole*.

COCO YAM. A perennial, tuberous plant with large, heart-shaped leaves which is extensively cultivated in the humid, tropical regions of the world for its edible root. This is a staple foodstuff in the Far East and Pacific, where it is prepared in many ways. Originally native to Southeast Asia, there are now more than a thousand species. The tuber varies in shape from round to elongated, is one to six inches in diameter and may be as much as 24 inches long, with colours ranging through yellow, white, orange, red or purple. All are rich in vitamins A and C.

COD. A salt-water fish with a very low social rating, yet one of the most important in the commercial fisheries. It is caught chiefly in northern seas. In Britain its reputation has suffered from some bad cooking, yet correctly cooked it can provide some excellent eating. Escoffier has written of cod that it ranks amongst the finest of fish for delicacy and flavour, and were it only as difficult to come by as salmon, it would be held in wide esteem.

COEUR À LA CRÈME. This is one of the simple country sweet dishes of France made from cream cheese and shaped in a heart-shaped mould. These little moulds are made of wicker or metal. This type of sweet is served throughout the country, although not always moulded into the heart shape.

2 lb. cream cheese
1 pint (1¼) heavy cream
4 egg whites
salt

Rub the cheese through a fine sieve and beat the cream into it. Beat the whites to a dry, foamy mass and fold these into the cheese. Add a little salt. Line a heart-shaped perforated mould or basket with muslin, and fill it with cheese. Stand the basket in the refrigerator overnight, letting any further whey drop through into a bowl. If neither a heart-shaped mould nor basket is available, use a round sieve.

When ready to serve, unmould on to a platter and take away the muslin. Surround (when possible) with fresh garden or wild strawberries, sprinkle with sugar and serve with cream or with French bread.

COFFEE. 1. A bush or small tree of the genus *Coffea*.
2. The seeds of species of *Coffea*.
3. A drink made from these seeds.

In the trade there are three main kinds of coffee, known shortly as milds, Brazils and robustas, each of which varies widely in quality. The milds and Brazils are from *Coffea arabica*, the robustas from *Coffea canephora*. The milds include coffees from Kenya, parts of Tanzania and from Central and South American countries other than Brazil. The finest are from Costa Rica, Colombia and Kenya. The milds are superior in quality to the Brazils, though Brazil produces a small amount of the mild category. The robustas have a marked flavour of their own quite unlike the *arabicas*.

The finest drinking coffees generally sold are blends, always with a proportion of superior milds. The superior milds are the product of coffee 'cherry' (the oval red fruit containing two seeds known as 'beans') which has undergone a careful preparation consisting of selective picking of ripe berries, pulping, fermenting, hulling, grading and removal of diseased and low-grade beans; followed by classification by expert tasters on shape, appearance, colour and flavour.

The roasted coffee bean contains an appreciable amount of caffeine and small amounts of minerals, vitamins and aromatic substances. Caffeine, an alkaloid, is a mild stimulant and is beneficial, having been found to give an increased capacity

131

for mental and muscular work. It is caffeine that gives coffee its chief value, but the pleasure of drinking it derives also from the aromatic substances which give the characteristic aroma and flavour of well-made coffee. It is only coffees made from fine blends or from straight premium mild coffees, such as those from Kenya, containing as they do a normal quantity of caffeine and a full range of aromatic and other substances, that are of real interest from a gastronomic aspect. Much of the aroma is lost during roasting and for the finest results care should be taken to obtain coffee that has not been over-roasted. It should be brown and not approaching black. A darker roast is often more popular on the continent of Europe.

Coffee may be deprived of most of its caffeine by certain extraction methods. This is like throwing out the baby with the bath water, but decaffeinated coffee may be of use in cases, fortunately rare, of people under medical advice to avoid caffeine. Another innovation is the production of soluble or instant coffee, the use of which has increased in recent years. Though varying in quality, none of it gives the pleasure of ordinary good coffee.

To make good coffee it must be freshly ground and infused or percolated with boiling water, but not boiled with the grounds present. The simplest way is in an earthenware jug, decanting the coffee from the grounds when they have sunk, but there are many varieties of satisfactory percolators that make good coffee. Four heaped dessertspoons (4 tablespoons) of ground coffee to a pint (1¼) of water makes strong coffee to which sugar and cream may be added according to taste. *Café au lait* (which see), coffee with warm milk, should be well made of a sound blend which for this purpose may contain chicory as an acceptable diluent.

Coffee is used in hot drinks fortified with spirits and many combinations have been tried. One of the most popular is Gaelic coffee, made of strong black coffee, sugar, Irish whiskey and whipped cream. Similarly Scotch whisky, Bénédictine, rum or other liqueurs or spirits can be used. Coffee can also be served iced as a cold drink.

Coffee is commonly used as a flavouring in cooking and it is here that in some cases a good instant or soluble coffee may find a place. Coffee ice-cream, coffee filling or coating for cakes and coffee ice-cream pudding known as a parfait (which see) are some of the ways in which it is used.

COFFEE HOUSE. According to legend, coffee was first drunk at the beginning of the 9th century A.D. by a Mufti of Aden; eight hundred years later it reached Europe and, from the reign of Queen Anne to that of George III, it was so popular amongst the English upper and middle classes that coffee houses were established all over London and in some of the larger towns. At the beginning of the 18th century there were known to be five hundred in London alone, and historians have noted the enormous influence they exerted on the social and business life of the literate classes, affecting politics, the arts and trade. The coffee house served not just as a place of refreshment, but as a club where, before the advent of the telegraph, telephone or comprehensive newspapers, information and news of every kind could be exchanged. Men of various professions or none had their particular coffee house, where they could be found regularly by clients or friends. Here political views were aired, opinions sounded, alliances made and bargains sealed, all in the comfortable yet stimulating atmosphere engendered by coffee drinking – and without the sometimes inflammatory effects of alcohol. Perhaps the most noteworthy and lasting result of the early coffee house came from one kept in Lombard Street by Edward Lloyd in the early part of the 18th century, for from this simple establishment grew the great insurance institution of Lloyds of London. By the 19th century the coffee house had been largely replaced by the club and the pub and, in a different sense, by the tea shop so popular in 20th-century Britain. But soon after World War II, when the Italian *risorgimento* brought that country's styles and ideas to Britain, espresso bars spread rapidly through every city and town in Britain and became again the indispensable coffee houses of previous centuries, but this time for the young to use as comfortable and inexpensive gathering points.

COFFEE LIQUEURS. Liqueurs with a basis of various spirits and different coffee extracts are made in a number of countries. The original coffee liqueur was called Crème de Café, a term still in use, but many varieties are now sold under brand names, such as Tia Maria, a Jamaican rum liqueur made from Blue Mountain coffee extract flavoured with local spices. Brazil has its Bahia, based on grain spirit, and Mexico its Kahlua, which is popular in the United States. Other examples are Aloha, a rum-and-coffee liqueur from Scotland, and the German *Mokka mit Sahne* with a 10 per cent fat content.

COGNAC. Only brandies distilled from wine from the vineyards of the Charentes, the region around the French town of Cognac, qualify for this name. There are nevertheless great differences among the Charentes brandies. The wine for the best cognac comes from the Grande Champagne vineyards, (so called because of the similarity of the chalky soil with that of Champagne). This is followed in order of merit by wine from the Petite Champagne and Borderies vineyards. These are all vineyards

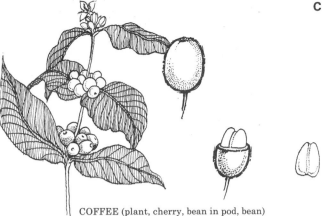

COFFEE (plant, cherry, bean in pod, bean)

close to Cognac itself and their soil is quite different from that of other Charentes vineyards such as *Fins Bois*, *Bons Bois* and *Bois éloignés*. Cognac as sold, however, is a blend of Charentes brandies; the greater the proportion of best (Grande Champagne or Petite Champagne) brandies, the finer the cognac. Time is also an important factor and the recognized tokens of age in the brandy trade are: one star for brandies when three years old; two stars when four years old; three stars when five years old. Older brandies often bear the initials V.S.O.P. (very special old pale) or V.V.S.O.P. (very very special old pale).

Cognac is distilled up to 72 per cent alcohol. When distilled to a higher strength, up to 84 per cent, it is called *esprit*; if over 84 per cent it is termed *alcool*. Old dates on labels of cognac should be treated with reservation; brandy loses strength with age very rapidly indeed and dark colouring can be artificial. The best age for brandy is between 20 and 40 years old.

COINTREAU. A colourless orange-flavoured liqueur, a very fine triple sec white curaçao.

COLA NUT. The seed of a tree which, when dried, provides a mild stimulant containing a small amount of caffeine: it is used in a variety of soft drinks all over the world. Originally the tree was indigenous to West Africa but is now widely cultivated in South America and the West Indies.

COLCANNON. An Irish country dish of potatoes and cabbage.

COLESLAW. An American salad now popular in many parts of the world as it is nutritious, easy to prepare and makes an excellent accompaniment to a variety of cold dishes. Shredded raw cabbage is mixed with a creamy mayonnaise and chilled.

COLLARD. Pickled or salted meat tightly rolled and cooked with herbs and spices. It is pressed and served cold.

COLLINS. Drinks comprising spirits mixed with fruit juices and soda water.

JOHN COLLINS

Gin with the juice of 2 oranges and 1 lemon and soda water. Iced. If other spirits are substituted for the gin, this gives other members of the Collins family – Tom Collins, etc.

COLLOPS. The collops of olden times were slices or lumps of meat, sometimes bacon; we read of collops and eggs. Beef collops are what today we would call steaks, and mutton collops are our mutton chops. In the Book of Job there is an allusion to the man who 'maketh collops of fat on his flanks', and Shakespeare talks of a 'collop of flesh'. At one time Shrove Monday was called Collop Monday because on that day people took leave of their diet of meat and prepared for Lent. The following Saturday was known as Egg Saturday for a corresponding reason.

However, whatever the origin of collops, many people associate them with Scotland.

COLOMBARD. See BORDEAUX WINES.

COLONIAL GOOSE. Not a goose at all but an Australian way of stuffing and roasting a leg of mutton. Formerly the meat was roasted in a camp oven which, it was claimed, possessed the virtue of making any mutton as tender as lamb.

COMBLANCHIEN. See BURGUNDY WINES.

COMFITS. A word of ancient origin meaning a sweetmeat of varying kinds. By the close of the 16th century men and women of fashion always carried with them a box of comfits. This custom was not confined to Britain. The courtiers of Henry III of France seemed unable to exist without the abundant use of comfits. When the Duke of Guise was shot at Blois, he was found with his comfit box still clutched in his hand.

In more recent years, comfits were small sweets or cachous carried in flat tins and chewed, rather like modern chewing gum.

COMMANDARIA. See CYPRUS WINES.

COMPÔTE. Basically this is the French culinary term for stewed fruit, but there is a world of difference between compôte and fruit stewed in water to which sugar is added. To make a compôte, fresh or dried fruit is cooked gently in a sugar syrup until the fruit is tender, and it is not allowed to break or lose its shape. When the fruit is cooked it is carefully taken out with a perforated spoon and the syrup boiled hard to reduce it and then poured over the fruit. Sometimes brandy or a liqueur is poured over the fruit just before it is ready, or perhaps thinly sliced orange or lemon peel or spice is added to the syrup for flavour.

COÑAC. See SPANISH WINES.

CONCASSER. A French culinary term which appears often in English cooking books. It means to chop roughly or shred coarsely and is usually applied to tomatoes. The tomatoes should be skinned and then gently squeezed to remove the seeds before being chopped.

CONCH. A term widely applied to a large number of marine snails found in all oceans and generally of the *Strombus* family. The flesh of the large pink conch is used extensively for fish bait and as a source of food in southern Florida, the Caribbean and the Bahamas. A chowder (which see) is made by the inhabitants of Key West from the conch; it is also tenderized by pounding, then breaded and fried. The flavour and texture is similar to that of the scallop and may be cooked in similar style.

CONDÉ, À LA. Many soups and sweet dishes, in which rice plays a vital part, are styled thus.

CONDIMENTS. This word comes from the Latin *condire*, to season or pickle. Substances of pronounced flavour used as seasoning agents, to give relish to food or stimulate the appetite are condiments. Many of them are essential.

The first stage in the important development of condiments was the discovery of salt, consecrated by the Greeks to their gods. Then came other condiments, anything with which man could add piquancy to his cooked food, particularly to some of those early dishes of sodden meat. Among the chief condiments today are salt and pepper, mustard and vinegar. The many and various spices and pickles, and items such as ginger, herbs and leaves of plants, are all condiments.

CONDRIEN. See RHÔNE WINES.

CONFECTIONERS' SUGAR. See ICING SUGAR.

CONFECTIONERY. Most confectionery is today made in factories and many processes in the making of some confectionery call for a high degree of skill and accuracy. The basic ingredient for all confectionery is sugar, sometimes dissolved in water and referred to as sugar syrup.

CONFITURE. French term for jams, also sweetmeats of sugar and fruits.

CONGER EEL. A seawater eel which can grow to a length of eight feet. Less oily than freshwater eels (which see), it may be cooked in the same manner.

CONSEILLANTE, LA, CH. See BORDEAUX WINES.

CONSERVE. There is considerable confusion between what is actually marmalade and jam; but there is even more confusion about what is jam, preserve or conserve. There is a nice description of the word preserve (a term also applied to conserve) which describes the former as a stupid, priggish sort of word employed by 'people who use the word residence instead of house'.

CONSOLANT. The French term for the glass of wine given to cooks and their assistants during the course of their work. According to the province, this can also be cider or beer.

CONSOMMÉ. Consommé is the French name for the strained liquid of any meat broth. It is made by simmering raw meat and bones in already cleared stock until all the goodness is extracted, and its flavour is decided mainly by the vegetables cooked with it. Clear stock, however clear, is not consommé; but if care is taken in removing all scum and fat from the stock, the result is as clear as and of as good a colour as most of us would want. For many soups the two are interchangeable and much of the pleasure we get from both good clear soup and consommé is that they are limpid.

There are innumerable varieties of consommé, some simple, others very elaborate.

COOK. The noun cook comes from the Old English *coc*, and this from the Latin, *cocus*.

At one time the cook was called *hominum servatorem*, the preserver of mankind. In Norman times the cook was styled *magnus coquus* or master kitchener.

In the days of our forefathers the cook's talents were recognized and appreciated. Cooks were well paid for their work and had the right to the title 'Esquire' by their office. Such was their position that from time to time lands and properties were bestowed upon them.

'Man is a cooking animal', declared Boswell,

GERMAN WINES: André L. Simon and S. F. Hallgarten tasting German wines.

COQUILLE ST JACQUES

'the beasts have memory, judgment and all the faculties and passions of our own mind in a certain degree; but no beast is a cook.'

COOKERY. Cookery is very much like music. Simple or difficult; pleasing to some, and not to others. Some nations are noted for their highly developed sense of music; others have a genius for cookery. Cookery, like music, has no frontiers. Its message is to the whole human race wherever there is a palate able to appreciate fine savours.

There are no limits to the variations in cookery. One may like a type of cookery better than any other, it is entirely a matter of personal taste and circumstance. English cookery, for example, may be called the plain-song of cookery. American cookery is bolder, striking unexpected sharp notes, and possessing greater individuality. France preserves the dignity and harmony of the great classical cuisine.

The nationality of a cook makes no difference, what matters is that he or she shall be blessed with a fair share of imagination and commonsense.

COOKERY BOOKS. Reading cookery books for many people is more enjoyable than reading thrillers. They make soothing bedtime reading, providing an escape from the harsher realities of the day and filling readers with a comforting nostalgia.

Since people began to enjoy food, rather than just eating to live, there have been cookery books. Apicius seems to have been the first recorded cookery book writer. But the first English cookery book came much later, in 1147, and was called *The Forme of Cury*. Both books repay study.

Since those earlier days there has been a steady and obviously welcome stream of books telling us in greater or lesser detail what to do with our food. Some of these books have become best-sellers and their authors' names household words, such as Mrs Beeton of England and Fanny Farmer of Boston, Massachusetts. To Mrs Beeton has been attributed the facetious instruction: 'First catch your hare'. Actually the instruction was 'First case

your hare', a perfectly normal one at that time, for to case in the 18th century was merely to dress. And the originator of that misunderstanding was not Mrs Beeton but the obscure Mrs Glasse, author of an 18th-century cookery book.

Many famous writers unexpectedly turned their hands to writing cookery books. Alexander Dumas was prouder of his culinary dictionary than of his novels. Dr Johnson at one time threatened to write a cookery book which, however, did not materialize: just as well, perhaps, since the doctor was a coarse eater.

COOKIE. The American term covering a large variety of small, filled or unfilled, sweet or semi-sweet cakes, usually round and flat in shape. The nearest British equivalent is the sweet biscuit.

COOKING. This is much older than cookery (which see). The primeval savage cut his slice of meat from the haunches of the animal and ate it raw. The discovery of fire and the art of cooking signals and authenticates the earliest stage in the refinement of man. When man became a cooking animal he raised himself to a new distinction which marked him off from all the rest of the animal world.

COQUILLE ST JACQUES. The French name for scallops, usually also applied to a recipe in which scallops are the main feature.

There is a delightful legend concerning the origin of the name. When the body of St James was being miraculously taken in a ship without sails or oars from Joppa to Galicia it passed the village of Bonzas, on the coast of Portugal, on the day a marriage had been celebrated. The bridegroom, a young knight, and his friends were riding horseback along the seashore when the knight's horse got out of control and rushed into the sea. The miraculous ship stopped its perilous course and as the rider and horse came close to it, the saint's disciples on board spoke with the knight. They told him it was the saint who had saved him from a watery grave and explained the Christian religion to him.

HAM: an uncooked joint.

He was convinced and was baptized there and then, and the ship resumed its journey while the knight returned at the gallop to his friends. He told them what had happened and they too were converted and were baptized together with the bride by the knight.

Perhaps the real point of this story is that when the knight emerged from the sea both his dress and the trappings of his horse were covered with scallop shells; therefore the Galicians took the scallop shell as the sign of St James. Since then the shells have been worn by pilgrims to the shrine of St James of Compostela.

COQUITO. *Jubaea spectabilis.* One of the most valuable palm trees of Chile. Its sap is used for making palm honey, the Chilean counterpart of the Canadian maple syrup. The seeds are eaten as sweetmeats and the fibre is made into cordage.

CORAL. The roe of a lobster, or the soft greenish matter which turns red in cooking. It is found in the hen lobsters only in the ovaries. It is greatly esteemed in French cooking to colour sauces, particularly to be used with lobster and butters.

CORDIALS. Cordials are spirits which have been sweetened and aromatized, also coloured in most cases. They owe their name to the fact or fancy that they steady or stimulate the heart (*cor*). They are sold under the name of their informing flavour, such as blackberry cordial, clove cordial, mint cordial, etc.

CORDOBAN. See SPANISH WINES.

CORDON BLEU. The blue ribbon of gastronomy, and in France the highest gastronomic order of merit given to women. It consists of a rosette of dark blue ribbon and is only bestowed on female cooks who are renowned for the excellence of their cooking. Culinary etymologists have not yet settled their dispute as to the precise derivation of the term cordon bleu.

CORGOLOIN. See BURGUNDY WINES.

CORIANDER. A delicate lacy-leafed annual whose leaves and seeds are both used. It is far more appreciated in Oriental cooking than in Western, although it was introduced into England a long time ago. In certain parts of Britain it has established itself as a wild plant. It is extensively cultivated throughout the Mediterranean countries, as well as along the northern coast of Africa and to a lesser extent in the United States. In India it grows profusely and its leaves are used as the British and Americans would use parsley.

Coriander seeds are tiny and yellowish, extremely aromatic, and when crushed emit a warm flavour which is a curious combination of sage and lemon peel. They are used in all curries, in pilaus, stews and other savoury dishes. Certain Continental pastries are flavoured with coriander seeds and so are some gins and liqueurs. It is sold both whole and ground. It is incidentally the seed which in the old days was sugar-coated and sold as comfits or Scotch candy. Sausages and wild game are frequently flavoured with this versatile herb.

CORK. Cork is taken from the bark of the cork oak which grows in the Iberian peninsula and the Mediterranean area. One of its uses is to stopper bottles, and the shorter the cork, the shorter the life of the wine in the bottle. Longer corks are used for wine to be kept for a long time.

The function of a cork in the neck of wine bottles is not only to stop wine from coming out of the bottle but also to stop impurities going in. Therefore, the quality of the cork is important if wine is to be preserved.

The amount of air which reaches wine in a bottle through the cork – a porous substance, but only just – is infinitesimal but by no means negligible: it is probably responsible for the way in which bottled wines improve with age, 'probably' because the behaviour of bottled wines has as yet never been explained to the satisfaction of scientists. Bottled wine 'put down' in a cellar or bin or laid on a shelf must be placed in a horizontal position so that the wine in the bottle is at all times in contact with the inside base of the cork.

Sometimes a cork breaks in the neck of the bottle, especially with old wine. With experience most broken corks can be removed cleanly, but if all fails and pieces of the cork reach the wine, decant the wine through a fine mesh or wine strainer.

CORKED or **CORKY.** Both words are often used to describe a wine which is not fit to drink because it has acquired the objectionable smell of a musty or otherwise faulty cork. Strictly speaking, however, this is the meaning of 'corky' only; 'corked' means a bottle with its cork stopper still in.

CORKSCREW. The modern version of the corkscrew was invented about 1700. It was different in shape and greatly improved on the early medieval corkscrew. Nowadays every possible variety of corkscrew is found on the market, from the simple spiral variety to elaborate models employing air pressure. However, the great secret of getting a cork properly out of a bottle is to screw the corkscrew well into the cork.

CORN

CORKSCREW

CORIANDER

CORN, INDIAN CORN, SWEET CORN, MAIZE.
Although corn means any kind of grain, either
wheat, as in 'corn and oil' in the Bible; or oats, the
'corn' in the horse's nosebag; it always means
maize in culinary parlance. There are two main
varieties of corn or maize grown for human consumption on a much larger scale than all other
varieties put together: they are the *indentata*
variety, or Indian corn proper, also called in the
United States 'dent' or 'field corn', and sweet corn,
which is more of a garden variety and is practically
the only one to be used as a fresh vegetable. The
grain of the first contains very little else but
starch and is well suited for the preparation of
various types of cornflours, hominy and similar
starchy foods. The grain of the second contains
both sugar and starch; it is excellent as a fresh
vegetable, picked and boiled before being fully
ripe, hence its name of green corn. It is also largely
canned at that stage for later use. When fully ripe
and dried, corn can be stored and used as cattle
feed during the winter months. Ripe and dried
corn is also ground and the meal or flour thus
obtained can be used to make many kinds of
pastries, cakes and breads. See also MAIZE
BREAD.

CORNAS. See RHÔNE WINES.

CORNED BEEF. See BULLY BEEF.

CORNET. The French name for small conical
pastries filled with cream. In Victorian England
they were known as cornucopias. A cornet is now
associated with ice-cream and also called an ice-
cream cone.

CORN FLOUR. This is corn meal which has been
ground and bolted until it is as fine as wheat flour.
It is used in baking and in sausage-making in the
United States.

CORNFLOUR or **CORNSTARCH.** An exceedingly
fine white flour used for thickening puddings and
sauces, and sometimes used in baking cakes etc.

The Chinese use it a great deal for thickening
soups.

CORNISH PASTIES. Squares of short pastry
rolled thin and enclosing a filling of uncooked
beef, calf's liver, potatoes, turnips and carrots, all
chopped and seasoned with salt and pepper. The
edges of the pasty are firmly sealed and it is baked
in a moderate oven to let the contents cook in their
own juices.

CORNISH SPLITS. A simple cake from Cornwall,
the county on the southwestern tip of England.
The splits are yeast buns, split into halves and
filled with Cornish cream and strawberry jam.

CORN MEAL. A type of flour which can be either
yellow or white. In the United States it is prepared
in two ways, known as the old and the new process.

In the old process the corn is stone-ground and
many people feel this produces a richer-flavoured
flour because the corn germ is retained. In the
new process the corn is crushed between steel
rollers and other machinery removes all the husk
and germ.

Because of the difference in the moisture content
of the two types, it is not always possible to inter-
change them in recipes.

CORN OIL. See OIL.

CORN POPPER. Any of the various utensils
used in popping corn. The basic implement consists of a closed wire cage with a long handle, but
more sophisticated modern versions are electrically heated, with a window for observation, and
enlarge the corn up to four times its natural size.

CORN STICK PAN. A baking mould, generally
of heavy iron and with cavities shaped like ears of
corn. It is used throughout the United States to
bake a maize bread known as corn sticks or
'chipmunks'.

CORN SYRUP. A syrup made by the reaction of

acid on cornflour (cornstarch) and resulting in a palatable and highly nourishing food. It varies from clear to amber in colour and is used as a table syrup or in cooking. One of its major uses is as a source of glucose in preparing infants' bottle formulas. It is extensively used in candy making as it does not crystallize when cooked, thus keeping the candy soft and at the desired consistency.

CORTESE. See ITALIAN WINES.

CORTON. See BURGUNDY WINES.

COS D'ESTOURNEL, CH. See BORDEAUX WINES.

COSNE. See LOIRE WINES.

COSTMARY. Alecost in Britain, this plant was once used for flavouring home-made ales. Today, it flavours salads, soups, game, poultry and veal.

COT. See LOIRE WINES.

COTEAU DE L'AUBANCE. See LOIRE WINES.

COTEAU DU LAYON. See LOIRE WINES.

COTEAU DU LOIR. See LOIRE WINES.

CÔTE BLOND. See RHÔNE WINES.

CÔTE BRUNE. See RHÔNE WINES.

CÔTE DE BEAUNE. See BURGUNDY WINES.

CÔTE DE BEAUNE VILLAGES. See BURGUNDY WINES.

CÔTE DE BROUILLY. See BURGUNDY WINES.

CÔTE DE DIJON. See BURGUNDY WINES.

CÔTE DE LÉCHET. See BURGUNDY WINES.

CÔTE D'OR. See BURGUNDY WINES.

CÔTE RÔTIE. See RHÔNE WINES.

CÔTES DE NUITS. See BURGUNDY WINES.

CÔTES DE NUITS, VINS FINS DE LA. See BURGUNDY WINES.

CÔTES DE NUITS VILLAGES. See BURGUNDY WINES.

COTIGNAC. A particularly good quince paste.

One of the best is commercially made in Orléans.

COTRIADE. A fish soup as prepared in Brittany. It can be called the Breton *bouillabaisse* and the more fish which can be included the better the soup.

COTTAGE CHEESE. This is made from skimmed milk with a starter of rennet, buttermilk or an acid. Cottage cheese resembles cream cheese, but has a lower fat content. It contains a high proportion of protein and calcium. See CREAM CHEESE.

COTTAGE PIE. A potato crust pie with a filling of ground, cooked left-over meat.

COTTONSEED. See OIL.

COUHINS. See BORDEAUX WINES.

COULÉE-DE-SERRANT, LA. See LOIRE WINES.

COULIBAC. See KOULIBIAC.

COULIS. A French culinary term which has undergone some changes in its career. In old English cook books the word cullis is found but this has fallen into disuse and coulis has taken its place.

At one time coulis were sauces and also the juices which flowed from roasting meat. Some cooks called liquid purées coulis, but only those prepared with chicken, game, fish, crustaceans and some vegetables. Today coulis denotes some thick soups made with crayfish, lobster, prawns and other crustaceans, the word being employed where *bisque* has formerly been used.

COUNTRY CAPTAIN. A type of chicken curry. The chicken is cut into serving portions, fried with onions in butter, and flavoured with curry spices. When the chicken pieces are brown, stock is added and the chicken is cooked until tender, then served with rice. It is an everyday manner of cooking in India. However, there is a little mystery attached to the name country captain, but it would seem that since so many captains in the days of the British in India travelled Up Country and were always served chicken curry in this fashion, it became jocularly known as country captain.

COUPE. This is a shallow cup made in glass or silver, usually on a low stem, like a champagne glass, and used for serving ices or fresh fruit salad.

COUPE JACQUES. A French culinary term for fresh fruits, sliced and steeped in various liqueurs, then covered in ice-cream and served in a coupe.

COURGETTE. See ZUCCHINI.

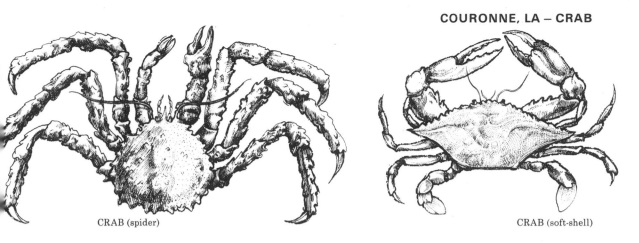

CRAB (spider)

CRAB (soft-shell)

COURONNE, CH. LA. See BORDEAUX WINES.

COURT BOUILLON. A savoury liquid, slightly acidulated, prepared for the cooking primarily of fish but also vegetables and veal, for example calf's head. A *court bouillon's* function is to give flavour, also to keep the flesh a good colour. There are several different ways of preparing a *court bouillon*, but all have either wine or vinegar.

COUSCOUS. This is the national dish of the Maghreb, the North African countries of Morocco and Algeria and Tunisia. Its origin is Berber but it has been adopted elsewhere by the Arabs who call it *maghrebia*, although this is quite different from the *couscous* of North Africa.

Couscous is a fine semolina made from wheat grain and until recently this was ground at home. Now *couscous* is bought ready-made.

There are infinite variations of this dish and all exponents maintain their version is the correct one. Basically it is semolina steamed over a stew which is made from meat, usually lamb but also chicken, and a variety of vegetables, chick peas and raisins often being added. Spices are used but sparingly. With the *couscous* a fiery sauce is served. Some versions of *couscous* are thin, others thick. But it should be prepared in a *coucousier*, which is a pot made in two parts, traditionally of earthenware but more recently of aluminium. The bottom part is large and round and in it the broth or stew is cooked; the top is a sieve with fairly wide holes, and this holds the semolina. The *couscous* is served piled on a large dish (preferably either wooden or earthenware), butter is worked into it, and then the meat and vegetables arranged round it. The peppery sauce is passed separately.

COUTET, CH. See BORDEAUX WINES.

COWFISH. The general term for any of the various boxfish which have horn-like projections over the eyes and a bony exoskeleton covering the body. They are related to the triggerfish and are sometimes called trunkfish. The cowfish is found in semi-tropical and tropical waters of the world and, in the western Atlantic, are sometimes caught as far north as the Carolinas. In the Bahamas, where they are considered a particular delicacy, they are baked whole in their shells. Local tradition has it that, caught when the moon is full, the fish possess aphrodisiac properties. The meat is white and flaky, resembling that of a young lobster.

COW HEEL. The foot of a cow, cleaned and with the hoof removed. It can be cooked as a stew but when used it is more frequently made into head cheese (which see) or used to make a rich, very gelatinous stock which requires much reducing.

CRAB. Probably most crabs are edible but many do not repay the trouble of extracting the meat. What are generally known as edible crabs are usually a pinkish-brown with almost heart-shaped shells, which can measure up to 12 inches across. The female or hen crab is considered better than the male and contains a brownish roe called the berry which gives the meat its characteristic flavour.

The American mussel crab has a shell less than one inch across, but its meat is worth several dollars a mouthful. The blue crab constitutes three-quarters of the fresh crab sold. The eastern and southern coasts of the United States produce the large horseshoe, king or casserole crab and a delicacy in that country, and the Mediterranean area, are soft-shelled crabs. These are crabs that have outgrown their shells and shed them; to be safe to eat they must be obtained alive.

The hermit crab lives in abandoned mollusk and other shells. It can be cooked like shrimps, or cleaned and returned to its borrowed shell and grilled or roasted on embers.

The long-legged thornback, a European spider crab, has good flesh, but in Britain it seldom reaches the markets.

The black crabs of the West Indies are land-dwellers that migrate annually to the sea to breed. As they are at their best at this season and are locally considered a delicacy, many never reach the sea.

CRAB APPLE. A tree native to Europe, Asia and North America. Many species and hybrid varieties are cultivated for culinary or ornamental purposes. *Malus sylvestris* is the common European crab apple; *Malus fusca*, or Oregon crab, is one of the American forms; *Malus baccata* and *Malus x robusta*, the Siberian crabs, are grown for their decorative qualities. The tree owes its English name to the sourness of its small apples, which are excellent for jams and other preserves.

CRACKERS. The American equivalent of the English dry biscuit. The cracker may be plain, salted or sweet and range from the hard, unleavened ship's biscuit to the Graham cracker (see GRAHAM FLOUR) used in puddings and especially popular with children.

CRACKLING. The scored skin or rind of a joint of pork after it has been roasted on a spit, or baked crisp in the oven.

CRACKNEL. A plain biscuit made of a paste boiled before being baked, thereby causing it to puff up.

CRADLE. Also called a decanting basket. It is a wicker basket designed to hold a bottle of wine in almost the same position as the bottle lay in the cellar, and this should not disturb the sediment. This is necessary only for old bottles of red wine where there should be sediment.

CRANBERRY. Also called the craneberry, this is the shrub and fruit *Vaccinium oxycoccos* which grows in turfy bogs in northern Europe and bears a small red berry with an extremely acid flavour. The American cranberry, *Vaccinium macrocarpon*, has a similar but larger berry. The fruit ripens from August to October and may be sold fresh or dried for making sauces, tarts, jellies and pies. In North America the cranberry is cultivated and sold in many areas, as it is the traditional accompaniment to roast turkey and chicken.

CRAPPIE. Common name given to two members (the black and the white crappie) of the sunfish family native to North America from Canada to Florida, and westward to Nebraska. Crappie have also been successfully introduced into California and are now to be found in all of the states except Alaska and Hawaii. The name is also applied to the closely related calico bass. Bugle-mouth bass, goggle-eyed bass, John Demon, chinquapin perch and newlight are just a few of the nicknames given to crappie.

CRAWFISH. See LANGOUSTE.

CRAYFISH. Generally known as the crawfish in the United States, this is a freshwater crustacean resembling the lobster but smaller in size. It is popular in many parts of the world eaten fresh and prepared in the same ways as other similar crustaceans; at the same time it is marketed extensively both frozen and in cans. Crayfish has been a source of food in Europe for centuries and is commercially bred in France. The smallest are potted, the medium-sized used mainly as a garnish and the largest are eaten in various ways as a main course. The salt-water variety is also known as the spiny lobster (which see).

CREAM. The fatter part of fresh milk. When fresh milk is left undisturbed for any length of time, the cream rises and may be easily collected on the top. Although this is the best way to get the best cream, there are many other devices to obtain more of the cream content of milk in much less time.

Cream is used in many ways, by itself or in conjunction with other foods; it improves practically all hot foods when added to them at the last moment, just before serving. It is no less excellent, however, by itself, either in the frozen form of ice-cream, semi-liquid with stewed or fresh fruit, in tea or coffee or in a hundred other ways. Most of the cream in milk is used to make butter and also some cheeses.

CREAM CHEESE. The mildest form of cheese and at one time the simplest kind to make at home. It is merely milk which has been soured by rennet or other curdling substances, such as lemon, and put into a piece of muslin and left hanging until all the moisture has drained through – usually overnight. To this can be added salt, if required, cream, herbs and other flavourings. Pasteurized milk is almost impossible to sour, thus rendering cheese-making at home difficult (see COTTAGE CHEESE).

CREAMING. This usually means beating butter and sugar together until the mixture is soft and light with a texture of cream. It is a preliminary stage for making cakes. Butter is also creamed with flour as a preliminary to making a *roux* for sauces and soups.

CREAM OF TARTAR. A substance found in the juice of grapes after they have been fermented in wine making. It is the deposit or lees at the bottom of the cask or barrel and is refined to give us one of the main ingredients in baking powder. It has been known for several generations.

CREAM PUFF PASTRY. In French *pâte à choux*, this is a quick and easy preparation which every cook should be able to prepare. It is simply a very

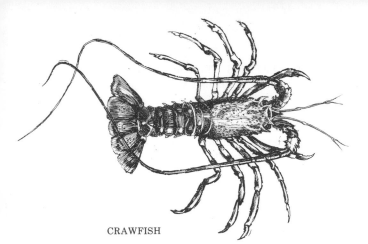

CRAWFISH

CRANBERRY

thick white sauce of flour, water and seasoning, into which eggs are beaten. The eggs cause the pastry to swell as it cooks. If making this kind of pastry for a sweet, sugar is also added. If correctly made, it is impossible to fail with cream puff pastry. The perfect puff pastry shell is firm to the touch, tender and dry inside.

CRÉCY. In France this means dishes cooked with carrot. The carrots of Crécy in France are considered to be some of the best.

CRÈME PÂTISSIÈRE. Also known as confectioner's custard or baker's custard, this is a thick French custard or cream used to fill tartlets, cream horns or puff creams, or to sandwich between halves of meringue.

  1 whole egg and 3 egg yolks
  1½ oz. (3 tablespoons) flour
  4 oz. (5 tablespoons) caster sugar
  ½ pint (⅔) milk
  vanilla flavouring

Beat the eggs into the flour, add sugar and continue beating until the mixture is smooth. Add the milk, still beating, and vanilla. Pour this into the top of a double boiler and cook over hot water until thick. Stir all the while to prevent curdling.

CREOLE SAUCE. See SAUCES.

CRÊPE. The French name for pancake.

CRÊPE SUZETTE. There has been much written about this famous pancake – so many legends, so many stories of princes and lovely ladies – that it is sad to have to explain that all it really is, is a pancake set aflame.

CRÉPINETTES. Small, flattish, square French sausages enclosed in caul but not encased in a gut or skin. Paper-thin slices of salt pork can be substituted for the caul (which see). Crépinettes are usually, but not necessarily, made from pork meat and a highly seasoned forcemeat, and the finest of them are studded with truffle.

CRÉPY. Light and pleasant white table wine from the hillside vineyards in the Haute-Savoie *département* of France, along the southern shore of Lake Geneva.

CRESS. The various members of the Crucifera family, cultivated and wild, which are common to Europe and North America. The best known are garden cress (which see) (or peppergrass) which is used for garnishing; winter cress and upland cress, both of which are annuals used in winter salads and sandwiches; watercress, an aquatic perennial which is used extensively in salads; and Indian cress, commonly known as nasturtium, whose leaves, buds and occasionally the blossom are used in salads, while the immature fruit can be used as a substitute for capers.

CRIMPING. This means to make crisp or brittle. When applied to pastry, particularly pies, it means pressing the tines of a fork or similar instrument down on the edges of the uncooked pastry. This provides a decoration and also seals the edges so that the filling is more firmly enclosed.

When crimping is applied to fish, deep cuts are made in fresh fish which is then left for a couple of hours in a mixture of water and vinegar. This renders the flesh firmer and makes it easier to cook.

CRIOTS-BÂTARD-MONTRACHET. See BURGUNDY WINES.

CROAKER. The name given in the United States to several kinds of fish supposed to produce grunting noises, chiefly the *Micropogon undulatus*, a small but gastronomically important fish of the Gulf Coast and the North Atlantic south of Cape Cod.

Other croakers valued as food are the Japanese croaker, abundant all the year round off the Pacific coasts of Japan; the slate-cod croaker of the Indian Ocean, available all the year round, but particularly abundant from February to June; and the yellow croaker, found from September to February along the coasts of China, Korea and southern Japan. It is the most important fish used in China for salting.

CROISSANT. This is a type of bread, crescent-shaped, light and appetizing, and deserving of high praise. It gives just the right amount of bread necessary for the *petit déjeuner* or French breakfast.

Croissants arrived in France from Budapest. In 1668 the Turks, besieging the city, began to construct tunnels to make their passage through the walls. Bakers, working as they did in those quiet hours between dusk and dawn, heard the sound of the tunnelling, gave warning and saved the city. They were rewarded with permission to make pastry shaped in the form of a crescent, the emblem of the Turkish flag. Or that is said to be the story. Later the croissant found its way to France to become the invariable accompaniment of the morning *café au lait* (which see).

CROIX DE GAY, CH. LA. See BORDEAUX WINES.

CROQUEMBOUCHE. This French word is also written *croche-en-bouche* and thus, it is contended, the term means all kinds of pastries which crunch and crumble in the mouth. The typical *croquembouche* is made from tiny cream puffs filled with cream, glazed with sugar and piled one on top of the other in gradually decreasing circles to form a pyramid. But they can also be made with meringues, various fruits, almond paste (marzipan) and Genoese pastries.

CROQUE-MONSIEUR. This is ham and grated cheese sandwiched between two slices of well-buttered bread, quickly fried in very hot deep fat.

CROQUETTES. Cone-shaped forms of ground meat, either fowl or game, or ground beef, lamb, veal or fish, and vegetables. The mixture is bound with eggs or a sauce, generally egg-and-bread-crumbed, and fried in fat or oil until golden brown and crisp.

Although croquettes are everyday fare and usually plain, there are some classical croquettes which are rich and even expensive. For example, *croquette Sevigné* includes cèpes, truffles and a *sauce soubise* in its combination. *Nimoise* is a mixture of salt-cod, truffles and a white wine sauce. *Gorenflor* is a croquette of soft fish roes, shrimps, mushrooms and truffles. *Judic* is celeriac, carrots, French beans and mushrooms, bound with a tomato sauce.

CROUSTADE. A fried bread shape or baked pastry crust, used in forming a base or foundation for serving delicately cooked fish, game, ragoûts, minces or other meat entrées.

CROÛTONS. These are sippets of bread fried and served as a garnish with soups, purées and other dishes.

CROWDIE or **CROWDY.** Traditionally a Scottish breakfast dish and a name applied to all foods of the porridge kind.

CROWN ROAST. An essentially American way of cutting, trimming, and presenting a whole loin of lamb, mutton or pork crownwise, that is to say roasted and served whole, with the inside of the 'crown' filled with mashed potatoes, and surrounded by green peas and small carrots.

CROZES HERMITAGE. See RHÔNE WINES.

CRUMB. As a culinary expression this means to coat an ingredient in breadcrumbs or cracker crumbs, having previously dipped it in beaten egg, milk or some other adhesive liquid.

CRUMPET. One of a typical kind of English teacake, once an almost essential part of the winter tea. They are round, about half an inch thick and studded with holes. Before World War I the muffin and crumpet man was a regular feature of winter afternoons and used to walk the chilly, often foggy, streets ringing his muffin bell, carrying a tray of his wares on his head.

Crumpets are toasted – and used to be toasted in front of the once typical English open fire with a grate – and served hot, spread thickly with butter which oozes through the holes on to the plate.

CRUST. The name has two different meanings according to whether it applies to bread or wine. A crust of bread is the outer, that is the hard-baked, part of the loaf. The crust of wine is composed chiefly of tartaric and other organic salts.

CRUSTACEAN. A class of the arthropods, the greatest division of the animal kingdom that ranges from the spider through the lobster and many other less familiar groups. Crustaceans are distinguished from the other arthropods by their aquatic method of respiration and by the possession of two pairs of antennae. The exoskeleton forms a hard shell in the larger forms. A great variety furnish a good amount of the sea food that we consume. Among the best known are the shrimp, lobster, crab and crayfish. They have an agreeable taste, solid small-grained flesh, are usually white in colour and are extremely perishable unless refrigerated.

CRYSTALLIZING. A sugary finish given to fruits, some flowers and fondants.

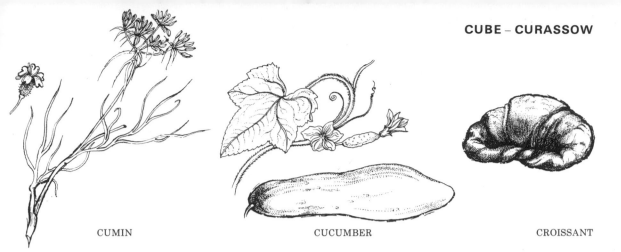

CUMIN   CUCUMBER   CROISSANT

CUBE. In a culinary sense, to cut any food, especially bread, into small squares, larger than dice.

CUBEB. The berry of a climbing plant or shrub native to Java. It resembles a pepper and has a pungent, spicy flavour used in Oriental cookery with great effect.

CUBE STEAK. A less tender cut of steak which has been treated in a machine designed to break down the tougher fibres and muscles and thus make the meat more tender and juicy. The machine impresses a number of small squares on the steak during this process, giving the surface a cubed effect and hence its name. Cube steak is generally grilled, fried or smothered.

CUCUMBER. The fruit of a creeping plant and native of northwest India, it came to Europe via Antioch and Egypt. Cucumbers finally arrived in Britain towards the end of the 16th century. They acquired a reputation for being indigestible; Evelyn, the diarist, wrote that they were considered poisonous.

Cucumbers are great mixers and blend well with tomatoes and lettuce, green peppers, indeed most green salads, and they make an excellent garnish for poached fish and other fish dishes. Cucumber sandwiches are among the most popular. They can be served as hors d'oeuvre, creamed as a soup, braised as a main dish, pickled, stuffed and baked, or sliced and fried.

In the East and the Middle East cucumbers are short, stubby, fat and sweet, with a lighter skin than is usual with the European cucumber, although even in Europe they do vary from very dark green to bright yellow. Some have a smooth skin, others are rough and ribbed. There is an apple-shaped cucumber which many people consider the finest of them all, and the Japanese climbing cucumber, which is one of the most prolific.

CUMBERLAND SAUCE. See SAUCES.

CUMIN SEED. An extremely aromatic seed with a slightly bitter flavour. It is the seed of the small annual herb cumin, which belongs to the parsley family and is called *comino* in Italy and Spanish-speaking countries. Native to Egypt, Asia and the Mediterranean, it resembles in appearance and flavour the caraway seed. It is used both in sweet and sour dishes, invariably in curries and often in pilaus.

CUNNER. Popular name of *Crenilabrus melops*, a small fish found off the Atlantic coasts of Europe. *Tautolabrus adspersus*, which is also known as the cunner, is a similar fish plentiful in New England waters. Both are species of wrasse. They are of real gastronomic value and may be prepared for the table like smelts.

CUP. Cups are summer drinks, which are mostly prepared in large jugs, and made up of practically any and every kind of wine and spirits, soda or seltzer water, sugar and fruits, and, of course, ice. The more straightforward cups are known by the name of the principal wine or other beverage used, examples being claret cup, champagne cup, cider cup and hock cup.

CURAÇAO. One of the most popular of the flavoured liqueurs, originally made in Holland with fruit from the island of Curaçao. During the 19th century Amsterdam was famous for its curaçao. It is now made in countries other than Holland and marketed under the name of a registered brand. Most curaçaos are white, but many are now available in other colours, for example pale blue, green, orange and brown. Triple Sec curaçao is a water-white highly rectified variety. There is also *sec, demi-sec*, and *surfine*, all different grades of strength and sweetness.

CURASSOW. A short, heavy, gallinaceous bird, with short wings and a strong bill. It lives in small flocks east of the Andes from Panama to Paraguay. It feeds on berries and insects and its flesh is white and palatable, not unlike that of the turkey. It has been domesticated in South America. It is prepared for the table like turkey and is considered the finest game bird of South America.

CURD. Curd is made by milk when it coagulates, either naturally when it sours, or artificially when an acid or rennet is added. It can be eaten as it is but is more frequently made into cheese.

CURD STRUDEL. See STRUDEL.

CURING. The process of preparing meat, fish or vegetables for immediate or future use by drying, salting, smoking or other methods of preservation. Examples of this are sugar-cured ham, smoke-cured bacon and flue-cured tobacco.

CURNONSKY, PRINCE OF GASTRONOMES. One of the great men in the French gastronomic world, he was born Maurice-Edmond Sailland in Anjou in 1872 and died in 1956. At the turn of the century things Russian were fashionable and Sailland rechristened himself. He took the Latin name *cur non* (why not) and *sky* to add a Slavic touch. Thus, Curnonsky was born. The title 'Prince of Gastronomes' was awarded in a contest conducted by one of the French newspapers. After his death it was decided that no other person could ever be worthy to bear the same title, so it was not given again. He was a gifted writer, and his taste in food and wines was impeccable.

CURRANT. There are two kinds of currants used for food. Those belonging to the *Ribes* which are black, red and white, are all cultivated and sold fresh. The red and white are related and have a characteristic odour which is not unpleasant, while the black has a distinctive and extra-pleasing flavour. The dried currant, used mostly in cooking, is a small seedless grape which was originally obtained from Corinth and called *raisin de Corinthe*, hence the anglicized form, currant.

CURRY. The origin of the word is debatable, but it probably comes from the Tamil *kari*, meaning a sauce. It also means spiced food and the sort of food the Indians have been eating for 5,000 years. The first 'modern' mention of curry was in A.D. 477.

Most of the spices used in Indian cooking were originally chosen as much for their medicinal or antiseptic properties as for their flavour. In the days when there was no refrigeration, antiseptics were of extreme importance. Modern tests have proved the correctness of the Indian's preference for spices.

The basic spices for curries are traditional. They are turmeric, used both as a flavouring and colouring; chillies, very hot to give a pungent flavour as well as colour (Indian curries are often a bright red); ginger to add a subtle flavour and also aid the digestion; garlic and onions (when used) for a heating effect; cloves crushed to a powder to give an aromatic perfume, or eaten whole after a meal – or, for that matter, at any time of the day to sweeten the breath; poppy seeds which are rich in oil and used for thickening; and tamarind because it is mildly laxative and has a slightly acid flavour. To these basic flavours are added variously cumin, coriander, cardamom seeds, neem leaves from the national tree of India, other flavouring leaves called ambiguously curry leaves, with coconut in the south, grated and squeezed to a coconut milk.

Most foreigners consider curries hot. Most Indians protest they are not. It is a matter of taste and region. In the south there are curries which use as many as fifty hot chillies. In the north, the Punjab for example, the curries are less hot, considerably so, and only half a dozen chillies will be asked for in a recipe. These differences between northern and southern curries should be borne in mind when ordering in Indian restaurants. In Bombay and West Bengal it seems it is simply a matter for family taste.

CURRY POWDER.
 ¾ oz. (⅓ cup) dark cardamom seeds
 6 large pieces cinnamon bark
 ¼ oz. (1 tablespoon) whole cloves
 ¼ oz. (1½ tablespoons) black cumin seeds
 a large pinch each of mace and nutmeg
Grind all these ingredients in the blender or, better still, in a coffee grinder (so long as it is not used for coffee). Pass this mixture through a sieve and store in an airtight bottle. It will keep for at least 2 or 3 weeks if the bottle is airtight.

CUSK. A large sea-fish, closely related to the cod. It is found in the North Atlantic off the coasts of Europe and North America and is prepared for the table like cod.

CUSSAC. See BORDEAUX WINES.

CUSTARD, EGG. One of the best known and probably the simplest of children's foods. It should be prepared with milk, flavoured with sugar, a little vanilla and thickened with beaten eggs.

CUSTARD APPLE. The common name given to the tree *Annona reticulata* and its fruit, found in tropical America. Successful transplantation has spread it throughout the tropics of the world and it has become an important product because of its large, sweet fruits which resemble small pineapples.

CUTLET BAT   CUTTLEFISH   CUSTARD APPLE

CUTLET. A chop cut from the best end of neck of lamb, mutton, pork or veal and fried, braised or grilled (broiled).

CUTLET BAT. A long wooden mallet or bat used to pound cutlets or meat before cooking them.

CUTTLEFISH. The name commonly applied to members of the *Cephalopoda* class of mollusks and, more correctly, to members of the *Sepiidae* family, of which the best known is the *Sepia officinalis* or European cuttlefish. This mollusk has a broad, distinctive head with two highly developed eyes and measures six to ten inches in length. The body is oval-shaped and supported internally by the leaf-shaped cuttlebone, and has ten arms or tentacles.

Generally found in shallow or shoreline waters, it rests horizontally near the bottom. The flesh is an important source of food in Japan, Italy and Greece and the cuttlebone is valuable for use as soft lime for feeding pet birds and as a dental abrasive. It contains a fluid which it uses when escaping from enemies and this is the basis of the pigment sepia which is used in water-colour painting.

CYPRUS WINES. Wine-making flourished in ancient Cyprus and even in those early days it was exported to Egypt, Greece and Rome. More than half of today's exports from Cyprus go to Britain. Cyprus can claim the oldest named wine in the world, its famous dessert wine Commandaria, so named by the Knights Templar in 1191. It is still made today. Story has it that Sultan Selim II (nicknamed The Sot) wanted to conquer Cyprus only to gain access to its wine. But Turkish rule did nothing good to wine-making and it was not until the beginning of British administration in 1878 on the island that viticulture started to recover and make progress. Cyprus was lucky to escape the phylloxera plague which swept the rest of Europe and so its vines have been growing on their old roots without interruption.

Cyprus produces both red and white wine, mostly of the table wine variety, but is best known for its Commandaria. The production of brandy in Cyprus, a twelfth of which is exported, has made much progress.

CZECHOSLOVAK WINES. Although wine has been made in Czechoslovakia since as early as the 9th century A.D., the history of viticulture has been as turbulent as the country's political history. Consequently the ravages of wars over the centuries were not made good until about 1920 when the whole national viticulture was reconstructed and the country became self-sufficient for ordinary wines. Both history and geography have influenced Czechoslovak wines, with the presence of Austria, Germany and Hungary on its borders, whichever power was dominant introducing its own grape and preferences. Slovakia produces perhaps three-quarters of the country's total production of wine, all of which is consumed at home.

D

DAB. The popular name for several species of flounder, found near the Atlantic seaboard of North America and off the coasts of northwest Europe. Dab is marketed extensively on both sides of the Atlantic for its delicate flavour and digestibility, though the flesh is less firm than that of the sole or plaice.

DAGWOOD. A sandwich named after the comic-strip character who is supposed to have invented this gastronomic bomb, which is a multi-layered construction containing every possible and impossible ingredient and is edible only to its designer. See SANDWICH.

DAHI. Indian name for curd (which see).

DAIKON. A type of radish. The daikon is known as

the Japanese radish and sometimes as the Chinese radish. It has long, thin, hard roots and is one of the most commonly used vegetables in Japan. In flavour it somewhat resembles the common radish known in the West, but is less sharp. It is considered to be an aid to digestion as it contains pepsin. It is also much used in the preparation of pickles.

Daikon was first used in Japan as a 'fragrant thing', to sweeten the breath and cleanse the mouth, all the better to appreciate wine.

DAIQUIRI. See RUM.

DAISY. The name given to a series of heavily iced alcoholic drinks. These 'tall cocktails' were the predecessor of the Collins series of drinks, all of which can be generically termed coolers. Generally served in goblets with large amounts of ice, they are garnished with various fruits, flowers or vegetables. Their popularity has, however, declined largely due to the complexity of the ingredients and preparation.

DALMATIAN WINES. See YUGOSLAV WINES.

DAMPER BREAD. A type of Australian bread made from a scone mixture in the shape of a loaf.

DAMPFKNÖDELN. German yeast dumplings also called *Dampfnudeln* or *Hefenknödeln*. They are cooked in sweetened milk and butter and served sprinkled with vanilla sugar, apple purée or other stewed fruit.

DAMSON. A small oval plum with a dark blue skin and a greenish flesh, ripening late. There are several varieties, all regarded as derivatives of *Prunus institia* or Damascus plum, and closely related to the sloes of the hedgerows.

Generally speaking the fruit, although by no means unpleasant to eat raw, is better cooked. Damsons can be cooked in any of the ways suitable for plums, and are specially good made into jams and cheeses, pies and tarts, jellies and pickles.

DAMSON BRANDY. This is simply damsons steeped in brandy to make a cordial which some people prefer to cherry brandy or sloe gin.

DANDELION. The popular name of this well-known weed of the field and the hedgerows means 'lion's tooth', a reference to its deeply notched leaves. When young the leaves are used for medicinal purposes and for making dandelion tea. They are also used in salads.

There are cultivated varieties of dandelion which

have lost much of the original bitterness. Many country people cook dandelion leaves as they cook spinach and consider them nutritious. In any case, they have a strong action on the kidneys, hence the French name *pissenlit*. Cultivated dandelion leaves are usually found on sale in country markets on the continent of Europe.

Dandelion wine is made from the petals of the flower, and the roots and leaves are used to give bitterness to herbal beers.

DANDELION AND BACON SALAD
fresh young dandelion leaves
salt, pepper
vinegar
diced lean bacon
Wash the leaves and shake well in a towel or salad basket. Mix enough vinegar to make a dressing with salt and pepper. Pour this over the dandelion leaves. Mix well. Fry and brown the bacon in a pan without adding any other fat. While this is still hot, pour it over the dandelion leaves.

DANISH BLUE (DANABLU). A round cheese about eight inches in diameter and four inches high, a copy of the French Roquefort. The paste of this cheese is chalk-white with a network of evenly distributed blue veins. It is buttery and its flavour very sharp. However, Danish blue produced in Denmark for home consumption is even sharper in flavour and more heavily veined.

DANISH CHEESE. Almost without exception Danish cheeses are copies of other cheeses, sometimes famous ones. To avoid confusion internationally and perhaps too because the Danes feel their cheeses can compete in their own right, Danish cheeses have been renamed. Danablu or Danish Blue (which see) was copied from Roquefort; Esrom was copied after Port Salut (Esrom is where it is made); Samsoe, or Danish Swiss, is similarly named after its place of manufacture, the island of Samsø.

DANISH PASTRY. A rich pastry, usually made with a yeast dough, garnished with sugar, spices, nuts, icings, etc. Danish pastries are intended as adjuncts to coffee but are often eaten after the main dish at lunch.

DANZIGER GOLDWASSER. A liqueur, the basis of which is some form of grain spirit, the flavour that of orange peel and various herbs, the colour white, the taste sweet, and its chief feature a number of specks of gold leaf, tasteless and harmless, which float about the liqueur when it is shaken or served. Originally made in the old port of Danzig, it has been copied in many other towns and countries.

DATE PALM (with fresh and dried fruit)

DANISH PASTRY

DARIOLE. This is another of those culinary dishes or terms which has rung the changes. In the England of 1664 it was a rich meat pie. Then it became a shell or cup of pastry filled with custard, cream etc. Mrs Beeton in 1861, and earlier cookery book writers, did not consider it necessary to explain its meaning. Grease a dariole mould was all they vouchsafed. And their dariole dishes were sweet.

Nowadays this name applies to a small cylindrical mould. A French recipe for filling a dariole mould is as follows: line as many dariole moulds as required with puff pastry, rolled out six times, and fill with a frangipane cream (which see) mixed with plenty of blanched almonds and flavoured with kirsch. Bake in a hot oven until the pastry is golden brown and sprinkle with caster sugar.

DARJEELING. A town in the province of West Bengal, India, where a variety of black tea is produced which is regarded by the experts as the finest in the world. See TEA.

DARNE. A French term for thick wedges of fish taken from the middle part of a large fish, in particular from salmon, cod or turbot.

DASH. As applied to food measurement, a dash means a scant one-eighth of a teaspoon.

DASHEEN. A type of taro little known in Britain, although it has been grown in the southern United States since 1913. The name is said to be a corruption of the French *de Chine*, 'from China'. See TARO.

DASHI. A light, clear fish stock which is indispensable to Japanese cooking and has a subtle and delicate flavour. It is made from flaked *katsuobushi* (dried bonito flakes) and *konbu*, which is dried seaweed. *Dashi* has been said to be the cornerstone of Japanese cooking, as well as being the basis of Japanese soups. It is the cooking liquid of many other dishes. There are in fact a number of *dashi* stocks, used for these various purposes. It is pale amber in colour, like a perfect chicken bouillon, and has not the remotest trace of fish or seaweed taste. Most Westerners mistake it for a superb chicken consommé. In fact, the only possible substitute for *dashi* would be this – but it is only a substitute, it does not and cannot give the same flavour.

In Japan *dashi* comes in packages of various sizes and qualities, including an instant one, which makes life very easy. In the West the ingredients for making *dashi*, as well as the packaged variety, will be found in stores selling Japanese foods.

DATE. A fruit of ancient origin, native to the northern shores of the Persian Gulf and now grown throughout the Arab countries. It is the fruit of the date palm, a tree which sometimes reaches to a height of 100 feet, but more generally grows to 20 or 30 feet. The dates grow in great hanging bunches which can weigh 30 lb. or more, the trees commencing to bear fruit at eight years and continuing to do so for over a century.

Dates are exceedingly rich and nourishing and have provided food for tribesmen in the deserts of Arabia for thousands of years. Dates fresh and warm from the palm are superb.

The three chief commercial varieties of dates are: the soft juicy dates, which are the best, the sweetest and the most usual type exported abroad; the dry hard dates which keep the best and are the Arabs' favourite; and the fibrous, rather dry hard dates, often sold in blocks, which are inferior and do not keep well.

HOW TO TURN OLD DATES INTO FRESH

This requires a red melon (watermelon). Take some old dates, cut a hole in the melon, fill it full of dates, cover and leave for 24 hours. When the melon is opened the dates will be found as fresh as if plucked straight from the palm.

DAUBE. A French culinary name which describes a method of cooking meat. The term *daube* without any qualification usually implies beef, but other meats can be cooked in the same manner, as well as poultry and game. Meat cooked *en daube* is braised in stock, generally red wine based, enriched with several other ingredients and well flavoured with herbs. *Daube à l'avignonnaise* is a dish of braised mutton cooked in red wine.

DAUBIÈRE. A variety of casserole, preferably of earthenware or copper, with a tight-fitting lid for braising. *Daubières* once had deep, indented lids which could be filled with hot charcoal, giving top and bottom heat in the vessel. See BRAISING.

DAUPHINOISE. This French culinary designation usually refers to a preparation which includes potatoes.

DAURADE. See SEA BREAM.

DECANT. Most if not all wines are best decanted into perfectly clean and well polished clear glass decanters, even for no better reason than that their colour shows off so much better when thus served. In the case of red wines, however, it is not merely a question of looks but of leaving behind in the original bottle every piece of sediment (or lees) which red wines cast off in the process of ageing. This operation must be carried out with great care, preferably over a lighted candle to make sure that the wine is clean and allowing none of the residue to get into it.

Butter is also said to be decanted when it is melted and purified by being transferred from one container to another.

DECANTER. A narrow-necked glass container used to hold decanted wine so that it can be served without any sediment from the bottle.

DECOCTION. The liquor resulting from the extraction of the soluble parts from a substance by boiling; for example, a clear soup is a decoction of meat and/or vegetables.

DECORATING. See GARNISH.

DEEP FAT FRYER. A deep fat fryer is or should be a deep heavy pan complete with a wire basket to fit inside it which can be lowered into the boiling fat during cooking. The basket has its own handle and it is often fitted with hooks that catch on the rim of the fat pan, thus keeping the basket off the bottom. The mesh is wide enough to allow ready access of the liquid but fine enough to retain food placed inside it. Some types of wire baskets are sold separately, others in combination with the pans. Particularly useful is the folding wire basket which can be used in a frying pan when small items of food are being fried. These fit into most pans.

DEEP FREEZING. See FREEZING.

DEER. Members of the mammal family Cervidae noted for beauty of form and swiftness of motion, these are the oldest of the ruminants, dating back to the Miocene period. The male is known as a buck, but the male of the European red deer is called a stag or a hart, when mature, while the female is known as a hind or doe. In medieval hunting terms every deer and each stage of life of the buck had a different name. All deer have a coat of fur or hair, short in the summer but heavier during cold periods. Colours range from reddish brown to grey on the surface, with white on the belly. Deer meat, known as venison (which see), is valued as food and in some areas is the main source of food, as in Lapland, Greenland and other Arctic regions. Representative types of deer are the red, fallow and roe deer in Europe, the whitetail and moose of North America, the reindeer of Scandinavia and caribou of Newfoundland.

DEGLAZE. This is an important culinary term and means to heat stock or wine together with the sediment left in the roasting or frying pan so that a gravy is formed. Before adding the liquid, all excess fat must be removed.

DEHYDRATION. A process of removing the water content from foodstuffs by:

1. passing heated air over the food at a temperature low enough to prevent changes in cell structure or in vital salts, yet high enough to remove the water; or

2. by exposing it to very low temperatures for a short period of time whereby the water content freezes while the tissues are not affected.

DELICATESSEN. A German word now adopted in England and America to mean a display of foods ready for the table, mostly of the hors d'oeuvre category. Also the shop or store department that sells such foods.

DEMERARA RUM. See RUM.

DEMERARA SUGAR. See SUGAR.

DEMIDOFF. The French culinary name of some of the richest garnishings named after a member of the Russian family of Demidoff, Prince Anatole Demidoff, who married Princess Mathilde but soon divorced her. He was one of the celebrated gastronomes of the Second Empire and many extravagant recipes have been named after him.

DEMI-GLAZE. Half glaze. A sauce reduced until it is almost thick enough for glazing.

DEMIJOHN

DECANTER

DEMIJOHN. A corruption of the French *dame-jeanne,* and the name for a large glass wine container, often straw-covered, with a short neck and small handles. It is found in most Mediterranean countries and can hold up to ten gallons. It is used a great deal in southern Spain where much sherry of the less fortified kind is drunk.

DEMI-SEC. A term used of a type of champagne which is distinctly sweet.

DEMI-SEL. A soft whole-milk French cheese, about 4 oz. in weight, similar to the Gournay. but with 2 per cent of added salt. It is made in many parts of France but the best comes from Normandy.

DEMI-TASSE. A small cup of black coffee, usually served after luncheon or dinner. In the United States, it is the accepted name for a small cup of coffee.

DENSITY. For gastronomical purposes the term density is synonymous with specific gravity, that is, the ratio of a given mass to an equal volume of water at a temperature of 4° C. (39.2° F.). For example, a pint of alcohol will weigh less than a pint of water, thus alcohol is said to be less dense or to have the lower specific gravity.

DEPOSIT. See SEDIMENT.

DERBY or **DERBYSHIRE CHEESE.** A hard-pressed English cheese which is more flaky than Cheddar but not so crumbly as Cheshire. It is an arguable cheese for many writers compare it to various other English cheeses, overlooking the fact that it is a cheese on its own. But after six months, when it is at its best, it deteriorates, losing its special characteristics, and perhaps this is the reason why comparisons begin.

There are variations of Derby cheese, the best known being Derby Sage. Fresh sage leaves are introduced to the curd which gives the cheese a sage flavour and colours it green.

DESSERT. The last course of a meal. Nuts and dried fruits and such small sweetmeats as chocolate truffles or dragées are included in the dessert. At the same time a dessert wine is served. Nowadays dessert very often means the sweet or pudding course.

DESSERT WINE. This is a full or sometimes fortified wine and is usually drunk with or after dessert. Some table wines, therefore, fall into this category e.g. Sauternes, Barsac etc. In America it is any wine that has been fortified with brandy or spirits.

DESICCATION. The process of dehydration (which see).

DEVIL. This means to apply a highly-seasoned paste to meat, fish or poultry before grilling or frying. Sometimes the paste is applied direct, sometimes mixed with breadcrumbs. It is particularly good with poultry, and at one time devilled turkey and chicken bones were a regular feature of household cooking as well as appearing on restaurant menus. The French culinary term is *diable.*

DEVIL-FISH. Another name for the angler fish (which see).

DEVITALIZED FOODS. Foods from which some or all of the natural elements have been removed either by deliberate action or by poor cooking. Normally foods should be cooked so that all the essential nutritional value is retained but, in certain scientifically planned diets, where an individual is medically restricted from ingesting a particular element, this will be removed by intense heat or cold or some chemical process.

DEVONSHIRE CREAM. A clotted cream made by separating cream from the milk and then scalding the cream in a pan of hot water. This produces a smooth cream with a crust on top. See CLOTTED CREAM.

DEXTROSE. A form of glucose or grape sugar.

DEZIZE. See BURGUNDY WINES.

DHAL. Also dal or dholl. Indian name for lentils (which see).

DIABLOTINS. Small cheese-flavoured croûtes served as a garnish for clear soups. Also called diablotins are small cheese-flavoured profiteroles and, curiously, chocolates sold in paper cases accompanied by a motto.

DIAMOND-BACK TERRAPIN. See TURTLES.

DICE. Food cut into small cubes or pieces.

DICKE BOHNEN MIT RAUCHFLEISCH. A Westphalian dish of pork and beans in which pork takes pride of place; it occupies the same position in the heart of every true Westphalian, for pork is called Westphalia's gift to mankind. See page 117.

DIEPPOISE. A French culinary term for a preparation of saltwater fish. The fish is served in a white sauce garnished with mussels and shrimps.

DIET. This may mean either an individual's normal daily food, or a particular regime of invalid fare prescribed by a doctor or dietician to combat a disease or correct a physiological deficiency or disorder. In modern times the problems of feeding the diseased and undernourished members of society have resulted in the art, science and profession of dietetics (which see), which deal with every aspect of the needs of the human body in terms of calories and nutritional values, including proteins, starches, minerals and vitamins, what foods supply them and how the body uses them.

Great names in the field of diet and dietetics begin with Hippocrates, who advocated the treatment of disease through diet, followed by Pythagoras, who recommended the exact measurement of food and drink. The oldest recorded cookery book, the Apicius, written in the 1st century B.C., contained many sensible principles for diet. Later came Miss Florence Nightingale, founder of modern nursing, who together with Alexis Soyer, originated the 'extra diet kitchens', first in the hospital at Scutari during the Crimean War and later in military hospitals throughout Britain and the Empire. From then on until the end of the 19th century the feeding of patients in hospitals became the responsibility of the nursing profession. In the eastern United States a series of cookery schools was established and Mrs Sarah Tyson Rorer, the principal of one of these schools, is generally regarded as the first American dietician.

Since then a great volume of knowledge has been gathered together by medical and scientific experts all over the world, and research continues on various unsolved problems of diet, such as causes of anaemia in women, many tropical diseases, the concern in the West over weight control and many others.

DIETETICS. The art and science concerning the application of nutritional principles to the feeding of human beings. It involves special knowledge and skills in (1) how the body ingests and uses foods; (2) the needs of the human body in relation to energy and chemicals and how foods supply these needs; (3) special requirements of the body under various forms of stress, such as disease or difficult climatic conditions.

DIGESTER. The forerunner of the pressure cooker. It was used in the 17th and 18th centuries for making broth and beef tea. It consisted of a heavy cast-iron cooking vessel, fitted with a lid which was securely slotted into grooves and formed a complete seal. The lid was fitted with a valve which allowed steam to escape.

DIGESTION. This is the intricate way in which food is dealt with by the stomach, intestines and certain juices in order that it may be assimilated into the body in the most beneficial manner. A sound and smoothly-working digestion may to a great extent be ensured in early childhood by providing regular meals eaten in a calm and cheerful atmosphere. The digestive system is affected by many factors but perhaps by the emotions more than any other, and it is essential to eat unhurriedly and in an atmosphere of relaxation and good humour. For older people it is also important to discover which foods tend to upset the digestion – it may be roast pork, cucumber, sherry or even the homely egg – and to keep to a diet which suits this complicated and important piece of the human machine.

DIGESTIVE BISCUITS. The trade name for a wholemeal biscuit which has no particular digestive qualities and is similar to the Graham cracker of the United States.

DIGESTIVES. French *digestifs*. These are liqueurs, or cordials in America, usually drunk after a meal. They have earned this name largely because of the herbs used in their manufacture, all intended to help the digestion.

DILL. An important herb in which both the leaves and the seeds are used. It is a member of the parsley family, with pale feathery leaves like those of the

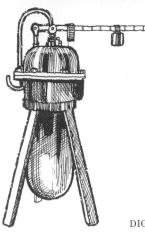

DIGESTER

DILL (flower and seed)

fennel, although the plant is smaller and has yellow flowers. The flavour of the leaves tends towards that of parsley, while the seeds resemble caraway.

Dill is not much used in British cooking, except perhaps in some fish dishes. In the United States its primary function is to flavour pickles. It is somewhat over-used in Scandinavian cooking, also perhaps in Russian cooking. The best known use of dill is in pickled cucumbers. It can be used in sauerkraut and is macerated in vinegar to make dill vinegar. It should be used with discretion.

DILUTING. To reduce in strength by adding water or other liquids. In cooking the term is synonymous with thinning, as of soups, gravies, stews, etc. For example, milk is used to dilute a thick gravy.

DINING TABLE. The dining table as such came to Britain in the 18th century. Until then the table had been a board upon which food was put to be eaten rather than admired.

The new dining tables were made by craftsmen and ornament was applied not only to the board upon which the food was placed but also to the legs. With the new tables came silver to replace the old pewter. At this time cooks began to think as much of garnishing their dishes as cooking them.

The 19th century brought further changes. Victorian influences arrived, bringing heavy tables, heavy cutlery, and ornate cruet sets. The decoration of the table became more important than the food. At the turn of the century dinner was served *à la Russe*, and menus were long and often tedious. Tables at times looked like ornamental gardens, with statues and fountains, flowers and small shrubs Everyone used tablecloths, great expanses of thick white patterned damask or lace. Tablecloths predominated well into the first quarter of this century, when practical and often attractive mats, which allowed the beauty of the table to be seen, began to be popular.

The Edwardians went in for centrepieces of silver and tall glass flower containers, which hid one's neighbours and certainly the guest opposite.

Changing conditions brought the dining table into the kitchen, sometimes even the kitchen table becoming the dining table, or corners of the kitchen were elevated and made into 'dinettes'. Between kitchen and dining room often there is only a bar, all for ease rather than elegance. Now again there is a return to the dining room and the dining table, and table decoration is once more coming into its own along with the tablecloth.

DINNER. Dinner-time has changed over the centuries, from the 11 a.m. Norman timing of the 11th century to the 20th century, when a main meal taken in the evening is generally accepted as dinner. What constitutes a good dinner is obviously both a matter of taste and education. Those who refer to their midday meal as their dinner are quite correct, since dinner at whatever time it is served is the main meal of the day.

DIP. Usually a soft savoury mixture which is served at a cocktail or wine party: a bowl of the mixture is placed in the centre of a platter and guests help themselves by dipping sticks of celery, carrot etc. into the mixture.

DIPLOMAT. In culinary language, this is a name given to several different dishes, including a pudding and a sauce (which see).

DISSECTING. A term sometimes used instead of jointing, e.g. 'dissecting a chicken'.

DISSOLVE. When a solid mixes with liquid so that no trace of the solid is left it is, in cooking language, dissolved. Sugar and salt, for example, will dissolve in water. Some solids dissolve in cold water, others need to be heated to make this happen.

DISTILLED WATER. Water that has been through a process in which all gases and minerals have been removed. It is flat in taste and only normally used as a beverage aboard sea-going vessels, where it is aerated to remove the flat taste. Its basic use in gastronomy is to dilute other liquids without altering the basic taste.

DITALINI. A variety of Italian pasta, small cuts of macaroni.

DIVINITIES. A confectionery of the fudge family, characterized by one or both of the following traits: crumbly texture or white appearance.

DOBOS TORTE. Pronounced dobosh, this rich layer cake is a speciality of Hungarian cooking, although the Yugoslavs and the Austrians claim it as well. Each layer is spread with chocolate cream, the thickness of which must equal that of the cake layers. The top is spread with caramel which is cut, while still hot, into sections. Otherwise it is impossible to cut through, it is so crisp. The sides of the *torte* are spread with chocolate cream.

DODS, MRS MEG. Mistress Dods was the hostess of the Gleikum Inn, St Ronans, Edinburgh. A book, *The Cook and Housewife's Manual*, was published in 1826 under her name, but the real author is believed to have been Mrs C. J. Johnstone, author of many well-known novels.

DOGFISH. The common name of several species of small shark of the *Squalus* and *Mustelus* genera, found on both sides of the Atlantic. The name dogfish is also applied to other unrelated fish, such as the dog salmon (*Oncorhynchus keta*) or burbot (*Lota maculosa*), a freshwater fish found in the Great Lakes and in Canada, and to the mudfish, found in sluggish warm waters of the southern and western United States. The preserved flesh of the marine dogfish is usually hard and dry, and requires soaking before eating. In Britain the dried flesh is sold under the name of 'Folkestone Beef' or sometimes 'Gray fish'. Freshly caught fish can be cooked in the same way as cod (which see) or any other large fish, or can form the basis of a thin but highly nutritious soup. Commercially the dogfish is valuable as a source of vitamin C from the liver oil, while the skin is used for polishing metal or wood and the flesh may be converted into an excellent fertilizer.

DOLCI. Italian for sweet dishes.

DÔLE DE SION. The best and best-known of the red wines made from Dôle grapes, a red wine from the vineyards of Sion in the Swiss canton of Valais.

DOLLARFISH. A small fish of the Stromateidae family, more widely known as the butterfish and found along the eastern coast of the United States. In the summer months it is found in tremendous numbers near shore along the Middle Atlantic and New England states, where it is netted in quantity. The fish is oval in shape and eight to ten in. long, with a blunt head and small mouth. The back is silvery blue and highly irridescent while the fish is alive. It is a popular fish because of its distinctive flavour and firm-textured flesh, and is cooked in the usual ways common to the smaller fishes.

DOLMA. The Turkish name for anything which is stuffed, from a finger-length vine leaf *dolma* to a whole sheep. *Dolmathes* is the Greek name for the same thing. The stuffing is invariably one of rice, spices, ground mutton or lamb and often currants. The *dolma* is used throughout the Middle East with slightly different spellings. Whether *dolmas* are of Turkish or Greek origin is one of the culinary mysteries, but they are more likely to be Greek than Turkish.

DOLPHIN. This name is applied not only to certain highly intelligent marine mammals but also, unhelpfully, to fish of the genus *Coryphaeua* found in warm, deep waters throughout the world. One of the most beautiful of the game fish, it is marked by a high forehead rising steeply from a large mouth located in the lower part of the head. Its sparkling, blue-green-yellow colour turns to yellowish-gold when dead. It can grow to six feet in length and weigh up to 75 lb., and is highly prized as a game and food fish. Smaller fish may be cooked whole, but is normally divided into steaks and fillets for a variety of recipes.

DOM PÉRIGNON. A Benedictine monk, cellarmaster at the abbey of Hautvilliers near Epernay, who, in the 17th century, achieved fame by discovering the process of making sparkling champagne. This is now the brand name for the best champagne from Moët Chandon. See CHAMPAGNE.

DOMAINE DE CHEVALIER. See BORDEAUX WINES.

DOMINIQUE, LA. See BORDEAUX WINES.

DOUBLE BOILER. This is really two saucepans, one of which fits snugly into the top of the other. The lower pan is filled with water which is kept boiling or at almost boiling point so that food placed in the top half is cooked without direct heat. It is useful for making sauces which might curdle or other mixtures which burn easily. See also BAIN-MARIE.

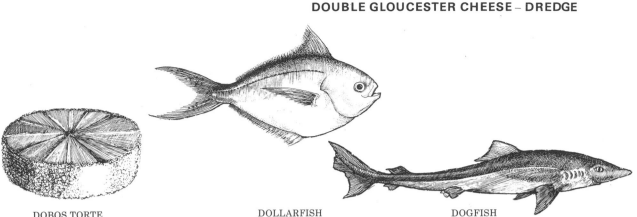

DOBOS TORTE   DOLLARFISH   DOGFISH

DOUBLE GLOUCESTER CHEESE. This is one of the finest West of England cheeses. Its flavour is milder than Cheshire cheese (which see), but has come down in the cheese world since the Gloucestershire farmers changed from cows which produced rich milk in small quantities, to breeds giving more but thinner milk. Double Gloucester is now factory made.

There is also a single Gloucester, the main difference being that it is smaller and is eaten younger, at about six weeks old.

DOUGH. This is a mixture of flour and other ingredients, the result being a soft mass or solid form of batter, thick but pliable enough to be shaped by hand or rolled out on a board and cut into shape. A soft dough is generally used for bread, scones or buns, while a stiff dough is used for pastry.

DOUGHNUTS. As far as the British are concerned, there is not much variety in the doughnut. They are made either from a yeast or baking powder dough and fried in deep fat until brown and crisp. Most have a small quantity of jam inserted into the middle, and there are also cream doughnuts. There is no great tradition of doughnut eating in Britain as, for example, in Germany, where they were an essential part of the New Year celebrations, everyone eating a hot doughnut for luck immediately after midnight.

According to American sources, doughnuts were eaten by prehistoric Indians and in some excavations petrified fried cakes were found which were thought to be doughnuts. They were round doughnuts, for the doughnut with the hole in the middle is of recent origin. It is said that these were invented by a sea captain who found that doughnuts gave him indigestion. As he liked them so much he made some experiments and finally discovered that the hole in the middle made the doughnuts more digestible, as they were more thoroughly cooked.

DOVE. See PIGEON.

DOVER SOLE. See SOLE.

DOWITCHER. An American seashore bird (*Limnodromus griseus*) which ranges from Western Alaska to Central Brazil and Peru. It is about 12 in. long, with a bill one quarter the length of its fat and chunky body. It is prepared for the table in the same way as the snipe (which see).

DRAGÉE. A sugar-coated sweetmeat or candy. Almond dragées, for example, are whole almonds coated with hard sugar, coloured pink or pale mauve, or left white. They are extremely popular in France and especially in Italy, where they are offered to guests at weddings and christenings.

DRAIN, TO. To remove liquid or fat from foods by means of a sieve, colander or by placing fritters etc. on absorbent paper.

DRAMBUIE. The oldest Scottish liqueur, it is made from Scotch whisky, heather honey, and a variety of spices and herbs. It is a secret formula belonging to a Scottish family whose ancestors are said to have been given it by Bonny Prince Charlie as a reward for their helping him to escape to France. The Gaelic, *an dram buidheach*, means 'the drink that satisfies'.

DRAW, TO. This means to remove the entrails of poultry and game etc.

DRAWN BUTTER. In the United States, this is clarified butter (which see). In Britain, it is melted butter, used as a sauce.

DREDGE. In the kitchen this means to sprinkle food with dry ingredients such as flour, sugar, cornmeal, or fine breadcrumbs. To dredge does not mean to coat thickly, but it does imply a heavier sprinkling than the term dust (which see). Special containers are sold for dredging. Meat, chicken or fish can often be dredged by placing them in a paper bag with whatever dry ingredient is being used for the purpose.

DRESS. This is the art of trimming, garnishing, cleaning and generally serving food in a pleasing manner. Where a recipe instructs the cook to dress a food, it usually means to garnish it and present the dish artistically.

DRESSING. In culinary language this means something that adds flavour, and there are several sorts of dressings. Salads are usually dressed, and dressings for these belong to two main schools, the French and the American. French dressings are the simplest, while American dressings are the most complicated.

DRESSING, BOILED. An American dressing for which there are a hundred or more variations. It is home-made and still commands approval. It can be used with fruit salads or blended with sour cream and used for cole slaw (which see) and potato salad.

VIRGINIA BOILED DRESSING

4 egg yolks
1 tablespoon (1¼) cold water
1 tablespoon (1¼) cider vinegar
¾ teaspoon (1) dry mustard
¾ teaspoon (1) each sugar and salt
¾ cup (1) sour cream

Beat together the egg yolks with the cold water, then add the vinegar, and, still beating, the mustard, sugar and salt. Put into the top of a double boiler and cook over hot, but not boiling water, stirring all the time until the mixture thickens. Cool, then fold in the sour cream.

DRIED FRUITS. All over the world housewives have dried fruit to keep for lean or out-of-season times. Today the drying of fruit is a huge commercial undertaking, and the United States leads the world in the production of several types of dried fruits.

The term dried fruits includes such fruits as apples, apricots, currants, dates, figs, peaches, prunes etc., used for puddings, cakes, fruit salads and other dishes. The food value of dried fruits lies in their sugar content. Also, quick cooking is the present day secret of treating dried fruit.

DRIED VEGETABLES. Because of modern manufacturing techniques, there is little or no difference in the food constituents of fresh and dried vegetables. But, because the water in the vegetables has been evaporated, we have a higher concentration of these constituents in the latter.

Dried vegetables must be thoroughly cooked, preferably in a well-flavoured stock. As they are highly concentrated, they can be blended with other foods.

DRINK STIRRER. A small slender rod to stir drinks, usually alcoholic, in the individual glass. It usually has a small knob at one end for crushing sugar granules, but should not be confused with either the muddler or the swizzlestick, two other stirring implements which have distinct uses. The stirrer is commonly used with highballs and similar drinks.

DRIPOLATOR. This is a coffee pot which in appearance resembles a double boiler. It is made in two separate sections, an upper and a lower. The bottom of the top section is perforated and to it is attached a third, smaller and removable container, which is also perforated and fits tightly into the top of the bottom section. The coffee, which should be finely ground, is put into this central container between the two sections which are then assembled and boiling water is poured into the top section and seeps slowly through the coffee to the lower half of the pot. When the water has finally percolated through into the lower section, the top section and the coffee container are removed and the lid, which fits both top and bottom sections, is placed on the bottom half which is now used as a coffee pot, equipped as it is with a handle and spout.

DRIPPING. This is the fat which has been separated from the meat during cooking. It can also mean fat melted from meat-fat especially for dripping. This latter process, however, is called rendering, and the flavour of the dripping is not the same. Dripping from roasting meat and other cooked meats often has small particles of gravy or meat in it, so it requires either straining or clarifying. The best dripping of all is beef dripping, with pork or goose close runners-up. Beef dripping spread on fresh bread (or thick and freshly made toast), put under the grill until it melts into the bread and lightly sprinkled with salt, is delicious and nutritious.

The drippings from bacon and fried sausages should be used in cooking for sautéeing potatoes or meat for a mince or hash, and for frying rice. Pork and chicken dripping, well strained, can be used for making pastry.

DRIPPING PAN. A pan placed under food, usually a roast, into which the gravy drips.

DRUMFISH. The name given to any of the fresh or salt-water fish which make a drumming sound by using the air bladder as a resonator. The three most important are the red drum or channel bass *(Sciaenops ocellata)*, a large, copper-coloured fish distinguished by a black spot near the tail; the black drum *(Pogonais cromis)*, sometimes copper-coloured and sometimes grey and easily identified by the barbels or whiskers on the lower jaw; and

DRUMSTICK

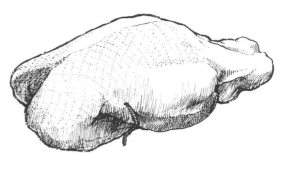

DUCK

the freshwater drum *(Aplodinotus grunniens),* which ranges in colour from metallic grey to a silvery pink. All have powerful throat teeth and feed on mollusks and crustaceans. The drumfish is found on the Atlantic coast of North America and in the Gulf of Mexico, and is important both for sport and for the table. All grow to a length of five feet or more and the sea drum may weigh more than 150 lb. The freshwater variety is found throughout the Mississippi basin.

DRUMSTICK. A colloquial Indian name for the long slender pods of the horse-radish tree, equally colloquial in nomenclature. The scraped roots of the tree make an excellent substitute for horse-radish. The drumstick, boiled, has the flavour of asparagus, while the seeds are dried and used in curries. The leg of a chicken or turkey is also referred to as a drumstick.

DRUPES. See FRUIT.

DRY. Dry has two meanings in gastronomy. When applied to food, it is the opposite to moist. Sometimes this is a fault, as in the case of meat and game dishes. Sometimes, as in dry biscuits, it is a desired quality.

When applied to wine, dry is the opposite of sweet; it may be a compliment, for instance when applied to an intensely clean sherry or other white wine. Or it may be a reproach, as when applied to an acid wine or a wine with too much tannin.

DRY ICE. This is crystallized carbon dioxide, prepared by pressure and used for long-term refrigeration. Its basic advantage over ice is that, instead of producing water when melting, it releases carbon dioxide gas, generally harmless and neither toxic nor corrosive. Important commercially, it is used to cool long-distance shipments of certain foodstuffs and to refrigerate iced foods and beverages sold on the streets.

DU BARRY. The French culinary name for a garnish for joints, featuring cauliflower with a

sauce mornay (see SAUCES). The Countess du Barry gave her name to many French dishes, the principal of which is the well-known *Crème du Barry* or cream of cauliflower.

DUBLIN BAY PRAWN. Also called the Norway lobster; its French name is *langoustine.* The mottled, yellowish-pink Dublin Bay prawn is like a small lobster with slender elongated pincers.

DUBONNET. A popular French proprietary aperitif made of a sweetened wine base, with bitter bark and quinine added to give its special flavour designed to promote the appetite. It is now also made in the United States. Much used in cocktails, it can also be drunk neat or diluted with iced water in hot weather.

DUCHESSE. This term usually refers to potatoes creamed with milk and butter and used as a garnish or an accompaniment. The puréed potato is piped on to greased baking sheets in rosettes, lightly brushed with beaten egg, and then browned in the oven. Duchesse potatoes can also be piped straight on to a serving dish as a border which is then browned in the oven and the centre filled with suprême of chicken or another similar dish.

DUCK. Many people regard the duck as an extravagant bird and it has not quite achieved the popularity of the chicken either in Britain or the United States, although in Long Island there is probably the largest duck-breeding industry in the world. The jibe 'too much for one and not enough for two' seems to have stuck.

French cuisine has a great regard for the delicacy of the flavoursome, succulent duck and almost all of the French duck recipes are internationally acclaimed. In Britain the culinary term duck is used both for the male and the female bird, just as in French culinary parlance canard and caneton (duck and duckling) cover all. In North America most duck is duckling, for the breeders, taking advantage of the voracious eating habits of the duck, feed them up and in a matter of weeks get a duckling to reach the required weight for a duck.

The Greeks sprinkled roast duck with wine from Chios, while the Romans, eating only the breast and, curiously, the brains of the duck, liked to garnish them with white truffles, doubtless from Piedmont. To the Chinese, when ducks are found in pairs, it indicates conjugal fidelity. Mandarin duck, with their exquisite colouring, develop a strong attachment to their mates and often pine and die when separated.

Fidelity, conjugal bliss or not, this has not prevented the Chinese cooks from developing a hundred-and-one different and often exciting ways of cooking and serving duck, from the whole duck to the tiniest morsels, many of which might well be discarded in the average Western kitchen. The Chinese were raising duck for the table long before the Romans. The finest of them all, the White Peking Duck, came from the Imperial Palace aviaries and were intended, quite rightly, for the Imperial chopsticks.

The duck, it is true, is not the most economical item in the poultry group, but it is usually lower in price, which makes up for some of the waste. Its bones make an excellent soup. A 5-lb. duck should serve four to five people.

In French classical cooking there are three distinct types of duck, the Nantais, a small duck from 3 to 4 lb., which is killed by having its head chopped off and is then left to bleed before it is cooked. The second is the Rouennaise, a larger duck from 5 to 6 lb., which is smothered so that it has lost none of its blood before it is cooked. And thirdly is the *canard sauvage*, wild duck, which is generally a sort of mallard, but may be any wild duck – sometimes reared in the barnyard from wild ducks' eggs.

In Britain the flavour of the Aylesbury duck or duckling, which are large and rather similar to the Rouen duck, is highly thought of.

In the United States it is the Long Island duck which is favoured, descended from the Imperial aviaries of old China. The first nine of these ducks were imported into North America in March 1873, a date still honoured by Long Island duck raisers.

ROAST DUCK (Normandy)

1 5 lb. duck
1 oz. (2 tablespoons) butter
1 cup (1¼) white bread, diced
1 lb. tart apples
powdered cinnamon
salt, pepper
½ cup (⅔) each white wine or cider and stock
2 tablespoons (2½) Calvados
½ cup (⅔) thick cream

Heat the butter in a pan, add the diced bread and fry this until it is lightly browned. Peel, core and chop the apples, add them to the pan with the bread, sprinkle with cinnamon, salt and pepper and just moisten with some of the wine. Cook until the apples are soft, then stuff this mixture into the duck. Truss it, sew up the opening and sprinkle lightly with salt and pepper. Place it breastside up on a rack in a roasting pan and roast uncovered in a moderate oven 25 minutes for each pound. Prick the skin several times to release the fat. At this stage the fat can be poured off from the pan. Heat the white wine and stock and pour this over the duck and continue to baste frequently. When the duck is tender take it from the pan and arrange on a hot platter. Keep hot. Skim off as much fat as possible from the pan, add the Calvados, stir briskly and then add the cream. Gently reheat then strain the sauce over the duck. Serve with red cabbage or peas, celery or spinach and potatoes.

DUCK, WILD. Wild duck are found and eaten all over the world. It is not practicable here to describe every member of this extensive family of wild fowl, but the following list is intended to be representative of this gastronomically delightful class of bird.

BLACK DUCK. A dark brown duck with white wing linings, called the black mallard in the United States. It ranges from Canada to North Carolina and winters from New England to Louisiana. Shot as a game bird, it is highly prized as food.

CANVAS-BACK DUCK. The most famous North American duck and the epicure's delight. It owes its gastronomic reputation to its diet of wild celery which is obtainable only by deep diving.

MALLARD. An omnivorous duck found throughout the world. The male is generally brightly coloured, with chestnut and blue-green, the female brown. Its abundance, size, availability and delicate flavour make it possibly the most important of wild ducks.

PINTAIL DUCK. This beautiful duck is as fine for food as for sport. It is recognized by its long slender neck and pointed tail, which have caused it to be nicknamed 'sea pheasant' in Britain.

TEAL. Among the smallest of wild duck, and often called puddle ducks, teal are widespread throughout Europe, Asia and the Americas and are found in freshwater streams, ponds and lakes. A distinguishing prefix describes the various species, examples being cinnamon teal, Chinese teal and green-wing teal.

WIDGEON. The middleweight of the duck family, this freshwater pond bird averages 20 in. in length and from 2 to 3 lb. in weight. Its food is mainly pond vegetable life and it is prized as a table bird for its delicate but distinctive flavour.

WOOD DUCK. The North American Carolina wood duck and the Asian mandarin duck are representative of this genus. They are among the

DUCK PRESS

DUNDEE CAKE

world's most colourful birds and their taste is comparable to their beauty. Wood duck once faced extinction in North America because of overshooting for plumage and meat, but intensive conservation efforts and careful regulation of hunting have restored them.

COOKING WILD DUCK

All wild duck should be plucked dry. This chore may be easily performed by melting a quantity of paraffin wax in hot water and pouring over the duck. When hardened the feathers and down are easily pulled from the carcass. The body is then singed, and wiped inside and out with a damp cloth. The duck should never be washed.

The breast should be larded to protect it against the heat and to improve the flavour, and the body cavity and the outside rubbed with olive oil and seasoned with salt and pepper. It is best spit-roasted or roasted in the oven. Duck must be basted frequently to prevent drying out. A good basting may be made by melting butter in hot water and adding lemon juice. All wild duck should be cooked rare, and served hot.

One note of caution. If the duck is not bled, it should be cooked within 24 hours. This precludes the possible development of dangerous toxins.

DUCK EGGS. Care must be taken that these are well cooked, as they may be infected with bacteria. While not recommended for light boiling, they are excellent in cakes.

DUCK PRESS. A device which is used to extract the juices from duck carcasses.

DUCRU BEAUCAILLOU. See BORDEAUX WINES.

DULCE. Another name for carragheen moss (which see).

DUMAS, ALEXANDRE. This prolific French novelist who lived from 1803 to 1870 was prouder of *Le Grand Dictionnaire de Cuisine* than of his famous novels.

DUMPLING. Dumplings belong to the best of home and country cooking in many parts of the world. Probably the ancestor of all of them is the Chinese dumpling. Marco Polo, when he returned from his travels in the Far East, brought back with him not only the secret of Chinese noodles, eventually (so we are told) to be developed into Italian pasta, but also of dumplings which became ravioli; the only difference between the two is in the stuffing.

Dumplings for the British means small balls of steamed or baked dough. Plain dumplings are cooked in soups and stews, while the sweet varieties are usually stuffed with fruit, currants, raisins etc. and served with brown sugar. Britain's most famous dumpling is the apple dumpling, which is baked.

Germany, with her *Klösse*, probably has the finest array. But Czechoslovakia has rich and delicious dumplings stuffed with *Zwetschgen* or heavily flavoured with poppyseeds; the Poles their potato dumplings; and so on. The word dumpling is said to be a diminutive of the word *dumpf*, meaning a thick, ill-shapen piece, or, in Low German, damp and moist.

DUNDEE CAKE. This is a rich fruit cake the top of which is generously strewn with blanched almonds.

DUNLOP CHEESE. A Scottish cheese, similar to Cheddar but more moist and of a closer texture. It originated in Dunlop, Ayrshire.

DUNMOW FLITCH. This is a flitch of bacon (side of bacon) awarded on Whit Monday in the Essex town of Great Dunmow to those married couples who claim never to have quarrelled or wished themselves single since their wedding. The custom is supposed to have been started in Henry III's reign by Robert Fitzwalter, and the first award recorded was in 1445. But the custom was mentioned by Chaucer a hundred years earlier as being well known in his day. It has been abolished and revived several times and today it is an amusing parody on the original trial, although there are still genine contenders for the flitch, as well as those who enter for the fun. Two flitches are offered, the first as the prize, and the second is divided among the contestants.

DURIAN. The fruit of a Malaysian tree which is grown extensively in other parts of the Far East. It is a seasonal and in some ways a freak fruit. It is as if a fairy godmother and an evil spirit had attended its inception, one giving it the flavour of the gods, the other maliciously the smell of the devil. Local inhabitants find it irresistible, and so does the Westerner once he has managed to overcome the repugnant smell possessed by the durian and tasted its ivory-tinted flesh. The flavour of the durian when it has reached the exact and correct degree of ripeness has been described as a mixture of full-flavoured cheese, mingled with peanuts, pineapple and apricots, a little garlic and a dash of sherry. The texture is that of a thick egg custard. The fruit is about the size of a coconut and the outside is completely covered with sharp prickles. The durian must be smelled and eaten to be believed.

DURRA. One of the sorghums, which are cane-like grasses cultivated for their sap, the source of molasses and sugar. It is found and grown throughout subtropical regions of the world.

It is also the name given to a variety of maize grown in India and used as a coarse foodstuff.

DURUM WHEAT. A variety of hard wheat, grown throughout the world, resistant to cereal rust and used mainly for making pasta (which see).

DUST, TO. A culinary term meaning to sprinkle food very lightly with a dry ingredient, which is usually flour or icing (confectioners') sugar.

DUTCH OVEN. This was a culinary contraption invented during the 19th century. Sometimes it stood on high feet and was set close to the fire, or in some cases it was provided with hooks at each side by which it could be hung on to the bars of the grate.

In the United States it is a kitchen utensil dating back to American colonial days. Originally made of iron, it is now made of cast iron and comes in different sizes. It must have a tight-fitting lid so that steam cannot escape from it, and several foods can be cooked in it at the same time.

DUTRUCH. See BORDEAUX WINES.

DUXELLES. This means a mince or hash of mushrooms, chopped shallots and herbs simmered in butter, used to flavour soups, sauces and stuffings. It is said the name *duxelles* derives from Uxel, a small town of the Côtes-du-Nord in France; others believe, and perhaps with better reason, that the dish was so called because it was a creation of La Varenne, a member of the household of the Marquis d'Uxelles.

E

EARTHENWARE. A term covering plates, dishes, bowls and vessels made from clay and generally functional when used in the gastronomic sense. Earthenware may be plain or glazed in a variety of colours and is an attractive and useful part of any kitchen. It is used as ovenware or for storing pâtés, pickles, etc. The more decorative pieces are often brought to the table, particularly vegetable and casserole dishes, or jugs for breakfast coffee.

EARTHY. Rather what the name suggests, an earthy flavour experienced usually in coarse wines that comes from the soil in which the grapes were grown.

EASTER. An important festival in the Christian Church which has both Christian and pagan origins. The date of the Christian Easter was fixed in A.D. 525 to be always the Sunday following the first full moon after the vernal equinox.

Those countries which observe Easter have their own traditions and customs and food plays an important role in most celebrations, mainly because it follows the long weeks of strict fasting. As the Italians say, a 'good meal praises the Lord'.

Eggs figure in many Easter festivals. At one time they were given to the congregation at Easter in English churches as palms were given on Palm Sunday, but the former custom has ceased. Eggs, banned during the Lenten fast, always return to the table at Easter, often coloured eggs for Easter Sunday morning breakfast. In the Midlands and the North of England, children still roll coloured eggs, called 'pace-eggs' (from Pasch), down the hillsides. The rolling away of the eggs signifies the rolling away of the stone from the tomb.

In Germany and Central Europe brightly painted eggs have been exchanged between families and friends for generations. The modern chocolate or pasteboard egg filled with presents is but a development of these more simple customs.

In the Orthodox Church Easter plays an important role in the life of the faithful and still today people flock to Athens to attend the moving Easter celebrations ending with a candlelit procession

(Opposite) HORS d'OEUVRE: an assortment of Spanish hors d'oeuvre.
(Overleaf) ITALIAN WINES: vineyard in Alba, Piedmont, showing Moscato grapes from which Asti Spumante is made.

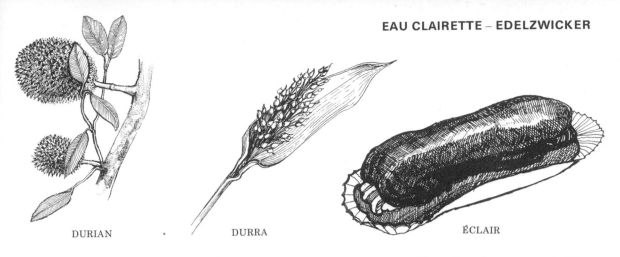

DURIAN   •   DURRA   ÉCLAIR

through the city. These celebrations are followed by a positive orgy of Easter eating, with roasted lamb or kid, special soups and cakes.

For the Russian Orthodox, Easter is not Easter without *pashka* or *kulich* (which see).

In Rome, not surprisingly, Easter is celebrated with a curious mixture of reverence and gaiety. Everyone goes to the churches and the city seems to be *en fête*. Shop windows are filled with brightly decorated cakes, sweets and candied fruits. At home, the traditional roast lamb or kid is served with the early artichokes, which go so well together. In other parts of the country boiled lamb is preferred, served with salami, or there are the special Easter pizzas, chocolate eggs and hard-boiled eggs and plenty of wine. Special pasta dishes appear, or rich rice puddings and cakes made from *ricotta*. Sicily is famed for an Easter cake made in the shape of a lamb, and for *cassata*, popular at Eastertide.

EAU CLAIRETTE. Said to be the first recorded French liqueur. It was sweetened with eau-de-vie (which see), scented with lemon, rose leaves and other aromatic herbs and decorated with specks of gold.

EAU-DE-VIE. Translated literally from the French, this means 'water of life' and in France it is the term commonly applied to brandy. In fact, however, it can denote any potable spirit including, but not necessarily limited to, spirits produced by the distillation of wine. It may be drunk as a spirit on its own or used in the preparation of liqueurs. A few of the various types are *eau-de-vin*, from wine; *eau-de-marc*, from *marc* (which see); *eau-de-grain*, from grain; *eau-de-cidre*, from cider; *eau-de-prunelle*, from the sloe (see SLOE GIN); and many others.

ECCLES CAKES. Originally regarded as a product of this Lancashire town, these cakes today are obtainable at any baker or confectioner in England, although the detailed recipe for the genuine Eccles cake is a prized secret of Messrs Bradburn & Co., a family firm that first made Eccles cakes

over 300 years ago. Then the cakes were part of the Eccles Wakes (festival holidays) held in Eccles to celebrate the dedication of the local parish church. As many people came long distances on foot, it was customary for stalls to be erected in the churchyard providing food and refreshment for the travellers. Eccles cakes were sold on the stalls.

True Eccles cakes made from rich butter puff pastry, are round and some 3 inches in diameter. They are filled with currants, butter and sugar which are wrapped in the pastry. The cake is rolled twice, dusted with sugar, and its traditional feature is three light diagonal cuts across the surface. The cakes are baked, sugar side up, on a greased baking sheet in a very hot oven for 12 to 15 minutes. They are served cold and their fame has spread throughout England.

Related to Eccles cakes are Banbury cakes (which see), Coventry Godshead, and Hawkshead and Chorley cakes.

ECHAUDÉ. A French pastry poached in water, then dried in the oven. It has been known in France since the 13th century.

ECHÉZEAUX, GRANDS ECHÉZEAUX. See BURGUNDY WINES.

ÉCLAIRS. Long finger-shaped *choux* pastry cakes usually filled with whipped cream or a *crème pâtissière* and spread with chocolate cream icing.

EDAM. A Dutch cheese made partly from skimmed milk, easily identified by its spherical shape and, if produced for export, its bright red rind. It is sometimes known in England as red ball. Colouring the rind has been practised in Holland since the 13th century. Edam is seldom used for cooking. It often figures in a typical Dutch breakfast.

EDELWEISS. A golden Italian liqueur, flavoured with *fiori d'Alpi*, the wild flowers of the alps, and sweetened with crystallized cane sugar.

EDELZWICKER. The name given in Alsace to

(Previous page) LAMB: crown roast of lamb, uncooked.
(Opposite) LAMB: saddle of lamb, uncooked.

white wine made from two or sometimes more different types of grapes, every one of them a 'noble' *(edel)* or fine quality grape.

EEL. For centuries eels were a mystery. No one knew how or where they bred. Some extraordinary theories were advanced. Aristotle declared that they generated spontaneously from mud, while Pliny offered the theory that it was from horses' tails.

Eels are migratory and at a certain time they have an urge to return home. Home is far away and, guided by some mysterious instinct, they slither from ponds overland to and down rivers until they reach the sea. Here they spend several months in the waters of the estuaries of European rivers gaining strength for further travels. Eventually restored they set out on their journey across to the deepest part of the Atlantic, mid-way between the Azores and the Bahamas. Here they breed and then die of exhaustion.

When the eggs hatch and the larvae reach a length of 5 in. they drift back, helped by the Gulf Stream, and make their way to the rivers or ponds of their parents. How this is achieved is still a mystery.

As far as British taste is concerned, eels have suffered a relapse. At one time they were eagerly accepted by both Church and Crown in lieu of money. They were always found on the tables of the rich, and no man was too poor to have an eel for dinner from time to time.

Eels continued in popularity until the 18th century, then suddenly they were no longer welcome at the tables of the rich, although they were sold in their thousands in the streets.

Hot stewed eels, once a favourite, are no longer in demand. But smoked and jellied eels are still eaten and are relatively expensive. Most of the eels eaten in London come from Ireland. Eel has remained popular in other European countries, especially the Netherlands, Germany and Denmark. The Channel Island of Jersey has a conger eel soup, garnished with marigold petals.

EELPOUT. This is a member of the cod family, more frequently referred to as the burbot and sometimes as the burbolt. It has a large mouth and its body, which is long and eel-like, may attain a length of over 3 feet. Its weight is never great, 8 lb. being exceptional. It is not a great favourite with the cook, but opinions of its culinary qualities are divided. The flesh is palatable but not easily digested, and the liver, when fried, is excellent. It can be used in soups, fish stews, or boiled and served with a fish sauce.

EFFERVESCENCE. The upward movement of bubbles of gas in fluid, as seen in boiling liquid. It is generally brought about by the introduction of carbon dioxide gas into the liquid either by natural or artificial methods. In wine it is achieved by allowing a small amount of controlled fermentation to take place, thus giving a pleasant tang or prickle. See CHAMPAGNE.

EGG. In the dawn of the world before the domestication of the hen, when wild eggs were among the first foods of ancient man, he saw them as symbols of fertility. Primitive people in Egypt, Greece and other countries believed that the universe was born from a great World or Mother Egg. Heraclitus, the Greek philosopher, said, referring to his then world: 'Here we are as in an egg'.

Eggs were believed to have magical powers to ensure fertility. German and Slav peasants used to smear their ploughs with a mixture of eggs, flour and bread on the Thursday before Easter to bring a good harvest. In 17th-century France a bride broke an egg on entering her new home, for eggs were a symbol of good fortune. To take eggs in or out of the house after dark was to court ill-luck.

Empty shells were unlucky. The Romans destroyed them so that no one could use them to make spells. Many people believed that witches wrote their spells in egg shells and flew about in them. This idea persisted for a long time and there are still people who turn their empty shells upside down and break them with a spoon. Usually they have no idea why they do this.

Birth, rebirth, fertility, magic, fortune, witchcraft – eggs meant all this. But today we think of eggs only in terms of their great importance in cooking.

Eggs are one of the most useful of the staple foods since they form a complete food in themselves. No other food product has such a wide and varied use. They are a valuable source of vitamins A and B, also a fair quantity of vitamin D. Eggs are low in calories, an important factor in a slimming diet, and are easily digested. They can be used at almost any meal, and as a main breakfast and supper dish they are unsurpassed, for they are easily and quickly prepared. This fact alone makes the egg a useful standby in any kitchen.

Besides their possibilities as a main dish, eggs are used in many kinds of baking, for soufflés, cakes, pies, etc. They are used as coating agents, for fritters, for custards, and for binding different vegetables or meats to turn these into cutlets. They make excellent garnishings and improve the flavour of frozen foods such as ice-cream for they act as a sort of wrapper around the ice crystals preventing these from collecting in colonies. Mayonnaise, salad cream and hollandaise sauce would not be but for the egg. They work as clarifiers

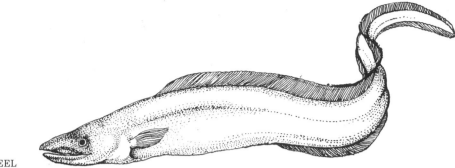

EEL

in soups and always improve the colour, flavour and texture of any dish in which they have been used, as well as adding nutritive powers.

Some people believe the brown egg is a fresher, finer egg than the white. This is not so. They may be prettier but the colour of the shell does not bear any relation to the egg inside and not even any fixed relation to the chicken species which laid it. In other words, the shell colour is no criterion of quality.

The colour of the egg yolk, however, is determined more by the hen's diet. A hen fed with plenty of greenstuff will produce eggs with a darkish yellow yolk, while one fed with castor oil in its diet and less greenstuff offers us a pale yellow yolk rich in vitamin A. For a good egg the yolk should be well-centred in the white and in a nicely rounded form. The membrane surrounding it should be firm and not break too easily.

The white of an egg should occupy our attention. If it is almost colourless, except for the two white cords extending from the yolk towards the end of the egg, it is fresh. The egg white is usually in three or four layers. The first layer is watery and surrounds the yolk. Then come two jelly-like layers, and lastly another watery layer. The jelly part should equal the watery layers, but often it does not. Summer eggs are always more watery than winter eggs; some hens simply lay watery eggs, and no one knows quite why, although research is being made into this problem.

One of the tests for eggs is to drop them in their shells into a bucket of warm water. If they drop to the bottom, they are fairly sure to be good. If they float, they will be stale and those which float determinedly on the top of the water are best thrown away or sent back to the shopkeeper. Another test is to take the eggs into a dark room and look through them against a light bulb or candle. If the egg appears clear, then it is good; if cloudy, send it back.

After the usual tests have been made, it is still not absolutely certain that the egg is good. Only after the egg has been removed from its shell can the cook really tell if it is fresh and this can be

too late. So, when using several eggs in a dish, drop each one first into a small bowl or cup and see whether it is bad – one's nose will tell one pretty quickly.

The principle involved in cooking eggs is the same as with meat. If meat is exposed to a fierce heat all its albumen will shrivel up. This happens to an egg if it is dropped into boiling water.

The make-up of an egg weighing 2 oz. is: $\frac{1}{4}$ oz. shell, $1\frac{1}{4}$ oz. white, and $\frac{1}{2}$ oz. yolk.

The treatment of eggs before cooking is also important. They will separate more easily when cold than when warm. But the whites beat up more easily if at room temperature. Also a generous pinch of baking soda added to the egg whites just before beating produces a firmer, smoother meringue. To boil a cracked egg, add vinegar, salt, lime or lemon juice to the water. A few drops are enough to seal the crack. When frying eggs, add a little flour to the pan to prevent sticking. This is especially important when cooking them in the dripping from bacon or ham previously cooked in the same pan.

It is interesting to know that an egg eaten raw is normally digested in the stomach in $1\frac{1}{2}$ hours, while a baked one takes 4 to 5 hours.

BAKED EGGS

One of the oldest methods of cooking eggs. Baked eggs are usually prepared in individual dishes, either cocottes or ramekins (which see) although several may be baked together in a small casserole dish. Put a tablespoon ($1\frac{1}{2}$) of cream into the dish, break in the eggs and put a small piece of butter on top of the egg. Bake in a low oven or, better still, a *bain-marie* (which see). See plate 95.

EGG AND BREADCRUMB. One of the most usual cooking operations. It means to dip an article of food, before frying, into beaten egg and then into fine breadcrumbs. This is done to give a crisp crust and to prevent the fat being absorbed into the food. Fish, veal, chops, rissoles etc. are treated in this manner.

EGG BEATER. See BEATER.

EGG CODDLER. This is a small china container with a screw top lid which holds one egg. It is placed into hot water and the egg when cooked served in the container.

EGG CUPS. These are small specially designed cups to hold one or two boiled eggs for eating. There are probably hundreds of different designs available, some very simple and traditional, others designed in strange forms of birds and animals for children. They are made of china, fireproof glass, metal, even silver and wood. Modern designers are now turning their attention to egg cups with some interesting results.

EGG DISHES FOR BAKED EGGS. These are shallow, round dishes with ears or handles on either side. They can be made from fireproof china, earthenware or cast-iron or they can be enamelled.

EGG HOPPERS. An everyday dish from Ceylon. Egg hoppers can be described as a variety of pancake made with flour which is mixed to a batter with coconut milk and cream. The batter is cooked until it is half set and then an egg is broken over the top; both pancake and egg are then cooked together. They are quite delicious.

EGGNOG. Sometimes called eggflip, this is a fortifying and easily digested drink made from varying combinations of milk, eggs, sugar, various flavourings and wine, beer or spirits. These are beaten together and served either hot or cold. During the last century it was a rather more concentrated concoction of eggs beaten up with hot wine, beer or spirits. Nowadays it is often prepared without alcohol.

PLAIN EGGNOG

Beat up an egg with 2 teaspoons (2½) of honey, 1 cup (1¼) of milk and ¼ teaspoon (⅓) of vanilla and serve chilled. Other flavourings, such as grated orange peel, or nutmeg, may be substituted for the vanilla.

EGG POACHER. A shallow, lidded saucepan to hold water, fitted with two or more small, shallow curved containers each holding one egg. This fits above the water.

EGGPLANT. See AUBERGINE.

EGG ROLLS. These are a kind of stuffed pancake sometimes called spring rolls. They belong to Chinese cooking and are very much 'small eats'. The filling can be ground chicken, shrimps, prawns, pork etc. Egg rolls can be served as an hors d'oeuvre or as part of a main course. There are several methods of making the pancakes, or wrappers, as they are more usually called, which are sometimes as thin as paper.

EGG SAUCE. See SAUCES.

EGG SEPARATOR. This is a device for separating the white from the yolk of an egg. They are made in metal, plastic or china.

EGG SLICER. An egg slicer is a device for cutting a hard-boiled egg into slices in one quick operation. While there are many different designs of egg slicers on the market, they are alike in principle. The shelled, cooked eggs are held in a depression while a grid of fine parallel wires equally spaced is pressed down through the egg, making the cuts.

EGG TIMER. A shaped glass container with two bulb ends joined together by a narrow waist. The top half of the container holds a measured quantity of sand. When the container is turned upside down the sand passes into the other end in a given time, between 3 and 4 minutes, which is the usual time allowed to boil an egg.

EGG WEDGER. This little gadget cuts hard-boiled eggs neatly into eight segments.

EGYPTIAN LOTUS. The edible water lily of Egypt and Asia. The leaves and root may be eaten as a vegetable, while the pod-like fruit contains kernels which are delicate and almond-like in flavour.

EIERKUCKAS. Alsatian pancakes which are very substantial served either sweet or savoury. They are rather rich but very good.

EISBEIN MIT SAUERKRAUT. This dish is a great winter favourite in Germany. It consists of knuckles of pork cooked with celery, parsnips, carrots, leeks, chopped apples and onion. It is served with sauerkraut (which see). See Page 117.

EIS-LIKÖRE. German equivalent of American-style drinking, German liqueurs on the rocks.

ELAND. A large member of the African antelope family, and valued both for its distinctively flavoured meat and as a sporting trophy. The flesh should be prepared in the same way as venison (which see).

ELBO. A Danish cheese, oblong in shape, about 18 in. long, 6 in. wide, from 11 to 13 lb. in weight. The paste is golden with a few 'eyes'; the rind is reddish brown.

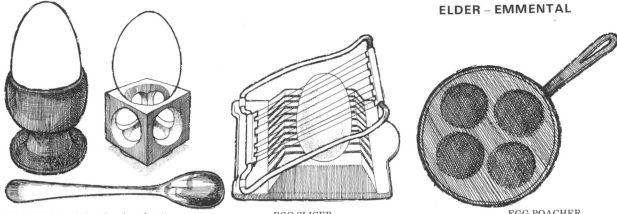

EGG CUPS (traditional and modern)   EGG SLICER   EGG POACHER

ELDER. A small wayside tree common in Europe, North America and western Asia. Elders are known for their large clusters of creamy-white flowers and later their masses of tiny purple-black berries.

Elder flowers, either fresh or dried, are the basis for many old-fashioned tisanes which are reputed to promote sleep and are useful as a flavouring, for they give off an aroma similar to the muscat grape. Elder flowers can be used to flavour stewed fruit and, added to fruit, such as gooseberry, when making jellies, to give a quite distinct but pleasing flavour.

The berries are best known as a basis for country wines, and on the continent of Europe they were once added (illegally) to some fortified wines to give them colour. Their flavour is strong and rather bitter, but in small quantities they can be added to stewed apples and other fruits. In Scandinavia elderberries are often used as a basis for fruit soups.

ELIXIR. The name given from early times to cordials or essences containing properties said to prolong life. Nowadays a few elixir recipes are still recorded and made in small quantities, the best known of which is the elixir of the *Grande Chartreuse*. This is a distillation of alcohol, angelica, melissa and hyssop leaves, cinnamon pods, mace, saffron and sugar.

ELK. The name applied to the species *Alces alces* or the great, flat-horned northern European deer. The American moose, *Alces americanus,* is a counterpart but is considered by naturalists as a distinct species. The American deer often incorrectly called the elk is in fact related to the European red deer; gradually the American Indian name of wapiti is replacing the misnomer, elk, for this species. The flesh may be bought in certain areas of Europe and North America, but at a high price as it is classified as a game animal. It is light, tasty and digestible and may be prepared by any of the methods used for beef or venison (which see). Three precautions are necessary, however: it must be well-larded as there is very little fat, cooked slowly to prevent toughening and, if marinated, this must be for not more than 24 hours.

ELVERS. Freshly spawned or very young eels, some so small as to be transparent. They are considered a delicacy by eel connoisseurs. In Spain they are cooked in hot oil well flavoured with garlic and served in a wooden bowl with wooden spoons. In other parts of Europe they are cooked until they turn to a jelly and are then eaten with bread and butter. They are caught in the estuary of the Severn in the West of England. Thin as threads, they are called locally 'the whitebait of the west'. At one time they were cleaned by the fishermen and carried round in baskets by street sellers who cried their wares around Gloucester. Today most of the Severn estuary elvers are exported to Holland alive to stock eel beds there.

ÉMINCÉ. This is the French culinary name for a dish of meat cut into thin slices, put into an earthenware dish and covered with some suitable sauce, which can be *sauce bordelaise, chasseur (hunter's), italienne, poivrade* or simply tomato or mushroom sauce.

COLD BEEF WITH TOMATO SAUCE (*Emincé de boeuf à la tomate*)

thin slices cold roast or braised beef

2 oz. (4 tablespoons) butter

1 heaped teaspoon (1½) plain or all purpose flour

3 tablespoons (3¾) gravy or stock

tomato sauce (which see)

Heat the butter in an earthenware pan, add the flour, stir until blended and gradually add the gravy. When this begins to simmer and the sauce is smooth add the pieces of meat. Cover and simmer for 1 hour. Turn on to a hot, deep plate and smother with hot tomato sauce.

It is essential that the meat is simmered and not cooked quickly so that it remains tender.

EMMENTAL or **EMMENTHAL.** One of Switzerland's 'big five' cheeses named after the Emme Valley in the canton of Berne. It has been made since the 16th century, although over the years its character has changed. Originally it was an Alpine cheese but it is now the essential part of a modern industry based on the valleys. One of its main characteristics is the holes – the cheese that is not there – which is something of a Swiss invention, begun in the Middle Ages but developed on a larger scale later. Emmental is made from cows' milk and will keep for many years, which is good for exports. Wheels for export must weigh not less than 145 lb. Some wheels exceed 220 lb.: these require at least a ton of milk (1,200 quarts). Wheels became bigger many years ago to escape tolls levied on cheeses in transit. The toll was fixed on the number of cheeses not the weight.

Emmenthal is perhaps the most copied of all Swiss cheeses, perhaps because of the holes. American Emmenthal, made in Wisconsin, is one of the best imitations, mainly because it was started by the Swiss settlers who went to the New World in 1845 and took their cheese secrets with them. But there is a Danish Emmenthal called Samsø, another made in Finland, and others in Germany and Holland. There is also an Argentine Emmenthal called *Queso Gruyère*.

EMU EGGS. Used in Australia, these are extremely oily and are usually broken into a bowl and left for several hours before using. The layer of oil that forms on the top is removed.

ENCHILADAS. A tasty Mexican dish consisting of cooked meat, vegetables, spices and cheese all rolled together in a tortilla (which see) and baked in a medium oven. This is one of the classic Mexican dishes.

ENCLOS, L'. See BORDEAUX WINES.

ENDIVE. This is a curly plant of a pale green colour with a somewhat bitter flavour. In salads it is prepared like a lettuce and, indeed, can be used as a substitute for lettuce when the latter is unobtainable. In France this type of endive is called *chicorée frissée* and in the United States it is known as curly endive or chicory. Apart from being useful in a salad, endive can also be cooked and served as a main vegetable. See CHICORY.

ENDIVE WITH A WHITE SAUCE

Pick off the wilted leaves from 1 lb. endives and discard these. Thoroughly wash the remainder and cook them gently in just enough stock to cover until tender and the liquid almost reduced to nothing. Take the endive from the pan, chop it finely and season with a little salt, pepper and paprika pepper. Prepare a white sauce (which see), using the remainder of the liquid in which the endive was cooked, and then add the chopped endive to it. Simmer for a minute or so, stir in 1

beaten egg, and serve hot, garnished with triangles of crisply fried bread.

ENGLISH BAMBOO. This is the name given to a pickle made from the young shoots of the elder tree. The shoots are peeled, salted and dried and a hot pickle poured over them.

ENGLISH BREAKFAST TEA. A name applied in the United States to all China-flavoured blends of black teas, although at first it was applied only to teas known as North China Congous. Such teas were popular at breakfast with the English in Colonial days, and the name was originated by Americans of the period. The name is not known in England.

English breakfast teas are aromatic, strong and without bitterness, and are popular in the United States.

ENGLISH DAIRY CHEESE. A very hard American cheese not unlike Cheddar used in cooking.

ENGLISH MUFFIN. See MUFFIN.

ENTRECÔTE. This is the French name for a cut of beef taken from between the ribs, but the term is sometimes used for a cut taken from the *contre-filet* or rump. The real entrecôte is usually grilled, whereas a slice of *contre-filet*, sometimes called rumpsteak in France (and sirloin in the United States), is often fried in butter.

ENTRECUISSE. A French cookery term for the fleshy thigh of poultry and game birds to distinguish it from the lower half of the leg or 'drumstick'.

ENTRE-DEUX-MERS. See BORDEAUX WINES.

ENTRÉE. The word entrée literally means the beginning, but not in the culinary sense. Louis Eustache Ude (who see) said: 'The entrée is any dish of meat, fowl, game or fish, dressed and cooked for the second course'. In any case, it is a term which is today somewhat out of date, and to many it means the third course, that preceding the roast and following the fish course, and usually a made-up dish with a sauce. For example, creamed sweetbreads in *vol-au-vent* cases would be regarded as an entrée by some. Nowadays, as far as restaurants are concerned, the word entrée signifies the main course.

ENTREMESES. These are Spanish hors d'oeuvre. Typical examples are: small black or green olives; prawns; small pieces of pork meat chopped into squares about $\frac{1}{2}$ in. square and fried in oil with

ENDIVE

ÉPERGNE

a little garlic; a salad made of chopped onion, tomato and red pepper served raw and covered with an ordinary vinaigrette dressing; and cold chopped potatoes in a vinaigrette dressing. *Entremeses* also include small squids or calamaries which are chopped in rings, dipped in flour and fried; small squares of goats' milk cheese or *manchego* (sheeps' milk cheese); radishes, cockles in sauce with chopped parsley; fried anchovies or sardines; and fried strips of whiting or hake.

ENTREMETS. This word means side dishes. They can be savoury dishes of fish, meat and vegetables, omelettes or cheese dishes, as well as sweet dishes. Louis Eustache Ude (who see) was said to be the first to distinguish clearly between entrées and entremets. The term entremets applies to all vegetable dishes, jellies, pastries, salads, prawns, lobsters, and in general to everything that appears in the second course, except the roast.

ENZIAN LIQUEURS. As the name suggests, liqueurs flavoured with the long roots of alpine gentian plants, made in Bavaria, West Germany, and also in the alpine regions of France and Switzerland. Enzian is considered to possess medicinal properties which relieve stomach pains.

ÉPERGNE. A table centre of three, four or eight glass, porcelain or metal bowls attached to an ornamental metal stem. In France, *épergnes* are still used as hors d'oeuvre sets for serving pickles such as gherkins, salted cucumbers, small pickled melons, capers and other similar delicacies. They can also be used for serving stewed fruit or iced petits fours.

EPICURE. According to some people, an epicure is one who indulges systematically and critically in the luxuries of the table. The name is derived from a celebrated Athenian teacher, Epicurus, and the accepted concept of the epicure is said to be an aspersion on Epicurus' character, for his mode of living was simple, temperate but cheerful. He held that human happiness was the ultimate end of all philosophy, and that pleasure constituted the highest happiness and consequently must be the end of all human exertions.

Because the true meaning of the teacher's words was little understood, people who gave themselves up to a life of sensuality came to be known as epicureans.

In today's sense, the epicure is a gourmet, one who is fastidious about his food and a connoisseur of food and wine. He gives special attention to food combinations and carefully considers what should form the basis of his meals, which he plans with equal attention to the accessories. The true epicure considers that the gourmand indulges to excess, and that gluttons need a doctor's treatment.

ÉPIGRAMME. A French name for two cuts of lamb, both cooked dry: a slice of breast of lamb and a cutlet, dipped in egg and breadcrumbs and either grilled or fried.

ÉPINARD. French for spinach.

ÉPLUCHAGE. In wine terminology, this is the picking over of the grapes, to eliminate any imperfect or bad ones. See page 96.

ERDBEERENKUCHEN. A German strawberry tart.

ESCABECHE. A Spanish and Provençal method of preparing small fish as hors d'oeuvre, very often fresh sardines, whiting, mullet or fresh anchovies. The fish is usually fried first, very often in boiling olive oil, then piled into a dish and covered with a hot, seasoned marinade and left for 24 hours, when the fish is ready to be served.

ESCALOPE. A French word which is used for a cut, slice or scoop of meat or fish without any bones in it, no gristle, and no skin.

The term is chiefly used of strips of veal cut from the cushion or fillet, but a concave slice of *foie gras* scooped out with a silver spoon is also called *escalope de foie gras*.

ESCARGOTS. See SNAILS.

ESCOFFIER, AUGUSTE. A great cook who earned the title 'The King of Chefs, and the Chef of Kings'. After early training in his home-town of Nice he came to London, where he gained celebrity. In 1890 in London he opened, together with two other great hoteliers, the Savoy Hotel. He left this later to take over the kitchens of the Carlton Hotel. It was here that he invented the Pêche Melba and, in 1920, as a reward for all he had done to enhance the prestige of the French cuisine, he was made a Chevalier of the Legion of Honour.

Escoffier commenced his career when he was 12 years old and continued working until he was 74, having practised his art for 62 years, surely a record. He died in 1935 when he was nearly 89. His books included *Le Guide Culinaire* and *Ma Cuisine*.

ESCOVEITCHED FISH. This is a form of pickled fish prepared and served throughout the West Indies.

    2 lb. king or cutlass fish
    olive oil for frying
    garlic to taste
    1 cup (1¼) mild vinegar
    1 small onion, finely chopped
    1 chilli, finely chopped
    4 pimento or allspice seeds

Clean the fish and cut into steaks. Heat enough olive oil to fry the fish until brown on both sides. Drain and place in a shallow dish, previously rubbed with garlic. Leave to cool. Bring the vinegar to the boil with the remaining ingredients. Take it from the heat, cool and then pour it over the fish. Leave for 24 hours to marinate, drain and serve with a salad.

ESPAGNOLE SAUCE. One of the three important sauces of the French cuisine, the other two being velouté and Béchamel (see SAUCES).

ESPRESSO COFFEE. This is an Italian invention which has spread throughout the world. No one knows exactly how the name espresso originated, but it was probably given because the coffee is quickly made. By many it is considered more delicate, aromatic and fuller of flavour than the everyday coffee of the average Italian. Café espresso coffee is made in a large electric urn in which steam under pressure is forced through the powdered coffee. There are espresso machines for home use. These come in different shapes and sizes and for use with electricity or gas, all instructions attached.

ESQUIRE TRENCHANT. In earlier centuries this term denoted the second in command of the domestic staff of a large establishment, next in rank to the majordomo. In smaller houses the two functions were often combined.

ESSENCES. These are essential flavours extracted and bottled. Unhappily, in extracting essences by maceration or distillation some of their fine overtones are lost. Some of the poorer quality essences contain cheap substitutes or synthetics and only those essences which are made and guaranteed by a first-class manufacturer should be used.

Among the more usual essences in use in the kitchen are the following: rose-water and orange-flower water; coffee essence; almond extract; peppermint oil. Vanilla essence is used by many cooks, but flavouring sugar with vanilla bean, or using the vanilla bean in cooking, is infinitely better.

ESTAMINET. French term originally used to describe a small restaurant, café-bar or coffee house which permitted smoking. Nowadays it generally refers to a basement tavern.

EST EST EST (IT IS, IT IS, IT IS). A story often told but worth repeating. In 1110 the German Bishop Johann Fugger was on his way to Rome for the coronation of the Emperor Henry V. Loving wine as he did, he sent his servant a day's journey ahead with orders to write on the door of any inn where the wine was good the simple word 'est'. How many inns were thus classified history does not relate. But in Montefiascone, a small hill town some 60 miles from Rome, the wine was so good that the enthusiastic servant wrote: 'Est! Est!! Est!!!' – and stayed. The bishop went no further. His retinue continued on to Rome but he (and his wine-loving servant) stayed behind tasting and drinking himself into his grave. Before he died the bishop willed that the town of Montefiascone should be his heir, on condition they poured a barrel of the local wine over his grave every year. And this was done, until a sensible cardinal ruled this to be a waste and that the wine should go to the local seminary for the benefit of the young. See ITALIAN WINES.

EVAPORATED MILK. See MILK.

EWE. The flesh of a ewe, when young, is used as mutton. In some parts of southwest France ewes' meat is pickled in the same fashion as pork. See MUTTON.

EXOCOETUS. The more common of the two families of flying fish found in the warmer oceans.

MACKEREL with Aïoli

FALLOW DEER

The fish does not actually fly but, by leaping from the water, is able to glide through the air by using its wing-like pectoral fins. The flesh is firm and can be cooked in the same way as other small fish.

EXTRACTS. These are obtained from many foodstuffs by varying processes. Meat extracts are natural juices and mineral salts, used to flavour soups etc. Yeast extracts are used in the same manner and are a good source of vitamin B.

F

FAGGOT OF HERBS. By this is meant a few sprigs of parsley, a sprig of thyme and a bay leaf tied together with thread. In other words, what we call today by its French name 'bouquet garni' (which see). The equivalent of these in dried herbs would be one dessertspoonful (1 tablespoon) mixed.

FAGGOTS. Also called savoury ducks, faggots comprise a savoury mixture of ground offal, pork, breadcrumbs and herbs. They are baked in square, round or loaf-shaped individual portions, each wrapped in a piece of pig's caul; or the mixture may be placed in a baking dish and covered with the caul. Faggots make a substantial dish and are popular in the North of England. They can be eaten cold, with a salad, or hot with vegetables and gravy and are sometimes served with apple sauce.

FALERNIAN WINE. This is the modern name for Falernum, a wine much appreciated by the ancient Romans.

It takes its name from Falernum, or Falerno as it is now called, where it is made. This wine was almost a legend in Roman times and inspired Horace and Virgil to sing its praises in verse while Martial spoke of it as *immortale Falernum*. It is said that the Romans used to keep the wine for anything up to 200 years without spoiling. It was a strong wine and they used to concentrate it to the consistency of jelly. It was served diluted with water and spiced with aloes, myrrh, resin, pitch, marble dust, perfumes and herbs.

Both red and white Falernian wine is still made with grapes from the same vineyards, but it is not appreciated today as it was in Roman times.

FALLOW DEER. A species of deer (which see) native to southern Europe, North Africa and countries east of Persia. Not originally native to Britain, they are found in the private parks of country houses and many live wild in British woodlands. They are smaller than the red deer and are named for their colour, which is a pale brownish yellow. The animal is prized as a sporting trophy and the meat is delicate and highly palatable. For methods of cooking see VENISON.

FARCE. French term for forcemeat or stuffing.

FARFEL. These are grains of dough and have been used in Polish–Jewish kitchens for several centuries. They serve as a soup garnish.

FARGUES. See BORDEAUX WINES.

FARINACEOUS FOODS. These foods have a high starch content.

The word 'farina' literally means meal or flour and applies to the starchy material obtained from vegetable products such as potatoes, beans and peas after grinding and milling.

Sago, arrowroot and tapioca are among the more common farinaceous foods which are extremely nutritious when cooked with milk. They give energy to the body; they are not fattening if taken in moderation.

FARINA DOLCE. An Italian sweet flour made from dried and ground sweet chestnuts.

FASEOLE. A type of shell or haricot bean, similar to and prepared in the same way as white haricot beans (see BEANS). It is smaller in size and the pod and bean are greenish in colour.

175

MARKET SCENE: a French poultry and game market.

FAT. Fats used in cookery are obtained from animal and vegetable products. They are compounds of carbon, hydrogen and oxygen. Fats are extremely concentrated forms of body fuel which supply energy and help in preserving and forming body tissues. Animal fats include lard and butter which are solid and melt at a low temperature. Vegetable fats include olive oil and other oils derived from seeds and nuts which are liquid at room temperature.

FAYE. See LOIRE WINES.

FECULA. This is a very fine flour usually extracted from potatoes. This term is also applied to starch extracted from manioc and yams. Fecula must not be confused with meals obtained from cereal grains.

It is used as a thickening agent for soups and sauces.

FELL. This is a thin papery tissue on the outside surface of a leg of lamb. In mutton it is better to remove this, but in spring lamb it should be kept on as it helps in basting and also keeps the lamb in better shape. The fell does not effect the flavour of the meat.

FENNEL. There are several varieties of fennel. It is a herb and a vegetable of ancient lineage and probably the Romans introduced it into Britain. Much later it was taken to the United States and, in California today, it is one of the most common naturalized weeds. The herb fennel is a tall plant with green stalks and feathery leaves used in both garnishing and flavouring.

The flavour of fennel varies according to type. Wild fennel is bitter without the anise flavour. Sweet or Roman fennel tastes strongly of anise but is not bitter. Bitter fennel is the type commonly grown in Russia and Central Europe, while sweet fennel is grown in Italy, France and Greece.

In England, cooking with fennel was well established before the Norman Conquest, but as a flavouring rather than as a vegetable. Fennel and fish went together, and on fast days it was the rich who had fish and fennel, and the poor who had fennel. It is still used in British cooking with fish. But fennel is equally good with pork and in marinades for pork or wild boar. It is excellent in soups and in salads. Italian cooks could hardly manage without fennel in some form or other.

Fennel is a digestive and some authorities say it is good when slimming. In Florence they flavour one of their salamis with fennel and call it *finocchiona*. Fennel seeds are cheap and easy to keep.

Fennel as a vegetable is important. It is a large bulbous root which looks like an overgrown celery and can be used in all the ways of using celery. For the *amateur* it is one of the most delicious of all vegetables, and delicately flavoured with anise.

There is yet another variety of fennel known as *carosella* or *cartucci*, the stems of which are cooked as asparagus and served with a white sauce or raw in a salad.

Fennel is used in many drinks where the flavour of anise is demanded.

FENNEL AU GRATIN. Wash two or three fennel bulbs thoroughly and cut into two. Cook in boiling, slightly salted water until tender. Drain. Place the fennel in a shallow baking dish, dot with slivers of butter, sprinkle with salt and pepper to taste, and cover with a layer of grated Parmesan cheese. Add a few more slivers of butter and bake in a hot oven until lightly browned.

FENOUILLET. Three varieties of French pears are given this name on account of their unusual aniseed flavour: the *fenouillet gris*, *fenouillet gros*, and the *fenouillet rouge*.

FENUGREEK. Both the leaves and the seeds of this curiously named leguminous plant are much used in Oriental cooking. In India it is served fresh in a salad but it is rather bitter. It is a native of Western Asia but gets its name from the Latin *fenugraecum,* which means Greek hay. It is an annual, rather like a tall clover, brilliant in colour and grown as a crop. The seeds are sand-colour and come in varying shapes and are reputed to be fattening, which might be the reason for their Asiatic popularity. Their flavour resembles that of celery seeds.

In the United States fenugreek seeds are used to impart a maple flavour to candies. But the chief use for fenugreek is in the flavouring of curries, or in flavouring commercial curry powder.

FERA. See SALMON.

FERMENTATION. In gastronomy this means the chemical reaction which produces changes in the characteristics of foodstuffs. It is caused by the action of bacteria upon sugar, lactose, etc. Examples are the fermentation of grape juice for wine, of yeast in bread (causing it to rise) and of milk for cheese-making.

FERMENTED TEA. See TEA.

FERNET BRANCA. An Italian brand of bitters with a world-wide reputation for bitterness. It is very dark in colour and of 40 per cent alcoholic strength. It is used in some cocktails, and also combined with water or soda water to make a long drink.

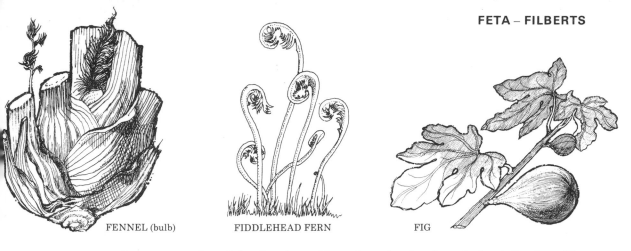

FENNEL (bulb)   FIDDLEHEAD FERN   FIG

FETA or **FETTA**. The most popular of the Greek cheeses, dead-white, soft, and well salted. It has its origin in the hills above Athens. It is a farmhouse, so-called pickled cheese, but distinct in flavour, and in the right setting extremely good to eat. It can be used in cooking – there is, for example, a dish of sucking pig stuffed with feta; also it is good fried in small squares *(saganaki)* to eat with drinks as an appetizer. However, perhaps the nicest way of eating feta cheese is with coarse, soft brown bread and black olives.

FETTUCINE. The Roman name for tagliatelle. See PASTA.

FEUILLETTE. A small wine cask, mainly used for Chablis, containing 136 litres or 30 (37½) gallons. When used in other parts of France the capacity varies from 112 to 144 litres; for example, when used for Burgundy, the cask will be large enough to hold only 114 litres.

FIASCO. The Italian word for flask, the plural of which is *fiaschi*. The *fiasco* is used for wine, and particularly, but not exclusively, for Chianti. It is round-bottomed and usually straw covered for with its round belly and bottom and long neck it cannot stand alone. See page 105.

FIDDLEHEAD FERN. An edible fern popular in the United States, but which originated in France. It is also called the cinnamon fern, and the finest comes from Maine, growing on the shores of lakes and streams. Fiddleheads have sturdy stems curving about the delicate fronds which look somewhat like a fiddle, hence the name. The soft budding stem of the fiddlehead fern has long been known as food in northern Maine and is collected in great quantities. After being washed, it is cooked like broccoli; its flavour combines something of broccoli, asparagus and artichokes. It is served with boiled bacon and also with Hollandaise sauce on toast with butter, and cold as a salad with a vinaigrette sauce. Fiddlehead ferns are best when cut young and tender and are also available in cans.

There is a pleasing legend about the fern. The original sense was doubtless feather. Ferns are sacred to the Archangel Gabriel because, stepping aside to let Adam and Eve pass the eastern gate of Eden down into the wilderness, he brushed his wings against a boulder and a feather dropped. It took root and grew like a fern.

FIG. Figs and fig trees are frequently mentioned in the Bible but they originally spread from Smyrna to Syria and then to Biblical Palestine. The Romans introduced fig trees in all temperate parts of Europe while the French, it is said, brought them to New Orleans and the Spaniards to California in 1750.

There are over 160 varieties and colours range from greenish-yellow to purple or black depending on the individual variety. Fig trees are long lived and some in California are said to be over a hundred years old. The fruit serves as a container for its flowers which do not appear externally.

Figs are best eaten raw when fully ripe and soft. They contain a good deal of sugar. In some parts of France and Italy they are served as an hors d'oeuvre, like melon, but in Paris they are usually eaten at the end of a meal. A salad of figs with thick cream and brandy makes an excellent dish.

Figs may also be dried by exposure to the sun. As the fruit dries, the sugar forms a deposit on the surface so it can be said the figs are preserved in their own dried syrup. They may be used in making cakes and various puddings and are also very good when stewed.

FIGEAC, CH. See BORDEAUX WINES.

FIGPECKER, FIGEATER, FIG-BIRD. These are the different English names given to the small birds which feed mostly on figs in the south of France and Italy. They are caught and cooked in much the same manner as ortolans (which see).

FILBERTS. These are nuts belonging to the same genus as the hazel-nut and cobnut.

The name is probably derived from St Philibert,

the saint whose feast is observed on August 22, the day on which nut picking usually starts.

The three main varieties to be found in England are the white, red and frizzled filberts. The white and red are similar in appearance but, as their designation implies, the kernel of the former is white, while the latter is covered with a reddish-brown skin. The husks of the third variety are frizzled and cut at both ends. All these varieties have an excellent flavour.

Other examples of these nuts include the Californian, Chinese and European, the giant, the Himalayan, Japanese, Siberian, Tibetan and Turkish filberts. There are several hybrid varieties as well.

Freshly gathered filberts are best when they peel easily from their skins, but they can be stored in their husks for use in winter. When dry they may be blanched by adding the kernels to boiling water. They are then turned on a rough cloth which removes the skins.

Turkey, Italy and Spain are leading producers.

FILÉ. This is a powder made from the young tender leaves of the sassafras tree which are dried and gently rubbed between the fingers. It was originally used extensively for cooking by Indians of the Choctaw tribe and it was from them that the early French colonists obtained it.

The sassafras leaves contain a certain quantity of mucilage which is both appetizing and healthy. The Creole French called it *filé* from the French *filer* to run, spin out or to pay out. *Filé* does exactly this when added to any mixture which contains water for as it is poured slowly or paid out and stirred into the liquid, it binds and thickens. The art of making gumbo (which see) consists in a judicious mixing and measuring of the *filé*. It is not cooked but added to the gumbo immediately before serving.

Filé is still produced and sold by the Choctaw Indians.

FILET MIGNON. This means in France a small cut taken from the end of the beef fillet. Such fillets are usually grilled or carefully fried.

FILLET. The French word (*filet*) which has become anglicized and applies to meat, fish, poultry and game. It is applied to undercut of the sirloin of beef, a thick slice of mutton, pork or veal, also the boned breast of chicken and game, and boned slices of fish.

FINANCIÈRE. The French name for a rich garnish, a ragoût of equal richness or a filling for *vol-au-vent* cases. As a garnish, *financière* is served with meat and poultry. It consists of all or some of the following ingredients: veal or poultry quenelles, olives, truffles, cocks' kidney and combs, and mushrooms. It is, as the name implies, an expensive garnish.

FINE. The French restaurant's professional name (pronounced feen) for any kind of brandy of unknown or unrevealed parentage. It is also called *fine maison* or *fine de la maison*.

FINNOCHIO or **FLORENCE FENNEL.** A cultivated variety of fennel, a native of southern Europe and the Mediterranean region. The first year's leaf rosette is used, the base of which is swollen to form a bulb or tuber. See FENNEL.

FINES HERBES. A mixture of parsley, chervil, tarragon and even chives, finely chopped. In earlier times mushrooms and truffles were also added. They are often mixed into an omelette to make *omelette aux fines herbes*, but an omelette flavoured only with finely chopped parsley is also thus named. *Fines herbes* can also flavour a grilled steak or a plain salad.

FINGER BOWLS. '. . . the diners made use of their fingers to dine with, but for the sake of cleanliness each person was provided with a small silver ewer containing water . . .' From a description of an Anglo-Saxon dinner . . .

Finger bowls today are usually of glass, although there are some of silver, brass and other metals. The bowls are half-filled with warm water and brought to the table at the close of the meal for the guests to cleanse their fingers. They are used at all formal functions and at any meal which involves the use of the fingers, in particular when game, poultry and fruit are served. The water in the bowl is sometimes faintly scented and a flower petal floats on the top. If the food served is greasy, the water can be flavoured with lemon juice to combat the grease.

FINING. In wine-making this is a process of clarifying wine known since Roman days. Certain substances are added to the wine in the barrels which gradually settle, carrying down in the form of sediment or lees the impurities that might have been held in suspension in the wine. White of egg, isinglass, gelatine, and other substances have been used in this way, including commercial powders, milk and even blood.

FINNAN, FINDON HADDOCK. See HADDOCK.

FINO. See SPANISH WINES.

FINTE. A shad-like marine fish that spawns in

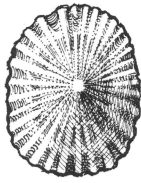

FISSURELLE

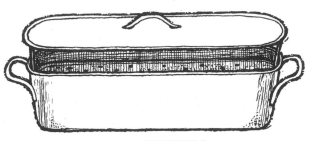

FISH KETTLE

European rivers, differing in shape from the shad in its elongated shape and possession of sharp teeth in both jaws. It is prepared for the table in the same way as the shad (which see).

FIOR D'ALPI. Mountains are the home of herb liqueurs, as the name (flower of the Alps) of this Italian variety suggests. Some of these liqueurs boast the extract from a thousand flowers, and distillers have been working on this process for nearly a century in Italy. The liqueurs are presented in white flute bottles each containing a 'tree' which consists of a small twig on which are suspended small crystals of sugar. They are smooth and reviving and, like other herb liqueurs, owe their existence originally to their medicinal properties.

FIORE SARDO. A Sardinian cheese made from ewes' milk. When it is young and still soft it is eaten; when fully cured and hardened, it is used in cooking.

FISH. Fish does not always receive the full measure of gastronomic attention it deserves. The Greeks and the Romans knew the value of fish and so did the Egyptians. And long, long ago the Church wisely enjoined its members to eat fish during Lent, not mentioning proteins or vitamins, but saying, curiously, that this food 'prevents idle chatter, since fish are themselves proverbially mute'.

Fish, like meat, contains large quantities of protein essential for body-building and body repair. Eating fish is, therefore, a splendid investment in health.

Freshwater fish and saltwater fish differ considerably in flavour. There is also a difference between fish caught in cold waters and those from tropical waters, or between fish caught in running rivers and in lakes. Brook trout, for example, is superior to lake trout. The food supply of fish also influences its flavour and both freshwater and saltwater fish are better when taken from a sandy and rocky bed than from a muddy one.

Habits also affect the flavour of fish. A lazy, sluggish fish will have a more watery, softer flesh than a fish which gives the fisherman a run for his money. Fish is never tough.

Fish deteriorates and decomposes more rapidly than meat. In selecting fish, see that its eyes are still bright and its flesh firm – and this also applies to frozen fish, although these are usually frozen as soon as caught. Frozen fish should be thawed slowly in cold water and cooked immediately.

FISH KETTLE. A fish boiler, this is an oval-shaped pan which contains a removable grid, thus enabling the fish to be taken out without breaking.

FISSURELLE. Any of the species of marine mollusks whose locomotive organs are found near the stomach. They are related to the snail, barnacle and limpet and there are more than a hundred varieties. In the Mediterranean a type known locally as St Peter's ear is common. Fissurelle are generally cooked in the same way as octopus.

FISTULINA HEPATICA. An edible fungus growing on oak trees, commonly called liver fungus in the United States, ox-tongue in Britain and *langue-de-boeuf* in France. It is used mainly in soups and stews.

FIXIN. See BURGUNDY WINES.

FIZZ. So called because of its effervescent nature, the fizz is a long, cold, slightly sweetish alcoholic drink usually made with a basis of gin and served as a refreshing summer drink.

FLAGEOLET. See BEANS.

FLAGEY-ECHÉZEAUX. See BURGUNDY WINES.

FLAKY PASTRY. See PASTRY.

FLAMBER. To flame food with a spirit i.e. brandy or other fortified wine. The spirit is heated, set alight and poured flaming over the food. It also means to singe.

FLAN. This is an open round pastry shell filled with fruit, custard or cream. Special flan tins or pans are available which consist of a ring set on a metal base. When the flan is baked, the ring is easily lifted off without any fear of breaking the pastry, which may be either short crust or biscuit pastry.

In Britain and the United States flans are usually sweet preparations, but in France they can be either sweet or savoury. In parts of France and Spanish-speaking countries, a flan may be a set cream, in particular *crème caramel*.

FLANK. The side below the ribs of a beef carcass. The best part is sold under the name of thick flank, that from the hindquarter as thin flank. Thick flank can be salted and pickled, then boiled or stewed, and used in pies. Thin flank of the best quality can be roasted but is best braised or stewed.

FLATBRØD. This wafer-thin Norwegian crispbread is made from rye, barley and wheat flour. It accompanies cheese, soup or salad and is still sometimes baked at home in country districts. The name means 'flat bread'.

FLATFISH. A name given to several saltwater fish, including the halibut, plaice, turbot and sole. Flatfish differ from other fish in having both eyes on the same side of the head. The two sides are generally referred to as the 'eyed' side and the 'blind' side. See under respective entries.

FLAVOURING. In the strict sense of the word, a flavouring agent is an extract or essence that is added to food to give additional or improved flavour. It differs from seasoning in that seasoning does not impart its own flavour but merely heightens or tempers the food to which it has been added.

FLEUR,CH.LA. See BORDEAUX WINES.

FLEURIE. See BURGUNDY WINES.

FLEURON. A French term to designate a small flaky pastry motif used to decorate certain dishes and the top of pâtés in a pastry crust.

FLIP. The name originally given to long, hot, sweet beverages containing alcohol and eggs. The alcohol ranged from beer through rum, wine and brandy or any combination of these, and the mixture was heated by placing a red hot poker in the bowl or glass. Today a flip is generally served cold and is prepared in a cocktail shaker or electric blender to ensure proper mixing.

FLIP GLASS. A glass especially designed for serving flips (which see). It is a stemmed tumbler of 5 oz. capacity, the mouth being slightly wider than the base. The glass is thicker than an ordinary wine glass so that heat or cold may be retained.

FLITCH. A side of bacon. Pigs intended for bacon are split down the back after they have been slaughtered, the chine bone removed and the ham or legs. The forelegs and shoulders are also usually taken off, although if the pig is small they are left on. See DUNMOW FLITCH.

FLOATING ISLAND. A light French pudding (*Ile Flottante*) made with steamed meringue and egg custard sauce.

FLOR. See WINE TERMS.

FLORENTINE. A method of cooking, used mainly for fish and eggs, which always includes spinach. The fish or eggs are set on a bed of cooked spinach covered with a Mornay sauce (see SAUCES), sprinkled with grated cheese and baked in the oven.

FLORENTINES. These are wafer-thin biscuits containing nuts and dried fruits, including glacé cherries, and coated with chocolate.

FLOUNDER. A small fish of the Pleuronectidae family of flatfish; also the name commonly applied to plaice in the United States. This delicate table fish seldom exceeds 2 lb. in weight or 12 in. length. In European waters the best months for flounder are from February to September. It is prepared by a variety of methods, one of the best ways being to grill the fish whole, basting frequently with butter and lemon juice mixed.

FLOUR. Any fine white powder which has been ground from grain or cereals such as rye and wheat; i.e. cornflour (cornstarch), rice flour or wheat flour. Wheat flour is the most usually used for culinary purposes and is one of the staple foods in most temperate climates. There are several grades of wheat flour, from fine white to coarse wholemeal.

Flour also varies according to the type of wheat grown. Hard wheat, as grown in Canada, produces strong flour. Soft wheat, grown in Australia and Britain, produces weak flour.

Cake flour is made from soft flour, from winter wheat. Wholemeal flour contains all the germ and much of the husk. White flour contains very little germ or husk, but it keeps longer than wholemeal. Graham flour is similar to wholemeal flour and ground from wholewheat grain.

FLOUR SIFTER

FLATFISH

FLOUR SIFTER. A sieve which has been especially devised for sifting flour and which can hardly be used for anything else. The American sifter is in the shape of a large cup with a mechanism at the bottom worked with a handle which forces the flour through the mesh. The British sifter is simpler, usually round and made of wood or metal with a particularly fine mesh at the bottom through which the flour is shaken.

FLOWERS IN COOKING. Cooking with flowers flourished during the time of Buddha, of Christ and of Mohammed. The Romans enjoyed flowers in their dishes and so did the Aztecs.

In many countries today flowers still play an important part in the kitchen. Rose petals and whole violets are candied at home and commercially. In Turkey and other parts of the Balkans rose petal jam made from the old-fashioned cabbage rose is a favourite preserve. Rose petals and acacia flowers are made into exquisite fritters, and rose brandy is a well-known flavouring for cakes and puddings. Germany has a rose petal wine cup. Primroses are used in salads and to flavour apple pies. Mignonette, lime and grape vine flowers are also used in wine cups. Chrysanthemums are an ingredient in Japanese and Chinese cooking. The petals of marigolds are dried to be used as a flavouring for soups and stews, puddings and custards. Country women pickle nasturtium seeds and use them as capers. The nasturtium flowers are used as a garnish for soups or salads and the large green leaves can be rolled and used as *dolmas*. Ground chicken breast with crushed violets is recommended as a sandwich filling and, for sheer exoticism there is little which can beat caviar and orchids spread between thinly sliced brown bread.

FLUMMERY, FLUMERY OR FLOMERY. An old-fashioned sweet which is a sort of jelly blancmange although over the centuries it has appeared in several guises.

FLUTE. As a culinary expression to flute means to cut fruit, vegetables and other foods in a decorative manner; or to press pastry dough round the rim of the pie or tart before baking. Flute is also a name for the 'yard of bread' or the long thin crusty French loaf, as well as the name of the long tapering champagne glass.

FOIE GRAS. The liver of artificially fattened geese, a speciality of Alsace Lorraine and Toulouse. There are also chicken and duck *foie gras*. Many rate the last-named as the finest. See PÂTÉ DE FOIE GRAS.

FOLD. To combine two mixtures, one light and containing air, such as creamed butter, sugar and eggs, or stiffly beaten egg whites, and the other heavier. The blending should be done with a downward motion and a careful turning over and over of the mixture to prevent air escaping, the bowl of the spoon just scraping the bottom of the mixing bowl each time.

FONDANT. Candies of French origin, made of sugar and water, plus an acid substance such as lemon juice and a flavouring. Fondant mixtures can also be used for coating fruits, nuts and other confections.

FONDUE. The best-known Swiss dish, which has many variations; each fondue cook claims his slight variation to be the secret of the perfect fondue. Some swear by a touch of finely chopped shallot, others insist that a little Sbrinz cheese must be added, others a couple of spoonfuls of cream. Some drink white wine with fondue, others only kirsch. Most fondues have alcohol as a main ingredient. The Fribourg fondue is prepared with wine and no kirsch is added. The usual mixture of cheese is half and half of two kinds, generally Gruyère and Emmenthal. On the other hand, a favourite mixture is half Emmenthal and half Greyerz cheese. Probably the best known of the fondue recipes is from Neuchâtel.

To make a fondue it is necessary to have a round earthenware dish with a flat bottom, so that it will stand firmly on top of a small spirit stove which is put on the table. The fondue is first cooked in the kitchen in the dish, which is then brought to the table, preferably a small, round one. Each person at the table is equipped with a long-handled fork and a plate of bread cubes. The idea is that each person spears a cube of bread and dips this into the fondue. Care must be taken not to lose the bread in the fondue, or a forfeit will be exacted. It could be a bottle of wine for the others at table or, if a pretty girl, a kiss for all the men. It is considered bad manners to spill the fondue on the cloth, and the best way of dealing with it is to swirl the fondue quickly round the bread on the fork. This catches the drips and also helps it cool off.

1¼ lb. mixed and grated Emmental and Greyerz (or Gruyère) cheese
1 cut clove of garlic
4 small wine glasses dry white wine
1 clove of garlic, finely chopped
nutmeg and pepper
1 heaped tablespoon (1¼) potato flour
1 tablespoon (1¼) kirsch

Rub the inside of the earthenware dish with the cut clove of garlic. Add the wine and warm it over a low heat, then stir in the grated cheese and continue stirring until the cheese is blended with the wine. Add the chopped garlic and freshly grated nutmeg to taste, and sprinkle with freshly milled pepper. Mix the potato flour into the kirsch and stir it into the cheese mixture. In about 3 minutes it will have thickened and can be brought to the table to be kept hot on the spirit stove. The fondue must be eaten at once, while still hot. Serve with kirsch or white wine.

FONDUE BOURGUIGNONNE. This is one of those dishes which the Swiss have so successfully adopted that many think it is indigenous. However, it is of French origin and its appearance in Switzerland is recent.

It is a meal best served for four people who can sit comfortably round a table, in the centre of which is a copper or iron pot, filled with hot oil, sitting firmly on a spirit stove. In front of each person at table is a small plate of steak cubes (only tender meat can be used in this manner) and a two-tined, long handled fork, Round the stove in easy reach of all are small bowls containing sauces, such as sauce Albert (which see), tomato flavoured with soy, often a curry sauce, a Béarnaise, etc. To eat, impale a cube of steak on a fork and plunge it into the boiling oil. Leave it there until the meat is cooked, a minute or so. Dip it at once into one of the sauces, and pop into your mouth (remember that the steak is hotter than you think). It is traditional to try all of the sauces in turn. Continue in this manner until all of the steak cubes are finished. See page 293.

FONDUE DU RAISIN. From the province of Savoy, a mild French cheese which is covered with grape pips.

FONDUTA. One of the famous dishes of Piedmont. To be successful it must be made with genuine Fontina cheese.

1 lb. Fontina cheese
milk
6 egg yolks, well beaten
2 oz. (4 tablespoons) butter
1 white truffle, thinly sliced
freshly milled white pepper

Cut the rind off the cheese and cut the cheese into small dice. Put it into a bowl, cover it with milk and leave overnight.

Put the cheese and milk into the top of a double boiler and cook over hot, not boiling, water. Add the egg yolks and the butter. Cook over a low heat stirring constantly but gently with a wooden spoon. As soon as the cheese and eggs have amalgamated and the consistency is smooth and creamy, pour it into heated plates and sprinkle with truffle and pepper. The combination of the cheese and truffle is perfect. Enough for 4 people.

FONRÉAUD. See BORDEAUX WINES.

FONTAINEBLEAU. A very light French triple-crème cheese available throughout the year. It is often served with sugar and cream or whipped with fresh raspberries or strawberries.

FONTINA D'AOSTA. One of Italy's great cheeses. The true and original Fontina comes from a rigidly defined zone, the Valley of Aosta, in the mountains of northern Italy near the Swiss border.

In appearance this cheese resembles Swiss Gruyère in that it has a light brown crust and comes in wheels 12–15 in. in diameter and three to four in. thick, The colour of the cheese is ivory, the texture fairly firm, broken here and there with tiny holes. For many, Fontina is a cheese-maker's dream come true. It combines the nutty sweetness of Emmental with the tang of Gruyére, plus a suggestion of Port-Salut. At room temperature it never liquifies but neither does it remain quite solid, being creamy.

Fontina d'Aosta has many imitators, known by names such as Fontal, Fontinella and Fantina which may be marketed in the United States as Fontina. The name is not protected there by law as it is in Italy.

FOOCHOW OOLONG. See TEA.

FOOD. The simplest definition of food is that which is taken into the body to maintain life.

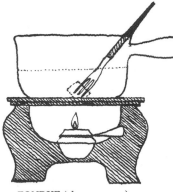

FONDUE (cheese server)

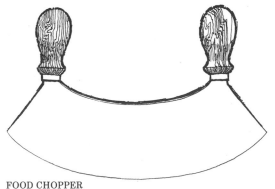

FOOD CHOPPER

Food can be divided into three main categories each making its own contribution to keeping the body healthy. They are carbohydrates, fats and proteins. In addition there is a group of inorganic minerals and a group of organic substances known as vitamins.

Collectively these foods build new tissues, maintain and repair worn out tissues, give energy for heat activity and growth and regulate body processes.

Carbohydrates and fats provide energy and include starchy foods, sugar and various fats. Proteins are building foods and include meats of all sorts, fish and cereals. Minerals and vitamins regulate body processes and these can be found abundantly in fruits and vegetables.

Since all these foods perform specific functions it is necessary that they all be included in a daily diet. Menus should be well balanced and contain appropriate quantities of each in the interests of good health.

Man has for long sought to discover the relationship between good health and food. It is said that the ancient Egyptians in the first century B.C. came to the conclusion that excessive eating was the cause of many diseases. Hippocrates during 460–359 B.C. said: 'Persons who are very fat are apt to die earlier than those who are slender.' Modern research into food, health and general wellbeing received its first impetus in the 19th century when Magendie, a French scientist, discovered when experimenting on dogs that proteins were essential to life. At about the same time a German scientist, Liebig, found that fats and carbohydrates were fuel foods. Since then research has made great strides and several vitamins and amino acids have been identified and their links with body needs established. Today a great deal is known about the needs of the body and the sorts of food that will fulfil them.

The aesthetic side of food should not be neglected. Well prepared and attractively served meals stimulate the appetite and aid digestion.

FOOD CHOPPER. A double-handled semi-circular or crescent-shaped knife used to chop or dice vegetables, fruit, herbs etc. It is made so that the handles are well above the blade of the chopper so that pressure can be exerted downward and the knife used with a rocking movement for greater efficiency. It can be used on the usual chopping board, also in a wooden bowl into which it fits.

FOOD MILL. A food mill is a device that forces vegetables and fruits through perforations, causing them to be puréed or riced. One typical design has a set of blades, operated by a crank, that presses the food against perforated metal shields.

FOOD PRESERVATION AND STORAGE. The quest for food has been an essential feature of man's struggle for survival from the beginning of human history.

Very early man probably spent most of his time in search of food for his daily needs, not knowing how to provide even for the next day. Gradually he discovered agriculture and found that he could store his cereals until the next harvest. He learned how to domesticate animals, stocking some of them for meat and others for milk which he found could be converted into cheese and stored for a reasonable period. The primitive hunter learned how to salt, dry and smoke his meat and fish as a means of food preservation and storage. Much later the use of spices for food preservation spread to the West after the European voyages of discovery.

For centuries little progress was made in developing food preservation techniques. The first break-through came with microbiology and the discovery of micro-organisms which explained why food spoils. Much of the pioneer work was done by Pasteur. These micro-organisms attack animal and plant life much as germs attack human life and, like humans, living animals and plants have a degree of natural resistance to these attacks. Once dead, however, the microbes take over and decay sets in. By studying the properties of these microbes modern microbiologists have evolved methods to neutralize or considerably retard or suspend the process of decay. Much of modern food preservation is based on these principles.

The relevant point is the behaviour of these micro-organisms in varying conditions of temperature, humidity and air. It is known for instance that most of the dangerous ones die in temperatures of over 176° F or 80° C, particularly if water is present. Food cooked at this or a higher temperature can be kept for a reasonable period but it would have to be re-heated to deal with any possible re-infection which may have occurred during storage.

All micro-organisms die in temperatures of over 284° F or 140° C and food exposed to this degree of heat becomes entirely sterile. Not all foods can be cooked at such heat. Re-infection must also be guarded against. Food may also be made sterile by irradiation but this is not permitted by law in most countries because of health risks. In Britain a Government Advisory Committee considers certain exemptions which are granted only in cases where hospital patients must have a sterile diet.

Pasteurization is the process by which milk and other liquids are heated to a certain temperature which is maintained for a specified time. This kills off most of the microbes and milk does not spoil easily after being so treated.

Canned foods appear on many a table and are gaining in popularity because of the convenience with which they can be used. Most of the organisms in question belong to the aerobe group which can only grow in the presence of air. Sterilized or pasteurized foods placed in airtight containers will keep because the absence of air will stop the micro-organisms from growing.

Probably refrigeration and deep freezing are the most important forms of modern food preservation and storage. The micro-organisms in their spore form can stand very low temperatures, but their growth is checked by the cold which renders them harmless. The modern refrigerator, therefore, enables the housewife to store quantities of cooked and raw foods and dairy produce for reasonable periods of time.

The same principle applies to deep freezing for commercial purposes. Ships that transport meat and other products over long distances are equipped with storage space maintained at very low temperatures which keeps the food from spoiling. Wholesale and retail establishments have similar storage facilities.

The time-honoured methods of preserving by pickling, salting, smoking and dehydrating are still employed although new techniques of dehydrating have been much used recently.

Certain chemicals may also be used as preserving agents but since they can also be harmful to humans their application is strictly limited.

FOOL. An old English sweet dish of puréed fruit, usually gooseberries or rhubarb. The name may have originated from the French *foule*, meaning pulped, but the term fool as used in cooking might equally have been suggested by the synonym 'trifle', a kind of clotted cream. Although gooseberries and rhubarb are the two fruits generally associated with fools, any fruit which can be stewed and puréed can be cooked in the same manner.

FORBIDDEN FRUIT. The proprietary name of an American liqueur made from grapefruit brandy.

FORCEMEAT. Stuffing, of which there are several types, used for chicken, hare, veal, hearts, fish etc.

FORESTIÈRE. The culinary name of a garnish for small cuts of meat or poultry consisting of wild mushrooms (morels), diced lean bacon and diced potatoes fried in butter.

FORK. This is the youngest member of the knife, fork and spoon trio, simply because the fork was not so essential to eating. The fork emerged from the kitchen, where it started its career, when present concepts of good table manners began to develop.

Like other implements, many varied and specialized forks have been developed. Table forks are usually flat with three or four tines. There are special forks for fish, for oysters or prawns, for salads, for puddings and meat. Kitchen forks are larger, built to stand heavy wear. For table forks, silver is still probably the preferred metal but steel is a good second favourite.

FORMOSA TEAS. See TEA.

FORTIA. See RHÔNE WINES.

FOUDRE. Large casks of varying sizes used to mature and store wine in the cellars or for transport of cheaper wine. See also FUDER, STÜCK.

FOURCAS DUPRÉ, CH. See BORDEAUX WINES.

FOURCHAUME. See BURGUNDY WINES.

FOURME DE CANTAL. Recorded in Roman times, cantal is one of the most Cheddar-like of French cheeses. It is made from cows' milk from the upland pastures of Cantal, in south central France, and hard-pressed in cylindrical moulds (*fourmes*).

FOURME DE SALERS. A hard, cows' milk cheese which is somewhat like Cheddar and historically one of the oldest of the French cheeses.

FRUIT FORK   SALAD FORK   PRAWN FORK

FOWL. In present-day usage, an edible bird, more particularly applied to a chicken which is suitable only for boiling or steaming.

FRANCONIA. An important German wine district centred in Würzburg. The wine is heady and usually sold in *Bocksbeutels* or flagons and is called *Frankenwein* or *Sternwein*.

FRANGIPANE. This name applies both to a type of French *choux* pastry or *panade à la frangipane* used as an ingredient in a stuffing, and also a rich cream. Originally the name applied to a perfume which came from the flower of the red jasmine. Then a sweet dish of almond cream flavoured with this perfume became the fashion. Cheap substitutes have gradually taken its place and it is now a thick cream of the *crème pâtisserie* variety, sprinkled with crushed macaroons. It is also used as a cream topping for tarts and a filling for cakes. There are also commercially prepared small tarts boasting the name frangipane tarts. The cream is said to be the invention of an Italian (some say a chef, others a nobleman) named Frangipani who was in Paris during the time of Louis XIII.

FRANKFURTER. See SAUSAGE.

FRAPPÉ. The French word for iced. *Frappés* are made from sweetened fruit juices frozen to a mushy consistency, and belong to the water- and fruit-ice category. They are not as rich as ice-cream and are usually served in a parfait or sherbert glass – often topped with whipped cream.

A *frappé* also means an iced drink. Various liqueurs, for example crème de menthe, are served over shaved ice in a cocktail glass. The resulting concoction is sipped through a straw as the ice melts.

FREEZING. A development of the last decade although it has been known for centuries that cold delays the decay of food. In the home, freezing means deep freezing or a slow drop of temperature which hardens or solidifies foods.

FRENCH COOKING. 'France is the gastronomic paradise of the universe', wrote Curnonsky, Prince of Gastronomes (who see).

French cooking has long been recognized as the finest in the world and more words have been written on French than any other form of cooking. It is the touch of genius in French cooking which has conquered the world. In almost every capital French cooking is offered in the best restaurants, at formal dinners and at grand receptions.

With good cooking comes the willingness to give time and talent to every detail of a dish and menu, and this the French do, famous chef and ordinary housewife alike.

There is no waste in French cooking and its variety is immense. Eggs, butter and cream with the discreet use of wine may sound extravagant but when a French cook tackles even a lesser piece of fish or meat with these ingredients, it results in a culinary masterpiece.

The great cities of France and its great chefs have given us the elegant cuisine, but it is the smaller towns and villages which have shown us *gastronomie sans argent*.

In a dictionary it is impossible to go into detail of French cooking, or even to attempt to mention more than a few classical dishes. Curnonsky tells us that he once drew up a complete list of the dishes and wines of France. It contained 380 pages – and these for titles only, not one single recipe.

FRENCH BREAD. See BREAD.

FRENCH DRESSING. See VINAIGRETTE.

FRENCH FRY. A term applied in the United States to foods cooked in hot fat deep enough to float them.

FRENCH TOAST. This is bread, sliced, dipped into milk and beaten eggs and fried. It is also called Bombay toast, German toast, Nun's toast, Spanish and Portuguese toast. It should be brown and crisp on the outside and soft inside. See POOR KNIGHTS OF WINDSOR.

FRIANDISES. The French name for a variety of small cakes or confections which include glazed fruits, petits fours etc.

FRICANDEAU. A larded cushion of veal braised whole and glazed with its own gravy. It is garnished with quenelles, sweetbreads, mushrooms and truffles. This recipe is reputedly the invention of Jean de Carême, an ancestor of the famous Carême (who see). The name is also applied to fillets or slices of fish, mainly of sturgeon, tunny or tuna fish, which are braised in fish stock.

FRICANDELLES or **FRICADELLES.** These are fried meat balls or cakes, made either with chopped beef or chopped veal.

FRICASSÉE. A kind of ragoût usually made from white meat or poultry. The meat is browned lightly and then treated as in a white stew.

FRIED BREAD. See CROÛTE.

FRITTER. The English equivalent of the French *beignet.* There have been fritters since the days of Pliny, when chick pea fritters were popular at Roman dinners. All fritters are made with a batter and are deep fried, but the batter may be prepared in so many different ways that the variety of fritters is beyond count. A really well-made and perfectly fried fritter should be light, golden brown and crisp outside, and full of rich creamy goodness inside. They can be an accompaniment to a meal, a meal in themselves, or served as a climax to a meal, sugar-sprinkled or with a sauce. They are made with fruit, vegetables or cheese, or they can be simply a light and frothy sweetened batter.

FRITTO MISTO. This has been described as the equivalent to the English mixed grill, while the literal translation is mixed fry. Neither description does justice to one of Italy's most famous dishes which is strictly indigenous and varies slightly from province to province. A *fritto misto* is a combination of meat, fish, poultry, game and vegetables. It includes small pieces, often mere mouthfuls, of tender veal, calf's liver, tiny chokeless artichokes, chopped brains, sweetbreads, flowerets of cauliflower, broccoli, cubes of courgettes (zucchini), aubergine (eggplant), mushrooms, olives etc. These ingredients are usually breaded, fried in deep fat and served hot, golden brown and crisp.

FROG. These unattractive looking amphibians have a long gastronomic history. The Romans, not usually lacking in the spirit of culinary adventure, seem to have ignored the possibility of frogs providing edible titbits, and it was not until the 16th century that they were on the table of the elegant French, although from time to time between the 11th and 16th centuries they received some attention, sometimes favourable, at other times distinctly sour. However, in the 16th century an enterprising Frenchman from Auvergnat amassed a fortune supplying frogs to the Parisians. Nowadays frogs are consumed in considerable quantities in many countries.

It is only the aquatic or pond frogs which are edible and only the hind legs are eaten.

Frogs' legs are usually sold in Europe prepared for cooking, although in the markets of the Far East the frogs are exposed for sale alive and firmly kicking in large buckets. The smaller legs are the most tender, and their flesh is white and delicate, with a flavour akin to that of young chicken. The flesh is digestible and each leg is little more than a titbit to be eaten with the fingers. In France frogs' legs are usually sold by the dozen and about 4 pairs make one portion.

FROMAGE BLANC. The simplest of all French cheeses, being simply thick curd drained of its whey. When it is eaten with salt and pepper, it remains *fromage blanc.* When it is served with sugar and cream, it is *fromage à la crème,* and when the curds are set to drain in a small heart-shaped wicker or metal container, and it is turned out on to a plate and served with cream and sugar, it becomes the classic French country dish *coeur à la crème* (which see).

FROMAGE DE BANON. See BANON.

FRONSAC, CÔTE DE. See BORDEAUX WINES.

FROSTED. A term applied to an ice- or frost-covered glass used to serve drinks. The frosting is accomplished by chilling a glass to the point where atmospheric moisture condenses on the surface as ice crystals, thereby suggesting coldness.

FROTHING. A very old practice of dredging meats or poultry with flour and salt just before taking them from the oven and applying a fierce heat to the bird or roast so that it appears encased in a crisp froth.

FROZEN FOOD. This is a general term to describe the wide range of foods which are frozen, commercially packaged and retailed to the public. The list of such foods has grown since the first garden peas were frozen and offered to an interested but sceptical market. Today not only are single items thus sold, but also complete meals.

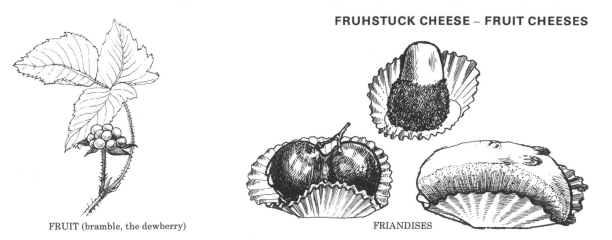

FRUIT (bramble, the dewberry)   FRIANDISES

The first experiments in freezing food were carried out by Lord Bacon, who tried freezing foods in snow. His experiments came to a sad end, however, when he caught cold and died.

Whether frozen foods taste like fresh food is a matter of opinion. They are time-savers and just as there is a case for using fresh foods, so there is, in this age where time is money, for frozen foods. There is no shelling of peas, nor washing of spinach, no trimming of meat or choosing of the fish for its bright eye and the chicken by its plump breast. There are no seasons either in the world of frozen foods.

FRUHSTUCK CHEESE. A small, round American cheese of the Limburger type (which see). The name is often anglicized as breakfast cheese.

FRUIT. Gastronomes accord a much more restricted meaning to the term fruit than do the botanists. Peas and beans are fruits to the botanists but vegetables to the gastronomes.

Fruits gastronomically speaking are the fleshy succulent seed-containers of fruit-bearing trees, shrubs, bushes, canes etc. They are divided botanically into the following categories:

POMES. The pip fruits. They are few in number but of great importance since they include the apple and the pear.

DRUPES. Stone fruits, bearing only one seed per fruit, encased within a hard stone. These include the apricot, almond, cherry, nectarine, peach and plum.

BRAMBLES. The fruit of the *Rubus* of which there are over 3,000 varieties. Most of us call them simply berries and their prototype is the blackberry.

CURRANTS and GOOSEBERRIES. The fruits of the *Ribes* genus all of which the French include in the single word *groseille*. Included among these are black, red and white currants as well as the gooseberry and similar berries.

HEATH FRUITS. These are a branch of the Ericaceae family and are also known as berries and include the cranberry, huckleberry, blueberry etc.

CITRUS FRUITS. These are the pulpy juicy fruits with a thick rind which is an outer cover and protection.

NUTS. One-seeded fruits with a fibrous or woody shell protecting the kernel or edible seed within. Among these are included the hazel-nut, chestnut, filbert, pecan, etc.

FREAK FRUITS. These are not regarded as fruits at all by the botanists although most other people do. They include the strawberry and the pineapple, and it may be a shock for many of us to be told that the fragrant strawberry is not a fruit but merely an enlarged receptacle terminating the flower stalk of the plant, the true fruits of which are the dry achenes borne on this enlarged receptacle.

Some fruits, such as the date and banana, afford sufficient nourishment to sustain life for a long time. Others, like the apple, recommended by some for keeping the doctor away, are now said to be merely wholesome. Some fruits are eaten simply for their fine flavour and to vary diet.

It is generally agreed that fruit as a common item of diet is beneficial and the vast improvement in transport as well as cultivation has made some varieties of fruit available over a wide area throughout the year.

FRUITARIAN. See VEGETARIAN.

FRUIT BUTTERS. These are made by cooking fruit to a pulp the consistency of a thick paste, suitable for spreading. Less sugar is used in fruit butters than in jam.

The fruits most commonly used for fruit butters are: tart apples, apricots, grapes, plums and quinces; or such combinations as apple and grape juice, apple and plums, or apple with quinces.

FRUIT CHEESES. Our grandmothers and their mothers before them would make fruit cheeses to help them out with their puddings throughout the winter. The jars in which the cheeses were stored were usually wide-mouthed and often brushed with a sweet oil before the cheeses were poured into them. Thus they turned out easily, to be served whole, as a spread, or as a filling for pies.

A fruit cheese is simply fruit cooked until very soft and thick with as little water as possible and as slowly as possible. Quinces, medlars, blackcurrants, apples and gooseberries can all be made into fruit cheeses.

FRUIT COCKTAILS. These are used as appetizers, and therefore they should be served in small quantities and not too sweet. The fruit can be fresh, canned or bottled, but such cocktails must be well chilled. Serve in stem cocktail glasses.

FRUIT KERNEL. The soft, usually edible part within the hard shell of the stone or nut of the fruit. The kernels of some fruits, for example apricots, are used as a basis for some liqueurs.

FRUIT KNIFE. For kitchen use these are small knives equipped with serrated edges.

Fruit knives for the dining table are supplied with matching forks and are smaller than the meat knife or even the fish knife. They are generally not part of the matching cutlery set but often rather ornate with carved ivory handles. Fruit knives and forks are somewhat out of fashion, together with finger bowls.

FRUIT PECTIN. See PECTIN.

FRUIT PIE. This term means different things to different people. The basic ingredients are the same, fruit and pastry, but the method of making varies. There are fruit pies with a lot of fruit made in a pie dish with a layer of pastry on top. Such pies are also known as 'deep-dish pies' or 'single crust pies'. Or there are pies in shallow pans or pie plates with pastry both top and bottom and fruit in between. This is known as a 'double crust pie' or tart. Then there is the open fruit tart cooked in a pastry shell, also called a flan.

FRUIT STORING. To keep fruit fresh for short periods it can be stored in a cool, preferably dark place, lying in single layers. It must be inspected at frequent intervals to see that none is deteriorating, because fruit infections spread rapidly.

For longer storing, fruit should either be bottled or deep-frozen. Apples and pears will keep for several months if wrapped in tissue paper and kept in a dark, cool but moist place with a temperature of 35°–40° F.

FRUIT SYRUPS. These are a practical addition to any store cupboard. Children like them diluted or they can be used in making fruit jellies, as well as for sauces poured over ice-creams or puddings.

Fruit which is too ripe for other forms of preserves is exactly right for syrups – but it must be fresh. Poor or decayed fruit will produce syrups of poor flavour.

The best fruit for making syrups are the berries – strawberries, raspberries, loganberries etc. – and the currants, red, black and white.

FRUMENTY. An old English country sweet not unlike porridge, but enriched with egg yolks, cream, honey and spices. In earlier times it was a popular everyday food and, in its richest form, was referred to as the Lord Mayor's Dish; today it is rarely encountered, and mainly eaten for its high content of vitamins A and B.

FRUTTA IN MOSTARDA. A speciality of Cremona (Italy) which is seldom, if ever, made at home. It consists of ripe mixed fruits, such as cherries, apricots, pears, almonds, figs, pumpkin and plums, cooked in a sugar syrup and heavily flavoured with French mustard. It is very good and served usually with cold meats.

FRY. See WHITEBAIT.

FRY, TO. This means to cook in hot fat. There are two ways of frying, deep frying and shallow frying. Shallow fat frying requires a wide shallow pan (skillet), and deep fat frying a deep fat bath or very strong saucepan with a wire frying basket. Shallow fat frying includes dry-frying when the only fat used in the pan is that which runs from the food, for example, from bacon or sausages, when only a slight greasing is required as when making omelettes or pancakes, or when using fat to come half-way up the sides of the food being fried. Frying is often done as a preliminary to a moist method of cooking, such as stewing or braising, especially in Italian cooking.

Deep frying requires a lot of fat or oil, but this can be used again and again if correctly strained and stored. After being used it should be gently warmed until all the bubbling has stopped which ensures that no water is left in it to hasten its decomposition. It should then be strained through a wire strainer fine enough to retain even the smallest crumbs of food, as these when cooked not only burn but also cause the fat to decompose.

FUDGE. A soft type of sweetmeat or candy, creamy and sweet. It is made with sugar, butter and milk and flavoured generally with chocolate, ginger or vanilla.

FUDER. Large casks used in the Moselle district in Germany for storage of wine at the vineyard or wine house. See STÜCK and page 118.

FUNGI

FUGU. The Japanese name of the globefish, blow-fish and balloon fish. In Japan only licensed vendors may sell this fish as, incorrectly treated, it can become a deadly poison. Its skin is sold to make globefish lamps.

FUMET. This is a strong concentration of essence of fish, meat or game. It is important to give body to both game and fish.

FISH FUMET

1 lb. bones and trimmings of any fish
1 carrot, chopped
1 small onion, chopped
4 tablespoons (5) chopped parsley
2 oz. (4 tablespoons) butter
1¼ cups (1¾) water
1 cup (1¼) wine
3 peppercorns, crushed
salt to taste

Heat the butter in a saucepan, add the fish bones and trimmings, the vegetables and parsley. Cover and cook gently for 10 minutes. Add the water, wine, peppercorns and salt and cook gently, still covered, for 30 minutes. Strain and use as required. For a game fumet, use game bones.

FUNGI. Under this name there is a wide variety of plants which are either parasites on living plants and animals or else feed on dead organic matter. They grow profusely in damp and shaded places, and are found on tree trunks, in caves and on decayed wood. There are about 2,000 species of fungi and some are edible.

The field mushroom, *Psalliota campestris*, is one of the best known edible fungi. The common mushroom, *Psalliota (Agaricus) hortensis*, is now widely cultivated in Europe and the United States. Many of the poisonous fungi are found among the *Amanita*, although Ceasar's Amanita *(Amanita caesarea)* is one of the finest edible fungi.

Before experimenting with unfamiliar species it is advisable to buy a well illustrated specialist book or, better still, to visit a museum which has pictures of fungi which can be used as a means of identification.

G

GAELIC COFFEE. Pour a generous tot of Irish whiskey into a tall glass, put a silver spoon in each glass to keep the glass from breaking, then add hot, strong black coffee almost to the top of the glass and sugar to taste. Take out the spoon and pour thick cream over the back of it into each glass to spread evenly over the top. The cream must not penetrate the coffee. Gaelic coffee is meant as a pick-me-up and is sometimes served as an after-dinner drink in Ireland.

GAFFELIÈRE, CH. LA. See BORDEAUX WINES.

GALANTINE. This was originally a cold preparation of boned, stuffed and pressed chicken served in its own jelly. Towards the end of the 17th century, however, other birds, also meat and fish began to figure in this dish. Now galantines are made from young turkey, guinea fowl, Nantes duckling, pigeon and game birds such as pheasant, partridge and grouse, in addition to the original chicken. Veal and fish are also prepared in this way.

The term galantine by itself implies galantine of poultry; if other meats or fish are used this must be indicated, i.e. galantine of fish.

GALICIA. See SPANISH WINES.

GALLIMAUFRY. The origin of this word seems to be unknown. According to one authority, it is an old English name for a hotch-potch or hodge-podge; in other words a dish made up of odds and ends from the larder. Another source explains that it was originally a magnificent dish created by Taillevent, master chef of King Charles VII of France.

GALLON. The standard wine measure which, until 1826, was the same in both Britain and America, i.e. 231 cubic in. for wine and 282 cubic in. for ale. The imperial gallon was introduced to Britain in 1826 and equals 277.3 cubic in. Its weight equals 10 lb. of distilled water. In America, the gallon used is the old English gallon of 231 cubic in. or 128 oz.

GALLWEYS IRISH COFFEE LIQUEUR. A smooth, dark brown Irish liqueur with a whiskey basis, flavoured with coffee and herbs and sweetened with honey.

GAMAY GRAPE. See BURGUNDY WINES.

GAME. This designation covers wild animals and birds which are hunted for sport and are protected in many countries by game laws. This means that the time of year during which they may be hunted is strictly controlled and it is an offence to shoot during the closed season, i.e., the nesting season. It is, however, usual to include under the heading game such animals as rabbits, which are not protected by game laws.

The chief British game birds are pheasant, grouse, snipe, partridge, and wild duck, and the chief game animals are hare, deer (venison) and rabbit. The chief American game birds are quail, turkey, pheasant, duck, grouse, dove, snipe and woodcock. The chief game animals are deer, bear, wild boar, rabbit, squirrel and coon.

Game is a luxury, although not necessarily an expensive one, but it demands care when cooking. Its chief merit is its gamey aroma and for most game lovers it should be hung (see HANGING) for at least a week before being cooked. The main difficulty in cooking is to counteract the often extreme dryness of the flesh.

GAME CHIPS. These are small thin slices of potato fried in deep fat until a golden brown, sprinkled with salt and served with game.

GAME SHEARS. Extra strong shears or scissors designed to cut through bone and used to divide fowl and game, into halves or small portions.

GAMMON. Gammon of bacon, although almost precisely the same cut of bacon as ham, lacks the latter's delicacy of flavour owing to the method of curing. It can be used in the same ways as ham (which see).

GARBANZO PEA. See CHICK PEAS.

GARBURE. A word of Spanish origin which means roughly the same as ragoût; the soup of this name so popular in the Pyrenees could easily be classified as a ragoût. It would appear to be a Basque soup with a history of several centuries. There are many different imitations of it throughout France. It is said to originate from Béarn where it is considered 'the jewel of the gastronomic crown'. But even in Béarn itself *garbure* is variously prepared, according to the season. Essential ingredients are cabbage, beans, potatoes and pork or bacon.

GARLIC. A member of the lily family and probably a native of the Kirghiz region of Central Asia, but cultivated in the Mediterranean area since early Egyptian times. Today it is grown in warm climates all over the world. There are several varieties. Some have bulbs covered in a white skin, others have a pink or mauve skin. The bulbs vary tremendously in size, as do the number and size of the cloves in a garlic bulb. The best garlic is grown in warmer climes.

Garlic as a flavouring excites much controversy. Socially it is not altogether acceptable in many countries, especially in northern Europe, although British attitudes are said to be changing. To tell non-garlic eaters that Roman soldiers ate garlic as a stimulant before going into battle is merely to bring a reply that doubtless it was the combined odour of garlic that won the Romans their empire. It was also said at one time that 'mariners would almost as lief go to sea without a compass as without a plentiful supply of garlic'.

The ancients regarded it as more than a spice. Pliny and Herodotus speak of it as an energy food and claim that the slaves who built the pyramids for the Egyptian Pharoahs subsisted mainly on a diet of garlic and onions. Aristophanes speaks of athletes eating garlic for physical fitness while the prophet, Mohammed, extolled its virtues as an antidote against poisonous stings and bites. In certain parts of India, however, garlic is associated with the devil and some orthodox Hindus are chary of it; but this aversion is by no means general and garlic is grown and eaten in India.

GARLIC SALT. This is simply garlic-flavoured salt which is prepared commercially but can be made quite easily at home, by rubbing a cut clove of garlic over coarse white table salt. Garlic salt may be substituted for ordinary salt to enliven the flavour of almost any savoury dish.

GARNACHA BLANCA GRAPE. See SPANISH WINES.

GARNISH. A garnish is the technical name for any addition made to a dish which not only improves its appearance but also its flavour. In the days of French *haute cuisine* the garnish was often more important than the dish. Each garnish has its name. A dish labelled *ambassadeur* means garnished with artichoke bottoms filled with a

MARKET SCENE: a Muslim market

GARLIC (bulb and clove)

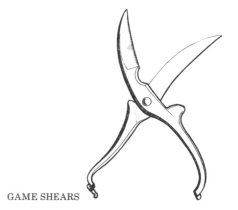

GAME SHEARS

mushroom purée, grated horse-radish and *duchesse* potatoes. *Forestière* means morels, lean bacon and *pommes noisettes*.

GASTRONOMY. The respect given to the art of preparing and serving food has been a measure of civilization throughout recorded history.

The Greeks held the cook in the highest esteem and gave him honour. He was also highly paid. The Romans were well known for their sumptuous banquets at which quantities of food were served to the accompaniment of visual entertainment.

Then followed the Dark Ages and European man returned to eating comparatively primitive food again, the purpose of eating being simply to keep body and soul together. The only literate and educated people were the monks in their monasteries and as they preserved the knowledge and philosophy of more enlightened times so they preserved the skills of the vineyard and the kitchen. When light returned to Europe and a new civilization began, the art of good eating emerged from the monasteries.

Food changes in character over the years. Some foods go out of favour, new dishes are invented, others modified. There are also periods when there is a creative outburst of activity and the culinary art flowers, along with other arts. The 19th century was such a period in France, and produced Brillat-Savarin, one of the greatest culinary artists in history.

The art of good eating, however, varies little because there are a few basic principles which seem always to guide the true gourmet. Much too often good eating and the word gourmet are woefully misunderstood. A gourmet is a connoisseur of good food and good wine more concerned with quality than quantity. He is a civilized person with a cultivated and educated palate capable of savouring and appreciating the food and wine given to him. As a music lover can discern the various instruments which constitute an orchestra, so a gourmet can discern the various flavours that combine in making a dish. Similarly he has the ability to savour the full flavour of the wine. The composition of a meal is also of importance to him. A test of a gourmet is what dishes he selects to compose a particular meal and the wines he chooses to go with them. He also insists on a well and attractively laid table. These powers of discernment and appreciation imply a delicacy of taste and moderation. It does not follow that a gourmet eats elaborate meals all the time (quite the contrary) but it does follow that a gourmet is a man of taste and judgment when it comes to food and drink.

The word gourmand is erroneously associated with gluttony. The French have no objection to it because it has no such overtones for them. A glutton is the very opposite of a gourmet. He is more concerned with quantity than quality though he may pretend otherwise. He eats and drinks far too much to savour good food and wine, and he is apt to be coarse in other ways as well. In fact, he is uncivilized in his approach to food.

GÂTEAU. French for cake. The word is usually applied in Britain to a cake made with a butter sponge and lavishly decorated with icing, cream, nuts, butter cream or jam.

GATTINARA. See ITALIAN WINES.

GAZPACHO. A speciality of Spanish cooking, particularly in Andalusia. Called both a soup and a salad, it is made with fresh cucumber, tomatoes, sweet peppers, bread and water, iced and served with diced hard-boiled egg whites, thinly sliced lemon, croûtons and ice cubes in each plate.

GEECHE LIME. A chutney-like relish originating in Savannah, Georgia, and made from a formula developed in Colonial times. It is prepared from a sour, olive-like fruit peculiar to the area of the Ogeechee river in southeast Georgia.

GEFILTE FISH. A dish from Jewish cooking. Gefilte means stuffed. This dish may have originated in Holland or it may have come from Russia or Poland, where it was commonly referred to as 'Jewish fish'. In some Jewish communities the

193

MEAT PIE: a raised meat pie.

filleted portion is chopped and stuffed back between the skin and backbone. In American Jewish families the filleted fish is mashed to a pulp and made into balls. It is now considered a traditional Sabbath and holiday dish.

GELATINE. Gelatine is a transparent substance made by boiling beef bones, cartilage and tendons.

It is used as a protective colloid in scientific research, has its industrial applications and is used to make glue. Its pure form is used in cookery for making sweet puddings, prepared meat products and confectionery. It contains protein. A characteristic of gelatine solutions is their gel-forming property. They melt on warming and set on cooling.

The first attempt to manufacture gelatine on a commercial basis was made by a French scientist in 1681 but it came to nothing. After the French Revolution the government was faced with the urgent task of alleviating mass starvation and the French Academy of Medicine declared gelatine a nourishing food. It was then commercially produced, added to soups and broths and served to people in hospitals and public institutions.

Two types of gelatine are available. Plain and uncoloured for jellied soups, meat and fish, and in crystal fruit-flavoured form mixed with sugar for making puddings.

GENEVA. An English term for Dutch gin or schnapps. The name has nothing to do with Geneva in Switzerland, but is a derivative of *genièvre*, a juniper with which gin is flavoured.

GENIPAP or **GENIPOP.** This is a gooseberry-shaped fruit which grows in bunches with a greenish-white skin. Found in the West Indies and the northern part of Latin America, it is sub-acid with a pleasant juice which is purple in colour. It can be eaten raw, but is mainly prepared as a conserve and a type of marmalade.

GENOESE. At one time this was descriptive of a rich sauce served with fish, but now applies to a sponge cake mixture made from eggs, sugar and butter beaten together to make a batter of a particularly light and even consistency.

GENOVOISE SAUCE. See SAUCES.

GENTIAN. Gentian is a herbaceous plant found in the Swiss Alps, the Pyrenees, and the Andes and other parts of America. There are over 200 species.

Gentian flowers are also used to make aperitifs in alpine regions of Europe. Gentiane, a digestive liqueur, is particularly favoured in France and Switzerland.

GERMAN CHEESES. Tilsiter, made for more than a century, is Germany's best-known cheese. German cheeses are classified as hard, semi-hard, semi-soft, soft and fresh. Most of these are acknowledged copies of French and Dutch cheeses and bear the name of the original. See page 78.

GERMAN FOOD. Germany is a country embracing several Teutonic but different regions. It is obvious, therefore, that much of its cooking varies according to region. The Silesian has entirely different ideas of what is good to eat from the man from Hamburg. But by and large the Germans are hearty eaters, preferring good substantial meals. There are dumplings, thick warming soups, plenty of meat dishes, sausages, heavy dark breads, vegetables of all kinds and sauerkraut (which see).

But it is an interesting cuisine, with some culinary combinations which are surprising. It makes heavy demands on butter, eggs, mushrooms, and cream. The Germans are great cake-makers and -eaters. Wine is used in their cooking, as is beer. The Germans have given the world the word delicatessen, for which they are famous. Most German menus include fish, many varieties being smoked, some salted or pickled, and others cooked with interesting sauces. Fruit soups are much in favour as a beginning to the main course. See page 117.

GERMAN TOAST. Another name for French toast, which see.

GERMAN WINES. Germany's viticultural area is very small. The total of approximately 70,000 hectares is only about 0.7 per cent of the world's total wine-producing area. The average crop of a German vintage produces about 1.8 per cent of the world production of wine, the average yield per hectare varying from year to year: the average yield for 1950 to 1959 was 52 hectolitres per hectare, and for 1960 to 1966, 81 hectolitres per hectare.

Germany's reputation as a wine-producing country lies in the variety of her white wines and their special character, a result of the climate of this most northerly of viticultural regions.

Nearly 30 different varieties of vines are planted and listed here are the most important, with their proportions expressed in percentages:

White grapes	Sylvaner	35%
	Riesling	26%
	Müller-Thurgau (a crossing of Riesling and Sylvaner)	14%
	Gutedel	2%
	Pinot Gris	1%
Red grapes	Portugieser	8%
	Trollinger	3%

GENTIAN

Blue late Burgundy	2%
Limberger	1%
Black Riesling	4%

The German wine districts are situated in the south and south west of the country. In order of size of area they are: the Palatinate; Rhinehessia; Moselle, Saar and Ruwer; Baden; Württemberg; Rheingau (or Rhinegau), with the Bergstrasse; Nahe; Franconia; Middle Rhine; Ahr.

Most intriguing for many people are the naming and labelling of German wines. The labels give, in addition to the vintage, information about:

1. The geographical situation of the vineyard. This may be simply the name of the village, or the village plus a site name. (Village names, such as Rüdesheim, Nierstein, Forst etc., are often written in the adjectival form with the suffix -er. Typical site names are Badstube, Berg, Domtal, Jesuitengarten.)

2. Species of grapes used.

3. Details of harvesting and special categories of wines. German terms used for this include:

Auslese. This designation is strictly limited to unsweetened wines produced entirely from carefully selected bunches, to the exclusion of any that are not fully ripe or are in any way damaged or diseased.

Beerenauslese. This denotes a wine made from specially selected single berries which have been allowed to become over-ripe or 'sleepy' in good vintages.

Edelbeerenauslese. Synonymous with *Beerenauslese*, this term is used when the honey-like bouquet produced by the *Edelfäule* or 'noble rot' is very evident.

Goldbeerenauslese. This is an *Auslese* (not a *Beerenauslese*) made from fully ripe golden grapes, that is to say grapes which have been attacked by the fungus *Botrytis cinerea* and have passed the golden stage.

Spätlese. This term is reserved exclusively for unsweetened wines from fully ripened grapes gathered later than the normal harvest period.

Trockenbeerenauslese. Term used of wines made exclusively from fully ripe grapes that have been allowed to become partly dried and raisin-like on the vine. Only *Beerenauslese* or *Trockenbeerenauslese* wines may be designated as *Spitzengewächs*, 'very best growth', or *Hochgewächs*, 'superb growth'.

Cabinet or *Kabinett*. Natural wine of good quality, but not entitled to *Spätlese*.

Dreikönigs-Wein. Wine from grapes gathered on January 6 (Twelfth Night) of the year following the actual vintage.

Eiswein. A wine produced from fully ripe frozen grapes, gathered and pressed in this state at minus 6° to 8° C. Great wines up to *Beerenauslese* standard.

Jungfernwein. 'Maiden wine' – the first wine produced from a newly planted vineyard.

Maiwein. A Rhine wine cup based on the fragrant herb, woodruff.

Perlwein. A sparkling wine with approximately half the pressure of a Sekt, bottled in the usual Rhine or Moselle bottle, in most cases on the sweet side (up to 40 grams per litre of unfermented sugar is permitted).

St Nikolaus-Wein. Wine produced from grapes gathered on December 6.

Schillerwein. A wine pressed from a mixture of red and white grapes (*schillern* means to shimmer).

Sekt. German sparkling wine, also known as sparkling hock. Produced by the *méthode champenoise*, or *en cuve close* or *gazéifié*.

Sylvester-Wein. Wine produced from grapes gathered on December 31.

Other descriptions to be found on German labels:

durchgegoren	fully fermented
echt	genuine
Fass Nr.	cask number
Fuder Nr.	
Gewächs, Eigengewächs	growth, own growth
Kellerabfüllung,	bottled in the cellar
Kellerabzug	of the proprietor
naturrein	purely natural
Naturwein	natural wine
Originalabfüllung,	
Originalabzug, or any	original bottling
combination with the	
word *Original*	

Originalwein	original wine
rein	pure
Schlossabzug	'castle-bottled'
ungezuckerter Wein	unsweetened wine
Wachstum, Kreszenz	own vineyard

CLASSIFICATION

It would not be possible to classify German wines on the basis of a comparison of village with village, site with site. The only valid comparisons would be *Spätlese* with *Spätlese*, ordinary wine with ordinary wine, and so on. In the old days classification was mostly according to the best cask produced, and the vineyard responsible for it was considered to be the best vineyard. Classification is therefore only possible by taste and quality of each single cask. There are of course specially favoured *Lagen* (sites) which enjoy suitable soil and lots of sunshine and therefore produce genuinely good wines. Among such sites are:

Palatinate	Forster Kirchenstück, Jesuitengarten Deidesheimer Herrgottsacker, Wachenheimer Gerümpel
Rhinehessia	Niersteiner Auflangen, Ölberg Oppenheimer Sackträger, Reisekahr Nackenheimer Rothenberg
Moselle	Bernkasteler Doktor Piesporter Goldtröpfchen Uerziger Würzgarten Wehlener Sonnenuhn
Saar	Ockfener Bockstein Ayler Kupp, Herrenberg
Ruwer	Maximiner Grünhäuser, Herrenberg, Kaseler Nies'gen
Rheingau or Rhinegau	Rauenthaler Baiken Johannisberg Schloss Vollrads Rüdesheimer Berg
Nahe	Schloss Böckelheimer Kupfergrube
Franconia	Würzburger Stein, Leisten Randersacker Spielberg

Although Germany produces more red wine than is perhaps generally realized, the total amount is not very large. Among the best vineyards are:

Palatinate	Dürkheimer Feuerberg Herxheimer
Rhinehessia	Ingelheimer Hundsweg, Steinacker
Baden	Affenthaler Klosterreberg
Württemberg	Brackenheim
Rheingau or Rhinegau	Assmannshäuser Höllenberg
Franconia	Klingenberg am Main
Ahr	Walporzheimer Honigsberg Neuenahrer Sonnenberg

GERVAIS. A soft French cheese, named after its maker but is now the generic name for French cheese of soft cream type.

GEVREY-CHAMBERTIN. See BURGUNDY WINES.

GEX, FROMAGE DE. A delicately blue-veined cheese from Bresse which has been judged by some connoisseurs as even finer than Stilton.

GHEE. A clarified buffalo butter used in the Indian subcontinent.

GHERKIN. Very small cucumbers, the best of which are not more than $1\frac{1}{2}$ inches long and especially grown for pickling and preserving in vinegar. They are mainly used for garnishing.

GIBLETS. The edible entrails of poultry and game, namely the heart, liver, gizzard and neck and, on occasion, the feet, which are stewed to make stock or made into a ragoût.

GIGONDAS. See RHÔNE WINES.

GIGOT. The term *gigot* is applied in France to a leg of lamb and is probably derived from the old French word *gigue*. Sometimes it is also spelled *giggets* and used to denote small slices of any sort of meat.

GIMLET. An alcoholic drink made from equal parts of gin and lime juice cordial poured over crushed ice and served in a special goblet sometimes called a gimlet glass.

GIN. A strong spirit distilled mainly from grain and flavoured with the berries of the juniper (which see). It was invented in the 17th century by Dr Franciscus Sylvius, or de la Boë, a professor of

GINGER

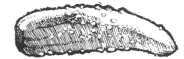

GHERKIN

medicine at Leyden University in Holland, in the course of experiments to find a prophylactic against certain tropical diseases. He called his discovery *genièvre*, the French word for juniper, from which the English name gin derives.

Englishmen returning from the 17th-century wars spoke of 'Dutch courage' when alluding to gin and the expression has remained in use for bravery inspired by alcohol. Before this time English distillers had used beer and wine lees to make spirits, for which there was an increasing demand, but they were not very palatable. Gin became a popular drink in England because of its refinement. Local distillers benefited when Queen Anne increased the tariff on imported wines and spirits and lowered excise duties on domestic products. It was also cheap, as the jingle shows:

> Drunk for a penny
> Dead drunk for tuppence
> Clean straw for nothing.

Most gins are colourless, although some have a pale straw tinge. Gin does not have to age to be potable. A good one should be smooth, crystal-clear and delicate in aroma. Although most spirit distilling countries have their own variations of and names for gin, there are only two basic types: the Dutch and the dry English or American. Dutch gins, variously referred to as *jenever*, Hollands and Schiedam, have a pronounced flavour which makes them unsuitable for cocktails; the Anglo-American gins may be drunk neat or used in a range of cocktails.

GINGER. The root or tuber of a sweet plant which looks like a tall iris. It is a native of India, China, South Asia and the West Indies. The root resembles a horny large potato which has started to produce small potatoes on itself. It has a light brown skin and the flesh is firm and pungent.

Ginger has long been prized for its flavour and it is said that the old kings of the Orient used to eat ginger boiled in honey – probably the precursor of crystallized ginger as we know it today. The ancient Greeks, Romans and Arabs used it extensively.

One of its most important uses today in Western cooking is in the making of gingerbread, which is perhaps the oldest sweet cake in the world. It is said to have been invented by a Greek from Rhodes about 2800 B.C. It soon became famous throughout the Mediterranean area and was known as *melitates*. Chaucer mentions it ('They sett him Roiall spicerye and Gingerbread') in 14th-century England. At about this time it became customary to make it into fanciful shapes representing men, birds, animals, letters of the alphabet, and some were coated with gilt hence the expression 'to take the gilt off the gingerbread'. Throughout the 16th century it was the custom to present gingerbread to honour the recipient on certain occasions. It often weighed 150 lb. or more but this depended on the nature of the occasion. There are many variations of gingerbread using different fruit flavours but all are made with fat, sugar, eggs, molasses, flour, ginger and other spices.

Preserved ginger and crystallized ginger are popular confections, and ginger biscuits are well known. Ginger is also used for flavouring drinks such as ginger beer, ginger ale and ginger wine. Small pieces may also be used in assorted spices for pickling.

GINGER ALE. A non-alcoholic effervescent drink flavoured with ginger.

GINGER BEER. A mildly alcoholic effervescent drink flavoured with ginger.

It makes a refreshing drink on a hot summer day. The ingredients are sugar, water, ground ginger, brewer's yeast and lemon rinds. The interaction between sugar and yeast results in the formation of alcohol, and carbon dioxide which makes ginger beer effervescent.

GINGERBREAD. See GINGER.

GINGER SNAPS. Sometimes these are called ginger nuts but in either case are a round, ginger-flavoured biscuit with a particularly firm yet crisp consistency.

GINGER WINE. This is an alcoholic drink made with ginger essence, water, tartaric acid, cream of tartar, sugar and yeast. It is served as a liqueur or mixed with other drinks. A drink consisting of ginger wine and whisky in equal proportions is much liked by some people.

Earlier recipes for making ginger wine included rum, whisky and brandy. Ginger cordial is an earlier variant of ginger wine; the recipe includes gin instead of brandy and whisky and sherry or madeira.

GINKGO. The ginkgo tree is grown in the United States for its handsome foliage, but in Japan its nuts are considered a great autumn delicacy and are much used in Japanese and Chinese cooking. The nuts, which are a gem-green colour, are cooked in a variety of ways. They are roughly the size of small green olives and not unlike them in appearance. Ginkgo nuts are supposed to aid digestion and to diminish the effects of too much wine drinking.

GIRDLE. See GRIDDLE.

GIRDLE or **GRIDDLE CAKES.** The northern English and Scottish name for drop scones. In the United States and parts of Canada they are called griddle cakes or pancakes and, as they are very popular in both these countries, there are many embellishments added to the basic cake, including both sweet and savoury fillings.

GIVRY. See BURGUNDY WINES.

GIZZARD. The second stomach of birds in which the food is ground. See GIBLETS.

GLASS. Evidence supports the view that the ancient Egyptians made glass as far back as 3000 B.C., but it was the Greeks who devised the blow-pipe method of producing glass which in its basic form survives to this day. Glass used to make bottles (which see) revolutionized wine-making in that in conjunction with the cork (which see) wine could be kept to mature for long periods. But it was not until the 16th century that glass completely replaced gold and silver wine goblets. By the 18th century glassware manufacture had made great strides and goblets, decanters and wine glasses were so beautifully made that they were considered objects of art. The first attempt to make glass in America was in 1608. It is thought that glass intended primarily for drinking water was first made in America, possibly as an outgrowth of the temperance movement.

Some of the later developments in glass-making include the manufacture of fire-resistant glass for cooking at high temperatures.

GLACÉ. The French for glaze. Glacé icing is sugar icing and *fruits glacés* are fruits dipped in a syrup which has been cooked to the 'crack' and hardens when cold. Another sense of the word is implied in meringue glace, which is *meringue glacée*, meringue with ice-cream.

GLAZE. A meat glaze is a strong gravy or bone stock reduced by long boiling almost to a brown syrup, which sets firm and hard when cold. A small nut of this can be added to a gravy or sauce to strengthen the flavour. It can also be melted down to be used for brushing over cold tongue etc. A mock glaze can be made by stiffening a clear brown stock with gelatine.

Jam glaze is made from either apricot jam or redcurrant jelly and is used for brushing over fruit flans, cakes etc.

To glaze means to make food shiny or glassy or to add lustre either with egg, water, sugar or the above glazes.

GLEN MIST. A liqueur with a basis of Scotch whisky, honey and flavouring herbs; it is not as sweet as other Scottish liqueurs.

GLOBE ARTICHOKE. See ARTICHOKE.

GLORIA, CH. See BORDEAUX WINES.

GLUCOSE or **DEXTROSE.** Glucose or dextrose is a natural sugar found in fruits, vegetables and other products. It is one of the sugars formed in the green leaves of plants under the action of sunlight. Some plants retain sugar as such in their tissues, as for example cane sugar and beet sugar. Others link the sugar units together chemically to form a starch polymer which is stored in special parts of the plant such as the grain in cereals or the tuber in potatoes. Glucose is also found in honey and in the form of a gum in dried fruits. It can be manufactured commercially by treating starch with sulphuric acid.

Glucose is used in confectionery, jams and syrups, and to increase the sugar content of wine. It is favoured by athletes as it is a source of energy which can be readily absorbed by the system.

GLUTEN. The part of any cereal flour remaining when the starch is removed by kneading the flour under running water. It is valuable in making starch-reduced bread for diabetics or others on low starch diets.

GLYCERINE. Also glycerin or glycerol. This is a sweet, colourless, odourless, syrupy liquid in its pure form.

It is found in all wines and beers in varying

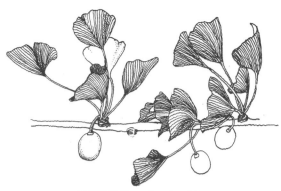

GINKGO (branch and nuts)　　　　　　　　GNOCCHI

percentages because of the fermentation of sugar by yeast. Glycerine is used to retain moisture in some types of confectionery, and in making cake icing to prevent excessive hardening.

GNOCCHI. One of the most interesting of the Italian pastas (which see) and adopted with modifications by the French. Gnocchi come in the form of small dumplings, usually about the size of a walnut, and are made either from a maize flour called *polenta* or from puréed potatoes. Small croquettes are made by mixing the flour or potato with eggs, butter, seasoning and one or more of a variety of flavourings such as cheese, spinach or nutmeg. These are poached in gently boiling water until they rise to the surface and are then dried in a hot oven after being sprinkled with cheese and butter. Plainer ones are served with chicken livers or some kind of rich meat or vegetable sauce.

GOAT. The domestic variety (*Capra hircus hircus*) is found all over the world and, though reared mainly for its milk in North America and northern Europe, where goats' milk cheeses are popular in certain areas, the young goat, or kid, is eaten as a delicacy in Mediterranean countries and parts of the Middle East. Roast kid is sometimes preferred to lamb, especially when cooked whole and, at festivities on certain Mediterranean islands, a young kid is wrapped in myrtle leaves and slowly baked in an underground oven. Kid stewed in wine and herbs is a popular Italian Easter dish.

GOAT FISH. A tropical fish found in the Caribbean and the Gulf of Mexico, so named because of the double barbel on its lower jaw. The spotted variety, *Upeneus maculatus*, is popular for its firm flesh and distinctive flavour.

GOATS' MILK. This has a higher percentage of fat and protein than cows' milk and has a stronger flavour.

GOBY. See GUDGEON.

GOLD LEAF. The art of reducing solid gold to thin leaves is an ancient one. Pliny the Elder observed that a small quantity of gold could be beaten down into 750 leaves each four digits square. Gold-beating has been known in the East for centuries.

The Italian cooks of the 16th century experimented with gold powder in cooking and it became a fashionable ingredient in recipes. The idea may have occurred to them because they also dabbled in medicine and alchemy and gold has associations with both. Gold was considered a universal cure and the key to long life during the Middle Ages. Gold dust was sprinkled on food given to patients who could afford it. It is also said that small grains of gold were mixed with corn given to chickens being fattened for royal households.

Tiny specks of gold leaf are a feature of Danziger Goldwasser (which see) and of the similar Elixir d'Anvers from Belgium.

Indian gold leaves are wafer-thin and made of 14 carat gold. They are used to garnish sweetmeats and sweet dishes. Silver is similarly treated.

GOLDBEERENAUSLESE. See AUSLESE and GERMAN WINES.

GOLDEN SYRUP. A pale, golden syrup produced by the evaporation of cane sugar juice. Less sweet than sugar, it is used to flavour puddings and gingerbread and as a filling for tarts.

GÖNEZ. See WINE CONTAINERS.

GOOSE. The favourite of our nursery rhymes. When one is called a 'silly goose' it may not be a compliment, but it is no insult either. 'He can't say boo to a goose' suggests that geese are cowards. When we have 'cooked our goose' it means all is finished and everyone knows what happens when we 'kill the goose that lays the golden egg'. According to Egyptian mythology it was a goose that laid the golden egg of all eggs, the sun. Even so, goose was a favourite dish with the Egyptians.

The Romans, like the French much later, crammed the unfortunate goose until its liver became enormous, and their webbed feet were cooked with cocks' combs to make a favourite Roman delicacy.

Goose pie was at one time the Christmas treat in Britain. During the 19th century it became the poor man's idea of a Christmas dinner and goose clubs were formed to provide this.

Formerly more honour was done to the goose at Martinmas and Michaelmas when the young stubble-fed goose appeared on the table, tender and juicy and quite distinct in flavour from the super-fatted Christmas goose.

In Central Europe today the goose takes precedence over the turkey and in Germany they say 'Eine gute gebratene Gans ist eine Gabe Gottes' (a fine roast goose is a gift from God).

France probably has the most by-products from the goose. Foie gras is one of them – although there are areas where the goose's by-products are more important than the bird itself. Geese bred for foie gras make poor eating. In goose-rearing countries goose-fat is a favourite item of diet. Smeared on soft fresh bread, sprinkled with salt and freshly milled pepper, it is gourmet's food. Goose necks are stuffed and eaten not only in France but also in Hungary, a great goose-rearing country.

The goose and the gander look alike and at a quick glance it is not easy to tell which is which. They are of similar size and marked alike. When trussed and ready for the oven the word goose is applied to both.

GOOSEBERRY. In northern Europe this thorny bush, *Ribes grossularia*, bears a small green fruit which varies in shape from round to oval and has a tart but distinctive flavour. In North America the *Ribes hirtellum* and *Ribes missourienses* are widely cultivated and bear a berry similar to the European variety. The gooseberry was brought to England from the Continent in the 16th century and soon gooseberry pie became traditional fare for Whitsuntide if the fruit ripened in time. It is still popular in jams, preserves, tarts and fools (which see) on both sides of the Atlantic. There is also a larger, hairy, purplish gooseberry which, when fully ripe, is sweet enough to make an excellent dessert fruit in its raw state.

GORGONZOLA. The most popular of the Italian blue cheeses, Gorgonzola is named after a village near Milan but it is now mainly produced in and around Milan. Credibly, the invention of Gorgonzola is attributed to one of those accidents which abound in cheese lore. The proprietor of a wineshop was often paid by the local farmers for their drinks by the cheeses they made. His cellar became piled high with them and there they ripened and became famous.

Because Gorgonzola keeps and travels well it enjoys an international reputation. It is unique for its creaminess. Nowadays it is stored in cool, damp caves, always in a draught, just after the salting process. At first a red mould sets in and grows over the cheese, eventually penetrating right through. It is at its ripest in about six months.

White Gorgonzola, slightly more bitter in flavour, is highly appreciated in Italy.

GOUDA. A smooth, mellow, yellow-rinded cheese made from whole milk, named after a Dutch town. It is not a good cooking cheese and is primarily to be eaten with fresh white or pumpernickel bread. Small Goudas have a red rind.

Most Gouda is exported young – good but not great cheese. When it ages the flavour is entirely different. Some people consider mature Gouda to be among the great cheeses.

GOULASH or **GULYAS.** A rich Hungarian stew or soup for which there are many recipes, some traditional. The word *gulyas* means shepherd and this was a shepherd's dish, sustaining and complete. In the remote parts of the country great cauldrons of goulash are cooked. The usual ingredients are beef, veal or pork highly seasoned with paprika and other condiments.

GOURDS. These belong to the Cucurbitaceae, a family which includes cucumbers, melons and all vegetable marrows and squashes. Gourds are among the oldest vegetables known to man and were familiar to the original inhabitants of North America. The genus *Cucurbita* numbers about 20 species of these trailing vine-like plants. They require little care and yield abundantly within a short period. See also MARROW.

GOURMAND and **GOURMET.** See GASTRONOMY.

GRAHAM FLOUR. Named after Sylvester Graham, the 19th-century reformer and dietician who invented the process. See FLOUR.

GRAM. See CHICK PEAS.

GRANA CHEESES. The generic name of a group of Italian cheeses. The word *grana* means grain and refers to the grainy texture of the cheeses when they age. There are two types of *grana* cheeses, both commonly called Parmesan outside of Italy. One is *Parmigiano-Reggiano*, the other *Grana Padano*.

GRANADILLA or **GRENADILLA.** This delicious fruit is a variety of the passion flower of which there are numerous species.

(Opposite) MINESTRONE.
(Overleaf) NUTS: Assorted nuts and raisins: clockwise from top, slivered and chopped almonds, pistachios and pine nuts, cashews, a bowl of assorted nuts, macadamia nuts, raisins (centre).

GOOSEBERRY

Several varieties are cultivated for their fruits in the tropics and subtropics. Some varieties were grown in hot houses in England during the 19th century. There is yet another variety which can be grown in England with excellent results on a warm south wall or a house wall. The small purple fruit is the juiciest and best. The type commonly grown in the United States is large with a seedy pulp similar to a pomegranate.

In some varieties the fruit is yellow with a viscous pulp which is eaten with a spoon. It is excellent mixed with sherry or fresh cream and sugar. It may also be used to flavour ice-cream.

The plant was called 'Passiflora' by the early missionaries to South America who likened the structure at the centre of its flower to a scourging post, the corona to the crown of thorns, the stamen to the five wounds and the stigmas to the three nails of Christ's Passion.

GRAND MARNIER. Popular brand of French Curaçao liqueur marketed in two kinds: *Cordon rouge* and *Cordon jaune*, the latter being sweeter and of lower alcoholic strength.

GRAND PUY LACOSTE, CH. See BORDEAUX WINES.

GRAND VENEUR. See SAUCES.

GRANITE (GRANITA). An Italian water ice formerly called sorbet in England. It is neither solid nor liquid and consists of either sweetened fruit juices, fresh strawberries or similar fruits, or coffee. Such ices in the old days of gargantuan eating were served half-way through a meal to relieve over-burdened stomachs.

In Italy *granita* heralds the first sign of summer. It is eaten at all times of the day and night, often with bread or brioche.

GRANITA DI FRAGOLE (Strawberry Water Ice)

2 lb. strawberries
juice ½ lemon
juice 2 oranges
8 oz. (1 cup) sugar
2½ (3¼) cups water

Wash and hull the strawberries and rub through a sieve. Add first the lemon juice, blend, then add the orange juice. Put the sugar and the water in a pan and cook slowly for 5 minutes, or until the sugar is dissolved. Cool the syrup then add it to the strawberry mixture. Pour it into a freezing tray and let it freeze until firm. It can be stirred from time to time, but if it crystallizes this does not matter, as the ice particles are part of the nature of a *granita*.

GRANULATED SUGAR. See SUGAR.

GRAPE. A vinous fruit which grows in clusters. Generally growers produce grapes for the table or the bottle but there are basically four main types, for wine, table, raisins and unfermented grape juice. Any kind of grape can be made into wine, used at table or made into grape juice. But in fact no good wine grape does well as a table grape, or vice versa, except for the *Petite Gamay* of the Beaujolais in France. Table grapes and wine grapes are two distinct categories of *Vitis vinifera*, the patriarch of 90 per cent of the world's cultivated vines, known to the ancients and first cultivated by the Egyptians who had brought wine culti-vation, wine making and cellarage to a high degree of perfection.

There were wild vines in Greece, France and Italy but cultivated varieties came with the Syrians, Phoenicians and Mesopotamians. It was the Romans who spread vineyards throughout Italy and France, and the Carthaginians who introduced them to Spain.

The Romans brought vines to Britain, but when is not quite certain. Bede wrote of English vines in A.D. 731, and vineyards were mentioned in the Domesday Book. The Normans called Ely the Isle of the Vines and at one time the Bishop of Ely used to receive, as tithes, wine made from the vines grown in the diocese.

It seems to have been usual for monasteries in England to cultivate vineyards, but with their

(Previous page) OMELETTE.
(Opposite) OMELETTE SURPRISE (Baked Alaska).

suppression and the imports of cheaper wines from the Continent, viticulture was neglected in England, although at a later date English hothouse grapes were recognized as the most luscious and beautiful grapes in the world.

There are immense numbers of different kinds of grapes grown throughout the world. The best of the European grapes come from France and include the golden *chasselas* of Fontainebleau, Napoleon or *Bicane Chasselas*, Royal Madeleine and the white Muscat. The last are seeded and peeled and used in the classical recipe *sole Véronique* (see SOLE). Many French grapes are sun-dried to make them into raisins and sultanas (white seedless raisins), while currants are obtained by sun-drying grapes from the Greek islands.

In the United States grapes are grown in every part of the country except the north. California grows the *Vitis vinifera*, the wine grapes. In New York it is the native *Vitis aestivalis*, while in the East and South most grapes are the progeny of the aboriginal *Vitis labrusca*, found in North America in A.D. 1000.

American favourite grapes include Flame Tokay, Emperor and Thompson Seedless, the Ribier, the Malagas of California. In New York State, also Ohio, the Concord, Isabella, Catawba and Delaware are preferred. In the South it is the Muscadine and many varities of Scuppernong which are favoured.

The naming of the colours of grapes is imprecise. White can mean anything from golden-yellow to ice-green. Red becomes almost purple, while black can mean deep blue or purple, rather than a true black.

GRAPEFRUIT. A citrus fruit that grows in many warm regions of the world. It was so called because it hangs in 'grapes', that is to say clusters, and seems to have been given this name in Jamaica. The name was certainly known there in the early 19th century. The grapefruit was probably originally a mutation in *Citrus grandis*, the large, very bitter, thick-skinned pomelo or shaddock (which see), taken to the West Indies from the East in 1696.

Grapefruit itself has not long been known in Europe, but has become quickly popular. It is a large round fruit, the skin varying from thin to very thick, in colour from pale almost green-yellow to a bright yellow or even pink-flushed. The flesh is pale yellow, although sometimes it is pink tinged and almost reddish. The flavour varies from acid to very sweet, according to climate, variety and even maturity.

The grapefruit is versatile, and it can be used in salads, served at breakfast or as an hors d'oeuvre. It can be grilled, made into a drink, a jam or jelly, and the skin can be candied.

GRAPEFRUIT JUICE. One of the most popular breakfast juices in the United States and Europe, whether freshly pressed or canned. It is generally pale yellow in colour, although a certain California grapefruit produces a soft pink juice, and it is considered to have mildly tonic properties as well as being rich in vitamin C.

GRAPE PRESS. A device which extracts juice from grapes by means of applied pressure. See PRESSOIR.

GRAPPA. An Italian spirit corresponding to the French *marc*. It is simply a distillation of the spent stalks, pips and grapeskins after the wine has been pressed. It is much to be avoided except when produced by a reputable distiller. California also produces a beverage brandy of the same name.

GRATE, TO. To reduce to small particles, granules or slices by rubbing on a grater. The form the substance takes depends on the shape of the perforations.

GRATER. These are made in different shapes, sizes and designs to meet all needs. Basically it is a thin sheet of metal or plastic with shaped perforations stamped in it. Some are round, others flat or curved, and they may have one or more types of perforations. Although the metal or plastic is thin, it must be firm enough to stand up to use

GRATIN, AU. A French term, now universally used for dishes with a rich sauce on which a layer of breadcrumbs is scattered before browning in the oven or beneath a salamander grill (broiler).

GRAVES. See BORDEAUX WINES.

GRAVES DE VAYRES. See BORDEAUX WINES.

GRAVY. The best gravy is that which consists of juices oozing out of cooking meat, but the name also refers to any form of concentrated stock in which meat, poultry or game is cooked.

GRAVY BOAT. The name commonly given to a low, boatshaped container used to dispense gravies, sauces etc. It is also called a sauceboat.

GRAYLING. A small freshwater fish found in the rivers and lakes of Europe, Asia and North America. It is prized by sportsmen as an excellent dry fly fish nearly as good to eat as trout.

GREASE. This means to rub a cooking utensil with grease, i.e. butter, oil, dripping or other

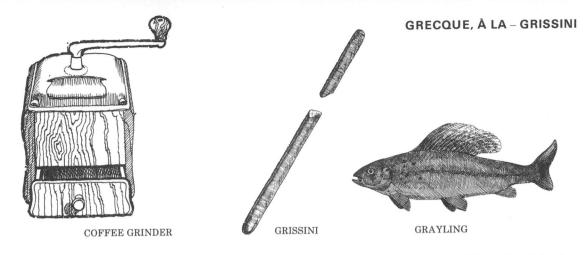

COFFEE GRINDER   GRISSINI   GRAYLING

cooking fats, before cooking to prevent food sticking to the pan. Most cooking pans are best greased with a brush or a wad of soft paper dipped in fat.

GRECQUE, À LA. Strictly speaking, dishes labelled *à la Grecque* should be of Greek origin, but this is not always so. Often the term applies to dishes of French origin. Vegetables are described as being cooked *à la Grecque* when cooked in a seasoned oil and water mixture.

GREEK WINES. Greek wines vary enormously, principally because the growers do not confine themselves to a particular kind of grape. This means that the wine producers must make their wine from the grapes as they come in. One vineyard alone will send six or more different kinds, so that it is impossible for the wine-producers to achieve a uniform quality. The only possible exception is the wine produced in Mesogeia, in the interior of Greece. Here there are large tracts under cultivation producing one variety of grape, the Savvatiano. This grape also produces a retsina wine of a fairly uniform quality, said to be the best in the country.

There are white, red and *rosé* Greek wines, dry and sweet, light and heavy. So great is the diversity in quality that when one finds a wine to one's liking and carefully notes the name and the year of vintage, another bottle of the same type can be a sorry disappointment. Equally, a bottle of wine which may seem displeasing can have a sister bottle which is quite good.

The most controversial wines of Greece are the retsinas (which see).

GREEN. See WINE TERMS.

GREEN PEPPER. See CAPSICUM.

GREENGAGE. See PLUM.

GRENACHE. A sweet dessert wine from Rousellon under the Pyrenees, made in the Banyuls district.

GRENADIN. Small slices of fillet of veal, larded and braised.

GRENADINE. A French *sirop* or liquid form of sugar made from pomegranate juice, brilliant scarlet in colour and absolutely free from any trace of alcohol. It is used as a sweetening agent, with iced water; in cocktails and bitters.

GRIDDLE. A round flat pan of heavy iron, made without sides and used for cooking scones, pancakes, etc., on top of the stove. One northern European form has a half-loop handle similar to that on a bucket, whereas in the United States the griddle has a long handle. Also called a girdle.

GRIDIRON. This is a metal frame used to cook meat or fish by grilling (broiling) over a charcoal fire. It is certainly one of the first implements for cooking used by early man, and is contemporary with the spit.

GRIGNOLINO. See ITALIAN WINES.

GRILL or **BROIL.** Undoubtedly the first cooked meat man ever ate was grilled or broiled. Even today this ancient and simple method of cooking is hard to surpass. It is a method of cooking in a gridiron over embers or in modern stoves under or over a grill or broiler. Formerly grilling was always on an open fire of wood or charcoal.

GRILLET, CH. A very scarce wine – dry, white and of great character – from the upper Rhône valley.

GRINDER. A piece of equipment which reduces food to small pieces or powder. The four main types are meat, pepper, salt and coffee grinders.

GRISKIN. Chine of pork, also a thin poor piece of loin.

GRISSINI. Italian salt sticks or thin sticks of bread about the thickness of a man's finger and 12 to 18 in. long. They are hard and crisp.

GRITS or **GROATS**. These are oats or corn from which the husk has been completely removed. This is done in a mill where the grain is hulled and ground to a coarse meal. Bran and germ are sifted out and the resultant product is known as hominy grits (which see).

GROG. Originally the nautical term for a mixture of rum and water and said to have been named after Admiral Vernon's grogram cloak; this officer of the Royal Navy had ordered water to be added to his sailors' rum ration as he considered neat spirit too intoxicating.

GROS PLANT. See LOIRE WINES.

GROSLOT. See LOIRE WINES.

GROUND CHERRY. Sometimes called Chinese lantern or strawberry tomato, this is any species of the genus *Physalis*, a plant which grows in tropical regions of the world and parts of the southern United States. The berry is the size of a large cherry, orange or red in colour and surrounded by a yellow, papery calyx resembling a lantern. It makes an interesting addition to the normal range of preserves as it has a tart but distinctive flavour.

GROUNDNUT. See PEANUT.

GROUND RICE. See RICE.

GROUPER. The name commonly applied to many members of the sea bass family and widely distributed throughout the warm waters of the world. These fish range in size from 2 to 12 feet in length and weigh up to 80 lb; the common size taken commercially is about 10 lb. Practically any method of cooking may be employed with this delicious fish as the flesh is firm, flaky and delicately flavoured.

GROUSE. Game birds found throughout the colder regions of the northern hemisphere, related to the pheasant and all of the subfamily *Tetraoninae*. They range in size from 15 to 20 inches in length, are of stocky build and have brown feathers. All grouse are extremely palatable as they are principally vegetivorous and are highly prized as a game bird and a table delicacy. Grouse have a special meaning for the British sportsman. The principal species found in North America are the ruffled grouse, considered to be one of the finest of game birds, the prairie chicken and the ptarmigan. In Europe the family is further represented by the capercaillie, the black and the red grouse.

GROWLER. An early 20th-century slang term in the United States for any vessel used to carry beer home for consumption from the neighbourhood saloon. In general it consisted of a quart pail, with a tight-fitting lid, and a wire bail handle.

GRUAUD LAROSE, CH. See BORDEAUX WINES.

GRUEL. A thin form of porridge which can be made from barley, oats, wheat or other cereals and was once considered essential for invalids, nursing mothers and children.

GRUMELLO. See ITALIAN WINES.

GRUNT. A marine fish of the family Haemulidae found in all tropical seas and so named because when alarmed it emits a curious sound made by rubbing their teeth together. Some grow up to 3 feet in length and can weigh as much as 20 lb. They are popular as a game fish and are delicious served in a variety of ways when freshly caught.

GRUYÈRE. There is a Swiss and a French Gruyère. The former is a favourite in Switzerland, where it has been made for centuries. It is named after the Gruyéres valley in the canton of Fribourg, although it is now also made in the cantons of Vaud and Neuchâtel.

Gruyère is often confused with Emmental cheese, which it resembles. There are several technical differences but for the layman it is enough to know that Gruyère has smaller and fewer holes, a greasier rind and a texture which, although quite firm, is creamier than Emmental. The taste is slightly acidulous.

French Gruyère has much in common with the Swiss, for it is made on the other side of the valley.

GUAVA. A medium round or oblong, yellow, greenish-yellow or pink-flushed fruit from $1\frac{1}{2}$ to 3 inches in diameter with a thick rind surrounding a mass of seeds embedded in a firm soft pulp. The flesh varies in colour from white to yellow to a pale pink. The fruit may be sour or sweet but it always has the same characteristic flavour.

Originally a native of Central America, it is now grown in most tropical countries. The guava tree, a member of a large family of 3,000 or more species of woody plants, grows up to 30 feet or more. It is hardy, nourishes in a variety of soil types and hardly needs attention. It is also drought resistant.

Guavas can be eaten fresh, stewed, puréed, and made into jams and jellies. Guava cheese is one of the finest of fruit cheeses.

A smaller dark red variety, known as the strawberry guava, is considered by many as superior to the ordinary guava. Its sweet but somewhat acid flavour has a vague resemblance to the strawberry.

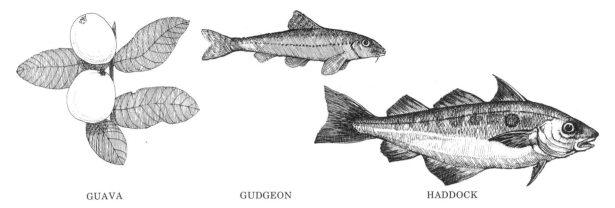

GUAVA   GUDGEON   HADDOCK

In Florida is another variety known as the pineapple guava because of a similarity in flavour.

GUDGEON. A small freshwater fish, *Gobio gobio*, which lives on lake and river bottoms throughout Europe and Asia. It measures 6 inches or less and is cooked in the manner of whitebait (which see).

GUIRAUD, CH. A first-growth Sauternes. See BORDEAUX WINES.

GUINEA FOWL. A family of birds (Numididae) related to the pheasant and originally indigenous to Africa. They were brought to Europe first by the Greeks, then the Romans, and re-appeared in the 16th century when the Portuguese returned with them from the West African coast of Guinea. The common guinea hen *Numida meleagris* has been reared domestically in many parts of the world for several hundred years as the flesh is tender and delicately flavoured, with a hint of gameyness. The most popular variety has dark grey feathers finely spotted with white, grows to the size of a large pheasant and is cooked in the same ways.

The eggs are small, pretty and a pale fawn colour, these are esteemed by epicures for their richness and flavour.

GUM SYRUP. Also known as simple syrup, syrup gum, bar syrup, gomme syrup. It is made with sugar, water and gum arabic.

GUM TRAGACANTH. This is produced by several species of plant found in Iran, Turkey and Greece; the gum exudes spontaneously from the bark. It has been known to man and used from pre-Christian times, mainly medicinally. Gum tragacanth is also used in cookery as an emulsifying agent, a thickener for sauces and a base for ice-cream powders and gelatinous desserts.

GUMBO. The word gumbo, or gombo, is a Creole patois corruption of the African word for okra (which see). It is now recognized as meaning a dish or a soup thickened with okra; to qualify the dish must have okra as a principal ingredient. There are many types of gumbo, all taking their name from the ingredient giving the dish its flavouring or taste.

GURNET (GURNARD). A fish of which there are several species, the best known being the grey, yellow and red. Its flesh is white and firm, its flavour good. It can be baked or poached and served with a sauce or in any of the ways of haddock.

H

HADDOCK. An important food fish of the North Atlantic – from Iceland to the Bay of Biscay and New Jersey – at its best from September to February. Of the cod family, the Gadidae, it is smaller than cod with rather firmer, drier flesh and a slightly more distinctive flavour. It is distinguished by dark marks on each shoulder, ascribed to bruises St Peter left when he took the shekel for the temple tax out of its mouth. In Britain the haddock is the *Gadus aeglefinus* (United States usage is *Melanogrammus aeglefinus*) and its French names are *aigrefin* and *eglefin*. Many other fish have been called haddock, including New Zealand's red cod, the golden haddock or John Dory (which see), the opah (Jerusalem haddock), hake and ocean perch. The popular Norway haddock is the red-fleshed *Sebastes marinus*, also called redfish or rosefish in the United States.

Smoked haddock come in two forms: flat finnans, which are split, and Arbroath smokies which, gutted and cleaned, are smoked closed, in the round. Finnan haddock or finnan haddie taking its name from the village of Findon near Aberdeen, won acclaim as the finest smoked haddock. Nowadays the name is increasingly applied to smoked haddock wherever it is caught and cured. Finnans emerge golden, smokies almost black and sooty.

To cook fresh haddock: Any recipe for cod or similar white fish is suitable. Fillets coated with well-herbed breadcrumbs and fried are good. So is haddock in quenelles and soufflés. An old English way is to stuff the haddock with a forcemeat of oysters or mussels or one flavoured with anchovies or anchovy essence and bake it on a bed of mushrooms and a little chopped onion. The liver and roe of fresh haddock have long been used in forcemeats for stuffing baked haddock, for making boiled dumplings and crappit heids (stuffed heads) of haddock which are then boiled in fish stock.

To cook smoked haddock: First skin the fish, finnans as well as smokies. The fisherfolk's simplest way is to steam the finnan, covered, with a nut of butter for five minutes, then add a cupful of milk slightly thickened with cornflour. It is ready when it comes to the boil and cooks a few minutes more. A way that delights Scotsmen and wins praise from sophisticated gourmets is to rub the skinned finnan with butter, grill (broil) it briskly and serve it with pats of unsalted butter. Finnans are also the ideal fish to give character to an English style kedgeree. And finnans fried with thin-sliced smoked pork or ham make a combination 'as perfect as the wedding of bacon and eggs'. Eggs marry happily with finnans too. Haddock Monte Carlo, for instance, is a notable dish. It is a finnan poached in milk and water, garnished with a poached egg on a cooked tomato-and-onion purée and served with a roux-thickened sauce made from equal parts of the fish liquor and cream.

Arbroath smokies, cooked by their long smoking, only need re-heating. The skinned smokies are heated on both sides, opened, filleted, spread inside with butter and fresh-milled pepper and closed – then browned each side briefly under a hot grill.

HAGGAMUGGIE. A Shetland fish haggis made in a washed fish stomach (muggie) tied at each end. The stuffing is fish livers with an equal quantity of fine oatmeal, toasted and seasoned. The haggis is boiled for half an hour and eaten hot with potatoes.

HAGGIS. The chopped, minced or ground innards of an animal cooked with other ingredients. Nowadays it is often simply made in a saucepan (pot haggis). The traditional haggis (most usually of sheep's pluck) is a pudding or sausage – the mixture boiled in the cleaned stomach bag of the animal. It was such a fat sausage that moved Robert Burns in the 18th century to compose his 'Address to a Haggis', declaring it worthy of a long grace and calling it the 'great chieftain of the pudding race'. It has become an essential part of the Scotsman's Burn's Night celebration.

The delights of haggis mixtures, however, were discovered thousands of years ago, possibly almost as soon as man cooked meat and certainly by the time he developed the mixing of flour foods with it.

Around 400 B.C. Aristophanes described the explosion of a 'stuffed sheep's paunch' incautiously attacked at table. There is a Roman recipe in Apicius. English recipes survive from the early 15th century and haggis was a popular dish in England down to the 18th century.

HAG HA'ASIF TZIMMIS. An Israeli harvest festival dish served at Succoth, symbolic of autumn fruits. It is a baked casserole of layers of sliced cooked sweet potatoes, raw apples and parboiled pumpkin, spread with a mixture of marmalade, water and white wine, juice and grated rind of a lemon, and fat.

HAKE. The name of many fish of the cod family, the Gadidae, though sometimes regarded as a separate family. Hake is very easy to fillet. Up to 4 feet long, and slender, it has soft white flesh which can be cooked in any ways suitable for cod. European hake, of the genus *Merluccius*, is an important food fish of the Atlantic and Mediterranean coasts – at its best from June to January. Other species of the genus come from Atlantic and Pacific coasts of North America, from southern South America, New Zealand and South Africa (where it is called stockfish or, in Afrikaans, *stokvis*). The silver hake of northern New England is rated very good eating. The other principal genus, the *Urophycis*, is sometimes called codling. It includes squirrel, gulf, Carolina, southern spotted and white hake – found along North America's eastern and southern coasts.

HALBSTÜCK. See WINE CONTAINERS.

HALB UND HALB. German name for a liqueur of half curaçao and half orange bitters.

HALF-AND-HALF. A drinkers' colloquialism meaning different things in different places. Whisky-and-water 'half-and-half' for instance. More generally, half-and-half is a mixture of beers. In the 18th century it was porter (strong) and ale (comparatively weak). Nowadays it can be mild and bitter ales or old and mild ales. 'Mother-in-law' is a Cockney term for stout and bitter half-and-half.

In the United States, 'half-and-half' denotes a very light cream – a mixture of equal quantities of milk and cream.

HALIBUT. A flat fish that inspired the poet William Cowper to an ode – to the 'immortal memory' of one he dined on in 1784. Its name, like the equivalents in Germany, Scandinavia and the Netherlands, means a holy fish, supposedly because it was so popular on holy days. Since it lies on the sea bed, it has two eyes on the right side of its head – a feat

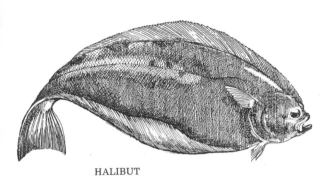

HALIBUT

of evolution which not all flatfish achieve and which some achieve with two on the left. It is the biggest member of the Pleuronectidae family, reportedly having reached 12 feet in length and 500 lb. But the younger fish, called chicken halibut and weighing 2 to 4 lb., have the finest flesh. They are at their best from March to October, whereas the larger fish are best in autumn and winter. Halibut flourish in the cold waters of the North Pacific (where nearly three quarters of the world's commercial catch is taken) and on both sides of the North Atlantic. Sometimes called ellbot and, in France, *flétan*, it is related to plaice and smear dab. The California halibut is different, of the Bothidae family and akin to turbot and brill. Halibut oil, made from the liver, is a good diet supplement to meet deficiencies of vitamins A and D.

HALIOTIS. See ABALONE.

HALLOWE'EN. The eve of All Saints' day, October 31, has its special foods.

A Hallowe'en cake is an iced cake containing little silver charms – thimble, ring, horse-shoe, wish-bone, coin – each with its superstitious significance. The Hallowe'en colours, orange and black, are simulated with orange icing and chocolate decorations or witches, cats, owls and bats. Other Hallowe'en cakes, marzipan-covered, imitate apples and pumpkins.

HALVA. A sweet dish popular from the Balkans to the Pacific and made from ground sesame seed, fruit or vegetables, such as carrots, and papaws. A Pakistani recipe fries semolina in plenty of butter, adds sugar syrup, cardamom seeds, raisins, chopped pistachios and almonds. The mixture is gently heated until it thickens. It is then set in moulds to cool, turned out and sprinkled with ground cinnamon. A similar Greek recipe includes beaten eggs and ground almonds.

HALVA, CARROT. The correct type of carrot for this sweet is a translucent red carrot.

1½ lb. carrots

8 cups (10) milk
good pinch saffron, soaked in milk for 30 minutes
¾ lb. (1½ cups) granulated sugar
sultanas (seedless white grapes)
2–3 oz. (4–6 tablespoons) unsalted butter
silver or gold leaf (optional) (see GOLD LEAF)
blanched almonds or cashew nuts to taste
2 cardamom seeds, crushed

Scrape the carrots and shred them into long thin strips. Bring the milk to the boil in a large saucepan, add the carrots and saffron. Cook this over a low heat until the carrots are thick and soft and all the milk has been absorbed. Stir from time to time; the more one stirs the better. Add the sugar, sultanas and butter. Now stir well and pour this mixture into another hot and dry pan and boil, stirring constantly until the mixture begins to solidify and change to a deep red colour. Turn it out on to a dish and garnish with silver or gold leaf as well as almonds or cashew nuts and crushed cardamom seeds. Carrot halva is served both hot and cold. It reheats easily.

HAM. Like gammon, ham comes from the hindleg of the pig, but it is generally cut off round the bone at the fresh pork stage and cured separately, which ensures its special flavour and delicacy.

In the past, similar cuts of beef, mutton or lamb were cured and cooked in the same manner as ham.

The following are the main types of ham:
AMERICAN HAMS
Kentucky ham: this is taken from Hampshire hogs fattened on wild acorns, beans and clover. Towards the end of their lives they are penned and fed on grain. The hams are dry-salted for about a month, smoked over apple and hickory wood for another month, then matured for 10 to 12 months.

Virginia ham: the true Virginia hams come from razorback pigs fed on peanuts and peaches, and are cured after secret recipes, then smoked over apple and hickory wood fires and left in the smokehouse till the proper flavour has been reached.

A variation of these hams is known in the United States as the Smithfield ham (this name has no connection with Smithfield meat market in London, but belongs to a small town in Virginia). The pigs feed in the woods on acorns and beech and hickory nuts for the first nine months, and after being turned into the peanut fields are fed on corn. The hams are dry-salted and spiced with black pepper, then heavily smoked with hickory, oak and apple wood, and matured for at least a year.

CONTINENTAL HAMS

The best known are: *jambon d'Ardennes*, from Belgium; *jambon de Bayonne* (see BAYONNE HAM); *prosciutto di Parma*, from Parma in Italy; and Westphalia ham from Germany. French *jambons de campagne* are locally cured hams for eating either hot or cold. They tend to be rather coarser than other hams, but often have an interesting flavour derived from treasured family recipes for curing. Prague ham is salted and cured in brine for several months; after which it is smoked with beech wood and kept in a cool cellar to mature until it is marketed. In the opinion of many this is the finest ham of all.

Danish hams: these are a subsidiary product of Danish bacon factories and are shipped green. They are also boned and canned for export.

German hams: apart from the Westphalia ham, the best known is that from Mainz, which may be eaten raw but is sometimes boiled whole and served in thin slices as a cold hors d'oeuvre.

Spanish hams: the most famous is the *jamon serrano*, a raw ham from the Huelva region, where traditionally the hams are left in the snow to mature. It has a very delicate flavour and should be a rosy pink at its best.

ENGLISH HAMS

Bradenham ham: a noble ham, distinguished by its black skin and pinkish flesh within. Produced by a firm in Chippenham, Wiltshire, it has a sweet and mild cure which dates back to the end of the 18th century and must be hung for many months after pickling so that its delicate and characteristic flavour can mature and develop.

Suffolk (Seager) ham: this ham's distinction also depends upon its secret sweet cure and maturity.

Wiltshire ham: in effect a gammon, as it is cured like bacon while still on the side of the pig. It is mild, but lacks the distinctive flavour of a ham cured separately. It does not keep so long as other, separately cured hams.

York ham: a firm and tender ham, famous the world over – indeed the name York is synonymous with all that is best in cooked ham. It is mild, but by no means insipid in flavour and its pink meat is appetizing and delicate.

IRISH HAMS

Irish hams are dry-salt cured and, after being boned, are peat-smoked.

HAMAN'S EARS. Jewish pastries simulating ears, eaten in memory of Haman's defeat by Esther and Mordecai. They are deep-fried in oil and served hot or cold with cinnamon sugar or honey. They are also called *oznei Haman* in Israel and *hojuelos de Haman* by many Sephardic Jews.

HAMAN'S POCKETS. Fried Jewish pastry – rounds with the edges folded over to enclose a poppyseed-and-honey filling.

HAMBURG. German city that has given its name to a variety of foods and drinks, some quite unassociated with it geographically or gastronomically. Hamburg meat in some European countries is salted and smoked horse meat. In Sweden, hamburg ribs are lightly smoked and salted ribs of pork. Hamburg brandy is potato or beet spirit coloured and flavoured in an attempt to imitate grape brandy. Hamburg grapes are black table grapes of German origin, suitable for hothouse cultivation. Hamburgs are small domestic fowl which, despite the name, are chiefly breeds of English origin.

HAMBURG BRISKET. One German dish, internationally appreciated, where hamburger is applied in its German sense, is *Hamburger Rindfleisch*. It is spiced beef brisket (sometimes called the shoulder cut in the United States and roughly the *poitrine* of France) in Hamburg style.

HAMBURGER. Also called a burger, this means many things quite unconnected with Hamburg. It is (1) a patty or flat cake made of chopped, minced or ground meat; (2) this patty served in a split roll with various garnishes; (3) the ground meat itself; and by a further extension, (4) any dish of minced meat whether formed into a patty or not.

The patty was originally fried or grilled (broiled). In its simplest form it is finely ground lean raw beef, formed into flat cakes. It resembles the long-standing English patty called, probably with slightly more accuracy geographically, a Vienna steak. The meat, which should be from the better cuts, can be moistened with tomato juice or a relish or bound with beaten egg. Finely chopped onion is often mixed in and indeed recipe variations, regional and personal, are almost infinite. Because of its variations and the ambiguity in the name itself, hamburgers made with beef tend more and more to be called beefburgers.

Garnishes for the hamburger in the roll or bun can be a slice of tomato or onion, ketchup or other relish, or indeed anything the roll can accommodate.

In many places any kind of finely chopped, ground meat is called hamburger – mutton, lamb, ham, pork, poultry or game beside beef. Indeed

HAMAN'S POCKETS

HAMPER

meat-loaf and fricandel recipes are also so called.

In the extension of the meaning of hamburger to other dishes of minces, one of the more logical makes it almost synonymous with meat ball. In this form, sometimes lightly fried and sometimes not, it is simmered in soup or sauce. The *albondigas* (which see) of Mexico, for example, are often called Mexican burgers. Casserole burgers are hamburger patties between layers of sliced potatoes and sliced onions in a casserole, all covered with soup and baked. But hamburger turnovers are simply minced or ground meat in a pastry turnover, and hamburger pies can be any sort of mince with any other ingredients. A burger chop suey can include cooked rice or pasta with almost anything else simmered with the mince. Closer to the original patty idea is the cheeseburger. It can be hamburgers fitted around a slice of cheese; egg-and-crumbed and deep-fried or shallow-fried hamburgers with a slice of cheese placed on top after the first side has browned; hamburgers with grated cheese mixed with the mince; or baked hamburgers split to take a slice of cheese for the last few minutes of baking.

HAMIM. A rich *cholent* or Jewish stew of boiling fowl, rice, pulses, other vegetables and spices. *Cholents* are cooked on Friday night to avoid the work of preparation on the Sabbath.

HAMINDAS. Eggs cooked 12 hours or more as a hot dish for the Jewish Sabbath. Sometimes they cook in the pan juices of an overnight stew. More typically they are casseroled in an oven on the lowest possible heat. The water in the covered casserole has added to it a little oil, pepper and an onion complete with its skin. The eggs emerge brown all through and delicately flavoured.

HAM OF BEEF. Also ham of mutton. Here ham is used anatomically – the thigh and the buttock, the rump or hindquarter. But like pig's ham (which see) these cuts are dry-cured in salt, sugar, saltpetre, and ground spices for about three weeks. They are also sometimes smoked – usually over peat, wood, sawdust or aromatic shrubs.

HAMPER. Our picnic basket derives its name from the hanaper, the wickerwork case which in ancient times protected drinking goblets.

HAND. 1. The foreleg, sometimes called shoulder of pork (which see), or the foreleg or forefoot of other animals. 2. Hand also means a cluster of bananas.

HANDKÄSE. German small cheeses originally made at home and shaped by hand. In Hesse they have *Handkäse mit Musik*, the 'music' being an accompaniment of finely-chopped onions in oil, vinegar, pepper and salt, which usually makes itself heard a few hours after the cheese has been consumed.

HANGING. To tenderize them and increase their flavour meat, poultry and game should be hung in a cool, dry, well-ventilated place. To avoid spoiling, the period of hanging should be carefully judged. It will be shorter in hot humid weather than in cold. Age and type of animal also count. Older birds, for instance, need to hang longer than young ones. Much meat nowadays does not hang long enough – unless it is slaughtered locally, when it usually hangs properly before it is offered in the shop. So, if the conditions are right, hanging butcher's meat, for 2–3 days at least, can pay dividends. Home-killed animals not cooked immediately after slaughter must be hung if they are not to be tough and insipid. Farmyard chickens and ducks and domesticated guinea fowl are hung, head down and undrawn, for two to four days; geese, five to seven days; and turkeys, three to seven days. Game birds are hung by the neck, unplucked and undrawn. For most tastes they are mature enough when tail or breast feathers pull out easily. Partridge and pheasant are usually well hung. Wild duck, widgeon and other water fowl are best hung for a few days only. Birds like snipe and woodcock, which are to be cooked with their entrails inside, should also hang only a few days. Game animals are hung in their pelts by their feet. Large animals like elk (moose), red deer and

PEPPERS: casserole of duck with green peppers.

reindeer can hang two to three weeks in cool weather; roe deer, four to five days; and hare and rabbit; two to six days.

HARD, HARSH. See WINE TERMS.

HARD SAUCE. See SAUCES.

HARD TACK. Sailor's name for ship's biscuit (also called hard crackers or pilot's crackers in the United States), now principally used for thickening hunters' and fishermen's stews.

HARE. A small wild animal with a rich, gamey flesh. It makes the best eating when young (when the 'harelip' is only faintly noticeable). It should hang, unpaunched, for six days if possible. Hang it, head downwards, with a bowl to catch the blood, which will be used in the cooking. A young hare needs no marinating but older hares, over one year old, need to marinate for at least a day. Young hares are good roasted or jugged, while older ones are best made into brawn, terrines, soup and forcemeat balls to garnish the soup.

HARICOT BEANS. See BEANS.

HARICOT OF MUTTON. A stew of turnips, potatoes and onions with mutton but no haricot beans. Some Frenchmen argue it is more correctly called *halicot* from *halicoter*, to chop.

HARLEQUIN. Name given to various dishes in which, theoretically at least, harlequin colours are produced. The Austrians have Harlequin Roast – a beef joint with strips of carrot, bacon or ham and pickled cucumber pushed through it to show, like mosaic pieces, when the roast is sliced. They also have Harlequin Cream, a brandy cream sauce with chopped angelica, candied peel, candied cherries and candied pineapple in it. South African Harlequin Sweet Potatoes are mashed sweet potatoes moistened with red wine, covered with pink and white marshmallows and briefly roasted; and Australians casserole lamb with carrots, peaches, peas and olives and call it Harlequin Lamb.

HAROSET. A Jewish mixed-fruit paste for Passover. Only its religious symbolism is constant, the recipes varying almost infinitely. It is usually uncooked, and it can include puréed dates, dried figs and raisins, all sorts of fresh fruits, citrus juices and grated rinds, egg yolks and spices. A Kosher red wine, usually dry, is in most recipes. It can be a rich pudding garnished with chopped nuts, or an hors d'oeuvre if the sweeter ingredients are minimized. Matzo meal can be added to make it easier to shape into balls or to use as a spread.

HARTSHORN RINGS. Norwegian cakes leavened with hartshorn salt (which see), especially associated with Christmas. They are deep-fried until golden brown. Their Norwegian name is *hjortetakk*.

HARTSHORN SALT. An ammonia salt or carbonate used as a raising agent.

HARZÉ. A semi-cooked cheese of Port Salut type made at Harzé, Belgium.

HARZKÄSE. A small soft German sour-milk cheese, hand-made in the Harz mountains.

HASH. Diced meat or fish, usually pre-cooked and reheated in a flavourful sauce, often served in a border of mashed potatoes, the hash covered with breadcrumbs and quickly browned under the grill. In France, where it is called *hachis*, it appears in a great variety of dressings and garnishes.

HASLET. Also spelled harslet. A countryman's favourite in which any or all of the heart, liver, lights and sweetbreads of a pig are used. It can be fried, stewed or casseroled. Or, ground with bacon, sage and onion, it can be sewn up in a caul to make faggots which roast hanging before the fire, or are baked in a hot oven for about 45 minutes.

HATTED KIT. Curds made by the Scots by adding to a quart of buttermilk a pint of warm milk, ideally milked straight from the cow into the bowl (the kit). The whey is drained off as the hat (the curds) forms. The curds are strained through a hair sieve, moulded and chilled. They are sprinkled with cinnamon or nutmeg and sugar and served with fruit or cream.

HAUNCH. Hindquarters of quadrupeds, especially game and particularly deer and wild boar, but also of mutton and beef.

HAUT-BAGES, CH. See BORDEAUX WINES.

HAUT-BRION, CH. See BORDEAUX WINES.

HAUT-BRION, CH. LA MISSION. See BORDEAUX WINES.

HAUTVILLIERS. A village overlooking Epernay in Champagne, France. Here rest the remains of Dom Pérignon, a 17th-century Benedictine monk and cellarer at the local abbey, who brought drastic changes to the methods of wine-making and bottling. Because of these improvements he is generally considered the father of sparkling champagne. At Hautvilliers an annual wine festival celebrates his achievements.

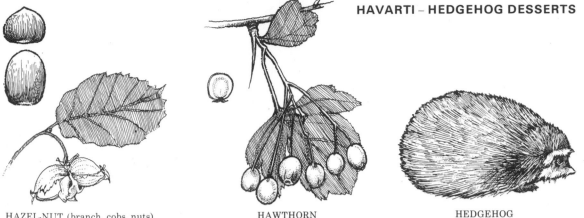

HAZEL-NUT (branch, cobs, nuts)   HAWTHORN   HEDGEHOG

HAVARTI. A mild Danish cheese, formerly called Danish Tilsit, which gets sharper as it matures.

HAVERCAKE. A Yorkshire type of oatcake. 'Haver' means oats; a haversack was originally a bag used to carry oats.

HAWAIIAN DUCK. 1. A way of roasting jointed duck in orange sauce with pineapple pieces. 2. A table duck (*Anas wyvilliana*) popular in Hawaii.

HAWICK BAKE. Scottish biscuit (cookie) flavoured with allspice.

HAWTHORN. The haws or berries of the hawthorn are used for jams and jellies. In England wine is made from the flowers and the haws.

HAY-BOX COOKERY. A once fashionable way of keeping pots of food hot for hours once they have been brought to the boil. They are embedded in an insulated box containing a material, originally hay, which is a bad conductor of heat.

HAZEL-HEN. A game bird from the mountain forests of Europe (north of the Alps, but not present in Britain) and northern Asia. It is also called hazel-grouse and, in French, *gelinotte*. It is esteemed wherever it is available – a plump-breasted bird (about partridge size) of tender white flesh and a subtle gamey flavour, sometimes of pine.

HAZEL-NUT. A nut which grows all over Europe and is cultivated commercially, particularly in southern Europe. Britain imports the filbert and cob varieties. Used as a dessert and in cake and biscuit cookery.

HEAD CHEESE. A brawn. In England it is usually prepared with pig's or calf's head. In Scotland it is called jellied head and in France there is the comparable *hure de porc* or *hure de sanglier* (boar's head). The French and Dutch words for cheese are also used of brawn: *fromage de tête de porc* and *hoofdkaas*.

HEART. Hearts of ox, calf, sheep and pig make flavoursome dishes in their own right (see also OFFAL). They also combine well in forcemeats and soups. The Hungarians, for instance, make a rich soup of calf's heart, lung and rice, thickened with sour cream.

HEARTH CAKES. English term for French round cakes, regionally specialized. Originally they were of unleavened dough and baked in embers on the hearth.

HEARTSEASE. A wild violet used in syrups, conserves and pastes.

HEATHCOCK. The male of the black grouse, also called, in Devon, heathpoult.

HEATHER ALE. A fermented liquor which apparently had its origin with the Picts and is still made in the islands and highlands of Scotland, from full-blooming heather boiled for an hour in water. Nowadays the strained water is reboiled with ground ginger, hops and golden syrup and then fermented with brewers' yeast. It is ready to drink in three days.

HEAVEN AND EARTH. A German and South African name for a mixture of equal quantities of cooking apples and potatoes boiled together, flavoured with salt, pepper and diced fried bacon.

HEAVENLY BREAD. See MANNA.

HEDGEHOG. Spiny little European quadruped named from its habitat (hedgerows) and the shape of its snout. Fat and succulent in the autumn, its flavour is variously likened to roast chicken and sucking pig. It is a favoured gipsy dish, spit-roasted or baked in clay. For hotchi, the clay bake, the animal is encased, spines and all, in clay and cooked on hot embers. Then the clay is removed, taking with it the skin and spines.

HEDGEHOG DESSERTS. Cakes or puddings

made (or cut) to the shape of a hedgehog, usually coated with icing or glaze into which split almonds or bits of angelica or other make-believe 'spines' are stuck.

HEDGE MUSTARD. A South African wild plant eaten as a green vegetable.

HEIGHT. The thinner air at altitudes above about 2,000 feet above sea level requires adjustments in cooking times and temperatures and often in the amounts in recipes used at lower altitudes. Water boils at nearly 10° F. lower at 5,000 feet than at sea level and the different stages in sugar cookery are reached about 10° F. lower. Even inside pressure cookers altitude materially affects temperatures for any given pressure-gauge reading. Similarly in baking the influence of altitude may demand a considerably hotter oven and variations in amounts of leaveners, water, flour or eggs.

HÉLÈNE. *Coupe Hélène, poire Hélène* or *belle Hélène*. Ice-cream and hot chocolate sauce with pears (which see).

HELZEL. A Jewish dish of the stuffed skin of the neck of chicken, turkey, goose or duck roasted in the pan juices beside the bird. The stuffing can be rich or simple – ground meat, chopped nuts, spices, chopped hard-boiled eggs, or merely matzo meal and soy flour with chopped onion and generous seasoning.

HEN. Female of domestic fowl and many other birds, also of crab and lobster. A grey hen is a stone liquor bottle. Hen and chickens is an old term for large and small pewter drinking pots.

HENWARE. See HONEYWARE.

HERB BEER. A fermented drink usually including hedge and field plants – young nettle heads, for instance – in addition to the recognized herbs.

HERB OF GRACE. Another name for rue, symbol of repentance. See RUE.

HERB PATIENCE. See SORREL.

HERBS. The history of herbs stretches far back into time, a history as soothing and pleasing as the plants themselves. There is mention of herbs in records of the ancient Egyptians who used to put bunches of them in the hands of mummies. Persians planted them with loving care in their gardens where things pleasing to nose, eye and taste were grown.

The Greeks too grew wondrous herbs and even

today they cannot enjoy a meal without the flavour of fresh herbs. The early temples of healing taught the value of herbs in medicine. Hippocrates, the 'Father of Medicine', had a list of 400 different herbs in regular use, at least half of which are still employed today. Herbs such as mint and anise are mentioned in the Bible, though there is some doubt whether these were the same as the modern herbs of those names.

The Hebrews obtained precious oils and herb plants from the East. Coriander is said by many to have been the manna of biblical days.

Herbs are basically plants – though some fruits from trees are also classed as herbs. Usually herbal plants are soft and juicy.

Herbs are still much used today for healing, especially in the East. In the West the use of herbs has tended to diminish as botany has become more of a science and the knowledge and control of medicine has spread.

Naturally with such an ancient history there are many legends, some charming, others lurid. For example, the curiously-named mandrake, with its distorted roots, was cultivated for its sedative properties and there was a story that whoever pulled it from the ground would collapse. Dogs were, therefore, set to do this job – and one reads that they died.

Tansy comes from the Greek, *athanasia*, meaning immortality. Sesame signifies immortality to the Brahmins; thyme was believed to be a source of courage. Coriander was used by the Arabs in love potions; the carrot, by the Greeks.

Mandragora, so one reads in the Old Testament, was useful in cases of sterility. Indian peasants wore sprigs of basil to enlist sympathy when visiting relatives or unsympathetic landlords. Chervil, said Pliny, was invaluable against hiccups. The Romans and the Greeks wore parsley to absorb the fumes of alcohol and, in more recent times, American colonists chewed dill to keep them awake during boring church sermons.

Herbs are undoubtedly rich in vitamins and the ancients also believed they were more valuable when picked under certain signs of the planets. Much of their curative reputation has been sadly discredited, but even today it is well known that many of them have an excellent effect on over-worked digestive systems and ease jaded nerves.

The early herbalists certainly knew a great deal about smells. *The Great Herbal*, published in 1526, advises: 'Against weyknesse of the brayne smel to Musk', and states that 'basil taketh away melancholy and maketh men merry and glad'.

Indeed, glancing through old records, it would seem that men were perpetually wilting with melancholy. But how much nicer to pluck a sprig of basil than to swallow a tranquillizing pill.

HICKORY (twig, nut in shell, shelled)

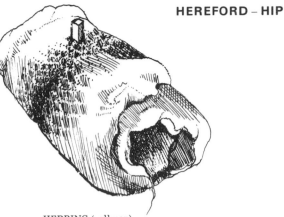

HERRING (rollmop)

HEREFORD. An English breed of white-faced, red-bodied beef cattle. Herefords have been introduced into many cattle-raising areas of the world.

HERKIMER CHEESE. Smooth, well-matured, Cheddar-type cheese named after the New York county where it began.

HER MAJESTY'S PUDDING. A rich custard – 1 pint (1¼) milk, ½ pint (⅔) cream and 8 egg yolks baked together in a mould and served with fruit compôtes or syrups. It was popular in Queen Victoria's reign and – who knows? – Her Majesty may well have enjoyed it.

HERMITAGE. See RHÔNE WINES.

HERMIT CRAB. See CRAB.

HERMITS. American nut-and-raisin cookies, variously flavoured, baked on a sheet in teaspoonful-size drops or in long narrow strips which are sliced when cooked.

HERRGÅRD. The word is Swedish, meaning manor. In culinary matters it is applied to foods in farmhouse or country-house style. *Herrgårdsost* is perhaps the most highly esteemed cheese in Sweden. The half-cream version tastes something like Gouda. The full-cream *Herrgård Elite* resembles a hard Emmental. *Herrgårdsstek* is a Swedish pot roast. A joint – usually of beef, but also of veal, elk or horse meat – is braised with onions, spices and vinegar. If anchovy fillets are added the dish is promoted from manor to palace and called *slottsstek*.

HERRING. A flavourful and highly nutritious fish abundant in the North Atlantic and the Baltic, with related species in the North Pacific. At their best from June to December, Members of the family include the alewife (which see), thread herring and California herring. Fresh herring have been an important food fish since prehistoric times and they have been salted and smoked for hundreds of years. Red herring, strongly salted and darkly smoked, gets its figurative significance from the fact that, dragged across a fox's trail, it destroys the scent and confuses the hounds.

Herrings are preserved as kippers, bloaters, salt herrings, rollmops and Bismarck herring (which see).

Cold herrings, pickled raw or smoked or cooked and cooled, are popular hors d'oeuvre, often served with chopped carrot, celery, olives and onion. Herring, fresh or smoked, are indeed most versatile. They are poached, stewed, stuffed and baked, made into pies, pancake fillings, spreads for sandwiches or canapés. The roes are good too, cooked with the fish or made into separate savouries.

HERVE. Soft Belgian rennet cheeses of Limburger type, often incorporating herbs and ripened in beer-soaked cloths.

HET PINT. A festive drink in Scotland of heated sweetened ale with grated nutmeg, beaten eggs and whisky. A typical recipe is 4 pints (5) ale, 3 eggs and ½ pint (1¼ cups) whisky. It is mixed by pouring from one jug to another.

HICKORY NUT. American nut of which the pecan is a type. Similar to walnut and like it used in cakes, cookies and, when puréed, in puddings.

HIGHBALL. A long drink of diluted spirits. Usually it is whiskey and ice in a tumbler, filled up with soda water. But there are as well, brandy, gin, vodka and rum highballs. The dilutant can be plain water or any aerated water. A cider highball – whiskey and ice topped up with cider – is called a stone wall. The name of highball has also been given to various cocktails.

HILSA. Also spelled hilsah. An Indian food fish allied to the shad (which see) and sometimes called Indian salmon.

HIP. The fruit of the rose, particularly the wild rose or dog rose (*Rosa canina*). Fully ripe and red hips make an agreeable preserve or a syrup for drinking or for pudding sauces. They are also rich in vitamin C.

HIPPOCRAS. A sort of medieval vermouth, also called Ypocras and Ipocras. These names were medieval forms of Hippocrates. Hippocrates' sleeve was a flannel used by vintners and chemists to strain liquids; hence Hippocras, the drink thus strained. It was a sweetened and aromatized wine – one of the most popular from the Middle Ages on at least into the 18th century. The wine, probably wine that was souring, was mixed with honey, herbs and spices. Its relationship with vermouth is implicit in the 1577 description of 'sundrie sorts of artificial stuff as ypocras and wormewood wine.' Some versions gained the reputation of having tremendous aphrodisiac power. In Holland, newly married couples are sent to bed with a bottle of white Hippocras for the bride and a bottle of red for the groom.

HOCHEPOT. One of the best ways of cooking oxtail – with flamed brandy, wine and stock.

HOCK. 1. Originally an English name for German white wine but now more generally applied. It began as hochamore, from Hochheim on the Main. It was much liked by Queen Victoria and thus was fashionable.
2. Hock of animals. Hock and hough are pronounced in the same way (hok) and mean the same thing, the leg portion between knee and fetlock. Strictly the words apply to the hindleg, but culinary usage has widened that. The hock of veal is the shin of the hindleg. But the hock or shin of beef is of the foreleg – a much underrated cut which makes good stews and brawns. In pork, bacon and gammon the hock is part of the pig's foreleg and is sometimes called forehock.

HOCK AND DOUGH. A traditional Northamptonshire farmhouse dish made with a fresh pork hock. A roll of suet paste (stuffed with minced or ground beef and sage) lines the sides of a roasting pan. The hock goes in the middle, surrounded by sliced potatoes and onions, with a little stock. It is baked in a hot oven (425° F., mark 7) for about an hour.

HOCKTIDE. The second Monday and Tuesday after Easter, celebrated in the English county of Berkshire with a traditional supper: Welsh rarebit and macaroni with watercress salad and plenty of punch to drink. See RAREBIT.

HODGE-PODGE. See HOTCH-POTCH.

HODGILS. Scottish dumplings for soups and stews.

They are made of seasoned oatmeal with chopped chives, bound with broth-top beef fat and boiled for 20 minutes.

HOGFISH. Name given to two fish. The Mediterranean one, with flesh so tough it is used only in *bouillabaisse* and other fish soups, is called also scorpion, toad and sea devil because of its ugly spiny head. The other one, a large West Indian and Floridian fish, is good eating.

HOGGAN. A Cornish variant of the classic Cornish pasty (which see) but without potato and closed at the top instead of the side.

HOGGET. A young sheep, usually a yearling.

HOGMANAY. Scots festival of New Year celebrated gastronomically with black bun (see BUN), shortbread and Athole Brose (which see).

HOGSHEAD. See WINE CONTAINERS.

HOLANDA. An Argentine cheese in Dutch style.

HOLLANDAISE, SAUCE. See SAUCES.

HOLLANDS. See GIN.

HOLLY. Merely decorative in England, holly berries are used in Corsica and elsewhere roasted and ground to make a drink somewhat like coffee. In Alsace they are fermented and distilled to make Houx, one of the most expensive spirits in the world. The young shoots of knee holly or butchers' broom are eaten on the continent of Europe, cooked like asparagus.

HOLSTEINER. A German, cooked, skimmed-milk cheese.

HOLYROOD PUDDING. An Edinburgh pudding of semolina, milk, butter, sugar and ratafia biscuits boiled together for five minutes. When it cools slightly, beaten egg yolks and a little marmalade are blended into the mixture. Stiffly whisked egg whites are folded in and the pudding is steamed in a buttered mould for about an hour. Turned out of the mould, it is usually served with an almond sauce.

HOMINY. Maize (corn in the United States) which has had the hull and germ removed and been ground to various degrees of coarseness rather as oats are in Scotland. Hominy grits are a coarse meal. Hominy is used in much the same way as rice for sweet puddings or as an accompaniment to savoury foods. It makes a breakfast cereal, cakes

HONEY (in comb)

HOPS

and muffins. Boiled, cooled and sliced, it can be fried as the Italians fry polenta.

HOMOGENIZING. A treatment of milk which breaks up the fat globules and keeps them in suspension so that they do not rise to the top as cream.

HONEY. Natural liquid sugar. The bees convert most of the sucrose of the flower nectar to invert sugar (dextrose and laevulose), which represents about 80 per cent of the weight of the honey. It is thus an easily assimilated source of energy. Until the development of cane sugar, honey was the cook's chief sweetener, highly appreciated. The honey mentioned in the Bible, however, was not always true honey. Often it was probably date juice boiled and reboiled until it was dark golden brown like maple molasses. Besides being used as a spread and a sauce, honey can replace sugar in many recipes. Honeys take their flavours from the flowers predominant in their production. There is thus a range of flavours to explore: wild rose honey from Greece, lavender honey from France, linden honey from Czechoslovakia, orange-blossom honey from California and gum or eucalyptus tree honey from Australia.

HONEY AGARIC. An edible fungus used like mushrooms.

HONEYDEW MELON. See MELON.

HONEYWARE. An edible seaweed (*Alaria esculenta*) gathered in Scotland and the Faroes. It is also called henware and badderlocks. The latter name is said to have derived from 'Balder's Locks', an allusion to the tragic Norse god.

HONGROISE. In French culinary terms, *à la hongroise* signifies dishes in Hungarian style, usually in a paprika-flavoured cream sauce.

HOOSIER. Indiana is the Hoosier State and hoosier fried chicken is a way of browning chicken

pieces in hot fat, then lowering the heat and simmering them, covered, for about 20 minutes. They are then given a final 10 minutes, uncovered, on raised heat to re-crisp them.

HOP. A climbing vine. In spring the tender shoots are a favoured vegetable, particularly in Belgium. Cooked like asparagus, they go well with poached eggs and in omelettes. The flowers of the female plant, when ripe, are used to make beer bitter.

HOPPIN' JOHN. The traditional dish of peas-and-rice of the Bahamas, also made in southern areas of the United States. The Bahamian way is to cook everything together, while some American recipes cook peas, rice and tomatoes separately.

HOREHOUND. A fragrant weed, common in Britain, used like a herb in salads and sauces and, in country cooking, to flavour toffees.

HORS D'OEUVRE. Easy-to-take foods, hot or cold, served before a meal or before the main part of the meal. They can be of any and every kind but ideally they are light and tempting – stimulating the palate without clogging it or dulling the appetite. They can be of fish, flesh, eggs, fruit, vegetable; simple or elaborate. They separate roughly into two main types – single or mixed. Single hors d'oeuvre include caviar, oysters, smoked salmon, shrimps, raw or soused herring, *pâtés, bouchées,* kebabs, smoked beef or chicken, hard-boiled eggs of various kinds, artichokes, melon and grapefruit. Mixed hors d'oeuvre are often smaller – bite-size or easily handled with a fork – whether served at table or buffet style. They include olives, gherkins, potato crisps (chips), canapés, small puffs of choux pastry stuffed with savoury mixes, sardines and anchovies, small meat balls, cocktail sausages, sliced salami and other sausages, smoked ham, croquettes, Russian and potato salads, asparagus tips, other chopped vegetables variously dressed, cooked peas and beans, and sometimes dressed rice or macaroni. See SMÖRGÅSBORD, ZAKUSKI and page 161.

HORSE. A very good meat in the opinion of peoples of many Continental and Latin American countries. It is judged by the same standards, cut in the same joints and cooked by the same methods as beef. Retail horse butchers in Britain are few and the meat goes largely to pet foods.

One recently suggested explanation of the deep-rooted English aversion to horse meat is that in pagan times the Anglo-Saxons ate it only once a year, at a fertility festival. When the Anglo-Saxons were evangelized, the Church was unable to assimilate this celebration into the Christian calendar (as it did with the Yule feast, for example) and simply prohibited the festival and the eating of horse meat associated with it. So sternly was the ban enforced that it became a taboo, exerting a profound psychological influence long after the original reason for it had been forgotten and later generations of Englishmen had grown accustomed to rationalizing it in terms of their feelings for 'man's best friend'.

The logic of its acceptance is that apart from its slightly yellower fat it is very much like beef in appearance and, age for age, as amenable to culinary skill and inspiration. Young horse, thoroughbred or cart-puller, killed in or after accidents, commands luxury prices on the Continent. Salted and smoked horse is also called Hamburg meat.

HORSE MACKEREL. Name given to several large fish, not all mackerel, including tuna (tunny), scad and tropical cavally. Some, like Maine tuna, are declared to taste more like pork than fish. The young of two European types of horse mackerel are canned as a substitute for sardines.

HORSE MUSHROOM. A coarse but edible mushroom with a hollow stem.

HORSE-RADISH. A free-growing plant whose thick taproot is grated or ground to be used as a condiment in sauces, vinegar dips and spreads. See SAUCES.

HORSE'S HEAD. English name for a food fish of Asian waters, from India to Japan, salted in large quantities by the Chinese.

HORSESHOE CRAB. See CRAB.

HORSE'S NECK. A long drink. Drape a long spiral of lemon rind over the rim of a tumbler and anchor with two lumps of ice. Add a generous measure of brandy and fill up with ginger ale.

HOSPICES DE BEAUNE. See BURGUNDY WINES.

HOT. See WINE TERMS.

HOTCHI. See HEDGEHOG.

HOT-CROSS BUN. See BUN.

HOTCH-POTCH. Sometimes called hodge-podge. In contrast to hot pot (which see), this is a soup or broth, though it has so much in it that it resembles a stew. Thackeray called *bouillabaisse* a hotch-potch and many an Irish stew could be so called too. Like the Arab *shorbah* it can be a meal in itself merely with bread. In Scotland, when it is made with meat and not simply with bones, the meat is sometimes taken out and kept hot in the oven to be served as a second course with mashed potatoes and greens. The Scots rate it highly as a traditional dish. They also call it hairst bree (harvest broth).

HOT DOG. A hot frankfurter (which see) eaten in a buttered roll with mustard or other relish and chopped fried onions or other garnish. The Americans, having extended the meaning of frankfurter, have invented many names for the hot dog.

HOT POT. Hot pot differs from hotch-potch (which see) in that it begins with much less water or stock and ends its cooking with little free liquid. Hotch-potch, by contrast, is a broth. The meat (or fish) of a hot pot is essential to its character. The hot pot ingredients are cooked in layers, with the top layer of sliced potatoes being oven-browned before cooking is complete.

There are many hot pot recipes, varying individually and regionally. Some use beef or other meats or fish. To the basic recipes can be added all or any of such things as oysters, mussels, mushrooms, green olives, celery, chopped kidneys and diced bacon besides relishes, herbs and spices.

HOT SLAW. Cold-weather cousin to coleslaw. Shredded cabbage heated in spicy white sauce.

HOT-WATER CRUST. See PASTRY.

HOUGH. See HOCK (2).

HOWTOWDIE. Scots for pullet, possibly related to the old French *hutaudeau*. 'Stoved howtowdie with drappig eggs' is a stuffed chicken pot-roasted with button onions, herbs and spices. Eggs are poached in gravy or broth and placed around the bird on the carving dish, each on a pat of spinach.

HRAMSA. A full-fat soft Scottish cheese flavoured with wild garlic. Hramsa is an old spelling of rams or ramson (wild garlic).

HORSE-RADISH

HUBBARD SQUASH. See SQUASH.

HUCKLEBERRY. See BILBERRY.

HUFFKINS. Buns made of bread dough with a little extra lard in it. Eaten hot from the oven with plenty of butter, they are farmhouse favourites, particularly in Kent, England.

HULL. To husk, remove or strip the hull or outer covering in particular from strawberries or corn.

HULLER. A pair of metal tweezers shaped specifically to hull strawberries.

HUMBLE PIE. This began as umble pie – umbles being the heart, liver, kidney and other innards of the deer. The umbles were anciently the servants' portion. So 'to eat humble pie' is a double pun. Umble pies and puddings are still made in hunting country in Britain and are ranked much higher nowadays, gastronomically and socially. A Highland version is called deer haggis.

HUMMING ALE. A strong beer, a stingo. Both humming and stingo are figurative words deriving from the effect – expected, alleged or actual – of the beer on the drinker.

HUMMUS BI TAHINA. A widely known, traditional and much appreciated Arab dish of cooked, puréed chick peas. The chick peas are worked to the consistency of a thick mayonnaise with lemon juice and crushed garlic and flavoured with *tahina* (which see). It is served as a *mezze* or appetizer in Arab countries, eaten with fresh soft Arab bread, which is used as a spoon.

HUNDRED-YEAR-OLD EGGS. Also called thousand-year-old eggs and Ming Dynasty eggs. All three names are exaggerations, since the eggs are some months old at the most. They are duck eggs, preserved by the Chinese in a casing of ashes, tea, lime and salt and rolled in dry rice husks and buried for the required time. When the eggs are

ready, the casing is broken off and they are shelled. The yolks have turned an orange yellow-green colour, the whites solidified like a dark green jelly or piece of semi-precious stone. They can be served as appetizers, impaled on a cocktail stick and with a thin slice of fresh ginger.

HUNGARIAN WINES. Hungary produces about 120 million gallons of wine a year, but its viticulture is more noted for the high quality of some of its wines. Wine is made in nearly all parts of the country; traditionally in the hills that surround the plain, the growing of wines on the barren plain east of the Danube being a more recent development.

The climate and soil are ideal for viticulture. Generally there is plenty of sunshine, and the prolonged fine autumn weather is conducive to the making of Hungary's best wines which depend on late harvesting. In some areas, local geographical conditions assist. Along the northern shores of Balaton, the vast inland lake, the hillsides receive the benefit of reflected heat and moisture rising from the water.

Nearly two-thirds of the production is white wine, and it is among the whites that the finest examples are found. Their qualities and character, although based on the particular grape varieties planted, are much affected by variations of soil, situation and amount of rainfall. The western hills get more than twice the amount of rain of the sandy eastern plain. Some of the vines with the greatest breeding are planted on volcanic soil and sand.

The best wines include those made on the shores of the Balaton lake, mainly from an Italian variety of Riesling grapes, which thrive in this particular type of soil and situation. Other varieties of grape used here are the *kéknyelü* (blue-stalk), the *szürkebarat* (grey friar) which is the French *pinot gris* acclimatized, and a few others. Individually and mixed they produce fresh, fruity, elegant and fragrant white wines of varying dryness. Examples are: Balatoni Riesling, Balatoni Furmint, Badacsonyi Kéknyelü.

Similar grape varieties and a few more, such as

Rhine Riesling, *Traminer* and *ezerjo* (literally 'a thousand times good') produce the excellent white wines of the small vineyard area of the Somló Hill, which at times were preferred even to Tokaj. The wine of Somló develops its full character of bouquet aroma by ageing and takes four to five years to reach its peak. At Mor, wine has only been made since the 17th century, but the wine made of the indigenous *mori ezerjo* is very pleasant, dry and delicate.

Near the Austrian border, near the town of Sopron, both white and red wines, have been made since Roman times, the latter from a grape variety called the *kékfrankos*. This can be dark red, or light red, almost *rosé*, depending on the vinification. In the south-west around Szekszard another red wine, rather sweetish, is made of the *kadarka* grape, while near Villány a bright red, full wine is produced.

The famous 'Bull's Blood' of Eger (*Egri Bikaver*) is made of *kadarka* and other vines imported from France. It is a deep red, full, serious wine with a fragrance of its own which develops by slow, long maturing. Near Debrö, another Hungarian vine, the *hárslevelü* (lime-leaf) makes a semi-sweet, aromatic white wine. On the sandy soil of the great plain, large quantities of pleasant, everyday drinking wines, mainly white, are made.

The greatest glory of Hungarian wine-making is the famous product of the 25 villages of the Tokaj district. This great wine is made of a blend of three grapes: *furmint*, *hárslevelü* and *muskotaly*. The superb flavour is due to very late harvesting after a hot, sunny autumn, when the grapes have shrivelled and the juice becomes concentrated in sugar and flavour, through the action of the 'noble rot' (which see).

The shrivelled grapes are known as *aszu* berries, and when they are picked out separately and added to the must of the rest, the renowned Tokaji Aszu is the result, luscious, sweet and long ago dubbed 'the wine of kings and the king of wines'. The *aszu* berries are added to the must in special hods called *puttony*, and it is the number of hods added to each barrel of must that determines the quality, thus there are three, four or five *puttonyos aszu* made. This wine is naturally expensive to make, but it has tremendous longevity.

The other kind of Tokaj wine is called Szamorodni. In this case the *aszu* berries are not separated from the rest, the bunches are used as they come. Fermentation, as with the *aszu* is very slow. The sweetness or dryness of this wine varies, depending on the proportion of shrivelled berries included; when there are few, the wine is Szamorodni dry, a delicious, fruity fragrant wine suitable for an aperitif; when they are numerous, a sweet wine results, second in quality only to Tokaji Aszu.

Tokaj Essence, the rarest of all, is made from the juice that trickles out of the *aszu* grapes, while they are kept during the harvest, waiting to be used.

One *puttony* (about 7½ gallons) of *aszu* berries may yield about three pints of essence, so its scarcity can be understood.

HUNTINGDON FIDGETT. A pie which is made of layers of sliced cooking apples, onions and diced bacon, covered with a short crust.

HURE. Culinary French for head (of boar or pig) and for jowl of salmon.

HUSBANDS. A Gloucestershire name for gingerbread men. Traditionally they are gilded.

HUSHÅLLSOST. Literally household cheese, from Sweden. Of varying fat content, it is mild, slightly sour and eaten quite young, at 1–2 months old.

HUSH PUPPIES. Fried cornmeal puffs from the southern United States normally of a batter incorporating chopped onion, to serve with fried fish. Also served with meats or salads and, leaving out the onion, with syrup. The name is said to have come from cooks at southern fish fries who cooked extra bits of batter to hush the dogs hungrily yapping when they smelled the fish.

HUTSPOT. A hot pot (which see) made in Holland from long-simmered beef, carrots, potatoes and onions. Legend associates this Dutch dish with the raising of the Spanish siege of Leyden in 1574.

HYDROMEL. A drink made with honey, water, herbs and spices. Fermented it becomes mead or vinous hydromel, from which spirit is sometimes distilled.

HYSSOP. A mint. Hyssop honey, from hyssop nectar, is highly rated for flavour.

I

ICE-CREAM. A most popular frozen pudding. Iced food and drinks have a long history. Roman emperors made their slaves fetch them ice from the Alps; 'hills candied with snow' Horace called them. Nero had a fondness for snow flavoured with honey and fruit, which probably tasted something like a sorbet. Marco Polo, to whom the culinary world owes so much, brought back from the Far East

HYSSOP

IGUANA

stories of slant-eyed men sitting on embroidered cushions eating dishes of ice flavoured with exotic fruits. The Italians, always quick to adopt something new gastronomically, began to make ice-cream, and the Medicis took their ideas to France. Greece also was famous for ice-cream making, and so was Turkey. The first ice-cream eaten in England was probably about the time of Dr Johnson when raspberries mixed with pure cream were frozen in a pewter bowl of ice.

Iced bombs are made by freezing ice-cream in a bombe mould.

ICE-CREAM FREEZER. A utensil for making ice-cream in the home without refrigeration. The traditional unit consists of a wooden outer container with an inner metal container which holds the ingredients. The metal container is rotated in a mixture of ice and rock salt by a crank and gear arrangement with fixed paddles inserted in the metal container to ensure even freezing and a smooth consistency. Nowadays the freezer is generally motorized, so that little effort is required, but the result is superior to any commercial product because of the ingredients and the technique used.

ICE-CREAM SODA. A beverage made from ice-cream, various flavourings, carbonated water or a soft drink and generally served in a 10-oz. glass. It is eaten with both a long-handled spoon and straws. The mixture is usually given the name of the flavouring, but some elaborate concoctions have been given correspondingly exotic names. The ice-cream soda is a truly American product, and practically every village and town has one or more 'soda fountains'.

ICING. A sugar coating used to decorate cakes and buns. There are five different kinds of icing.

1. Butter icing: a combination of butter and icing (confectioners') sugar used for filling cakes and sponges.

2. Fondant icing: a soft icing of velvety texture used to decorate light cakes.

3. Frosting: the American term for icing which is made with egg white and icing sugar.

4. Glacé icing: this is icing sugar worked to a thick cream with syrup or water and flavoured.

5. Royal icing: a hard white icing used mainly for wedding, birthday and Christmas cakes.

ICING (CONFECTIONERS') SUGAR. See SUGAR.

IGUANA. A large lizard found in the forests, dunes and on the rocky coastlines of South America and the West Indies; there is a similar species in the Fiji Islands and Madagascar. It grows up to five feet in length and, as the flesh is tender and extremely palatable, it is looked upon as a delicacy in South America and other regions.

ILES DE LA GIRONDE. The main vineyards of the islands of the Gironde are the Iles Bouchard, Fumadelle, Margaux, du Nord, Nouvelle (sanspain), Patrias, and Verte.

IMPÉRATRICE, À LA. Puddings, usually of rice, flavoured with vanilla, crystallized fruit previously soaked in kirsch, and whipped cream.

IMPERIALE. A large bottle (claret) containing eight ordinary bottles or six litres, *after* decanting, which means an initial capacity of eight and one half bottles.

IMPÉRIALE, À LA. Dishes garnished with truffles, *foie gras*, kidneys and other similar garnishes.

INDIAN CORN. See MAIZE.

INDIAN FOOD. Cooking in India has its rules and food is governed by more than climate. Hindus believe that food was created by the Supreme Deity for the benefit of man and while they make the art of cooking a sacred rite attended by some ceremony, they also include a few taboos. But there is a tradition of good cooking, with perhaps more for Western tastes in the Punjab and West Bengal.

All Indian cooking is regional and the man from Madras neither knows nor cares what his Punjabi compatriot eats. In the north the cooking has been influenced by neighbouring countries, by foreign invasion, by the Muslims and, as elsewhere, by the weather. It includes pilaus and birianis, tanduri dishes, grills and kebabs.

There is the fiery curry cooking of the south, linked with vegetarianism and the use of coconut, and here the staple food is rice. In the deep south, however, rice is eaten less and tapioca comes into its own, but with coconut prominent still. There is the elegant cooking of Hyderabad, where curries are milder and with a Persian air.

On to Gujarat, where they add a type of solid molasses to their curries, and Maharashtra where mustard seeds and plenty of dried herbs are added and fish is popular. In Bombay are congregated the Parsis with such dishes their ancestors brought with them over 1,000 years ago. Goa, farther south along the coast, has both Portuguese and Christian tradition, using plenty of spices and coconut, but bringing a softer more gentle touch to its curries.

All in all, Indian food is varied above all things, which makes it difficult to say exactly what it is. Generally, though, it is true to say that the best food is found in Indian homes.

INDIAN PUDDING. A slowly baked cornmeal pudding flavoured with molasses, ginger and cinnamon. It is served with ice-cream, is considered as American as maple sugar and popcorn and is one of the best of the real American puddings. It is believed to be of American Indian origin.

INDIENNE, À L'. Dishes flavoured with a curry sauce, and served with rice.

INFERNO. See ITALIAN WINES.

INFUSE. To steep herbs or other flavourings in boiling liquid and leave until the liquid has absorbed this flavour. Milk is often flavoured by infusing vanilla bean, cinnamon stick or lemon or orange rind in it. Wine is flavoured for sauces and other dishes by the infusion of mushroom peelings, truffles or various herbs.

INTERLARD. See LARD, TO.

IRISH MOSS. See CARRAGEEN.

IRISH STEW. The classic stew of Ireland. It is a dish of mutton, potatoes and onions, flavoured simply with salt and pepper and simmered for two or three hours.

IRISH WHISKEY. See WHISKY.

ISINGLASS. Isinglass is the dried bladder of certain fish, especially the sturgeon. It is an extremely refined form of gelatine and has the same uses, but animal gelatine is rapidly replacing isinglass. See also GELATINE.

ISRAELI WINES. Palestine was probably one of the first countries to enjoy wine and the history of Jewish wine is long and fascinating. One is told in the Bible that Canaan flowed not only with milk and honey, but with wine. Wine was easier to obtain than water and was used in all kinds of ways other than for drinking (washing houses and dyeing clothes, for example).

Vines grew everywhere, and production was at its peak at the time of the destruction of the Second Temple at Jerusalem in A.D. 70. After that, wine making was neglected and with the advent of Muslim rule every vine was forcibly pulled up.

Modern wine-making began in 1870 with the foundation of an agricultural school which received a grant from Baron Edmond de Rothschild in 1882. New vineyards were then planted at Richon le Zion. The Israelis are a wine-drinking nation and some 80 per cent of their wine is consumed in the country. Exports are growing, though, and with it a change in the type of wine produced.

Israel produces all types of wine: red, white and *rosé* as well as sparkling wines. Recently the Israelis have paid attention to the production of dessert wines as well as brandy. Wines are drunk young in Israel and they do not follow the same pattern as European vintages. It has been observed that a bad year in Europe might well mean a good one in Israel and *visa-versa*.

ISSAN, CHÂTEAU D'. See BORDEAUX WINES.

ITALIAN FOOD. Many say that Italian food is Mediterranean cooking at its best. It is not complicated cooking; much of it distinctly earthy. Also it is not all cooking with olive oil, although this is an important ingredient. Where the olive tree does not flourish though, milk and butter are used instead of the oil.

The tomato, which the Spaniards introduced into Europe, has been adopted by the Italians to such an extent that it is hard to conceive of an Italian meal without some touch of this 'fruit'.

An important part of the Italian meal is the antipasto or hors d'oeuvre, which varies from region to region as well as from season to season. *Pastas* (which see), of course, are always in season, and figure as a beginning to a meal on most Italian menus.

There is a splendid diversity in the Italians' use of meat and they use all parts of the animal. Tripe, brains, spleen, liver, offal and kidneys all find

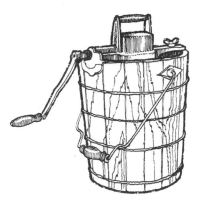

ICE-CREAM FREEZER

their way into Italian dishes. An Italian *fritto misto* runs the whole gamut of meat, fish, and offal, blended with the different flavours of herbs and with garlic. There is an Italian saying: 'What does not kill you, fattens you'. Which means that anything edible is worth eating if properly cooked.

Italian soups are worthy of mention, and minestrone is not the only soup the Italians have. As no point in Italy is more than 100 miles from the sea, obviously fish represent a harvest that is hard to beat, embracing everything the Mediterranean has to offer.

With so much abundance of meat, fish and pasta, one wonders where the Italians find time for vegetables. But they do, and have a vast choice, for Italy stretches from alpine coldness to the warm south. Many popular vegetables are the invention of the Italians as their names show – broccoli for example.

ITALIAN WINES. A constant climate has helped to make Italy one of the largest wine-producing countries in the world and wine-making there is almost as old as history. Most regions of Italy make wine but the most important quantitatively are Apulia, Sicily, Veneto, Emilia, Piedmont, Tuscany, Campania, Abruzzi and Lombardy in that order.

Quality of Italian wines in recent years has been in question but government legislation enacted in 1963 introduced regulations which controlled and protected production and brought reliability to those who drink Italian wine. Despite heavy production, on the whole Italian wines have been mainly consumed at home, some not reaching beyond their own region. What export there was has been mostly to West Germany, Switzerland, the United States, and even to France. Apart from a few well-known names, not much Italian wine has been imported into Britain.

Piedmont, the most westerly region of northern Italy, is perhaps vinously the most important and stretches from the Alps down to the plains. Asti Spumante, often known as the champagne of Italy, is grown here. This wine, often too sweet for English tastes, is best served with fruit or dessert at the end of a meal, for mid-morning drinks or for parties. Barbaresco, an excellent ruby-red wine, is ideal served with game. It keeps moderately well. Barbera has three wines each named after the place where it is produced, d'Alba, d'Alessandria and d'Asti; all are of a dark-ruby colour, with a dry genuine taste. Barolo is often called the 'King of Wines' in Italy. It is dry, full-bodied and harmonious, excellent with roasts. It matures after four years and is perfect at eight. The bottle should be opened several hours before serving, or, as the people of Piedmont do, the previous evening. Bracchetto is a sparkling red wine, light and sweet but becoming rare. Cortese is a dry white wine to be drunk young and with fish. There is some sparkling Cortese and a semi-sweet version called Gavi. Gattinara is a magnificent dry red wine which matures at five years and correctly accompanies truffle dishes, typical of the area.

The most important wines of Lombardy, situated in the middle of northern Italy, include Sassella, Grumello and Inferno, often considered as a trinity. They are wines of a similar type. Sassella is a vivid ruby-red wine with a delicate aroma which increases with age and is considered the best of the three. Next is Grumello, also a lively ruby-red colour with a slight, almost imperceptible strawberry flavour, dry yet slightly sweetened. Inferno is a dry, warm and mellow wine that matures in two years and reaches its best in four or five years. It has a deep ruby-red colour and is served with game and roasts.

Veneto, the northernmost region of Italy, makes some good wines. Bardolino is a dry and pleasantly bitter tasting wine, ruby-red in colour but very clear and bright. Recioto produces two types of red wine, a dry and a sweet, made with the *recie* or the ears of the bunches of grapes which have had more sun and ripening than most. Soave is a dry white with a pale straw colour and one of the most highly regarded wines of Italy. Some of the best Soave is made in the French manner and is sometimes likened to Chablis. It should be drunk when fairly young. Valpolicella is one of the best-known Italian wines outside of Italy and is becoming popular in Britain. It is a pleasant red wine with a bright ruby-red colour and fairly dry. It matches most red wine menus.

Emilia, one of the most interesting gastronomic regions of Italy, where the best Italian cooks come from and which has given birth to the term Bolognese, also produces wine. Lambrusco is something of an oddity in that it is a dry sparkling red wine which produces some curious reactions, although not to the Bolognesi who find it perfectly normal. It is particularly recommended with local dishes, especially *Zampone con Tenticche* (which see). There is also a dry and a semi-sweet Lambrusco, both with a thick froth. Albana is a fine table wine with a deep, golden colour, described as dry, light and fresh, sweet but not so sweet that it cannot be served with fish, although some Albana is yet sweeter and better for the sweet course.

Tuscany produces Chianti, one of the best known of the Italian wines and one of the most controversial. Basically there are two or three kinds of Chianti, some to be drunk very young, some almost as soon as it is bottled, and some when aged. The young wines are fresh and fruity, the old full-bodied and fragrant. The first growths of Chianti are designated by a black cockerel on the neck label of the bottle, a *fiasco*.

Umbria is the country of St Francis of Assisi. It produces Orvieto, a white wine of which there are two types, a dry and a semi-sweet, both a pale straw colour. Of the two, the sweet is better known, it has a pleasantly sweet flavour and is of good body. However, the dry is the better wine with a somewhat bitter aftertaste. A good wine to drink with fish.

South of Ravenna, in the Marches, an area of beautiful beaches and the calm Adriatic sea, Verdicchio is produced, pale straw in colour, fresh and good to drink with fish. It is dry or semi-dry with a slightly bitter taste, and keeps moderately well.

The region of Lazio claims Rome as its capital and Est Est Est (which see) as its best-known wine. This excellent dry white table wine is a good companion to the eels caught in nearby Lake Bolsena. There are two main types. One is dry with a pleasant, slightly bitter touch and pale straw in colour; the other is limpid, golden yellow in colour and served with fruit.

Campania, with Naples as its capital, produces Lacrima Christi del Vesuvio Bianco, a pale straw-coloured wine suitable for keeping. It is dry wine with a not unpleasant 'volcano' scorched taste that goes well with fish. Lacrima Christi del Vesuvio Rosso is the red equivalent, a good table wine that accompanies white meat roasts.

Apulia produces the largest quantity of wine, although most of it is used for blending and is often sold when still fermenting. Aleatico di Puglia is a rich ruby-red wine which loses its strength with age and turns orange in colour. It is exuberant with a pleasant aromatic bouquet, and should be served cold as a dessert wine. Primitivo di Manduria is a full-bodied, sweetish red wine mostly used for blending. Rosato de Salento, a good table wine, some of which is outstanding, should be served cool. Squinzano is another wine mainly used for blending, but with light wines. It is a warm, full violet-red wine.

Calabria, the toe of Italy, produces Ciro, a deep ruby-red wine that keeps well, is sweetish but generous and alcoholic, and matches strong cheese.

Sicily produces strong and powerful wines, rich in flavour. One writer has described them as 'wines which flash like a knife and which leave an unprepared drinker more dead than alive'. Faro is one of the island's better red wines and is produced near Messina. It is a wine with a bouquet of oranges and rather pale in colour, and goes well with roasts and game. Marsala, created by the English brothers Woodhouse, is Sicily's famous wine. It has been a well-known name in Britain since the 18th century. Nelson victualled his fleet in Marsala and a great deal of its wine was exported to Britain at one time, although now it is a little out of fashion. There are four main types, Marsala Fine, Marsala Superiore, Marsala Vergine, and Marsala Speciale. Like sherry and port, Marsala is a fortified wine. As a dessert wine, it has the virtue that it does not deteriorate after the bottle is opened. It is also one of the main ingredients in Italy's famous *zabaione* (which see). The lower slopes of Etna produce the appropriately named wine, Etna, both red and white of moderate quality. Cerasuolo is a wine produced in the southeast corner of Sicily; the name means cherry-red. It is a full-bodied wine which goes well with rich food. Moscato is a good sweet wine made from the Moscato grape, the best of which comes from Syracuse.

Sardinia, Italy's other well-known island, produces a good deal of wine. Giro is a topaz-coloured, lightish dessert wine; Nuragus is a light dry wine mainly used for blending; and Vernaccia, which needs to be kept for ten years before drinking, is a golden-yellow, dry and with something of the character of a natural unfortified sherry. In Sardinia, Vernaccia is drunk before and after meals.

ITALIENNE, À L'. Culinary term for dishes garnished with spaghetti or other pasta, or meat, poultry, fish or vegetables cooked with finely chopped mushrooms.

IZARRA. The best liqueur of the Basque country of southwest France. It is an aromatic, digestive

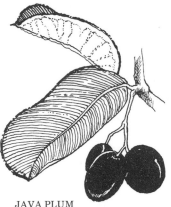

JAVA PLUM

JACK FRUIT

liqueur made in two grades, namely green and yellow, the latter being sweeter and of a lighter alcoholic strength than the green.

J

JACK FRUIT. There are many varieties of this tree but the honeyjack is the sweetest and best. It is native to India but is now cultivated throughout southern Asia. The fruits, which are irregularly oblong or round, weigh about 50 lb. and sometimes more. Jack fruit is eaten raw, boiled or fried: it is used in curries and pickles and is often dried, like figs, for winter use. If the pulp is boiled in milk, strained and then frozen it makes a palatable blancmange. The mature seeds, which resemble chestnuts in size and shape, can be roasted.

JAGGERY OR PALM SUGAR. A thick brown sugar made from palms, usually in the form of round cakes. Its flavour is nearest to maple sugar, molasses or black treacle.

JALEBI. A rich Indian sweetmeat made of a saffron-flavoured batter which is fried in hot fat in rings, drained and placed in a rose-water flavoured syrup for two minutes, and served either hot or cold.

JAM. A preserve in which the whole fruit or its pulp is cooked with sugar. The best jams are made with fresh fruit and refined sugar, the ratio being 1 lb. fruit to 1 lb. sugar. Sometimes vegetables such as marrow are made into jam.

JAMAICA PEPPER. See ALLSPICE.

JAMBALAYA. One of the traditional New Orleans Creole dishes using rice as the basic ingredient combined with meat, fish or shellfish to give it its distinctive flavour.

JAPANESE ARTICHOKE. See ARTICHOKE.

JAPANESE HORSE-RADISH. See WASABI.

JAPANESE RADISH. See DAIKON.

JAPONICA FRUIT. The slightly scented fruit of the ornamental Japonica tree, used to make jams and jellies, either alone or combined with apples.

JARDINIÈRE, À LA. Culinary name for a garnish for meat and poultry dishes, made of vegetables cooked separately and served round the joint or bird.

JASNIÈRES. See LOIRE WINES.

JAVA PLUM or **JAMBOLAN.** A small dark-maroon or purple-coloured fruit from the Malay Archipelago about the size and shape of an olive. There are several varieties. There is a small variety with dark flesh and a larger type with white flesh. The white-fleshed fruit is sweeter and less astringent than the dark-fleshed type.

JELLY. The name applies to three very different culinary preparations.

1. A soft, usually semi-transparent article of food obtained by boiling bones and animal tissue rich in gelatinous matter, such as cow's heel or calf's foot. It is used for glazing, decorating and garnishing meat, fish or poultry dishes.

2. A preserve in which fruits, especially those rich in pectin or to which pectin is added, are cooked with sugar, in a similar manner to jams, then strained and allowed to set. Such jellies are bottled and stored as jams.

3. Jelly (jello) puddings made from fruits with artificial aids such as gelatine or edible sea-weeds like agar-agar or carrageen (which see).

JELLY ROLL. The American name for Swiss roll, a sponge roll filled with jam and dusted on top with icing (confectioners') sugar.

JENEVER. See GIN.

JEREZ. Jerez de la Frontera, the home of Sherry. See SPANISH WINES.

JERKY. See BILTONG.

JEROBOAM. Normally a double magnum (four bottles) of champagne, although it can be up to six bottles.

JERUSALEM ARTICHOKE. See ARTICHOKE.

JEW'S MALLOW. This is a potherb which grows throughout the Middle East and parts of Africa. It is a rather glutinous vegetable resembling both chard and spinach and is a very important item of food in these countries. It matures quickly, is well branched and is about a foot tall.

JIGGER. A liquid measure equivalent to 1½ fluid oz. and now in general use for dispensing spirits. It may be made from metal, glass or plastic.

JOHANNISBERG. Probably the most famous vineyards of the Rheingau (see GERMAN WINES), crowned by Schloss Johannisberg, still owned by the Metternich family and making classic wines under scrupulously controlled conditions.

JOHN DORY. A European marine fish of real gastronomic worth, also called golden haddock. Like the haddock it has the 'finger and thumb' mark on each flank. A French legend has it that when the fish was caught it groaned so loudly that St Peter threw it back again, leaving his mark on it. As the John Dory has an ugly head it is usually offered for sale decapitated. The flesh is firm, white and delicate in flavour, almost resembling lobster meat. It can be grilled, poached or baked.

JOHNNY CAKE. One of the classic corn (maize) breads, originating in the state of Rhode Island, the basic 'secret' ingredient of which is water-ground corn meal made from white sweet corn.

JOINT. As a verb this means to cut into pieces or, with poultry, to sever at the joint. The carcasses of animals intended for human consumption are cut into portions called joints.

JORDAN ALMOND. See ALMOND.

JUG. A game stew, especially of hare, which uses the blood of the animal. It should be cooked in an earthenware or stone cooking vessel probably originally called a jug.

JUICE. The natural liquid found in meats, fruit and vegetables. The juice of some fruit is obtained by pulping and straining the fruit. In others it can be pressed or squeezed out. Juice from meat and poultry is usually extracted by means of a specially designed presser.

JUJUBE. The small egg-shaped reddish-yellow fruit of a tropical plant, also known as *t'sao* or Chinese date. The plant is native to southern Asia, but now grows in the South of France and California as well. It belongs to the same genus as the lotus.

The name is also given to a sweet (candy) made of gelatine, water, sugar and flavourings (either scented or medicated).

JULEP. A long, sweet, alcoholic drink flavoured by the leaves of or extract from an aromatic plant. The name is derived from the Arab *julab* or rose-water. Juleps are now widely known, with the American mint julep possibly the most famous.

JULIÉNAS. See BURGUNDY WINES.

JULIENNE. The culinary name for a consommé or clear soup to which a mixture of finely shredded vegetable is added; also applied to the finely shredded vegetables themselves. There can also be a julienne of chicken or turkey breast, of mushrooms, truffles, gherkins etc.

JUNEBERRY. Also called serviceberry, this is the fruit of the shad bush. It is sweet and juicy, ranging in colour from dark red to purplish-black, and grows wild in many of the western United States. It played an important part in the diet of the early American Indians and is now cultivated for use, both fresh and dried, in pies, tarts, jellies etc.

JUNGFERNWEIN. See GERMAN WINES.

JUNGLE FOWL. The popular name of more than one species of those birds from which our domestic fowl is supposed to be descended.

JUNIPER. An evergreen tree the ripe berries of which are aromatic and used to flavour spirits (chiefly gin), cordials, and many game dishes.

JUNKET. Milk which has been artificially thickened. It is sweetened and served as a cream.

JURA. Wines made on the French side of the Swiss frontier. They are very dry and include Château Chalons wines.

JURANÇON. An uncommon, luscious dessert wine from vineyards near Pau. Very little is made and it is correspondingly hard to obtain.

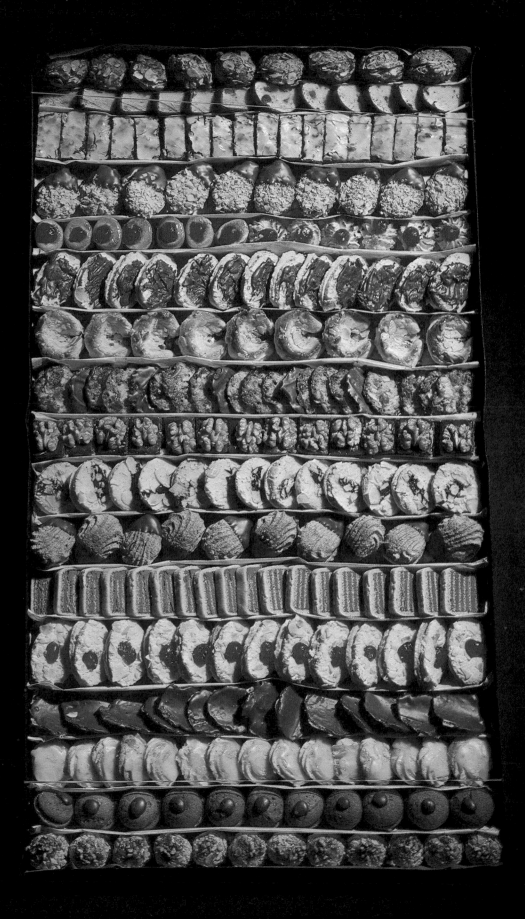

KANGAROO

KALE

K

KADAYIF. A sweet Balkan baklava-type pastry.

KAHLÚA. See COFFEE LIQUEURS.

KAISERSCHMARREN. A sweet pancake, rather thick and served torn apart with two silver forks. It is a favourite German sweet dish.

KAKAVIA. This is the Greek *bouillabaisse*. According to the Greeks, they are the originators of *bouillabaisse* which, they say, is a relic of an ancient fish soup introduced by the Greeks to their colony of Massilia (Marseilles). It takes its name in Greek from *kakavia*, the type of communal earthenware pot placed amidships in which fishermen used to cook their fish.

KALE. Also known as borecole, an anglicized form of the Dutch *boerenkool*, 'peasant's cabbage'. It is one of the earliest vegetables, known in England since Anglo-Saxon days, and has always been popular with country people. A winter vegetable, it is sometimes known as winter greens.

KALTE ENTE. The literal translation of the German is cold duck, but the term is used to describe a type of cold punch made both in Germany and Switzerland.

   3 lemons
   sugar to taste
   2 bottles dry white wine
   1 bottle champagne, sekt or asti spumante

Slice two of the lemons and prick the slices with the tines of a silver fork to allow the juice to flow freely. Put the lemon slices into the bottom of a punch bowl or a large crystal jug and sprinkle with sugar. Pour in the white wine, stir until the sugar has dissolved, and then chill. Add the champagne immediately before serving, and garnish the bowl

or jug with long thin strips of lemon rind from the remaining lemon.

KANGAROO. An Australian marsupial. Most Australians have never eaten either kangaroo or the related wallaby, nor even tasted the famous kangaroo tail soup, although it is exported as a connoisseurs' soup.

KASHA. In Russia a coarse meal of cracked buckwheat, barley or millet (which see).

KASHKAVAL. A smooth, slightly elastic cheese made throughout the Balkans from sheeps' milk. It can be used in cooking and takes the place of Parmesan cheese.

KASSERI. A firm white, mildly flavoured, soft-textured Greek cheese, eaten fresh as a table cheese but also dried for grating.

KAVA. Also called ava, arva and yava, a beverage much used in the South Sea Islands and by the Maoris in New Zealand. It is non-alcoholic, but if drunk in sufficient quantities it can have an intoxicating effect, making the drinker weak in the legs but not, it is said, in the head.

KAYMAK. A type of clotted cream. The name is Turkish but the cream is known by this name more or less throughout the Balkans. It can be prepared at home and often is, but usually it is bought commercially prepared, at least in the cities. The best *kaymak* is produced from sheeps' milk but cows' and goats' milk will produce a good *kaymak*. 'Unripe' *kaymak* is cream which is used fairly soon after it has been made and has a mild and very pleasant flavour. 'Ripe' *kaymak* has a sharp, almost cheese flavour and is so thick it cuts like butter.

KEBAB. There are several spellings for this word, the origin of which is obscure. Kebabs mean for most people grilled (broiled) meat, preferably done over charcoal. It is a method of open-air cooking which can be traced back to the mountain people

233

PHEASANTS: roasted and garnished.

of the Caucasus, who impaled their meat on their swords and roasted it on the open fire. In Turkey the word means, more broadly, small pieces of meat which are cooked in different ways, although one of the most famous kebabs in that country is the *döner kebab* or ever-turning kebab, which is lamb cut into long strips and wound like an immense bandage round a vertical spit. This revolves continuously a few inches from a charcoal fire, and the browned meat is sliced off in thin layers.

Cubes of vegetables are also called kebabs; there are kebab ragoûts, and a favourite Turkish recipe is lamb kebabs grilled and served on slices of coarse brown bread over which warmed yoghourt is poured. There are also fish kebabs.

KEDGEREE. Also spelt kichery or, in Hindi *khichri* it was, originally, 'a mess of rice, cooked with butter and dal (lentils) and flavoured with a little spice, shred onion, and the like; a common dish all over India and often served at Anglo-Indian breakfast tables'. In England kedgeree today has come to mean re-cooked fish served with rice for breakfast.

KERNEL. Literally a seed, but especially a seed contained within any fruit, i.e. the soft edible portion inside the hard shell of a nut or stone fruit. The body of a seed such as wheat, barley and other grains is also known as the kernel.

KEROPAK or **KRUPUK.** In Malaysia and Indonesia a savoury wafer made from tapioca or sago flour and variously flavoured, but usually with dried prawns or shrimps. Keropaks are grilled or fried, when they puff up and resemble the Indian pappadums (which see).

KETCHUP. A popular sauce or condiment. Its earlier name was catchup (still used in the United States) and Steele wrote of catsup. The word more than likely comes from the old Chinese word *ke-tsiap* which means a fish brine. Today ketchup usually refers to a somewhat salty extract of fish (especially anchovy), walnuts, mushrooms or tomatoes – although this last is used as a sauce, rather than as a flavouring like the other named ketchups. Old English cookery books give several recipes for elderberry, oyster, mussel and even cucumber ketchups among others.

KETJAP. A hot sauce and an indispensable ingredient in Indonesian cooking. The name probably comes from Chinese *ke-tsiap*, as does ketchup.

KETTLE. Today usually applied to a covered pot with a spout. There are electric kettles, whistling kettles for the absent minded, enamel kettles, which are often brightly coloured and easy to keep clean, and aluminium kettles.

Formerly the word kettle was applied to any vessel used for boiling water and is still applied to a pot in which fish is cooked, i.e. fish kettle. A kettle of fish in the north of Britain is a dish of stewed fish cooked *al fresco*, and the expression when used colloquially means an awkward state of affairs.

KHOYA. This is a very solid cream used in North Indian and Pakistani cooking.

KIBBEH. No Sunday lunch in the Lebanon or Syria is considered complete without one form of this popular dish of ground meat and cracked wheat, of which there are several varieties. The meat is always lamb and is heavily pounded, then mixed with cracked wheat and again pounded. It is served in several ways, raw, fried as small meat balls, or as a large 'tray' *kibbeh*. Green salad, a bowl of thick yoghourt or sliced radishes are the usual accompaniments.

KICKSHAW. In culinary terms, a small, fancy dish of food. The word originally denoted small luxury items and is probably a corruption of the French *quelque chose*.

KID. See GOAT.

KIDNEY. The kidneys of beef, veal, lamb, mutton and pork are all excellent food. They should be bought as fresh as possible and preferably in their surrounding fat. Grilled kidney once was a traditional breakfast dish, and a steak pie without kidney is a sorry thought. The French work lovingly with kidneys, masking them with rich and delicious sauces or serving them *en flambé*; one of the best known of the Dutch soups is *niersoep* (kidney soup).

In Britain kidneys are lumped together with offal (variety meats). There are many people who will not eat kidneys, yet once they were reserved for chiefs and warriors, since they were believed to give courage as well as strength to those who ate them. There is a phrase 'a man of my own kidney' which means someone after one's own heart.

KIDNEY BEAN. See BEANS.

KIMCHI. A Korean pickle which could be called the sauerkraut of the Orient. For many people Korean food is *kimchi*. There are a hundred different varieties of this controversial pickle which finds its place on every Korean table at all meals. Some *kimchis* are hot, others mild; some are fermented, others hardly at all. A lot goes into a

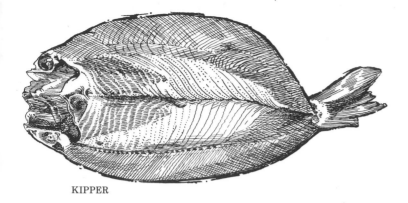

KIPPER

good *kimchi*. Cabbages, radishes, cucumbers, onions and garlic, red peppers galore and often pickled shellfish. All this is fermented in earthenware jars filled with salted water. When the weather is warm fermentation takes place rapidly and the *kimchi* is ready in a few days. The winter *kimchi* jar is buried deep in the earth and taken out as required at each mealtime.

Autumn is *kimchi* time, a period of household excitement. *Kimchi*, of course, is the answer to the lack of fresh vegetables during the long lean winter months. It supplies a large amount of vitamin C, plenty of protein, calcium, carbohydrates and vitamin B1.

KINGFISH. See CERO.

KIPFEL. In Austria a crescent-shaped roll or croissant.

KIPPER. A herring split open, salted and smoked. They can be poached, grilled or baked.

KING HARRY'S SHOESTRINGS. A pastry in the shape of a Maltese cross, decorated with glacé cherries.

KIRSCH. A liqueur distilled from fermented juice of small, black, and very juicy cherries and the crushed kernels of the fruit. *Kirschwasser* is a German speciality made in the Black Forest, and elsewhere.

KIRWAN, CH. See BORDEAUX WINES.

KISSEL. Russian *kisyel*, a soft pudding made from fruit and thickened with potato flour or cornflour (cornstarch).

KISSEL, STRAWBERRY

1 lb. strawberries
½ lb. (1 cup) sugar or to taste
2 tablespoons (2½) cornflour (cornstarch)
2 cups (2½) water

Hull the strawberries, wash them if necessary and rub through a sieve. Put aside. Put the sugar and

water into a pan, bring to the boil and cook to a syrup. Mix the flour with enough of the hot syrup to make a thin paste, pour this back into the syrup, bring once again to the boil, cook for a minute or two, and take the pan from the heat. Pour the cornflour syrup into the sieved strawberries, stirring all the while, and leave until cool.

This recipe can be prepared equally well with raspberries or other berry fruits.

KISSES. Hardly known in Europe, these miniature meringues (which see) are popular in the United States and are made with a variety of flavourings and embellishments. Aunt Rosa's Kisses, containing pecan nuts and dates, and Creole Kisses, flavoured with brown sugar and chopped, are only two of the many varieties.

KISSING CRUST. That portion of the crust of a loaf of bread that has touched another loaf during baking. It is also the soft cracks that appear on the surface of the bread when the loaves are left to cool.

KITCHEN. In most western European languages the word for the part of the house where food is cooked is derived from the Latin *coquina*, although the connection between English kitchen, Dutch *keuken* and German *Küche* on the one hand, and Italian *cucina* and French *cuisine* on the other may no longer seem very obvious.

KITCHEN EQUIPMENT. Since the turn of the century there has been a quiet but bright revolution in the realm of kitchen equipment. Our heavy iron pots and black kitchen stoves have been relegated to the museums. Although sometimes one might feel in a slightly bewildered Mad Hatter's world with so much variety offered, one should be grateful to those designers who try to help one get the best possible results in the kitchen with good, well-made and often gay-looking equipment. And when buying, remember it is usually false economy to buy things just because they are cheap and that only commonsense and experience can really be the guides.

KITCHENER, DR. A non-practising physician with three main hobbies – cookery, music and optics. He was born about 1775 the son of a rich coal merchant, went to Eton and took a degree of medicine at Glasgow. He never practised as he inherited his father's fortune and devoted himself to science and the two arts, cookery and music. He wrote *Apicius Redivivus or The Cook's Oracle*, published in 1817. It became a bestseller and went into several editions.

KLODNIK. (Iced Beetroot Soup). Basically ingredients for this famous soup, popular both in Russia and especially in Poland, are 'to taste'. The quantities given are approximate.

12 servings:
2 pints (2½) light, strained stock
1 pint (1¼) kvass, beer or white wine
1 pint (1¼) sour cream or milk, strained
1 lb. cooked, finely chopped beet greens
4 tablespoons (5) finely chopped fresh dill
finely chopped chives and fennel to taste
4–6 hard-boiled eggs, each cut into 8 pieces
1 slice cooked cold veal, diced
1 large pickled cucumber and 1 small fresh cucumber, diced
about 1½ dozen crayfish or lobster tails, cut into halves
1 large cooked, peeled and grated beetroot
salt, pepper
ice cubes

It is as well to start with all these ingredients cold. Mix the first ten ingredients together in a large tureen. When well blended, add the grated beetroot, to give the soup a pleasant pink colour. Add salt and pepper to taste, a few pieces of ice and serve as cold as possible.

KNEAD, TO. The process by which dough ingredients are thoroughly blended with a pressing movement of the hands, stretching the dough and then folding it over on itself.

KNUCKLE. The ankle joint of pork, veal and other meat, used to make stews and pies, while the bones can be used to make a soup stock.

KOFTA. Turkish *köfte*, Greek *keftethes*. A type of rissole or meat ball popular throughout the Balkans, the Middle and Far East.

KOHLRABI or **KNOL-KOHL.** The origin of this vegetable is obscure. It is a hybrid of the large Brassica family with a swollen stem and somewhat like a turnip. It has long been a favourite vegetable in the Far East, but the date of its introduction into Britain is unknown. The famous herbalist Gerard mentions it and so does Abercrombie in his *Gardener's Dictionary*, 1786, where he calls it the turnip cabbage.

Its flavour is delicate, a little nutty, slightly reminiscent of the turnip, and it is greatly appreciated on the Continent. It can be cooked in most ways in which the turnip is cooked, but it should not be peeled before cooking, as this ruins the flavour.

KOLACHKY BREAD. A small, light bun which originated in Bohemia and became popular in parts of the United States. It is usually made from a lightly sweetened dough which contains eggs and milk, and is folded into an envelope shape. When baked it may be powdered with sugar or filled with various fruits or nut purées.

KOLA NUT. See COLA NUT.

KOMBU. One of several varieties of Japanese seaweed (see SEAWEED). A large species growing more than 1 foot wide and 10 feet long, it is used at weddings, Shinto and other festivals as a symbol of prosperity and long life. Dried *kombu* is used as a soup stock, as a seasoning, and as chewing gum.

KÖNIGSBERGER KLOPS. One of Germany's simple but classic dishes.

1 lb. stewing meat
2 oz. (4 tablespoons) suet
2 oz. (4 tablespoons) butter
1 large onion, grated
2–3 slices crustless white bread
1 large cooked potato, mashed
4 teaspoons (5) capers, chopped
8 anchovies, chopped
1 egg
2 bay leaves and 1 clove
juice ½ lemon
1 tablespoon (1¼) flour

Pass the meat and the suet twice through a grinder. Heat the butter and fry the onion until soft but not brown. Soak the bread in water and then squeeze it dry. Mix the meat, bread, potato and onion to a smooth paste, add half the capers and half the anchovies. Mix well and bind with the egg. Break off pieces and shape these into balls, somewhat larger than a golf ball.

Bring a little water to the boil in a large pan; add the bay leaves, clove, the remaining capers and anchovies, and the lemon juice. Carefully arrange the meat balls on the bottom of the pan. Bring the water once more slowly to the boil, lower the heat and cook gently for 30 minutes.

Take the meat balls out of the pan with a perforated spoon and put them to one side but keep warm. Mix the flour with enough water to make a thin paste. Stir this into the stock, bring

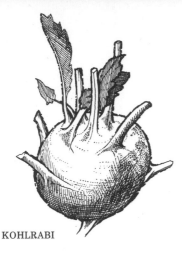

KOHLRABI

KUMQUAT

again to the boil and cook for 10 minutes. Return the meat balls to the pan and continue cooking for 5 minutes. Serve the meat balls in their sauce in a deep serving dish with rice or boiled potatoes.

KORMA. See QOORMA.

KOSHER. Food prepared in accordance with traditional Jewish ritual and dietary laws (*Kashrut*) contained in the Talmud.

KOULIBIAC. A Russian type of pie. Unlike most European pies, it is not made in a dish but is placed upside down on a baking sheet. The pastry is leavened and there are various different fillings, always arranged in layers. A typical filling would be rice, followed by ground meat and sliced hard-boiled eggs; salmon or other strongly flavoured fish and sliced hard-boiled eggs; shredded white cabbage and sliced hard-boiled eggs etc.

KROMESKI. Of Polish origin, this is creamed mixture of chicken, game or veal divided into small pieces and wrapped in thin rashers of bacon. These are dipped into batter and fried in deep fat.

KUGELHUPF. A yeast cake studded with raisins, soaked in rum or kirsch, which belongs to Alsace. It is rather dry and needs an unstinted supply of Alsace wine to be duly enjoyed. See BABA.

KULICH. Russian Easter cake baked in the shape of an Orthodox priest's hat, iced and decorated with the Cyrillic letters X-B, for 'Christ is Risen'. It is cut in rounds for serving.

KÜMMEL. A popular liqueur with digestive qualities, flavoured with caraway seeds and cumin, but not coloured. Riga kümmel was for many years the best, but nowadays much is made in Germany, Holland and elsewhere.

KUMQUAT. A native of China where it was called ·*Chin kan* meaning 'gold orange'. It is a citrus that grows to an oval or round fruit about 1 in. in diameter and is cultivated throughout the Far East. It can be eaten raw but it is best preserved whole, or combined with fruit salads to add piquancy. It has a sweet-sour flavour.

KUMYS. A cultured sweet-sour, fermented, mildly alcoholic drink made from mares', asses' and camels' milk in the Uzbek, Bashkir and Kirghiz regions of Russia. Its origin is pre-Christian and both Pliny and Xenophon have written of its merits. Marco Polo compared it to an excellent white wine. He wrote that Genghis Khan drank it and, for his supply, maintained a stable of about· 10,000 horses, all as white as snow. It was claimed that only direct descendants of the Khan were allowed to drink milk from the white mares.

At one time a type of kumys was available in drug stores in the United States, but prepared from cows' milk, which doubtless would have made a good Tartar weep. The advent of yoghourt put the sale of kumys out of fashion. Outside of Russia, it is difficult to get the right culture to make it.

KVAS. A fermented liquid used both as a drink and as a basis for some Russian soups. Made from rye bread, water, sugar-syrup, yeast, white flour, raisins and lemon juice, it has been described as a type of light beer.

L

LABARDE. See BORDEAUX WINES.

LACRIMA CHRISTI. See ITALIAN WINES.

LACTIC ACID. This is produced by the fermentation of milk sugar. It is found in sour milk and is used to make cheese. Milk is nearly always acidified by innoculating it with strains of lactic acid-producing bacteria. The amount of acid produced varies with the type of bacteria used and this is one of the main reasons why it is impossible to make a wide variety of cheeses. The culture of the bacteria used in making cheddar-type cheeses is known as the 'starter'.

Lactic acid is also found in animals and fish. When an animal is well-rested, the glycogen in its muscles breaks down into lactic acid and when slaughtered this acts as a preservative agent and delays the process of decay in the meat.

It is never possible to have a 'properly rested' fish because it keeps on struggling to the very last and thus consumes its glycogen. This is one of the reasons why fish spoils so quickly.

LACTIC FERMENTS. These are minute organisms which when introduced into milk cause the fermentation of milk sugar, resulting in the production of lactic acid (which see).

LACTOSE. Also known as milk sugar, this occurs in milk and is an important part of the diet of a growing infant, who needs an easily assimilated form of carbohydrate.

LADIES' FINGERS. See OKRA.

LADLE. A large spoon with a cup bowl and a long handle used mainly for serving liquid food, more particularly soups and punches.

LADOIX-SERRIGNY. See BURGUNDY WINES.

LADY FINGERS. Small, light, finger-shaped pieces of sponge cake usually served with ice-cream or used as a foundation for sweet puddings.

LAFITE, CH. and **LAFITE-ROTHSCHILD, CH.** See BORDEAUX WINES.

LAGER. One of the most popular types of beer, originally produced in Germany. Light in colour, clear and slightly carbonated, it is served cold.

LAGUNE, CH. LA. See BORDEAUX WINES.

LAKE HERRING. Another name for the cisco (which see).

LAKKA. See SUOMUURAIN.

LALANDE. See BORDEAUX WINES.

LALANDE DE POMEROL. See BORDEAUX WINES.

LAMB. For the farmer a lamb is a young ovine animal before it gets its permanent teeth, after which it is a hogget until it reaches the period when it has to be clipped. In culinary parlance there are two sorts of lamb: milk-fed lamb and then the young animal up to the age of 12 months, when it becomes a sheep. Breed, age and feeding are the three main factors responsible for the quality of lamb. The best joints are the saddle and the shoulder, but they are also the least economical as they carry a greater proportion of bone to meat than other cuts. Then come the loin, cutlets or chops, the neck, the best 'small cuts', then the leg. There are also the innards and other odds and ends, from the tongue to the tail.

LAMB'S FRY. The liver, heart, sweetbread and inside fat or 'leaf' of the lamb.

LAMB'S LETTUCE. Also known as corn salad, this is a hardy annual plant used as a salad vegetable in winter.

LAMB'S TAIL PUDDING. A traditional British country dish made from the tails of lamb docked from March to June. The tails are collected, skinned, washed and stewed until the meat, fat and the more or less cartilaginous bones form a mass. This is then mixed with batter and potatoes and baked in the form of a pasty.

LAMB'S WOOL. A hot, alcoholic drink to which Pepys and many of his contemporaries were partial. It was made with hot ale, sweetened with sugar, thickened with roasted apples and flavoured with grated nutmeg or ground ginger. See also BRASENOSE ALE.

LAMPREY. A neglected fish in Britain. Many people have read that Henry I of England died of a surfeit of lampreys, and Alexander Pope, the poet, suffered the same fate in 1744. Although lampreys are no longer popular in England they are eaten in Eastern Europe and in France. Their flesh is delicate but fatty and considered somewhat indigestible. The most highly prized is the eel lamprey.

At one time in Britain ships carrying lampreys were granted special protection. Also it was customary for the town of Gloucester to present the reigning monarch with a lamprey pie.

Today lampreys are objects of scientific interest as living fossils. In general appearance they resemble the eel but differ from other true fish in having no scales, no paired fins, a circular suctorial mouth and a cartilaginous backbone.

LAMPRIADAS. An ancient Greek said to have been the inventor of brown sauce.

LANCASHIRE CHEESE. The softest of the hard-pressed cheeses, which even at three months old

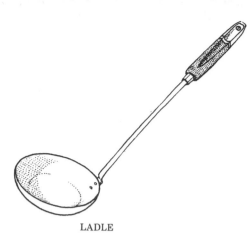

LADLE

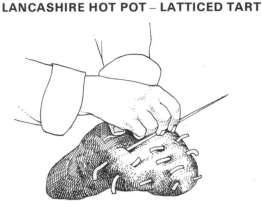

LARDING NEEDLE

spreads like butter, but with a stronger flavour than either Cheddar or Cheshire. As it does not travel well, nearly all of it is consumed locally.

LANCASHIRE HOT POT. One of the traditional dishes of England. It consists of neck of lamb and sheeps' kidneys cooked in layers with potatoes, flavoured with onions and herbs and sometimes oysters. It is usually baked in the oven and served in the dish in which it is cooked. See also HOT POT.

LANGOA BARTON. See BORDEAUX WINES.

LANGOUSTE. See SPINY LOBSTER.

LANGOUSTINE. See DUBLIN BAY PRAWNS.

LANGUE DE CHAT. A type of biscuit (cookie) which derives its name from its shape: thin, long and flat, like a cat's tongue. Usually served with certain liqueurs, sparkling wines and ice-creams. It is also used as a basis for sweet puddings.

LAPWING. See PLOVER.

LARD. The white fat from the inside of a pig, melted and clarified. Lard is considered by many as the best fat for pastry making, certain breads, shallow and deep-fat frying. Pure lard is 99 per cent fat and therefore does not splutter when heated. It has a high 'smoking' temperature.

LARD, TO. This means to introduce narrow strips of fat larding bacon or pork through the surface of uncooked meat in order to nourish or tenderize it and give it fat and flavour. Liver, tenderloin of beef and certain game birds are often larded.

LARDING NEEDLE. A long steel needle with a large eye into which narrow strips of pork fat or larding bacon are threaded.

LARDING PORK. Pork fat used to lard, bard or wrap round food. Very dry game birds are usually barded with thin slices of larding pork.

LARDY CAKE. Country-style bread-dough cakes which appear in several English counties: Sussex, Wiltshire, Oxfordshire and Cambridgeshire. The dough is saved from bread-making or bought from the baker, rolled out, spread with lard, sugar and currants, then folded and re-rolled three times. It is then cut into squares, brushed with milk, lightly sprinkled with coarse sugar and baked until it has risen and is a golden brown colour.

LASAGNE. Wide ribbons or squares of Italian *pasta*. It can be purchased commercially but is one of the easier *pastas* to make at home. It is usually boiled in salted water until *al dente*, that is almost soft, and then placed in layers in a deep baking dish alternated with ground meat, cheese, cooked tomatoes, peas etc. It is then covered with a white sauce and baked until brown.

LASCASES, CH. LEOVILLE. See BORDEAUX WINES.

LASCOMBES. See BORDEAUX WINES.

LAS PALMAS. Chief wine mart of the Canary Islands, whose wines were known in Shakespeare's England as Palm wine and Palm sack. See also CANARY WINES.

LASSI. This is sour milk, whipped until smooth, flavoured with sugar and mixed with water or soda water to make a long, cool drink. It is popular in the Middle and Far East.

LATEX. All parts of the papaw plant have small vessels which when cut secrete latex. This latex contains papain which is an aid to digestion and a meat tenderizer. It is a colourless, sticky fluid soon getting milky; it coagulates. See PAPAIN, PAPAW.

LATOUR and **CH. LATOUR.** See BORDEAUX WINES.

LATTICED TART. A filled pastry shell covered with a narrow criss-cross of pastry.

239

LAUDUN. See RHÔNE WINES.

LAUJAC. See BORDEAUX WINES.

LAVER. The name of two sorts of edible seaweeds, the fronds of which are eaten stewed or pickled.

LAVERET. A salmonoid fish related to the char (which see) and found in both salt water and in the deep, cold lakes of Europe. Its delicately flavoured, firm flesh makes it one of the most prized fish for the table.

LAVILLE-HAUT-BRION. See BORDEAUX WINES.

LAYER CAKE. A cake consisting of two, three or more layers spread with a cream filling or jam.

LAZY SUSAN. A revolving tray, many of which are made to fit a particular table. They were useful in large families at breakfast time as each person at table had only to revolve the tray to reach the marmalade or honey. There are also lazy susans made with separate compartments in which different foods are placed.

LEAVEN. A form of soured wheat paste which, when kneaded into dough for bread or pastry, produces fermentation and thus causes the dough to rise and become lighter and more digestible.

LEAVENING AGENTS. These include brewers' yeast, baking powders and sodas, all of which cause bread, cake and pastry dough to rise and are known collectively as leaven (which see). Such factors as steam and hot air also make substances light and porous. The addition of egg whites will act as leavening with some ingredients as, when beaten, they contain air which is released during the baking process.

LEBKUCHEN. Small German spice cakes (cookies) particularly associated with Christmas. The name comes from *Libum*, a flat cake. They have been made in Germany for 700 years and at Christmas markets are sold under the wings of tinsel angels, and often used as a Christmas tree decoration.

LECKERLI. A Swiss type of biscuit (cookie), usually cinnamon-flavoured and eaten on festive occasions.

LEEK. An important member of the lily or onion family, so ancient that its origin is obscure. It was grown in Egypt at the time of the Pharoahs and later was used by the Romans who probably brought it to Britain. There are many types of leeks grown all over Europe, although they are less popular in the United States. They vary from the enormous bulbous types grown in Britain to the mild, aromatic tender varieties favoured on the Continent.

The flavour of the leek is similar to the onion, but milder and sweeter. But leeks must be used with discretion unless their flavour is intended to predominate. They are much used in soups, as in Vichyssoise soup (which see); in Eastern Europe they figure in hors d'oeuvre; the Greeks cook them with black olives. Young tender leeks can be thinly sliced and used in salads, a use that dates back to the Romans. The plant is also the national emblem of the Welsh.

LEEKS, GLAZED

Trim off the root ends of about 12 leeks, trim the green leaves, cutting off about one-third of these. Cook the leeks in boiling water for 10 minutes, rinse well in cold water. Drain and put into a casserole with plenty of butter, $\frac{1}{2}$ pint ($1\frac{1}{4}$ cups) stock, 1 teaspoon ($1\frac{1}{4}$) fine sugar and a little meat glaze. Cook this gently until the liquid is reduced. Serve on a hot dish, with the sauce poured round the side, and garnish with pitted, halved black olives.

LEES. The settling of any liquid, also the sediment or dregs resulting from wine or liquor manufacture.

LEFT-OVERS. Abundant left-overs no doubt mean that the administration of the kitchen is poor, but some of the best traditional dishes of the world are the result of their skilful utilization. They may not rank among the culinary heights of *grande cuisine* but they have a place in good *bourgeoise* cooking. See BUBBLE AND SQUEAK.

LEGUME. The fruit or edible part of a leguminous plant, i.e. beans, peas or pulses. They are important as a food as they have a high percentage of protein and carbohydrates, but they are also exceedingly starchy and require thorough mastication to avoid digestive disturbances.

LEICESTERSHIRE CHEESE. A hard cheese made in the same manner as Cheddar but of a flamboyant yellow colour. The colour has no effect upon its flavour, which is rich with a slight tang associated usually with lemon.

LEMON. The yellow, aromatic acid fruit of a citrus tree which probably had its origin in the Himalayan mountains, where it still grows wild. It has been called the fruit with a thousand uses.

Lemons were introduced in Britain 400 years ago but they have been known in other parts of Europe for over 1,600 years. West Asian excavations have

(Opposite) PIG: a roast sucking pig.
(Overleaf) LE PINOT NOIRIENNE.

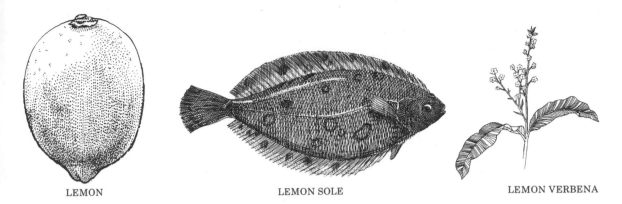

LEMON   LEMON SOLE   LEMON VERBENA

brought to light pips said to have been from lemons or limes existing 4,000 years ago. Ancient writings often confused lemons and limes.

Lemon juice, which is greatly used in cooking of all kinds, has very little aromatic flavour and is used as a souring agent, taking the place of vinegar. The main flavour comes from the skin which contains the essential oil of lemon, known as the zest. This is obtained from the lemon by grating the skin or firmly rubbing a knob of sugar over it.

Lemons vary from small, smooth and even thin-skinned varieties, to those which are large and with a thick coarse skin. Lemons for export are picked green and ripen off the tree. Those left to ripen on the tree have a finer flavour.

LEMON BALM. A herb with many names. It is native to southern Europe and has been in cultivation for over 2,000 years. The Romans appear to have brought it to Britain. It is today grown all over the world as a garden plant.

Lemon balm grows to a height of one to two feet: its leaves are oval with midly serrated edges and small yellowish or whitish flowers. It is a perennial. It has a pleasing lemon scent and is useful to blend with other herbs. In Belgium and Holland it is used in pickling herring, but it cannot be claimed as a herb of great culinary importance. A leaf is pleasant in iced tea, lemonade, and fruit and claret cups, and it is used in several famous liqueurs, including Benedictine and Chartreuse. It is greatly loved by bees: one of its names, Melissa, comes from the Greek name for the bee.

LEMON CURD or **CHEESE.** A soft, spreading preserve made from lemons, eggs, butter and sugar and used mainly in tarts.

4 juicy lemons
1 lb. (2 cups) granulated sugar
4 oz. (8 tablespoons) unsalted butter
4 egg yolks, well beaten

Scrub the lemons, grate the rind, cut into halves and squeeze out the juice. Pour the juice into the top of a double boiler, add sugar, butter and the grated rind. Cook over a moderate heat until the

sugar dissolves. Pour this mixture over the egg yolks, stirring all the while to prevent curdling. Return the mixture to the pan and continue cooking over a gentle heat until the mixture thickens. Put into jars and seal at once.

LEMON ESSENCE or **EXTRACT.** A flavouring agent made from the oil expressed from lemon rind and alcohol.

LEMON FISH. See AMBER FISH.

LEMON GRASS. A lemon-flavoured grass common in Southeast Asia, but now grown in parts of Florida. It contains a great deal of essential oil called citral. Lemon grass is a popular ingredient in Indonesian and Malaysian food and where this is not available citral can be used instead.

LEMON OIL. A pale yellow liquid expressed from the skins of fresh lemons and used as a flavouring.

LEMON SHERBET or **WATER ICE.**

1½ cups (1⅞) strained lemon juice
grated rind 1 lemon
1 cup (1¼) fine sugar
3 cups (3¾) water

Combine the juice with the rind. Cook the sugar and water together for 5 minutes. Cool. Stir in the juice. Pour into an ice cube tray and freeze in the usual manner, stirring from time to time.

LEMON SOLE. One of the best of the flatfish, found in all northern seas and corresponding to the yellowtail flounder in the United States. The flesh is firm and white with a delicate flavour. It is a favourite in Britain and America, but less well thought of in France.

LEMON SQUASH. A commercially bottled, lemon-flavoured liquid.

LEMON VERBENA. A delicate aromatic herb with lemon-flavoured leaves used in salads, some puddings and as a substitute for lemon grass.

245

LEMONADE. A generic name for all long drinks which are strongly flavoured with lemon juice. The simplest form of lemonade is made with lemon juice, water and sugar. In more elaborate forms the water is replaced by aerated or sparkling water and the sugar by sugar syrup.

LENGTH. See WINE TERMS.

LENTIL. Lentils or pulses are seeds of leguminous plants. They are native to Central Asia, where they have been cultivated since prehistoric times. There are numerous varieties and India is a leading producer and consumer. Lentils are there known by the generic name *dal* or *dahl*. A few varieties are also grown in the Middle East, Greece and some other European countries.

Lentils are an extremely nutritious food and are served at least once a day in most Indian homes. They are rich in protein, vitamin B, iron and phosphorus. Some authorities suggest lentils may possibly have made Esau's 'mess of pottage'.

LÉOGNAN. See BORDEAUX WINES.

LÉOVILLE, CH. See BORDEAUX WINES.

LETTUCE. It is not known when lettuces were first introduced into Britain, but they are mentioned in John Gardner's *Feate of Gardening, circa* 1440. There are several varieties but the two main types are the cos and romaine.

The lettuce is chiefly used as a salad. It should be freshly picked (not always possible), washed and carefully dried. The best way to dry a lettuce is to swing it in a wire basket – out of doors. When this is not possible, the lettuce can be put into a rotating basket especially made for this purpose. To pat a lettuce dry in a cloth is to ruin it. If gently swung in muslin it is not ruined but depressed. Lettuce should be plainly and discreetly dressed with oil and vinegar or lemon juice, salt and pepper and nothing else. It should not be cut with a knife or scissors, but simply pulled apart with the hands.

Lettuce can be cooked in a number of ways, in soups and stews or simply as a green vegetable.

LEVARET. A young hare.

LEVURE. This is a firm paste made with flour and water and used for sealing the lids of pots and casseroles in which poultry, game or highly seasoned *pâtés* are being cooked. The sealing prevents some of the rich flavour escaping with the steam. It is a method of cooking still much used on the Continent and in the Far East where many of the traditional pots and pans do not have tight-fitting lids.

LEYDEN GREEN. A Dutch spiced cheese made in two grades, one from whole cows' milk the other from skimmed milk. The paste is a light yellow, shot with green.

LIAISON. A thickening agent, designed to give body to a liquid food, sauce, soup or broth. An example of liaison is a roux (which see), a butter and flour mixture which forms the base of a sauce. There are many other liaisons all of which can be found in good instructional cookery books.

LIEDERKRANTZ. See AMERICAN CHEESE.

LIGHTS. The lungs of an animal. In Britain and the United States they are generally used for animal food but in many other European countries they are used to make savoury dishes for the table.

LIMA BEAN. See BEAN.

LIMBURGER CHEESE. A semi-hard, fermented, full-flavoured, strongly smelling cheese first made in Limburg, Belgium, but generally attributed to Germany. There is also a Limburger made in the United States.

LIME. A small, oval-shaped, thin-skinned, greenish-yellow fruit of the citrus family and a close relation of the lemon. It probably originated in India but is also grown in Italy, the West Indies and Florida. There are many varieties.

Its juice is extremely acid and an average lime, about half the size of a lemon, contains about one-third more citric acid than an average lemon. It is used exactly as a lemon and in most tropical countries serves as a substitute.

There is a flowering tree much used for roadside planting known also in Britain as the lime. This is in fact the linden, which belongs to quite another genus, namely *Tilia*.

LIMPETS. Small unprepossessing looking mollusks which are chipped off rocks with a knife or a sharp blow of the fist. They are of real gastronomic worth.

Wash them in water until free from sand and put into a pan with cold water, bring to the boil and drain. They are then ready for eating.

LINDEN or **LIME FLOWERS.** These have nothing to do with the citrus lime but are the flowers of a large tree which frequently decorates avenues and drives in town and country. The flowers, which are a yellowish white, are still used to make a *tisane* or linden tea which is considered good as a cure against nervous headaches and hysteria. The flowers are also used in green salads.

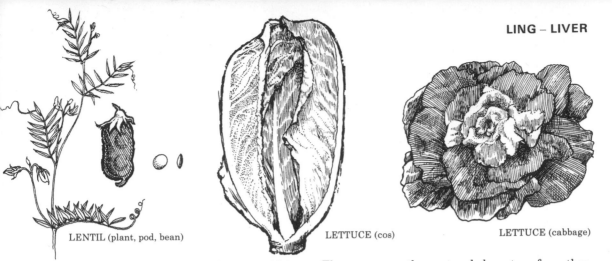

LENTIL (plant, pod, bean)　　LETTUCE (cos)　　LETTUCE (cabbage)

LING. A long, slender member of the codfish family. Its average length is three to four feet. In colour it is greenish-brown above and white below. Its flesh is fine and its liver rich in oil. It is a prolific fish, producing up to 50 million eggs. It is mainly dried or salted. In North America and New Zealand it is also called burbot or cultus cod.

LINZER TORTE. A favourite and well-known Austrian hazel-nut cake, spread with jam.

LIPTAUER. A Hungarian goat cheese, rather oily but with a fine granular texture. It is mixed with half its quantity in butter and various flavourings, such as finely chopped anchovies, caraway seeds, chopped chives and capers, enough Hungarian paprika to give it a pale pink colour and beer to moisten it.

LIQUEURS. Known as cordials in the United States. A dictionary entry, which prosaically but correctly describes a liqueur as an alcoholic beverage flavoured with aromatic substances and usually sweetened, pays little reverence to an ancient drink that is a medicine, digestive and after-dinner drink all in one.

Originally liqueurs are believed to have been based on wine, not spirit; but this was in the 5th century B.C. when Hippocrates was practising the art of distillation. Liqueurs as we know them today are based on spirit and were, it is thought, the invention of monks who, acting as herbalists and medicine men combined, manufactured liqueurs to restore and revive over-worked monks.

The spirit base for liqueurs varies according to the country where liqueurs are made. Brandy, which is made from grapes, is used in France; East European countries favour potato or grain spirit; Scandinavian countries mainly use grain spirit but some potato spirit; the British Isles uses gin and whisky; while Italy mainly uses a grape brandy as well as other spirits. Others use alcohol distilled from fruits, such as cherries, plums, apricots etc. or from spirit distilled from nuts and kernels.

Flavours are the natural bounty of mother nature but which herbs, kernels, seeds, flowers, fruits etc. are used generally is a carefully guarded secret held by the manufacturers. Usually it is a mixture, and one liqueur maker claims to use 130 different peels, roots, herbs, spices and so on to create his special flavour.

Italy is considered to be the 'modern' home of liqueurs, i.e. up to the 15th century. The Italians called them *liquori* from which the word liqueur is derived. But, as mentioned elsewhere in this dictionary, Catherine de Medici brought with her to France on the occasion of her marriage a number of culinary 'secrets'. Among these were receipts for liqueurs. The French were not slow to learn and today perhaps more *digestifs*, as the French still call liqueurs, are now made in France.

See liqueurs under their own names.

LIQUORICE. This herbaceous perennial plant with blue flowers and long sweet roots is found mainly in Spain and Sicily, but grows well in English gardens also.

The evaporated juice of liquorice roots makes excellent confectionery with a characteristic bitter-sweet flavour of its own. It is black and has medicinal qualities.

LIRAC. See RHÔNE WINES.

LISTRAC. See BORDEAUX WINES.

LIVAROT. A pungent French cheese with a dark red crust, usually banded by reeds. It is a ripened cheese of the Camembert or Gorgonzola type made from cows' milk and is at its best from January to March.

LIVE FOODS. By this term is meant such foods as whole-grain bread, rennet, sour milk, yeast, bean shoots, wine and sauerkraut.

LIVER. The most important, both in volume and excellence, of the innards of mammals, particularly of the calf. Lambs' liver can be used in garnishing.

Ox liver, although coarse, can be used as a substitute for calves' liver. Pigs' liver is often used in sausages. Calves' liver may be prepared for the table in many ways, but should never be over-cooked or it will toughen. Fish liver, such as that of turbot and skate, is also eaten.

LIVER PASTE. A type of soft Continental sausage used as a spread or an hors d'oeuvre.

LOAF. A moulded mass of foodstuff such as bread, cooked meat, sugar and the head of a cabbage.

LOBSCOUSE. A seaman's dish of meat stewed with vegetables and ship's biscuits. The name is of obscure origin but occurs in several countries. In Sweden *lopskojs* is mashed potatoes mixed with salted meat, ham or onions; there is a Danish version called *labskovs*; and the Germans have two similar dishes known as *Labskaus*, one claimed as a speciality of Oldenburg, the other of the Rhineland.

The dish is represented in England by the lobscouse of beef, potatoes and onions fried together which is, or was, served in Cumberland to celebrate Twelfth Night. It is still eaten in Liverpool, where the word has been shortened to 'scouse' and is familiarly applied to the people of that city and their dialect.

LOBSTER. A salt-water crustacean with large claws and several feelers. When caught, lobsters are mottled blue-black, but turn bright red when cooked. They grow to about 18 in. The minimum length at which they may be taken in British waters is 9 in. British legislation also forbids the sale of hen lobsters carrying spawn or eggs. Before this law was passed the eggs from the hen were used extensively for lobster butter. It was pounded together with the creamy parts of the head and some of the shell and passed through a sieve. The butter was also used for flavouring soups and sauces.

Lobsters are best bought alive and can be kept for a short time in the least cold portion of the refrigerator. If buying a lobster ready-cooked, pull back its tail. If it springs back into position the lobster is fresh. See SPINY LOBSTER.

LOCUST BEAN. See CAROB.

LOGANBERRY. A cross between a raspberry and the American blackberry, originally raised by Judge Logan of California. The fruit resembles the raspberry in character, but is larger, darker coloured and more prolific. Loganberries are delicious but highly perishable and their chief use is for bottling or canning, although they can be used as a dessert fruit. The berry has a large core which comes away from the vines when gathered. They were brought to England by Frederick P. Norbury in 1907.

LOIN. That part of an animal which extends along the backbone, between the ribs and the tail.

LOIN CHOP. A chop taken from the loin of an animal.

LOIRE WINES. The Loire is the most varied French wine river, with the emphasis on white wines: dry at both ends, and sweet to medium-dry in the middle. The vineyards generally do not press on the river banks, and are considerably dispersed throughout the wide valley, as well as along the tributaries, including the Cher, Vienne, Loir and Layon. Throughout the whole area about one million hectolitres of *AC* wine are produced. The total vineyard area is about 110,000 hectares spread through seven main *départements*. With one or two notable exceptions Loire wines are *vins de consommation*, to be drunk young and fresh.

THE GRAPES

In the Upper Loire the *sauvignon* is used for the best dry white wines, the *chasselas* for lesser wines. In Touraine and Anjou the finest white wine grape is the *chénin blanc*, otherwise known as the *pineau (pinot) de la Loire*. The best red and *rosé* wines are made from the *cabernet franc*, with a small proportion employing the superior *cabernet sauvignon*. The less good *rosés* come from the *groslot, cot* and *gamay* grapes; the last of these is also used for lesser Anjou reds. Muscadet is a grape name, also known as the *melon de Bourgogne*. Less good Muscadet may be made from the *gros plant du pays Nantais*.

THE WINES

Pouilly. If the wines are taken roughly in order from the upper reaches of the Loire downstream, the first well-known dry Loire white is Pouilly Fumé, grown on the right bank north of Nevers. Its popularity, particularly in Paris, has led to a considerable rise in output since World War II. It is not to be confused with Pouilly Fuissé, the leading wine of the Mâconnais. There the second word is that of a place, but Pouilly Fumé is named after the local name for the *sauvignon* grape. Only wine from this grape is entitled to the Pouilly Fumé *AC*. A lesser wine, sold as Pouilly-sur-Loire, comes from the *chasselas* with a various proportion of *sauvignon* added. The area is subject to frost, so production varies greatly. The Pouilly Fumé is a wine of distinction, with a real *goût de terroir* that persists, but tends to lose its charm after a couple of years in bottle. The most famous Pouilly Fumé is Ladoucette's du Nozet, no longer

LOBSTER

confined to the château vineyard of that name. More supple than many Pouillys, it is entirely estate bottled.

Sancerre. This old town on the left bank of the Loire is opposite the Pouilly *commune* of Tracy. Like its neighbour, production has greatly increased recently, and the wine is a favourite in Paris *bistros*, but it may be doubted whether all wine sold under this label is authentic. Also made from the *sauvignon*, it is sweeter and fuller then Pouilly Fumé, with an attractive honey nose, though a similar 'strike' is clear on the palate. Thirteen *communes* produce Sancerre. The best known are Sancerre, Chavignol, Bué and Amigny. Red and *rosé* Sancerre are also made, but they are of much less interest.

Quincy and Reuilly. These two isolated wine areas west of Bourges are associated with the Cher and its tributary the Arnan. Both are made from *sauvignon* grapes, with some admixture from lesser varieties. Quincy is similar in style to Sancerre, but drier and less fragrant. Less then 4,000 hectolitres are produced; a little medium sweet and red wine is made. Reuilly's production of white and red is even smaller. In style Reuilly is like Quincy. A non-*AC rosé* is also made here. Both Quincy and Reuilly wines are for early drinking.

Jasnières and the Coteau du Loir. This tiny area north of the main river puts the Sarthe *département* on the wine map. The dry to medium dry wine is made from the *chénin blanc* grape, and except in fine years when it can develop well it may be somewhat hard. Jasnières is the best wine here, but less than 200 hectolitres are normally made, and the total of other red and white Coteau du Loir wines does not exceed this.

TOURAINE

Vouvray. There are nine *appellations contrôlées* in this heart of the region, four of them Touraine designations. The most prolific and famous white wine is Vouvray, which may be still, *pétillant* or sparkling. The grape is the *chénin*. The still wine can vary from fairly dry to rather sweet, depending on the year and vinification. An attractive fruity nose and a generally slightly sweet flavour often masks a surprisingly alcoholic wine of up to 14°. It can improve with age and lasts well. Opposite Vouvray is Mont Louis on the south bank. This is a much smaller area producing similar but lighter and less expensive wines, which until 1937 were usually sold as Vouvray. Vouvray, Rochecorbon, Vernou and Ste-Radegonde are the most important Vouvray *communes*. The vineyard area, to the east of Tours, is about 1,500 hectares.

Chinon and Bourgueil. These two leading Loire reds are produced below Tours. Chinon comes from the town of that name on the southern tributary of the Vienne. Bourgueil is on the northern, right bank. Bourgueil is alleged to smell of violets or alternatively of raspberries. Both wines come from the *cabernet franc* grape. They can be rather hard except in good years, which may be rather rare in this northern climate for red wines. However, the Chinon wines are usually rather softer, while Bourgueil, astringent in youth, can soften and mature with age. The latter has two *AC*s, St-Nicolas de Bourgueil, which generally produces the finer wine, and Bourgueil. A little *AC* white Chinon is made, but the red is superior.

Other Touraine Wines. The basic *AC* here is Touraine and about 60,000 hectolitres are produced, divided more or less equally between white and red or *rosé* wine. There are three sub-districts: Touraine Amboise, Touraine Azay-le-Rideau and Touraine Mesland. The better wines are dry white, but Mesland produces more red and *rosé* than white. Amboise has rather more white, and Azay white only.

ANJOU

This district includes a greater variety of wine types than any other Loire region. It is the most prolific region, with an output of 500,000 to 600,000 hectolitres from 32,000 hectares. About three-fifths of this is *rosé*. The best comes from the *cabernet*, with a minimum strength of 10°, while the ordinary Rosé d'Anjou need only be 9°. Nearly all white Anjou wines are made from the *chénin blanc*.

Saumur. These wines from eastern Anjou may be called either Saumur or Anjou, but this does not apply equally to the Anjou wines outside the

Saumur area. Saumur produces the only red wine of any quality in Anjou, Saumur Champigny *AC*, made almost in the suburbs of Saumur. A light-coloured *cabernet rosé* is also produced in the district in relatively small quantities, and most wine is white. Much of this goes to produce sparkling Saumur, probably the best French sparkling wine after champagne, but it has been over-shadowed in the last 50 years by the vast expansion of champagne production and marketing and also, in recent years, by the development of cheap sparkling wines produced by the tank method. Sparkling Saumur entitled to the *AC* must be made by the champagne method, and may include up to 60 per cent of wine from black grapes. Both dry and sweet are made.

Coteaux du Layon. This area to the west of Saumur produces some of the finest sweet and medium sweet wines of France, including at least one of international repute: Quarts de Chaume. The Coteaux includes six main *communes*: Rablay-sur-Layon, Faye, Beaulieu, St Lambert-du-Lattay, St Aubin-de-Luigne and Rochefort, which is on the Loire. All wines from these villages are sweet. The two special vineyards of Quarts de Chaume and Bonnezeaux each has its own *AC*. Both make wine from sun-dried grapes caused by the *pourriture noble* of Sauternes, but they have more acidity than the sweet Bordeaux white wines. Quarts de Chaume is the more luscious.

Coteaux de l'Aubance. The white wines here are less distinguished than those of the Coteaux du Layon. Many are *rosé* (Brissac is one of the main centres of Anjou *rosé*), but only the white wines are entitled to this local *AC*. The other main centre is Mûrs on the Loire.

Coteaux de la Loire. Situated on the right bank, this small area of 11 *communes* includes some of the best moderately dry white wines of the whole valley. The grape is the *chénin blanc*, and the wines vary from dry to semi-dry according to the style of vinification. The most celebrated *commune* is Savennières, entitled to its own *AC*. It contains two of the most famous of the Loire vineyards: La Coulée-de-Serrant and Roches-aux-Moines. Both produce dry wines of considerable style and elegance.

Muscadet. This is the popular, inexpensive, dry white wine of the lower Loire, and production extends intermittently from the borders of Anjou into Brittany. The wine is named after the grape. Although grown widely there are two special areas with their own *AC*: Muscadet des Coteaux de la Loire and Muscadet de Sèvre et Maine. The first is near the Anjou border: the latter, much more prolific area is nearer to Nantes, the centre of the trade. Opinions differ as to which is the better of these two areas, and much depends on the variable standards of viticulture and wine-making where small growers predominate. This fresh, pale wine can be refreshing and clear, but also may be excessively acid. It should be drunk when young, for it can soon take on colour and become dull.

LOLLIPOP. A large, clear toffee or candy, usually impaled on a stick.

LONDON BUNS. Plain buns, long and finger-shaped, covered with a white sugar icing. They have been made in the English capital for so long their beginnings have been forgotten.

LOQUAT. A delicate little fruit which grows in clusters and comes both egg-shaped and round. It has a somewhat downy, yellowish to white flesh which encloses a few large seeds. It is extremely acid when half-ripe but sweet when ripe. Originally a Chinese fruit, it has been developed by the Japanese.

It is best peeled, cooked and served with cream or combined with other fruits in a salad or fruit cup, but it can be made into a jam or jelly.

LOTUS. The lotus known to antiquity is said to belong to the buckthorn family. It was found in the Mediterranean and its fruits were the size of sloes, containing a mealy substance used for making bread and a fermented drink. The Romans knew a species which they called the Libyan lotus, and the Greeks applied the term to a bush found in southern Europe whose fruit was used to make bread and fermented wine for the poor. The lotus wine was said to produce a feeling of contentment and forgetfulness, hence the term *lotophagi*, or lotus eaters.

The lotus as we know it today is a water-lily found in the Mediterranean, Asia, Australia and the United States. From Japan to India it is a much used vegetable. As sold in the market it looks like a decayed root of no interest and one wonders who first thought of eating it. It is extremely good, crisp and versatile. It is cut diagonally and running through its entire length is a circle of five holes which the Chinese cook stuffs with glutinous rice and serves as a sweet. Thinly sliced, the lotus root can be served raw in salads, boiled or fried.

LOTUS SEEDS. Like small hazel-nuts, these have a delicate fresh flavour. They can be eaten raw or soaked in water and cooked in sugar and made into a stuffing for puddings, dates and duck. Asians chew them as a digestive.

LOUDENNE, CH. See BORDEAUX WINES.

LOUPIAC. See BORDEAUX WINES.

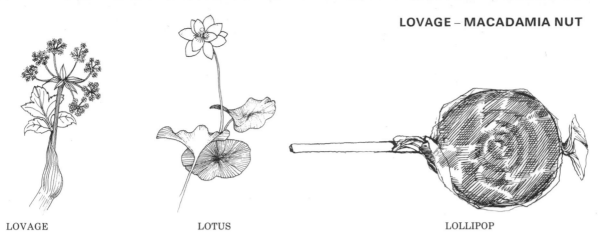

LOVAGE   LOTUS   LOLLIPOP

LOVAGE. True lovage is a native of southern Europe, although another species, also known as lovage, sea or Scottish lovage in the United States, grows wild in the north of Britain. It is a large herb with a thick stalk and looks like a large celery plant. All parts of the plant can be used, leaves, seeds and roots. Its flavour is distinct but difficult to describe. Tom Stobart, in his *Herbs, Spices and Flavourings*, says 'pleasantly musky, lemon-scented celery'.

LOVE IN DISGUISE. It was a Frenchman who wrote '*On aime, en Grande-Bretagne, les plats aux noms imagés. L'amour Masqué, enfin, n'est autre qu'un coeur de veau enrobé de bacon roulé dans la chapelure.*' And that is exactly what it is, calf's heart wrapped in bacon, a traditional British country dish.

LUAU. A Hawaiian traditional feast which has become a tourist attraction and something of a travesty. Originally it was prepared by the local people for special occasions. A pig, its body stuffed with hot stones, is roasted in a heated pit, covered with banana leaves, spread with a mat and then covered with earth. It is left for several hours and when ready to eat is served with sweet potatoes, breadfruit and banana, which have been thrown into the pit, to be baked at the same time. Poi (which see) is a traditional accompaniment.

LUDON. See BORDEAUX WINES.

LUMPIA. Also spelt *loempia*, this is the Indonesian and Filipino version of the Chinese egg roll (see EGG ROLL).

LUNCHEON. The modern midday meal which varies from a sandwich and salad to an elaborate formal meal. The word luncheon is said to be derived from the old English word, lunch, meaning a lump.

LUTING. A paste used for fastening lids on pie dishes or game which is potted in covered dishes.

LUXEMBOURG WINES. The vineyards of the Grand Duchy of Luxembourg are on both sides of the River Moselle for about 20 miles and are some 2,000 acres in area. The best wines of Luxembourg are white, rather thin in most years, but elegant and refreshing and capable of reaching a high degree of perfection. There is also some white sparkling wine, and a petillant wine called *perle*.

LYCHEE. A small oval fruit about $1\frac{1}{2}$ in. in diameter. There are several varieties but most have a thin, red outer skin, hard and almost crisp, encasing a soft, white, transparent flesh which encloses a single large brown seed. Lychees have a slightly sweet-acid flavour reminiscent of the Muscat grape.

Lychees are native to South China, where they have been cultivated for centuries. The lychee is one of those fruits almost as good canned as fresh. Fresh lychees are eaten as they come but they can also be shelled and pitted and served in salads.

LYONNAISE, À LA. Lyons style. This usually means a garnish in which fried, shredded onion is a main ingredient.

M

MACADAMIA NUT. This nut, native to Australia, is also called the Queensland nut. It was introduced into the southern part of the United States, the West Indies, South Africa and the Mediterranean. Although the Australians at various times have done much to stimulate interest in it, it is only in Hawaii that the production from cultivated trees is important.

Two main forms of the nut exist: one has a thick shell, and the other, usually smaller, a thin one, which makes it better for dessert purposes.

The nut itself is white, crisp, sweetish in flavour and rich in oil. Many claim it is superior to other dessert nuts in general use, having a finer flavour and aroma than either the hazel or the Barcelona nut.

An excellent nut butter can be made with the macadamia nut.

MACARONI. One of the more widely known types of Italian *pasta* which comes in long tubular forms. The characteristics of good macaroni are a creamy colour, a smooth appearance, and freedom from discolouration or mottled specks. It must break with a clean snap and when cooked should be firm, without stickiness and remain unchanged in shape.

There is a legend to account for the name. Neapolitans declare that one of their cardinals, on being presented with *pasta* in this form for the first time, exclaimed in joy *'Ma caroni'* (the little dears), and thus the name stuck.

At the end of the 18th century a group of London fops, having recently returned from Italy where they discovered macaroni, founded a new club, The Macaroni Club, with the idea of introducing this new dish to Londoners. The members were later nicknamed macaronis. This was no compliment as macaroni had come to signify a foppish young man. See PASTA.

MACAROON. A small round cake made of almond paste, sugar and egg whites, and baked on rice paper. The origin is unknown but some authorities suggest it came from Italy to France where it achieved unique distinction. In the Italian version, called *amaretti*, the same ingredients are used in different proportions, plus a dash of salt.

However, the French city of Nancy claims to be the originator of the macaroon. By the 17th century, Nancy was famous for them, a renown the city still enjoys. Several generations of a Nancy family have specialized in this confection and their product is known as Macaroons of the Macaroon Sisters.

Several kinds of macaroons have evolved over the centuries. A particular favourite is the coconut macaroon, which is made in the traditional way except that the fresh or dried coconut takes the place of almonds.

MACAU. See BORDEAUX WINES.

MACE. The filmy, lace-like outer covering of the nutmeg. In its natural form it is reddish in colour but as it dries it becomes orange. Its origin is Indonesian.

Mace is a mild and fragrant spice, combining the flavour of nutmeg and cinnamon, and can be used for both sweet and savoury dishes. It enhances the flavour of fish sauces, stuffings, gravies and soups, and a wide range of sweets. A teaspoonful of ground mace will do much for a pint of whipped cream.

MACEDOINE. A French culinary term which describes a mixture of vegetables or fruits of different colours, either sliced or cut into various shapes. They can be cooked and served hot or cold in a cocktail or salad, or in a sauce as a garnish.

This term also applies to sliced fruit or vegetables set in a mould in jelly.

MACERATE. To soak or infuse in liquid. Usually applied to fresh fruit moistened with brandy, rum or liqueur, or to chopped glacé fruit to be added to a cake mixture.

MACKEREL. One of the best and cheapest of the sea fish which can be cooked in several ways, although probably at its best grilled (broiled) and served with clarified butter.

Mackerel must always be eaten when absolutely fresh for it spoils rapidly. A fresh mackerel is firm with bright and distinct markings, clear eyes and a pearly-white belly. April, May and June are the best months in Britain for this fish, and it is advisable not to eat it during August and September.

This is a fish with a long history. The ancient Egyptians knew it in 1200 B.C. and some temple officials were said to be masters of the art of pickling it. Romans prized mackerel as a food which they salted and sent all over the Empire. More recently mackerel was an important item for the American settlers, as both a food and as an article of commerce. In 1671 the laws of the Colony of Plymouth proscribed strict penalties for indiscriminate mackerel fishing.

Closely allied to the mackerel is the Spanish mackerel and some larger American species.

MACO. See MAMMONCILLO.

MÂCONNAIS and **MÂCONNAIS BLANC.** See BURGUNDY WINES.

MADEIRA. This is a mountainous, subtropical island in the Atlantic, 400 miles off the northwest coast of Africa and 600 miles from metropolitan Portugal, of which it is a part. Its delicious wines are its most famous product.

Four kinds of vines are grown, giving four classes of Madeira wines, ranging from dry aperitifs to sweet dessert wines through all the gradations in between:

Sercial is the driest wine. It is made from Riesling grapes originally transplanted from the Rhineland.

Verdelho is the next in classification and less dry than Sercial.

Bual (or *Boal*) ranges from medium-sweet to sweet, but is less sweet than malmsey.

Malmsey (or *Malvasia*), the most famous of all the wines of Madeira, is sweet and made from grapes

PORTUGUESE WINES: the Douro vintage.

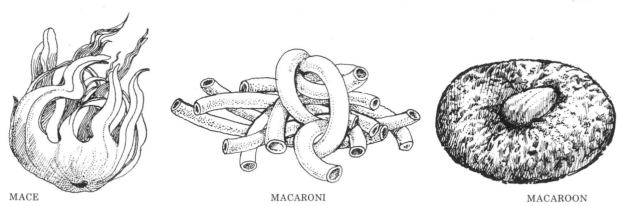

MACE   MACARONI   MACAROON

grown on vines originally imported into Madeira from the eastern Mediterranean 500 years ago.

Most of the wines produced in Madeira fall into one or other of these categories, although a few are blended specially and do not exclusively belong to any of them. Several of these special blends are very dry, but perhaps the most famous exception is Rainwater, originally blended for the American market and still largely imported there.

Although Britain has played the most important rôle of any foreign country in the evolution of the Madeira wine industry, the United States has had a big part too. Madeira has sent its wines in substantial quantities to North America since the early settlers developed a taste for them. George Washington is said to have favoured Madeira and when he died a good stock was found in his cellar.

Madeira is fortified, and the brandy is added when fermentation has run the course required by the particular kind of wine. The dry wines are allowed to ferment longer than the sweet. The brandy will stop fermentation abruptly if added in sufficient quantity. But in repeated small doses it will slow down fermentation and bring it to a halt gradually.

When the wine has fermented enough, the heating process follows. This is a process unique in wine-making. The only other wine known to have had a comparable preparation was the Falernian of ancient Rome. This heat treatment occupies a period of not less than six weeks, in a large tank or in a heated chamber, and the temperature of the wine is gradually raised to about 140°F. Here it is held for a further six weeks and then slowly reduced to normal. The chamber or tank in which the wine is heated is known as the *estufa*, and the wine is said to be *estufado* when the heating process is complete. It is said that the *estufa* is a device for reproducing the effects of a slow journey through the tropics. In the days of sail, it was found that Madeira wines transported through the tropics in the sun-baked hold of a ship were greatly improved. It is thus that the *estufa* was born.

The effect of this heating is to give the wine its caramel-like flavour and its unmistakeable tang.

It also gives it its amazingly longevity, for it seems that the wines of Madeira will live for ever. Many people claim to have tasted wine made in the 18th century, and a Madeira wine over a hundred years old is quite common.

On the other hand, vintage wines (that is wine of a particular year) do not exist in any great quantity nor are they laid down every year by any means. When it does happen, the amounts are comparatively small. No vintage wines of this century have yet been shipped to Britain. In the view of the exporters, no vintage wine made since 1899 is yet old enough to be sent out of Madeira.

Madeira wines are nearly always blended and the solera system is often used, as in Jerez. The solera is a means of maintaining an even quality of wine from year to year without regard to the weather or the success or failure of the harvest and a system by which newer wines are used to refresh older ones.

Madeira wine can claim three other remarkable qualities:

In nearly every instance, however sweet at first impact, it tends to dry out on the palate finally. There are no cloying Madeiras.

It does not deteriorate in the bottle after it has been opened, like other fortified wines. If the cork is replaced after some wine has been poured it will still be as good as ever many weeks later.

Madeira is almost impervious to ill-treatment, whether by climate, ignorance or carelessness.

MADEIRA CAKE. A rich plain cake, always topped with two thin slices of candied peel. In the 19th century it was served with a glass of Madeira wine, just as today wine biscuits (sweet crackers) are often served with sherry.

8 oz. (1 cup) butter
½ lb. (1 cup) castor (superfine) sugar
5 eggs
½ lb. (2 cups) plain flour
castor (superfine) sugar for sifting over the top
2 thin slices candied citron peel

Cream the butter with the sugar. Beat the eggs, add to the mixture. Sift in the flour. Pour the mixture into a buttered 8-in. cake pan, thickly sift castor sugar over the top and bake for 1 hour in a moderate oven. Place the peel over the top of the cake as soon as it has set (but without taking it out of the oven) and continue baking.

MADEIRA SAUCE. See SAUCES.

MADELEINE. A small French teacake made of flour, butter, eggs and sugar and baked in shallow shell-like moulds.

Some say madeleines were invented by Anice, Talleyrand's great pastrycook, others that they were known long before Anice and were made in the small town of Commercy; they were a favourite at the court of Versailles about 1730. Stanislaus Leszcynki, father-in-law of Louis XV, introduced them to Paris. It is said that the recipe was long secret but eventually sold to Commercy bakers for a large sum of money. This cake is also celebrated in French literature because it was the taste of a madeleine dipped in tea which sparked off a train of thought in Proust's mind and led him to write his famous novel, *À la recherche de temps perdu*.

Madeleine is also a garnish consisting of artichoke bottoms filled with onion purée and topped with haricot beans.

MADERISÉ. The polite French name for the stink which wines acquire when kept too long in the bottle.

MADRILÈNE. A clear soup usually served cold and flavoured with tomato juice. The term is also applied to other dishes flavoured with tomato juice.

MAGDELAINE, CH. See BORDEAUX WINES.

MAGNUM. A bottle containing the content of two ordinary bottles of 75 or 80 centilitres.

MAIDS OF HONOUR. A rich confection made of puff pastry filled with a curd flavoured with eggs, almonds, butter, rennet, brandy, sugar, salt and cinnamon. The town of Richmond, in Surrey, is famous for this confection which is said to derive its name from the maids of honour who attended Elizabeth I when she lived at Richmond Palace.

MAIGRE. 1. A large, scarce Mediterranean fish of excellent flavour with a white, firm and bloodless flesh.

2. A French culinary term denoting a vegetarian dish, usually applied to Lenten dishes.

MAÎTRE D'HÔTEL. Cooking *à la maître d'hôtel* implies dishes quickly and plainly cooked, with parsley as a main flavouring.

It is also the French term for head waiter, in former times the steward of a large household. The *maître d'hôtel* is in charge of the dining room and should have a good knowledge of cooking. Dishes which are finished at table, such as steak *au poivre* or dishes *flambé*, are his responsibility.

MAÎTRE D'HÔTEL BUTTER. A seasoned butter.
2 oz. (4 tablespoons) butter
finely chopped parsley to taste
salt, pepper
lemon juice
Beat the parsley into the butter, add salt and pepper and enough lemon juice to moisten. The butter should be firm, but soft. Serve with grilled (broiled) meats, grilled or fried fish, as well as with vegetables, in particular young boiled carrots.

MAIWEIN. See GERMAN WINES.

MAIZE. See CORN.

MAIZE BREAD (AMERICAN CORN BREAD). Commonly identified with the southern United States. Local names and variations are hoe cake, corn pone, egg bread, spoon bread, shortening bread and ash cake, from the method or ingredients used in cooking. The best known in the deep South is hoe cake. This term is attributed to the method used by slaves to cook in the field, as the flat side of a hoe was used as a skillet (frying pan). The cake is now made by mixing a thin gruel of ground corn (maize), water and salt. The skillet is brought to a medium heat, greased and the mixture poured on quickly. It spreads rapidly. When browned on one side, it is turned to brown on the other. The edges are lacy and the whole cake crisp.

Shortening bread is a thick mixture of corn meal (which see), salt, either water or buttermilk, and pork cracklings. It is made into a small oval loaf about 6 in. long and 1 in. thick and baked until the crust is hard. When baked in an open hearth it is called corn pone or ash cake.

Egg bread and spoon bread are made of a mixture of corn meal, eggs, baking powder, salt and a milk and water mixture, and baked in a greased pan.

MAJORCA. The largest of the Balearic islands, off the east coast of Spain; its many vineyards produce much wine of the *ordinaire* class.

MALAGA. See SPANISH WINES.

MALARTIC LA GRAVIÈRE, CH. See BORDEAUX WINES.

MALAY ROSE APPLE. This fruit comes from Malaysia and neighbouring countries and the best

MANGO

MADELEINE

is obtained from trees near fresh water where the soil is moist and drainage good. Its flesh is thick, juicy and fragrant.

MALBEC GRAPE. See BORDEAUX WINES.

MALESCOT, CH. See BORDEAUX WINES.

MALLARD DUCK. See DUCK, WILD.

MALMSEY or **MALVASIA.** See MADEIRA.

MALT. The name given to barley after it has germinated and the germ has been eliminated from the grain. By this process the grain starch is converted into sugar which is known as maltose. The end product is pure malt which is principally used for brewing beer and distilling spirits, but also makes a highly nutritive beverage when mixed with hot water. Another variety is the pale yellow or amber malt which is used to make malt extract and various foods for babies and invalids.

MALT BREAD. A sweet, soft dark bread prepared with malt and flour etc. and flavoured with raisins.

MALTED MILK. A powder made of dried milk plus wheat and malted barley extracts. Mixed with fresh milk it makes a nourishing drink.

MAMALIGA. A type of corn meal mush and the staple food of the Rumanians, who revere it as a gift from God and call it *mamaliga de aur* (bread of gold). It is similar to the Italian polenta. Besides being eaten as bread it is prepared in various ways, cooked in layers with cheese, served hot or cold with cream or with sauerkraut, dipped in beaten egg and fried or made into dumplings.

MAMMONCILLO. A tropical fruit which grows in the West Indies and Puerto Rico. It looks like a bunch of large green grapes. Inside the tight thin skin, which can be easily broken, is a layer of sweet-sour, yellow pulp surrounding a large egg-shaped seed. The seeds may be eaten roasted.

It is also known as Spanish lime, *quenepa*, honeyberry and *maco*, and by other local names.

MANCHEGO. A well-flavoured, exceptionally nourishing Spanish cheese. It is salted, fermented and left to ripen in moulds lined with esparto grass, which leaves a clear imprint on the rind. The quality of cheese varies according to the facilities for making it and the skill of the makers. All the cheeses are cylindrical in shape, about 2–5 in. in diameter and 5 in. high. The colour of the paste varies from dead white to golden yellow. Some manchegos have many small holes, others none.

MANDARIN ORANGE. See ORANGE.

MANDOLIN. The French name given to a knife set in a piece of wood rather like a plane, and used for the rapid slicing of vegetables, in particular cucumber. In Victorian kitchens they were called cucumber slicers.

MANGE-TOUT. The French name for some varieties of French beans and green peas, the pods of which have no parchment lining and can therefore be eaten when the bean or pea is fully grown.

MANGEL-WURZEL or **MANGOLD-WURZEL.** A field variety of the common beetroot, mostly used as cattle feed. Its leaves may be cooked like spinach; its roots treated in the same way as turnips. In Britain a country wine is made from mangel-wurzel.

MANGO. A good mango is the choicest of all tropical fruits and among the best fruits in the world. Its sweet-sour pulp is delicious when properly ripe: when not, it is indifferent. It was first known in India some 4,000 years ago and has become a part of Indian tradition and folklore.

There are some 500 varieties, but among the best known are the alphonso, bangalora and dueshri. At the other end of the scale are some varieties hardly worth bothering about. The fruit varies in size, shape and colour. Generally it is about the size of a large pear, but some varieties are smaller and others, bigger. Some are round, others are long and narrow. It is generally yellow, orange, red or green.

Mangoes are usually served chilled and in the same way as cantaloupe (which see under MELON).

They are also used to make drinks and various sorts of pickles and chutneys, both sweet and sour. The dried shreds of a green variety make an excellent condiment in Indian cooking.

Mangoes are now grown in most parts of Southeast Asia, Egypt, the West Indies and tropical Australia. The Portuguese brought the tree to Africa about 500 years ago where it flourished, but the fruit there is inferior in quality.

A large variety of mango trees have been planted in Florida, and government experts have improved some stocks by selective breeding.

MANGOSTEEN. This comparatively rare and exotic fruit is found in Malaysia, Indonesia, Ceylon and the West Indies. Reddish-purple in colour, it is of the same size as a mandarin orange. The rind is thick and hard and has to be cut with a sharp knife. The fruit consists of five to seven segments which are white to ivory in colour and have the consistency of a ripe plum. They are so delicate that they melt in the mouth like ice-cream. The flavour is likened to a blend of pineapple, apricot and orange. Mangosteen is best eaten chilled; puréed it also makes an interesting topping for ice-cream and sherberts.

This fruit is comparatively rare because it is difficult to grow even under ideal tropical conditions. The seedlings take 10 to 15 years to flower and the budlings another 8 to 10 years to mature. Although fertilizers and chemicals can hasten the process, there are still no large-scale plantations in Southeast Asia.

There are two big mangosteen orchards in the Western hemisphere. One is owned by the United States Department of Agriculture at Summit in the Panama Canal Zone; the other is a commercial venture in Honduras which produces 40 to 60 tons of fruit a year.

MANIOC (CASSAVA). The name given to a plant, the tubers of which produce tapioca. It is native to South America, and Brazil is the world's largest grower. Manioc has been introduced into Africa, India, Southeast Asia and the Pacific Islands.

Manioc may be eaten boiled or roasted, much like a potato. But there are other uses as well. There is a famous Brazilian dish known as *farofa* made with flour ground from the manioc root or plant. Brazilians are very fond of manioc flour lightly cooked in butter with a pinch of salt. They also sprinkle manioc flour as a flavouring on any dish they may happen to be eating.

MANNA. Manna, or the Bread of Heaven, was miraculously provided for the Children of Israel in the wilderness as they fled Egypt. The Bible refers to several species of the plant but there is much speculation about the variety connected with this event and reported in Exodus XXI: 13-15. It is thought, however, that it may have been the edible wind-borne lichen, found commonly on rocks in the Sinai Desert, which blows off in storms and collects in the valleys.

A manna shower fell in Iran during the drought and famine of 1854, and a heavy fall was also reported in Turkey in 1891. In times of drought lichen curls into lightweight flakes or balls which are carried great distances by strong winds.

The term manna is also applied to a number of plant exudations. The sweet exudation obtained from the manna ash tree is used as a mild laxative and most of this is collected in Sicily.

Tamarisk, which yields a honey-like exudation, and camel thorn, which yields sucrose, are among other species found in the Middle East. The manna from the tamarisk tree drops from the leaves. Insects puncture the leaves and the heat of the day softens the rather resinous exudation so that it drops to the ground. This manna is held to be of superior quality to that extracted from the tree itself. It must be well cleaned of the twigs, soil and leaves embedded in it; in its crude form it is an uninviting mess. It is used to make *gaz*, a kind of nougat, in Iran.

MANZANILLA. See SPANISH WINES.

MAPLE SYRUP (SUGAR). Made from the maple, a sugar-yielding tree belonging to the sycamore family. Although maple trees are found elsewhere, only the American and Canadian varieties are economical sugar producers. There are two main species: the black maple and the sugar maple. The former is considered the better sap yielder.

Maple sap collecting goes back to early Americana. A $\frac{1}{2}$ in. spigot is inserted in the trunk and the sap is collected in large galvanized buckets. It is then treated and its water content removed by evaporation; the finished product is maple syrup. Children love to pour the syrup on snow or crushed ice and eat the resultant hard sweet. Maple syrup is chiefly eaten with hot biscuits (scones), griddle cakes and French toast.

Maple syrup may also be processed into sugar and used with boiled rice, hot and cold breakfast cereals and in sweets and other confections.

MARASCHINO. A sweet liqueur with a highly concentrated flavour distilled from fermented maraschino cherries and their kernels, used a great deal as a flavouring in certain sweet dishes.

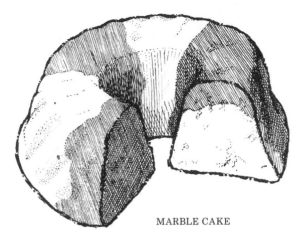

MARBLE CAKE

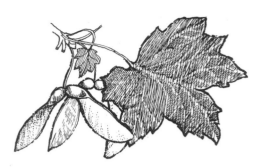

SUGAR MAPLE (leaf and keys)

Maraschino was first produced over 200 years ago in Zara, Yugoslavia, and exported in distinctive shaped bottles. It is now also produced in Italy.

MARBLE CAKE. A cake made of two or three different coloured mixtures cooked together in the same pan so that they mingle together to produce a marbled effect.

MARBUZET. See BORDEAUX WINES.

MARC. Spirit or *eau-de-vie* produced from the mass of skins and seeds left in the press after the wine has been extracted. *Marc* is usually sold with the indication of its origin, for example *marc de Bourgogne* (which see under BURGUNDY WINES) or *marc de Champagne*. It is also made from apples and marketed as *eau-de-vie-de-cidre* or Calvados.

MARÉCHALE, À LA. The French culinary name for preparing small cuts of meat and poultry which are dipped in egg and breadcrumbs and fried in butter. They are usually garnished with green asparagus tips and truffles.

MARENGO, CHICKEN À LA. One of those dishes which, being a success, eventually finds a place in gourmet cookery.

This dish was invented by Dumand the Younger, Napoleon's chef when the Emperor defeated the Austrians at Marengo in 1800. Napoleon had not eaten all day and ordered Dumand to prepare him a meal. The chef foraged in the nearby Italian village but could produce only 3 eggs, 4 tomatoes, 6 crayfish, a small hen, some garlic and olive oil, and a saucepan. The chef used his brain, and his bread ration to make a panade; jointed the chicken and browned it in the oil; fried the eggs in the same oil together with the tomatoes and the garlic. He poured some water laced with Napoleon's brandy over the ingredients and cooked the crayfish on top of them in the steam. Napoleon, we are told, enjoyed the meal and ordered a repeat performance after every battle.

Once Dumand left out the crayfish and substituted mushrooms. Napoleon would have none of it. He felt the dish had brought him luck and must not be changed.

The term marengo also applies to a dish of fried pulped tomatoes with mushrooms, truffles, onion or garlic. Eggs *à la marengo* are fried in oil and served with fried ham and Madeira sauce.

MARENNES. Green Marennes are delicious French oysters which take their name from the small town of Marennes where they are bred.

They have a rich, pale flesh and are famous for their green gills, caused by some minute organisms which the oysters eat in these beds.

MARGARINE. A manufactured substitute for butter made from animal or vegetable fats and oils. It was invented by the French chemist Mège-Mouriés, who conducted his researches at the behest of Napoleon III, there being a serious shortage of butter at the time. Mège-Mouriés experimented with beef fat and produced the world's first margarine in 1867. He soon obtained a French patent, and a British one followed in 1869. His invention was at first sold as butterine in Britain, but the term margarine (from the oleo-margarine of the chemists) was later adopted. The British Food and Drug Act, 1928, defines margarine as 'any article of food, whether mixed with butter or not, which resembles butter and is not milk-blended butter'. In the United Kingdom all margarine for household use must contain vitamins A and D in specified quantities. In the United States, margarine is also vitamin enriched and the contents are listed on the label.

Margarine may be used instead of butter in most cooking operations.

MARGAUX, and **CH. MARGAUX.** See BORDEAUX WINES.

MARIGOLD. A well-known garden flower with bright orange petals and pale green leaves. Marigold petals, dried and fresh, have been used as the poor man's saffron for centuries. Marigold petals are used to flavour certain soups, for example conger eel soup and some meat soups in Holland, and to colour cheese. See FLOWER COOKING.

MARIGOLD PIE. A very old country dish made with a short pastry crust and savoury egg custard generously flavoured with fresh marigold petals, baked until set and served with English cheese.

MARINADE. The word marinade comes from the Spanish *marinada* meaning to pickle. It is a seasoned liquid in which certain foods are soaked either to impart flavour or to tenderize. All marinades include an acid and it is this which works on the game, meat or fish soaked in it before cooking, adding new flavour, softening tough fibres and increasing their natural sapidity. It ensures a certain preservation and lifts food out of the commonplace.

Some marinades are used uncooked: this is better for smaller portions of food. Others are cooked.

MARINIÈRE. A method of cooking shellfish using white wine. It is used particularly for mussels (*moules marinières*). The name is also given to dishes garnished with mussels.

MARJORAM. A herb native to the Mediterranean areas but now widely cultivated throughout the world. Its flavour is spicy, sweet and scented and akin to thyme, which it often replaces in many dishes. If grown in Mediterranean regions it is a perennial; but in colder climates it is an annual.

It can be used in a variety of recipes. In omelettes, sauces, stews and soups; with carrots, spinach and courgettes (zucchini), clams, onions and turtle. It is good mixed with a green salad or lightly rubbed on the inside of poultry, and with game such as hare and venison. It dries easily and well.

Pot marjoram, as its name implies, is marjoram which grows indoors in a pot. It is also a Mediterranean plant with light green leaves and tiny purple-tinted flowers. It has not so good a flavour as the sweet marjoram and may sometimes be even slightly bitter. It can be used rather in the same manner as sweet marjoram, and especially with strongly flavoured dishes.

There are a large number of different kinds of wild marjoram, many of which grow in Britain, but when consulting the older books on this herb it is often difficult to decide which type is meant.

There is also a variety of marjoram known as winter marjoram which grows wild in Greece.

MARMALADE. An indispensable breakfast item in Britain. The French and other Continentals call jam marmalade. Exactly the difference between jam and marmalade is hard to define. To some it means a method of cooking. Others feel all citrus fruit preserves are marmalades. Jams are made from soft fruit and take a lot of sugar; marmalades require longer cooking and less sugar.

The word marmalade comes from the Portuguese word for quince, *marmelo*, which in the 16th century was made into *marmelado*.

In Spain a *marmelade* is a type of stiff fruit cheese (which see), cut into squares and served as a sweetmeat. In France the word *marmelade* is applied also to fruit stewed for a long time until reduced to a thick purée and used mainly as a filling for tarts and flans.

MARMITE. A metal or earthenware pot with or without feet, depending on whether it is used on the hearth or the stove. Straight-sided marmites for stove cooking are also made in large sizes for big establishments. The classical French *marmite* is the earthenware one in which the *pot-au-feu* is made.

MARMITE, PETITE. A clear soup served from the marmite in which it is made. Served on the side usually are grated cheese and oven-dried slices of French bread, sometimes spread with bone marrow. Made well, this is a rich consommé prepared like a beef *pot-au-feu* with a chicken (or carcass and giblets) added. It takes its name from the marmite, the saucepan or stockpot. Traditionalist French home cooks insist that the pot should be earthenware, but most professionals prefer enamelled or other metal pots; they claim constant use gives the earthenware an impregnation of aged fat which affects the soup.

MAROILES or **MAROLLES.** This cheese was first made in A.D. 960 and has been affectionately known by French cheese lovers as *vieux puant* or old stinker, an indication of its pungency. Its 1000th anniversary was celebrated with due ceremony in the medieval village of the same name. One of the best French cheeses, it is square in appearance, like a Pont l'Evêque, with a thick red rind. This rind is brushed frequently while the cheese is ageing and then rinsed with beer.

MARQUIS DE TERME, CH. See BORDEAUX WINES.

MARRON. The French name of the large French chestnut which differs from the Spanish chestnut or *chataigne* by never having more than one seed per pod. Being very starchy, *marrons* are usually preferred for stuffings. They were originally known as 'acorns of Sardis' because they were grown in Sardis, Lydia.

MARJORAM

MARSHMALLOWS

MARRONS GLACÉS. The French name for glazed chestnuts. Large whole chestnuts, peeled and cooked, are poached for hours in pans of sugar syrup of increasing density so that the chestnuts become permeated with the syrup and almost transparent. To give a final glaze, a thicker syrup is lightly beaten until white and the chestnuts coated with it.

MARROW (VEGETABLE). One of the Cucurbitaceae, the family that includes cucumbers, melons and squashes. In Britain it is a late summer vegetable and best eaten when small, when the flesh is still delicate and tender. Marrow can be gently stewed in butter and garnished with finely chopped parsley or green herbs; or stuffed with a savoury filling and baked; or made into a jam.

MARSALA. See ITALIAN WINES.

MARSANNAY, ROSÉ DE. See BURGUNDY WINES.

MARSHMALLOW. A fluffy sweet confection made with egg white or gelatine, coated with powdered sugar.

MARTILLAC. See BORDEAUX WINES.

MARTINI COCKTAIL. The straight martini, oldest and simplest form of this cocktail, is half gin and half French vermouth, thoroughly mixed. A dry martini is two-thirds gin and one-third vermouth. An American martini has a higher proportion of gin.

MARZIPAN. A sweet confection of ground almonds, sugar and egg white much used in making rich sweetmeats of fancy shapes. When correctly made it should be as pliable as potter's clay.

The origin of marzipan is disputed; some say it dates back to ancient times when made by nuns. The French *massepains* are *petit fours* of different shapes.

MASCARPONE. An Italian soft cheese, like ricotta. In Italy it is served with chocolate cake, strawberries or with bread. It is butter-coloured, made from fresh cream and tastes like whipped cream. It is sometimes beaten with a liqueur or brandy and sprinkled with sugar.

MASGOOF. An Iraqi dish of Tigris salmon. The fish is spread-eagled on a stick frame and several are set in a circle all equidistant from a fire of mimosa twigs. The grilling takes about 1 hour. The fish are then laid on large platters and either covered with chopped tomatoes or spread with a curry sauce. The hot fish is pulled off with the fingers and eaten with soft Arab bread. A *masgoof* ceremony in Baghdad takes place in summer, in the evening on the dried-out bed of the Tigris.

MASKING. To cover food with a sauce, jelly or mayonnaise after it has been cooked, or for serving.

MASSENA, À LA. The French culinary name for the garnish served with tournedos, fillets and noisettes. It is composed of artichoke hearts filled with thick Béarnaise sauce and strips of poached beef bone marrow. It can also be made with artichoke bottoms filled with Périgueux sauce and with slices of poached marrow on the tournedos.

MAS ST LOUIS. See RHÔNE WINES.

MASTIC. These are small clear crystals from an evergreen resinous shrub and are much used in Balkan cooking. Mastic is an important Greek export. In the days of the Turkish occupation the ladies of the Sultan's harem were allowed the proceeds from the sale of mastic gum as pin-money. The sales in those days were considerable, and as the main growing area was the island of Chios, the crop became an important money-earner and the island was granted its own parliament. Today there are some 4 million mastic bushes in Chios; but no parliament. The flavour of mastic is faintly like liquorice, a word of Greek derivation which means sweet root. It is used to make *raki*, a strong spirit (see ARRACK).

Mastic gum is produced by making incisions in the bark of the main trunk and branches to make the bush 'cry'. On the ground around the shrub a layer of fine sand is sprinkled, a carpet on which the 'tears' drop. These tears are the crystals and the work of sorting them out for size, colour and quality is still done by hand.

MATÉ. A Paraguayan tea – its full name *Yerba de Maté* – made from the powdered leaves and young shoots of a species of holly bush. It makes a beverage similar to green tea and is both a stimulant and a tonic. In most Latin American countries it is more popular than tea or even coffee.

Maté is brewed like ordinary tea, using 1–2 teaspoons ($1\frac{1}{4}$–$2\frac{1}{2}$) to a cup of hot water or milk, depending on the variety used. It is strained and and served with sugar, and may also be iced.

MATELOTE. A rich fish stew flavoured with red or white wine and herbs. This is also called *meurettes* or *pochauses* depending on the district and method of preparation. It is usually prepared with freshwater fish like carp, tench, pike and eel. *Matelote à la Normande* is the exception for it is made from sea fish, for example sole or gurnet. The preparation is moistened with cider and thickened with a *velouté* sauce based on fish stock and fresh cream.

MATZO. A type of unleavened bread which dates back to biblical days when the Jews fled from Egypt and in their haste had only time to bake bread made with flour and water and no yeast. Matzos have become symbolic of the bread of affliction and are always eaten by the Jews at the festival of the Passover. Over the centuries, Jewish cooks have learned to incorporate the matzo mixture into other dishes, such as dumplings for soup, and to make such Jewish specialities as *matzo crimsel* (which are fried matzo cakes), matzo meat loaves and *matzo kugel b'yayin*, a matzo wine pudding.

MATZO WINE PUDDING

8 matzos

$\frac{3}{4}$ pint (2 cups) red wine

4 oz. ($\frac{1}{2}$ cup) margarine, melted

$\frac{1}{4}$ lb. each seedless raisins and chopped nuts

6 oz. ($1\frac{1}{2}$ cups) sugar

2 teaspoons ($2\frac{1}{2}$) powdered cinnamon

6 egg whites, stiffly beaten

Soak the matzos in half the wine. Rub a casserole with margarine and cover with a layer of soaked matzos. Sprinkle with melted margarine, nuts, fruit, sugar and cinnamon. Spread with beaten egg whites. Repeat this operation until all the ingredients are used up, the top layer being of beaten

egg whites, raisins, nuts, sugar and cinnamon. Bake in a moderate oven for 30 minutes, take from the pan, pour the remaining wine over the top and continue to bake for a further 5 minutes.

MAUCAILLOU, CH. See BORDEAUX WINES.

MAYONNAISE. An emulsion or thick, rich sauce consisting of oil, eggs and vinegar or strained lemon juice, flavoured with salt and pepper and sometimes mustard and other similar ingredients. It is served with salads, meat, chicken and eggs.

MEAD. An alcoholic beverage of great antiquity.

MEAL. Grain or pulse ground to a powder.

MEAT. This is the general term for beef, mutton, lamb, veal, pork and game flesh, together with offal, kidneys, sweetbreads, hearts etc. Good meat has a firm and elastic texture and any with a doubtful odour or which is flabby and moist should be avoided. There should not be an undue proportion of fat or lean; and the lean should be finely grained with a marbling of fat and the fat free from spots.

For roasting (which see), a joint should not be smaller than $2\frac{1}{2}$ lb.; smaller portions should be braised or pot roasted.

Meat is cooked to bring out its flavours, to improve appearance, and to make it easier to digest. Meat should not be eaten too fresh as it lacks flavour and is tough.

MEAT BALLS. Any combination of meat, raw or cooked, shaped into balls. There are hundreds of ways in which to prepare them since they are part of almost every cuisine.

MEAT EXTRACT. See EXTRACTS.

MEAT GLAZE. See GLAZE.

MEBOS. Apricots dried in the sun and served as sweetmeats or comfits (which see).

MÉDAILLON. French culinary name of small, round and flat cuts of meat or fish, or a cut of moulded and enriched ground preparation. Round slices of *foie gras* are also called *médaillons*.

MEDLAR. A fruit about the size of a small apple with a brown skin and firm flesh. The medlar tree is cultivated in Britain but also grows wild in southern Europe and some parts of Asia. It is also found in America where it was taken by the Jesuits. The fruit of the cultivated variety is the best.

The fruit is edible for only two weeks after being

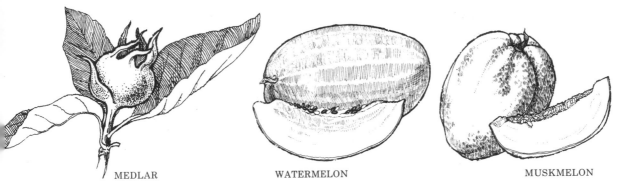

MEDLAR   WATERMELON   MUSKMELON

picked, when disintegration, or bletting, as it is called, sets in. It is chiefly used for preserves, medlar jam being particularly good.

MÉDOC, BAS MÉDOC, HAUT MÉDOC. See BORDEAUX WINES.

MEGRIM. A deep-water flat-fish found all round the British coasts. Among flat-fish it does not rank high as a food fish, its flesh being rather coarse and dry. It is frequently sold as sole, but with some qualifying, often erroneous, term such as witch sole or even lemon sole.

MELBA. The name of a sauce made from fresh raspberries and named after Dame Nellie Melba, the noted singer, who was fond of good eating. Many dishes have been named after her of which probably the best known is Peach Melba, ice-cream served with peaches and a raspberry sauce. See PEACH.

MELBA TOAST. Very thin slices of bread baked in a slow oven until crisp. Originally it was made for Dame Nellie Melba.

MELILOT. This tall plant, known in America as sweet clover, has yellow lupin-like flowers. It is dried and used to flavour stews, stuffings and marinades. In Switzerland, blue melilot flavours Schabzieger cheese.

MELON. Musk melons and water melons are two distinct genera of the Cucurbitaceae or cucumber family. Both bear hard-skinned, juicy fruits of 4 to 12 in. in diameter.

MUSK MELONS

Native to the Indian subcontinent, these were grown by the early Egyptians and their cultivation has spread to most warm or temperate regions. The chief varieties are:

Cantaloup. A round, rough-skinned variety named after the castle of Cantalupo, near Rome, where it was developed in the 17th century, after introduction from abroad. The sweet flesh varies from a pinkish yellow to pale green. In trade usage the name is commonly applied to other musk melons as well.

Casaba. A large American melon with a tough, lightly ribbed and much wrinkled skin. The flesh is soft, creamy white and sweet, but aroma-less. The two most common types are the golden and the pineapple.

Charentais. A small melon with a deliciously flavoured, deep orange flesh.

Honeydew. Used for desserts, hors d'oeuvre, and pickles, this popular melon has a greenish flesh, sweet and fragrant.

WATER MELONS

These are smooth-skinned, with pink flesh that is, as the name implies, very juicy but with less flavour than musk melons. Water melons are widely cultivated in warm and temperate countries.

MELT, TO. To liquefy by heat.

MELTS. The spleen of animals. Ranked as offal, it is perfectly edible but usually sold as pet food.

MENDIANTS. Common French name for a sweet made of almonds, figs, hazel-nuts and raisins the colour of which recalls the habits of the four Roman Catholic mendicant orders.

MENU. Tradition has it that the first modern menu was devised by the Duke of Brunswick in 1541 to give his friends a choice among the dishes his chef could prepare.

The use of the menu is common now but there is an earlier European version of it which served an entirely different purpose. It was not a menu in the sense of a bill of fare at all, but a set of instructions for the kitchen staff of a royal or princely household and also a rendering of accounts to the chamberlain. The menu, or *escriteau* as it was known in old French, told the staff the order in which various courses were to be served. The cost of buying food-stuffs was also indicated on the menu for the convenience of the chamberlain.

The menu came into its own in Europe at the time of the first French Restoration in the early 19th century. When individual menus first came into vogue some of Europe's great artists illustrated them and these were later sought as collectors' items.

The menu as used today serves two purposes. It indicates what food is available and in public eating places at what cost. There are two types of menu, the *à la carte* and the *table d'hôte*.

MERCUREY. See BURGUNDY WINES.

MERINGUES. The history of this sweet is obscure but some say meringues were probably first made in 1720 by Gasprini, a Swiss pastrycook who worked in Mehrinyghen. French royalty liked them and Marie Antoinette is said to have made and baked them herself.

Essentially a mixture of egg whites and sugar, there are three varieties of meringues:

1. *Meringue Chantilly:* egg whites beaten until stiff with castor (extra fine) sugar folded in; used for meringues baked in half-shells and sandwiched together with whipped cream, or to garnish the top of a sweet dish.

2. *Meringue Cuite:* egg whites and sugar whisked together until very thick, preferably over a gentle heat, and used for meringue baskets and *petits fours* and as a base for creams.

3. *Meringue Italienne:* whisked egg whites on to which a sugar syrup boiled at 260° F. is poured. This is whisked until thick and used to cover such dishes as baked Alaska or iced bombe and for certain pastries.

MERLOT GRAPE. See BORDEAUX WINES.

MERRYTHOUGHT. Fanciful name for the furcula between the neck and the breastbone of poultry also called the 'wishbone'. Both names refer to the custom of two persons making a wish and pulling the bone. The holder of the larger broken portion will, it is said, be granted his wish.

MEUNIÈRE. French culinary name for a method of cooking fish in which the fish is dredged with flour and fried in foaming butter until a golden brown. It is then taken from the pan and put on a serving plate. The pan is wiped clean, fresh butter is fried in it until a pale brown; lemon juice and finely chopped herbs are added and, while the butter is still foaming, it is poured over the fish, which is served immediately.

MEURSAULT. See BURGUNDY WINES.

MEYNEY, CH. See BORDEAUX WINES.

MIGNONETTE. The French culinary name for coarsely ground white or black pepper. It resembles mignonette seeds.

MILANAISE, À LA. Literally, according to the style of Milan. The food is dipped in egg and breadcrumbs and cooked in clarified butter.

MILK. Milk is an almost complete food, invaluable for growing children and a source of nourishment for adults. It contains protein, sugar (lactose), fats and salts, as well as vitamins A, C, D and certain B-vitamins. Milk has been used for thousands of years, and together with the cow that provides most of it, it has formed part of folklore and even of the religion of ancient civilizations.

Cows' milk is universally used, but in some parts of the world milk is also obtained from buffaloes, goats, camels, sheep and reindeer.

Milk is one of the foods for which there is no substitute and probably there is no human being who does not consume it in one form or another. It is drunk hot or cold, added to tea or coffee, or used to make a large variety of other hot or cold drinks. It is an ingredient of many puddings. Milk is the basis of the other dairy products such as butter, cream, cheese of all sorts, buttermilk and yoghourt.

Goats' milk has about the same composition as cows' milk except that the fat globules are smaller and it is therefore easier to digest. It can be fed to infants who find cows' milk difficult to digest. It is sweet and agreeable but different in taste from cows' milk. After long years of neglect outside of certain mountain areas, goat farming for milk is once again coming into its own in the United States and Europe.

CONDENSED MILK. This is produced by gradually reducing the water content of milk by evaporation. Only a part of the water is allowed to evaporate and the result is a whole milk with the consistency of honey to which sugar is added. A valuable food, it will keep for a reasonable time after the container has been opened.

EVAPORATED MILK. In this the water content is reduced much as in condensed milk, but the resulting liquid is thinner. Sometimes small amounts of vitamin D concentrate are added, but no sugar. If canned when hot and sterilized, evaporated milk keeps for a long time. If diluted to restore the original water content, its nutritional value is about the same as fresh pasteurized milk.

SKIMMED MILK. This is milk with the fat content removed by a separator. A useful source of protein, it is used in making bread, cakes, biscuits (cookies) and ices.

MILK BREAD. Bread in which milk, rather than water, is used to prepare the dough.

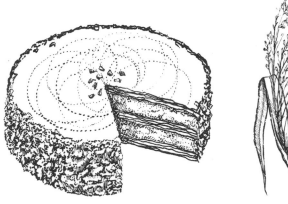

MILLE-FEUILLE GÂTEAU

MILLET

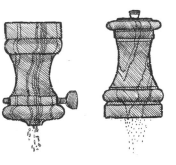

MILLS (salt and pepper)

MILK SHAKE. Cold milk, flavoured with coffee, chocolate, banana, strawberry or other essences and whisked until frothy, often topped with a scoop of ice-cream. The ice-cream may also be whisked with the other ingredients.

MILL. A gadget to grind coffee, breadcrumbs, pepper, block salt, etc.

MILLE-FEUILLE. Literally 'a thousand leaves'. The name given to the French *pâtisserie* made of layers of puff pastry baked until crisp and layered alternatively with whipped cream and raspberry or strawberry jam. The top is iced with a thin layer of fondant.

MILLÉSIME. 'The year of the vintage.' When a wine is said to be *millésime* it means that it bears the date of its vintage.

MILLET. A term used of a number of food grains which although similar do not strictly belong to the same genus. Millets were probably cultivated in India in prehistoric times, and certainly the Romans used the cereal in a sort of milk porridge. Various types of millet are grown in Asia, Africa, some parts of Europe, and the United States.

Millet flour is white and used in cakes and puddings and said to equal rice in food value.

MILT. The soft roe of a fish, as of the male herring, for example. It is the equivalent of the spleen of the animal, so-called because at one time it was thought to have the same function as the soft roe.

MIMOSA. A garnish of thinly sliced, fresh green beans and coarsely grated yolks of hard-boiled eggs, usually added to clear soups or salads to give a 'mimosa' flower look.

MINCE. In the United States, to grind. It means to put through a mincer or to cut into very small pieces with a knife or food chopper.

MINCEMEAT. A preserve, the recipe for which has changed over the centuries. The first recipe seems to date back to 1486 and contained 'a hare, a pheasant, two partridges, two pigeons and two conies strongly spiced and cooked' and then 'made craftily into the likeness of a bird's body, the meat stuffed into a pastry shell and feathers placed over all'. Early recipes include meat.

Two centuries later the mincemeat of the traditional British Christmas fare as we know it today began to evolve. Eggs, raisins, orange and lemon peel were added along with meat and spices. The American version usually contains meat.

There were some modifications over the years and meats of all sorts were excluded: the contemporary version consists of chopped apples, dried fruits, orange and lemon peel, and sugar and suet. It is matured in rum or brandy and used as a filling for pies and tarts.

MINERAL WATERS. Mineral waters can be divided into two broad categories, aerated and still, but all have one thing in common – they contain no alcohol. Aerated water can further be subdivided into natural and artificial types,

Natural mineral waters are produced in the depths of the earth by leaching minerals from rock by tremendous heat and pressure. The water, washing out these free minerals, reaches the surface sometimes as hot thermal springs. Over the years medicinal spas have sprung up round these mineral springs, good examples being Wiesbaden in Germany, Bath in England, Warm Springs, Georgia in the United States, and many others.

Aerated waters are effervescent because of the presence of carbon dioxide gas. In natural waters this results from the passage of water through limestone rock; in artificial waters it is introduced in the bottling process.

Still mineral waters contain minerals but are not carbonated.

MINESTRA. An Italian word for a thick soup. In days when inns were few and far between, travellers found shelter in monasteries. The monks, accustomed to receive guests at all hours, as part of their routine had a cauldron of meat and vegetables simmering on the stove for instant service. This was known as *minestra*, derived from the Latin *ministrare*, to serve.

MINESTRONE. Literally a large *minestra*, a soup of beef stock in which is cooked a combination of many vegetables and *pastas*, with just enough stock to float both. In Italian households the meat which gives the stock its flavour is usually left in the soup, thereby making the *minestrone* a one-course meal.

MINNOW. Tiny fresh-water fish (the tiddler of British schooldays) which is often substituted for gudgeon. It also resembles whitebait and should be cooked in the same way.

MINT. This is such a large family of ancient lineage that it almost needs a book to itself, with so many kinds of mint, both wild and cultivated. The natural habitat is the Mediterranean area and western Asia.

The name mint derives from the Latin *mentha*, and there is a legend that this name in turn comes from Mintha, a daughter of Cocytus, who, rather unkindly, was turned into a mint plant by Prosperina. Legends apart, mint has been recognized as a useful herb since earliest times and the New Testament has a reference to a tithe of mint, cumin and anise.

The Romans used mint in their cooking and they probably brought it to the British Isles. In the Middle Ages it was a favourite herb – in days when strongly flavoured herbs were necessary. Throughout the centuries it has remained a popular culinary herb – although it is not much used in France.

The best-known species are as follows:

Apple mint. A mint of delicate flavour with a hairy, roundish leaf of a cool green. Its flavour is almost fruity with overtones of mint. It can be used in fruit cooking and in fruit soups.

Bergamint or orange mint. Also known as eau de Cologne mint and lavender mint. This is a mint with an almost lavender-like fragrance, although it strikes people differently as its various names imply. Its leaves are broader than the other mint leaves. Its stems are almost reddish and the leaves have a purplish tinge. This too can be used in ice-creams, apple sauce, fruit cups etc.

Spearmint. This is the everyday mint of the garden, often referred to as curly leafed mint. It has deep green leaves which are slightly crinkly with a tendency to fold within themselves. This is the mint for sauces, jellies, drinks and salads.

Peppermint. A mint of a delicate fragrance, with deep green, spear-shaped leaves with toothed edges. It is the mint used in herbal teas and can be used in almost all non-alcoholic beverages, including a glass of water. Oil of peppermint is distilled from this member of the mint family, from which are made sweet confections such as peppermint cream. Certain liqueurs are flavoured with it.

MINT JULEP. See JULEP.

MINT SAUCE. See SAUCES.

MINUTE. A name given, more in the United States than in Britain, to dishes which have been cooked quickly. The most usual of these is MINUTE STEAK (which see).

MINUTE STEAK. A boneless steak, cut $\frac{1}{4}$ in. thick, grilled (broiled) or fried for no more than 2 minutes.

MIRABEAU. A dish which takes its name from Mirabeau, the French revolutionary and son of the Marquis of Mirabeau. It consists of grilled (broiled) meat, with strips of anchovy fillets arranged in a criss-cross pattern on the meat and served with pitted olives, blanched tarragon leaves and anchovy butter.

MIRABELLE. A small, golden-yellow plum (see PLUM). The name is also given to a strong liqueur made chiefly in Alsace from this fruit. It is pure white and kept in glass rather than casks.

MIRACULOUS FRUIT. A berry-bearing shrub or tree which occurs wild in West Africa but has been cultivated in the United States by the Department of Agriculture. The first taste is somewhat tart, but the 'miracle' is that this soon changes into a pleasantly sweet taste. Its uniqueness lies in the fact that anything sour eaten or drunk after the berry will taste sweet for an hour or two, sometimes longer. Thus lemon juice will taste sweet. Miraculous berries may be used to take the tartness out of grapefruit, rhubarb and other similar fruits. The sweetness induced by this fruit appears to be preferable to that of any known synthetic sweeteners. Salty and bitter flavours are affected to a lesser degree.

MIREPOIX. A garnish that takes its name from a French duke who lived in the reign of Louis XV. It is a mixture of diced carrots, onions and celery with or without blanched belly of pork or ham. It is used in the preparation of meat, fish, and shell-fish dishes to enhance their flavour and as a foundation for some soups and sauces.

MIROTON. A sort of stew from left-over boiled beef warmed with plenty of sautéed onions and served with rich Espagnole sauce (called brown

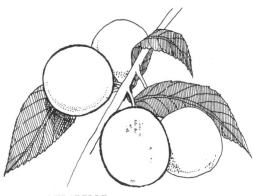

MIRABELLE

sauce). This dish dates back hundreds of years but its exact origins are not known. In some old French recipe books it is referred to as *mironton*.

MISSION-HAUT-BRION, CH. LA, See BORDEAUX WINES.

MIX, TO. In culinary terms, to combine ingredients by beating or stirring.

MIXED GRILL. A combination of grilled (broiled) meats. These may include lamb chops, lamb kidneys, farm sausages, tournedos, rashers of bacon, veal noisettes and chicken, garnished with tomatoes and mushrooms and served with fried potatoes.

The French version, *friture mixte*, usually has some calves' liver, brains and sweetbreads, while the Italian version, *fritto misto*, also contains such vegetables as artichoke bottoms, aubergine (egg-plant) and French beans.

It takes a certain skill to make this dish because of the need to allow for the varying lengths of time required to grill each meat so that all are done at the same time and ready to serve.

MIXED PICKLES. A mixture of vegetables, cut into small pieces and preserved in a clear spiced vinegar.

MIXER. An electrical gadget to beat, mix etc.

MOCHA. A fine quality of coffee which takes its name from the Yemeni town of Mocha. Mocha beans are extremely fragrant with a distinctive flavour. Coffee from such beans should be served in very small cups.

The term mocha is often used to describe coffee dishes of all sorts, as well as combinations of coffee and chocolate.

MODE, À LA. A French culinary term for large cuts of braised beef on any dish prepared in the current French style of cooking, the word *française* being understood.

In America, pie *à la Mode* is the description given to all sorts of fruit pies topped with ice-cream.

MOISTENING. In cooking this means adding a liquid of some kind to dishes such as ragoûts, stews, braised meat and poultry etc.

MOLASSES. A dark syrup, produced during the manufacture of sugar, which normally comes in three grades: first-boil molasses for table use; second-boil, which is darker, less sweet and has a pronounced flavour; and third-boil, commonly called blackstrap, which is used in the manufacture of cattle feeds, alcohol production and other industrial processes. Once widely used as a household sweetener, the principal use of molasses now is for flavouring confectionery, puddings and in general cookery. See also BLACKSTRAP.

MOLLET, OEUF. French term for a soft-cooked egg, the white of which is just set but the yolk is still quite liquid.

MOLLUSK. A term that embraces squids and octopuses, as well as oysters, mussels and scallops.

MONAL. A magnificent rainbow-coloured pheasant, a native of the Himalayas, western China and the eastern part of Afghanistan.

The monal is polygamous and gregarious and can have a life span of about 30 years. It is known to crossbreed with other pheasants, and can be bred in captivity if the right climatic conditions are provided. It is regularly imported into Europe and America and there are quite a few specimens in Western aviaries that help to preserve this unique game bird.

There are two other varieties, the Chinese monal and Sclater's monal. The relationship of the three is obvious but the Himalayan monal is the most beautiful of all the pheasant family. The other two are extremely rare and very expensive, if indeed they can be obtained at all. Moonal and monaul are other spellings of the name.

MONBAZILLAC. A rich, golden, dessert wine from the vineyards of three *communes* of the Dordogne *département*; Monbazillac, Colombier and Pomport.

MONKEY PUZZLE TREE. This is *Araucaria araucana*, also called the Chile pine, the tree which bears the Chile pine nut (which see).

MONKFISH. An alternative name for both the angel-fish (which see) and the angler fish (which see).

MONOSODIUM GLUTAMATE. Monosodium glutamate is the chemical name of *Ve-tsin* which is widely used in Chinese cookery and may be used equally effectively in Western.

This white powder stimulates the taste buds and enhances the flavour of many foods. It should not, however, be used for sweet and egg dishes.

Use about half a teaspoon ($\frac{2}{3}$) for each pound of meat or fish and each quart ($1\frac{1}{4}$) of stock or cupful ($1\frac{1}{4}$) of gravy. It may be added at any stage of cooking but it is better to rub it into meat before cooking.

MONPELOU, CH. See BORDEAUX WINES.

MONSTERA (*Monstera deliciosa*). A fruit that lives up to its botanical name. When ripe it suggests a large ear of corn whose great plump kernels arranged round a central inedible cob become loose as they ripen and when fully matured may be extracted and eaten. It tastes like a luscious fruit salad, and is suggestive of a variety of flavours including bananas, strawberries and pineapples which blend together but nonetheless remain identifiable.

Monstera should not be eaten unless fully ripe because in its earlier stages it contains a substance irritating to the throat. This fruit does not always ripen naturally, in which case it should be cut and placed in a refrigerator for about 24 hours and then left at room temperature until it softens.

Its deep cream blossom is beautiful. It is grown in the West Indies and Queensland, Australia, and has also been successfully planted in southern Florida.

MONTAGNY. See BURGUNDY WINES.

MONT-BLANC or **MONTE BIANCO.** The French and Italian names for a popular Continental pudding of sweetened, puréed chestnuts, flavoured with brandy, piled mountain-wise and covered with whipped cream to simulate snow.

MONT REDON. See RHÔNE WINES.

MONTÉE DE TONNERRE. See BURGUNDY WINES.

MONTHÉLIE. See BURGUNDY WINES.

MONTILLA. See SPANISH WINES.

MONT LOUIS. See LOIRE WINES.

MONTMAINS. See BURGUNDY WINES.

MONTMORENCY, À LA. Montmorency is a variety of cherry originally grown in a district of Paris. When a dish is described as *à la Montmorency* it means that it contains these particular cherries, for example, canard *à la Montmorency*.

MONTRACHETS, LES. See BURGUNDY WINES.

MONTROSE, CH. See BORDEAUX WINES.

MONTS DE MILIEU. See BURGUNDY WINES.

MOONFISH. This name applies to two different fish:

1. *Mola mola*, a marine fish of warm and temperate seas, called *poisson lune* by the French and *Mondfisch* by the Germans. Sunfish is another English name.

2. *Lampris guttatus*, a large spotted deep-sea fish known to feed below depths of 600 feet. It is purple and silver in colour with salmon-red flesh. Because it is found in most seas it is known by several names, including opah, Jerusalem haddock and, among English fishermen, kingfish. *Gudhlax* (God's salmon) and *glansfisk* (shining fish) are the Icelandic and Danish names which reflect the internal and external qualities of this fine fish.

MOOSE. See ELK.

MOREL. One of the most flavoursome fungi, whether freshly picked or dried for winter use. Morels grow in woods and on mountain slopes, the best being found in alpine country. They look like little pointed pieces of brown or black sponge and must be washed carefully. They can be cooked in the same way as mushrooms and also used to garnish fricasees, soups and sauces.

MORELLO CHERRY. See CHERRIES.

MOREY-ST-DENIS. See BURGUNDY WINES.

MORGON. See BURGUNDY WINES.

MORILES. See SPANISH WINES.

MOREL (*Morchella esculenta*)

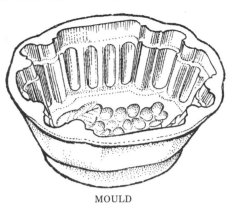

MOULD

MORNAY, À LA. A method of preparing food, usually fish or eggs, with a Mornay sauce. See SAUCES.

MOROCCAN WINES. Although viticulture on an extensive scale did not start in Morocco until the beginning of the 20th century, it has progressed at a great rate and there are now over 180,000 acres of vineyards, of which a part is devoted to table grapes. Many of the Moroccan red wines, particularly those from around Meknes, are light and of quite good quality, considering the southerly latitude at which they are grown. France is the principal market for these wines, where they are extensively used for blending as well as being sold as *ordinaires* under their own name.

MORTADELLA SAUSAGE. This is often called Bologna and is of Italian origin. It is still made in Bologna, which has the reputation of making the best. A similar type of sausage called *mortadelle*, served as an hors d'oeuvre, is produced in Lyons and Paris.

MORTAR. See PESTLE.

MOSELLE WINE. See GERMAN WINES.

MOSTELLE. Also called *moutelo, mutele, motelle* and *mustella*. A scarce but delicious fish found in the Mediterranean and highly prized for its liver. It should be eaten very fresh and may be cooked in the same way as burbot.

MOULD (MOLD). A container in which food is packed so as to retain the shape of the container when turned out. The word often refers also to a dish so produced, for example fish or chicken mould. Moulds may be hot or cold.

(2) A woolly or furry growth consisting of minute fungi growing on the surface of jams, preserved fruits, meat and other substances in contact with the moist air. This does not actually spoil food (except bread) or make it unfit to eat but ruins its appearance, but in the case of cooked foods, especially meat, it suggests staleness. Mould should be scraped off cheeses and skimmed off jams and preserves etc.

Moulds which form on certain cheeses to give a particular flavour and turn them blue are deliberately introduced.

MOULIN-À-VENT. See BURGUNDY WINES.

MOULIS, CH. See BORDEAUX WINES.

MOUSAKA. Called the cottage pie of the Balkans, this is a casserole dish with many versions, but usually consists of layers of vegetables (which vary according to the season), alternating with layers of minced (ground) meat. The meat may be pork, lamb, beef or veal. Sometimes the mousaka is covered with a layer of white sauce, as in Greece, but more often simply with breadcrumbs or grated cheese or left *au naturel*.

MOUSSE. The French word for foam or froth and this is the key to a mousse, the essence of which is lightness. As entrées, main dishes for lunch, or a fine addition to a buffet, savoury mousses of puréed meat or fish, poultry, game or vegetables can be served hot or cold. They can be made in a ring-mould and turned out to be served with various garnishes and sauces.

As a sweet, cold mousses are based on separated eggs, and a flavoured egg-and-cream custard or fresh fruit purée.

MOUSSELINE. The name given to various preparations which have whipped cream added to them. It is used in particular for little moulds of fish, poultry, game, shellfish or *foie gras*, enriched with cream. They are served hot or cold. See SAUCES.

MOUTON-BARON-PHILIPPE, CH. See BORDEAUX WINES.

MOUTON-ROTHSCHILD, CH. See BORDEAUX WINES.

MOZZARELLA CHEESE. A soft Italian curd cheese which comes in a creamy butter ball, or as

269

a tan-coloured, smoked variety in a number of shapes. Mozzarella is a classic filling for pizza and is suitable for melting in a casserole or for use as a table cheese.

MUDDLER. A pestle or thick heavy rod used to crush and mix fruit slices, mint, sugar etc. in drinks. Thus to muddle in this context means to use one of these implements.

MUFFIN. This is a light, circular, spongy, flat unsweetened cake baked in a muffin pan. Muffins are made with milk, butter, flour and yeast and are toasted, buttered and served hot. They used to be sold in the streets of English towns by the muffin man carrying his tray and bell.

MUFFIN, AMERICAN. A type of quick bread or scone, made with a batter, poured into well-greased muffin pans, which are similar to the British deep patty tins, and baked in a hot oven. They are turned out as soon as they are baked and served piping hot. A standard American recipe (with American quantities) is as follows:

2 cups sifted all-purpose flour
2 teaspoons baking powder
½ teaspoon salt
2 tablespoons sugar
1 egg, beaten
1 cup milk
2 tablespoons shortening, melted

Sift the dry ingredients, then moisten with the eggs, milk and shortening. Stir only enough to blend, pour into well-greased, deep muffin pans or patty tins and bake in a hot oven for 20 to 25 minutes.

MUFFIN DISH. A large, flat, usually round dish which is fitted with a cover. It is used at table to serve hot muffins, toast etc., the cover keeping the contents warm until required. They can be of silver or other metal, or of porcelain.

MUFFIN PAN. This is an American baking dish made of thin metal with a number of cavities of some depth shaped to hold individual muffins, cupcakes or gems.

MULARD. A cross between a Rouen and a Barbary duck, and unable to reproduce its kind. In some regions of France *mulards* are fattened for their livers which are made into delicious *foie gras*. The flesh of these ducks is preserved in fat and is held by epicures to be even better than *confit d'oie* made by the same methods.

MULBERRY. The Romans are said to have enjoyed this fruit, while Pliny, the Greek scholar, also refers to it in some of his writings. The mul-berry tree was first introduced into England in 1648 and planted at Syon House, near London.

The two main varieties are the white and black mulberry. The former is meant to feed silkworms while the latter is a sweet, aromatic and juicy fruit which, like most berries, can be used in a variety of ways. Mulberries should be eaten as soon as ripe as they are quick to spoil. A particularly interesting way of preparing this fruit is to pour a mixture of chartreuse, ginger syrup and strained orange juice over the sugared berries before serving. Mulberries may also be used for making jams, jellies, pies and tarts.

The black mulberry is also interesting because of its association with some famous people. A mulberry tree now in the garden of Buckingham Palace dates back to 1609, when James I planted 400 acres in St James's Park with the object of founding a silkworm industry. It was the wrong mulberry and his project foundered, but this part of St James's became a fashionable resort and both Pepys and Evelyn wrote about it. Milton is said to have planted a black mulberry tree at Stowmarket in Suffolk when he lived there and planted another one in the garden of Christ's College, Cambridge. Shakespeare planted a black mulberry tree at New Place, Stratford-on-Avon, but when the Rev. Gastrell acquired New Place he had it cut down, much to the fury of the public. A carved casket made from the wood of Shakespeare's mulberry tree is now in the British Museum, London.

MULLED WINE. Any wine, although red is the more usually chosen, which is brought almost to the boiling point, then poured back into a jug in which some sugar lumps have been melted in a little hot water. A slice or two of lemon are added, and the wine is stirred and sprinkled with a little grated nutmeg.

MULLET. There are three varieties of this fish, but the best is the red mullet, found in the Mediterranean and northward to British waters. It is a white-fleshed fish with a bright red skin weighing between 2 oz. and 12 oz. When mullet are cleaned their liver, which is considered a delicacy, is retained and cooked with the fish. Some cooks hardly clean the inside of red mullet at all. For this reason it is sometimes called the 'woodcock of the sea'. One of the nicest ways of cooking red mullet is *en papillote*, but it can be fried or grilled (broiled) and served with a *maître d'hôtel* butter (which see).

The grey or striped mullet is not related to the red mullet and is caught on both sides of the North Atlantic and along the coasts of the North Pacific. It is a larger fish with a coarser, but white and firm flesh, cooked in many of the ways used for salmon.

PROFITEROLES: a French wedding cake, composed of a tower of profiteroles.

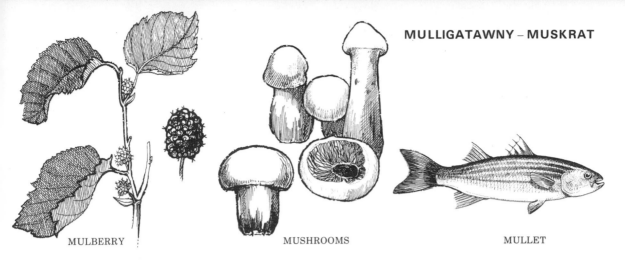

MULBERRY   MUSHROOMS   MULLET

The eastern grey mullet is found along the coasts of North China, Australia and East Africa, and is excellent fried and grilled (broiled). It is superior to another similar fish of Far Eastern rivers, known as the blackhead.

RED MULLET EN PAPILLOTE

4 red mullet, cleaned

2½ oz. (5 tablespoons) butter

salt and freshly milled pepper

lemon juice

Cut an oval of wax paper for each fish, large enough to enclose it completely. Spread the centre with butter, place the fish on it, season well and add a good squeeze of lemon juice. Wrap up the fish, crimping the edges together, i.e. making small pleats, and completely enveloping the fish. Place on a baking (cookie) sheet and bake in a moderate oven for 15–18 minutes.

MULLIGATAWNY. By origin this is an Indian soup but it has been so 'worked upon' by successive generations of British housewives in India that it has lost its identity. The word mulligatawny is a corruption of the Tamil *molegoo tunee*, 'pepper water'.

This soup is made with a boiling fowl or breast of lamb cooked in water until tender with onions, garlic, spices, herbs, coconut cream or milk of almonds, cream or milk. Rice and slices of lime or lemon are usually served as a garnish to this soup as well as the meat, cut into small slices.

The custom of adding rice to the soup is an old Anglo-Indian one, dating from the time when the British in India had rice served with everything they ate.

MUSCADELLE. A small sweet grape from which the Cape (South Africa) wines were made in the 19th century and still used in France and elsewhere for making sweet wines.

MUSCADET. See LOIRE WINES.

MUSCAT. The name of the most highly scented variety of *Vitis vinifera*, the wine-making parent grape. It is popular both as a dessert grape and for making a sweet dessert wine. There are many types of Muscat wines, and most of them are sold under the name of their place of origin, such as Muscat de Frontignan, Muscat de Samos, etc.

MUSH. A kind of porridge made from Indian corn (maize) rated for its satisfying and nutritive qualities.

MUSHROOM. This is the name given to a wide variety of edible fungi. Hippocrates in his writings around 400 B.C. referred to the popularity of mushrooms and also mentions that they were exported to other countries. They have been used in French, German, Italian and Russian cooking for centuries and were known to the Chinese and Japanese cuisines from very early times. See also FUNGI, MOREL.

MUSIGNY. See BURGUNDY WINES.

MUSK DEER. This primitive species of deer lives in the high altitude forests of Mongolia and Siberia and southwards to the Himalayas. A smaller version of this species is also to be found in Korea.

The male has a bag-like gland which contains a substance of a powerful scent and aromatic flavour. This substance is called musk and it is so highly prized that the musk deer has been hunted to near extinction.

There is a Turkish recipe for cakes which are made of wheat starch, butter, syrup, blanched and skinned almonds, rose-water and musk. These confections are known as musk cakes and are cut in diamond shapes and dusted with castor sugar.

Another use is in a musk-flavoured cream and musk drops and in infinitesimal quantities to flavour some liqueurs.

MUSKRAT. This is a North American aquatic rodent, a pest as far as farmers are concerned, but a delicacy described as marsh rabbit on restaurant menus in some parts of North America.

Negroes who settled along the east coast after

REMUAGE

the American Civil War were so desperately poor that they caught these plump, furry animals for food and sold the skins, for which there was a market. By some chance it was discovered that muskrat was delicious when properly cooked, and muskrat breeding was soon a thriving industry.

It is roasted, baked, stewed or made into a pie.

MUSSEL. An edible mollusk found in the English Channel, the North Sea and the coastal waters of the United States. Mussels also occur in fresh water and are sometimes known as the 'oysters of the poor' because of their excellence and relative cheapness.

There are several varieties but the common mussel is the popular one. It has a long shell which is slightly rough along the back. When cultivated, breeding in hurdles makes them tender, delicately flavoured and small but plump.

The best way to open mussels is to steam them. Before being steamed they must be thoroughly washed and scrubbed for they contain sand which makes them gritty.

Mussels may be eaten raw, stewed, baked, pickled, smoked, stuffed, fried, in chowders and soups and as a garnish for fish dishes.

MUSSEL CRAB. See CRAB.

MUST. Unfermented, expressed grape juice.

MUSTARD. A widely used condiment known from biblical times and much appreciated by the Romans.

Mustard as we know it today is the innovation of an obscure old lady simply known as Mrs Clements of Durham. In 1729 she hit on the idea of grinding mustard seeds in a mill exactly like wheat and selling them in the form of a fine powder. This was most successful locally, and it is said she made a small fortune selling what became known as Durham mustard all over England. She also managed to secure the patronage of George I.

There are two main varieties of mustard plants. One is known as white mustard and yields reddish-yellow seeds; the other is black mustard with smaller blackish-red seeds. The mustard powder usually sold in Britain is a mixture of both varieties, sometimes flavoured with *curcuma* or other aromatic substances. The best mustard seeds come from Britain, France, the Netherlands and California.

There is a third variety known as wild mustard whose oily seeds are mainly used to adulterate the other two. In England mustard is prepared mainly by moistening the powder with water which gives a creamy paste. But English mustard may with good effect be mixed instead with vinegar, wine,

ale, cream or cider. To give flavour, infusions of herbs, spices, ground shallots or garlic may be added and to improve its consistency oil may be used in its making. In France *moutarde de Dijon* is made by moistening the powder with verjuice and *moutarde de Bordeaux* with unfermented wine.

MUSTARD AND CRESS. This is really garden cress, an annual native to Persia but now established in Britain and North America. It is pungent and can grow to a height of 18 in. with white flowers. As a very young plant it is used as the so-called mustard and cress as a garnish and in salads and sandwiches.

MUSTARD PICKLE. A mixture of vegetables, cut into small pieces, preserved in a yellow mustard sauce.

MUSTARD SAUCE. See SAUCES.

MUTTON. Mutton is the flesh of mature sheep usually about a year to 18 months old. Sheep are mentioned in ancient writings and the Bible in particular abounds in references to them, but it is not certain when man first ate mutton.

Mutton was a favourite of the French-speaking Normans, who gave this name to the choicer cuts. 'Sheep' is of Old English origin and was the word used by the Anglo-Saxon hinds who tended the animals in the fields. The terms 'mutton chops' and 'sheeps' tongue' show how the meat was apt to be apportioned.

There are many ways of cooking mutton, mostly depending on the cuts used. In France the best quality mutton is the so-called salt meadow, from sheep reared along the coast where aromatic plants grow.

Best quality mutton should be bright red, close-grained and firm. It has a great deal of firm white fat evenly spread over muscular tissues and in the tissues itself.

MUTTONFISH. Australian name for abalone.

MYCELLA. A type of Gorgonzola made in Denmark. The paste is more yellow than white and the flavour is somewhat milder than the genuine Gorgonzola.

MYRTLE. This is a handsome evergreen shrub which grows all over Europe. It has a pleasant fragrance, particularly the variety grown in Italy.

The ancients used it in their cookery and *myrtalum*, a sort of stew, took its name from the myrtle berry. They also used myrtle berries as a substitute for pepper. The leaves are used to flavour roast pork and the small birds which are

MYRTLE

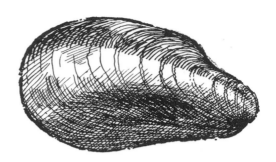

MUSSEL

a delicacy in Mediterranean countries. The shepherds put myrtle branches on the fires over which they roast lamb and kid.

N

NAARTJE. South African tangerine which can be served as a dessert fruit. It is also crystallized or made into a preserve.

NANTUA. French culinary name for sauces and garnishes in which crayfish are used.

NAPOLEON. The French name for a cake made with layers of puff pastry filled with *crème patissière* (which see).

NARBONNE HONEY. A honey which is made in Narbonne, France. It is rosemary scented and has been known since the days of the Romans. Its reputation was good then and it has not faltered since.

NASEBERRY. See SAPODILLA.

NASI GORENG. Fried rice usually cooked together with a number of other ingredients. Served throughout Indonesia and Malaysia, it is rather similar to the Chinese fried rice dishes. *Bami goreng* is a similar fried dish with noodles instead of rice.

NASTURTIUM. A common garden flower usually grown for its brilliant flowers, also known as Indian cress or canary creeper. The young leaves of the plant can be used in sandwiches and salads while the buds are often pickled and used as capers. Nasturtium vinegar can be made by packing fully blown flowers into a bottle and covering them with vinegar flavoured with a little garlic, shallot, red pepper and salt.

NATURE. See WINE TERMS.

NAVARIN. The French culinary name for a ragoût of mutton (not lamb) made either with small onions and potatoes or with different vegetables such as carrots, turnips, new potatoes and green peas in which case *à la printanière* is added to its name.

NAVEL ORANGE. See ORANGES.

NÉAC. See BORDEAUX WINES.

NEAPOLITAN ICE-CREAM. Any plain or fruit cream ice made in a simple 'brick' mould. It can be of one colour, but several layered colours are more usual.

NEAT. An old English name for ox or cattle, retained only occasionally for neat's tongue, meaning ox tongue.

NEBBIOLO. A black grape grown in Piedmont and Lombardy and used to make red table wines. Among these are Barolo and Barbaresco, two of Italy's best-known wines. See ITALIAN WINES.

NEBUCHADNEZZAR. See BOTTLES.

NECTAR. In classical mythology, the wine of the gods, a distillation of refined dew. Today the name is given to any particularly delicious beverage and to the honey of plants.

NECTARINE. A delicious late summer fruit grown under glass in Britain. It is a variety of the peach, smooth-skinned, but flushed with red; the flesh is firm but fragrant and melting. It is made into jams and preserves. Nectarines are at their best when freshly picked and served as a dessert fruit, with a glass of chilled Sauternes.

NEGUS. The name given during the reign of Queen Anne to several types of punch. One was a rather liverish mixture of port wine, sugar, lemon and water. There was also one made with melted calf's foot jelly, white wine, sugar, lemon and spices. Another, described as 'genteel', used cowslip wine instead of white wine and was sweetened with 'broken clear candy sugar which tinkled and splintered as it melted in the thin glasses. It was served after a ladies' card-playing evening, before the short walk home through the summer twilight'. The name negus comes from its reputed inventor, Colonel Francis Negus.

NESSELRODE. The culinary name of one of the classical iced puddings, invented by Mouy, chef to the Russian Count Nesselrode, and at one time fashionable. The base is ice-cream, flavoured with maraschino and mixed with chestnut purée and candied fruits. This mixture was frozen in a tall mould and turned out for serving garnished with *marrons glacés*.

NETTLE. A troublesome weed commonly called stinging nettle, but nourishing to eat if picked when young and tender. Country housewives cook nettles as spinach, and, in Eire, nettle soup is a speciality of the country. Nettle beer is also made in some country districts in Britain.

NEW ENGLAND CODFISH CAKES or BALLS. Simply codfish and potato mixed, shaped into balls or patties and either fried or sautéed.

NEWBURG. Hot lobster cooked in a sherry sauce, served with a thick rich cream sauce and said to be the invention of a chef of New York's famous Delmonico Restaurant.

NIÇOISE. The name given to dishes composed of foods common to the Nice region, mostly fish and vegetables. Dishes cooked *à la Niçoise* have as main ingredients tomatoes, garlic, black olives, anchovies and olive oil. See SALADE NIÇOISE.

NIERSTEIN. The most important wine-producing region of Rhine-Hesse, from which come fine quality white wines. See GERMAN WINES.

NOBLE ROT. *Botrytis cinerea* to the botanists; *pourriture noble* in French; *Edelfäule* in German; and *aszu* in Hungarian; all high-sounding names for a parasitic fungus which develops on grapes, ruining some but ennobling others to produce some of the greatest white wines in the world. This extra natural gift to vines depends on the weather, which must be just right, and means that pickers must work through vineyards several times choosing individual grapes. The fungus penetrates the grape without puncturing the skin. If all goes well, the grape withers and becomes desiccated: the remaining juice retains a higher proportion of sugar. The wines produced are of fine quality but the extra work entails higher prices.

NOISETTE. French for dishes flavoured or made with hazel-nuts. Also a term to describe small round, choice pieces of meat, usually lamb; these may be the eyes of chops, or meat rolled and cut without the bone.

NOISETTE POTATOES. Potatoes scooped out in the shape of a hazel-nut and browned in butter.

NONPAREILLE. The name given in France to small capers, pickled in vinegar, and to 'hundreds and thousands', the coloured granulated sugar used to decorate sweets and cakes.

NOODLES. See PASTA.

NORMANDE, À LA. In the Normandy style. The French culinary name for a garnish of fish, also a sauce for fish. Fish braised in white wine, garnished with poached oysters or mussels is one example. It also means small cuts of meat and feathered game cooked in cider and served with a Calvados enriched sauce, or poultry cooked in Calvados or cider, cream and apples. See SAUCES.

NORVÉGIENNE. A name given to various preparations in cooking but more precisely an ice-cream. This is a so-called 'surprise' pudding of ice-cream inside a hot soufflé or sponge cake casing.

NORWAY LOBSTER. See DUBLIN BAY PRAWN.

NORWEGIAN BLUE (NORMANNAOST). This cheese has only recently come on to the world markets. It is a good-looking cheese, pleasing to eat, and emulates Roquefort far more than any other blue cheese of its type. It is not as sharp in flavour as Danish blue and, although not as creamy, has more character.

NOUGAT. There are two main types of nougat:
1. White nougat, for which Montélimar is famous. This is a confection of boiled sugar and egg whites mixed with nuts and dried cherries. The mixture is set in shallow pans between sheets of rice paper before being cut into small rectangles.
2. Caramel or almond nougat. In this preparation castor sugar is melted to a caramel with chopped almonds browned in it. This is turned out on to an oiled sheet and can be moulded as required. —

NOUGATINE. A round orange-coloured sweet with a delicate honey flavour and a speciality of Troyes in the Haute Seine, France.

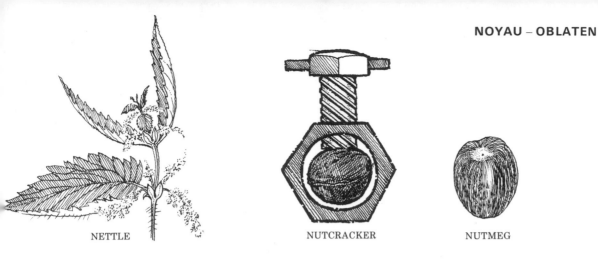

NETTLE   NUTCRACKER   NUTMEG

NOYAU. A strong, sweet, almond-flavoured liqueur, made from extracts of peach and apricot kernels.

NUITS-ST-GEORGES. See BURGUNDY WINES.

NUT. The name for a number of different types of fruit with a woody outer casing and a soft inner skin enclosing an edible kernel. Nuts have been the food of man from earliest times and are still an important item of diet in many parts of the world. Although in some countries nuts are served as a dessert, there is a growing tendency to recognize that they are a basic food rather than a mere adjunct to a meal.

In the United States the production and consumption of nuts is considerable and there is evidence of their growing importance in the diet.

NUT BRITTLE. A type of toffee or candy heavily flavoured with nuts.

NUT BUTTER. A thick butter-like spread made by pounding or grinding and then pressing a variety of blanched and roasted nuts. The most generally known is peanut butter, but similar butters can be made with cashew nuts, pine nuts, hazel-nuts and brazil nuts among others. Kept in a cool, dry place, such butters will keep for months.

NUTCRACKER. An instrument designed to open or break nuts by bursting their shells through applied pressure. There are many elaborate versions of nutcrackers, but the basic pattern is a pair of levers hinged together at one end to form a fulcrum. The nut is placed between the levers as near to the fulcrum as possible, and the inside of the levers is serrated to hold the nut which is cracked by firmly squeezing the levers together. Nutcrackers are made of metal as a rule, but many are also allied with a hard wood.

Served with nutcrackers should be a small pick with a sharp metal point which is used to take the nut from the shell. Nutcrackers and picks are also used to extract the meat from lobster claws.

NUT GRATER. These graters consist of a metal drum bearing small teeth which is enclosed in a cylinder. A wooden block which exactly fits the feed hopper serves to press the whole kernels against the teeth while the handle is turned.

NUTMEG. The hard, dark aromatic kernel of the fruit of the nutmeg tree, indigenous to the Moluccas or Spice Islands in Indonesia and now also grown in the West Indies. When the nutmeg is taken from the fruit it is encased in a lacy covering or aril, known as mace, which has the same flavour.

Nutmeg is a pungent spice and should be used with discretion, grated straight into the dish in which it is required. It can be used both in sweet and savoury dishes and often flavours hot punches and other warming drinks.

NUT PASTES. These are made by combining sugar with the ground kernels of nuts and are much used by confectioners. Almond paste is the most usual and its most general use is as marzipan.

O

OATMEAL. Hulled oats ground into flour or meal, generally prepared in three grades: coarse, medium and fine. Oatmeal is used in the preparation of bread, puddings, porridge, oatcakes and scones.

OATS. A principal cereal (which see) and one of the earliest cultivated by man. A food source for both man and his domesticated animals, its uses are now mainly confined to breakfast cereals and feeding stuffs.

OBLATEN. These are large, plate-sized wafers which were a speciality of Carlsbad (now Karlovy Vary) in Czechoslovakia. One of the best Austrian *torte*, *Pischinger Torte* (which see), is made with *oblaten* and chocolate-hazel-nut cream. *Oblaten* are also made in the United States.

OCCA, OKA-PLANT. This is a South American plant the tubers of which are eaten as a vegetable. It was imported into England in the early 19th century from Peru. In Britain it grows best in greenhouses. The pulp is white and floury, and the outer skin yellow, red or brown. Occa tubers should not be eaten fresh because when green they contain a certain acid which masks their flavour. In South America they are left to dry in the sun for a few days. They are then boiled.

Occas are also grown in France and are mentioned in the *Cuisine Classique*. They are used to make an excellent thick soup known as *purée péruvienne*.

OCTOPUS. A cephalopod mollusk with a dark brown fluid which can be squirted out to form a protective screen. It is eaten in many parts of the world, particularly in Italy and Greece. The octopus has eight tentacles linked at the base, large eyes and a 'beak' like a parrot. One of its peculiarities is its power to change its colour rapidly. It appears to have complete control over these changes, and is able to pass through pink, yellow, brown and black to blend with its surroundings.

Although octopuses can grow very large, in temperate waters they rarely exceed a yard long. Fishermen in the Mediterranean kill octopus by beating them slowly and systematically on a rock. The unfortunate creature dies hard and when killed in this manner, they say, its flesh will become tender. Octopus flesh resembles lobster in taste.

OFFAL or **VARIETY MEATS.** An animal's offal consists of the skin, feet, tail, horns, head and tongue, the lung, liver, spleen and pancreas known as the pluck, the intestines and any other internal organ.

Such offal was in daily use among the Englishman's ancestors, for pigs' feet and head, sheeps' trotters, the maw or paunch, and intestines of the wild and domestic pig and other animals are included in many 'receipts' of the 14th century.

OÏDIUM. See WINE TERMS.

OIL. A fluid grease extracted from animals, vegetables and minerals. The word oil in early use meant that expressed from ripe olives; later the word came to mean any viscid liquid. Oil falls into three categories: mineral oils, which have no place in the kitchen; the cooking and salad oils; and essential oils which are flavoured substances contained in flowers, herbs, fruit and spices.

The different cooking oils all have their distinct flavours and aromas and leave their impact on local cooking. Olive oil is generally preferred in *haute cuisine*, and throughout the Mediterranean, Turkey and Greece. Each area, almost each district has its own variety of olive oil, some heavy and strong-flavoured, others finer and less strong.

Walnut oil is of delicate flavour and aroma. Corn oil is a vegetable oil. Cottonseed oil, purified and rendered, is used as an ingredient in vegetable cooking fats and margarine. Peanut, sesame, mustard and sunflower seeds yield favourite Far Eastern oils and all are good cooking mediums. Safflower is expressed from the seeds of the safflower (bastard saffron) and is favoured by many, while almond oil expressed from bitter almonds and kernels is used only in specialized cooking. Other edible oils of local use are coconut oil, heavy and with a strong aroma, and palm nut oil, used in African cooking, as well as many other oils expressed from nuts, all of them important.

OKRA. Also called *bamya*, *bamies*, ladies' fingers and *quimbombo* etc. It is a mucilaginous and aromatic bean and the seed pod of a plant belonging to the marrow or hibiscus family. It was probably taken from West Africa to the United States, where it has flourished in the southern States. It thrives in most tropical countries, including India, where it is a popular vegetable. In the Balkans it appears almost daily.

OKROSHKA. A well-known cold white wine and vegetable soup from Russia.

OLD-FASHIONED. See WHISKEY, BOURBON.

OLEO. Short for oleomargarine, an older name for margarine (which see).

OLIVE. The real mystery of the olive is where, when and by whom it was first cultivated. These are questions no one has answered. It would seem to have been an almost unconscious pruning and development over an immense space of time, a fortuitous domestication of the wild olive and its gradual development. Whatever its origin, it does seem that the olive, of Mediterranean origin and always close to the sea, is one of the oldest fruits known to man and has been cultivated since prehistoric times. Olives are mentioned in ancient Greek and Roman writings as well as in the Bible, and there is evidence to suggest that the olive has been used for over 5,000 years. Olive oil seems to have been an article of commerce worthy of mention in Egyptian records.

Olive trees, with gnarled trunks and silverygrey foliage, grow everywhere around the Mediterranean. In the spring the trees are covered with tiny flowers; later come the berries, which turn green and then black as they ripen.

OKRA   OCTOPUS

There are many varieties of olives and size has nothing to do with their flavour. Some of the nicest olives are small and often grow in rough-looking locations on remote hilltops. The flavour of the olive is greatly influenced by locality.

The first man who ate an olive must have been, in the culinary sense, brave or foolhardy, for the olive on the tree is bitter and inedible. Not until they have been pickled in brine do olives lose this bitterness: some olives, usually grown for oil, never lose it.

Green olives are those which are picked unripe; the black ones are those which are left to ripen on the trees. Those who only know olives packed neatly in jars or cans would be surprised to see them in the Mediterranean markets in vast quantities, sold in tubs from which the buyers are expected to taste before bargaining.

Olives are not merely something to nibble with drinks in the countries where they are grown. They are cooked in savoury dishes, used as garnishings, mixed with stuffings and are an important ingredient in many salads, such as *salade niçoise*. In Sicily large green olives are stoned and stuffed with a savoury filling, rolled in egg and breadcrumbs and fried in olive oil (see OIL).

OLIVES, MEAT. These are small rolls of meat enclosing a stuffing, usually fried and braised.

OLIVIER, CH. See BORDEAUX WINES.

OLLA PODRIDA. This soup, stew or hotch-potch is a Spanish speciality, particularly in Andalusia. It is made with whatever meat is available, including poultry, and all kinds of vegetables, but *garbanzos* (chick peas) and *chorizos* (Spanish spiced sausages) are obligatory.

OLOROSO. See SPANISH WINES.

OMELETTE. Among the recipes of Apicius is one for *ovemele*, a dish of eggs and honey, and probably the father of all omelettes. Names of dishes are always conjecture. Some people say that the name omelette came from the French *amelette*, meaning a blade, via *alumette*, thus describing the long, flat shape of the omelette. A recipe for 'An Amalet of Eggs' given by Mrs Ann Cook in *Professed Cookery*, 1760, called for 12 eggs with 50 asparagus to produce an omelette an inch thick, garnished with parsley and served with a butter sauce.

Alexander Dumas said that the omelette is to *haute cuisine* what the sonnet is to poetry.

For a good omelette fresh eggs at room temperature are essential. Also important is a special heavy pan, reserved for the purpose, never washed but always rubbed with salt and oil after use.

PLAIN OMELETTE

3 eggs

½ oz. (1 tablespoon) butter

salt, pepper

Heat the butter until almost nut-brown. Lightly beat the eggs while the butter is cooking. Add salt and pepper. Tilt the pan to distribute the butter evenly round the pan. Add the egg mixture and move the pan around to spread it evenly. As the egg sets, gently move the pan back and forth over the heat. Take the pan from the heat, tilt it forward and fold over one side of the omelette with a fork, then the other side. Serve at once on a hot plate.

ONION. A member of the lily family, a most adaptable vegetable and worshipped by the ancient Egyptians. Onions may have originated on the shores of the Mediterranean or, according to some authorities, in the Hindu Kush. In any case, they are older than recorded history. The Babylonians taught the Egyptians that the onion is a symbol of perfection because it is a circle and one can travel the line around a circle throughout eternity.

The Egyptians gave the onion the honours reserved for the immortals and placed a bouquet of onions in the mummy's hand to get him through the after-world.

By the beginning of the Christian era the onion of Egypt had become so sacred that the priests forbade the eating of it. Horace, Pliny and Xenophon were among those who paid their written tribute to the onion.

There are several varieties of onion. The warmer the climate the larger the onion and the milder its flavour. As climate becomes sterner, so the onions become hardier and more strongly flavoured, and keep better. Where onions grow all the year round, they tend to be of poor quality.

Colours vary through white, yellow to a purple red. The colour is also an indication of flavour. White onions usually are milder than either red or yellow and are better for making creamed soups and sauces.

There is a belief that onions planted in a rosebed will mean sweeter roses.

Types of onion:

Button onions. Small onions picked before they have reached full size and which can be pickled or used in cooking as a garnish.

Potato onions. These owe their name to the fact that they multiply by offsets from the parent bulb in the same way as potatoes. They are said to have originated in Egypt and should be treated in the same manner as shallots.

Rocambole. A distinct species of onion with a garlicky flavour. Sand leek is its old name.

Spanish onions (Bermuda). These are not a distinct variety; the name is given to any large mild onion. In the United States it means any imported onion. Spanish onions have a glossy brown skin.

Tree or Egyptian onions. These onions have bulbs both at the root and the top of the stem. Both sets of bulbs can be used in cooking.

Welsh onions. Natives of Siberia so called because they were once grown extensively in Wales. They form no bulbs, the parts used being young growths, in salads and flavourings. They can be used instead of chives.

Other types include the various hard varieties, such as Polish onions, which are very good; Canary onions, rather flat and difficult to peel; and shallots and spring or green onions (which see).

OPORTO. See PORTUGUESE WINES.

OPOSSUM. General name of the American marsupial family Didelphydae, and popularly applied specifically to the Virginia opossum. This animal, about the size of the domestic cat, is omnivorous, eating insects, fruit, birds' eggs, meat and ferns. During the autumn and winter, when it is at its fattest, the opossum makes a most palatable dish, baked and served with sweet potatoes.

ORANGE. Oranges originated in Asia, probably South China and the former Indo-China. Sailors and other travellers brought them to the Mediterranean; some writers advance the theory that the golden apples of classical mythology were oranges, not apples. In the 14th century a Spanish ship brought the first citrus fruits to Britain, 15 citrons and seven oranges. Oranges were served at a banquet given by Henry IV in 1399. Cardinal Wolsey used an orange studded with cloves to ward off smells, and during Elizabethan times oranges were sold in baskets in the streets. Nearly a century later one orange-seller, Nell Gwyn, became a king's mistress, which probably helped to promote their sale. They became so popular they were thought to be a cure-all. Queen Anne of England squeezed orange juice on her lamb; and oranges and lemons were served between courses at gargantuan banquets to aid digestion.

Oranges are said to have been brought to the West Indies by Columbus. The first orange orchard started in California in 1805 and, later, orchards were established in Florida. Both had climates favourable for orange cultivation.

The usual classification of oranges is thus:

Sweet oranges (Citrus sinensis). These are tight-skinned oranges and are the usual types for eating. These can be further divided into the Spanish, which are large and coarse-grained; Mediterranean oranges, which are fine-grained; blood oranges, which are either dark red or of mixed colours; and navel oranges, seedless and with a 'navel' at one end.

Bitter, Seville, sour or Bigarade oranges. The bitter orange is similar to the sweet orange, except for the pulp which is too acid and bitter to be eaten raw. It is usually made into marmalade and is much grown for its strongly scented flowers which form the basis of orange-flower water and the oils used in perfumery. The rind of bitter oranges is aromatic and used in making bitters.

Mandarin oranges. The mandarins, tangerines and satsumas are loose-skinned oranges which are easily peeled and pulled into sections. There are many types. The flavour is less acid than the sweet orange and the skin, though highly aromatic and full of oil, has the distinctive tangerine flavour and a smell unlike other oranges. Clementines, known as 'Oh My Darlings' in the trade, are related to the tangerines. Seedless, tight and smooth-skinned, with a flavour more orange than tangerine, they come from Italy, Spain and Israel.

See also KUMQUAT.

ORANGEADE. A drink made with the juice of sweet oranges and plain or sparkling water.

ORANGE BITTERS. These are used to add flavour and bouquet to mixed drinks and cocktails. See ORANGES, *Bitter*.

ORANGE-FLOWER OIL. An essential oil produced from orange blossoms, used in confectionery and pastry.

(Opposite) RIJSTTAFEL.
(Overleaf) ROLLS: an assortment of rolls.

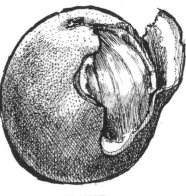

ORANGE

ONION

ORANGE-FLOWER WATER. A fragrant liquid collected from the distillation of orange-flower oil It is used as a culinary flavouring.

ORANGE POMANDER. An orange, studded with cloves and used to perfume clothes.

ORCHIS. The name given to the whole orchid family which grows in many parts of the world. Orchids have long been known and used by man: the Greek philosopher Theophrastus speaks of orchis tubers as an aphrodisiac. This belief persisted into medieval times, when a new mystique was added to it. It was thought that the sex of the unborn child could be predetermined with the help of orchis tubers. The belief was that a preparation made from a younger tuber would result in a boy, while that of an old tuber would produce a girl.

Various orchids are much prized as food while others are used medicinally in many parts of the world. But the best known is the vanilla (which see) an edible variety which has a superb fragrance and is used to flavour a large number of dishes.

OREGANO or **ORIGANO.** The name by which wild marjoram is commonly known. It is a difficult herb to discuss at length since its species or family ramifications are enormous. In fact, the classification of this popular herb is being studied at this moment.

One of the problems when talking of oregano is not only the number of species, but also the fact that plants of the same species when grown in different climates and soils produce quite different flavours. The best we can say is that, in general, the flavour of oregano is stronger than sweet marjoram, and it is pleasant and aromatic.

Oregano can be used in most of the ways in which sweet marjoram or pot marjoram is used, but it must be remembered that its flavour is stronger, therefore discretion is urged. However, the Italians use it with abandon in almost all of their savoury dishes, ragoûts, stews etc., and in pizzas. In Greece where it is called *rigani*, it is used in savoury dishes, but mainly with grilled meat and fish.

ORGEAT. A French *sirop* made from an emulsion of almonds and sugar. It is used to flavour iced water as a long drink or in the mixing of some cocktails.

ORION. Greek inventor of white sauce.

ORMER. A gastropod mollusk, *Haliotis tuberculata*, an abalone (which see) found in the Channel Islands and the neighbouring coasts of France. Ormers are a great delicacy. By convention they are usually classified among the fish dishes, but they are much more akin to meat and are often partnered by a red wine.

ORTANIQUE. A cross between an orange and tangerine. It is of Jamaican origin.

ORTOLAN. A European bunting of exceptional flavour which has enjoyed the favour of gastronomes so long and so widely that its numbers have seriously decreased and outside France it is rarely found on a menu. Ortolan can be cooked in any manner in which quail is cooked. It should not be drawn as its trail is esteemed for its flavour.

ORVIETO. See ITALIAN WINES.

OSSOBUCO. A typical Italian dish of shin of veal cooked in wine with vegetables and flavoured with finely chopped parsley, garlic, lemon rind and anchovy fillets which are sprinkled over the meat just before serving. The dish is usually served with a risotto dressed with melted butter and grated Parmesan cheese. An important part of this dish is the marrow inside the bones and for this a marrow fork is supplied with which to dig it out.

OSTRICH. A large swift-running bird whose flesh was much prized by the Romans. The second Apicius dedicated a special sauce to it. Its flesh is dried and eaten in South Africa. An average bird yields about 60 lb. of meat and 40 lb. of fat.

Ostrich eggs are a delicacy. To extract the

(Previous page) SALADE NIÇOISE.
(Opposite) SAUCES: roast of beef with sauce Béchamel.

contents, bore a hole in each end and shake into a bowl. If used in place of hens' eggs, add 1 tablespoon ($1\frac{1}{4}$) of water to each of 4 beaten eggs. Two tablespoons ($2\frac{1}{2}$) of this mixture equals 1 hen's egg.

OTAHEITE APPLE. Also called Malay apple, a native of the Pacific. It was introduced into Jamaica at the same time as the breadfruit. It probably came, as its name suggests, from Otaheite, the earlier name of Tahiti. The fruit is pear-shaped, pink or red, with a slight rose flavour. It grows in clusters and is in season in June and July only.

OUZO. See ARRAK, ARRACK, RAKI.

OXIDIZED. See WINE TERMS.

OX-TAIL. Ox-tails have been used in cooking for centuries, in soups, stews and ragoûts.

OX-TAIL SOUP. One of the most popular of the winter soups in Europe. It is said the first ox-tail soup was made by a starving French nobleman during the Reign of Terror in Paris in 1793. In those days the tanneries received hides complete with tails, which they threw away. One day this hungry nobleman begged a tail, which he was given. He took it home and made it into a soup. The word got around and resulted in a heavy demand by other beggared and starving noblemen for tails.

OYSTER. The oyster is an edible bivalve shellfish known to man for centuries as an exquisite delicacy.

The first known oyster farm was founded by Sergius Aurata in southern Italy in 102 B.C.

Ancient shell mounds found in America indicate that the Indians ate oysters long before Europeans colonized that continent. The Greeks prized the oyster as food and used its shell as a ballot paper, the voter scratching his choice on it with a sharp instrument. The Celts knew the oyster and after the Roman occupation oysters were sent from Britain to Rome packed in snow and ice for the Imperial capital's feasts and banquets. Cicero is said to have enjoyed them. Oysters were believed to be good for the brain and it is said that Louis XI of France invited the Sorbonne professors to an oyster feast once a year 'lest their scholarship should become deficient'.

The largest oyster farm in the world is in the Bay of Arcachon in France. French oysters were threatened with extinction as recently as the 19th century because of indiscriminate gathering by dragnets for a great part of the previous century. The situation was so serious that in 1840 the French Government sent a naval vessel to protect the Arcachon oyster beds. The subsequent rehabilita-

tion of these beds owes much to a person by the name of Coste who went to Italy to study Italian methods of maintaining oysters.

In Europe the English Colchester and Whitstable oysters and the French *marennes vertes*, *marennes blanches* and the *belons* are the best. These and similar high quality oysters are best eaten raw and in their own liquor. They are far too delicately and exquisitely flavoured to be eaten in any other way. At the very most a bare squeeze of lemon is all that may be added.

The other good quality oysters are Blue Point, Cornish, Loch Ryan and Zeeland. There is another variety known as Portuguese oysters. These, and deep-sea oysters, may also be eaten cooked, because they do not compare with quality oysters. The three American varieties are the native Eastern oyster, the Olympia and the Japanese oyster, originally imported from Japan. These are good enough to eat raw, but not so good that they ought not to be cooked. They may be used in patties, pies, sauces and stews. Australia produces good oysters.

Edible oysters are not pearl-producers: these breed in warm tropical waters.

OYSTER, BLUE POINT. Correctly, this is an oyster grown in a certain section of Long Island waters. The name is used commercially and indiscriminately to designate a good-sized oyster which may come from any of the Atlantic waters or the Gulf of Mexico. Formerly the blue point oyster came not only from a certain section but from certain beds and a certain depth. For many people it is the best eating oyster on the East Coast of the United States.

OYSTER OF POULTRY. Two oyster-shaped pieces of meat on the back of a bird, situated in the bone cavities on the lower part of the carcass and the only good meat on the back.

OYSTER PLANT. See SALSIFY.

P

PADDLEFISH. Also called the spoon-billed catfish or spadefish, this member of the sturgeon family is named for its extraordinary spoon-like upper jaw which is approximately one-third the length of its body. It abounds in the lower Mississippi and other rivers of the southern United States, reaching a length of six feet and weighing as much as 100 lb. The flesh is similar to that of the sturgeon and is smoked and sold under that name, while the roe is in demand as a source of caviar.

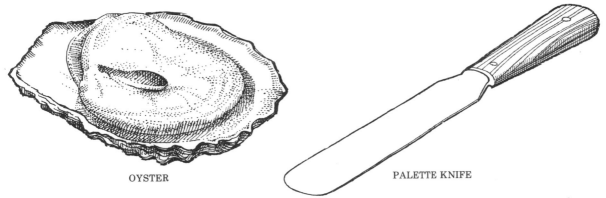

OYSTER

PALETTE KNIFE

PADDY. From the Malay *padi*, another name for rice (which see) before it has been husked.

PAELLA. A traditional Spanish dish of rice, shellfish, chicken and vegetables cooked together and generously spiced with garlic. It is usually served in the large, shallow metal pan in which it is cooked.

PAIN PERDU. See FRENCH TOAST.

PALESTINE SOUP. The term used for a soup made of Jerusalem artichokes.

PALETTE KNIFE. A wide-bladed, flexible knife of different sizes. It has many uses in the kitchen, usually for the spreading of icing (frosting) and creams.

PAMPLEMOUSSE. The French for grapefruit but a term which should properly be applied only to the Riviera type which is smaller than the American grapefruits. However, the distinction between grapefruit and *pamplemousse* has almost disappeared and both turn up in France under either name.

PALMIER. A Parisien speciality of small strips of puff pastry which are rolled in granulated sugar, folded and baked in a moderate oven until the sugar caramelizes.

PALM NUT OIL. See OIL.

PALM WINE. An alcoholic drink made by fermenting the sap of the coconut or date palm. There are other palms which produce a similar wine or toddy.

PALOLO. A type of sea-worm which appears on the surface of the sea in South Sea Island waters twice a year and then only for two hours. When cooked, palolos are a greenish colour and taste faintly like oysters.

PANADA. Culinary term of Spanish origin: a thick

sauce to bind *quenelles*, forcemeats and rissoles. It can be roux-based or otherwise made with various flours, crumbs of fresh or toasted bread or rusks, rice or potatoes. Enriched with egg yolks and butter it is called frangipane panada.

PANADE. A homely French broth thickened with stale bread soaked in water, stock or milk and simmered until it is a gruel. Butter, pepper and salt and, optionally, a beaten egg are then added. *Panade* is also French for panada (which see).

PANADÉS. See SPANISH WINES.

PAN-BROIL. An American cooking term meaning to cook meat in a hot pan with almost no fat, pouring off fat as it accumulates.

PANCAKE. Food historians say the pancake was the first 'made' dish, the original formula being probably a mixture of meal and water cooked on a hot stone. Since then pancakes have been made everywhere, many assuming a seasonal significance. In Britain it is traditional to eat pancakes on Shrove Tuesday to use up the milk, butter and eggs once forbidden during the Lenten fast.

In Holland there are *pannekoeken* and the thinner *flensjes*. Russia has its *blinis*. In France there are *crèpes*, in Germany *Eierkuchen*. Alsace Lorraine is famed for its *eierkuckas*, Mexico for its *tortilla* and Hungary for its *palaçinta*, a stuffed pancake which can be sweet or savoury. The Swedish *fläaskpannkaka* or bacon pancake is a good breakfast or luncheon dish.

PANCREAS. See SWEETBREADS.

PAP. Soft food which is fed to infants and invalids.

PAPAIN. This is an enzyme which decomposes proteins and is found in papaws. Because of this property it is an excellent digestive, particularly when a diet consists of mostly meat, eggs, milk and other protein-rich foods. It is also a tenderizer. See PAPAW.

PAPAW, PAWPAW, PAPAYA. A large and delicious fruit which grows on a sub-tropical tree (*Carica papaya*). Its shape is globular or oval, but it varies considerably in size; a really fine specimen can reach a weight of 20 lb. It is rapidly coming to the fore as a source of useful products. In countries where it grows, meat is wrapped in the large cut-out leaves to tenderize it.

The skin of the fruit is smooth, shading from dark green to a deep orange. A dark green colour does not indicate unripeness. The papaw is hollow inside, its flesh varying in colour from a pale yellow to a deep salmon, and in thickness between 1 and 2 in. There are hundreds of grey to black seeds crowding its inner wall, each enclosed in a gelatinous membrane. These are considered good for the digestion and are chewed by people living in papaw-growing countries. Both the flavour and the fruit are distinctive. Papaws are best eaten raw, with a spoon, sprinkled with lime or lemon juice. Unripe papaw can be cooked as a vegetable, also preserved with whole ginger. The half-ripe papaw is a source of papain (which see), while the ripe fruit has little or none.

Papaws grow rapidly; the male tree flowers but does not produce fruit, while the female yields a dozen or more specimens of this luscious fruit on a slender trunk. The various similar sounding names of the papaw are said to come from the Carib word *ababai*.

Also called papaw and pawpaw is the fruit of a small tree (*Asimina triloba*) of the southern and middle United States. This is a member of the custard apple family with purple flowers and a yellow edible fruit.

PAPAYA. See PAPAW.

PAPE CLÉMENT, CH. See BORDEAUX WINES.

PAPER COOKERY. A way of baking (also frying) foods by wrapping them in greaseproof paper, buttered or oiled with its edges folded securely to retain juiciness and aroma, called in France *en papillote*. This method is commonly used for red mullet, trout, pilchards, and like-sized fish, for smallish cuts of meat or for halved small game birds. Foil wrapping, buttered inside, achieves the same results, but the paper envelopes puff up to release to each guest at table a gentle explosion of appetizing smells.

PAPILLOTE. French word (derived from *papillon*, butterfly) for paper frills decorating the end of a cutlet or other bone.

PAPILLOTE, EN. The French culinary term for paper cookery (which see).

PAPPADAMS. An Indian form of bread in the shape of a wafer made of pulse or lentil flour variously seasoned. They can be grilled, baked in a hot oven or fried in deep fat until they are crisp. Served with curry.

PAPRIKA. A red-powder condiment prepared from one of the varieties of capsicum (which see). Although it is also called red pepper and is cousin to cayenne and chilli peppers, paprika is not related to the true pepper. The paprika popular in Britain and the United States is relatively mild. Other grades are considerably hotter. Long favoured for its pungency, paprika flavours sauces, sour and fresh cream, butter, potatoes, rice and meat dishes – notably Hungarian goulash.

PARBOIL. To partially cook food in water or stock.

PARE. To remove an outer coating, such as the skin or peel of fruit.

PARFAIT. Commonly a dessert mousse or ice-cream pudding but also, in Escoffier's usage, *foie gras* in jelly. The dessert was originally based on a coffee cream, but parfaits are now made with fruits, nuts, chocolate or marshmallows and flavoured with essences, liqueurs or sweet wines. The usual basis is sugar syrup with eggs and cream. Large types are moulded and frozen. Parfaits in individual glasses can be merely thoroughly chilled.

PARKIN. A North of England cake made of oatmeal, flour, sugar, powdered ginger, spices and candied peel, mixed with black treacle, fat and water, baked in a shallow pan, and cut into square slabs for serving. It should be kept for a week before using to gain a pleasant moist texture.

PARMENTIER, ANTOINE-AUGUSTE. A French agronomist whose name is given to many potato dishes. For over 200 years Frenchmen had regarded potatoes with suspicion until Parmentier popularized them in the late 18th century.

PARMESAN CHEESE. One of the finest cheeses in the world, made in Italy for more than 900 years. The full and correct name is Parmigiano-Reggiano and it comes from a small area of the country comprising Parma, from which it gets its name; Reggio-Emilia, where most of the cheese is produced; Modena; and certain sections of Bologna. It is made from mid-April to precisely November 11. Although Parmesan can be eaten fresh, it is best known as a hard grating cheese which has the quality of bringing out the essence of every other ingredient with which it is matched. It is a cheese which has never been duplicated outside of Italy

PASSION-FRUIT

PAPILLOTE

PARTRIDGE

and belongs to a group of cheeses known by the generic name of *grana* (which see), or grain, which refers to their grainy texture.

PARSLEY. One of the most common and popular herbs of which there are several varieties. In Britain and the United States it is mainly the curly leaf type which is preferred; but in many countries the plain leaf parsley is better liked. The latter is used more in cooking than as a garnish, for which it is not so suited as the bright-green curly variety.

Parsley probably comes from the eastern Mediterranean and was known to the ancient Greeks and Romans. It seems not to have been much known in Britain until the 16th century and it travelled to North America with the early settlers.

Hamburg parsley is grown as a root vegetable although it is botanically a true parsley. Its white, fleshly taproot can be eaten uncooked like raw carrot, or cooked in the ways for carrot. Its flavour has been likened to a cross between celeriac and parsnip. Its leaves can be used as parsley.

PARSLEY SAUCE. See SAUCES.

PARSNIP. This vegetable has a peculiarity not shared by many others; it is uneatable in its wild state, but very palatable when cultivated. It has been cultivated for centuries as food both for man and beast. There are several different kinds of parsnip, the round or turnip parsnip and the long carrot-shaped varieties being the best known.

PARSON'S NOSE. Also called Pope's Nose. The extreme end portion of the tail of a fowl and considered by many to be extremely tasty.

PARTRIDGE. The name properly designating a common game bird, *Perdix cinerea*, but is also applied without discrimination to many types of gallinaceous fowl. In the United States it is also incorrectly applied to certain grouse and quail family species (which see). The partridges of the Old World are not as clearly distinguishable as a group as those of the New World, and are found in most temperate and tropical countries from Britain to Australia. Typical, but not all-inclusive of the Old World partridges are the common or grey partridge, *Perdix cinerea*, and the red-legged *Caccabis rufa*. The common partridge chiefly inhabits cultivated fields in Britain and on the Continent. The red-legged partridge, nicknamed 'Frenchman' in some counties of Britain, is found in France, southern Europe and on the Channel Isles. The flesh, however, is not as tender and juicy as that of the grey partridge, although its habits are similar.

Partridge are readily domesticated and even when wild will feed with barnyard fowl when food is scarce. Young partridge should never be hung for more than three days, nor should they be served with a highly seasoned sauce as the flesh is distinctively but delicately flavoured. An older bird may be served with a garnish which is fairly assertive to complement its gamey flavour.

PASHKA. The Russian traditional Easter cheesecake, shaped like a flowerpot. The cheesecakes are packed in special wooden moulds like a four-sided pyramid, embossed on the sides with Christian symbols (the Orthodox cross and the Cyrillic letters XB for 'Christ is Risen').

PASSE-TOUT-GRAINS. See BURGUNDY WINES.

PASSION FRUIT. A plum-sized fruit, purple when ripe and native to South America. The inside of the hull contains small black seeds surrounded by yellow pulp which has a delicious flavour. It may be eaten raw as a fruit or its juice used in cocktails or punch. The juice may also be added to a fresh fruit cup but sparingly, no more than a drop or two. Main edible varieties are the purple passion fruit, the yellow, the bell-apple, the sweet calabash and the granadilla. The name was given because of the supposed resemblance of the flower to the instruments of the Passion (see GRANADILLA).

PASSOVER BREAD. See MATZO.

PASTA. A magic name in Italian cooking, covering several hundred different ways of mixing flour and eggs or water to produce *pasta* of many different shapes and sizes: long and short, fine as 'angel's hair', thick as 'pipes', and long narrow ribbons or short squares. *Pasta* is boiled and baked, stuffed, or served with a rich sauce or simply with melted butter. It should be served as a first and not as a main course.

Legend has it that Marco Polo brought *pasta* to Italy from China, but it is known that the Romans ate *pasta* and, in the Pompeii Museum, ancient equipment for making it is exhibited.

PASTEURIZATION. A treatment of food to kill harmful micro-organisms without impairing its quality. Mild controlled heat is applied to milk and other foods and drinks. Radiation pasteurization is the application of low doses of beta or gamma rays. The process is named after Louis Pasteur who developed the heat treatment from his work on fermentation in wine and beer in the 1860s.

PASTICCERIA. The Italian word for pies, cakes, pastries, tarts etc. of which there is a considerable range, all quite different from the usual British and American equivalents. There are many which are similar to French pastries, such as the delicious Sicilian *cannoli* (crisp tubes of pastry filled with a custard cream). *Strogliatelli* is a little reminiscent of the Austrian *Äpfelstrüdel*, and there are buns and cookies of all descriptions. Included are *torrone*, which is a special delicacy, a type of nougat massed with nuts and flavoured with honey; *panforte*, or the 'strong' bread of Siena; the *panettone* of Milan; *zuppa inglese* (which see), a rum-flavoured tipsy cake eaten in Rome; and the Sicilian *cassatas* all come under the general name of *pasticceria*.

PASTILLES. Small lozenges flavoured with concentrated fruit juices.

PASTIS. French aniseed-flavoured aperitifs.

PASTRAMI. Highly seasoned smoked beef, especially shoulder cuts, originally from the Near East. The beef is cured in spices for ten days, then smoked for eight hours. It is eaten hot or cold.

PASTRY. A paste, usually a fat-and-flour mixture with water or other liquid added to make a dough for shaping and baking. Also the product of the baking. Canadian pastry is a name sometimes given to crumble topping for pies – a rubbed-in plain cake mixture of butter, flour and sugar used instead of pastry on top of fruit. Equally loose usage gives us nut pastry (fine-ground pecans, Brazils or other nuts), wafer pastry and crumb pastry (bread, cake or biscuit crumbs), when such things are used to form cases for pies or tarts.

Pastry-making is a centuries-old art, certainly known to the ancient Greeks and Romans, though its major development in the Western world dates from the late 18th century. The flour used today is normally plain wheaten, but it may be replaced or supplemented by other flours or admixtures of things such as mashed potatoes. It may have baking powder, yeast or other leaveners. Butter remains the favourite fat for the gastronome but efficient results are also achieved with a mixture of fats, or even with lard, proprietary shortenings or vegetables oils. Almost all types of pastry call for maximum convenient coolness in the ingredients, for minimum handling of the dough and, at least to start with, a hot oven. Most recipes call for a little salt to be sifted with the flour. All liquids should be added carefully lest the dough become sticky and unmanageable.

The most commonly used pastes are short (shortcrust, flan, cheese pastry and suetcrust) or flaked (puff, rough puff and flaky). Shortcrust (basically 1 lb. flour to $\frac{1}{2}$ lb. fat) is crumbly when cooked, popular for all sorts of pies, tarts, turnovers and pasties, sweet or savoury. Flan pastry, also called biscuit crust, is richer (1 lb. flour to $\frac{3}{4}$ lb. fat and 4 beaten eggs). It is used most for sweet pastries. Cheese pastry, when used for pies or tarts, includes fine-grated cheese in the basic shortcrust mix. Suetcrust replaces the usual fat in basic shortcrust with shredded suet. Since suetcrust tends to bake hard it is usually steamed or boiled for sweet or savoury puddings. Another short pastry is fork-mix pastry, made with flour beaten into an emulsion of oil and water, and one version, sometimes called Boston piecrust, is made with rather more oil.

In contrast to short pastries, flaked pastries seek to keep the butter in separate layers from the layers of dough. The French call them *pâtés feuilletées*. Reducing the layers to the thinness of leaves requires patient rolling, folding and re-rolling. The lightest puff pastry is used for vol-au-vents, bouchées, mille-feuilles and other fine pastries. Less fairy-light to eat but quicker to make are flaky pastry (for meat pies, jam slices, Eccles cakes) and rough puff (for sausage rolls, pies etc.).

Two other pastries in common use are hot-water crust, also called raised-pie crust, and *choux* pastry. Both boil the fat in water or milk before combining it with the flour. The hot-water crust is a stiff dough moulded to make a filling of meat or game which bakes in the crust. The *choux*, with eggs beaten into it, is a thick batter, piped from a forcing bag on to baking sheets to make cream buns, sweet or savoury éclairs and *profiteroles*, or deep-fried as *petits-choux* or cheese *aigrettes*.

PASTRY BLENDER

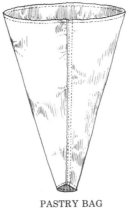

PASTRY BAG

PASTRY BAG. A cone-shaped bag more often called in Britain a forcing bag or piping bag, usually of plastic but also of paper or fabric. The point of the cone is cut off to accommodate a tube through which soft foods are forced by squeezing the bag. Suitable foods include creamed potatoes, savoury pastes, eclair, meringue and biscuit mixtures, icings and whipped cream. Decorative shapes are achieved by the size and configuration of the mouth of the tube – plus the skill of the user.

PASTRY BLENDER. A gadget for cutting fat into flour in pastry-making. Usually it is a straight handle with stiff wires (or a slotted strip of metal) joined at each end to form a deep curve.

PASTY. A savoury meat or vegetable filling wrapped in pastry and baked in the oven.

PATACHE D'AUX. See BORDEAUX WINES.

PÂTE. French for pastry, not to be confused with *pâté*. It also refers to *pasta*.

PÂTÉ. *Pâtés* to a Frenchman are an indispensible part of the *haute cuisine. Pâté de foie gras* is a beginning to a dinner in the grand style. A *pâté de veau et porc* is found in the Frenchman's *pique-nique* basket, while the *pâté maison* is the pride of every French restaurateur wherever he may be, proving his skill in the subtle blending of various sorts of finely minced or ground meats.

There are *pâtés* and *pâtés*, and it has become usual to describe as a *pâté* a mixture of any finely ground meats, liver, game etc. seasoned and flavoured and baked as a *pâté*. Strictly speaking these are *terrines*. Both the *terrine* and the *pâté* mixture is the same. However, when the mixture is placed in a dish which has been lined with pork or bacon fat it is a *terrine*, and when it is baked in a pastry crust or as the French say *en croûte* it is a *pâté*. When the mixture is of finely ground fowl or game bird meat and steamed it is a *galantine*.

In Renaissance days, *pâtés* were made of all kinds of meats. Badger, porcupine and dormouse all wound up as *pâté* or *terrine*. *Pâtés* composed of giblets, heavily peppered, were a lower-class Parisian delicacy of the 17th century.

PÂTÉ DE FOIE GRAS. One of France's most delectable dishes. It is reputed to be the invention of an 18th-century Norman pastry cook, Jean Joseph Close (or Clause) who was taken by his master, the Marshal of Contades, to Alsace, where he had been appointed Governor. There Close is supposed to have created the dish which became world-famous, goose liver combined with finely chopped veal and truffles, enveloped in a rich pastry. When Jean Joseph Close retired he put his creation on the market and made a fortune.

PÂTISSERIE. The French term for pastry or pastry-cook's shop.

PATTY. Small round pastry cases filled with savoury filling.

PAUILLAC. See BORDEAUX WINES.

PAUPIETTES. Thinly sliced pieces of meat used as wrappers for various meat or forcemeat fillings. Also, in Escoffier's usage, fillets of sole and cabbage leaves used in the same way. The meat slices are spread with a well-spiced forcemeat and rolled up. Wrapped up in thin slices of fat bacon, they are tied up with cotton thread to be braised, baked or casseroled. Bacon and thread are removed before serving.

PAVEIL DE LUZE, CH. See BORDEAUX WINES.

PAVES DU CAVES. A speciality of the French town of Cauterets. They are a burnt-sugar confection which imitate to perfection the pebbles of the Pyrenees mountain streams.

PAWPAW. See PAPAW.

PAYSANNE. When used as a culinary term this means food cooked peasant style.

PEA. Before the advent of the potato into Britain, peas were the chief vegetable (not our precious fresh pea, but a dried split pea). Dried split peas have been used as food since times immemorial and are mentioned in the Bible. In ancient Rome, they were cooked by the plateful at the circus. In fact, people liked peas so much that at political elections they were issued free, for a consideration of a vote. A 15th-century gardener called Michaux gave us the peas we know today, and until he died peas were known as *michaux*.

There are several varieties of green peas, but all can be cooked in the same manner.
See also PETITS POIS.

PEA, SPLIT, or **SPLIT PEAS.** Peas which have been dried and the outer skin removed, thus making them easier to cook. Like lentils and dried beans, dried peas have been known since earliest times. They are easily stored and will keep for a long period. They can be cooked in the same ways as for lentils, but the manner in which they are best known to the British is as a soup or, as one writer has written, 'the immortal pease pudding', a traditional dish handed down by our forefathers, which has formed a staple food among country people for generations. Many housewives have their own special recipe for this pudding, but it might be interesting to try the recipe from *The Cook's Oracle* (see KITCHENER, DR).

'Put a quart of split peas into a clean cloth; do not tie them up too close, but leave a little room for them to swell; put them on to boil in cold water slowly until they are tender; if they are good peas they will be boiled enough in about two hours and a half; rub them through a sieve into a deep dish, and add an egg or two, an ounce of butter, and some pepper and salt; beat them well together for about ten minutes, when these ingredients are well incorporated; then flour the cloth well, put the pudding in, tie up as tight as possible, and boil it an hour longer. It is as good with boiled beef as it is with boiled pork; and why not with roast pork? This is a very good acompaniment to cold pork or cold beef.'

PEA BEAN. Also known as French kidney bean, this is one of the varieties known in France as *mange-tout* (which see). The beans are small and round as peas, hence the name. Pea beans should be gathered before they begin to swell in the pods and cooked whole. Only the 'top and tail' need be removed. This is an excellent vegetable and must be eaten when fresh and tender; it is much too delicate to store even for a short period.

PEACH. A luscious fruit probably of Chinese origin and, as one authority has concluded, 'one of the most beautiful gifts the Orient has given to Europe'.

The peach has been cultivated in China for at least 1,500 years or possibly longer. It is thought probable that at some point the Chinese peach may have been influenced by strains imported from Iran. There have been exchanges of varieties between the countries if not of species. There is a record of some sort of fruit entering China from Iran during the reign of Emperor T'sai Tun of the T'ang dynasty. The fruit is referred to as 'Kwan-ta'o' or 'Kin-tao', meaning yellow or golden peach, but this could easily have been a sort of plum or apricot.

It seems the peach began in China and spread westwards along the caravan route through Asia to the Mediterranean lands and then to Europe. The Greeks and Romans knew the peach and introduced it to countries under their influence. The peach was brought to America by the early Spanish explorers and by 1600 it was common in Mexico and soon spread to the north. America now accounts for almost one-half of the world's production. Most of the commercial varieties were developed in America and the Elberta, developed in 1870, is still the most widely grown free-stone variety. Italy is the leading producer in Europe, followed by France, Spain and Greece.

There are no less than 2,181 varieties. The peach is the third most important of deciduous tree fruits after the apple and pear.

The skin of most peaches is downy and fuzzy but there is a variety with a smooth skin known as nectarine (which see). In all other respects, however, the two are identical. A yellow-fleshed peach is four times richer in Vitamin A than an orange.

A good quality peach is about the size of an orange. It should be firm, free of blemishes, fresh looking and whitish or yellow in colour. This fruit spoils easily.

Freshly picked peaches are delicious as a table fruit or in a fruit salad. They are also used in confectionery, jams, jellies, conserves and liqueurs.

The peach is historically associated with ice-cream because when Dame Nellie Melba, the great Australian singer, gave a party at the Savoy Hotel in London in 1892, Escoffier, who was then the chef at the Savoy, created the famous *Pêche Melba* in her honour. A swan carved of ice (symbolic of the swan in *Lohengrin*) was in the centre of this work of art and around it were arranged poached peaches in syrup on a bed of vanilla ice-cream. Later he improved upon this by adding a purée of fresh raspberries and a sprinkling of shredded green almonds. This version first appeared on a menu of the Carlton Hotel on its opening in London on 15 July 1899.

SAUCES: with Fondue Bourguignonne.

GARDEN PEA (plant, pea, pod)   PEAR   PEANUT (plant, shell, nuts in shell)

PEACH BRANDY. The established name for a sweet liqueur made from peaches, used only when 20 per cent of the spirit content is brandy.

PEACOCK. Male of the peafowl and most splendid of the pheasants. Its flesh when young is tender, not unlike turkey or goose in flavour, but cooked like pheasant (which see). A native of South and Southeast Asia, it was raised in Europe for the table and still is in a small way. But it reverted largely to ornamental duties soon after the turkey was introduced from Mexico. One of the recorded extravagances of Roman times was the killing of 500 peacocks to make a dish of their brains. It held pride of place at medieval banquets in Britain and on the Continent, and was often served in full feather, tail erect, feet and beak gilded. This was made possible by skinning the peacock and by wrapping head and feet in cloth kept constantly wet during roasting. Charlemagne served several thousand peacocks at one of his banquets.

PEANUT. Also known as the groundnut, monkey nut and goober, and by many other names. This is a plant which grows in tropical and subtropical areas and is widely cultivated for its diverse uses. It is not a nut but a pea which has a high protein and iron content and is one of the world's most valuable sources of oil for cooking and the manufacture of margarine. What remains after the oil has been processed is used as animal feed. In some countries, particularly the United States, the peanut is marketed in quantity for consumption whole, either roasted or plain, for use in confectionery and for the manufacture of peanut butter.

PEANUT BRITTLE. A brittle toffee flavoured generously with roasted peanuts.

PEANUT BUTTER. A thick paste, made from peanuts, with a texture ranging from smooth to coarse. It can be used as a spread and in biscuit (cookie) and cake-making.

PEANUT OIL. See OIL.

PEAR. Next to the apple the pear is cultivated more extensively than any other fruits, except in tropical and subtropical lands. Named varieties run into hundreds. All are descended from the *Pyrus communis* or common pear. Another species called the Chinese sand pear furnishes a score of other sorts and a third species, the snow pear, is grown on a restricted scale for the making of perry (which see).

Pears may be dumpy, lumpy, oval or round, as well as what is thought of as pear-shaped. The French have their own descriptive names: the *besi* is egg-shaped; the *bergamotte*, ball-shaped; the *calabash*, a bludgeon; the *colmar*, a spiny-top etc. Skins vary from pale green to a yellow and russet-brown, striped or flushed or dotted with red.

It is hard to describe the flavour of a pear. Some say it has a hint of a full-bodied wine, others of a spice or a trace of almond or rose-water. It has a subtlety of flavour which is individual. In texture some are smooth and so soft (the French call them *fondant*) that they melt in the mouth. Others are crisp and firm, some almost gritty and others like cotton wool.

The British have long been pear *amateurs*, but most of the better pears today are of French and Belgian origin including the *bosc* (Belgium) and the *doyen du comice* (France), probably the finest pear in the world. Nothing ever goes wrong with the comice whereas that other favourite, the William (the Bartlett in the United States), is often floury. In England, the Conference, a good all-rounder, provides the greater proportion of the pear crop. Other good pears are the Anjou, popular in the United States, the Louise Bonne, Seckel and Winter Nelis.

Eating pears must be watched carefully and eaten as soon as ready for they can turn sleepy overnight. Juicy sweet dessert pears are meant for eating raw and putting into salads; but cooking pears can be poached, stewed, bottled or made into pear butter.

PEARL BARLEY. Barley (which see) reduced to rounded small grains.

295

PECAN. The most valuable of the tree nuts in the United States. Native to a restricted area of the South and Mexico, it has been successfully cultivated in California, although it rarely grows north of the 39th parallel. Pecans are eaten as any other dessert nut, and are sold ready salted, toasted or uncooked for use in confectionery, candies, pies or other sweetmeats.

PÊCHE MELBA. See PEACH.

PECORINO CHEESE. Pecorino is the generic name for all Italian cheeses made with sheeps' milk. Pecorino Romano is a hard grating cheese used for *pasta*; Pecorino da Tavola is a sharp and pungent table cheese, but milder than the grating Pecorinos.

PECTIN. A carbohydrate in fruits and vegetables which with sugar makes jams and jellies set or gel. Since the amount of pectin varies from fruit to fruit and from stage to stage of the fruit's life, extra pectin has sometimes to be added. This can be done by adding pectin-rich fruits or an extract made by long boiling of such fruits – among them, sour apples, cranberries, gooseberries, under-ripe blackberries or raspberries, and black- or redcurrants. Such extracts can be bottled and stored. Commercially produced extracts can be bought.

PEEL. To pull or peel off the outer covering of such fruits as oranges, grapefruit or bananas.

PELLEJOS. See SPANISH WINES.

PEMMICAN. A food, devised by the North American Indians, which would remain edible for long periods so that it could be used in times of war and on long journeys. They cut venison or buffalo meat into strips, dried it in the sun, pounded it to a paste with fat and mixed this with wild berries. The mixture was formed into cakes which were packed tightly into rawhide bags. In more recent times a similar concoction has been used on Arctic expeditions, using beef and raisins, as this provides a food of maximum nutritional value which requires the minimum of space while travelling.

PENGUIN EGGS. These are usually cooked hard before being used. The white becomes firm, but remains translucent. They have a strong fishy flavour and are often mashed with anchovy to disguise this.

PENNYROYAL. A perennial mint used in wine cups and juleps and as a herb in cookery. Nothing to do with pennies, the name comes from Latin *pulegium* (thyme), so called because it allegedly discouraged the flea (*pulex*).

PEPPER. The berries of a climbing vine of the tropical forests of monsoon Asia. They grow in strings, first green then bright red. To produce black pepper the berries are picked green and dried in the sun, thus turning into the black peppercorns we know. There are several kinds of black peppercorns, varying in size, colour and aroma. Good peppercorns should be hard, even in size and colour and free from leaves, stalks etc. They keep indefinitely, so can be bought in large quantities and stored in a jar. White peppercorns, more costly, are produced from the berries after the outer husk has been taken off just before the final ripening or, in some processes, washed off at a later stage.

CAYENNE PEPPER. A type of chilli pepper said to have come from Cayenne in French Guiana. It is used mainly to flavour oysters and game dishes, and is ground finer than chilli pepper.

NEPAUL PEPPER. Ground from yellow peppers and somewhat less pungent than the red.

PEPPERCORN. See PEPPER.

PEPPERGRASS. Species of cress, including garden cress, used in salads, soups and stews like watercress.

PEPPERMINT. See MINT.

PEPPERMINT GLACIAL. Another name for the digestive liqueur *crème de menthe*.

PEPPERPOT. A highly spiced dish which traditionally is a very wet stew or soup. The name is now also applied to stews with comparatively little sauce though still well spiced. The West Indian pepperpot, a stew, has classically cassareep and hot peppers in a stock of fresh beef or mutton, salt meat and a crab or lobster, plus okras and other local vegetables. Dumplings are cooked in it and served with it. Jamaican pepperpot soup is thickened with yam or coconut. The Philadelphia pepperpot is said to have been created by George Washington's army cook at Valley Forge at a critical stage of the war, after Washington had complained that the troops were deserting because of the monotonous food. It has developed many variations since then but correctly it includes shredded tripe and veal knuckles or diced bacon. It is sometimes thickened with flour, sometimes served with dumplings. In northwest Germany a similar beef stew is called *Pfefferpotthast*. The Chinese have a stew of chicken sometimes translated as chicken pepperpot – with a sauce made from the mild Szechuan pepper (*hua-chiao*), soy sauce and hot pepper.

PENNYROYAL   PECAN (shell, shell and nut)   PERIWINKLE

PEPPER STEAK. Beef steak rubbed liberally with freshly-ground black pepper before cooking. Thick steaks can be fried or baked with wine and stock added to the pan juices.

PEPPER WATER. A South Indian hotly spiced water served with rice. It was from this mixture that mulligatawny soup (which see) developed.

PEPPER WINE. Not a drink but a 'condiment' to 'pep-up' soups. Fill a bottle with fiery tiny red peppers and cover them with sherry. Leave covered for three weeks. Only a few drops are needed and the 'wine' keeps indefinitely, needing refills of sherry from time to time.

PEPSIN. An enzyme in the stomach which is important in digestion. There is also a commercial form of it, usually from pigs' stomachs, used as a digestive and as a ferment in the making of cheese.

PERCH. Member of the family Perca, this fish is found in fresh water throughout the world. While the average size is about 9 in. long and ½ lb. in weight, the giant perch of Lake Rudolph in Africa grows to 8 feet and 150 lb. The perch is one of the commonest and one of the best of the small freshwater fish for the table. It may be prepared in the same way as grayling or catfish (which see).

PERCOLATOR. See COFFEE.

PÉRIGUEUX SAUCE. See SAUCES.

PERIWINKLE. The common name for a small sea-snail, *Littorina littorea*, found on the shores of Europe and North America. In Britain it is abbreviated to winkle. They are abundant along the British coasts and are in season all the year round. Inside the shell is the edible snail which has a delicate flavour. Winkles can be roasted in their shells – this is said to be the best way to keep their flavour – but the usual British manner is to poach them in water or *court bouillon* for 20 minutes.

They are sold on shellfish stalls on British beaches and traditionally they are picked out of their shells with a long pin, after the cap or operculum has been removed. They are usually served with thin bread and butter, the snails first being sprinkled with salt, pepper and lemon juice.

PERLWEIN. See GERMAN WINES.

PERNAND-VERGELESSES. See BURGUNDY WINES.

PERNOD. When absinthe was banned in its original form, Pernod Anis, in many countries, became the most widely distributed substitute. It is a water-white aniseed-flavoured liqueur taken with ice and water which turns it milky.

PERRIER WATER. A natural mineral water from the south of France.

PERRY. This is fermented pear juice and is made in the same way as apple cider. In 1676 a much-travelled English gentleman and connoisseur of wine wrote a book on wines extracted from fruits in Britain entitled *Vinetum Brittanicum* in which he says, 'the richest wine this world affords is made from the grape, but for the English climate perry and cider are better'.

PERSILLADE. French culinary name of a mixture of finely chopped parsley and garlic added at the last moment to garnish a dish which is then termed *à la persillade*.

PERSIMMON. A tree fruit, notably of two species – the wild American (also known as Virginian date) and the Japanese, (also called the kaki plum). Gastronomically the kaki species is the important one. It has been grown in China and Japan and in Mediterranean countries for centuries and is now cultivated in the United States. Its fruit when ripe is about the size of a large hen's egg, quite soft and golden-orange. Ripeness is important since immaturity means extreme astringency. By contrast the ripe flesh is so very sweet

297

that it is often served with lemon wedges, French salad dressing, *eau de vie* (which see), dry wine or, in Japan, *sake* (which see). It can be cooked in cakes and puddings, or used to garnish them. Puréed, it can be incorporated in ice-creams, milk drinks and pudding sauces. It cooks like the apricot for compôtes, jellies and jams.

PERUVIAN WINE. A small production (about 2,000,000 imperial gallons yearly) of Spanish-type table wines, some of them fortified to emulate sherry, port and Madeira. Peru originated South America's Pisco brandy (distilled from muscat wine made in the Ica valley near the port of Pisco), which is the basis of the Pisco punch now marketed in the United States.

PESSAC. See BORDEAUX WINES.

PESTLE AND MORTAR. An important piece of kitchen equipment used for pounding ingredients to make them smooth or into a paste. The mortar is a thick bowl of marble or wood, stone or metal, and the pestle usually of wood or wood and stone combined.

PÉTILLANT. A French word to describe sparkling; *frizzante* in Italian and *Perlwein* in German. The sparkling wines of Vouvray and Saumur in France are perhaps the best known although Bourgogne Mousseux is another favourite. The sparkle is man-made in the vinification and there are three processes, the champagne method, the *cuve close,* and the impregnation method.

PETIT SALÉ. A joint of pork pickled 3–6 days in brine. It is boiled and served either cold as hors d'oeuvre or hot as a main dish, usually with cabbage and potatoes.

PETIT SUISSE. A French unsalted cream cheese, cylindrical in shape. It is made in two sizes, the larger one being called *gros* and the smaller *demi.*

PETITS FOURS. Bite-size fancy cakes, biscuits and other dainties, usually served with the dessert course. They include small macaroons and short-breads, little cubes of Genoa cake dipped in icing and decorated with cherries, angelica, ginger, candied violets or nuts, sugar-glazed grapes and other fruits, dates variously dressed and miniature 'fruits' of moulded and painted marzipan.

PETITS POIS. Very young, sweet and tender green peas of some high-quality varieties.

PETIT VERDOT. See BORDEAUX WINES.

PETIT-VILLAGE, CH. See BORDEAUX WINES.

PÉTRUS, CH. See BORDEAUX WINES.

PETS'AI. A newcomer to the cabbage family as far as the West is concerned. It looks like a large romaine or cos lettuce with almost white leaves and crisp stalks and gives out little odour while it is cooking. Its other Chinese names are *pai-ts-ai* or *wong bok*.

PETS DE NONNE. Soufflé fritters made with choux pastry. Some consider the name vulgar and call them instead *soupirs de nonne*, 'nun's sighs'. A nun at the ancient abbey of Marmoutier on the Loire is credited with their invention.

PETTICOAT TAILS. A type of shortbread made into thin crisp round cakes which the ladies of the court in the days of the Auld Alliance (the union of the crowns of France and Scotland) called *petits gâtels*, an earlier form of *petits gâteaux*.

PETTITOES. See PIG.

PEZ, DE, CH. See BORDEAUX WINES.

PFEFFERKUCHEN. A kind of gingerbread, supposedly invented by the Franks who migrated to Silesia from the region of Nuremberg. It is traditionally a German Christmas confection and hardly ever made at any other time. Honey, flour, sugar, lemon rind, rum and ginger are the main ingredients. *Pfeffernüsse* are German ginger biscuits (cookies).

PHEASANT. Considered by most shooting men as one of the finest game birds, it takes precedence over the partridge when their relative flavours are considered. They may be distinguished from other game birds by their long tail and by the fact that the cocks, no matter what their colouring, have a large red wattle surrounding the eye.

Its origin in Britain is obscure, some saying that it was introduced by the Romans. In the United States, Mongolian pheasants were introduced during the presidency of General Grant. Varying species were introduced later and have multiplied. However, they are becoming somewhat rare in the United States although one can easily buy those raised in captivity. These are often considered a better and safer bet, defying the axiom 'the wilder the pheasant, the better the flesh'.

Most pheasant lovers demand that a pheasant be well hung, often forgetting that highness in game varies within wide limits.

PHÉLAN-SÉGUR, CH. See BORDEAUX WINE

PESTLE AND MORTAR

PETS 'AI

PHYLLOXERA. A beetle-like creature that brought devastation to the European vineyards. A native of the eastern United States, it long prevented the growing of grapes within its territory. No one understood what was happening, only that all the European vines planted withered and died. There was, however, a vine native to the United States which gave bad wine but was immune from these attacks.

The beetle found its way to Europe, probably on an experimental vine, and its progeny swept through the vineyards doing terrible damage. Someone realized that the roots of the despised American vine were immune, and after much argument millions of American vines were grafted on to the surviving European stock. The new roots resisted the scourge and although there have been endless arguments since as to whether the pre-phylloxera wines were better than those produced after the disaster, everyone acknowledges that but for the American vines there would have been no wine – and but for the American beetle there would have been no phylloxera.

PHYLO. A plain, paper-thin, flour and water pastry used in Greek and Turkish sweet and savoury pastries and pies. It is made by experts and is available in Greek shops throughout the world.

PICCALILLI. A mixed-vegetable pickle in a mustard sauce. See PICKLES.

PICHON LONGUEVILLE, CH. See BORDEAUX WINES.

PICKLES. Preserves of vegetables or fruits in well-seasoned and spiced vinegar or similar liquid (see PICKLING). Herbs, notably tarragon and dill, are often added. Catsup or ketchup (which see), chutneys and other relishes are often included in the definition of pickles. Popular 'straight' pickles include olives, onions, walnuts, gherkins and other cucumbers, red or white cabbage, cauliflower florets, beets and other roots, melon rinds and almost any fruit. Mixed pickles are usually of chopped vegetables – piccalilli (which see), for instance. Mustard pickles are brined, chopped vegetables incorporated in a boiled sauce including mustard, vinegar and turmeric. Dill pickles are cucumbers with dill leaves and seed heads, all matured in brine for several weeks.

PICKLING. A process of flavouring or preserving meat, fish, vegetables, fruits and other foods in brine, spiced vinegar, lemon juice, brandy, wine, beer or cider mixtures. For pickling pork, beef and other meats saltpetre is usually added. Pickled eggs, also called bar-room eggs, are shelled hard-boiled eggs matured in spiced vinegar for about four weeks. Chinese hundred-year eggs (which see) and brine-cured duck eggs (*sen ya tain*) are also pickled eggs. Pickling periods can be a few days, weeks or months – or simple marinating.

Northumberland's pickled salmon, for instance, is boiled salmon steeped overnight in a mixture of equal parts of salt water, vinegar and white wine, reheated in this marinade and served hot.

PIDDOCK. A bivalve mollusk found in holes it bores in wood, clay and soft rock. Plunged, as in Sussex, into boiling water for a few minutes it is eaten like whelks. In Normandy piddocks are vinegar-pickled or cooked in butter and dressed with chopped herbs and breadcrumbs.

PIE. A dish of meat, fish, fruit, vegetables or other foods covered with a crust and baked. The crust is usually pastry (which see) but it can be of mashed potatoes (as in cottage pie) of bread, biscuits or cake crumbs, of rubbed-in cake mixtures, or of whipped egg white (as in lemon meringue pie). Pastry dishes without a crust or lid are normally known as tarts or flans in Britain, though Americans apply the name pie to them all – including the traditional pumpkin pie. Raised pies, moulded from hot-water pastry, have their top crust, base and walls of pastry. Envelope pies are flat squares of pastry with their corners folded in to enclose meat, poultry or other contents – more strictly a form of pasty. Then there are unbaked pies – for instance, refrigerator pies, usually a pie shell of crumbs with chocolate or butter, set firm in the ice box and then filled with ice-creams or cream-and-fruit mixtures. The Americans have confections like Boston cream pie and Washington pie both of which the British would describe as richly filled sponge sandwiches. But nomenclature varies. Italy's famous *pizza* would, if English, be a savoury flan, but *pizza* simply means pie.

From the Middle Ages to early in the 19th century the English pie often mixed both savoury and sweet ingredients, but since then it has been a homogeneous affair, definitely one or the other.

PIÈCE. See WINE CONTAINERS.

PIÈCE DE RESISTANCE. This French term has come to have the general meaning of something of great importance, a speciality or main item. In French culinary language it means the main joint or dish at dinner. *Pièces montées* mean decorative centre pieces, set pieces or even mounted pieces.

PIERRE BIBIAN, CH. See BORDEAUX WINES.

PIG. A swine or hog. Formerly the word applied, in the culinary sense, only to young swine before sexual maturity. Flesh of the adult pig is called pork when fresh, ham or bacon when cured. Sucking or suckling pig is ideally little more than a month old and 8 to 15 lb. in weight. This delicacy can be boiled and braised and made into terrines and galantines, but it is more usually spit-roasted whole. It can also be oven-roasted on a grill or grating so that the crackling is properly crisped. In central Sardinia it is roasted over a wood fire and then enclosed with myrtle leaves to absorb their flavour.

The odds and ends of the pig make many popular dishes and garnishes. The rind, finely chopped, is much used to enrich sauces and stews. Pigs' brains are poached in a court bouillon, fried in butter or incorporated in a sauce. Pigs' fry (heart, liver, lights and sweetbreads) and kidneys can also be prepared like those of other animals. Pigs' head, minus tongue and brains, can be boiled – or marinated and served as boar's head (which see). It also provides brawns and head cheeses (which see). The cheeks are usually cured like ham or bacon – Bath chaps (which see) are the most famous example – but they can be served baked or roasted. Pigs' trotters, also called pettitoes, are boiled for eating hot or cold (jellied), grilled, fried, fricasseed or stuffed. Pigs' ears and tails, similarly cooked, complete the list of edible parts.

A Sussex pig is a drinking vessel which stands on its tail when full, on all fours when empty.

PIGEON. Any of the species of birds belonging to the Columbidae, the doves and pigeons; there is no sharp distinction between the two names. Pigeons are found wild in most parts of the world and are reared domestically in some countries as pets and for sport and the table. (See SQUAB for young pigeon.) Domestic pigeons should be kept without food for 24 hours before killing, and should be hung head downwards in order to bleed correctly and thus keep the meat pale in colour. Feathers should be removed while the carcass is still warm.

PIGNOLI. These are the kernels of pine cones used extensively in Turkish and Balkan cooking as well as in many Italian dishes. They keep fresh for a considerable time.

PIG-NUT. Sometimes called hog-nut, these are the edible nut of North America's brown hickory tree; also another name for the ground chestnut.

PIKE and **PICKEREL.** Members of the family Esocidae and the single genus *Esox* which include some of the best-known game fish found in fresh water. The pike is classed as a coarse fish in Britain; in North America the various kinds of pike, pickerel (name applied there to several species, not to young pike as in Britain), and the muskallunge, or great North American pike, are highly prized game fish. All are predators. The muskallunge has been recorded as growing to more than 6 feet in length and weighing 70 lb. Pike in Britain has a bad reputation among cooks because of its allegedly dry flesh and superfluity of bones; but on the Continent and in North America it is esteemed for its firm, white, flaky meat. It is particularly good when boiled in a court bouillon and served with Hollandaise sauce. All recipes for bass, carp or perch (which see) are adaptable to the pike.

PIKELET. The word in the Midlands, the North of England, and Scotland for the crumpet (which see).

PILAU. Rice cooked in the eastern manner – or, more accurately, in one of the ways used from the Balkans to Burma. The name is also applied in the Middle East to *burghul* (cracked wheat) similarly cooked. The essential quality is that the rice be light and fluffy. It can be savoury or sweetened rice on its own. More usually it has other ingredients which qualify the name: mutton pilau; French *pilaff de crevettes*; Greek quail or octopus pilau (*pilafé mé ortikia* or *mé octapothi*); Iranian apricot pilau (*geisi pelo*); Iraqi lentil pilau (*mejedrah*, also called Esau's favourite); and the Turkish chicken-liver pilau (*iç pilav*). The different pronunciations throughout the East account in part for the various spellings.

PINEAPPLE   PIG'S TROTTER   PILCHARD   PIKE

PILCHARD. The name given to the fully grown sardine. Plentiful off Devon and Cornwall and the facing Continental coasts, pilchards are related to the herring and sometimes called gypsy herring. Best between July and Christmas, they do not travel well and are usually available fresh only near the coasts off which they are caught. There they are popular broiled or cooked in any way suitable to fresh herrings or sardines and they also appear in the Cornish star-gazy pie (which see). Filleted, they are also enjoyed *en paupiettes* (which see) or stuffed and baked in oiled paper (see PAPER COOKERY). Much of the catch is home-pickled or commercially canned in oil, brine or tomato sauce.

PILOT WAFERS. Also pilot crackers. Both terms are American names for a type of hard tack or ship's biscuits. Once common afloat and in the armed forces, they remain in use in New England for thickening chowders. See also CRACKERS.

PILSNER. A lager, strictly only the renowned one produced in Pilsen (now Plzeň) in Czechoslovakia. However the name has been freely borrowed by brewers everywhere to describe the best lager beer they produce.

PIMENTO. See ALLSPICE.

PIMIENTO. A capsicum of the same variety that gives us paprika (which see). The bulbous fruits, used as vegetables, are called Spanish peppers or, according to type and degree of ripeness, green, yellow or red peppers. With their seeds scooped out they are often stuffed with rice mixtures or forcemeats and baked. Sliced, they add colour and distinctive flavour to stews, sauces and salads. They should not be confused with pimento (allspice or Jamaica pepper).

PIMMS. Speciality drinks, known by numbers, based on gin, whisky, brandy, rum, rye and vodka. They are served as long drinks diluted with sparkling lemonade, garnished with sliced fruit and cucumber, mint and borage.

PINCH. In culinary terms, the amount of powdered condiments, spices etc. that can be held between the thumb and forefinger.

PINEAPPLE. A succulent and flavoursome fruit grown in most tropical and subtropical countries. The first account of the pineapple was given by Christopher Columbus and his men, who landed on the island now known as Guadeloupe on their second voyage of discovery. Much later it was also found in Hawaii where it was known as *holakahiki*. In Hawaiian *hola* means screw pine, and *kahiki* means from a foreign land. It would seem to follow that the pineapple is not a native of Hawaii but how and when it arrived there is a mystery. At any rate it came to a suitable soil and climate and flourished. Today Hawaii supplies more than one half of the world's demand for pineapples. It is also grown in large quantities in Brazil, Cuba, Mexico, Formosa, Ceylon, Malaysia, the Philippines and South Africa.

There are many varieties of cultivated pineapple which differ in size and shape of fruit and in taste and colour of the flesh. It takes six to seven months for the fruits to mature after flowering and it ought to be allowed to ripen attached to the plant in order to develop maximum flavour.

There may be a hundred or more separate fruits arranged spirally round a thick centred axis and the whole forms a broad, almost cylindrical multiple fruit tapering at the top, surrounded by a rosette and short, stiff, spirally arranged leaves known as the crown.

The pineapple is one of the finest table fruits and should be eaten uncooked. Pineapple juice makes a pleasant and refreshing beverage. The fruit itself is excellent in salads and makes a good flavouring for ice-creams, jellies and other confections. Canned pineapple and pineapple juice are also available, the first plant for this purpose having been established in Hawaii in 1892.

PINEAPPLE CHEESE. The credit for creating pineapple cheese goes to Lewis Morton, a dairy farmer of Litchfield, Connecticut, who first made it in the 19th century. It is a hard cheddar-type cheese which was extremely popular in America for the best part of the last century. Lewis Morton hung the cheese in a net that created corrugations similar to those of a pineapple as it drained to firmness. The rind was hard shellacked to the colour of a pineapple. The top was sliced off and replaced by a silver top to look like pineapple leaves and the cheese itself, weighing 1 lb., was pressed into the shape of the fruit. He first served it dramatically on a silver platter.

People liked to help themselves by digging in with a silver scoop. The cheese finally consumed, the shellacked rind was used as a salad bowl.

PINEAU DES CHARENTES. This *vin d'elegance française* is a natural liqueur made with fresh grape juice and *eau-de-vie de Cognac* according to strict rules. It can be white or rose tinted with true glints of gold. Its strength must be at least 17°. It has a characteristic bouquet which is due both to the quality of its components and its long maturation in oak casks. When served very cold, it makes a delectable and invigorating aperitif.

PINOLE. A concentrated food devised by the American Indians and consisting of parched, ground cereal grains. Like pemmican (which see), it is ideal for lightweight, long lasting, highly nutritious emergency rations. It can be eaten dry but is more palatable when mixed into a mush with twice its own bulk of water. Pinole made from parched corn maize is the most nutritious and was standard emergency fare of the early pioneers.

PINOT BLANC and **PINOT NOIR.** See BURGUNDY WINES.

PINTAIL DUCK. See DUCK, WILD.

PINTO BEAN. See BEAN.

PIPE. See WINE CONTAINERS.

PIPERADE. One of the ancient recipes of the Basque country. There are several versions of this dish, but the following recipe is typical of them all. It can be garnished with lightly fried bacon.
  2–3 tomatoes
  2 sweet peppers, green, red or yellow
  1 tablespoon (1¼) olive oil
  6 eggs
Peel and quarter the tomatoes and peppers and remove seeds and hard cores. Heat the oil and slowly cook the peppers and tomatoes until they are soft. Beat the eggs exactly as for a plain omelette and pour this over the vegetables. When the eggs are just set, serve the *piperade* at once.

PIPERINE. An alkaloid found in black pepper which gives it its pungency. If taken in sufficient quantities, it causes perspiration which on evaporation has a cooling effect on the body. This is probably the reason it is so widely used as a seasoning in hot climates.

PIPING. Decoration or ornament, usually icing or creamed butter on cakes. Mashed potatoes can also be piped round dishes of meat, chicken or fish.

PIPING BAG. See PASTRY BAG.

PIQUANTE SAUCE. See SAUCES.

PISCHINGER TORTE. An Austrian speciality made with *oblaten* (which see).
  1 packet or 10 *oblaten* wafers
  5 oz. (10 tablespoons) unsalted butter
  8 oz. (1 cup) fine sugar
  10 oz. (10 squares) cooking (bakers') chocolate
  vanilla flavouring to taste
  1 cup (1¼) finely grated hazel-nuts
  4 egg whites, stiffly beaten
  6 oz. (1½ cups) icing (confectioners') sugar
Place one *oblaten* wafer on a round cake plate. Beat the butter until creamy and gradually beat in the sugar. Melt 6 oz. (6 squares) of the chocolate in a bowl over boiling water. Add the melted chocolate to the butter and, when blended, add vanilla and nuts. Beat well, then fold in the egg whites. Spread a thin layer of this cream over the wafer, cover with a second wafer and another layer of the chocolate-nut cream. Continue in this manner until all the wafers and the cream are used up. The top layer must be left plain.

Melt the remaining chocolate in a bowl over boiling water, add the icing sugar, a little vanilla flavouring, and about 2 tablespoons (2½) of tepid water. Beat until the mixture is smooth and blended and then spread the icing over the top of the *torte*. Leave for 48 hours at room temperature.

PISSALADIÈRE. A Provençal-type *pizza* and often so-called. Traditionally the flat tart base is of bread dough, spread with chopped onions, tomatoes and garlic fried together in olive oil. The filling is covered with a pattern of anchovy fillets and stoned black olives and the *pissaladière* is baked in a hot oven. Roman cooks possibly introduced it to Provence when the popes reigned at Avignon.

PISTACHIO. A small deciduous tree, a species of turpentine tree. The nut has a delicious green kernel which it is best to roast, salt and cool before eating. The unsalted pistachio is a good flavouring agent for ice-creams and a large number of confectioneries. Grated pistachio nuts are also sprinkled

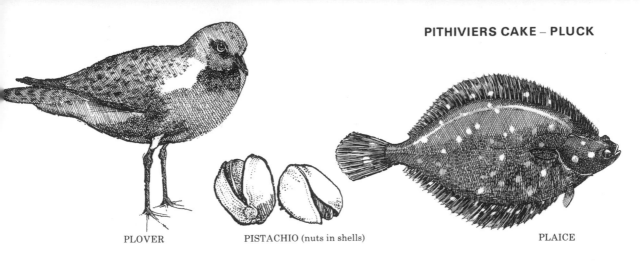

PLOVER   PISTACHIO (nuts in shells)   PLAICE

over rice and similar milk puddings. Pistachio nuts are rich in iron content.

PITHIVIERS CAKE. A French cake made from puff-pastry mixed with sweet and bitter ground almonds. It is light with a delicate almond perfume.

PIZZA. The word means pie in Italian, but in its most primitive form *pizza* is a round of yeast dough spread with tomatoes and mozzarella cheese and baked in a hot oven. The most famous of the many *pizze* is the Neapolitan *pizza* and it is very substantial. However, there is enough variety in pizza-making to write a book about them. The Roman *pizza*, for example, has plenty of onions but no tomatoes; the Ligurian *pizza* has onions, black olives and anchovies.

PIZZERIA. A type of simple eating house in southern Italy where a quick and small meal, usually a *pizza*, is served. Such institutions have spread to northern Italy, as well as to cities outside Italy.

PLAICE. A member of the flat-fish family in season throughout the year. The upper side of the fish is greyish-brown with orange and scarlet spots. If the spots are not bright the fish is stale.

The flesh of the plaice is not very interesting and a thick, plump fish makes the best eating. Small plaice are best fried in butter; larger fish filleted and baked in the oven, although they can be cooked in any of the ways for sole.

PLANKING. A method of cooking popular in the United States. It was invented by the Indians and adopted by the early settlers who found it both a convenient and delicious way to cook their meat and fish. It is not a difficult method of cooking. The plank should be well made of well-seasoned hard wood, hickory, maple or oak, and either oval or oblong in shape. It should also be grooved so that the juices will not escape. Any fish suitable for grilling (broiling) may be baked on a plank, and any kind of steak, from the hamburg to a fillet mignon. A plank used for meat should not be used for fish. It should never be washed but scraped, wiped with bread, and then rubbed with kitchen paper until clean. The older the plank the better it is, and for a planking expert, a really old and charred plank is considered a kitchen treasure.

PLANTAIN. A fruit similar to the banana and not always clearly distinguishable. However, a plantain is larger and harder than the banana. The two look alike but at the fruiting stage the difference becomes obvious. The plantain is best taken before it is ripe and eaten, roasted or boiled.

Plantains are grown in South America, the Caribbean Islands and India. They can also be dried in the same way as figs. The Mexicans also use the fragrant flesh as infant or invalid food.

PLANTER'S PUNCH. A long rum drink originating in the West Indies.

Put a liqueur glass of fresh lime juice into a tumbler, add 2 liqueur glasses of sugar syrup and 1 of rum. Fill the tumbler with crushed ice and stir. Add a strip of lime peel and grate nutmeg over the top, a dash of Angostura bitters; and serve with a straw.

PLATTER. A flat round or oval plate or dish.

PLOVER. Wading birds of the subfamily Charadriinae, and related to the phalarope and sandpiper, the plovers consist of approximately 60 species, distributed throughout the world. They are plump-bodied, with a large head, thick neck and strong, short bill; the legs are shorter and thicker than those of the average wader. They are migratory birds and are capable of flying great distances, but cannot swim well. Gastronomically, the best known are the lapwing and the golden plover. The plover is prepared in the same way as teal (see DUCK, WILD), while the eggs are considered a great delicacy and may be roasted or lightly boiled.

PLUCK. This word has two main culinary meanings:

1. To remove the feathers of a bird after it has been killed.

2. To draw or remove the heart, liver and lights (called the pluck) of an animal after slaughter.

PLUM. A late summer to early autumn fruit of which there are many varieties, both wild and cultivated. The important commercially grown varieties belong to the *Prunus domestica* species. The plum is a delicious fruit with a sweet, light flesh, pleasant aroma and a flat stone. The finest of all eating varieties is the Imperial Epicure, but being the worst cropping plum known it is not grown commercially. The chief dessert plum is the oval Victoria, with a red-to-yellow, transparent skin and superb flavour. It can also be cooked, used for jam-making and for canning. Then there are the Laxtons, similar in appearance to Victorias but coarser skinned. Pond's Seedlings, large and golden when ripe, are very sweet. The purple Belle de Louvain is popular for its size. The Zwetchgen, the small, dark-purple plum from which the Yugoslavs make their potent *slivovitz* (which see), is well liked in continental Europe.

Possibly the smallest plum ever to be cultivated is the golden-yellow Mirabelle. It is round like a large cherry, sometimes with a few red spots. Grown in Alsace, Germany and other parts of the Continent, it is sometimes known as the 'Cloth of Gold' in England.

The greengage is a variety of plum said to be named after the Gage family who first imported it into England from France at the end of the 18th century. In France and many other continental countries it is known as the Reine Claude, or by some variant of this name. It is sweet and delicately flavoured and may be eaten fresh or cooked.

The damson (which see) is a *Prunus institia* and thus a member of the plum family.

The United States has much the same range of commercial plums, with the addition of the beach plum. Texas plum and the American sloe.

PLUM PUDDING. A pudding which in most countries would be made of plums, but in British usage is made with every sort of dried fruit, but not usually prunes. The rich brown British Christmas pudding (which see) is a plum pudding. Related to the plum pudding is the simpler plum duff, which is also aptly called spotted dick or dog – a steamed or boiled suet pudding with raisins and currants.

POACH. To cook gently in simmering liquid. The temperature should not exceed 190–200°F., i.e. when the liquid is trembling. Eggs, fish and fruit may be cooked in this manner.

POI. A Hawaiian paste made by pounding cooked taro (which see) and allowing it to ferment. It is a pale grey colour, thick and sticky, and with no particular flavour. It was at one time so popular in Hawaii that men and even women are said to have eaten as much as 15 lb. daily. It is made in three 'thicknesses': 'one finger', 'two finger' and even 'three finger'. In other words, if the poi is so thick that a portion can be swirled round with one finger, it is 'one finger' poi. Two finger poi is thinner, as it takes two fingers tightly closed to scoop enough up for a mouthful; and three finger is the thinnest of all. Poi is an acquired taste and is usually served accompanied by such dishes as salted salmon, onions, tomatoes etc.

POKEWEED. A highly aromatic perennial herb, also known as pokeberry, pokeroot or pocan, which grows in the United States from Florida to Maine and west to Texas. The young shoots are eaten like asparagus and the seedlings like spinach. The root is extremely poisonous and must be removed before cooking the rest of the plant, while the purple berries are inedible and toxic.

POLENTA. A porridge, mush or pudding made, usually, of maize flour. In Renaissance Italy it was made of barley meal or chestnut flour and is still made of the latter in Corsica. The porridge can be eaten hot or cold with various additions, sweet or savoury. More often it is cooled, cut up and re-cooked in various ways – toasted, pan-fried or deep-fried in a batter or egg-and crumb coating, baked in rich layer pies or in the pan juices of roasts.

POLLACK or **POLLOCK.** A salt-water food fish related to the cod, but having a protruding lower jaw, like the kindred coalfish (which see). Other names for the pollack are green-fish and lythe.

POLLAN. A whitefish, sometimes called a fresh water herring, plentifully netted in Irish loughs. It is closely allied to the powan of the Scottish lochs and the vendace of Derwentwater and certain other British and continental lakes.

POMEGRANATE. A delicious and refreshing fruit mentioned in the Old Testament and known to the ancient Greeks and Hindus. It is probably a native of Persia but has been grown in Africa and throughout the East for centuries. More recently it has been grown in America, particularly in California and Florida.

The pomegranate is about the size of a large orange with a thin but leathery rind, pale yellow to purple in colour. Inside there are large seeds enclosed in pulpy flesh. The flesh is bright red or crimson, full of refreshing vinous and sub-acid juice. In good quality fruit the seeds within the

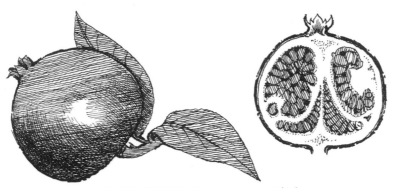

POMEGRANATE (fruit on stem, cross-section)

flesh are tender, juicy and easy to eat.

Pomegranate juice is used in beverages and ices and is particularly valuable in making grenadine.

The pomegranate is a very common fruit in Persia where in addition to being eaten raw it is also used in soups, sauces and sweets. The soup is particularly popular in winter and is made with ground beef, onions, spinach, sugar, rice and either pomegranate seeds or juice. A jelly, *Gelée Annar*, is a simple and favourite summer pudding, made by mixing pomegranate juice with isinglass or gelatine to set it and is served with cream. The Jamaicans also use pomegranates in general cookery, particularly jellies.

POMELO. The pomelo, also known as the shaddock, is the largest of the citrus fruits and a native of Malaysia. It is a coarse thick-skinned bitter fruit with a tough pink flesh. It is not grown on any scale anywhere as it is not a particularly palatable fruit, although it can be used in salads. The pomelo is sometimes taken for a kind of grapefruit, but modern authorities distinguish between the two.

POMEROL. See BORDEAUX WINES.

POMFRET. A sea fish found along the Indian coasts and highly esteemed. At first glance it is not unlike a smooth silvery plaice with a rounded snout and a small mouth, but its flavour is more delicate and could be likened to turbot. There are silver, white and black pomfret. In Pondicherry the French called it *pample* and in old recipe books it was called *pomplet*, possibly from the Portuguese *pampo*. Pomfret may be fried, grilled, poached etc.

POMMARD. See BURGUNDY WINES.

POMPANO. Considered by many to be the finest of all eating fishes, whether fresh or salt-water. It is found chiefly in the Atlantic, mainly in the warmer southern waters. Related to the mackerel, it grows to a length of 18 in. and weighs up to 3 lb. Pompano *en papillote* (which see) is one of the most highly prized sea food dishes.

PONT L'ÉVÊQUE. One of Normandy's finest cheeses, ranking fourth among the great French cheeses. It was originally called *Angelot* and in the 13th century was already reckoned an old cheese. Small and plump, the cheese has a crust with criss-cross markings from the strawmatting on which it lies. Its texture is soft with countless holes and a pale yellow colour, and its flavour is sweet. Pont l'Evêque cannot be imitated and is at its best in autumn and winter.

PONTET CANET, CH. See BORDEAUX WINES.

POOR KNIGHTS OF WINDSOR. Slices of bread soaked in liquid fried in butter and served with jam or sugar and sprinkled with cinnamon. It is the type of recipe which appears again and again. In France it is *pain perdue*; in Austria *arme Ritter* (poor knights); and Sweden has Rich Knights. There is an Argentine and a Portuguese version and even Bombay Toast is similar. See FRENCH TOAST.

The real Poor Knights, now called Military Knights, were created by Edward III in 1348 and live in Grace-and-Favour houses in the precincts of Windsor Castle in Berkshire, England.

POPCORN. A type of Indian corn with small pointed or rounded kernels and very hard endosperm; when exposed to dry heat the kernels are 'popped' by the explosion of the moisture within, producing a white mass of starch several times as large as the original kernel.

POPE'S EYE. The name given to the small circle of fat found in the middle of a leg of lamb or pork. In Scotland the primest rump steak.

POPOVER. The American equivalent of an individual Yorkshire pudding (which see). It is made by preparing a creamy batter from flour, milk, egg and salt. This is then baked in well-greased earthenware pots in a hot oven until the mixture rises golden-brown high over the edges of the pots. See page 243.

POPPY SEED OIL. An oil extracted from poppy seeds and used for cooking and salad dressings.

POPPY SEEDS. The seeds of a large variety of poppy grown in Holland and used extensively in continental and oriental cooking. Originally this poppy, which is different from the opium-yielding variety, was a native of Asia. The seeds may be either black or grey in colour, with no fragrance but of a distinctive flavour. They are extremely tiny and it is said there are more than 900,000 to the pound.

Poppy seeds may be eaten roasted or browned in butter. Seeds may be mixed with candied fruit, sugar and spices and ground to make a fat- and flour-free cake. Whole they are used also to coat loaves of bread. They make a filling for strudels and ring cakes, and they impart a pleasant flavour to noodles, pickles, preserves and beverages.

PORCUPINE. A rodent with stiff spines mingled in its hair, also called quill-pig. It is large (up to 40 lb.), fat and makes good eating.

PORGY. The name applied to several different species of salt-water fish in different locations throughout the world. In European waters and on the Atlantic coasts of North America, the *Pagrus pagrus* is called the red porgy; in the United States the scup and the menhaden are so called. It is prepared in the same way as catfish (which see).

PORK. The flesh of swine, hog or pig eaten fresh, not cured as ham or bacon. Cooked plainly its meat is white or palest pink, the lack of colour being due to the pork butcher's techniques: the drained blood goes into black puddings. Pork has long been a staple food though religious and social taboos have limited its use. Now improvements in pig-breeding, hygiene, transport and spoilage-control have combined to make it a widely enjoyed year-round meat. Pork is best when young and when the pig-feeding has been carefully programmed. The young porker's meat is firm and fine-grained, its fat white, its skin thin and smooth.

Pork is always thoroughly cooked and usually, in Western cuts, the better for slow cooking. Pork joints in Britain have the skin or rind still on them and for roasting or baking the skin is scored in narrow strips; in the United States they are usually sold without the skin. The slashes in the rind allow the rubbing-in of condiments, herbs and spices, and also let the rind develop into crackling, which at its best is a dry, crisp honeycomb of bubbles. In most pork dishes the fat emerges as a complement to the lean, with a texture and flavour which make it something to be enjoyed in its own right. In China and many European countries the rind of pork, usually chopped small, is a valued addition to the smoothness and consistency of stews and soups.

The Chinese are perhaps the most expert cooks when it comes to pork, their most universally used meat. Most commonly, the Chinese chop it into matchstick shreds or equally thin little squares and then 'stir-fry' it: they cook it, stirring constantly, in minimum fat and minimum liquid for only a minute or two. The Chinese enjoyment of spare-ribs of pork and sweet-and-sour pork has spread across the world. Sweet-and-sour pork is cooked in various ways and finished in a sauce including vinegar and sugar.

In Western cuisines pork is cooked much like other meats. Names of cuts vary from region to region, country to country. Britain's leg of pork means the fillet and knuckle – the half-buttock and a hind leg. Hind loin, immediately forward of the buttock, is called tenderloin in the United States and middle loin is called loin. In British general usage fore loin is further forward, spareribs for'arder still beside the blade bone. Right below them, as the pig stands, is the shoulder (shoulder butt in America) or hand and spring (American picnic shoulder and pork hock). Because of its richness, pork is usually accompanied by sharp-flavoured sauces: apple sauce, apple marmalade, tart redcurrant jelly, cranberry purée or jelly. Garnishes are similarly contrasting: boiled potatoes, sauerkraut, pickled peaches or braised celery.

PORPOISE. A mammal sometimes called the sea-swine and at one time a popular item of diet in England. It was once a favourite at the tables of the great, but is no longer eaten by the British, although it still has adherents in other countries. The Anglo-Saxons rated it highly, and the antiquarians tell us that at the 'coronacion of King Henry the ffifte' there was porpoise – and minnows. A curious combination surely, the one so large and the other so small. King Henry VIII was also fond of this archetype of obesity. If it was too large for a horse-load, the purveyor was given an extra allowance. It was cooked in various ways and one sauce recommended to be served with porpoise was made with vinegar, breadcrumbs and sugar. In the last century from time to time a porpoise would be brought to London's famous Billingsgate Fish Market, 'but instead of being food for kings, not even the beggar will touch it; it is bought only for show by the fishmongers'.

PORRIDGE. Once the staple dish of Scotland but now served largely at breakfast. In Scotland it is served hot with cold milk and sprinkled with salt; south of the border, with milk or cream and sugar.

PORRINGER. A small dish in which porridge

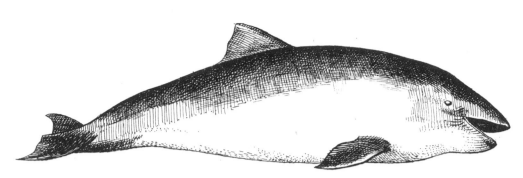

PORPOISE

used to be served to children. Silver porringers were often given as christening presents.

PORT. A wine made from the grapes grown in the valley of the Upper Douro, fortified at vintage time and shipped from Oporto, Portugal, mainly to the United Kingdom. When the grapes are pressed their sweet juice begins to ferment; but before fermentation has transformed the whole of the grape-sugar into alcohol, brandy is added to it and all further vinous fermentation is immediately checked. At that stage port is a blend of wine (fermented grape juice), brandy and unfermented grape juice. But of such materials time fashions two different and equally seductive wines: vintage port and tawny port. Vintage port is a wine made in one year, shipped usually two years after it is made and bottled in England soon after it is received. It is then aged in the bottle from 12 to 20 years to get the desired strength, delicacy, sweetness and flavour. Tawny port is not a wine made from any one year's grapes, but a blend of wines of a number of years. It is kept at Oporto in the shippers' lodges for many years and is matured in wood. It ages more rapidly than early-bottled vintage port and is shipped when ready to drink.

Ruby port may be the wine of one vintage kept in cask long enough to lose some of its 'fire', but not long enough to lose much of its colour. Or it may be a blend of wines of different years and style, a blend which may be made at Oporto by the shipper or in England by the wine merchants. There is also a white port which has many admirers.

Good port is taken seriously in Britain but at one time less good port was the 'pub tipple' for old ladies who drank a 'port and lemon'. Today it is recognized that these old ladies were not so odd. Port experts now admit that port can be taken as a long drink, diluted with tonic water and ice. Both white and tawny port can be mixed with gin or vodka, well chilled and served as a short drink.

PORTERHOUSE STEAK. A thick steak cut from the thick end of the sirloin. Its name originated from the old porterhouses where it was served.

PORTMANTEAU STEAK. A thick steak with a deep pocket cut along one side into which oysters are inserted. The steak is then sewn up and cooked in the usual manner.

PORT-SALUT. A French semi-hard cheese, made from whole milk and fermented. At one time it was only made by Trappist monks at the Port-du-Salut monastery but it is now produced in other parts of France and also in Belgium.

PORTUGAISE, À LA. Culinary French name for a dish featuring tomatoes above all else, but usually also garlic and onions.

PORTUGAISES. See OYSTERS.

PORTUGUESE WINES. While most of the table wines exported from Portugal are either simple beverage wines shipped in bulk, or lavishly advertised branded, pink, slightly fizzy ones in pretty bottles, it must be remembered that some extremely fine wines are made in several regions, which reach their full maturity only after a number of years in bottle. The latter kind will only be found in Portugal; they are hardly ever exported.

For a small country Portugal is very lucky in the varied range of wines it produces. Being further south than France, there is plenty of hot sun to ripen the grapes, but this in itself would not make for fine wines if it were not for two moderating influences. From the west the winds and atmospheric changes blow in straight from the Atlantic, and from the east the high mountains exercise a cooling influence.

From the north to south, wines are made in most parts of the country which can be divided very broadly into three main regions. In the furthest north the Minho region is the area of the *vinho verde*. The literal translation 'green wine' simply describes freshness and youth, but not the real colour of the wine, which is yellowish rather than green, or red (although it can also be white). The vines are grown, planted around and between other crops, climbing on trellises and sometimes trees, with the grapes forming at a minimum height of eight feet off the ground. This reduces the intensity of the reflected sunshine reaching them.

The *vinhos verdes* have a low alcohol content, but are rich in malic and lactic acids and subject to a slight, secondary (malolactic) fermentation which gives them their characteristic slight prickle, almost a *pétillance*. They are basically very dry and refreshing. The reds are hardly ever exported and the whites are sometimes blended with sweeter grapes to reduce the acidity when intended for export.

The Dão wine region is concentrated in the valleys of the Mondego and its tributary the Dão. The vineyards are mostly at 1,500 to 2,000 feet above sea-level, cultivated in steep terraces on the granitic soil. The *tourigo* is the most common grape variety: it is black, as is the *tinta pinheira*, while the *arinto* is white. The inclusion of *arinto* grapes does not reduce the deep ruby colour of the red wines; when it is used on its own it makes the white Dão – full, fruity and dry, and although of a different character, comparable to white Burgundy or Rhône wines.

The ordinary reds are big, full wines. They have to be kept in wood for up to four years before they are shipped abroad to be bottled and sold under regional or branded names. The better wines are never bottled before they have had at least four years in wood, and need another four years in bottle before being drunk under the name *Dão reserva*. The finest red wines are allowed to age for eight or more years in bottle; these wines, described as *garrafeira* are hardly ever encountered outside Portugal. *Reservas* and *garrafeiras* have great bouquets, fruitiness, a certain elegance and a long-lasting vitality, with a character very much their own.

In the Barraida district, just south of the Dão, good ordinary wines are made, and also some whites which are used to make sparkling wines by the *méthode champenoise*.

In the past, the products of the districts around Lisbon have often been lumped together and simply called Lisbon wines, as they were always shipped from that port. In fact, there are a number of different individual wines made in this area between Alcobaça, with its fairly ordinary whites, and Setubal in the south.

The most famous and unusual of these vineyards is Colares where the method of cultivation is unique. The vines grow practically on the beach and must be protected by earthworks. The roots are deep down in the sand, and the shoots appear to grow practically on the sand. These vines escaped the phylloxera through this protection of the roots by the marine sand. The bunches of grapes have to be supported by little wooden pegs. Colares is a small production, perhaps the best of all the Portuguese red wines. Bucelas, northeast of Lisbon, makes a straw-coloured white dry wine. Carcavelos nearby makes a richer, fruitier white, used as an aperitif in Portugal after about five years of maturing.

At Setubal to the south of the Tagus river a classic, luscious dessert wine is made of Moscatel grapes. There is no *pourriture noble* here; the rich sweetness is produced by the intense sun. Fermentation is arrested with brandy when a suitable balance of sugar and alcohol is reached. The typical Moscatel flavour is imparted to the wine by soaking fresh Moscatel grape skins in the wine for several months. See also MADEIRA, PORT.

POSSET. An old-fashioned concoction which was served either after a meal or instead of a meal. It varied from a simple treacle cure for a cold to an elaborate confection. Possets were served in china posset dishes with covers. Pepys writes of a 'good sack posset' he gave his guests which sent them away 'highly pleased'. Sir Kenelm Digby's recipe for a sack posset was sack, cream, egg yolks, sugar and spices and 'amber-greece' to be poured 'from a great height' and served hot or cold.

POTATO. A plant with tubers grown for food. Some authorities believe it is a native of the Peruvian-Bolivian Andes. Potato cultivation in South America goes back at least to the beginning of the Christian era, if not earlier. Pottery decorated with potato motifs has been found in graves of that date which would seem to confirm this view.

The potato was introduced into Spain in the early years of the 16th century by returning Spanish explorers and there are references to it in the literature of that age. One of them describes the potato as 'this ground nut which when boiled becomes as soft as a cooked chestnut but has no thicker skin than a truffle'.

The word potato is derived from the Spanish *patata* which in itself is a variant of a South American Indian word *batata*. Strictly speaking *batata* is the name given to the sweet potato.

It was probably introduced into Ireland at about the same time as in Spain and some authorities allege that it was from Ireland that Sir Walter Raleigh brought the potato to England. They dispute the legend that he carried it from Virginia because, they say, the potato was not grown there at the time. In the 16th century only the sweet potato was known in England but at the end of the century the potato, common potato, white potato or Irish potato, as it was variously known, was being grown in Italy, Flanders and Germany as well as Spain. Some herbalists of the day believed it to be an aphrodisiac and a cure for rheumatism.

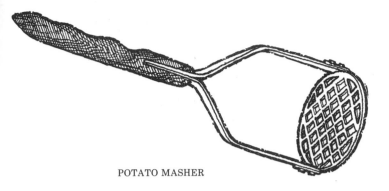

POTATO MASHER

The potato began to be grown as a commercial crop in England towards the end of the 18th century. It was first grown in Essex and offered for sale in London. In 1739 potatoes began to be cultivated extensively in Scotland. Before this, potato cultivation was frowned upon by Scottish preachers who believed potatoes unfit food for Christians as there was no mention of them in the Bible.

Gradually potato cultivation spread throughout Europe and became a major crop. It had also become a staple item of food in Ireland and it is said that a typical Irish peasant family ate about 8 lb. of potatoes each per day. This explains why the notorious potato famine of 1843 caused such havoc.

Today the potato is one of the eight major world food crops. There are four main culinary varieties: new, second early, mid-season and late crops. Their skins vary in colour from brownish-white to purple but the flesh usually varies from white to yellow. In general potatoes with a waxy, yellowish flesh are best fried, while the whiter and softer ones are best baked or boiled. The famous Idaho potato of America is excellent for baking. Potatoes can be cooked in an endless number of ways, but care should be taken to choose the right variety to go with a particular recipe. In addition to starch, potatoes contain a useful quantity of vitamin C, amino acids, protein, thiamin and nicotinic acid.

POTATO CHIPS (FRENCH FRIES). Potatoes, peeled and cut into strips about ½ in. wide and thick and the full length of the potato. They are soaked in cold water for 30 minutes, thoroughly drained, dried in a towel, and fried in deep fat or oil until crisp and a golden brown.

POTATO CRISPS. See GAME CHIPS.

POTATO FLOUR. A very fine flour prepared from cooked, dried and ground potatoes. It is nutritious and is used mainly to thicken soups, sauces and gravies. It can be used in puddings and in combination with other flours in breads and cakes.

POTATO MASHER. This implement is used to mash cooked potatoes to a creamy mass. Mashers are made of either wood or metal and come in many shapes. Some are used with a straight thrusting motion; others are also adapted for beating.

POTATOES, STRAW. These are potatoes grated and fried to look like straw. Wash and peel as many potatoes as required. Grate them, using the largest cutter in the grater. Drop them in cold water, leave for 30 minutes, then dry thoroughly. Have ready a large, deep pan with plenty of boiling fat and fry the grated potatoes quickly to a delicate brown. Take from the fat and drain on paper.

Straw potatoes can be prepared in advance and reheated in a hot oven.

POT-AU-FEU. A broth made from beef and vegetables and served in the *cocotte* or pot in which it is made. The meat is served separately surrounded by the vegetables as a main course, the broth as a clear soup. There are countless versions of this dish.

POTEEN or **POTHEEN.** From the Gaelic *poitín* or little pot, this is illicitly distilled whiskey made in Ireland from nearly everything that will ferment, but generally from barley or malt. This was common practice in the 18th century when the British government stopped the licensing of small stills, but poteen varying in strength and quality is still made in many parts of Ireland because of heavy taxes on spirits.

POT LIQUOR. The juice obtained when vegetables such as beans or peas are boiled with meat. Traditionally served in the United States with crisp corn bread (which is crumbled into the bowl), this is a Southern favourite and is highly nutritious.

POT PIE. A pie made of meat or poultry with vegetables and covered with a thick crust of short pastry, similar to the traditional English meat pie.

POT ROASTING. A process of cooking which combines frying and steaming and requires a heavy pan. It is usually done on top of the stove over a gentle heat. This method is used for tougher meats and is a good way of roasting smaller meat joints, as there is less shrinkage.

POTTED MEAT. Meat, poultry, game (or fish) cooked and pounded and preserved in pots or jars. Potted meats are covered (or should be) with a thick layer of clarified suet or butter to exclude air. Over the top is laid a sprig of parsley or other green herbs to assist in the preservation and flavour.

The best quality meats used to be served in this manner and it was a common practice for seamen and travellers to carry this long-keeping, compact food on journeys.

The difference between English potted meat and the French *terrines* is that in the former the meat is cooked before being preserved, and in the latter the meat is cooked in the *terrine* in which it is to be stored and served.

POUILLY-FUISSÉ. See BURGUNDY WINES.

POUILLY-LOCHÉ. See BURGUNDY WINES.

POUILLY-VINZELLES. See BURGUNDY WINES.

POUJEAUX. See BORDEAUX WINES.

POULTRY. A term which includes all farmyard birds bred especially for the table.

POWAN. See POLLAN.

POYFERRÉ. See BORDEAUX WINES.

PRAIRIE OYSTER. An American invention, imported into Britain. There is a story which recounts that a member of a hunting party on the Texas prairies fell sick and clamoured for oysters, of which there were none for hundreds of miles. However, an inventive fellow member of the party thought up a substitute. He dropped some shelled, but unbroken prairie hens' eggs, one at a time, carefully into a wine glass containing some vinegar, sprinkled freshly milled pepper over the top and added a pinch of salt. The patient took them and recovered.

Today a turkey's egg is recommended or, failing this, an ordinary hens' egg. A Worcester oyster is made in the same manner, substituting Worcestershire sauce for the vinegar.

PRALINE. Almonds or pecans covered with a coating of sugar syrup, flavoured and coloured.

PRALINER. French term meaning to add pralines, usually crushed, to creams, ices, souffles, etc.

PRAWNS. In Britain the name of small crustaceans, larger than shrimps. When fresh, they are a translucent grey colour but turn bright pink when cooked. Most prawns sold in England come from Norway, usually cooked on the ships, and arrive either fresh or frozen, peeled or unpeeled, to be sold by the pint or the pound.

Dublin Bay prawns. See separate entry.

Mediterranean prawns. Not often seen in Britain, these are red when raw and have a nutty flavour.

Pacific or king prawns. These are larger than ordinary prawns and are sold singly in their shells.

PREIGNAC. See BORDEAUX WINES.

PREMEAUX. See BURGUNDY WINES.

PREMIÉRES CÔTES DE BORDEAUX. See BORDEAUX WINES.

PRESSAC. See BORDEAUX WINES.

PRESERVES. This includes all manner of foods, fruits and vegetables preserved in various ways, i.e. bottled, pickled or made into jams, marmalades, conserves etc. Today one can buy any preserve and few women emulate their grandmothers whose larder shelves were lined with home-made preserves of every kind. The advent of frozen foods and the home freezers has somewhat lessened the need for home preserving in the bottled form.

PRESSED BEEF. Boned, salted and pressed brisket beef.

PRESSURE COOKING. Cooking by steam acting under pressure in a cooker made usually of steel or aluminium, with a lid which locks into place and is made airtight by a rubber gasket fitted between the edges of the lid and pan. On the lid is a control valve which allows a little steam to escape when food and liquid is inside it and cooking, and a safety valve which opens automatically if the pressure inside becomes too great. There are several types of pressure cookers on the market, and with each comes a leaflet of instructions, which should be carefully followed.

PRETZELS. Rings of water and flour paste baked in a very hot oven until hard, then glazed and sprinkled with coarse salt or caraway seeds. Common in Germany and the United States, they are now becoming more popular in Britain. Pretzels were known at the time of the Romans and have, over the centuries, gathered for themselves a good collection of traditions. According to one authority, their name is derived from a Latin word

SPANISH WINES: classifying Sherry.

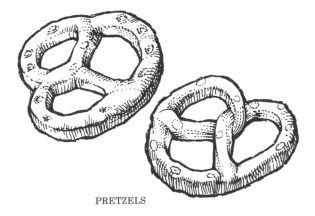

PRETZELS

which meant 'little reward', while another authority says that the word has the same derivation as prayer. A third story says pretzels were given to small children as a 'little reward' for learning their prayers.

However, they also seem to have been connected with good old-fashioned superstitions. People wore pretzels round their neck to ward off evil spirits (they ate the pretzels later), and they were hung on trees with the curious hope they would cause them to bear well. Even today there is a superstition, similar to the breaking of the wish-bone that to ceremoniously break a pretzel with someone will make a wish come true.

PREUSES, LES. See BURGUNDY WINES.

PRICKLY or **BARBARY PEAR.** The fruit of two varieties of cacti which grow in the United States, the Mediterranean area and parts of Africa. As its name suggests, the fruit is pear-shaped and prickly skinned. But it makes good eating both raw and cooked, although to eat too many causes constipation. During World War II the Sicilians discovered that the thick, watery leaves also could be cooked and eaten.

In Israel these pears are known as *sabras*, a word which is a compound of the Arabic *sabrus* and the Hebrew *saba*, both of which mean cactus. *Sabra* is also a term applied to native-born Israelis because, like the fruit, they are reputed to be prickly outside but of sweet disposition within.

Prickly pears are sold on street corners in Israel; the barbs are removed by rubber-gloved vendors and the fruit put on ice to cool and sprinkled with lemon juice.

PRIEURÉ, CH. LE. See BORDEAUX WINES.

PRIORATO. See SPANISH WINES.

PRISSEY. See BURGUNDY WINES.

PROFITEROLES. Little balls of *choux* paste which may be filled or not with various savoury or cheese mixtures and added to clear soups as a garnish.

There are also large *profiteroles* filled with fresh whipped cream and coated with chocolate.

PRONGHORN. An American game animal, the only representative of the separate Antilocapridae family. Found mainly in the western United States, the pronghorn is both a sportsman's trophy and highly esteemed table fare all the year round, though the meat is rather dry in the summer months, It is not as gamey in flavour as venison but may be cooked by any of the recipes used for the latter.

PROOF. See WINE TERMS.

PROVENÇALE, À LA. French culinary term for dishes flavoured with garlic, and usually tomatoes and black olives as well.

PRUNE. This is the name given to a dried plum, also to varieties of plum trees whose fruits are particularly suitable for drying because of the high sugar content and firm flesh. These varieties are specially cultivated for this purpose.

The art of drying plums has been perfected in California, a major prune producer. Most American varieties are of European origin, the first plum pits being brought to Massachusetts by the Pilgrim Fathers and by early French settlers to Canada. But the finest quality prune plums come from France, grown in Agen, Sainte-Livrade, Villeneuve and Tours. In France the fruit is boiled soon after picking and when cool is exposed on trays to dry in the sun. English plums dried by artificial heat compare favourably with most imported products. A variety also grows in Portugal.

Prunes may be eaten the same way as dried figs or dates, cooked in red wine and sugar, and served as a compôte or as a filling for tarts and puddings.

PRUNES IN RED WINE

1 lb. dried prunes

½ pint (1¼ cups) red wine

4 tablespoons (5) vanilla sugar

Put the prunes into a pan, cover with boiling water

and leave for 1 hour. Bring to the boil, lower the heat and cook for 20 minutes. Pour off half the liquid and put this aside, then add the sugar and wine to the pan. Continue to cook gently until the prunes are very soft, returning some of the reserved liquid if required. Drain the prunes from the liquid, cool and then take out the stones. Press the prune pulp through a sieve or put into a blender. Add enough of the syrup to bring the prunes to the consistency of a custard. Pour into glasses, chill and serve with whipped cream or yoghourt.

PRUNELLE, CRÈME DE. French and Dutch liqueurs made from plums and a small quantity of other stoned fruit, including the kernels.

PTARMIGAN. Of the grouse family, ptarmigan differ from the common grouse in that the legs have feathers down to their claws. In the northern hemisphere they are represented by about eight species. They feed on buds, berries, mosses and lichens, making the meat sweet and tender, with a delicate but definite aroma. Ptarmigan should be prepared in the same way as grouse (which see).

Other members of the family include the American willow grouse, the rock ptarmigan (found from Alaska to Labrador), and the red grouse.

PUCHERO. Also called *cocido* or *olla podrida*. A Spanish stew-soup – with many variations, particularly in Latin America – rather like a hot-pot (which see) or the French *pot-au-feu*. Like these the broth can be and usually is served in a separate dish from the meats and vegetables. Basically it is chunks of meat simmered on minimum heat until about half-cooked. Then, while the simmering continues, other things are added according to the time they need to cook.

PUDDING. As a culinary term this usually means a sweet dish, but there are a large number of savoury puddings, i.e. those cooked inside a suet crust and steamed or boiled, and those such as fish puddings which are made from pounded fish, eggs etc., filled into a greased bowl and steamed.

PUFF PASTRY. See PASTRY.

PULASSAN. A tree fruit from Southeast Asia, related to the lychee (which see). When its thick pebbly skin is removed it looks like an outsize peeled grape and has the hauntingly delicate flavour of the mangosteen.

PULIGNY-MONTRACHET. See BURGUNDY WINES.

PULSES. The dried seeds of leguminous plants, such as beans, peanuts, peas and soy beans. As they have no vitamin C or A, they cannot take the place of fresh vegetables in a diet.

PUMPERNICKEL. A dark, wholemeal rye bread from Germany also called *Schwarzbrot* (black bread) and Brown George. Originally associated especially with Westphalia and made from coarsely ground, unbolted rye flour, it is full-flavoured with a faintly acid aftertaste. Its firm texture makes it useful for canapés and open sandwiches.

PUMPKIN. A member of the gourd family in a wide range of sizes. Some are quite small and these are the best, while others become enormous. In Europe it is regarded more strictly as a vegetable and used for soups, although the French make pumpkin jams, and the Italians use pumpkin as a filling for sweet ravioli. In the United States it is used to make the famous pumpkin pie, as well as soup. In the Balkans pumpkin is sliced and made into fritters.

PUNCH. In a culinary sense this means hot or cold drinks. The name is supposedly derived from the Hindi word *panch*, meaning five, because five ingredients – arrack, lime, sugar, spices and water – were used.

PUNCHEON. See WINE TERMS.

PURÉE. This name is given to meat, fish, vegetables or fruit which have been pounded or mashed and sieved. The word when used as a verb means to press food through a sieve or ricer and then thin with a liquid.

PURIS. These belong to the Indian breads and there are many varieties. Some made with plain flour and water dough, others with yeast; some are stuffed, others plain, and finally there are sweet puris, All are fried in deep boiling fat until they puff up like balls.

PURSLANE. An annual succulent herb which grows in the Far and Middle East and in southern Europe. It is eaten cooked, in salads and as a pot-herb or for pickle.

Q

QOORMA. This Pakistani dish of stewed mutton or lamb starts in much the same manner as a *ragoût* but is rather more heavily spiced and is allowed to cook until the meat is almost dry.

QUAHOG

PUMPKIN

QUAHOG (QUAHAUG). A hard-shelled clam found chiefly along the New England coast. The yield is small compared with the soft-shelled clam, but quahogs are of fine flavour and of exceptional quality. They can be used in all the ways of soft-shelled clams, made into chowders, or served raw on the half shell.

QUAIL. Technically, the quail is a migratory bird related to the partridge family in the Old World, and to several gallinaceous birds found in the New World. However, the quail is more than simply another game bird. It is both the sportsman's and the epicure's delight, being as tasty on the table as it is honest in the field. So many members of the family are found throughout the world that it is impossible to list them here. Representative of the family are the European common quail, the Blue quail of Africa and the American quail.

In the United States, the names quail and partridge are used interchangeably in different parts of the country. It is also known as the 'bobwhite' from the sound of its call. Generally, however, the various species carry a descriptive word as part of their nomenclature, such as California quail, mountain quail and the crested quail.

Quail should be eaten not later than the day after being killed. They must be dry plucked, singed and drawn from the neck. The head and neck are removed and the wings trussed as squab.

Quail eggs have great delicacy and a velvety creaminess; they are usually served hard-cooked.

QUARK. The German name for curd or cottage cheese.

QUARKKLÖSSE (Curd Dumplings)
¾ lb. curd or cottage cheese
3 oz. (6 tablespoons) butter
3 whole eggs
4 tablespoons (5) soft white breadcrumbs
grated rind ½ lemon
2 tablespoons (2½) fine sugar

Beat the butter to a cream, then add the rest of the ingredients, adding each egg separately. Beat well. Break off pieces of the mixture, shape into dumplings, and cook in boiling water for 10 minutes. Serve with melted butter or with a vanilla sauce.

QUATRE-QUATRE. The 'Four Quarters Cake', is a true Breton speciality. It is made with a light firm dough and has become popular throughout France.

4 eggs
their weight in butter, castor sugar, flour
Weigh the eggs – if large they will weigh about 2 oz. each. Separate the whites from the yolks. Warm the butter to almost melting point. Beat the whites into a stiff froth. Beat the sugar with the yolks, add the butter and finally the flour. Beat until smooth, and then fold in the whites carefully so that they quite disappear below the surface of the batter. Butter a cake pan, half fill it with the mixture, and bake in a moderate oven for 1 hour. The cake will rise to the extent of the mould.

QUEEN OF PUDDINGS. A delicious Victorian pudding which is still popular. It consists of a mixture of milk, beaten egg yolks, breadcrumbs and sugar placed on the bottom of a buttered pie-dish and covered with a layer of strawberry jam. This is baked in the oven until set. The egg whites and sugar are beaten to make a meringue and piled on top of the pudding, which is then returned to the oven to brown.

QUEENSLAND NUT. See MACADAMIA NUT.

QUEJO DE SERRA. A generic name of the Portuguese sheep cheeses, which have a soft, oily and rich texture. They are considered by connoisseurs to be the best of their kind.

QUENELLES. A type of dumpling made with chicken, fish or veal forcemeat and bound with eggs. Some are poached in special moulds, others shaped in spoons and then dropped into boiling liquid. They are drained and served with a cream or a sauce. The traditional shape is oval.

QUENELLES OF COD, SALMON ETC.
Remove the skin from a thick slice of cooked cold cod or salmon, flake the flesh and rub it through a sieve or grinder. To each ½ lb. of fish add ¼ lb. of

butter and ¼ lb. of panada (which see). Season with salt and cayenne pepper and beat or pound to a paste. Gradually add 1 whole egg and then 2 beaten egg yolks. Pound again until the mixture is thoroughly blended. It can then be put into a refrigerator until required or used at once.

To cook quenelles, take a spoon, any size, fill it with the quenelle mixture and smooth over the surface with a knife, which has been dipped into hot water. Dip another spoon of the same size into hot water and with it slip the fish mixture out of the first spoon and place it in a buttered dish. Continue in this manner until all the quenelles are made. When all are ready, slip them carefully into a large shallow pan of lightly boiling, salted water and boil them until quite firm.

QUENEPA. See MAMMONCILLO.

QUESO BLANCO. An assortment of fresh, skimmed milk cottage cheeses in the Argentine come under this name.

QUESO BLUE. A blue cheese from the Argentine.

QUETSCH. A spirit distilled from the fermented juice of plums, chiefly in Alsace. It is sold pure white neither coloured nor matured in the cask.

QUICHE. An open-faced flan or tart of ancient origin. Originally it was made of bread dough but gradually this was replaced by pastry. The fillings vary from sweet fruit to savoury mixtures of fish, potatoes, onions, spinach etc. The most famous is *quiche Lorraine* with its filling of eggs, cream and bacon.

QUICHE LORRAINE
¾ lb. rich short pastry
8 slices streaky bacon
2 eggs
½ pint (1¼ cups) cream
salt, pepper

Roll out the pastry and line a well-greased shallow, round baking pan or, if available, a *quiche* pan. Cut the bacon into small pieces and fry it lightly in its own fat. Sprinkle the pieces of bacon over the pastry. Beat the eggs until smooth, add the cream, salt and pepper to taste and pour this mixture over the bacon. Put the *quiche* into a hot oven and bake for 30 minutes.

QUINCE. One of the earliest known garden fruits, but today one of the least cultivated. Some say it was the fragrant quince which lured Eve. In ancient times there was a superstition that quinces at a marriage feast assured love and happiness.

The quince spread through Europe by way of Greece and Rome, and to England from Austria in the 16th century. It was probably brought to North America in the 17th century. In France a quince sweetmeat, *cotignac*, has been made for centuries. It was a favourite sweet of Joan of Arc; when she made her famous entry into Orleans the towns-people had some ready for her. The French also make a quince syrup, a liqueur and compôte.

When raw the quince is tart and astringent, but cooked it is delicious and is often added to apple pie.

There are many varieties of quince, the most usual being pale gold, pear- and apple-shaped.

R

RABBIT. Compared to the hare, the rabbit is a comparatively modern importation into Britain. Its original home is believed to have been Spain and the Balearic Islands. The first mention of it is made in A.D. 230 by Athenaeus. In Roman times, the inhabitants begged Emperor Augustus to send a body of troops to wage war on the rodents.

It may have been the first time rabbits were in disgrace, but not the last. At one time they were part of the staple diet of the British but, due to their excessive breeding, extermination was their official sentence. After the ravages of myxomatosis wild rabbits fell out of favour in the British kitchen, although they appear to be making a come-back.

Wild rabbits vary considerably. One killed after a meal of garlic is uneatable, while one that has just fed on shrubs, tree bark and our garden lettuces, makes good eating. The corn-fed rabbit is fatter and bigger, and generally the doe is larger and better flavoured than her mate.

Wild rabbits are smaller than their domesticated cousins, but their flesh is superior. Tame rabbits, although bred for the table, have a white flesh which can be without flavour.

A young rabbit can be roasted or cooked in most of the ways for chicken; older rabbits are best stewed or used for pies and soups.

RACE. See WINE TERMS.

RACKING. See WINE TERMS.

RACLETTE. A splendid dish and one that cheese fans feel is a good reason to visit Switzerland. To make a *raclette* a wheel of semi-soft cheese – Bagnes or Conches – is cut in half and placed close to a crackling wood fire. As the cheese melts, which it does very quickly because of its high fat content, it is skilfully scraped off the wheel and onto a plate and served with potatoes boiled in

RACLETTE QUINCE RAMBUTTAN

their jackets, pickled onions and gherkins. It earns its name from *racler*, to scrape. Originally *raclette* was made in the Valais canton but is now served throughout Switzerland and elsewhere.

RADISH. A small, bright, purple-red root with a crisp white flesh and slightly peppery flavour. It may be round or tapered. There is also the Spanish black radish which has a better flavour and is slightly bigger. Radishes are usually served raw as an hors d'oeuvre or in a salad; in Eastern Europe they are served raw with fresh butter.

Radishes are among the oldest known vegetables and are thought to have originated in China, where they were cultivated in the 7th century B.C. They were favourite eating in Egypt's pyramid-building days, also in ancient Greece and Rome. In the latter city, they were used to pelt offending politicians, as we use rotten eggs today.

The radish came to the other countries of Europe in the 9th century A.D. and by the Middle Ages it had already become a common vegetable. At one time it was raised in every garden because of the swiftness and ease of its growth.

RAGI. An important small grain cereal also known as finger millet and African millet. It grows widely in Central and South Africa and extensively in Asia. Used in the form of flour, cakes or porridge, it stores well and seems immune to most pests.

RAGOÛT. One of the oldest known dishes, in which the simple use of meat with condiments is suggestive of the cooking of ancient Greece and Rome. The word *ragoût* is derived from the French word *ragoûter*, which means to re-awaken the taste. A white or brown spicy stew, it may be made with meat, fowl or fish, with or without vegetables. Navarin (which see) is the classic French version.

The term *ragoût* is also used to denote a garnish.

RAGUSANO. A Sicilian hard table cheese. When young it is sweet; after six months, when it is sharp and tasty, it is used for grating. Occasionally it is smoked.

RAILWAY PUDDING. A simple, baked jam pudding once frequently served on long-distance trains in Britain, hence the name. Also called Manchester pudding.

RAISED PIE. See PIE.

RAISIN. In France the term designates a fresh grape, but it also means a grape which has been dried by the sun or by artificial means for storage for later use. Not all grapes are suitable for this treatment. Up to the latter part of the 19th century, raisins were almost exclusively from grapes grown in the vineyards of Malaga and Greece and the districts bordering the eastern Mediterranean. Now grapes are dried on a very large scale in California, South Africa and Australia.

There are two main reasons for using raisins: flavour and texture, and high nutritional value.

RAISING AGENTS. Substances which produce a gas when acted on by heat or other substances, and make flour mixtures rise. These include baking powder, baking soda and yeast.

RAKI. See ARRACK.

RAMBUTTAN. A thirst-quenching fruit common in Hong Kong, Malaysia, Singapore, Indonesia, Thailand and elsewhere in Southeast Asia. The pulp is white, sweet and translucent, similar to the lychee. It is eaten raw. Its brittle, almost bright red skin, is covered with soft curled hairs like chestnut burr.

RAMEKIN. Known in Britain and the United States as a small fireproof china casserole in which savoury dishes such as cheese souffle, eggs etc. are baked. In France a *ramequin* formerly meant toasted cheese, but is now a tartlet filled with cream cheese, although this designation has different interpretations in different regions. As far back as the 18th century ramekins were made in Britain. These were cheese and egg dishes baked like a cheese custard. Such ramekins were not, however, always

317

small. Mrs Beeton baked ramekins in a saucer. It would seem to be a dish which travelled as there are German and Dutch recipes. The origin of the name appears obscure but it could come from the German *Rähmchen*, 'little cream'.

RANCID. Said of foods with a high fat content, such as butter, cheese and oils, when they produce a rank taste and smell.

RAPE. A root vegetable related to the turnip and cultivated for its oil-producing seeds.

RARE. In culinary terms this means to cook meat underdone; it applies in particular to the grilling of steaks or roasting of beef.

RAREBIT. Popularly known as Welsh rarebit, this is a savoury dish basically made with cheese and toast. The original rabbit or 'rare-bite' has now become rarebit. This dish has existed for a long time in England, Scotland and Wales but the English version has been modified. The earliest English way of making rarebit is described in a Georgian cookery book dated 1747: toast was placed in a plate before a fire, a glass of red wine was poured over it to soak in, thinly cut cheese laid on the toast and it was then put in a tin oven.

Toasted cheese dishes, using single and double Gloucester, Leicester and Cheddar cheeses, were very popular in the South of England during the 19th century. The Welsh version known as *caws pobi* is made of grated cheese, milk, butter, pepper, salt (mustard and beer are optional), slowly cooked and then poured on toast. The only difference between Welsh and Scottish rarebit is that the Scots butter their toast and the Welsh do not always do so.

RASCASSE. One of the ugliest and toughest of the Mediterranean fishes. Its only use is as one of the odd company boiled together to make *bouillabaisse*, the Marseilles fish stew or soup.

RASHER. A slice of bacon or raw ham. Rashers are sliced on a bacon slicer in varying thicknesses, each having a number. Nos 3 to 4 are classed as thin, 5 to 6 medium-thick, and 7 thick.

RASPBERRY. One of our most delicious fruits. According to legend, the Greek gods went berrying on Mount Ida and returned with *Rubus ideaeus* and the world has been gratefully eating raspberries ever since.

Raspberries did and still do grow in profusion all over the temperate zones of Europe, Asia and the United States. American Indians ate them as did the early settlers. During the American War of Independence, when substitutes were sought for tea, raspberry leaves were used, and the tea deemed by patriots as excellent. Fine though the cultivated raspberry is, the aroma of the wild raspberry surpasses it.

Raspberries have been cultivated for centuries. It is a composite fruit consisting of small seeds containing fruits which may be red or yellowish-white. The part of the flower carrying the fruit remains as a white core in the raspberry when it is ripe.

Mindful of the flavour of fresh raspberries picked straight from the bush, it is a matter of surprise that they have not reached the popularity of strawberries. Can any fruit taste nicer than crushed, chilled raspberries served with rich cream and a glass of Sauternes or champagne?

RASPBERRY VINEGAR. A sweet concentrate with many uses. It can be used as a flavouring or diluted with water and ice to make a long drink.

RASPINGS. Very fine crumbs from stale bread.

RATAFIA. A name given to spiritous liquor when flavoured with the kernels of fruits, such as peaches, apricots and cherries. It is no longer common either in Britain or the United States, but during the Victorian era such flavoured cordials were prepared at home. In old cookery books there are often a dozen or more recipes which include ratafia as a flavouring. There were even ratafia coffee liqueurs, curaçaos, ice-creams, cheesecakes etc.

Also called ratafias are small macaroon type cakes.

RATATOUILLE. A delicious stew from Provence, in France. It is a mixture of aubergine (egg-plant), sweet peppers, tomatoes and courgettes (zucchini), all diced, fried in just enough olive oil to cover the bottom of the pan, and then gently stewed until they form a rich soft mass. The dish is liberally flavoured with garlic, salt and pepper.

RAUSAN-SÉGLA, CH. See BORDEAUX WINES.

RAUZAN-GASSIES, CH. See BORDEAUX WINES.

RAVIGOTE SAUCE. See SAUCES.

RAVIOLI. Small squares or rounds of *pasta* filled with a mixture of ricotta, egg and one other cheese. They are neatly made into 'envelopes', cooked in boiling water for 10 minutes and served with brown butter and grated cheese as a sauce. For many people they are the ultimate in *pasta* dishes. When the squares are stuffed with savoury

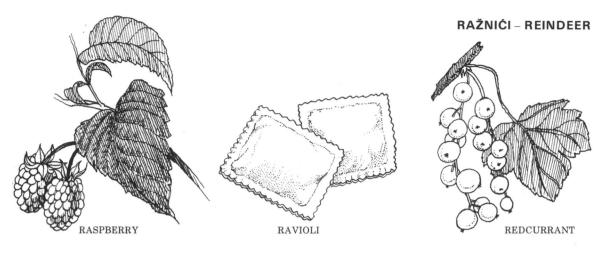

RASPBERRY   RAVIOLI   REDCURRANT

mixtures, they should properly be called agnolotti.

RAŽNIĆI. Small pieces of pork and veal alternately threaded on to skewers and grilled over charcoal. Yugoslavs usually serve them together with *çevabçiçi* (which see).

REBLOCHON. A semi-hard cheese made in the Haute Savoie from Tarentais cows' milk. *Reblochon* means second milking, and this cheese is made from the second yield. A round, flat cheese with a reddish rind and a soft, creamy texture, it should be eaten when young.

RÉCHAUFFÉ. Literally re-heated. Cold food warmed up or re-dressed. Some *réchauffé* dishes are better than their originals.

RECIPE. The term given to any formula setting out details for the preparation of food. Originally it applied to a medicinal formula and the earlier word was receipt rather than recipe.

No recipe except those which are absolutely basic should be considered unalterable. It should be tried as given, kept thus if it pleases: if not, changed. The varying of recipes is an amusing art and an infinite variety can be evolved by a judicious admixture of flavours and seasonings. As it was once neatly expressed, 'Every recipe is waiting expectantly to be improved upon; this immortal genius might be you.'

RE-CORKING. See WINE TERMS.

RED CABBAGE. A cabbage with dark red leaves used mainly in Britain for pickling. In the United States and elsewhere it is cooked in a number of different ways.

REDCURRANT. The cultivated varieties of this bush originated in Northern and Central Europe from several related bushes and were first grown in Britain in the Middle Ages. The red berries are soft and transluscent, growing in clusters. In the United States and Britain they are usually made into jelly, jam and beverages but they are no mean dessert eaten raw with fine sugar or together with raspberries and cream. They are superb also as a main fruit in summer pudding (which see), one of the best of British sweets, and in the Danish *rødgrød med fløde* (which see).

RED HERRING. See HERRING.

RED SNAPPER. This is one of the most important food fishes on the eastern seaboard of the United States. Related to the sea bass, it is found in deep water in the warm seas of the Gulf coast to New Jersey. Its average length is 2 feet and its weight about 6 lb. While not carnivorous, it is a greedy feeder and this, combined with its colour, gives it its name. The flesh is white and flaky and is prepared as bass, tunny (tuna) or pike.

REDUCE, TO. A culinary term meaning to boil down in order to concentrate flavour and thicken a liquid to the consistency of a sauce.

REFORME, À LA. The name given by Alexis Soyer, the great French chef, to certain dishes he created for the Reform Club, London. The best known is Cutlets Reforme: cutlets coated with egg and breadcrumbs, garnished with thin strips of carrot, truffles, ham and the whites of hard-boiled eggs slivered and served with *sauce poivrade*. See SAUCES.

REFRIGERATOR. Throughout the ages man has been concerned with refrigeration, always with one idea in mind: to preserve food. Snow and ice have been rushed from mountain tops at vast expense and buried in the earth or caves. From such primitive beginnings developed the simple but effective ice-box, in vogue until the home refrigerator was invented. This comes in all sizes and types, worked by electricity, gas or oil. There are also models for cars and camping.

REINDEER. A species of deer, similar to the North American caribou, inhabiting Arctic regions

319

and recently re-introduced into Scotland. It is domesticated in its own habitat, especially by the Lapps. The flesh of the female makes excellent eating, similar to venison in flavour, and the three-year-old beast is considered the best. The flavour of the buck is too strong for most people.

RELISH. A highly flavoured pickle which gives zest to food with which it is served and also stimulates the appetite. It is usually composed of different, tart fruits and its flavour is sweet-sour.

REMOULADE SAUCE. See SAUCES.

RENDER. To melt fat down into a dripping; a simple operation of putting pieces of fat into a pan either in the oven or on top of the stove and cooking until the dripping runs freely and the pieces of fat are brown. The dripping is drained off and the pieces of fat can be used to flavour certain dishes. If pork fat is used, the left-over pieces, called in French *grattons*, can be served as hors d'oeuvre.

RENNET. A substance extracted from the inner membrane of the fourth or true stomach of the sucking calf. It is used for coagulating milk for cheese-making, and making certain puddings, i.e. junket. Rennet for puddings can be obtained from grocers, but the type needed for cheese-making is bought only from dairy suppliers.

RESTAURANT. The name comes from France and meant at one time simply a soup. During the 16th century in France one popular soup was called a *restaurant* because it was supposed to have restorative properties. The chef, Boulanger, who served this soup had the word *restaurant* written over the door of his eating house. Gradually the word acquired its present connotation and the restaurant became the establishment we know today, and Boulanger founded a profession.

RETSINA WINE. The most controversial of the Greek wines, although drunk throughout the country, but locally, as it does not travel well. A *retsina* is a wine (either red or white but usually white) which has been deliberately and heavily resinated. To those who acquire a taste for it it can be an agreeable wine.

Its origin is interesting. In the days before casks the Greeks kept their wine in goatskins and then poured pitch pine on the top to preserve it. They came to expect wine to have the flavour of resin or pitch pine, and after casks had been invented the Greeks continued to add this flavour. Critics of the wine say that resin spoils it. It depends. *Retsina* wine drunk on the seashore beneath the pines or in pine woods is a pleasure

which remains long in the memory. The fragrant scent of pine needles mingles with the taste of the wine and enhances it.

Retsina wines belong to the tavernas of the towns and villages, and it is on the quality of its *retsina* that the reputation of a taverna is made or lost. If the *retsina* is good the word flies swiftly throughout the distict – and with equal speed if bad.

RÉVEILLON. In French-speaking countries a supper eaten after Midnight Mass on Christmas Eve. Also the supper eaten on St Sylvester's Night (New Year's Eve) after the stroke of midnight.

REYNIÈRE, GRIMOND DE LA. An amusing culinary writer, barrister-at-law and gastronome of the late 18th and early 19th centuries. In his *Manuel des Amphitryons* he wrote that a good meal is one of the greatest enjoyments of life.

RHODES. One of the islands of the Greek Archipelago which has made wine for centuries but in more recent years was influenced by the Italians who occupied it. Generally its wine is cheaper than on the mainland and follows an Italian pattern, more especially the liqueurs and aperitifs.

RHÔNE WINES. As a wine river the Rhône really begins its career in the Valais in Switzerland, but internationally the term Rhône wine refers to the districts beginning south of Lyons, where the Rhône is joined by the Saône, and ending in the region of Avignon, a distance of 125 miles.

Basically there are three main areas, two of them fairly closely linked in the northern part, the third in the south after a 40-mile gap in the vineyards. Allied to these, as the river valley broadens out towards the south, are some lesser areas. The lighter types of wine come from the north, the heavier from the south.

The Grapes. The most famous Rhône grape is the *syrah*, suspected of Near Eastern origin. It produces a firm, fruity wine. The other leading red wine grape is the *grenache*, less exclusive to this part of the world and chiefly associated here with Châteauneuf-du-Pape. Another red grape is the *cinsaut*. The leading white grape, unique to the northern part of the region, is the *viognier*. There are a number of subsidiary varieties.

Côte Rôtie. The first area south of Lyons is the tiny but distinguished red wine area of Côte Rôtie. Lying on the west bank, south of Vienne, and only 3 miles long, it is divided into two: the Côte Brune, producing red wines; and the Côte Blonde, making rather lighter reds. The soil is different, but the two are blended together, and about one-fifth of white wine from the *viognier* grape is added. Only

(Opposite) SOLE: paupiettes of sole with prawn sauce.
(Overleaf) SOUTH AFRICAN WINES: a harvesting scene at Stellenbosch.

REINDEER

3,000 hectolitres of wine is produced from the narrow strip of terraced vineyards overlooking the river; so the wine is expensive. Though lighter than other leading Rhône wines, it is a wine that keeps and improves for ten or more years. The centre of the trade is the right-bank town of Ampius, but there are only about 60 growers. Vidal-Fleury is the chief firm.

Condrieu. A few miles south of Ampuis is this even smaller white wine area, with a production confined to 300 or 400 hectolitres, although output is slowly expanding in a vineyard increasing from a 10-hectare base. For a white Rhône wine Condrieu is fairly light and fresh, though it has a certain earthy 'strike' in the taste. Nearly all is consumed locally, particularly in one or two celebrated restaurants, although its fame has led to some exports to the United States. The leading Condrieu, but entitled to its own *AC*, is Château Crillet, lying to the south of the village. The rarity of this wine, somewhat heavier than most Condrieu, but in good years with a distinctive flavour that somewhat resembles Rhine wines, has led to its particular *réclame*. Although the 300-year-old vineyard is being extended, production does not much exceed 10 casks of 300 bottles apiece. All the output is bottled on the estate in Alsace-type bottles.

Hermitage. Named from the bold vineyard-covered hill which overlooks the river at Tain, Hermitage was a famous wine in 18th- and 19th-century Britain, where its full-blooded qualities found favour. The wine was also used to 'strengthen' claret, then said to be *hermitagé*. The red wine is fuller than Côte Rôtie, lighter and more distinguished than Châteauneuf-du-Pape. Generously flavoured, it needs more bottle age than it usually receives; in a good vintage it is not at its best at least until 10 years old. Output totals only 4,000 hectolitres. Adjoining the Hermitage hill is the lower-lying Crozes-Hermitage, a fairly large vineyard, where agreeable but much less distinguished wines are produced. White Hermitage is a full flavoured but distinguished wine that some prefer to the red; it keeps well.

St-Joseph, Cornas and *St-Peray.* These three districts are on the west bank, opposite and to the south of Tain. The first is a recent *AC*, covering production in half-a-dozen villages including Tournon and Mauves. Both red and white wines are made. Cornas wines are bigger, more powerful. St-Peray was a favourite, inexpensive Victorian 'sparkler' made by the champagne method, but fuller and fatter in flavour in this southern climate. There is also a still St-Peray.

Châteauneuf-du-Pape. One of the few world-wide wine names of the region. Much the largest leading Rhône wine area, producing 80,000 hectolitres annually and due to expand to 100,000 hectolitres owing to world demand. A maximum production of 35 hectolitres per hectare is allowed, and a recent regulation ordained that output in excess of this figure would lead to a vineyard losing its coveted Châteauneuf *AC* for that vintage. This powerful, sometimes acid-short wine is made chiefly from the *grenache* grape, but a further 12 varieties are employed, including the *syrah* and the *cinsaut*. Sometimes the wine is quite naturally as alcoholic as a fortified wine, and normally it averages 14°, considerably stronger than burgundy. The richness of the wine is in contrast to the infertile, boulder-strewn hot vineyards. A small amount of white wine is made, a dry but often rather dull wine whose popularity partly depends on its colour. There are about 300 proprietors, some of them with very large estates, including La Bernardine, Fortia, Mas St-Louis, Mont-Redon. Clos des Pape and Rayas.

Côtes du Rhône. This basic *AC* covers a very large production of over 900,000 hectolitres in the wide river valley surrounding Orange and Avignon, chiefly in the Vaucluse and Gard *départements*. In addition first six, and then another eight villages won the right to add their names to the Côtes du Rhône *AC*. The first six included Gigondas, the best known, Cairanne, Vacqueyras, Vinsobres, Laudun and Chusclan. Since 1967 the wines of the 14 name *communes* may be blended and sold as Côtes du Rhône Village. Both red and white wines are made, with red predominant. Sweet Muscat wines, made at Rasteau and Beaumes-les-Venises, are entitled to their own *AC*.

325

(Previous page) STRUDEL: making the pastry.
(Opposite) TANDOORI CHICKEN.

Rhône Rosés. In Tavel, to the west of Avignon, the Rhône produces the most celebrated *vin rosé* in the world. Much drier than most others, and more alcoholic (about 12·5°), it has more distinction and flavour. In spite of its fame the area is quite small, with some 30 private growers and a co-operative of 120 members producing 18,000 hectolitres from about 600 hectares. Seven grapes including the *grenache* and the *carignan* are involved. Area under vines and output are expanding to meet world demand. Adjoining Tavel is the much less well-known Lirac, whose *rosé* is similar in style. The Tavel *AC* cover *vin rosé* only; Lirac produces red and white wine also.

RHUBARB. Although regarded as a fruit, rhubarb is really a vegetable. It was introduced into Britain in 1573 from the Volga, but it remained for two centuries simply a gardener's curiosity so that its use as food is recent. In 1810 a Deptford market gardener sent some rhubarb to a London market but was unable to find a buyer. However, since those days the cultivation and use of rhubarb has made rapid progress and it has been found to be one of the most easily grown vegetables.

The story of the Volga origin is interesting. Rhubarb, a species of *Rheum*, was long used in medicine for its purgative and astringent qualities. It grew wild in China and Tibet and was imported into Europe by way of the Volga region and the Levant.

Rhubarb is one of the more wholesome vegetables, mostly used in sweet dishes, preserves and pies. It is given to those suffering from constipation. There are several varieties but the two main types in England and America are the garden and the forced rhubarb. The long fleshy-leafed stalks of garden rhubarb are a deep red with dark green leaves; the forced is almost pink and its leaves a pale yellowish green. The leaves of the rhubarb are generally considered unsafe for eating since they contain a toxic element. In parts of the Himalayas, where rhubarb grows wild, the leaves are cooked and eaten.

RIBS OF BEEF. There are four joints which come under this heading: wing ribs, top ribs, back ribs and flat ribs. The wing rib is the cut generally most esteemed and commands the highest prices.

RICE. There is romance, legend and history behind the cereal we call rice, the staple food of more than half the world's population. For centuries it has meant life for millions and even today at least half the world gets 80 per cent of its calories from rice; for many it is the only source of food.

Rice is considered to be one of the oldest cultivated crops and most authorities accept that it is South India's gift to the world, brought to Europe by the returning armies of Alexander the Great. However, records show that rice was cultivated in China in 5000 B.C. and ancient writings in Thailand, Burma and Japan mention rice. It was cultivated in Egypt and Syria from 400 B.C., and the Persians grew it; the Arabs carried it to Spain and Spanish explorers and settlers introduced it into the United States.

There are reputedly 7,000 different types of rice, each differing slightly from field to field, as grapes from vineyard to vineyard. But these differences, although important to the growers, seldom enter into the calculations of even a rice-eating people like the Indians, let alone the Western buyer.

The function of rice in the East is that of an important main dish to which must be added a vast number of side dishes. In Thailand, an invitation to a meal is proffered thus: 'Come and eat rice,' and the side dishes on the tables are called collectively 'with the rice'. In Japan the three main meals are called *asa gohan*, meaning morning rice; *hiru gohan*, afternoon rice; and *yoru gohan*, evening rice.

In the Far East rice has been linked with the gods. In Java no girl would be considered eligible for marriage unless she could cook a good bowl of rice. The tradition of throwing rice at newly-weds indicates a wish they will be blessed with many children, and is a survival from the Hindus and Chinese who believed rice to be the symbol of fertility.

All rice-eating peoples have different ideas on how to cook rice. Some wash rice; others do not. The Iranians wash their rice, even soak it overnight to produce their variety of *pelo* or pilau. The Italians neither wash nor soak their rice and produce splendid *risottos*. It all depends on the type of rice used and the manner in which it is cooked. Only by trial and error can one really learn how to cook a particular rice.

The edible rice kernel is found in a hard shell-like hull surrounded by several layers of bran, some of which are removed, depending on the nature of the product required. In the case of brown rice, for instance, almost all of the bran is retained. This gives it more flavour and makes it nutritionally more valuable than unpolished white rice, which has practically all of the bran removed.

Polished (milled) rice has all of its fine dust taken away. There is also a quality known as converted rice which has some bran in it. It is yellowish in appearance but turns white when cooked. Par-boiled rice is rice that has been subjected to steam or water treatment before milling. It retains more vitamins and minerals because of this process.

Rice generally can be divided into long, medium and short grain types.

RHUBARB (plant and stalk)

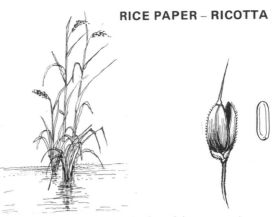

RICE (plant, husk, grain)

Long grain rice has grains 4–5 times as long as they are wide. When cooked the grains will separate and the rice looks light and fluffy. It is preferred for pilaus and for serving as a side dish with curry, stews, chicken or meat dishes: it can also be allowed to get cold and used for salads.

The shorter, plumper grains of the medium and short types cook tender and moist but tend to cling together. These types are favoured for risottos, croquettes, puddings, rice rings or moulds.

Rice was introduced to North America in 1685, into North Carolina, and later this rice became the standard of high quality for the cereal throughout the world. The Carolina regions abandoned rice growing at the end of 1865. Even so, European consumers still purchase so-called Carolina rice, although no rice has been exported from this area for at least 165 years. What the buyer gets is Carolina seed type. Similarly, what we call Patna rice is Patna seed type. Very little of so-called Patna rice comes from Bihar, but the name is reserved for good quality long grain rice.

Rice bran is the first major by-product removed from the rice kernel during the milling process. It is relatively high in protein and is primarily used for livestock feed.

Rice cereal is rice that has been converted into various forms. There are rice flakes or puffs that may be eaten cold, or pulverized rice which may be cooked in boiling water and served as a hot cereal.

Rice flour is milled rice ground into flour. One of its uses is to replace wheat flour in cakes and breads for those who have an allergy to wheat.

Ground rice, slightly coarser than rice flour, is used mainly in puddings, cakes etc.

Rice oil is the oil extracted from rice bran and polish. It is a stable natural oil which is adaptable to the manufacture of some margarines, cooking oil, salad oil, industrial oil and a wide range of other products.

Rice polish is the final layers removed from the rice kernel during the polishing process. It is a finer, heavier material than bran and is high in fat and carbohydrates. It is blended in various process foods. Rice polish is also used as a livestock feed.

Wild rice (which see) is a quite different North American plant.

RICE-PAPER. Made from the pith of a Formosan tree and edible. It is white, smooth and glossy. Macaroons and similar biscuits (cookies) are baked on it. It is much used in China and Japan to make artificial flowers and for painting.

RICER. This is an instrument to force cooked potatoes and similar vegetables, including chestnuts, through perforations giving them a granular shape that resembles cooked rice. The ricer is usually built in the shape of a metal basket with a snugly fitting metal plunger which exerts pressure on the vegetables within as they are pushed through.

RICE WINES. These are made in China and Japan. There are many types: both sweet and dry, potent and quite mild. A favourite so-called yellow wine is usually compared with a sherry, while a strong, colourless one is reminiscent of vodka. Most rice wines are served lukewarm. In Japan, sake (which see) is the rice wine of the country.

RICHEBOURG. See BURGUNDY WINES.

RICHON LE ZION. See ISRAELI WINES.

RICOTTA. A white, creamy, bland cottage variety of cheese made from the whey left over from other cheeses, such as Provolone, Pecorino and Mozzarella. It is on the borderline of cheese, but is an important ingredient in much of Italy's cooking. It is used as a filling for ravioli, and many lasagne and cannelloni dishes as well as for sweet dishes.

RICOTTA AL CAFFÈ (Sicily)

1 lb. ricotta

$\frac{1}{2}$ cup ($\frac{2}{3}$) castor (superfine) sugar

$\frac{1}{4}$ cup ($\frac{1}{3}$) finely ground coffee (Turkish grind)

$\frac{1}{2}$ cup ($\frac{2}{3}$) rum

Beat the cheese until it is light and then rub it through a sieve. Mix thoroughly with the remaining ingredients. Chill for several hours before serving. Serve in glasses with sponge fingers and, if liked, with cream. Some Sicilian cooks sprinkle the top with grated or powdered bitter chocolate.

RICOTTA SALATA. Salty, dry, hard ricotta, rather mild and grated for use as a seasoning.

RIDGE CUCUMBER. See CUCUMBER.

RIESLING. One of the oldest known and the greatest of the white wine grapes, which has become a great traveller in modern times. It was first known in the Rhine valley but has been successfully transplanted in countries as far apart as Chile and California, Australia and several European countries. Coming from a northern home, it produces good wine in cooler climes and on stony soil. All the best wines produced in the Rheingau and Moselle vineyards are from the Riesling grape. It does well in Alsace, Austria, Switzerland and the Italian Tyrol.

RIEUSSEC, CH. See BORDEAUX WINES.

RIJSTTAFEL. The word is Dutch for 'rice table'. This is an extravagant colonial interpretation of the simple Indonesian rice table, a luncheon or dinner feast that consists of rice and some 40 side dishes, which are served with it. See page 281.

RILLETTES. French *rillettes de porc* are similar to chitterlings. They can be made from chopped pig intestines or small strips of pork. They are fried in pork fat and when cold are pounded and put into small glazed pots. They are served as a first course and their preparation varies from district to district. Tours and Le Mans are famed for their *rillettes*.

RILLONS, RILLAUDS, RILLOTS. These are the same as *rillettes* (which see), except that the pork is not pounded but left in large pieces.

RIOJA. See SPANISH WINES.

RISI E BISI. One of Italy's famous dishes, an ultra-thick soup of rice and peas which was always served by the Doges of Venice at banquets given on the feast of St Mark. It is eaten with a fork and the peas should be equal in quantity to the rice.

RISOTTO. An Italian dish of rice, totally different in nature to pilau. It is made with thick short-grained Italian rice and meant to be thick and creamy. It can be variously flavoured, with mushrooms, tomatoes, truffles, or onions for example, and is usually served generously sprinkled with grated cheese.

RISSOLE. Ground meat, usually cooked, duly seasoned, and wrapped in a thin envelope of short or flaky pastry folded to form a turnover. Rissoles are fried in deep fat and served hot.

RISSOLER. A French term meaning to brown food slowly in fat.

RIZZARED HADDIE. A Scots term for sun-dried haddock.

ROACH. A fish of the carp family inhabiting the freshwater rivers of northern Europe. Of fair gastronomic value, it is cooked like grayling.

ROAST. This used to mean, and still does to some extent, a course in the menu after the sorbet and before the entremets. Strictly speaking, to roast is to cook in front of or over a fierce glowing heat, with the food rotating on a spit, called a roasting jack. Today the term is loosely used to mean the cooking of meat and potatoes in an oven. There is a modern return to true roasting with the rôtisserie or revolving spit operated by electricity.

ROBERT SAUCE. See SAUCES.

ROCAMADOUR CHEESE. A small, flat goat cheese made in the Causse mountains in France and named after the pilgrimage town.

ROCAMBOLE. See ONIONS.

ROCKFISH. The colloquial name for any of the fish living along the rocky ledges of the sea bottom. applied particularly to the striped sea bass of North America.

ROCK SALT. See SALT.

RØDGRØD MED FLØDE. A popular Danish summer pudding, remembered by tourists as having a name impossible to pronounce.

    1⅔ lb. redcurrants
    1⅔ lb. raspberries
    8 cups (10) water
    sugar
    ¼ cup (⅓) potato flour
    vanilla
    blanched, chopped almonds

Wash the currants and raspberries. Put into a pan, add water, bring to the boil and continue cooking until all the juice is boiled out. Strain the berries through a fine sieve and return the juice to the pan; add sugar to taste and bring to the boil. Take the pan from the stove, add the potato flour to thicken – a ¼ cup (⅓) of potato flour to every 4 cups (5) of juice. Add vanilla to taste and stir well. While still hot

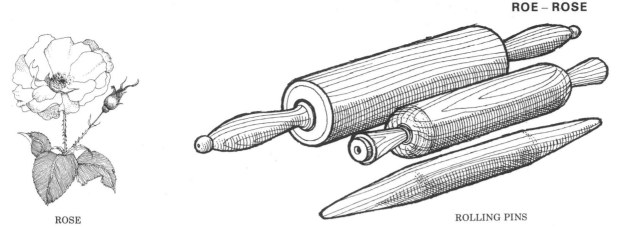

ROSE   ROLLING PINS

pour into a glass bowl. Leave it to set; when the pudding begins to stiffen decorate the top with the almonds. Serve with sugar and cream.

ROE. The name is given to both the milt (soft roe) of the male and eggs (hard roe) of the female fish. Soft roes are a popular savoury and a garnish to fish dishes. Hard roes can also be cooked and are used in hors d'oeuvre. The finest hard roe in the world is from the sturgeon and is called caviar. The dried hard roe of the grey mullet, called botargo, also has its admirers as does the roe from cod which is smoked and can be used to make a kind of *taramasalata* (which see).

ROLL, TO. In culinary terms this means to spread flat dough or paste with a rolling pin. It also means to roll up as with a Swiss or jelly roll.

ROLLING PIN. An instrument used to flatten dough into smooth sheets; there are several types. The simplest is a plain wooden rod. There are those tapered at each end. There are hollow glass rollers which can be filled with ice, those on which a series of designs have been carved to make fancy shapes for biscuits or cookies and some exceedingly thin for rolling *phylo* (which see) or other specialized pastry.

ROLLMOP. See HERRING.

ROLLS. These are best described as individual small loaves. Any kind of dough suitable for bread-making can be shaped into rolls. There are soft as well as crusty varieties. See page 282.

ROLY-POLY. A suet crust pudding filled with jam and rolled like a Swiss or jelly roll. It is either baked or boiled. Roly-poly is a traditional nursery pudding in Britain.

ROMAINE. See LETTUCE.

ROMANÉE-CONTI and **ROMANÉE-ST-VI-VANT.** See BURGUNDY WINES.

ROMANO. A black-rinded Italian cheese that resembles Parmesan. Sometimes it is blended with grated Parmesan as the latter has better staying powers.

ROQUEFORT. A French cheese made from ewes' milk; it is the only ewes' milk cheese which has won international recognition. It is also the only French cheese which has challenged the right of Brie to be called the King of Cheeses. It even claims it is the *fromage des rois et des papes*.

Its name comes from the village of Roquefort in the Aveyron *département*, although much of the milk comes from all over France. Much of the cheese is made – only during the lambing season – from the milk of several thousand sheep, reared in one of the poorest agricultural areas of France. It is made from the morning and evening milks, mixed and curdled with rennet from the lambs' stomachs. After it has been coagulated it is piled in layers with mouldy breadcrumbs between each layer, on which a culture, the *Penicillium glaucum* (var. *Roqueforti*) has been grown and which is responsible for the blue veining of the cheese. After salting and pressing, it is later matured very slowly and carefully in the caves of Roquefort where the temperature is about 46°F. and the humidity very great because of the existence of an underground lake.

ROSE. Most roses are grown for their beauty and there are several thousand varieties. A few are grown for their perfume and flavour. In both France and Bulgaria, roses are grown for perfume. The French use the cabbage rose, the Bulgarians, the damask. Although Bulgaria at present is famous for its export of roses, Persia was exporting rose-water to China at the time of Christ.

Drinks have been perfumed with roses for centuries. The Bulgarians have a rose liqueur which is very sweet, and the French their *parfait d'amour*. Rose petals are used for jam-making in Turkey and the Balkans; honey is also flavoured with roses. Rose petals are crystallized and in some countries people sprinkle rose petals on top of cherry pie before closing it.

ROSEMARY. This is the herb of remembrance. There is a charming legend that the Virgin Mary spread her linen cloak over a white-flowered bush of rosemary, and ever after the flowers were as blue as her own robe. It is an old favourite in herb gardens. The pungent and refreshing scent of the leaves is welcome in cooling drinks, stuffings, garnishes and soups, and with lamb and sautéed potatoes. It is obviously best fresh but it can be bought dried. It was taken by colonists to North America and now grows in profusion in North Carolina and Virginia.

ROSE-WATER. An extract of rose petals, used in Balkan, Middle Eastern and Indian cookery, particularly in sweet dishes, creams and cakes.

ROSÉ WINE. Pink or pink-coloured wine. The best *rosé* is considered to come from Tavel near the Rhône estuary, but some good *rosé* is made in Bordeaux, Anjou and other wine-producing areas of France, as well as in California. If *rosé* is correctly made, it comes from red grapes fermented for a few days on the colour-imparting skins and husks and must be drawn off at the precise moment when sufficient colour has been absorbed to give the wine the required hue.

ROSSINI. The name of a well-known Italian composer who is supposed to have invented a dish of tender steaks, garnished with sautéed *foie gras* and sliced truffle, and served with a Madeira sauce.

RÔTISSERIE. A rotating spit used with gas or electricity. Meat, poultry and game can be cooked on such spits and the result is much closer to the effect produced by old-time roasting spits in front of the fire than so-called roasting in an oven. Meat cooked on a rôtisserie is very succulent.

ROUENNAIS. See DUCK.

ROULADE. A meat roll.

ROUNDNESS. See WINE TERMS.

ROUX. Most sauces start with a roux, which is a mixture of butter and flour cooked together over a low heat. Slow cooking is important not only to concentrate flavours but to expand the starch in the flour gradually as it cooks. When the two ingredients are blended the liquid is gradually added and continually stirred over a low heat until the mixture is the consistency of a good thick cream. Many thick soups also start with a roux, the liquid being added in the same manner as for sauce-making.

ROWANBERRY. See ASHBERRY.

ROYAL ICING. See ICING.

ROYALE. An egg custard cooked in a mould and allowed to set before use. When it is firm and cold it is cut in various shapes and added to clear soups. It is usually cream, but when coloured it becomes *royale Crécy* (carrot-orange); *royale à l'écarlate* (lobster-red); *royale vert-pré* (spinach-green) etc.

RUBY. See PORT, WINE TERMS.

RUE. An old-fashioned and interesting plant: it has powerful medicinal substances which are extracted commercially. In small quantities it is a stimulant and some people chew a leaf of rue on a hot day; in large quantities it is dangerous. In tiny quantities it is possible to use it with fish and eggs, and in vegetable juice and cocktails. Rue was used in the old drink, sack, and today the Italians put it in Grappa, for the sprig of herb in Grappa bottles is rue, although of a less bitter species.

RULLY. See BURGUNDY WINES.

RUM. A spirit distilled from molasses: it can be distilled from the fermented juice of the sugar cane but this is not generally a commercial proposition except in Hawaii and Martinique. Rum is essentially a West Indian product, first recorded in Barbados in 1600. It was popular in America before 1776 and British sailors once sailed the seas on their rum ration. In colour it varies from water white, its natural colour, through amber to mahogany. The only colouring used is sugar caramel which does not affect the flavour.

There are many types and styles of rum, most of which may be classed in one or the other of the following three main categories: (1) the very dry, light-bodied rum of which the Cuban is the prototype and from which Daiquiri is made; (2) the rich, full-bodied rums of which Jamaican rum is the acknowledged standard; (3) the more aromatic rums such as those made in Martinique, Puerto Rico, Trinidad, Barbados, Demerara and many other island and mainland sugar cane districts.

A strong, heavy rum is made in New England from blackstrap molasses. A few private cellars contain some 'vintage' rums which rival old Bourbon and cognac, it is claimed.

Besides cocktails, rum is used as the basis of many short and long drinks, such as Collins, Daisies, Flips, Shrubs and Toddies.

The famous Jamaican rum punch is made from one part sour lime juice, two parts sweet syrup, three parts strong rum, four parts weak fruit juice and a dash of bitters.

RYE   ROSEMARY

RUMANIAN WINES. These are some of the most important wines of the Communist world. Even though Russia annexed Bessarabia after World War II, which had 40 per cent of Rumania's wine production, total output in the country has nearly doubled in the past 10 years. Vintage wines are rare, but the general quality of wine is good and improving.

RUMP ROAST. A cut from the leg. It is always boned and should be tender and juicy if cooked in a moist heat after being well seared. It requires slow roasting and frequent basting.

RUNNER BEAN. See BEANS.

RUSKS. These consist of twice-baked cake or milk-bread dough, sweet or plain. To make them, the dough is baked in a square pan and cut into slices when cold, and then re-baked in a slow oven until brown and crisp right through.

RUSSIAN SALAD. A mixture of cooked vegetables diced and masked with a salad dressing. The Russians called it a *vinaigrette* and there are a hundred or more versions of the recipe.

RUSSIAN WINES. The Soviet Union is possibly the world's largest grape producer, but as a wine-maker is not rated highly. What wine is exported is not as good as that of her European satellites. The best is produced in Moldavia, that part of Bessarabia annexed by the Russians after World War II from Rumania, but little is known of modern developments.

RUTABAGA. See SWEDE.

RYE. One of the most important of the cereals grown in Central and Northern Europe. It was introduced into North America at an early date and was at one time cultivated in New England on a much larger scale than wheat for bread and is still grown extensively for the distillation of rye whiskey. Rye flour is almost the equal of wheat flour in nutritive value, but is much darker. Black bread is made from rye flour with or without wheat, barley or oat flour mixed with it (see also PUMPERNICKEL). Rye whiskey is a straight whiskey distilled from a fermented mash of grain, of which no less than 51 per cent must be rye grain.

S

SABLE. A rich French short paste made with as much butter as flour. It is usually sweet but sometimes cheese is added to make a savoury mixture. The paste is generally made into small biscuits (cookies) and sandwiched together with jam or a cream cheese.

SACCHARINE. A commercial product 500 times as sweet as sugar, for which it is a widely-used substitute. It is produced from coal tar and there are several varieties. It has no food value as it passes through the system unchanged. There is no evidence that it is in any way harmful.

SACHER TORTE. Vienna's most famous cake, rich, elegantly simple and for which there is no shortage of 'authentic, original one-and-only' recipes. It was invented in 1832 by Franz Sacher, then Metternich's chef, when asked by his employer for 'something new'. He could not have known what a success story he was producing at the time, as he is reported to have said, 'I just flung together some ingredients – and there you are.'

The cake is a rich chocolate sponge, sliced in half, spread with apricot jam, the pieces sandwiched together and given a chocolate icing.

SACK. Dry and amber, this was one of the most popular of the Elizabethan wines. It was immortalized by Shakespeare through the mouth of Falstaff: 'If I had a thousand sons the first humane principle I would teach them should be to forswear thin potations, and to addict themselves to sack.'

The word was originally spelt seck and may have

applied at first only to dry wines of the sherry type. The drink does not seem to have come into use until early Tudor times. It became increasingly popular, an honoured wine among the people and poets.

The best sack, 'series' or sherris-sack, came from Jerez or Cadiz. Other sacks came from Malaga and the Canaries. The latter type reached such popularity that James Howell in 1534 called it the richest, best-bodied, and most lasting wine. See SPANISH WINES.

SADDLE. The upper portion of an animal including the loins not cut asunder, complete with kidneys and reckoned the finest part of the animal.

SAFFLOWER. A thistle-like plant cultivated for the orange dye obtained from its flowers and whose seeds yield an oil. It has been cultivated fairly extensively for centuries in India, the Middle East, Africa and Turkestan. Safflower seeds were found in some Egyptian tombs dating back at least 3,500 years. It is now also grown in America and some parts of southern Europe.

The flowers are used for colouring cakes and sweets and also as a dye, although this function is being taken over by synthetic dyes. The oil is used in Indian cookery.

Safflower is sometimes passed off as saffron to which it bears a resemblance, but it is brighter in colour than the more costly saffron.

SAFFRON. This comes from the orange-coloured stigmas of a mauve-flowering crocus. It is a native of southern Europe but since ancient times has been cultivated in France, Spain, Turkey, Greece, Iran, Kashmir and China. In the past this crocus was extensively cultivated in England. The English town of Saffron Walden was an important producer and its town arms still have three saffron flowers pictured within the turreted walls. Also, Saffron Hill, now a London thoroughfare, once formed a part of Ely Place Gardens where the saffron crocus was cultivated. It was much used as a spice and flavouring agent and said to have beneficial qualities. Sir Francis Bacon once said: 'What made English people sprightly was the liberal use of saffron in their broths and sweetmeats.'

In ancient times it was used in food, medicine and for making dyes. The Greeks and the Romans prized it, and Moghul Emperors of India held saffron blossoms in high esteem.

It is an expensive spice because the stigmas have to be picked by hand and over 200,000 of them are required to make 1 lb. of saffron. But only a small quantity is needed in cookery. Its aroma gives certain dishes their traditional flavour and yellowish colour. It is used in the classic French *bouillabaisse*, in *arroz con pollo* and in *paella*. It also enhances some sauces, breads, cakes (Cornish saffron cakes), fish, chicken and rice dishes, and is widely used in Iranian and Moorish cooking.

SAGE. A powerful herb to be used with discretion. There are several species varying greatly in flavour, some of which are more decorative than culinary. For cooking, the narrow-leaved sage with blue flowers or the broad-leaved sage (of which there are non-flowering varieties) are perhaps the best.

It is not clear when sage entered into European cooking. The Romans used it medicinally but not, it seems, in their kitchens. By the 16th century it was a well-known European herb.

In the United States sage is used with stuffings, stews, onions, veal, fish and bean dishes. In England sage has been limited to sage and onion stuffing and to flavour certain sausages. In Germany and Belgium it is used in eel dishes. The Italians are great sage lovers, using it in *saltimbocca* and dishes of small birds and kebabs.

SAGO. Sago is a starch extracted from the sago palm tree which grows in Malaysia, the Philippines, Indonesia and India. It takes 15 years for a sago palm to mature and when it blossoms the pith of its stem is packed with starch. The palm is then cut down and the starch extracted. The starch is moistened and mechanically shaken until it turns into globules. These globules, when roasted and dried, yield sago.

Similar globules are now made from the roots and tubers of various other plants, for instance, the tapioca root. Chemically, root starches and palm starches come in the same category and nutritionally they are of the same value. In fact, sago globules can be made from any starch and the name is applied to a variety of starches. Used mainly for puddings and soups.

SAINT-AMOUR. See BURGUNDY WINES.

SAINT-AUBIN. See BURGUNDY WINES.

SAINT-CROIX-DU-MONT. See BORDEAUX WINES.

SAINT-ÉMILION. See BORDEAUX WINES.

SAINT-ESTÈPHE. See BORDEAUX WINES.

SAINT-GERMAIN. The French culinary name for a popular soup made from fresh young peas.

SAINT-HONORÉ. A favourite French *gâteau* which consists of a circle of cream puffs filled with *crème pâtissière*, dipped into a caramel sugar and arranged on a cake base round the edge. The

TA PIN LO.

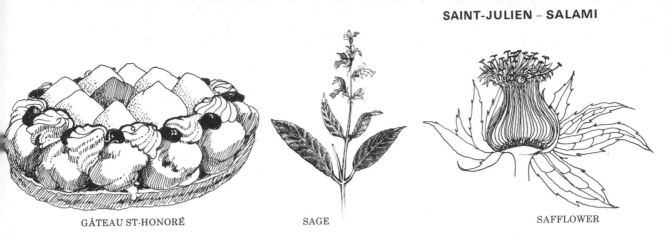

GÂTEAU ST-HONORÉ　　　　　　SAGE　　　　　　SAFFLOWER

spaces between the cream puffs are filled with glacé cherries or *marrons glacés* and the centre with a rich cream.

SAINT-JULIEN. See BORDEAUX WINES.

SAINT-LAURENT. See BORDEAUX WINES.

SAINT RAPHAEL. A French aperitif from the town of the same name. Its basis is white wine and its after-taste is that of quinine. It is usually served chilled and undiluted.

SAINT-SEURIN. See BORDEAUX WINES.

SAITHE. Another name for coalfish (which see).

SAKE. The traditional wine of Japan, made from white rice, malt and water. It is to the Japanese what champagne is to the French or whisky to the Scots. *Sake* is pale amber in colour, sweet and rich in flavour, and is the one traditional beverage taken with meals. At one time no one would consider drinking *sake* alone, so the word came to mean drinking parties. It is served in tiny porcelain cups not much larger than an egg cup. Formerly it was drunk cold, but when *sake* of inferior quality began to be served, it was warmed to disguise its poorness. The habit became fashionable so today it is always served warm or even hot. Therefore the little cups are the most convenient way of serving it. Apart from being a popular and national drink, it is offered to the shrines of ancestors, and a marriage is celebrated by the drinking of *sake*. When dining the Japanese exchange *sake* cups between host and guests, but the cup is rinsed afterwards as a sign of respect to the guests. Not to exchange is considered bad manners. If more *sake* is wanted, one offers one's cup, otherwise it is turned upside down.

SALAD. The French definition of a salad is *une réunion des choses confusément assemblées* . . . an accurate description of all too many salads but an odd thought from the French who still favour the simple green salad of lettuce or watercress.

Salads have been known to men for centuries. Shakespeare's plays prove that 'sallet' was already a common dish and a 'sweet lady' was likened to a salad, with the comparison intended as a compliment. Yet a hundred years later the 'sallet' was looked down upon and even today in Britain has not completely regained favour.

Salads are variously composed: those with one type of green leaf, those with a combination of green leaves, those made with vegetables and fish or poultry and other meats, and those which are flights of fancy, such as one finds in the Far East and often in the United States, and curiously in Russia.

Fruit salads: the word salad is surely a misnomer when applied to mixtures which do not have a piquante or savoury dressing.

SALAD BASKET. A woven wire basket about the size of a colander in which salad greens, particularly lettuce, are washed and drained.

SALAD DRESSING. This takes various forms to match the dish with which it is served. A light dressing, usually called French, consisting of oil, vinegar or lemon, plus seasoning is considered ideal for a plain green salad. More substantial dishes are served with creamier dressings, such as a mayonnaise.

SALAD OIL. In France, olive oil is the classic salad oil; while any edible oil can be used, only the finest quality should be used for salads and salad dressings.

SALAME or **SALAMI**. The sausage speciality of Italy. Nearly every province in the country has its own ideas on what constitutes the perfect salame. They differ in the kinds of meat used, the shape and size of the salame, the salting and maturing. Italian salame is always good. Milan salame is the one most often found in Italian stores outside of Italy, although there is an increasing variety nowadays. The Milan salame consists of equal

335

proportions of lean beef, pork and pork fat, seasoned with pepper, garlic and white wine. Florentine salame is a large sausage made from pure pork in which the meat and its fat are cut into fairly large pieces. It is tender and delicate in flavour. Some varieties of this salame are fennel-flavoured. Felino salame is made from pork meat with pork fat, lightly garlicked and flavoured with white wine of the area. It is an expensive sausage, even in Italy. Genovese salame is made from pork, veal and pork fat and is fairly strongly flavoured. Sopresse salame is from Verona and made with a mixture of beef and pork. Napolitano salame is also pork and beef in equal proportions, well seasoned with black and red pepper. Salame Sardo is a country type of sausage made from pork and well flavoured with red pepper. There are two or three Sicilian types of salame, salame flavoured with peppers, etc.

Other countries also produce excellent salame.

SALLY LUNN. Towards the end of the 18th century a bun by the name of Sally Lunn became popular in Britain, said to have originated from a young woman of that name who 'cried' them in the streets of Bath. Dalmer, a baker and a musician of the town, bought Sally's business and wrote a song on the bun, which became popular and increased sales. This story may be true or legend. There may have been a Sally Lunn but what the girl called out is also said to have been a West Country pronunciation of the French 'Sole Lune, Solielune' aptly describing the round, flat buns, gold on top and white underneath. Eliza Acton in 1855 gives a recipe for the buns, 'Solemena' or 'Solel Lame'.

SALMAGUNDI. An old English supper dish consisting of a meat salad, mixed and garnished with hard-boiled eggs, anchovy, pickles and beetroot. The food was diced and carefully arranged to form a particular pattern and it was served on a bed of green salad plants, with a dressing.

SALMI. A ragoût or stew made from partly cooked or sometimes left-over roast game. Correctly made it is a good dish.

SALMI OF DUCK

1 lb. cooked duck meat
1 oz. (2 tablespoons) butter
salt, pepper
$\frac{1}{2}$ cup (scant $\frac{2}{3}$) red Burgundy wine
1 tablespoon ($1\frac{1}{4}$) water
2 egg yolks
$\frac{1}{2}$ cup (scant $\frac{2}{3}$) fresh or sour cream

Heat the butter in a pan, add the duck meat, salt, pepper, Burgundy and water. Bring to the boil, lower the heat, cover the pan and simmer for 10 minutes. Beat the egg yolks, add the cream and

thoroughly blend. Pour this mixture over the duck, stirring all the while to prevent curdling. When the sauce is thick, the salmi is ready for serving.

SALMON. A member of the Salmonidae family, and recognized as the most perfect specimen of the true fish. In the northern hemisphere it rarely occurs south of latitude 40° but is found in quantity in suitable waters in both the Atlantic and Pacific oceans, and in the sea lochs or fjords and certain rivers of northern Europe. The salmon is marked by four distinct stages of growth. In the first the young fish, called a parr, grows up to 8 in. in length and its skin is marked with dark bars and red spots. At approximately two years the skin becomes silvery and the fish, now termed a smolt, migrates to the sea from its freshwater birthplace.

When it has grown much larger and weighs from 2 to 6 lb., it returns to its birthplace and is called a grilse. It now resembles the mature fish (the fourth stage) differing only in colour and markings, and with a shorter head and slighter form.

Broadly speaking, the salmon are divided into those of the Atlantic (the species *Salmo salar*) and those of the Pacific (five species belonging to the genus *Oncorhyncus*). The Atlantic salmon is brownish above and silvery below when fully grown, and the adult averages 10 to 20 lb., although fish weighing up to 80 lb. have been recorded. The five species of Pacific salmon are: the quinnat, which is also called the king, tyee, or chinook; the sockeye, which is also known as the red or blueback; the humpback or pink; the coho or silver; and the dog or chum. The king, or quinnat salmon, is the largest member of the family, usually weighing over 100 lb., and is found in the Yukon river in Alaska.

In all waters of the world salmon are regarded both as splendid game fish and a source of valuable and highly palatable food. All salmon may be prepared freshly caught, or preserved by drying, smoking or canning. The freshly caught fish may be cooked whole in a variety of ways, or cut into steaks. The classic way of preparing a fine salmon for the table is to poach it in a *court bouillon* or to bake it in kitchen foil, carefully timing the process according to weight so that it is tender without being dried. It may then be served hot or cold and with a variety of sauces and garnishes.

SALMON, SMOKED. These are salmon of over 10 lb. in weight, brined and then cured in a dense smoke for several hours, or left in a light brine for up to 12 hours. The best salmon for smoking is Scotch, then Norwegian and finally Canadian, that of the Atlantic being superior to that of the Pacific.

SALMONBERRY. An American wild raspberry

SALMON (sockeye)   SALSIFY

or bramble found from California to Alaska; it bears red, attractive flowers and large berries which are either salmon-red or wine-red when ripe. Like raspberries they can be eaten as a dessert fruit, cooked for a pie or tart filling, used in fruit salads or made into jams and jellies.

SALMON TROUT. The name of the European sea trout, one of the finest marine fishes for the table, hot or cold, served in any way suitable for salmon. It is in season from March to August. In the United States the name is colloquially applied to the char and the lake trout.

SALPICON. The French culinary name for a mixture of foods, such as game, fish, poultry, *foie gras*, truffles and mushrooms, all separately cooked and then bound in a sauce of appropriate flavour. Sometimes the *salpicon* is filled into small cases of puff pastry, *bouchées* or *vol-au-vents*, or served in dishes, the different items divided by strips of toast or fried bread. *Salpicons* are used mainly for garnishings or hors d'oeuvre.

SALSIFY. The long edible root of a plant which is supposed to resemble the oyster in flavour. It is a delicately flavoured vegetable in two varieties, the white and the black. The black is known as scorzonera and has black-skinned tapering roots and considered the better of the two by most people. Scorzonera is said to be a native of Spain and the word is derived from the Spanish *escorzo* which means serpent. It is said to be an antidote for snake bites.

The easiest way to cook salsify is to scrape the roots well, then boil them in salted water for 45–50 minutes or until tender. Drain and rub off the skin (this applies particularly to the black variety) and serve hot with melted butter. Both varieties make excellent soup. (If not used immediately, salsify must be dropped in lemon-flavoured cold water to prevent discolouration.) Salsify leaves, if fresh, can be cooked or used as a salad.

There is a related French variety grown only for its leaves which make an excellent salad.

SALT. Prosaically salt is a substance of sodium chloride extensively prepared for use as a condiment or as a preservative of animal food; but the discovery of salt was one of the earliest and most important developments of the culinary art. Since earliest times it has been an important nutritional item of man's diet and over the centuries has become the most important seasoning in the world. It is a necessity of life, and continued lack of salt leads to serious malnutrition.

Like so much concerned with the nutrition of mankind, salt has its history, not always pleasant. It was an early form of punishment and torture to be sent to the salt mines, for a living death. Taxes have been levied on it, and caused trouble. More pleasant is the *Via Salaria*, a street in Rome so named because salt was transported along it. In Tibet and Abyssinia it was once used for money; and salt was given to Roman soldiers in part payment for their dues, or their *salarium:* the origin of the modern word salary.

There is hardly a dish in the world that is not improved by that 'pinch of salt', including cakes for it makes the gluten in the flour more elastic and thus help the mixture to rise. Salt is added to the water used for cleaning vegetables to free them from grubs etc.

Bay or *sea salt.* This is obtained by evaporation of seawater and is *gros sel*. It can be bought in various degrees of fineness.

Cooking salt. This is a less refined salt and can be used for general domestic purposes. The best is the block salt. As it easily absorbs moisture, it must be kept in a dry place.

Freezing salt. A variety of salt sold for mixing with the ice used in ice-cream freezing machines.

Table salt. This is common or household salt finely ground which contains a proportion of magnesium carbonate and calcium phosphate to keep it dry and make it run more easily. Iodized table salt is also made.

SALT-CELLAR. From the medieval word *saler* or *salière*. The English of that time acknowledged the importance of salt by placing it with due ceremony in the middle of the table, exactly halfway down. Below the salt sat retainers and hangers-on. To be below the salt was to know one's place and woe betide the man who tried to creep up. He was liable to be pelted with half-gnawed bones. Salt-cellars gained in beauty and design and there are some fabulous ones in collections.

SALT FISH. Many fish, particularly cod, ling and other large fish, are salted when caught and either kept in a pickle or dried by air. The dried fish need soaking in cold water up to 36 hours before using, although nowadays dried salted fish is sold pre-soaked. The fish salted in a pickle need only 12 hours soaking. Salt fish is popular in the Mediterranean countries and parts of the West Indies.

SALTPETRE. Potassium nitrate. Used with salt for pickling and preserving meat.

SALZGURKEN. Small salted cucumbers. A German pickle made of cucumbers soused in salt water.

SALT HERRING. See HERRING.

SAMBOLS (SAMBALS). These are side dishes to rice and play the same role in Far Eastern cooking as chutneys in Indian cooking.

SAMBUCA. A water-white Italian drink with an aniseed flavour that can be drunk either as an aperitif or as a liqueur.

SAMPHIRE. A plant which grows on cliffs and rocks near the sea, often on shingle, and has a distinctive odour, some say like sulphur. For centuries its fleshy green leaves have been used in salads and pickled in vinegar. Shakespeare mentions the picking of samphire in King Lear: 'One who gathers samphire – dreadful calling'. Its name is said to be derived from St-Pierre or in Italian *herba di San Pietro*. It is sometimes confused with glasswort. Samphire is also called the poor man's asparagus and it can be steamed or boiled in the same way as asparagus.

SAMPIGNY. See BURGUNDY WINES.

SAND CAKE. Dry Madeira-type cake.

SANDWICH. The simplest definition is a piece of meat or other food, cooked or uncooked, pressed between two slices of buttered bread, often with the crust cut off. On the basis of this definition it is possible to claim that this form of refreshment has been known to man since early times although the term sandwich is of recent origin. It was an early French custom to provide farm workers with a meal consisting of pieces of meat stuck between two pieces of wholemeal or black bread. The Mediterranean countries had their own versions too.

The sandwich as such came into its own in the 18th century when John Montagu, Earl of Sandwich, gave it his name and elevated it socially. It is said that he was an inveterate gambler who hated to leave the gaming table, so his chef hit on the idea of serving him a sandwich. Others say he was a keen sportsman who did away with the usual set meal and ate two slices of meat spread between two slices of bread. Whatever the truth, the glamour of its new name gave the sandwich an honoured place at 18th-century buffets. The French quickly took it up and made it a part of their fare.

Since then the sandwich has evolved. Today sandwiches serve many purposes and the variety of fillings used is endless. There are small dainty sandwiches served with afternoon tea: those made with watercress and cucumber are favourites in England. A larger sandwich with bread cut diagonally and filled with more substantial food such as roast beef, ham or cheese may be eaten instead of a set lunch. English pubs serve these with beer. The American sandwich is enormous and a single one suffices. It may be a two- or three-decker sandwich filled with an assortment of foods.

The Scandinavians have a great variety of open sandwiches (see SMØRREBRØD) with special emphasis on sardines, herrings and similar fish. The fillings are placed on a single slice of bread. There is no limit to the variety of fillings and most meats, poultry, vegetables, cheese, eggs and fish make excellent sandwiches.

It is also claimed that a form of sandwich was made by the learned Rabbi Hillel who lived at the beginning of the 1st century A.D. He made it his custom during Passover to symbolize the suffering of his people and their deliverance from Egypt by taking two pieces of unleavened bread, *matzo*, and filling them with bitter herbs, chopped nuts and apple as his ritual food. This custom has since become a traditional part of Passover observance.

SANGAREE. A summer weather drink attributed to the southern United States and derived from the Spanish drink *sangria*. The classic sangaree consists of lemon juice, claret, a small amount of sugar, ice, and spring water to taste. Nowadays the word has come to mean any sweetened wine drink. Some cocktails have been concocted under this name using various spirits, wine and sugar.

SANTENAY. See BURGUNDY WINES.

SAPODILLA. The fruit of a tree native to Mexico and the South Americas and now widely cultivated in southern Florida, Bermuda, the West Indies and

SAUCE-BOAT

SALT-CELLAR

the Far East. It is called naseberry in the West Indies and North America, and chickoo in many parts of the Far East. The fruit is brown, egg-shaped or round, resembles at first glance a potato and is about 1½–3 in. in diameter. The flesh is sweet and apple-yellow to brown in colour. Its texture is soft like fudge. It is usually eaten raw, either peeled or cut in half round the middle with the one or two black seeds removed and the pulp scooped out with a spoon. It can be peeled, sliced and mixed into a macedoine of fruits, or sieved, made into a fool and served with cream.

SARDINE. The true sardine is the young of the pilchard and is only found off the coasts of Europe. In the Atlantic and the Pacific small fish are caught and called sardines, but are the young of herrings and are related to pilchards and anchovies.

Fresh sardines are delicious with quite a different flavour from the canned varieties – which vary in flavour and quality according to the olive oil used to preserve them and the amount of time they are matured. Sardines are caught in large quantities off the coast of Sardinia, hence their name.

SARDO or **SARDO ROMANO.** A grating cheese of the Pecorino type, made on the island of Sardinia.

SARSAPARILLA. Central and South American plant with cord-like roots which are dried and used to flavour carbonated and other so-called mineral waters.

SASHIMI. One of Japan's specialities. It is fish, sliced paper-thin and served quite raw. The most usual fishes prepared in this manner are tunny (tuna), bream, carp, abalone, and certain other shellfish. The slices of fish are garnished with shredded carrot, lettuce, or cabbage and served with grated fresh ginger and horse-radish. It is dipped into small bowls of sauce immediately before it is eaten. *Sake* (which see) is always served with *sashimi*.

SASSATIES. South African mutton kebabs. The meat is cut into cubes and put into a bowl with sliced orange and onion, lemon leaves, milk, sugar and salt. A cooked marinade is made from more sliced onion, curry powder, vinegar and chutney. This is poured while hot over the meat and left overnight. Next day the meat is threaded on to skewers and grilled (broiled) over charcoal.

SATSUMA. See ORANGE.

SAUCES. The British look to the French for sauces, remembering wryly the jibe that 'France has three religions and 300 sauces, while England has three sauces and 300 religions'. The French také sauces seriously, whether in *haute cuisine* or simple family cooking. They are the soul of French cooking and to assess their place, note their position in the average French cookery book – at the beginning. All French cooks would agree with Alexander Dumas that no cook can be a good cook until he has mastered the art of sauce making.

Sauces perform three main functions. They enhance flavour; they mask the lack of flavour; and they act as binders.

WHITE SAUCES. These are basic sauces made from a *roux* (which see) cooked long enough to eliminate the raw flour flavour yet remain white. The two main sauces of this group are Béchamel, prepared with a white *roux* and milk which can be flavoured with onion, carrot, herbs and seasoning; and velouté, which is similarly prepared but with a white stock of chicken, veal or fish.

BROWN SAUCES. For these sauces the *roux* is cooked until it is dark, and a basic brown sauce added. Brown sauce or Espagñole is the main sauce of this category.

TOMATO SAUCE. Made from tomatoes, bacon ends, onion, seasonings and stock. It is served either strained or unstrained.

EGG YOLK AND BUTTER SAUCES. Typical of this class is Hollandaise (see below).

OIL AND VINEGAR SAUCES. These include the dressings, vinaigrette etc.

FLAVOURED BUTTER SAUCES. Hot butter sauces or creamed butter flavoured with herbs.

The following list of sauces gives those in common use but does not by any means begin to cover the entire world range of sauces.

Agro-dolce. A sweet-sour sauce from Italy used with rabbit, hare or braised meat. It consists of brown sugar, currants or raisins, chocolate, candied peel, capers and vinegar, and gravy or juices from the meat with which it is to be used. Almonds and pine nuts are often added.

Aïoli. The mayonnaise of the Mediterranean, heavily garlicked. Recipes vary throughout the area.

Almond. These are of many varieties, usually prepared with crushed almonds and breadcrumbs and used with fish, chicken and turkey.

Albert. Horse-radish sauce with cream, butter, breadcrumbs, mustard and vinegar. For beef.

Allemande. Velouté with eggs.

Admiral, à l'. A butter-based sauce for boiled fish.

Anchovy. Most countries have their own versions of anchovy sauce, Italy in particular. Fresh or salted anchovies are used, often added to a basic sauce or *roux* and flavoured with wine.

Apple. A thick purée of apples used with pork.

Aurore. Béchamel sauce tinted with tomato.

Barbeque Sauce (American). Recipes for this sauce vary but most are highly seasoned with chilli and Worcestershire Sauce.

Bâtarde. Béchamel sauce with eggs; very like an Allemande.

Bavaroise. Wine vinegar, butter and horse-radish, seasoned, flavoured with nutmeg and served hot with fish and shellfish.

Béarnaise. A mixture of fresh herbs, chopped and cooked with shallots in white wine. It is thickened with egg yolks. One of the famous sauces, served with grilled meats.

Bercy. Velouté sauce flavoured with fish *fumet*, chopped shallots, parsley, white wine and butter.

Bigarade. Duck's gravy reduced, flavoured with orange and lemon juice, julienne of orange rind, and thickened with arrowroot or duck's liver.

Bolognese. An Italian sauce of mixed, diced vegetables and tomatoes, flavoured with herbs and white wine. A *pasta* sauce.

Bordelaise. Red wine sauce, mixed with meat glaze (which see), flavoured with shallots, parsley, mignonette pepper and herbs. Served with grills.

Bourguignonne. Chopped shallots, parsley, bay leaves, mushroom trimmings, cooked in red wine, strained and thickened with a *beurre manié* (which see). Served with meat.

Brandy sauce. A hard butter, brandy-flavoured sauce (also known as hard sauce) used mainly in Britain and the United States for mince-pies and Christmas pudding.

Bread Sauce. There are several recipes for this but basically it is made from breadcrumbs cooked in milk, flavoured with shallots or onion, ham, parsley, lemon and seasonings.

Brown butter sauce. This is butter cooked until it bubbles and variously flavoured with herbs, capers or lemon and served hot with fish, cabbage, broccoli, asparagus and grilled meat.

Cambridge. A variation of mayonnaise made of pounded egg yolks, anchovy fillets, capers, herbs, mustard, oil and vinegar. Served with mutton or lamb.

Caper. There are at least a dozen recipes for this sauce. They range from a bâtarde to a plain butter sauce, a brown *roux* or capers mixed with a dressing. Served with lamb, salmon or white fish according to the type of recipe.

Caudle. A hot rum or brandy sauce, sweetened and flavoured with lemon rind and served with plum, carrot or similar puddings.

Chantilly. A sauce *suprême* (which see) to which thick cream is added. For eggs, poultry, sweetbreads and brains.

Chasseur. A white wine sauce with minced mushrooms, chopped shallots, butter, chopped parsley and a meat glaze. Used with small cuts of meat, chicken, rabbit, game etc.

Chaud-froid, brown. Half-glaze sauce (see below) with aspic or gelatine, flavoured with truffles and Madeira. Used to coat cold meats.

Chaud-froid, white. Velouté sauce set with aspic or gelatine. Used with eggs, white meat and fish.

Cranberry. Stewed cranberries, seasoning, port or white wine; sometimes combined with oranges. Served with turkey, chicken etc.

Diable. Chopped shallots, mignonette pepper, white wine, cayenne pepper, meat stock and tomato purée. Served with meats and turkey bones.

Diplomat. Sauce Normande (which see) with lobster butter and brandy. For fish dishes garnished with diced lobster meat and chopped truffles.

Financière. Madeira sauce flavoured with truffles and chicken livers.

Genevoise. Mixed diced vegetables, fish stock, butter, pepper, herbs, red wine, sieved and finished with butter and anchovy essence. For fish, especially trout and salmon.

Grand Veneur. Poivrade sauce with venison gravy, mixed with redcurrant jelly and cream. Used for game.

Gribiche. Chopped gherkins and capers mixed into a sauce made from pounded hard-boiled egg yolks, seasoning, oil and vinegar, garnished with strips of hard-boiled egg white. For cold fish and shellfish.

Half-glaze. A basic sauce, which is an Espagñole sauce reduced with meat stock until one-tenth its original volume and finished off with a good sherry.

SAVARIN MOULD AND SAVARIN

Hard Sauce. A butter and confectioners' sugar mixture, served on fruit puddings.

Hollandaise. A butter sauce made with egg yolks, plenty of butter, peppercorns, lemon juice, and used mainly for fish, eggs, and vegetables.

Lyonnaise. Onions cooked in butter, white wine and vinegar, mixed with a half-glaze and sieved. Used with ragoûts, left-over and braised meats.

Madeira. Madeira, stock, gravy, butter and concentrated Espagñole sauce are the ingredients. Served with braised or roast meats in small cuts.

Matelote. Fish stock, red wine, mushrooms, half-glaze mixed and sieved. Served with fish.

Mayonnaise. A cold sauce made of egg yolks, olive oil, wine vinegar and seasonings. Served with cold chicken, fish, eggs, salads, etc.

Mint. Chopped mint, lightly sweetened, seasoned and moistened with vinegar. Served with lamb.

Mornay. Béchamel sauce mixed with butter and grated cheese (usually Gruyère and Parmesan).

Mousseline. Mayonnaise or Hollandaise with whipped cream or a fantasy of the imagination made from many eggs and cream. Served with fish, asparagus, broccoli or cauliflower.

Moutarde (Mustard). Hollandaise heavily flavoured with mustard.

Nantua. Mixed diced vegetables with crayfish (crawfish in the United States), butter, moistened with white wine and cognac, fish velouté, seasoning and tomatoes. Served with shellfish.

Newburg. Made from butter, sherry, cream, egg yolks, paprika and salt. Served hot with lobster.

Noisette. Hollandaise sauce with browned butter.

Normande. A fish sauce with variations. Basic ingredients are velouté, fish *fumet*, mushroom stock, mussel or oyster liquid, egg yolks and cream. If truffles soaked in Madeira are added, or poached oysters, it becomes Laguipière.

Onion. See *Soubise.*

Parsley. Butter sauce with chopped parsley. Used for fish.

Périgueux. Diced truffles and Madeira blended into a half-glaze. A famous classical sauce.

Piquante. Brown sauce flavoured with capers, shallots, white wine, sieved and garnished with gherkins and chopped herbs, and heavily seasoned with pepper.

Poivrade. Another famous sauce which varies but, generally speaking, the ingredients are wine vinegar, white wine, peppercorns, diced vegetables, herbs, light stock and Espagñole sauce. It is used for meat, game (when game essence is added) and ragoûts.

Poulette. Béchamel base with shallots, mushrooms, egg yolks and cream.

Provençale. Generally tomatoes, seasonings, always garlic, sometimes mushrooms, seasoning and oil. For fish, small cuts of meat, or vegetables.

Ravigote. There are two ravigote sauces, hot and cold. The cold one is a mayonnaise with capers and hard-boiled eggs, The hot one is a variation of Béchamel with white wine, chopped herbs, in particular chervil, chives, tarragon etc. The hot sauce is served with poultry and offal (variety meats).

Réforme. Equal quantities of half-glaze and poivrade, garnished with a julienne of egg whites, gherkins, mushrooms, truffles and tongue.

Remoulade. Mayonnaise with mustard, garnished with capers, parsley, gherkins, chervil and tarragon, finished with anchovy essence.

Robert. Brown sauce to which is added onions cooked in white wine, seasoned with mustard and pepper.

Soubise. Basically a purée of onions with Béchamel sauce lightly flavoured with nutmeg. Served with roast pork, eggs, chicken or mutton dishes.

Suprême. A velouté mixed with cream.

Tartare. Mayonnaise made with hard-boiled egg yolks garnished with chives and onions. Served with fish, cold chicken or other cold meats.

Verte (Green). Mayonnaise mixed with a purée of blanched herbs and sieved.

Vin blanc. Fish velouté, thinned with fish stock, thickened with egg yolks and finished with butter.

SAUERKRAUT. Shredded, crisp white cabbage fermented in salt and flavoured with caraway and juniper berries. Although almost everyone associates sauerkraut with the Germans, it was the Austrians who gave it its name. They learnt the recipe from the Chinese via the Tartars. The workers who built the Great Wall of China lived on cabbage with rice through the summers. In winter rice wine was added which soured the cabbage and gave it a delightful new flavour. When the Tartars swept through China they perforce ate the soured cabbage, liked it and devised their own improved method of salting cabbage. They left China and swept their imperious way west to Europe carrying their soured cabbage with them.

A nice tale and probably as true as many other culinary stories. People in the Balkans, when not attributing their longevity to eating yoghourt, give credit to sauerkraut.

SAUSAGE. A sausage is ground meat enclosed in a case of thin membrane, usually eaten grilled, fried or boiled. The Greeks spoke of *oryae*, their name for sausage, and the Romans called it *salsus*, from the Latin word for salted. Sausages were a great favourite with the Romans and the Emperor Constantine the Great thought them much too good for plebeian consumption.

The sausages of classical times were plain and unspiced, and it was not until the Middle Ages that experiments were made with various meats and spices which led to the modern sausage. Those that became famous took the name of the city in which they were invented: the *Wienerwurst*, for instance, was invented in Vienna; the frankfurter in Frankfurt; and the bologna in Bologna. The frankfurter is the ancestor of the American hot dog, which came to the United States over a hundred years ago.

Sausages have been called little 'bags of mystery' and in late Victorian times this term seems to have been used derisively because of the inferior quality meat used in their making.

There are various types of sausages and many countries have their own specialities. Among others, Germany has the *Bratwurst* with its 600-year-old history; there is the pork-and-blood filled smoked sausage of Poland; the Corsican sausage of pork fat; the sausages of Toulouse. They also come from as far afield as China, where the pork sausage *lop chong* is most popular although sometimes it is made of liver. The Chinese steam their sausages with rice, serving them sliced as an hors d'oeuvre or as a side dish, also in their stir-fried dishes.

Sausages vary in flavour and may be unspiced, spiced or highly spiced. The usual meats are pork, beef, veal and liver or a mixture of some of them. Small-sized sausages are known as chipolatas (which see), and the extra large are country style.

SAUTÉ or SAUTER. A method of cooking and browning food in a small quantity of very hot fat in a frying pan (skillet). The food may be sautéed simply to brown it or to cook it through, i.e. when sautéeing liver. It is one of the important cooking techniques and the following points must be noted.

1. The fat used must be a mixture of oil and butter, fat or oil, or clarified butter. It must be very hot before the food is added; otherwise the juices will not be sealed and the food will not brown. Butter alone cannot be heated to the required temperature without burning; hence the oil being added, as this acts as a fortifier.

2. Before the food is put into the pan it must be absolutely dry. If there is even the slightest dampness a layer of steam is created between the food and the fat, thus preventing both from browning and searing.

3. Never crowd the pan – there must always be plenty of air between each piece of food. Overcrowding means the food will steam rather than brown and the juices escape and burn in the pan.

SAUTÉ PAN. Similar to a deep frying pan (skillet) but with straight sides. (French: *sauteuse*).

SAUTERNES. See BORDEAUX WINES.

SAUVIGNON. See BORDEAUX WINES.

SAVARIN. A cake made with a yeast dough similar to the *baba* (which see). It is baked in large or small ring moulds, soaked in syrup and flavoured with kirsch or rum.

SAVELOY. A type of smoked pork sausage, lightly seasoned and coloured red with saltpetre. It is sold cooked and is usually skinned and sliced for serving.

SAVIGNY-LES-BEAUNE. See BURGUNDY WINES.

SAVOIE. The French part of the mountainous country between the Rhône valley, Switzerland and Italy known as Savoy. There are many vineyards in Savoie which produce wines, both red and white, still and sparkling, of local fame.

SAVORY. A rather bitter herb vaguely like thyme, used in sausages, stuffings and as flavouring for beans and peas. There is winter and summer savory. Their flavours are alike.

SAVOURY. Used in contradistinction to sweet, of food having a stimulating flavour. Also to describe a piquant morsel served as the last course at dinner. The object being to clean the palate after the pudding in preparation for the port to follow.

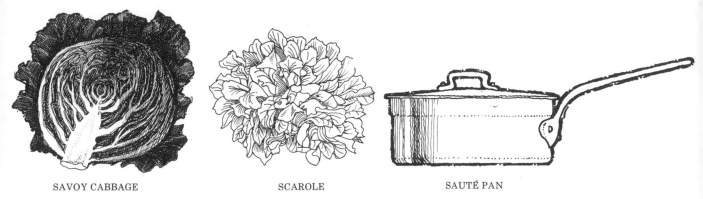

SAVOY CABBAGE   SCAROLE   SAUTÉ PAN

SAVOY BISCUITS. Small sponge biscuits used in making Charlotte Russe etc.

SAVOY CABBAGE. A variety of cabbage which comes into season in the middle of autumn and lasts throughout the winter. Its varieties include Dwarf Green Curled, Early Dwarf Ulm, Perfection, Best of All and Drumhead. It has crinkled leaves and is a hardy vegetable.

SBRINZ. The hardest of the Swiss cheeses. It is usually served sliced into thin shavings with a cheese plane and spread on buttered black bread. It is also an excellent grating cheese and does not become 'stringy' when cooked. It can be used instead of Parmesan in *risottos* and *pasta* dishes. It is a speciality of central Switzerland and owes its fine aroma and good digestibility to a 2–3 year drying process.

SCALLION. Another name for the Welsh onion or ciboule. See ONION.

SCALLOPS or **SCOLLOPS.** See COQUILLE ST-JACQUES.

SCAMOZZA or **SCAMORZA.** A soft, mild cheese originally made in Abruzzi. It can be eaten fresh, for it is essentially a table cheese, but it is also used in cooking.

SCAMPI. Originally the Venetian name of the giant Adriatic prawn which grows up to 6 in. in length. The body is pale amber, almost colourless, with a thin shell and no claws. The flesh is tender with a shrimp-like flavour. A similar type of large prawn is also caught in the Bay of Gaeto where it is called the *mazzacuagno*.

In Venice scampi are boiled like shrimps and served with sauce or fried in deep oil, either plain or first dipped in egg and coated in fine breadcrumbs. Before World War II real scampi were flown from Venice to London. Today when scampi are ordered in Britain it is almost invariably Dublin Bay prawns (which see) that are served.

The confusion with the Dublin Bay prawn or Norway lobster (*langoustine* in French) is interesting. This crustacean, which is not a prawn, reaches up to 10 in. in its cold native waters, but is two or three inches shorter in warmer seas; Dublin Bay prawns inexplicably migrated south just before World War I, were caught in large numbers off the Brittany coast and were encountered as far south as the Mediterranean, where they were promptly dubbed scampi. This has become the fashionable name in Britain for salt-water crustaceans of this size whether they are true scampi or not.

SCAROLE or **ESCAROLE.** A broad, wavy-leaved salad of the endive family.

SCHERIS. See SPANISH WINES.

SCHILLERWEIN. See GERMAN WINES.

SCHLOSSABZUG. See GERMAN WINES.

SCHNAPPS. See SNAPS.

SCHNITZEL. It might seem sacrilegious to doubt the origin of the so-called *Wienerschnitzel*. But the Vienna State Archives contain an account by Count Attems, adjutant to Emperor Franz Joseph, of Field Marshal Radetsky's report on the development of the Italian campaign in which he praised the Milanese cuisine, in particular the *scallopine alla Milanese*. The Emperor called for a demonstration and the chefs of the Imperial kitchens copied the dish so well that the Field Marshal said he wished his military orders were executed with the same accuracy. At any rate, the Emperor and his court so appreciated the Milanese dish it made a victorious entry in all the fashionable Viennese restaurants and was finally claimed as *echt Wienerisch*.

However, further research on the schnitzel by the Viennese brought to light that it was the Spanish troops of Emperor Charles V who imported the dish into Italy; one Cardinal Gattinari wrote that he had been served a 'costoletta in the Spanish manner'. The trail then continues into Andalusia, but after this becomes confused.

Whatever its origin, the *Wienerschnitzel* is simply a thin slice of veal, gently beaten, dipped in egg and coated in breadcrumbs and quickly fried on both sides in butter.

SCONE. The etymology of scone (pronounced skonn, which is an early spelling) is uncertain. Chambers Dictionary suggests the Gaelic *sgonn*, a shapeless mass; other authorities quote Low German *schoonbrot* and Dutch *schoonbrood* 'fine bread'; or it might have been the favourite cake of the people of Scone where once the Scottish kings were crowned.

White or brown flour is mixed with sour milk or buttermilk to a stiff dough. This is shaped into a cake or farl (round) roughly 8 in. in diameter and cut into four. It is baked on a girdle (griddle) or in a hot oven.

SCORE. To cut or slash parallel gashes over the surface of meat or fish to let out some of the surface fat so that it will cook crisply. This is done to fish before grilling. Pastry is also scored.

SCORZONERA. See SALSIFY.

SCOTCH BUN. Also known as black bun. It is a highly spiced bun baked inside a pastry shell. 'Bun' was an old term in Scotland for plum cake and the black bun was baked for festive occasions.

SCOTCH EGG. Hard-boiled egg encased in sausage meat and fried.

SCOTCH WOODCOCK. A savoury consisting of thin slices of toast spread with anchovy butter, topped with scrambled eggs and garnished with anchovy fillets.

SCRAPPLE. Name given to an American dish invented by the early German settlers in Pennsylvania. It was originally known as 'ponhaws' and was devised to use hogs' heads and other scraps which would otherwise be wasted. It is made with half a hog's head with the eyes and brain removed. Scrape clean, put into a pan, cover with water, simmer until the meat falls from the bones. Skim off the fat and chop the meat finely. Return it to the pot and season with salt, pepper and sage. Sift in cornmeal until it is the consistency of a soft mush. Cook slowly for an hour then press the mixture into greased oblong tins. This makes 3 lb. of scrapple which will keep for several months if properly stored. When required, thin slices are cut and fried until brown.

SCUP. Also known as the porgy, the two closely related species of this North American food fish are among the more important members of the Sparidae family and are found in abundance from Cape Cod to the Carolinas. Scup have an average length of 10 in. and weigh ¾ lb., but they can grow considerably larger when they find food plentiful. One of the most widely eaten of American fish, scup are prepared in the same way as catfish (which see).

SEA CUCUMBER. See BÊCHE-DE-MER.

SEA DATES. These are shellfish with something of the shape of a date, found off the coast of Genoa. They have a good flavour and are cooked in the same manner as mussels and made into soups and stews.

SEAGULL EGGS. These are similar in shape to a plover's egg and have a slightly green-blue shell. The flavour is rather fishy, but is eaten in coastal areas. Mashed with bloater or anchovy and spread on toast, they make quite pleasant eating.

SEA KALE. A vegetable found growing wild on the English, Continental and parts of the Irish coasts. From earliest times country people have cut the young shoots in spring and boiled them as greens. The exact date when sea kale was first cultivated in gardens is not known but probably it was not until the middle of the 19th century. Although it grows easily it has not become popular either in the United States or on the Continent. Even in England it is regarded as a luxury vegetable. It is better known as a forced vegetable to be eaten in midwinter when the shoots are pure white and some 8 in. long. It is cooked tied in bundles in salted water for about 20 minutes, drained and served hot like asparagus with a melted butter sauce. It forms a separate course in the menu. The fresh fronds are curly and green with a nutty flavour and can be eaten raw as a salad or like celery with cheese. Sea kale is also known as silver beet.

SEA MOSS. A name for carrageen (which see).

SEA SLUG. See BÊCHE-DE-MER.

SEAR. To brown the surface of meat through cooking by the application of fierce heat. This 'seals' the juices in meat and improves the flavour. At one time all meat was seared, but today there is a tendency to sear less and cook meat slowly.

SEASONINGS. Seasonings improve and enliven food, but cooks should take care not to over-use them. The main seasonings are salt, pepper, mustard, garlic, onions etc. Such seasonings,

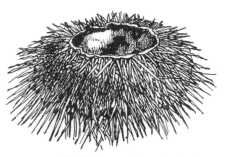

SEA URCHIN (prepared for eating)

SEA KALE

including the many herbs, spices, dressings and even sauces, are added not only to impart flavour but also to excite the taste buds to a better appreciation of the dishes presented. Pepper is not used for its biting quality, nor wine to give the flavour of wine. But both are used to produce a happy culinary blend of flavours. Correctly used, seasonings should bring about an aroma and flavour so subtle that even the epicure hesitates to name it.

SEA PIE. A beef stew with a suet crust.

SEA URCHIN. There are several varieties of sea urchin which, although a menace to bathers, are a joy to eat, with a flavour between oyster, mussel and lobster. They live in clusters, clinging to the rocks and can only be collected with wooden pincers or gloved hands, for they are covered with sharp spines. They are served cut into two on the half shell and their delicate coral roe is scooped out with a spoon. They are at their best eaten within the smell of the sea, served in large quantities (for the spiny urchin has little flesh), sprinkled with lemon juice and served with local white wine. In Japan a sauce is made from sea urchins.

SEAWEED. Few people make as much use of edible seaweed as the Japanese. It is one of Japan's most popular items of food and appears in many recipes, sometimes in the form of delicious biscuits (cookies) and, of course, in *sushi-meshi* (which see). In Japanese stores it is draped over counters and overhead rails like party streamers. There are some species a foot wide and several feet long. Seaweed is used at weddings and is a symbol of longevity. Some species of seaweed are sold in small packets and chewed by the Japanese as other people chew gum. Seaweed is used in making soup stocks as well as all kinds of flavourings.

SEDIMENT. Many wines after a while tend to throw deposits of varying kinds. This is part of the wine, and there is nothing necessarily wrong with it although it does indicate bottle-age. The wine

should be poured leaving the sediment in the bottle. In white wine, sediment takes the form of crystals but these can be dispersed by shaking the bottle and leaving it in a warm room for a few days. When sediment is heavy, as with full-bodied red wines, the bottle should be decanted and rebottled if it is to be kept longer. An old bottle of red wine that has no sediment is probably not what it is said to be.

SEEDLESS WHITE RAISINS. See SULTANAS.

SEELACHS. Smoked, dyed coalfish from Germany, used as a substitute for smoked salmon. It is sold as saithe, another name for coalfish.

SEKT. The German name of the German imitation of champagne.

SELF-RAISING FLOUR. This has 3 to 4 per cent of raising agent added and mixed in during manufacture. It is considered convenient by many housewives but it should not be used for rich mixtures where eggs are sufficient for raising, for bread where yeast is used, for batters which rise by steam or for plain pastries which are not meant to rise.

SÉMILLON. See BORDEAUX WINES.

SEMOLINA. Semolina, the purified middlings of wheat, was at one time much favoured for making bread. A writer at the end of the 14th century wrote: 'The best kind of wheat was called in old time *silogo* whereof was made the finest bread called *panis siligineus* which we call manchet and was plentiful among the Romaines.' An early French writer also says: 'Coarse wheatflour is that which to the Latines is called *similago* and is made of wheat excellent good having the greatest bran only lifted from it.' *Silogo* and *similago* both refer to semolina.

Semolina is used to thicken soups and make milk puddings, moulds and fruit whips. It also forms the basis of several *pastas*. A creamy variety is also made from maize.

SERCIAL. See MADEIRA.

SESAME OIL. See OILS.

SESAME SEED. Sesame is an aromatic and lovely annual herb, very important in Far Eastern cooking and native to India. The seeds when toasted and ground have something of the flavour of toasted almonds. Both in India and China the plant is cultivated on an enormous scale. The seeds vary in colour between so-called white to greyish-black and there is one grade which is a fine orange colour. Apart from being a popular ingredient in Asian cooking, sesame is used considerably in the Balkans and in Middle Eastern cooking (see TAHINA) and has become naturalized in the United States where it is used in cakes and pastries – following the Central Europeans who make sesame rolls and breads as well. Sesame can be purchased whole or ground, but it is far better bought whole.

SETUBAL. See PORTUGUESE WINES.

SEVE. See WINE TERMS.

SEVILLE ORANGE. See ORANGE.

SHAD. Popular name of fish of the genus *Alosa*. They are akin to herring but are rather larger and swim up rivers to spawn. Two species, the allis and the twaite, occur in British waters but are rare. The common shad of North America is a valuable food fish popular in the United States for its roe. Native to the Atlantic seaboard, it has been successfully introduced to the West Coast. It may be prepared to any recipe suitable for herring or mackerel.

SHADDOCK. See POMELO.

SHALLOT. A member of the lily family, which covers a wide range of flavours: the onion, garlic, leek and chives among them. The shallot is one of the milder members. It grows in the manner of the onion, with one difference. Instead of being one main bulb the shallot looks rather more like garlic with a series of sections or cloves which come apart easily. It is native to Western Asia. The name is a corruption of Ascalon, the city of the Philistines. It is believed that shallots were introduced into Britain by the returning Crusaders. Those shallots which grew in the Ascalon area were famed in Pliny's day for he mentions them in his writings. Shallots can be used in the same way as onions and are particularly suitable for pickling.

SHAND, P. MORTON. A much-quoted writer on food and wine of the 'twenties. His two best-known books are *A Book of Food* and *A Book of Wine*.

SHANDYGAFF. A long drink for thirsty summer days made by mixing beer and cold ginger beer. The origin of its name is unknown.

SHARKS' FIN. This is used in Far Eastern cooking and the best comes from the Philippines. When fresh it has no flavour and only after it has been sun-dried or cured does this develop. The cooking of sharks' fin used to be laborious with long soaking and simmering, but nowadays it is sold in pre-prepared form. It is expensive though and is often in fairly short supply. The traditional method of cooking sharks' fin is in the famous Chinese Shark Fin Soup on which a Chinese cook is prepared to stake his reputation.

SHASHLYK or **SHASHLIK.** Lamb grilled on a skewer sometimes served in restaurants on flaming swords. In Moscow shashlyk is served with lettuce, chopped onions and fresh parsley. Correctly milk lamb should be used for this dish.

SHEEPSHEAD. A greatly valued food fish, found off the Atlantic coasts of the United States. It received its name from the resemblance of its teeth to those of a sheep. It feeds chiefly on shellfish, which give it a delectable flavour. Its body is thick and chunky, its flesh white and flaky, and it weighs from 8 to 10 lb. It can be considered the supreme fish of American waters.

SHELLFISH. The name given to edible crustacea of which clams, crabs, crayfish, lobsters, mussels, prawns and scallops are typical examples. As shellfish deteriorate rapidly, they must be bought fresh and in season. Generally, all shellfish should feel heavy in proportion to their size.

SHEPHERD'S PIE. A dish consisting of cooked sliced meat baked in a pie-dish with a 'crust' of mashed potatoes. Sanders are miniature shepherd's pies.

SHERBET. Sherbet or sorbet is an iced sweet made with either fruit juice, syrup and lemon juice or with syrup flavoured with lemon juice and a fortified wine or liqueur. It is softer than ice-cream, and after freezing is served in chilled glasses. It is said that sherbet first came to Europe centuries ago from China through India and the Arab countries to Italy and France. Saladin, it is believed, offered iced sherbets to Richard I during the Crusades. The Romans used to flavour snow as their first attempt at making an iced sweet.

In modern times credit must be given to the Italians for helping the world to discover or re-discover the delights of these confections; *granita* or *spumone* are the Italian names. Procopio Cultelli,

SESAME (pod with seeds, leaf)　　　　　　　SHAD

a Sicilian who gallicized his name to Procope, opened a shop for ices and sherbets in Paris. These became the rage. By 1676 there were no less than 250 ice-makers in the French capital. Literary personalities such as Voltaire and Diderot flocked to the famous Café Procope to eat this new and exciting confection.

After 1780 techniques were developed to make a better product. The evolution of ices and sherbets had begun and today the varieties available are numerous and delicious.

SHERRIS. See SPANISH WINES.

SHERRY. See SPANISH WINES.

SHIRAZ VINE. Persia, 'the fountain of culture and civilization', claims the distinction of having given wine to the world. The shiraz vine or *sirrah*, or *petite sirah*, as it is called in California, has been planted and has prospered in different parts of the world. Wines are also made from the shiraz vine in Australia and South Africa, and the *syrah* of the Côtes du Rhône is said to be another of the family.

Omar Khayam wrote of it: 'I sometimes wonder if what the vintner buys, is one-half as precious as the stuff he sells.' Legend has it that the Shah Djemsheed always kept a dish of grapes by his bedside. One day he noticed that some of them had become over-ripe and had begun to ferment. Believing that the fruit had turned rotten and therefore poisonous, he ordered it to be thrown away. A discarded mistress hearing of this ate the 'poisonous' grapes as a means of committing suicide and ending her sorrows. The Shah was surprised to find her suddenly gay and happy. When questioned she confessed about the grapes. The Shah discovered the secret of the grapes, the wine industry thus began and the discarded mistress was reinstated in the royal affection.

Shiraz red or white has a pungent, spicy and perfumed flavour. In Persia, the shiraz vintage is in August and the wine can be made only under a licence. The country has 300 square miles of vineyards producing about 40,000 gallons of wine a year.

SHIRR, TO. To cook in a small shallow casserole, the best-known example being shirred eggs, i.e., baked eggs.

SHORTBREAD. This is a rich, slightly sweet biscuit-type cake served at Hogmanay, the Scottish New Year's Day (also called Cake Day). Immense quantities of shortbread are sent from Scotland every year to relatives and friends in every quarter of the globe for the festive season. It is a Scottish confection and although said to owe much to the French, it has been known in Scotland for three or four centuries. It is made in the form of a rich short crust pastry in a round mould, the edges crimped and baked in a slow oven until lightly browned.

There is also a shortcake which is somewhat richer and is of American origin. A homely Southern American variety known as 'shortnin' bread is made with all-purpose flour, soft brown sugar and butter. The mixture is cut into circles $\frac{1}{2}$ in. thick and baked till golden brown.

SHORTENING. A culinary term used more in the United States than in Britain and it applies to fats used in making breads, cakes, pastry etc. All fats, even oils, come under this nomenclature and are used because they make mixtures 'short' or tender. Fats with the greatest shortening power are lard, cooking fats and dripping, but as they are apt to flavour, mixtures are preferred i.e., half butter and lard.

SHRED. To slice so finely that the slices curl, or into the finest strips, or to grate so that thin strips are formed.

SHRIMP. In Britain this means only the small crustaceans never more than 2 in. long. There are two kinds caught off British shores, the pink and the brown. The pink shrimp (*Leandersquilla*) is a reddish-grey when raw and turns a bright pink when cooked. It looks like a baby prawn. The brown shrimp (*Crangon vulgaris*) is a grey-speckled brown when raw and becomes pinkish-speckled-brown when cooked. Both types are usually boiled in sea water on the fishing boats while still at sea. Shrimps have the same nutritive value as prawns and can often be cooked in the same manner. They are rather tiresome to peel, but the fresher they are, the easier the operation.

Shrimps in the United States are what are called prawns in Britain. For example, a butterfly shrimp, would be called, in Britain, a large prawn.

SHRIMP PASTE. The British variety of this paste is a mild mixture of pounded cooked shrimps, flavoured with salt, onion juice, Worcestershire Sauce and cayenne pepper. It is used usually as a sandwich filling, although it can be served on a bed of lettuce with toast. The Far Eastern variety is a pungent condiment used particularly in Indonesian cooking.

SHRIMPS, POTTED. A British speciality – brown shrimps preserved in clarified butter. They became popular in London clubs during the 19th century, and this led to a private mail-order organization and finally to world-wide distribution.

The correct way to enjoy potted shrimps is to warm them gently until the butter just begins to flow. Arrange the shrimps with their butter on lettuce leaves and bring at once to the table. Serve with thinly sliced brown bread.

SHRUB. A home-made cordial or liqueur with a rum or brandy base mixed with lemon and orange peel. The mixture is allowed to stand for about two months, sweetened, strained and bottled.

SILD. This is the Norwegian and Danish word for herring. Canned, lightly smoked herring imported from Scandinavia is often sold under this name in Britain. The related North of England and Scottish word sile is applied locally to young herring.

SILVER BEET. See SEA KALE.

SILVER FIR LIQUEUR. (Liqueur de Sapin.) A product of the Jura mountains made in the Pont-parliers area from the budlets of 'Christmas' trees. It is bottled in a wooden flask, considered almost as a tonic and has the balmy essence of the Franche-Comte forests.

SILVER LEAF. See GOLD LEAF.

SILVERSIDE. The outer part of the round of beef, also called the half-round. It is usually salted and boiled but it also makes an excellent joint when stewed with vegetables and herbs.

SIMMER. To cook foods in liquid and sauces at just below boiling point (195°F.) so that the surface barely ripples.

SIMNEL CAKES. The word simnel probably derives from the name of a very fine wheat flour used by the Romans. This cake as we know it today came to be baked on the fourth Sunday in Lent or Mothering Sunday, now called Mother's Day. It is said this was the day when servant girls were given a day off each year to go and see their mothers. Their mistresses allowed them to bake a cake and take it home. It was usually a simnel cake.

It is now more or less an Easter cake with a small marzipan egg and a little chicken on top, and consists of almond paste baked between two layers of a light fruit cake.

SINGE. To pass a flame over a chicken or other bird to burn off the fine hairs left after plucking. A gas taper or a wooden spill gives the least smoke.

SINGING HINNIE. A Northumberland girdle cake thus named because of the hissing sound the dough makes when dropped on to the hot girdle.

SIPPET. See CROÛTONS.

SIRAN, CH. See BORDEAUX WINES.

SIRLOIN. See BEEF.

SITGES. See SPANISH WINES.

SKATE. A large flatfish of which there are more than a dozen varieties. Skates and rays are recognized by their great wing-like pectoral fins. Not all species are edible. Only the side pieces of wing are eaten (except for the liver, obtainable only where the fish is landed) and these weigh between 1 and 2 lb. Unless caught young, skate can be tough and are kept for a couple of days before cooking.

In England skate is always sold cut into fairly regular-sized pieces and crimped. In France, where the skate are smaller, they are sold whole or cut into varying sized pieces. The usual method of cooking skate is to cut the wing into wide strips right through the gristle which forms the bones. Skate can be fried in batter (a popular method in British fish and chip shops), but is at its best poached in a *court bouillon* or water, drained and served at once with a hot black butter sauce.

SKIRRET. A herb said to have been brought to Europe from China. Its clusters of tuberous roots are sweet and tender and may be cooked like salsify. The plant has small, whitish flowers on a cluster of small branches and round or oval-shaped leaves. Since it is hardy, its dahlia-like roots may be left in

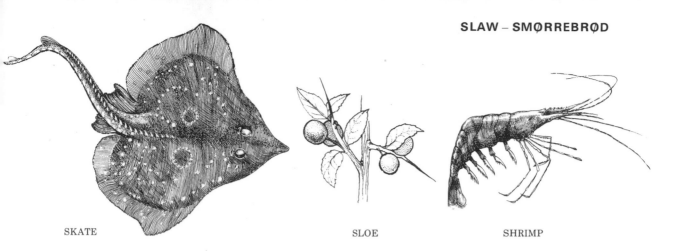

SKATE   SLOE   SHRIMP

the ground during the winter months and dug up when wanted to be used as an agreeable vegetable.

SLAW. See COLESLAW.

SLING. Strong, simply prepared, long cocktails generally garnished with fruit and served in tall, slender glasses and taking the name of the spirit used. Dissolve 1 tablespoon ($1\frac{1}{4}$) of sugar in a little water, add 1 jigger of the spirit desired, the juice of $\frac{1}{2}$ lemon or lime, 2 ice cubes and carbonated water, and garnish with a slice of orange or lemon.

SLIVOVITZ. An aperitif made throughout the Balkans from plums. It is called *šljivovica* in Yugoslavia.

SLOE. The fruit of the blackthorn which grows wild in woods and hedges in most parts of the British Isles. It bears fruit around September and is related to the plum; the fruit is small and hard, resembling damsons. It is not much used in the kitchen although when the fruits have been exposed to the frost they become less sharp in flavour and may be turned into jam. The most common use is as a flavouring to make the popular sloe gin.

In the United States the name sloe is given to the fruit of a native plum which is cultivated for the sake of the jams, jellies and conserves which can be made from its fruit.

SLOE GIN
1 lb. sloes
$\frac{1}{2}$ cup ($\frac{2}{3}$) castor sugar
3 cups ($3\frac{3}{4}$) gin

Remove the stalks from the sloes, wash and dry them. Prick with a large needle and put them into a jar, add the sugar and leave for 3 days, shaking from time to time. Add the gin and cover tightly. Leave for 3 months, shaking occasionally. Strain, bottle and cork and keep for one year.

SMELT. A small delicate trout-like fish, often used as bait. It has a curious smell and a flavour which many say resembles cucumber. Smelts require careful cleaning: pull out the gills (this will also remove the entrails), wipe the fish gently but do not wash it. Smelts can be fried or baked in the oven and garnished with lemon.

SMITH-HAUT-LAFITTE, CH. See BORDEAUX WINES.

SMOKING. A method of preserving meat and fish by drying them in the smoke of a wood chip fire over which sawdust is thrown to give a dense smoke. The flavour of the food depends on the type of wood used. Oak chips are considered by some as the best but juniper, hickory, and beech are also favoured. Some fish are brined before being smoked, such as kippers.

SMOKO. An agreeable institution of the Falkland Islands, a fairly substantial 11 a.m. meal consisting of sausage rolls, cream cakes and strong, sweet tea.

SMÖRGÅSBORD. Literally translated this Swedish term means 'sandwich table', but in reality it is a gargantuan display of hors d'oeuvre. The *smörgåsbord* is an old tradition said to have originated with country parties at which each guest brought along some kind of food. All these foods were arranged on a long table round which the guests walked, filling their plates. It is still a popular and indeed famous institution (a full-blown *smörgåsbord* is served on some Swedish passenger ships and in certain restaurants), but today, when people have less time for preparing food, it is served at home only on special occasions and varies greatly in extent.

When eating from the *smörgåsbord* one should begin with bread and butter and herring, accompanied by a small glass of ice-cold *snaps*. Beer is also served. After the herring other cold fish dishes are taken, followed by the cold meats and vegetable salads. If a hot *smörgåsbord* is offered the dishes are eaten in the order herring au gratin, omelettes, meatballs, kidney sauté, etc. The *smörgåsbord* is usually finished with cheese.

SMØRREBRØD. The Danish name for the open

sandwiches for which the Danes are famed. These delicious sandwiches may be served as snacks, as a preliminary to a meal, or several of them may make a complete meal. There are hundreds of varieties and new ones are turning up all the time. The sandwiches range from the simple ones, which office workers take for their lunch, to glorious 'technicolour' compositions available in delicatessens and restaurants. One well-known restaurant in Copenhagen boasts a list of over 250 varieties of smørrebrød.

Most Danish sandwiches are made with dark rye bread, which is whole-grain and firm, so that it can be thinly sliced. White bread of a heavy texture is also used, and sometimes toast. When making a complete meal of sandwiches, it is usual to start with a fish sandwich, then go on to meat and salad sandwiches, and almost inevitably finishing with a slice of buttered white bread spread with a thin slice of cheese.

Snitter are the Danish equivalent of canapés, often served at parties.

SMØRREBRØDSJOMFRU. The Danish name for a woman who is specially trained to make Danish open sandwiches, smørrebrød (which see). Literally translated it means 'sandwich maid'.

SNAILS. The only land mollusk popular among gastronomes in France and other parts of Europe, notably Italy. The best snails (*escargots* in French) are considered to be those that feed on vine leaves in the French vineyards, more particularly in Burgundy. They are at their finest at the beginning of winter (after the vintage) when the snail has sealed his shell and retired inside for a winter sleep and fast. At other times of the year the snails must be left to fast and purge themselves for a few days after they have been gathered and before they are cooked. Snails need a lot of preparation, difficult to carry out at home, so it is wiser to eat them in restaurants where the chef thoroughly understands the ways of dealing with them. It is also possible to buy canned snails, and in France they are available cleaned and ready for cooking, complete with garlic butter sauce.

SNAPPER. Fish of the genus *Lutianus*, inhabiting the warmer waters of the Atlantic and the Caribbean, some of which have considerable value as food fish. They attain a length of 3 feet and a weight of 30 lb. The three best known are the red snapper (which see), the grey or mangrove snapper and the pargo or mutton-fish, all commercially important. They are all game fish when caught on hand-held tackle and make a favourite table delicacy. They may be prepared by any of the classical methods of cooking fish, and the red snapper is particularly suited to baking whole.

The name snapper is also given to a valuable food fish of the Sparidae family in Australia and New Zealand.

SNAPS. In Scandinavia another name for akvavit (which see). Although usually flavoured with caraway an old custom has recently been revived and myrtle and mixtures of other suitable herbs is used to make *snaps* even more bitter. *Snaps* is usually served with food and ice-cold, in a glass which holds exactly one mouthful so that it is swallowed in one gulp.

SNIPE. Name often applied to any member of the Scolopacidae family of waders, characterized by long bills and streaked plumage. The principal genus is *Gallinago* found throughout the world. Snipe feed on marshy ground, using their bills to probe for worms and snails, a diet which gives this much prized table bird its distinctive flavour and slightly fishy quality. A North American cousin of this gamebird is Wilson's snipe, *Gallinago delicata*, so named for its delicate flavour. Throughout the northern hemisphere snipe are at their best in autumn and are prepared in the same way as woodcock, although the tastiest method is roasting.

SNOEK. Name given in South Africa to the barracouta (which see).

SNOW PEAS. These are small green peas which the French include in the *mange-tout* category (which see). They are also called Chinese Peas in the United States.

SODA. When used for food this is generally known as bicarbonate of soda or baking soda and is a by-product of common soda. It is sometimes added to green vegetables to keep their colour but this is now frowned upon as it nullifies their vitamin C content.

SODA BREAD. An Irish bread in which the raising agent is bicarbonate of soda with buttermilk.

SODA WATER. Water rendered sparkling by the introduction of carbon dioxide, produced preferably from bicarbonate of sodium.

SOLE. One of the most familiar of the European flat-fish and member of a family of fish that has twisted skulls so that both eyes are on the same side of the body, i.e. on the right side of the head. Their bodies are flat and somewhat elongated. Of this family the common sole (*Solea vulgaris*) holds a high place in gastronomy.

INDIAN THALI (curry).

SNOW PEA   SNAPPER

Soles live in temperate inshore waters, and their flavour varies according to the district from which they come. There are four species of sole met with in British waters. Of these the common sole predominates.

The Dover sole is simply the common sole, but so named by fish retailers and restaurateurs to distinguish it from inferior flat-fish, such as lemon sole, witch sole, Torbay sole and the megrim (which see). It usually grows from 10 to 20 in. long and weighs 1 to 1½ lb. Its flesh is white, fairly firm, with a delicate flavour and high nutritional content. Its colour varies slightly according to the area from which it comes but usually the 'upper' side is brownish with black blotches, the right pectoral fin tipped with black. It is fished in the North Sea.

The French or sand sole is very like its near relative, the common sole, but somewhat yellower in colour and covered with small black blotches and dots. Its home is the Mediterranean but it strays sometimes into the North and Irish Seas and occasionally finds a place on British fishmongers' slabs. The thickback or variegated sole is a reddish brown with bands of darker brown across its body. It seldom exceeds 9 to 10 in. in length and its range is from the Mediterranean to the southwest coasts of the British Isles. The solonette is a small, common flat-fish of the sole family found all round the British coasts. Its length is between 4 and 5 in., and it is considered too small to be marketed. It is often mistaken for a young sole as its colouring and habitat are the same.

Soles of the genera *Synaptura* are caught off Portuguese and Moroccan coasts, and a Portuguese sole, known as the *azevia* (*Solea azevia*), is occasionally seen in British shops. There is also a rare deep-water sole, *Solea profundicola*.

American species of sole are too small to be of value. They mostly belong to the *Achirus* and *Symphurus* genera.

SOLE VÉRONIQUE
4 servings:
8 sole fillets
salt, pepper
¼ cup (⅓) white wine

¼ cup (⅓) fish stock
1 oz. (2 tablespoons) butter
1 oz. (¼ cup) flour
2 tablespoons (2½) cream
¼ lb. Muscat or white grapes, skinned and the pips removed

Sprinkle the fillets with salt and pepper and fold over. Place in a sauté pan, add the wine and fish stock and cook slowly for 10 to 15 minutes. Carefully take out the fish with a long fish slice and place it on a hot serving dish. Strain the stock. Melt the butter in a pan, stir in the flour and, when well blended, gradually add the strained stock and stir until it boils. Test for seasoning and add the cream. Put one grape on top of each piece of fish and the rest around the side. Add the sauce.

SOLERA. See SPANISH WINES and WINE CONTAINERS.

SORBET. See SHERBET.

SORGHUM. The 35 species and many varieties of sorghum are an important cereal crop in Africa and Asia (see DURRA), and have been introduced into many other parts of the world. Sorghums are a source of human and animal food, of molasses and of an alcoholic drink made from its seeds. Bread and a kind of porridge can also be made with it.

SORREL. Sometimes called herb patience or patience dock, this herb grows wild but is also cultivated for its acid-flavoured leaves that add a distinctive touch to soups, stews and sauces. It is thought to have been introduced into Britain from France. Some believe that Mary Queen of Scots took cultivated sorrel seeds to Scotland, although it grows there in its wild state and is known as sourock. The Scots make a soup of sorrel leaves, butter, chicken or veal stock, chopped potato, salt, pepper and cream, with whipped cream to garnish.

It was listed as an English herb in the 13th century but then seems to have been forgotten. An old Cornish name for sorrel is sour sauce, and sour sauce pastries are still made there. A 16th-

353

VEAL: breast of veal with pimiento.

century English recipe uses sorrel to make a decorative green sauce with orange marigold leaves and slices of oranges and lemons floating in the pungent liquid.

Continental sorrel is less acid than the English variety and is used in salads and as a vegetable. Sorrel is good cooked like spinach and served with fish. At one time it was used as a salad with lamb and veal cutlets, and as a sauce it was customarily served with duckling, young geese and lamb. It grows abundantly in English meadows and country people still use it to make cooling and medicinal drinks.

SOUBISE. See SAUCES.

SOUFFLÉ. The culinary name of both a sweet and savoury confection, the chief ingredient being eggs. The yolks and whites are separated; the latter is whipped to a firm snow before being folded into the rest of the ingredients. Soufflés may be hot or cold and their flavours can be varied: lobster, spinach, asparagus, broccoli, cheese, vanilla, chocolate etc. In every case the technique is the same to attain the desired lightness.

A soufflé should be put into the oven to bake just as soon as the ingredients are blended, and the time planned so that it will be cooked as nearly as possible at the moment of serving. A soufflé must not wait; if it does, it sinks in the middle.

As a good soufflé should rise to almost treble its original bulk, a band of paper is always tied round the dish before the mixture is poured in, and the dish should never be quite filled. On the other hand, if making a cold puff or whip type of soufflé with a gelatine base, it must give the appearance of having risen, so that the dish, after it has been wrapped round with paper, must be filled 1 in. above the edge before it is left to set.

SOUP. One of the most widely accepted forms of food. The word comes from the Latin *suppa*.

Soups are basically water in which all manner of solid foods – flesh, fowl, cereals, vegetables and fruits – have been cooked. They can be divided broadly into two classes, clear and thick. Thick soups can be divided into those which are puréed or creamed, and those which are not. Clear soups can be hot or cold, liquid or jellied. Both clear and jellied soups give a *cachet* to a formal dinner; thick soups are intended more for lunches or for serving as a main course.

The line between soups and broths is hard to define. Many soups are as thick as a ragoût; boiled beef started in the stockpot. Soups and stews have developed together in the world's cuisine, their origin lost in antiquity. When the subject is explored, a curious relationship between soups and

puddings emerges. One of the earliest references to English soups states, 'it is a kind of sweet, pleasant broth made rich with fruit and vegetables and spices'.

Soup has been described as being 'to a dinner what a portico is to a house'. It should announce the full tone of the dinner 'as an overture of an opera announces the subject of the work'. Gourmets consider soup-making the ultimate accomplishment of the chef. Much of the culinary wisdom of the East has been deployed in making soups. Through the ages soups have played a rôle similar to bread. As a basic food every country, every civilization has had its soup: France its *pot-au-feu*; Italy its *minestrone*; Russia its *borsch*; China its sharks' fin soup; Britain its brown or Windsor soup; the United States its black bean soup; Switzerland its gravy soup; and Scandinavia, its fruit soups.

Soups have a similar task to hors d'oeuvre, but a different approach. They stimulate the salivary glands and the flow of gastric juices by their heat and moisture. Hors d'oeuvre is served before soup, although the two are not often offered at the same meal. It is better to follow the French custom of serving hors d'oeuvre at lunch and soup at dinner. If wine is served with soup, it should be at room temperature and of fairly high alcoholic content, such as brown sherry or old Madeira.

The choice of soups is important. Clear soup and consommé should precede a dinner of several courses, its purpose being to put the diners in the right mood, the 'overture' as it were. Thick soups on the other hand are no overture: they are the theme. Fruit soups can be served either before or after a meal. The Chinese serve soup half-way and all through a meal.

SOUR CREAM (SMYETANA). There is a lavish use of sour cream in Russian and other Slav cooking. It must be remembered that refrigeration is a comparatively recent innovation and cream spoils quickly. Instead of throwing soured cream away, the Slavs utilized it in their cooking and became so accustomed to its flavour that they now prefer cream this way. It is used in almost every kind of dish, with meat and poultry, with vegetables, fish, pancakes and noodles. Many delicious cakes and puddings owe their flavour entirely to sour cream.

SOUR MILK. In many countries sour milk is considered a refreshing and nourishing drink. It is simply milk which has gone sour and there is nothing cranky about using it. It has much the same flavour as yoghourt (which see) and, although the two are not identical, they are in certain culinary circumstances interchangeable.

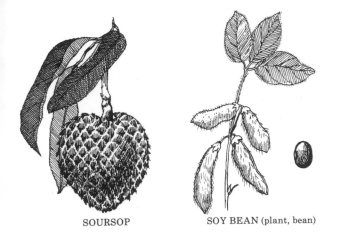

SOURSOP   SOY BEAN (plant, bean)

In Russia, milk is left in glasses and allowed to become sour and firm and to form a thick skin. This is served chilled, sprinkled with grated cinnamon and/or nutmeg, together with slices of black bread.

SOURSOP. A large almost kidney-shaped fruit with a rough skin covered with short soft spines. It is particularly popular in the West Indies and in Malaysia where it is sometimes called the *durian blanda.* Although it has none of the unpleasant odour of the *durian*, in appearance it is similar. The pulp is tart with an acid flavour, the texture resembling cotton wool soaked in some pleasant flavoured liquid. It is generally used to make drinks and blends well with other flavours, such as banana, orange or pineapple, and is perfect for making ice-cream.

SOUSING. Soaking or marinating and cooking in a pickle of vinegar and spices, salt etc. Used mainly for herrings and mackerel, although other types of fish can be soused.

SOUSSANS. See BORDEAUX WINES.

SOUTH AFRICAN WINES. The Dutch when they landed at the Cape recognized a land and climate ideal for the growing of grapes and within three years the first vines were planted, just over three hundred years ago. Another four years and the first wine flowed. After a further 30 years French Huguenots seeking religious freedom settled there, many of them bringing French wine-making skills with them. By the early 19th century South African wines were known throughout Europe, although Britain was the main customer. In 1918 the Co-operative Wine-Growers Association (K.W.V. – the initials of the Afrikaans title) was formed which controls nearly all the growing vinification and distilling in the country.

The wine country is concentrated mostly in the western region of Cape Province, within 150 miles of Cape Town. Experts state that while the wines are reliable, they are not outstanding in comparison with the best produced in Europe. They are classi-fied as 'standard' wines. The best red wine comes from the Constantia district close to Cape Town.

The over-abundance of sun has produced a debilitating effect on white wines, contributing to a loss of delicacy in flavour. Even so, more white wine than red is produced.

Where South Africa has made its mark in wine-making is in the field of fortified wines: the port, Madeira and sherry types. Perhaps it is here that the future lies. As much as 47 per cent of South African wines are now fortified, and the sherry has established itself as a rival to Spanish products commercially, if not in the arena of the connoisseur.

SOWENS. A traditional dish for Hallowe'en. It is a kind of oat porridge which is served with milk and was once a ploughman's dish, very common in Scotland, Northumberland and Northern Ireland.

SOY BEAN. See BEAN.

SOY BEAN CURD. An ingredient in Far Eastern cooking made from cooked curdled soy bean. It requires a complicated process of preparation which only experts attempt. The result of the curdling is a white substance which looks like a soft but firm white cheese. It is sold in several forms.

SOY BEAN SAUCE. According to a 19th-century recipe, this was made of boiled soy beans and bruised wheat, with common salt (dissolved in warm water) added. It was left to stand loosely bunged for 8 or 10 weeks, the liquid squeezed out and bottled. It enhances some dishes: a few drops in a vegetable soup adds considerably to the flavour. It also strengthens sauces and stews.

Both the Japanese and Chinese make soy bean sauce and in varying qualities, including light and dark sauce.

SPAGHETTI. The best known and probably the most popular of Italian *pasta*. It is made from hard wheat and eggs (if of good quality), mixed to a paste and dried in long thin strings. It is boiled for 12 minutes in fast boiling, salted water, drained, served with a sauce and generously sprinkled with grated cheese such as Parmesan or Pecorino.

There is even an Historic Museum of Spaghetti in the small Ligurian town of Pontedassio, near Imperia. It contains a fascinating collection of documents, ancient decrees, engravings, old machines and unique instruments all connected with the art and evolution of pasta-making.

SPANISH BRANDY. See SPANISH WINES.

SPANISH LIME. See MAMMONCILLO.

SPANISH OMELETTE. A true Spanish omelette is made with a base of onions and chopped potatoes which are cooked in oil and generously flavoured with garlic. The consistency is firm but light, and the omelette is not folded in the French manner. Instead it is cut into wedges, like a cake, for serving.

SPANISH WINES. The wines of Spain can be divided into three main classes: the great wines of Jerez de la Frontera, known as sherry, and similar types of wine; secondly, the heavy, sweet wines of Malaga (once called Mountain) and Tarragona; and finally, those sound table wines which are found throughout Spain – the best come from Rioja, but they can be bought at almost any local *bodega*.

Wine has been made in Spain since time immemorial. Certainly it was there before the Romans came. The art of wine-making has been developed and, in the case of sherry wines, specialized, so that ancient custom and modern techniques produce excellent wines throughout the Peninsula. They are mostly tables wines, made in enormous quantities, and they are fairly strong, rarely going below 10° of alcohol and sometimes as much as 14°, or in the case of the Priorato wines from the north of Tarragona, to an astronomic 20° of alcohol. Some districts make red wine which will be served with any kind of meat or fish; other districts make white wine which again will be served with any kind of meat or fish. A few make red, white and *rosé*, like Valdepeñas, and this wine is indeed so complete in itself that any one of the three sorts can be drunk with any food.

With Spanish wine, the date of the vintage is comparatively unimportant, and although it is true that some fine Rioja wines can be found with the date on the label, it is unwise to place much reliance on this. In any case the sun shines in Spain – except in very odd years like 1968 – pretty well the same on the same day of every year, and the wines, since they are made from grapes grown from the same soil, tend not to alter in their quality. This is not to say that some of the old wines are not now worth drinking, but generally you will have to travel to Rioja and carry with you some very

powerful introductions to Spaniards if they are to open their private cellars and give you wine which can go back to the middle of the last century.

Spanish wine was never very much more than honest wine until the phylloxera hit the vineyards of France, and the *vignerons* faced with ruin came to Spain to buy wine to mix with what they could save from their own crops. As the replanting of the French vineyards took a decade or so, they took the trouble either to buy vineyards or to instruct Spanish wine-growers in the noble art and modern technique of vinification. This led to a general improvement in quality.

Foremost among Spanish wines, and possibly Spain's greatest export, is sherry, sometimes called Sherris, Scheris, Xérès, Jerez or sack. Since 1968 sherry can only come from Jerez de la Frontera, Sanlúcar de Barrameda and Puerto de Santa Maria, which is the port for sherry. Up to a year or two ago, sherry was also made in Montilla, but this is now forbidden and the wine must be sold under its own excellent *denominación de origen* of Montilla and Moriles. Sherry was also made in the district round Niebla, which is a great hardship for the Nieblese who make a wine as good as sherry, yet cannot ship it as such. They have to accept a lower price for their wine, excellent though it is, simply because nobody knows about it.

Sparkling wines are made extensively in the northeast of Spain, mostly in the Panadés district, by all three methods, *méthode champenoise, cuvée close* and alas, by the infusion of carbonic acid gas into otherwise respectable and decent wine. Some good sparkling wines are made: the Spaniards claim that the largest manufactory of sparkling wine by *méthode champenoise* is that at Cordoniu, which family has been making wine there since 1551, long before Dom Pérignon. They further claim that they are the biggest manufacturers of sparkling wine in Europe, not excluding champagne. Spanish sparkling wine is certainly not champagne, and while it has some things in common, it should never be called such. Nevertheless, the Cordoníu *Non Plus Ultra* is very good indeed.

Spanish brandy

Brandy is distilled everywhere in Spain and it is correspondingly different in its flavour and quality. Mostly it appears under the label *coñac*, which is Spanish for cognac, and this it certainly is not. The best brandies – an excellent one by Torres in Villafranca del Panadés, and most of the commercial brandies like Fundador and Veterano – are very good. The cheap unbranded brandies are recommended only for black coffee on a cold day.

Although the vine is grown throughout Spain, the principal wine-growing districts are as follows.
JEREZ

Sherry is that incomparable wine, so deservedly

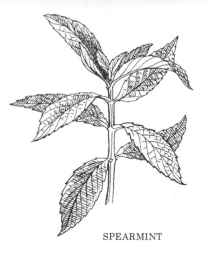

SPEARMINT

popular as an aperitif; or, in the case of the sweet *olorosos*, as a substitute for port after a meal; or, in the case of the fine *amontillados*, as good company for soup. Aperitif types start with the *fino*, which is pale, very light and should be extremely dry sherry made from grapes grown in the Jerez district. The great *finos* are delicate, charming and not, as most of the export brands, fortified with the addition of grape brandy. They reach a degree of vinosity up to about 20° alcohol. The secret of sherry is in its blending. The *bodega* system, which is the true wealth of Jerez, is built on hundreds of casks of the best *fino* added every year to an existing *solera*, and from the combination of the old and the new wine are blended specimens of such famous *marques* as the *Tio Pepe* of Gonzales Byass or the *Macharnudo Fino* and *Las Palmas* of La Riva. *Soleras* go back about two centuries; there is at La Riva one which started life in 1770 and is still in use, though only for very fine *amontillado* type of wine. It is tapped rarely and refreshed from wine almost equally old, and it is not generally sold. *Finos* and *amontillados* are made from the palomino grape; the richer *olorosos* and richest Pedro Ximénez or P.X. from the grape of the same name. The true Pedro Ximénez wine is very sweet and has the consistency of fine engine oil. The quality of sherry comes from two things, the palomino grape and the *albariza* soil: neither are found anywhere else in the world.

MONTILLA and MORILES

Sometimes known as Cordoban wines (Córdoba is the headquarters of this wine-growing district). These wines are all but identical with sherries, and only wines of the sherry type are produced. Up to recent years, they were nearly all exported as sherries, but this is now unlawful and they must be sold under their own *denominación de origen* of Montilla and Moriles. Very good wines indeed and in most cases as good as sherry and somewhat cheaper.

RIOJA

The home of the finest red wines in Spain, halfway between Burgos and Madrid. The River Ebro flows through the district. The wine-growing centres are based on Haro in the north, a very pleasant historic town entirely devoted to wine, and the rather larger capital of the Rioja, Logrono. The two dominating vineyards of Rioja are the famous two Marquises: the *Marqués de Riscal* and the *Marqués de Murrieta*; both make very fine wine indeed and about as near as can be got to the great French wines of the Médoc, but they have a quality of their own. They are much cheaper than the finest French wines and when found should be bought. The Rioja was the district from which those French wine-growers bought and developed their wine during the phylloxera scourge of the 1880s and 1890s.

LA MANCHA and VALDEPEÑAS

La Mancha wines (Valdepeñas is the principal wine-growing town in La Mancha) are the good common wines of considerable integrity and no little strength grown in the district south of Madrid. In La Mancha wine is still made as it has been since Roman days, in great pots like Ali Baba jars, called *tinaja*, containing anything from 3,000 to 12,000 litres. It is probably one of the most primitive and honest ways of making wines extant and the wine from it is neither fine nor great, extremely variable but generally excellent and very cheap. The best Valdepeñas wine has a vinosity of 13·5° alcohol for the white wine and as much as 14° for the *tintos* or red wines. They are much more heady than the roughly comparable wines of the Midi in France, which vary between 9° and 11°. It is Valdepeñas which is usually served in Madrid restaurants and wineshops and sometimes it is transported in pigskins called *pellejos*, similar to those which the famous citizen of La Mancha, Don Quixote, tilted with. Some wineshops in Madrid insist on these *pellejos*, and they say the wine is so much better when kept thus.

MÁLAGA (or MOUNTAIN)

The wines of the Mountain, as they were almost universally called up to the mid-19th century, are heavy sweet wines made and collected in the mountains some 40 miles north of Málaga. They are brought to Málaga, which has become the centre of distribution and blending, but the wine is essentially a peasant wine, made from grapes in thousands of small vineyards, mostly trodden and sold by the vineyard owner to the Málaga *bodegas*, either as must or in casks as fully fermented wine. The wine is also refined and sold as communion wine throughout Spain and elsewhere after inspection by the Catholic authorities. Málaga is very much the product of the local climate and is made from the Pedro Ximénez grape (rather more than half), together with moscatel, Jaén blanco, Jaén doradillo and Rome. It is a splendid sweet wine with some affinity to port (except that it never throws a crust) and keeps to a great age.

LEVANTE

These wines are mostly red but a good deal of ordinary white is produced too, and the alcoholic content is very high – 13° to 16° if the wine is allowed to age. The best wines are Benicarló, dark, rich and red, and the wines of Murcia, based on Jumilla and Yecla. Vast quantities of this wine are exported to other countries who make fine wines. Presumably somewhere between the original grape and the final bottle there is a change of nationality: in other words, these wines, because of their high strength, are considered good for blending.

CATALONIA

Tarragona. There are two kinds of wine made here. One is the sweetish, heavy wine termed Tarragona and this includes a special variety rarely met with in Britain or America, called Priorato. The other type consists of a group of excellent clean table wines produced throughout the large Tarragona district, by reasonably up-to-date methods and to some extent blended and matched to suit export markets.

The original Tarragona became notorious in Britain around the turn of the century, largely because it was a ferocious liquid, highly laced with brandy, and known as 'red biddy'. True Tarragona today is an excellent wine. Priorato, which has its own brand of Tarragona, and its own *denominación de origen*, is the product of grapes grown on a former volcano, making wine of incredible vinosity, very black, with an alcoholic content of about 18° to 20° after fermentation. It is a perfect wine for blending and giving body to lighter wines.

Panadés. The wines are made in the district covered by the *denominación de origen* centred on the town of Villafranca del Panadés, half-way between Tarragona and Barcelona. There is a very good wine museum in Villafranca del Panadés. Excellent wines are made throughout the Panadés district by every kind of method including that of maturing the wine by exposure in *bombonas* – large 30-litre pear-shaped glass bottles, which are left out in orderly ranks in fields to mature under the sun and rain. These are largely dying out and probably it is only the old firm of Torres who keep

them going, more for tradition than any other reason. Undoubtedly Torres wine is very good. At Sitges on the coast are made some very sweet dessert wines which are better than most. There are two types, a Malvasia, or Malmsey as it is known in England, and a Moscatel.

Alella. This is a very small *denominación de origen* area centred on a small town of the same name about 20 miles north of Barcelona. Garnacha blanca and Xarello grapes, from which the wines are made, are grown on a gritty, granite soil. This means that the wine, which is almost exclusively made at a large co-operative in the town of Alella, is not produced in great quantity but has both character and charm and a most delicious bouquet. Made in red, white and *rosé*, it is necessarily hard to come by.

GALICIA

The wine of Galicia has a character all its own, and is distinguished by a slight greyness in colour and a freshness and sharpness of taste unusual in Spanish wine. The wines are sometimes sold with their secondary fermentation incomplete and the corks lightly tied on the bottles with string. When opened the wine pops and is, because of the secondary fermentation, fizzy. They are a somewhat heady but quite delicious drink, if served cold. Galician wines are usually difficult to find outside Spain, and indeed in most places in Spain, although they are well known in Madrid.

CASTILE

The wine-producing area of Castile is centred round Valladolid and the village of Rueda, together with La Seca and Nava del Rey. Very good wine is made, with some affinity to the Rioja wines.

SPARKLING WINES. See WINE-MAKING and WINE TERMS.

SPÄTLESE. See GERMAN WINES.

SPEARMINT. See MINT.

SPICES. The story of spices is romantic and violent, its beginnings lost in the mists of time. The Babylonians are known to have grown spices which played an important part in their economy. They and the Assyrians compiled long lists of spices for use of doctors and were well informed on their medicinal properties. Their spice trade became so lucrative that men were willing to pay any price for the bark, buds, stems, roots or seeds of aromatic plants and trees – for spices are not derived from a particular part of a tree or plant but from any part rich in flavour and aroma. The demand for spices exceeded the supply and the spice trade found itself the most profitable in the world. The same spices for which today we pay a

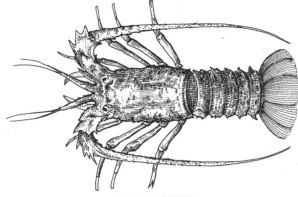

SPINY LOBSTER

few pennies were once worth their weight in gold. So precious was a cargo of spices that the loss of several hundred men on a single voyage was not reckoned too high a price to pay.

Most spices are of tropical origin. Cinnamon and cardamom, or 'grains of paradise', are from Ceylon and India; cloves and nutmegs from the volcanic shores of the Moluccas. Many spices were indigenous to China and were carried on the arduous and dangerous overland routes to India and beyond. Men died of heat, exhaustion or were murdered by highway robbers, but the trade flourished.

Many were the stories of fabulous wealth to be gained from spices. The Venetians held the spice monopoly for centuries, to lose it to the Portuguese.

The Dutch were hard on their trail, the French and English not far behind. They fought, whole islands were wiped out. It is hard to believe this fierce and bloody history when we see our spices today, all so neatly packed. Their romance has gone, but not their flavour and aroma. And once again their worth is becoming known.

What are spices? The word has come to mean 'hot' or 'sharp'; but there are sweet, spicy-sweet and hot spices, and more of the former than the latter. Cinnamon is a sweet spice; ginger a spicy-sweet, and cayenne is hot. Spices are nature's own products and should be in every kitchen. For us spices are perfumes trapped in glass jars. Sooner or later their perfume or aroma will evaporate. To keep properly the jars must be tightly sealed. Spices should be bought in small quantities and often, and the spice shelf checked frequently.

SPINACH. A deservedly well-liked vegetable, though less than universal in popularity. Turner's *Herbal* described it as 'a herb lately found and not much in use'. The Dutch introduced spinach to European cookery. It came originally from Asia. The classical cuisine evolved a number of ways of preparing spinach, among them several fine soups; the spinach Florentine, a purée of spinach, with a cream and nutmeg flavouring; spinach Livonien, Viroflay and Vert Pré, the last of these a cream of spinach, watercress and chicken velouté garnished with asparagus tips. Spinach is also prepared as a mousse, soufflé, salad and pâté.

During the 1920s spinach went through an unpopular phase because of its association with the nursery and the notion that it was meant for children for its high iron content. Fortunately spinach has shaken off this distaste and is now a vegetable enjoyed throughout the year.

Its three main varieties are summer, winter and perpetual. It must be carefully washed to remove sand and needs only the water clinging to its leaves to cook in. It must be well drained before serving.

SPINACH BEET. See CHARD.

SPINY LOBSTER. This is the crawfish or langouste and is one of the most popular crustaceans on the Continent. It may weigh up to 8 lb. and has flavoursome if rather coarse flesh, most of which lies in the tail. In the United States spiny lobsters or lobster tails, as they are called, are frozen and marketed in great quantities. It has no claws, its legs are uniform in size and it is cooked in the same ways as lobster.

SPIRITS (POTABLE). Alcoholic liquids obtained by distillation from certain wholesome materials such as wine in the case of brandy, sugar in the case of rum, grain for gin and whisky, and rice for arrack and *sake*, etc. In all spirits the nature but not the proportion of ethyl alcohol is the same. The great differences among them all is due to the by-products or impurities, which vary according to the nature of the 'mash' or fermented liquid from which they were distilled.

SPIT-ROASTING. See ROAST.

SPLIT PEA. See PEA.

SPONGE CAKE. A light cake made from well-beaten eggs, sugar and flour. No fat is used as this would result in too close a texture.

SPOT. The American name of a small marine fish

of some gastronomic repute which is caught off the North American Atlantic coasts. The name is also given to two other and quite different fishes, the red drum and the pinfish.

SPRAT. A small herring of the western coasts of Europe. A silvery fish 3–4 in. long, it is very good when fresh. Sprats can be grilled and served with a mustard butter, or coated in seasoned flour and fried until brown in deep hot oil; they are also smoked. Sprats are in season from October to March.

SPRING ONIONS (GREEN ONIONS). These are little green onions, the undeveloped thinnings of the onion crop, or a crop grown for salad purposes. They are usually served uncooked, cleaned and with salads, but the slightly larger spring onions are also excellent when cooked, giving a somewhat milder flavour than the bigger, older onion.

CREAMED SPRING ONIONS

Wash some spring onions, not too small and with the green ends cut off. Cook the onions in boiling, salted water until tender. While they are cooking, prepare a rich white or Béchamel sauce, well flavoured with mace and a pinch of freshly grated nutmeg, finishing with $\frac{1}{2}$ cup ($\frac{2}{3}$) of cream. The sauce should be thick and highly flavoured. Drain the onions and turn them gently into the cream. Reheat but do not let the sauce boil, and serve.

SPRING ROLL. See EGG ROLLS.

SPRITZIG. German name for a white wine which has a slight tendency to be effervescent or 'lively'.

SPROUTS, BEAN and **PEA.** Pea sprouts are more commonly encountered than soy bean sprouts, despite the fact that the latter name is often applied to both varieties. These sprouts are the roots which issue from the pea or soy bean, each carrying a little hood. It is usual to remove this hood, but it is a tedious process and one simply removes as many as possible when washing the sprouts in water. Pea sprouts are usually fine, white and tender. Soy bean sprouts are crunchy, more strongly flavoured than the pea sprouts and a golden-yellow colour.

SPUMANTE. See ITALIAN WINES.

SPUMONE. See SHERBET.

SQUAB. Squabs are young pigeons, just fledged to the point where they are about to leave the nest. They are never more than 4 weeks old and never weigh more than 14 oz. At this stage they are fat and delicate. They can be cooked in any of the ways for pigeon (which see), but they are best split and fried in a good olive oil, or oil and butter mixed. There is not much meat on such young birds but what there is is good.

SQUASH. Squash is an American term for a wide variety of marrows, pumpkins and gourds which grow throughout the Western Hemisphere. Quite a few varieties were known to the American Indians long before the voyages of discovery.

There are six main varieties of squash, three of which are available in the summer and the remainder in winter. The summer pattypan or cymbling squash is flat, disc-shaped and white. The yellow squash (usually called summer squash) is generally long and crook-necked although efforts are now being made to develop a variety with a straight neck. The green or green-striped variety is known as vegetable marrow, Italian squash, zucchini or courgette.

Summer squashes are usually picked and sold before they are fully ripe. The skin and seeds are therefore tender and the whole squash may be cooked without paring. These varieties should never be allowed to ripen too much as the rind and seeds harden and the flesh becomes fibrous.

The winter squashes include the small, fluted dark green acorn squash (which see). The sweet potato squash, marrow and other similar squashes are pale green, streaked with white and medium in size. The Hubbard squash is the largest and has a rough, dark green skin. One of the best winter squashes is butternut squash. It is sweet and nutty, must be pared and have the fibrous centre removed, and is usually served boiled and mashed with butter and seasonings. In Canada, a sweet squash pie, rather like a pumpkin pie, is made from butternut squash. Winter squashes have hard rinds and seeds. These varieties should be stored in a dark, cool place for some time.

The blossom of the squash can also be used as a vegetable, prepared by dipping in a batter before frying in deep fat. An unusual garnish, composed of unopened squash buds which are sautéed and which open while being cooked, may be served with omelettes and other egg dishes.

See also GOURDS, MARROW, PUMPKIN.

SQUID. A cephalopod mollusk which, like other members of its tribe, secretes a dark brown fluid called sepia.

Squids that are eaten are mostly between six and eight in. long, made up of a long sac with a transparent inner shell and ten tentacles, all with suction discs. They are active creatures, voracious feeders, and lay great quantities of eggs. They are caught and eaten all round the Mediterranean, under different names, and when properly cooked, make good eating.

STAR APPLE   SQUASHES (summer, butternut, Hubbard)   STAR ANISE

SQUIRREL. An arboreal, chiefly vegetarian animal not commonly eaten in Europe but relished throughout the United States. Its meat is white and in taste resembles chicken crossed with rabbit. It can be prepared by any recipe used for either.

STALKY. See WINE TERMS.

STAR ANISE. A kind of aniseed, the seed of an evergreen tree of the magnolia family grown in Japan and China. The tiny seeds are contained in a star-shaped dark brown pod, whence its name. It is curiously different from true aniseed and imparts a delicate flavour to cooking.

STAR APPLE. A medium-sized tropical fruit, a little like an aubergine (egg-plant) in appearance. There are two varieties: one with a green skin, the other a purple skin. The flavour of both is much the same, although there are those who maintain the green is better. When the top of the apple is sliced off it reveals cells forming a star. The flesh is delicious, of a custard-like texture in which black seeds are embedded. It is not a fruit which can be cooked or made into jams.

STARCH. A substance obtained from flour and some vegetables, such as corn, wheat, rice, potatoes and arrowroot, by removing some of its constituents. When heated it swells and is useful as a thickening agent.

STAR-GAZY PIE (A Cornish recipe). This pie is so named because of the way the fish heads gaze upwards.

  6 herrings or pilchards
  butter
  breadcrumbs
  3 eggs
  1 tablespoon (1¼) tarragon vinegar
  salt, pepper and parsley
  ½ lb. short pastry

Thoroughly clean the herrings, cut off their tails but retain their heads. Rub a deep pie dish with butter and line it thickly with breadcrumbs. Arrange the fish like 'mermaids', their heads held high in the middle of the dish. Beat the eggs with vinegar and pour over the herrings. Add salt and pepper to taste. Cover the pie with pastry, making a central hole for the herring to peek out their heads. Bake for 10 minutes in a hot oven, reduce the heat to moderate and continue cooking a further 30 to 40 minutes or until the herrings are cooked. Place a small sprig of fresh parsley in the mouth of each herring before serving.

STEAK. A cut from the fillet, rump, sirloin or other lean and meaty parts of the animal. Thick cuts of fish, such as cod, hake, salmon, swordfish, tuna etc., are also called steaks. Sometimes cakes of ground meat, i.e. Vienna Steak, are so named.

STEAM, TO. A method of cooking which retains the mineral salts, vitamins and flavour of the food. There are several ways of steaming but the following methods are the most usual: 1. in a steamer with a perforated base placed over a pan and fitting perfectly; 2. in a tiered steamer, a very useful utensil, but care must be observed; 3. in a large bowl standing in a pan of boiling water which comes half-way up the sides of the bowl; 4. in a compartment steamer which has several compartments fitted into the pan, and 5. pressure cooking.

STEEP, TO. To soak in hot or cold liquid.

STERLET. A small sturgeon found in the Caspian Sea and the rivers flowing into it. A fine caviar is produced from its roe, isinglass from the bladder, and the flesh is greatly appreciated by connoisseurs.

STEW. A stew may be made with meat, fish and vegetables; it can be brown or white. For the former the meat is browned before the vegetables and liquid are added. In a white stew the meat is put into the pan with cold water or stock and brought to the boil before the vegetables are added. Generally beef is used for a brown stew; mutton, lamb or veal for a white stew.

STEW, TO. A mode of cooking which must not be confused with boiling and is much practised by the French. It is a method of slow cooking by moist heat and can be done in a stewpan, casserole or saucepan, on top of the stove or in the oven. The method of cooking differs from boiling in the comparatively small quantity of liquid used and the prolonged action of a uniformly low degree of moist heat. There is an old saying, 'A stew must smile, never laugh.'

The aim of stewing is to render meat (or other ingredients) tender and it is therefore suitable for cooking either cuts of meat and elderly fowl which are tough, or coarse vegetables. Essentials for success are the use of vessels with close-fitting lids to prevent evaporation; cutting the meat into neat pieces to expose as much of the surface as possible to the solvent action of the water; and the correct proportion of liquid – ½ pint to 1 lb. of meat.

STILTON. A double cream, blue-moulded, semi-hard English cheese made, from May to September, from the richest milk and innoculated with a mould, the *Penicillium glaucum*, which is responsible for the blue veining. It is semi-hard because it is not put through the curdmill or pressed like Cheddar cheese.

Stilton is now legally protected by a trademark (a crown surmounting a Stilton) which can be used only for cheeses of a required standard made by members of the Stilton Cheesemakers Association in Leicestershire, Derbyshire and Nottinghamshire.

Three women are given credit for having 'invented' Stilton: a Mrs Paulet, on the strength of a statement in *Rural Economy*, published in 1790, that 'Mrs Paulet of Wymondham first made Stilton cheese'; a Mrs Orton of Little Dalby, Leicestershire; and a Mrs Stilton, who worked for the fifth Duchess of Rutland in 1800. Again it was alleged that the cheese was sold at the Bell Inn, Stilton, Huntingdonshire, for the *first time* in the last decade of the 18th century by one Cooper Thornhill, a kinsman of the 'inventor', Mrs Paulet.

However, there is documentary evidence that Stilton cheeses were known much earlier. There is a long passage in R. Bradley's *Country Housewife and Lady Director* (6th edition p. 77), published in 1736, concerning Stilton cheese and two lines in Sat. VI of Pope's *Imitation of Horace*.

'Cheese such as men in Suffolk made
But wished it Stilton for his sake.'

Stilton should be white with a blue mould evenly distributed over the whole of the surface. The rind should be well crinkled and regular, free from cracks and a drab brown colour. It is at its best when fully ripe, not less than six months old and preferably nine months. Never scoop a Stilton cheese; this is wasteful and extravagant because after a while the outer crust of cheese dries up and becomes spoilt. It should be cut level and the knife should be drawn straight across the face of the cheese. Stilton traditionally is served with port and biscuits (no butter, since a good cheese does not need butter), and it can be accompanied by a really crisp tart apple.

STINGO. See HUMMING ALE.

STOCK. Stock, the foundation of almost all good soups and many sauces, is the liquid obtained by simmering down various nutritious substances. Simmering is important since good stocks cannot be made quickly. Alexander Dumas called this simmering *faire sourire le pot-au-feu*, to make the pot smile.

A stock can be made and used the same day, but is better if at least one day old. As soon as a stock is made it should be strained, poured into a non-metal bowl and put into a cold larder or refrigerator. This preserves the stock, keeps it fresh and causes the fat to rise to the top and form a thick layer. This is removed before using the stock.

There are old-fashioned rules for stock-making which still hold good. The quality of the bones and flavourings should be good, and the former should be broken for this causes the gelatine to be released quickly. If a large piece of meat or a fowl is used to make stock this can also be used as a main dish.

There are slight variations in stocks but in the main the following three are the basic ones.

Brown Stock. For this meat, bones and vegetables are all browned before being put into the pot.

Brown Bone Stock. Bones only are used, with the vegetables, all browned before being put into the pot.

Light Stock. The meat and vegetables are put directly into the pan without previous browning.

STOCKFISH. See SALT FISH.

STOCKPOT. There was a time, not so long ago, when a stockpot simmered on the kitchen stove in every household. Often such stockpots became culinary dustbins breeding bacteria. As a result stomachs suffered and the stockpot fell into disrepute.

The stockpots of those days were made of well-tinned iron or copper. They were filled with water and into them were thrown all the bones and trimmings of meat and poultry, either dressed or undressed.

STOUT. A very dark ale brewed from well-heated, full-flavoured malts to which a quantity of roasted malt or barley has been added to give the drink its

GARDEN STRAWBERRY

WILD STRAWBERRY

distinctive taste and colouring. It is a strong and highly hopped beer with an alcoholic strength of about 6 per cent by volume. Stout shares with other ales and beers an honourable niche in English social history. Until around 1900 water supplies were often contaminated, and milk was not only expensive but was mostly used to make butter and cheese. Brewing sterilized stouts, ales and beers so that they were often the safest drinks available, stout having the merit of being nourishing as well.

STRACCHINO. A generic name applied to several types of soft whole-milk cheeses made in Italy.

STRAWBERRY. A favourite soft fruit of world fame. It does not seem to have been cultivated by either the Greeks or Romans but even so it has a fascinating history. When William Butler (1535–1618) wrote: 'Doubtless God could have made a better berry but doubtless God never did,' he was referring not to the superlative garden strawberry, but to the small wild or wood strawberry which many consider has greater flavour and fragrance than any of the finest modern cultivated strains. Although this strawberry was at one time cultivated on a large scale, and for centuries was the only variety cultivated in Europe, it is not considered to have been of importance in the development of today's strawberries.

Our present-day strawberries are descended from two main types, the Virginian or Scarlet strawberry, and the Chilean strawberry. It was the large fruit of the latter variety which caught the eye of a French naval officer near Quito in Ecuador. He carried back plants to his native country; two survived and the story of his struggles to keep them alive is fascinating.

Systematic strawberry breeding developed in France, based on the Chilean strawberry; and in Britain rather more on the Virginian. The influences of the two strains can be seen in the different characteristics of the Continental and British varieties.

One of the best ways to eat the cultivated strawberry is gently mashed with sifted sugar and cream. Some people like to dip them into a little salt, declaring this brings out their true flavour and sweetness. Wild or wood strawberries are best served in deep plates, with fine sugar sifted over them and claret or champagne poured over the top.

The wine brings out the flavour and also acts as an antiseptic. Cream does not mix well with the grainy texture of wild strawberries.

Maybe the Romans did not cultivate strawberries but one of the delights of the long Roman summer today is that there are always wild strawberries, served with sugar and often with wine or lemon or orange juice.

Although strawberries have been canned and frozen, still the best way is to eat them fresh and raw. They can be made into jam.

STRAWBERRY TOMATO or **ALKEKENGI**. A yellow, diminutive, tomato-like fruit enclosed in the leafy calyx of several varieties of *Physalis*, the 'Chinese lantern' flower of many English gardens.

STRAWBERRY TREE. See ARBUTE.

STRING BEAN, See BEAN.

STRUDEL. A rich pastry composed of paper-thin dough with a filling, either sweet or savoury. It is usually considered to be an Austrian speciality but in Hungary, where it is called *retes*, it is claimed as Hungarian. The pastry, which can be of flour, egg, water etc., or a yeast pastry, is rolled thinly on a floured cloth on a very large table. The dough is then stretched until it is so thin that print can be read through it. On this is spread a filling: stewed apples with walnuts and raisins, cherries with curd or, if it is to be a savoury dish, cabbage with eggs or fish. The tablecloth is then tilted away from the cook and as the cloth is pulled the strudel forms into a roll. This is placed on a buttered oven sheet and baked in a hot oven. See page 323.

STÜCK. See WINE CONTAINERS.

STUFFINGS. These are made with a variety of

ingredients: ground meats, sausage meats, bread-crumbs, fruit, rice, etc. A wide variety of foods is stuffed, sometimes to give flavour where this is lacking, sometimes to make a main dish out of a minor ingredient and often to correct fattiness or dryness.

When poultry or game is stuffed, every empty corner is filled with stuffing to upholster the bird and help it retain its shape while cooking. A goose is stuffed with bread, apples, onions and herbs in order to correct its excessive greasiness; turkey is stuffed with chestnuts and butter to correct dryness.

Many of the world's most famous dishes are those in which the stuffing rivals the flavour and value of the ingredient being stuffed. The stuffed vine leaves of the Balkans are an example.

STURGEON. Members of the family Acipenseridae of the order *Chondrostei* and among the oldest of the fishes. There are more than 20 species and sub-species all having more or less important value as food fish. Some are landlocked, some entirely maritime and some live in salt water but spawn in fresh water. The most common is the *Acipenser sturio*, which is found on both sides of the Atlantic. It is a bulky, long fish with a tapered, conical nose and a small mouth placed near the lower part of the head. Normally about 8 feet in length, the sturgeon has been known to grow up to 18 feet in the New England area of the United States, while a monster of 14 feet, weighing 2,250 lb. was caught in the Volga river in Russia in 1912. The female, when ready to spawn, carries eggs of greyish-black approximately one-tenth of an inch in diameter and such quantity that they make up one-third of the fish's weight. These make, when sorted, salted and packed, the famous delicacy, caviar (which see). The flesh of the sturgeon, while attractively white, is coarse in texture and inclined to be hard. Generally, like game, it should be hung and marinated before cooking. The best ways of cooking are sautéeing or grilling steaks of the fish in un-salted butter, or gently baking it whole with herbs and flavourings. Known as a 'royal' fish in Britain, it is usually encountered only during wartime food shortages or for special celebrations. Sturgeon caught in British waters are traditionally offered to the monarch.

SUBTLE. See WINE TERMS.

SUCCOTASH. A traditional American dish which is a combination of sweet corn kernels and lima beans. There are slight variations in different parts of the country.

SUDUIRAUT, CH. See BORDEAUX WINES.

SUET. The fat around the kidneys and loin of animals used for food. It applies specifically to sheep and bullocks, and is brought either in solid form or packaged and grated ready for use. It is used in stuffings, mincemeat, puddings, and in suet-crust pastry. Unprepared suet must be cleaned, skinned and finely chopped before using. Covered with flour, it will keep for some days.

SUGAR, BEET. During the 18th century, sugar crystals were first obtained from beet by a German chemist, Andreas Marggraf; but the commercial development did not flourish until the Napoleonic Wars. Napoleon worried about supplies from the sugar areas and gave money and encouragement to his scientists to produce sugar. The result was that by the end of the 19th century beet had replaced cane as the principal source of sugar in continental Europe.

SUGAR, CANE. The first reference to sugar is found in Far Eastern mythology, where it is told that man and woman emerged from sugar cane. Ancient records show that it was used as a food by the Polynesians and found its way to India in 300 B.C., where later one of Alexander the Great's admirals described it as 'reeds which make honey without bees'. The use of sugar spread through to Persia and Egypt, then to the warring Arabs who carried sugar with them as they pushed westwards.

By the 15th century, sugar refining was a lucra-tive business confined to Venice. It was such a precious commodity that a shipload brought to England was considered worth £1 million. Today London is the centre of the sugar trade, a position she has held since the 17th century.

One of the reasons for the high price of sugar was the difficulty of growing it in the Mediterranean region. Christopher Columbus took some sugar cane roots for trial planting in the West Indies; these thrived in the heat and plentiful rain, and for the next 300 years European nations fought to get a hold on the sugar-growing areas. Sugar was called 'white gold'.

Sugar cane is not an easy crop. The cane grows up to 12–15 feet high and as it deteriorates quickly after cutting, handling the crop must be done with almost military precision. Sugar refining is centred in metropolitan areas for ease of marketing and transporting.

The types of sugar available are as follows:
Ordinary granulated sugar is for everyday use.
Finest granulated is a sugar with a bright sparkle. Its crystals are smaller and more regular in size than ordinary granulated, and the sparkle makes it good for cake decorating.
Castor sugar, called superfine in the United States, dissolves quickly and therefore is popular

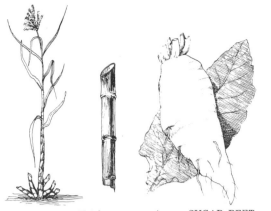

SUGAR CANE (plant an_ane)   SUGAR BEET

STURGEON

for use with fruit and cereals. It is a useful sugar for puddings because it is easily absorbed, and is used in cakes and pastry.

Icing sugar is called confectioners' or powdered sugar in the United States, and is used to make icing (frosting) and meringues.

Coffee crystals are large and were produced for coffee connoisseurs who like the first sip of their coffee to be bitter. The crystals dissolve slowly and only gradually sweeten the coffee. They come in clear white, light brown and a mixture of colours.

Cube sugar has succeeded the so-called loaf sugar which was produced in the shape of a conical loaf, then broken into pieces for easy use. Cubes are popular for hot drinks and are convenient to use as an exact quantity can be measured into the cup or glass. Cube sugar is available in different sizes.

Preserving crystal sugar has smaller crystals than coffee crystals but larger than granulated and is used for preserving fruit, jams and pickles. When in the pan the crystals do not settle on the bottom in a thick layer and therefore need less stirring to prevent burning. They also produce virtually no froth and therefore less skimming is required.

Refined brown sugars range in colour from golden to dark brown. They are used with cereals, coffee and in the making of fruit cakes and puddings. The darker the colour of sugar, the stronger its flavour. This sugar must be distinguished from the brown crystal sugar popularly known as Demerara.

Demerara sugar is merely raw sugar from which only the coarse impurities have been removed.

Barbados, almost black, is the darkest of brown sugars and is soft and moist.

Sand or *soft sugar* is pale brown and is indeed like damp sand.

Foot sugar is a raw sugar containing a large proportion of molasses; like Barbados, but coarser.

SUGAR, SPUN. This is sugar and water boiled together to the crack or brittle stage, worked to give fine glass-like threads, and used for certain puddings or confectionery. The sugary mixture is pulled and worked into baskets, flower shapes and other ornaments.

SULPHUR. See WINE TERMS.

SULTANA. The name of the dried grape of a vine producing long cylindrical bunches of small, round seedless grapes, golden-yellow and very sweet. They are called seedless white raisins in the United States. These are first sun-dried, then cured to bleach and preserve. They were originally shipped from Izmir in Turkey when the town was called Smyrna and thus named Smyrna raisins. Some sultanas still come from Turkey. California produces two or three varieties, and the vineyards of both Australia and South Africa produce large quantities of excellent sultanas. See GRAPE.

SUMMER PUDDING. Probably one of the best of the British puddings, but one which can only be made perfectly during one month of the year, the brief period in mid-summer when raspberries and redcurrants are picked at the same time. The classic recipe of bread and fruit is easily digested and the Victorians called it 'Hydropathic Pudding'.

1 lb. each redcurrants and raspberries
sugar to taste
8 thin slices of stale crustless white bread

Wash and prepare the fruit and gently cook it in a very little water until just soft. Sweeten to taste. Line a medium-sized pudding bowl with two-thirds of the bread, wedging the slices so closely together that they slightly overlap. Completely fill the bowl with the cooked fruit and cover the top with the remaining bread. Cover with a saucer, put a heavy weight on top and leave overnight. Turn out to serve, accompanied by whipped cream.

SUNDAE. An ice-cream served with a topping of fruit or syrup and a sauce. A truly American creation, it is supposed to have been invented when the State of Massachusetts enforced stringent laws on the sale of soft beverages on a Sunday. One enterprising salesman simply omitted the soda water from the ice-cream soda and thus complied with the law and produced a new dish appropriately named sundae. The combinations are endless and fabulous.

SUNFLOWER OIL See OIL.

SUOMUURAIN. A Finnish liqueur, sometimes called *Lakka*, made from cloudberries, which are grown in the Arctic North and have a delicate, bitter-sweet flavour.

SUPRÊME. A culinary term used when the breast and wing fillet of a game bird or poultry is removed in one piece, while uncooked, from each side of the bird. This dish is cooked and served with a *sauce suprême* (which see). It also applies to fillets of sole, *foie gras* or veal or any particularly chosen piece.

SURINAM CHERRY. A fruit of South American origin which takes its name from the country of Surinam, formerly Dutch Guiana. In this area it is also called *pitanga* but its botanical name is *Eugenia uniflora* and it should not be confused with the West Indian Cherry (which see).

The cherry is small and when not yet ripe is a bright red, gradually deepening until a dark red when quite ripe. It is distinctly eight-ribbed, oblate in shape and about 1 in. in diameter with a single seed surrounding a juicy soft flesh. While one does sometimes meet a Surinam cherry which has a sub-acid kind of sweetness, in general the fruit is acid and slightly bitter.

Surinam cherries can be cooked, sweetened, and used as a fruit sauce, or a filling in pies and tarts, or made into jellies and sherbets for serving with meat and poultry dishes. They are also frequently combined with other fruits, and a sliced cherry can be added to a fruit cocktail with good effect.

The tree grows in Florida and California and at one period was taken to Hawaii where it grows prolifically and is often cultivated as much for its great beauty as for its fruits.

SUSHI-MESHI. This is Japanese vinegared rice. Starchy polished rice of the finest quality is used for it. Originally *sushi* meant pickled fish and it was made by placing fish between layers of rice. After a while the rice fermented and became sour. The fish was considered good eating; the rice was thrown away. Now *sushi* has come to mean thin slices of fish or vegetable, and other edible small bits such as seaweed, beautifully arranged on small portions of vinegared rice, each portion looking like a small open sandwich. *Sushi* is served as a snack and there are *sushi* bars throughout the country; or exquisitely arranged boxes of *sushi* can be bought to take home, as Westerners buy boxes of chocolates. *Sushi* always forms part of any picnic lunch.

SWAN. Known in Britain as royal birds, these seldom appear on modern menus except on special occasions, such as the annual swan feast held by the Vintners Company. Even then, it is the cygnet which is served and the breast only is eaten. The flavour resembles that of a goose.

SWAN EGG. More delicate than the swan's size and tendency to eat fish would suggest, they are usually hard-boiled, but can be poached.

SWEAT. To cook gently in melted fat until the food, usually vegetables, 'sweats' or exudes juice. It is a preliminary for stewing and soup-making and should not be confused with frying. Sweating is also called 'fat-steaming'.

SWEDE or **RUTABAGA.** Also called Swedish turnip, this is a species of turnip with yellow-orange flesh (although there is a variety called *chou navet* with white flesh). Swedes are much larger and firmer, and less watery than turnips and make an excellent and palatable vegetable. They can be cooked in any of the ways of turnips. Boiled until tender, mashed with plenty of butter and seasoned well with black pepper, they are delicious.

SWEET AND SOUR. The Chinese sweet-sour dishes are the best known, although there are a large number of Italian ones. In Chinese cooking sweet and sour means sugar and vinegar with a good flavouring of soy sauce. In Italy raisins and chocolate are also used in sweet-sour dishes.

SWEETBREADS. Each animal possesses two kinds of sweetbreads, one found in the throat (throat sweetbread) and the other in the body proper, called heart or belly sweetbread. The latter are the best and the more expensive. Usually only calf's and lamb's sweetbreads are used in cooking although beef sweetbreads may be used when mixed with other meats in a filling or garnish. Throat sweetbreads are small and elongated in shape; heart sweetbreads are rounded. Both veal and lamb sweetbreads are white and tender. Sweetbreads are the glands of the animals.

Sweetbreads used always to be bought in pairs, but are now sold by weight and it is essential that they are bought very fresh as they quickly spoil. They should be plunged immediately into cold water to draw out the blood, and kept in it for one or two hours, with the water changed frequently. Certain preparation is necessary always before the actual cooking. To cook, drop the sweetbreads into a pan of fresh, salted cold water (just enough to cover), flavoured with lemon juice. Bring the water to the boil, then simmer for 15 minutes. Take the sweetbreads from the pan, drain well, again plunge into cold water and leave for a few minutes. Drain and carefully pick out the membranes and tubes

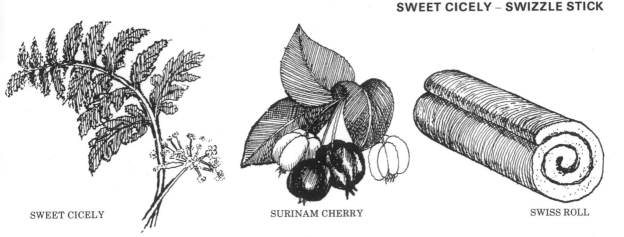

SWEET CICELY   SURINAM CHERRY   SWISS ROLL

without breaking the tissues. The sweetbreads can then be left in the refrigerator but not too long for they quickly absorb other flavours. Sweetbreads should be bought and used on the same day.

SWEET CICELY. An aromatic and beautiful herb also called giant chervil (French *cerfeuil*) or fern-leaved chervil. It is used in salads and stews.

SWEET CORN. See CORN.

SWEET PEPPER. See PIMIENTO.

SWEET POTATO or **BATATA.** The sweet potato is grown in the southern United States and in the West Indies. It is a tuber of a creeping vine and a member of the convolvulus group. It is usually long, reddish to purple skinned and has a sweet yellow flesh. Sweet potatoes were introduced into Britain and other European countries some three hundred years ago and were, at the time, popular. As far as Britain is concerned they have lost their early popularity and now are scarcely known, except as a vegetable eaten by the West Indians. There are actually hundreds of varieties of sweet potatoes, which although sometimes confused with yams belong to a different family. In the United States sweet potatoes are a popular vegetable and can be bought fresh, canned or dehydrated. They can be boiled, sliced or mashed, made into a sweet dish with milk, sugar and grated coconut, or spiced. They are also roasted in hot ashes or baked in the oven. A favourite tropical and North American method is to candy them.

SWEET SOP. A member of the Anona or custard apple family. Its skin is yellow-green, thick and rough and the flesh custard-like and sweet.

SWISS ROLL. Called jelly roll in the United States, this is a variety of sponge cake baked in a shallow baking pan, spread with jam and rolled while still hot.

SWISS WINES. While not claiming to make the best wines in Europe, Switzerland does boast the highest vineyard, 3,600 feet above sea level in the Valais. Another curious statistic claimed by Switzerland is that although only 22nd in the world list of wine-growers, with an annual production of 22 million gallons, she tops the table of wine importers, mainly with red wine from Italy. The mountainous nature of the country does not lend itself easily to vineyards. However, there is hardly a canton in Switzerland that does not have its own vineyards, and between them there is a varied output of different types of wine. But only four cantons grow grapes on any appreciable scale: Valais, Vaud, Neuchâtel and Tessin. Vaud claims to make the best white wines in Switzerland, between Vevey and Lausanne, but the Chablais district in the Rhône valley makes wine with a higher alcoholic content. Higher up the Rhône valley in Valais the vineyards there are the white Fendant and the Dôle, the latter considered to be the best red wine in Switzerland. The white wines of Neuchâtel are light but sparkling and not intended to be matured over a number of years but to be drunk sitting in the sun on the shores of Lake Neuchâtel. Tessin has emerged from a bad period and now produces good and cheap red wine mostly consumed by the local population and the tourists who flock to this region.

SWIZZLE. A long, cooling drink originating in the West Indies and consisting of spirits, bitters, lime juice and sugar, twirled with crushed ice to make it intensely cold. The swizzle takes its name from the spirit used, such as gin swizzle, rum swizzle, etc.

SWIZZLE STICK. These are made of hard wood or silver and are used by people who do not care for highly-aerated waters or fizzy drinks. If swizzled round in champagne, for example, it releases the gases and reduces the effervesence. In the West Indies there is a bush with radiating roots known as the swizzle stick bush. The bark is stripped off to the joint where there are five little offshoots, making a swizzle stick for use in all swizzles as well as for soups, custards and egg whisking.

SWORDFISH. One of the best of eating fish, related oddly enough to mackerel. It is a large meaty fish which can weigh from 60 to 300 lb. Its upper jaw is prolonged to make a vicious sword which has cost many a fisherman his life or a limb. The flesh is firm, with something of the texture of veal. It can be cooked in any of the ways of cooking tunny (tuna) fish but is perhaps at its best grilled or skewered in the Turkish manner. Another Turkish swordfish speciality is *lâkerda* which is salted and sliced thinly, rather like smoked salmon.

SYLLABUB. Variously spelled sillebub, sillabub, this is an old-fashioned sweet dish made from wine (or beer and cider) and fresh milk. The name supposedly comes from a combination of Sille or Sillery, part of the Champagne country and once the best-known wine name in England, and bub, Elizabethan colloquial for a bubbling drink. As a syllabub was made by mixing frothing milk and alcohol the name was a natural.

SYRUP. The French *sirop* and the American sirup; basically a thick solution of sugar in water. Add 4 cups (5) of sugar to one cup (1¼) of water and bring to the boil. Let it simmer till the liquid clears, then cool and bottle. This is the simplest sort of syrup also known in America as bar, gomme or gum sirup. The degree of its sweetness can be altered by varying the quantity of sugar.

Syrups may also be flavoured with fruit juices and other substances. In France, for example, almond, cherry, strawberry, raspberry, lemon, orange, coffee, rose and violet syrups are available and most are made at home, particularly by provincial housewives. Syrups make a refreshing drink when mixed with water or soda water, and syrups of red fruits mixed with a new white wine make a drink popular in France.

Maple syrup is much appreciated in America and used with griddle cakes of all sorts.

SYRUP, GOLDEN. A light sweet syrup which is made from the liquid left over after the sugar crystals have been removed during the refining process. It is processed and evaporated to give the required consistency.

T

TABASCO. A red pepper of the prolific capsicum or pepper family. It was introduced into the United States from the state of Tabasco, Mexico.

Tabasco sauce is a famous and proprietary brand of peppery sauce made of spirit, vinegar, red pepper and salt. It was marketed in 1868 in the United States and is now also made in Britain under licence. Because of its fiery nature only a few drops are needed to give zest to soups, gravies etc.

TÂCHE, LA. See BURGUNDY WINES.

TAGLIARINI. Very narrow Italian egg noodles, not more than about ⅛ in. wide.

TAGLIATELLE. Italian egg noodles cut into ribbons about ¼ in. wide.

TAHINA or TAHENEH. This is a rather thin paste made from sesame seeds crushed in a mill. A great Middle Eastern favourite, it is served there as an appetizer with Arab bread and various other ingredients to make a form of salad.

TALBOT, CH. See BORDEAUX WINES.

TALENCE. See BORDEAUX WINES.

TALMOUSE. The culinary name of a small individual soufflé usually flavoured with grated cheese and served as an hors d'oeuvre. Also a small, cheese-flavoured tartlet.

TAMALE. Mexican food is usually chilli-hot and the *tamale*, one of that country's best-known dishes, is no exception. It is made with *nixtamal*, a special cornmeal, in a number of ways but chiefly as a casserole, *tamale de cazuela*, which always calls for freshly-boiled chicken. However, in Central America left-overs are also used.

A *tamale* pie is another form it may take. A recipe for this calls for two roasting chickens which are combined with garlic, oil, onions, a lavish 1 tablespoon (1¼) of chilli powder, red and green peppers, corn pulp and lime or orange juice baked in a casserole lined with a paste crust of seasoned cornmeal and eggs.

TAMARIND. The fruit or pod of a handsome tree which grows to a great height, size and age. The pods, even on the same tree, vary in size and shape; some are long, like beans, others sickle-shaped. They start life green, then are covered with a thin film which turns them brown. Fresh from the tree the pulp, which has a pleasant sweet-sour flavour, is white and crisp and said to contain more acid and more sugar than any other fruit. After exposure it becomes a reddish brown. The tree is cultivated throughout India and Burma, as well as in other parts of the East and the West Indies. It is believed that the acid pulp, which is laxative and cooling, is also good against fevers. It is used in Indian cooking to flavour curries, in chutneys, for pick-

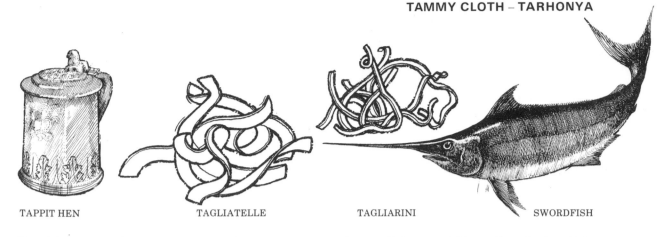

TAPPIT HEN   TAGLIATELLE   TAGLIARINI   SWORDFISH

ling fish and to make sauces. Tamarind sauce with pork is particularly good. Diluted tamarind pulp is made into a cooling drink and it sometimes flavours guava jelly. It is available in England in Indian shops, and it is sold as *tamarindo* in Mexican shops in the United States.

TAMMY CLOTH. A thick cloth made of some rough textured material (Dr Kitchener recommended worsted) through which liquids are strained. Nowadays, it has largely been replaced by a sieve.

TANDURI CHICKEN. Marinated and spiced chicken threaded on a long skewer and roasted in a hot primitive oven *(tandur)* (see page 324).

TANGELO. An American cross between the dancy (a sweet tangerine) and a grapefruit. Tangelos are about the size of an orange, juicy, sweet-smelling and easily peeled. They are a delicious eating fruit, used as tangerines. The flavour is sweet-tart.

TANGERINE. See ORANGE.

TANGLEBERRY. A sort of huckleberry which grows wild in some parts of America. Tangleberries are sweet and piquant in flavour and may be eaten fresh in fruit salads, pies and puddings.

TANNIN. See WINE TERMS.

TANSY. 1. A decorative herb which grows wild in Britain and other parts of Europe and in the United States, where it is also grown commercially. Its flavour is bitter but, like many other herbs, varies from place to place. Some claim it resembles rosemary in flavour, while others, camphor or lemon. It is not much used in cooking today although there are advocates of it as a flavouring for omelettes, meat pies, freshwater fish and salads.
    2. A sweet dish made from eggs, cream, breadcrumbs, sugar, lemon juice, and juice from pounded tansy leaves. It can be flavoured with brandy, sherry or orange-flower water. Tansy pudding was eaten on Easter Day.

TA PIN LO. Chinese and Mongolian chafing dish.

TAPIOCA. This is an easily digested, almost pure starch used to thicken soups and broths and also to make a pudding dressed with cream or fruit. It is produced in South and Central America, Africa and the West Indies, in the Far East and parts of India. It is made from the fleshy root of cassava, manioc or manihot, which is a common temperate and tropical plant. Tapioca flour is used as widely as wheat flour as a staple part of local diets in regions where it flourishes. Tapioca, when roasted and sifted, is graded and sold as flake, bullet, medium and pearl.

TAPPIT HEN. The Scottish name for a hen with a crest or top-knot and also for a pewter drinking vessel having a lid with a knob.

TARAMASALATA. A 'salad' from Greece, made from the roe of mullet or tunny (tuna) fish. The roe is mixed in a bowl with an equal quantity of bread, previously soaked in water and squeezed dry. When completely blended, olive oil is gradually added until the mixture has the consistency of a soft, but not too soft, purée. A little lemon juice is added to loosen it slightly. It is served as an appetizer.

TARGOLA. A fruit of the *tar* or *tad* palm, the same palm which gives its name to toddy (which see), and grows in India. *Gola* means a ball. It is a large fruit, which when sliced open reveals lumps of cool, translucent jelly about the size and shape of a flattened chestnut. These lumps are embedded in several inches of whitish pith and the jelly is protected from the pith by a yellowish skin which is easily peeled off. Targolas can be chilled and served with cream or eaten alone, as they come from the palm. They are pleasant to eat, although tougher than jelly.

TARHONYA. This is a type of *pasta*, i.e. flour

mixed with eggs, kneaded to a firm dough and then grated to make tiny pellets. It is lightly fried until a golden brown, when a little water is added. It is then cooked for 5 minutes, by which time the water has evaporated. More water is then added and the *tarhonya* cooked for a further 30 minutes. It is used as a garnish for meat or game dishes.

TARO. A vegetable widely cultivated in tropical regions which forms the staple food for many Pacific Islanders. It is a stemless plant with wide and exceedingly long leaves. Its chief value lies in its starchy root, which can be boiled or baked and made into a pudding or bread. The stalks are also cooked in the same manner as asparagus. The leaves are cooked like spinach (although they lack the bitter spinach flavour) and dressed with coconut milk. The root can be cooked, pounded and pressed into a firm mass which will keep for months.

TARRAGON. One of the great herbs, the best type of which is the French tarragon. It is used in many dishes of French origin and is essential in *sauce Béarnaise* or *Poulet à l'estragon*. It is part of the *fines herbes* for an omelette, is used in butters etc., and often in salads. Tarragon also flavours vinegar and certain liqueurs.

TARRAGONA. See SPANISH WINES.

TART. A dish of ancient origin. Chaucer mentioned it in *Canterbury Tales*; Pepys recalls a meal which included three tarts. Generally tarts are considered those dishes with an undercrust only and no crust covering the filling. But, looking through old cookery books, one sees that pie and tart are used indiscriminately. For example, from the 18th century are recipes which say, referring to tarts: 'If you bake in Tin-patties, butter them and you must put a little Crust all over, because of the taking them out: If in China or Glass, no Crust but the Top-one.' And one is surprised at the use of baking glass in those days.

In *Kettner's Book of the Table*, published in 1877, we read an interesting theory. 'A tart has nothing to do with tartness; it is identical with the French *tourte* and *tarte*, the old name for a kind of loaf, and with *tartine*, which still exists as a name for a slice of loaf. It is the Latin *torta* (from *torqueo*), which answers nearly enough to our roll of bread. Now, our fathers in the Middle Ages were rather deficient in plates, and it is curious to read of the little odd contrivances by which at grand feasts they tried to supply the want, and to make one plate do for two or three guests. Some genius discovered that the undercrust of bread would serve for a plate, and for a long period in France the undercrust of the *tourte* or *tarte* was the most common of dinner plates – at which period a family were wont, after eating their dinner, to eat their dinner plate. These dinner plates, made of dinner rolls, were in course of time specially prepared, were made more cakelike, were filled with dainty food, and were called, according to their size, tart or tartlets. The strict meaning of a tart, therefore, is an open crust of the nature of a plate . . . .'

TARTARE SAUCE. See SAUCES.

TARTARIC ACID. One of the most common vegetable acids and the chief acid of wines. It is also found in berries, in particular the rowanberry, and in certain other fruits, but can be obtained in powdered (and pure) form from chemist shops. It dissolves quickly in water and is used in some home-made wines and in lemon squash.

TASTEVIN, CONFRÉRIE DES CHEVALIERS DU. See BURGUNDY WINES.

TAVERNA. Briefly, a Greek eating house, but really a way of living for the Greeks. Tavernas exist for every type of appetite, every type of purse, every type of temperament, even for every type of food. A taverna to the Greek is what the pub is to the Englishman, and the *bistro* to the Frenchman. It is convivial, full-blooded and noisy with a buzz of talk and the clatter of waiters. A traditional taverna is small, with one room which is kitchen and dining room combined, a courtyard, and just a few tables and enough customers to make it amusing.

TAWNY. See PORT and WINE TERMS.

TEA. Legend has it that one day in 2737 B.C. Emperor Shen Nung of China was resting by a camp fire waiting for a pot of water to boil. Some scorched leaves from the open fire fell into the pot giving a pleasant aroma, which intrigued the Emperor because of his great interest in herbs and concoctions for medicinal purposes. He decided to taste this boiling water with the leaves in it and he liked what he tasted. He experimented further and the world's tea or 'ch'a' industry was thus born.

The Indians and Japanese have their own versions of the discovery of tea. In both cases an Indian Buddhist monk named Darma or Dharuma is believed to have vowed to contemplate for nine years without sleep, but in the course of his meditation he began to feel drowsy. He plucked a few leaves from a nearby bush and chewed them whereupon, say the Indians, he was refreshed and able to keep his vigil. The leaves were said to be tea leaves. The Japanese say that when Darma felt drowsy he was disgusted with himself and tore off

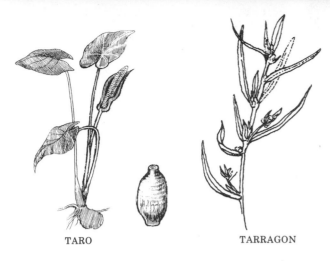

TARO TARRAGON

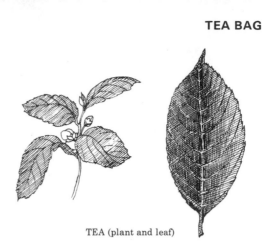

TEA (plant and leaf)

his eyelids and threw them away and where they fell they sprouted as tea plants. The astonished Darma boiled the leaves and drank the brew. It so refreshed him that he was able to fulfill his vow.

Tea is referred to as Tcha, Ch'a, Chaun, K'u t'u, Meng, T'e and T'u. Some of these may be references to a plant of a similar character, but by the 8th century tea in China, apart from its original medicinal use, had become a popular social drink and an important commodity of trade. A self-educated scholar, Lu Yu published a three-volume treatise, 'Ch'a Ching', on tea in A.D. 780, which testifies to its importance. By A.D. 800 tea drinking had spread to Japan, where the tea ceremony, whose rules had been laid down in China, is still an elaborate ritual.

Tea was first brought to Europe in the 17th century by the Dutch, who purchased it from Chinese trading junks reaching Java and Sumatra. From Holland it was re-exported to England and France, and in 1658 Thomas Garway published this announcement: 'That excellent and by all Physicions approved drink called by the Chineans Tscha, by other nations Tay alias Tea is sold at the Sultaness Head of cophe house in Sweetings Rents by the Royal Exchange London.'

Tea rapidly gained in popularity, ousting coffee. By the middle of the 18th century it was the principal beverage in England with Dr Johnson among its ardent champions. Tea consumption steadily increased and today Britain, the world's largest consumer, annually imports 500 million lb. and an average Briton drinks about 2,000 cups a year.

Robert Bruce of the Bengal Artillery, and then his brother Charles, also a soldier, discovered indigenous tea plants in Assam in 1823. The Government of India eventually decided to develop the industry and the first consignment of eight chests of Assam tea arrived in London in 1839. In the same year the government handed over the industry to private enterprise. Tea was planted in other parts of India as well with Darjeeling and the Nilgiris (South India) among the famous centres. Indian tea began to capture the British market and

India is now the leading supplier to Britain. Ceylon and Indonesia emerged as producers in 1869 and 1878 respectively.

Today India, Ceylon, Indonesia, Pakistan and East Africa are the main suppliers. The best tea comes from India and the highlands of Ceylon.

There are three basic sorts of teas: black or fermented; green or unfermented; and oolong or semi-fermented. Black teas are the most common in use. There are several varieties and sub-varieties of tea. The leaf grades include Orange Pekoe, Pekoe and Pekoe Souchong, which has large leaves. The broken grades have smaller and broken leaves and are quick brewing and strong. These include Broken Orange Pekoe, Broken Pekoe Souchong and Fannings or Pekoe Fannings. Then there is a tea known as Dusts which is suitable for blending purposes. These gradings are not based on quality but on the size of the leaf.

The flavour of tea varies from one tea estate to another and also from season to season. Most teas available in the market are blended teas: it is not unusual to use 25 different grades of tea to make a single blend. Almost every blend contains a substantial quantity of Indian tea.

Green tea is completely unfermented and the leaf is plucked without its stalk and steamed instead of being allowed to wither naturally. Most of the teas made in China and Japan are of this type but China also has black teas such as Panyon and Ichang.

Oolong teas are a cross between black and green teas. The leaf is allowed to wither slightly before panning and a slight ferment is allowed to develop. These teas are very popular in America and are made almost exclusively in Formosa.

Black tea is usually drunk with milk and sugar but it may also be taken with lemon. Iced tea is a refreshing summer drink. Tea ice-cream and punches are also growing in popularity. To make hot black tea allow one teaspoon for each cup and one for the pot. Pour boiling water into a well-warmed teapot and allow it to infuse the leaves.

TEA BAG. Small bags made of special paper which contain just enough tea to produce one cup. The flavour is barely distinguishable from tea made with loose leaves.

TEA-CADDY. A container in which tea was formerly kept. The word is a corruption of the Malay and Indian word *kati*, a measure of weight. When tea was expensive it was the custom to keep the family tea locked up in boxes, a practice which continued for some time after tea became commonplace. The caddies were often divided into two sections, one for 'green' or China tea and the other for 'black' or Indian tea.

TEA CANNISTER. A japanned or metal container with a well-fitting lid in which tea was kept.

TEA INFUSER. A sort of double spoon with holes in it formerly used when a quick cup of tea was wanted. It was the forerunner of the tea bag (which see).

TEAL. See DUCK, WILD.

TEAL, CAPE. Also known as the Cape widgeon, this is a small wild river duck, found from Ethiopia to Botswana and is good for the table.

TEAPOT. A lidded pot with a spout and handle made to contain an infusion of tea. The first teapots were of Chinese origin, made of stoneware of different colours either plain or decorated. These were the models for the earliest European teapots, first made in Holland and later in the 17th century in Staffordshire. The first-known English teapot is a tall cylindrical one with a conical cover, a short tubular spout, and the handle set at right-angles. It looks more like a modern coffee pot. But it is inscribed as a 'tea Pott . . . presented to ye East India Company'. Gradually over the years different shapes were created and teapots were made from silver, porcelain and red earthenware.

TEASEED OIL. An edible oil extracted from a plant of the tea family.

TEMPURA. Japanese deep-fried foods.

TENCH. In many parts of Britain the tench is called the 'Doctor Fish' because it is believed its slimy skin exudes a fluid which will cure any sick fish that rubs against its sides. It likes sluggish, muddy waters, but Izaak Walton wrote amiably that 'it eats pleasantly'. A fairly common fish in Britain, the tench is a smaller member of the carp family and makes quite good eating when cooked *au bleu* or grilled.

TEQUILA. The national drink of Mexico. It is named after a small town in the state of Jalisco, where the blue or *tequilana* agave grows in profusion and from this the drink is distilled. It is believed the Spaniards were the first to distil tequila from the agave plant.

TERRAPIN. See TURTLE, TERRAPIN and TORTOISE.

TERRINE. An earthenware dish, oval or round in shape with a cover. *Terrines* are fairly deep, of varying dimensions and with ears. By extension the word has come to mean also the food cooked in them: *terrine de foie gras* or *terrine de gibier* (game *pâté*), or *pâté en terrine*, which means that the *pâté* has been cooked in a *terrine* rather than in a crust (this would be *pâté en croûte*).

TERTRE, DU. See BORDEAUX WINES.

TÊTE DE CUVÉE. The best part of any particular pressing or vatting, from the best picking of the grapes in any good vintage.

THALI. Deep round metal tray used in India on which is served different foods in small metal bowls.

THICKENING. A term applied in cookery to the adding to sauces, soups etc., egg yolks or certain farinaceous substances either to thicken or to bind them.

THIMBLEBERRY. An American species of raspberry which grows wild from northern Michigan to the Pacific coast. The berries are light red when ripe and have a pleasant flavour.

THORNBACK. See CRAB.

THYME. An important culinary herb of which there are several varieties (among them lemon, caraway and orange), all with different flavours. Basically the plant is small, bushy, with tiny dark green leaves and purple flowers. Thyme is used in bouquet garni and in such famous dishes as *boeuf à la bourguignonne, estofat de boeuf*; also in soups and stews, with a large number of vegetables, in fish and in a *court bouillon*. It flavours stuffing, is used in *terrines, salmis*, game dishes including rabbit and hare.

TIFFIN. A word which at one time in India and neighbouring countries meant luncheon or a light repast. There was also the verb, to tiff, or to take luncheon. There have been many theories as to the origin of this word, but the derivation would appear to be English. The word goes back to the middle of the 18th century.

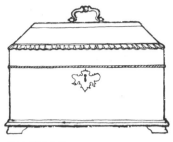

TEA CADDY

TEA INFUSER

TILAPIA. A genus of fish of the family Cichlidae of which several species from East African lakes are important as food. There is a large commercial fishery in Lake Victoria; they are found in smaller lakes and dams, and in the Nile.

TILSIT CHEESE. A German cheese, although also made in Switzerland. It is of the Port Salut type, well-punctured with tiny holes. The United States also produces a tilsit, which is milder than the original.

TIMBALE. This may be a pastry shell with a wide variety of sweet or savoury fillings; the term describes an egg dish akin to a soufflé or custard, although it may be made of brioche, genoise or baba dough. The timbale owes its name to its generally round shape: the word derives from Arab-Persian *atabal*, meaning a kettledrum.

There are French dishes made of copper, tin or china, round in shape with straight or sloping sides, also called timbales, which were made to imitate the appearance of a pie crust. Those foods which are cooked in such dishes have taken their name from them, i.e. *timbale de macaroni*, or *timbale de riz*.

TINAJA. See SPANISH WINES.

TIPSY CAKE. An old English sweet pudding. For this a moulded sponge or light cake, some 2 or 3 days old, is required. Make sure it is quite level at the bottom and place it in a shallow glass dish. Pierce it several times with a skewer. Pour over it as much red wine, mixed with 2 wine glasses of brandy, as it will absorb. Take up the liquor that flows into the dish and pour it over the cake again and again until it is quite soaked. Stick split almonds in the cake and cover with cold custard. The soaked cake often tumbles drunkenly sideways – hence the name.

TISANE. A French term to denote a herbal tea made by pouring boiling water over a wide variety of either fresh or dried flowers. More medicinal than culinary, it can be a refreshing brew with a mild tonic. Tisanes have been known for a long time and were made in China. Delicate ladies of Europe and America in the 18th and 19th centuries drank them; they were held to be beneficial if taken before retiring or after an evening meal.

A tisane made of camomile, a small daisy-like plant belonging to the aster family, is one of the better-known kinds. A level teaspoon ($1\frac{1}{4}$) of dried or 2 heaped teaspoons ($2\frac{1}{2}$) of fresh camomile are used to a cup of boiling water. It may be flavoured with a little lemon juice or sweetened with honey. The French have long drunk tisanes made of various herbs such as *vervaine* and *queues de cerises*, using them to stimulate or to soothe.

TISANE DE CHAMPAGNE. A second-class or second pressing champagne wine which is light in colour and alcoholic strength.

TOAD-IN-THE-HOLE. A fanciful folk-name for pieces of tender meat, lamb cutlets, sausages or even kidneys baked in batter.

TOAST. Generally one means by this term slices of bread browned on both sides. Not so long ago toast was made in front of a bright coal fire, with the bread impaled on the end of a toasting fork. Often the toast fell into the fire or suddenly burst into flame, but these were natural hazards which frightened no one. With the coming of electric and gas grills bread was toasted under these. Automatic toasters have taken all hazards (and fun) out of toasting. One can pre-select the degree of brownness one wants the toast to be, and the moment it is done the machine stops operating and up pops the toast. It is then either immediately buttered, if a soft toast is preferred, or put into a rack for a crisp toast; the brief stay in the rack allows the moisture to escape.

TODDY. Two sorts of drink are called toddy. The first is the fermented or unfermented sap of palm trees which grow in tropical and subtropical countries. In northern latitudes toddy is a hot drink made with spirits, hot water, sugar and lemon.

TOFFEE. One of the most popular forms of sweet-meats in Britain. It is a preparation of ancient origin and has been variously spelt as taffy or toffy. The derivation of the name seems obscure. It could be a corruption of tafia, a variety of rum made from molasses: toffee was originally made from black treacle, and perhaps flavoured with rum. Old cookery books all give many recipes for toffee, usually for something called Everton toffee and for butterscotch (which see), a type of toffee that differs mainly in being divided into small squares and packed in boxes.

The basic toffee recipe is sugar, butter and water boiled together, spread out on a well-buttered pan to thicken and then cut into portions.

TOHEROA. A Maori name for a New Zealand shellfish similar to the oyster and very like the Channel Island ormer. Its shell is as large as a man's hand, the flesh pearly-white and fat. The toheroa burrow firmly in the sand and the only notice they give of their presence is a tiny hole through which they breathe. A sackful of toheroa is too heavy a load for most men. Like the oyster it is an expensive item of diet and it is now protected to save it from extinction. Not more than 20 may be taken in any one day by any one person; a car-load of 5 or more persons may not take more than 100 among them; they must be dug from the sand with the hands and no implement whatever may be used. Neither may they be taken unless they are at least 3 in. long.

TOHEROA SOUP. One of the finest of the fish bisques. It is a pale green colour with a flavour which Eric Linklater, the Orkney writer, once described as tasting as though made from oysters fed on asparagus. It is exported in cans.

TOKAY. See HUNGARIAN WINES.

TOMATILLO. See GROUND CHERRY.

TOMATO. The fruit of a plant which is a member of the deadly nightshade family. Its exact origin is in doubt. Some people think it began in India, others in Africa or China; but generally it is thought it was first cultivated in Peru where Spaniards searching for gold came across the 'golden apple' instead. The Peruvians, who had been propagating the tomato from a humble red berry, gave so much thought to it that it became a theme in the decoration of their pottery. Its present name is of Mexican origin, but it has had several names on its way to becoming a success story.

Curiously its red beauty alarmed people, like shying away from a beautiful but dangerous woman. It was recorded that only a hapless lover or a potential suicide would toy with a tomato. This must have been because of the nightshade connection rather than the colour.

It was the Spaniards who brought tomatoes to Europe during the 15th century, more as a decoration than as a food. Tomatoes travelled via Morocco into Italy and were called *pomi de Mori* (apples from the Moors), which became *pomodori* or golden apples. The French, ready as always to take culinary risks, called the tomato *pommes d'amour*, perhaps because red is the colour of love; but the more prosaic explanation is that it was their version of the Italian *pomi de Mori*. While France was busy cooking her new-found discovery, Sir Walter Raleigh was presenting his Queen with tomato plants for decoration.

Today the tomato is grown throughout the world, in tropical and temperate climes, and the number of varieties is enormous. In the United States, which hardly knew tomatoes until the middle of the 19th century, recipes for cooking them are 'as the sands on the seashore for multitude, and the fruit appears in every kind of salad'. This applies equally to Italy and in lesser degree to Greece and Portugal. The Italians dry tomatoes in the sun and preserve them in olive oil to develop a flavour which cannot be imitated.

Tomatoes cannot always be 'bought by the eye'. Some of the large, untidy, tropical (or for that matter Mediterranean) kinds have an incomparable flavour. And for eating raw, like apples, many people swear by the sweet English tomato. But it is important to use the right tomato for the right dish – even when in an Italian recipe canned tomatoes are demanded (which is quite often, since their particular qualities are appreciated) then use Italian canned tomatoes, for only then will the true flavour of the dish be there.

Among the lesser-known varieties are the yellow tomatoes which have an extra sweetness and delicacy. The pear tomato, named for its shape, is of excellent flavour and keeps well. It is good for preserving and in salads. The sugar or grape tomato is a bush variety, prolific, ornamental and well flavoured. The fruit hangs in long, thick clusters, like large grapes and is very sweet. It is useful in preserves, salads, or with sugar and cream. The Tiny Tim currant tomato is a dwarf bush variety grown in pots. In fact it can be treated as a pot plant as it is ornamental, hung with tiny fruits which it bears freely. The fruit is good in salads, soups and savoury dishes.

TOMATO SAUCE. See SAUCES.

TOM COLLINS. The original Tom Collins was made by mixing a glass of dry gin and half a glass of lemon or lime juice, adding a teaspoonful of powdered sugar, shaking the lot with some cracked

TOHEROA

TOMATO

ice and straining it into a long glass which was then filled with cold soda water. See COLLINS.

TONGS, BOTTLE. These are used to deal with obstinate corks. The tongs are heated until red hot and the bottle neck is gripped just under the flange. When the glow has passed, about 1 minute, remove the tongs. Dip a piece of rag in cold water and apply it to the neck. It will break off cleanly where the tongs have held it . See page 244.

TONGUE. Beef, ox, mutton, lamb and calf tongues are classed as offal (variety meats).

They are sold fresh, smoked or otherwise cured. Some of the smaller ones are canned. Ox tongue is the best-known variety of tongue and is considered superior to all others.

TONKA BEAN. The fruit or bean of a tree which grows wild in the tropical forests of South America, containing an aromatic essential oil, *coumarin*. It is an egg-shaped fruit with a hard coat and a single seed embedded in a soft, pulpy flesh. The seeds are dried, and the oil extracted is used to manufacture bitters. It is also widely used as a substitute for vanilla.

TOPPING. A culinary term applied to the ingredients sprinkled as a topping or garnish over cakes, buns, puddings etc.

TORTILLA, MEXICAN. A thin flat cake or bread made with ground maize flour. Tortillas are filled with a meat mixture, beans and chilli to become *tacos*, and can be served as they are; or sometimes they are fried until crisp, masked in a sauce, and served as *enchilladas*. They are also served as a kind of scoop for eating thick beans or meat stews, and are even served as a pudding mixed with nuts, sugar and spices.

TORTOISE. See TURTLE, TERRAPIN and TORTOISE.

TORTONI. An Italian ice-cream, named after

Tortoni, an Italian whose café flourished in Paris at the end of the 18th century and who is credited with having brought ice-cream made with cream and fruit to that city.

TOSS. (Fr. *faire sauter.*) This is to turn food in a pan by tossing the pan up with a quick but decisive jerky movement so that the food is slipped over. The classic example is the tossing of a pancake so high that it turns a complete somersault in mid-air. Food cooking in a covered casserole can also be tossed. Grasp the casserole by its handles and toss it up and down with a jerky circular movement.

TOUR CARNET, CH. LA. See BORDEAUX WINES.

TOUR DE MONS, CH. LA. See BORDEAUX WINES.

TOUR-DU-PIN-FIGEAC, CH. LA. See BORDEAUX WINES.

TOUR HAUT-BRION, CH. LA. See BORDEAUX WINES.

TOUR-MARTILLAC, CH. LA. See BORDEAUX WINES.

TOURNEDOS. Small but fairly thick slices of beef cut from the fillet. They may be plainly grilled or fried, but they also lend themselves to a number of more elaborate preparations.

TOURNEDOS ROSSINI

Season and grill (broil) the required number of tournedos. Dip an equal number of slices of *foie gras* into milk, then into flour and gently fry in butter. Place the grilled tournedos on a hot serving plate, add the *foie gras*. Put aside but keep warm. Add to the meat gravy as much port wine as desired, sliced truffle to taste and simmer gently for a few minutes. Serve the tournedos (with the *foie gras*) on slices of fried bread, crowned with truffle. Surround with the gravy and serve at once.

TOURTEAU FROMAGER. A very unusual but

typical Vendée (France) cake made with fresh goat cheese. It is baked in a very hot oven, and when ready it has a blue-black crust and is creamy-yellowish inside.

TOWEL GOURD. A gourd-like fruit of a high climbing plant, *Luffa aegypticum*, which grows freely in the Nile Valley and in India and other parts of the Middle and Far East. It has several local names. The fruit is encased in a very hard fibre which is largely used for cleaning purposes. The fruit can be cooked like vegetable marrow.

TRAIL. The collective name for the entrails and intestines of certain birds and fish (snipe, woodcock, red mullet). It is cooked and eaten with the flesh.

TREACLE. Pure cane treacle is a dark, almost black syrup, sharp in taste, which is produced during the manufacture of cane or moist sugar. Because of its sharp flavour and dark colour, it is used in rich fruit cakes, gingerbread, and for baking ham, apples and other foods. It is high in calories and a good sweetener.

TREACLE TART. A tart made with short pastry filled with fresh breadcrumbs and golden syrup, flavoured with lemon rind and orange juice.

TREE TOMATO. This is not a tomato but the fruit of an entirely different species. Originally from Peru and Brazil, it now grows freely in New Zealand, mainly in the north of North Island. The fruit, which is about 3–3½ in. long and about 1¼ in. in diameter, is elongated like an egg, dark in colour and thin skinned. It grows in clusters on a tree some 6 to 8 feet in height, hanging like small red eggs. The fruit is eaten raw and is cut in half, sprinkled with sugar and scooped out with a small spoon; or chopped and lightly stewed, then served sweetened; or made into jams and chutneys.

TRIFLE. A very English sweet pudding, today made with sponge cakes or fingers, flavoured with jam, soaked with sherry, and topped with custard. The following recipe is taken from *The Ladies Companion*, 1753, and is one of two recipes:

'Take a Quarter of a Pound of *Naples* Biscuits, put them in a deep *China* Dish, with as much Red Wine as they will take to soak them: smooth them with the back Part of a Spoon, then whip Half a Pint of Cream, as for a Syllabub, with Sugar, Lemon-juice, and a Spoonful of White Wine, and lay on the Froth by Spoonfuls till covered thick. If it dont froth stiff, add the Whites of two Eggs. You may garnish, when you serve it, with Apples, peeled Walnuts, or any Fruit that is in Season, as you like.'

TRIPE. The first and second stomachs of all ruminants, but more particularly those of the ox. The first stomach is smooth and the second honey-combed; both should be represented in a dish of tripe. The classical way of preparing tripe in France is *Tripe à la mode de Caen*. Its preparation is a matter of labour and time, but it emerges as a culinary triumph.

TROCKENBEERENAUSLESE. See GERMAN WINES.

TROTANOY, CH. See BORDEAUX WINES.

TROTTER. The foot of an animal, usually applied to pig or sheep. Trotters are stewed or braised and appreciated by many gourmets. See PIG, PORK.

TROTTEVIEILLE, CH. See BORDEAUX WINES.

TROU NORMANDE. See CALVADOS.

TROUT. Any of the smaller freshwater species of the family Salmonidae, usually comprising three genera, *Salmo*, *Christivomer* and *Salvelinus*. This fish is found throughout the world and is one of the most delicate, beautiful and sought after for the table. The many kinds of char (which see) are members of the *Salvelinus* genus. The true trout native to Europe is the brown trout, *Salmo trutta*, and is found from Iceland to the Mediterranean countries. At one time the Loch Leven trout was considered to be a separate species but has now been classified as an adaptation. In North America the rainbow trout, *Salmo gairdneri*, represented in a sea-run variety on the Pacific coast by the steel-head, is common to the colder, fresh-water streams on both coasts. The rainbow trout also inhabits some lakes and streams of central and eastern Europe. The most widely found North American trout is the brook trout, *Savelinus fontinalis*, ranging from Labrador to Georgia on the east coast of the United States. This fish lives only in cold running streams where temperatures do not exceed 60° F. (16° C.).

TROUT COOKED WITH ALMONDS
freshly caught trout
salt, pepper
butter
blanched and sliced almonds
½ cup (⅔) dry white wine

Clean but do not wash the trout. Make a light incision down the back of each then lightly rub with salt and papper. Heat a shallow pan, add a large piece of butter and fry the trout for 4 minutes on either side. As soon as the fish are cooked, arrange them on a hot plate. Reheat the butter and the moment it becomes hot throw in enough

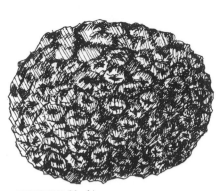

TRUFFLE (black)

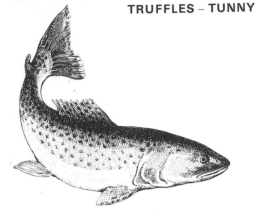

RAINBOW TROUT

blanched and sliced almonds to cover the fish completely. Shake the pan, for almonds burn easily. When a golden brown pour the wine over them. Pour this sauce immediately over the fish and serve at once.

TRUFFLES. An underground variety of fungi which grows 1 to 2 feet deep in the ground under a tree, usually the oak but also the birch, elm, willow and aspen. It refuses to be cultivated.

Both dogs, usually intelligent mongrels, and pigs are trained to scent out and dig up truffles. The former are preferred since, being obedient, they scent and wait; the pig scents and eats unless watched.

The finest truffles are the French black or Périgord variety, and the Italian white or Piedmont truffle.

Truffles are not handsome. The white truffle looks like a yellowish, badly-shaped, small potato, usually that size, although giant truffles are sometimes found. Its perfume is strong and difficult to describe. The flavour is slightly peppery. In Italy truffles are sliced paper-thin with a special knife and usually sprinkled on the dish as it comes to the table. They are used with rice dishes and together with Parmesan cheese. But even in Italy truffles are expensive and the season is short – November only.

The Périgord truffle is coal black and covered with warty knobs which make it difficult to clean. It is more plentiful than the white truffle, with plenty of aroma but no flavour. The best-known method of serving black truffle is in *pâté de foie gras*, but there are many other ways, not least in an omelette.

There is also an English truffle, black and warty with a pleasant but not lasting aroma which appears in some parts of England.

Finally there is the *terfez* or 'lion's truffle', the desert, sand or Arab truffle, plentiful in North Africa and parts of the Middle East, which is in fact a large mushroom that grows underneath the soil. Its flavour is closer to mushrooms and said to be the only type of truffle known in classical

times. Whitish in colour and shaped like a pear, desert truffles are sold by the basket in local markets and, unless there has been a bad season, are very cheap. The best are said to come from the area around Palmyra. The desert Arabs believe that truffles arrive with the storms. What really happens is that the storms break up the hard sand and reveal the hidden treasure below. Even Pliny thought truffles were sown by the thunderbolts of the autumnal storms. The darkest, hardest and largest truffles are the best of the desert kind. They are not as good as either the French or Italian truffles.

These are the main truffles. Scattered around Europe are several varieties of lesser character. Knowledge of truffles is limited, since they are not easy to find, so probably there are still many more kinds buried deep in the earth of which we as yet know nothing.

TRUFFLES, CHOCOLATE. These are one of the culinary specialities of Flanders.

8 oz. (8 squares) bitter-sweet chocolate
2 tablespoons (2½) rum, cream or black coffee
2 egg yolks, well beaten
3 oz. (6 tablespoons) butter, diced
chocolate powder or cocoa

Put the chocolate (broken into pieces) with the liquid into a saucepan and melt over a low heat. Take the pan from the heat and beat until smooth. Add the yolks, beating all the while, then the butter. Continue beating until the mixture is smooth, about 3 minutes. Leave to cool, then chill for several hours. Break off pieces the size of a caramel, roll these between the hands into round balls, roll in powdered chocolate, put into small paper cases and eat within 48 hours.

TRUSS. To secure poultry and game with skewers or string, to keep their shape during cooking, make their appearance neat, also to facilitate carving when cooked. Large joints of meat can also be trussed.

TUNNY or **TUNA.** The largest and most useful

member of the mackerel family. Its flesh is delicate and very popular; it lends itself admirably to being canned in oil. Tunny is found in all warm seas but chiefly in the Mediterranean, where it is a favourite fish. It grows to an enormous size and some species weigh as much as 1,000 lb. In the Pacific another species is valued chiefly as a game fish. The little tunny of the Mediterranean, the long-finned tunny or the albacore, and the bonito are smaller related fish.

Fresh tunny can be cut into steaks and grilled, poached or put on a bed of sliced vegetables, white wine added and cooked in the oven for about $1\frac{1}{2}$ hours – according to the thickness of the steaks.

TURBOT. A flat fish which has both eyes on the left side of its head and often weighs up to 40 or 50 lb. It is a fish of considerable value and was once rated higher than the sole. The smaller turbot, which are sweeter-flavoured, are called chicken turbot. The flesh of the turbot should be firm and white; it may be poached in a *court bouillon*, braised on a bed of vegetables, moistened with white wine, baked in the oven or fried in butter.

TURREEN. A large deep vessel with a lid, usually oval-shaped and made from earthenware or a ceramic material, and sometimes of silver. The lid has a slot carved out to allow for the ladle to rest. They are used for serving soup at table. Soup is ladled from the turreen into soup bowls. Smaller tureens of a similar shape were made for sauce or gravy. Many of the old tureens are beautifully designed and are museum pieces.

TURKEY. The short form of turkey-cock, turkey-hen and turkey-poult (the young turkey). It is a large bird which has been domesticated for several centuries and is one of our most valued table birds.

The name turkey was first given in England to the guinea fowl, which was originally introduced into the country from West Africa. Turkeys (in the present sense of the word) were discovered in Mexico, where they had been domesticated for some time by the Spaniards who are said to have brought them to Europe in 1530; but the matter seems not at all clear for there is a famous jingle:

Turkeys, carp, hops and beer,
Came into England all in one year.

And that year was 1520. Then it is recorded that by 1555 the turkey (guinea fowl?) was a prized table bird in Europe. When Shakespeare talked of turkeys, he was talking of guinea fowl, and even as late as 1633, when we read Dr Hart's *Diet of the Diseased*, the mention of turkey obviously refers to the guinea fowl. It seems that not until the reign of Queen Anne was the turkey as we know it today.

The turkey cock is larger than the hen and less economical, as its bones are heavier. A large specimen is better stuffed by the taxidermist than the cook. The best is the hen from 7 to 8 months old reared in semi-liberty, given plenty of food but made to scratch for at least some of it. Its legs should be black, the neck short, the breast broad and plump, and the flesh snow-white and firm, with thin layers of fat over the back.

Turkeys in the United States are by 'stern and inflexible tradition' eaten at Thanksgiving as well as at Christmas; while England still considers turkey as the Christmas bird although available throughout the year.

Turkey eggs are large and delicate of flavour, can be used in all the ways of hens' eggs and are especially good in sauces, cakes and puddings.

TURKISH COFFEE. Turkish coffee is served in small cups and traditionally should be 'as black as night, as bitter as Hell, and as sweet as love,' As there are degrees of love, so there are of Turkish coffee: very sweet, half-sweet and bitter.

To make coffee in the Turkish manner, the coffee must be ground as fine as flour and boiled in a long-handled, lipped coffee pot. Each cup should be made individually but up to 3 cups can be made at the same time with success. To make 1 cup of coffee, put 2 teaspoons ($2\frac{1}{2}$) of finely ground coffee into the coffee pot and 1 teaspoon ($1\frac{1}{4}$) of sugar. Add 1 coffee cup of water. Do not stir. Put the pot on the heat and bring once to the boil. Take quickly from the heat, let the froth subside, return the pot to the heat and bring again to the boil. Repeat this performance once more, boiling the coffee three times in all. Stir and pour into the cup. For extra sweet coffee, add twice as much sugar; for bitter coffee, omit sugar altogether. Real Turkish coffee addicts drink their coffee down to its dregs, then sit happily for hours chewing the grounds.

TURKISH DELIGHT. The popular English name of Turkey's sweetmeat *rahat lokum*. It has a marshmallow-like texture and is made from sugar, water and cornflour, flavoured usually with rose-water and often with such nuts as pistachio.

TURKISH WINES. Thought by some to be the cradle of the vineyard and its products, it took a modern revolution, first to deal it a near-death blow and then to provide the climate to bring Turkey again into the wine-making nations. Wine was made in Anatolia before the Hittite invasion, some scholars saying an old Anatolian word *Waiyana* is the origin of both the Indo-European *woino* (wine) and West-Semitic *wainu*. During the Roman Empire Anatolian wines were brought to Rome.

The cultivation of the vine for wine-making might have vanished for all time during the long

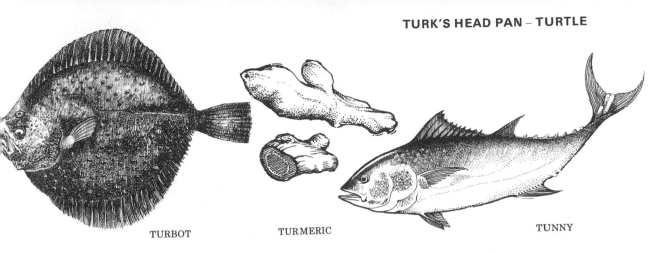

TURBOT   TURMERIC   TUNNY

period of Islamic domination but for the Christians resident in Turkey who were great wine producers. They were permitted to export and in the 19th century production reached 360 million litres a year. With Atatürk's revolution and the large-scale population exchanges the wine industry was vitally affected, almost again to extinction. However, Atatürk was no slave to the Koran and he reintroduced wine-making as part of his policy of reform and westernization.

Today wine is produced both by State monopolies and some private owners. Primitive viniculture, poor production methods and inadequate storage facilities have had a bad effect on quality wine but the potential is there, and methods are improving. One can look forward to seeing Turkey regaining some of the laurels she wore in ancient history.

TURK'S HEAD PAN. A circular cake pan with a central tube and spiral-shaped indentations in the walls. It is thus named because it supposedly resembles an early type of Turkish headdress.

TURMERIC. The fleshy root stalk of a brilliant tropical plant which belongs to the ginger family. It contains a bright yellow dye and is one of the principal ingredients in curries and other Far Eastern dishes. It is native to the Far East generally, and to parts of Africa and Australia. Even the colour of the flower when grown in hot countries is a bright yellow, although that grown in China is a dull green. The root of the turmeric is irregularly shaped; the aroma is clean but the flavour is rather bitter and faintly resinous. It has been used for centuries because of its colour and its warmth of flavour. If used in moderation, i.e. a pinch, it can be used instead of saffron to give colour to food. It is best bought in root form, but is also available powdered. Turmeric also adds colour to mustard pickles and prepared mustards.

TURNIP. Although widespread cultivation of turnips in England dates from the 17th century, and Viscount Townshend became forever associated with them through his experiments in the 18th century, it is probable they were grown earlier in monastery and other gardens. The Romans and the Greeks certainly ate turnips, cooking them with a considerable quantity of spices.

There are several varieties of turnips, all belonging to one or other of the two main varieties, the round and the long-rooted. The first is sweeter and better flavoured than the second. They are in season most of the year, although towards winter they are spongey and not so good for eating. They are at their best when so young that they can be eaten raw, as they are in Greece, as hors d'oeuvre.

Turnips can be boiled and mashed, cooked *au gratin*, glazed, beaten with eggs to make croquettes, or thinly sliced and served with a dressing or added to stews. The young shoots, known as turnip tops, are boiled as greens.

TURNOVER. A round of pastry folded over a filling to make a semi-circle and then baked. The fillings can be sweet or savoury; probably apple turnover is the best known of the tribe.

TURTLE, TERRAPIN and **TORTOISE.** These are all members of the reptilian order *Testudinata* or *Chelonia*, easily recognizable by their horny carapaces, which are generally saucer shaped. There are approximately 300 species of the two orders, most of which inhabit fresh water. The sea-going members are pelagic, living near the surface of all the warmer seas of the world, the greatest majority being found, however, in the tropical archipelagos. Probably the best-known turtle is the green turtle, *Chelone midas*, which, contrary to its name, is brown rather than green. The fat, however, is a rich green and is used to make the famous green turtle soup. This turtle can attain a weight of 1,000 lb. or more, though it normally averages 400 lb. Ruthless commercial exploitation has unfortunately heavily reduced their numbers, but stringent methods of conservation are being enforced in order to restore the population. Next in popularity is the diamond black terrapin, *Malaclemmy centrata*, which is found in the salt marshes of the Atlantic coast lines. The terrapin feeds largely on vegetation, fish and other aquatic animals. Its flesh is highly prized for the table and is much used as the basis of the famous Maryland terrapin soup in North America.

Many species of turtle are regarded as a source of delicious food and, although not marketed widely on a commercial basis, they are often available locally. Most turtles marketed commercially range in weight from 15 to 20 lb., but the smaller ones are preferred for their tenderer flesh.

TURTLE À LA KING
6 hard-boiled eggs
2 tablespoons (2½) butter
2 cups (2½) single cream
¼ teaspoon (⅓) each of nutmeg, pepper, allspice
½ teaspoon (⅔) salt
1 lb. cooked, diced turtle meat

Separate the yolks from the whites. Sieve the yolks, mix with the butter and beat until creamy. Scald the cream in a double boiler, add the spices, salt and the creamed butter and stir well. Add the meat and cook it gently until tender. Finely chop the egg whites. Serve the turtle with triangles of toast and garnish with the chopped egg whites.

TUTTI-FRUTTI. A type of preserve consisting of a medley of fruits which can be used as a sauce for puddings, ice-cream or even with some meat dishes.

Pour into a large crock 1 pint (1¼) of brandy (marc will do). Fruits are added in season, but the season starts with strawberries. Equal quantities of sugar and fruit are required. All the fruit is not placed in the crock at once; it can take a month or so if necessary. The following is the order in which the fruit is put into the crock: strawberries, cherries, raspberries, fresh currants, gooseberries, peeled and sliced fresh apricots, peaches and fresh pineapple. The tutti-frutti should be stirred each day until the final batch of fruit has been put into the crock, and never have more fruit than can be covered by the brandy. Always tie the crock down securely after each addition of fruit, and do not forget the sugar. When the crock is full it should be tightly covered and stored in a cool, dark place.

U

UDDER. The udder of a young cow or heifer is used sometimes for wrapping up croquettes or kebabs to be grilled over charcoal.

UDE, LOUIS EUSTACHE. A well-known chef and culinary writer of the last century, who is said to have been the first to define the difference between entrées and entremets. Ude said that an entrée was 'any dish of meat, fowl, game or fish dressed and cooked for the second course', and entremets applied to 'all vegetable dishes, jellies, pastries, salads, prawns, lobsters and in general to everything that appears in the second course – except the roast'.

For a time Ude was *maitre d'hôtel* to Madame Letitia Bonaparte but he left, we are told, on a little matter of 'arithmetics' and entered the service of the Earl of Sefton, with whom he remained for 20 years. He had a rather florid style of writing.

UGLI. The name given in Jamaica, where it originated, to a hybrid, a cross between a grapefruit and a tangerine. It is indeed ugly, with a loose, wrinkled, yellowish-red skin which has a green tinge, even when ripe. The skin peels off easily to reveal a juicy, orange-like fruit which is almost seedless. It is sweet and easy to eat.

UGNIBLANC. See BORDEAUX WINES.

UITSMIJTER. A popular and sustaining quick meal served in Dutch sandwich bars and restaurants. It consists of a round of bread and butter covered with ham or cold roast beef on which one or two fried eggs are placed. The name means 'bouncer' or 'chucker out'.

ULLAGE. See WINE TERMS.

UMBLES. The edible entrails of any mammal, but chiefly of the deer. See HUMBLE PIE.

UNLEAVENED BREAD. Bread that is made without a leavening agent.

UPSIDE-DOWN CAKE. A popular cake in the United States in which the fruit is placed at the bottom of a pan, then covered with batter, baked and turned out, and upside-down, for serving.

UPSIDE-DOWN CAKE
1½ oz. (3 tablespoons) unsalted butter
½ cup (⅔) maple syrup
2 medium-sized red apples
2 oz. (¼ cup) butter or shortening
½ cup (⅔) sugar
2 eggs, separated
6 oz. (1½ cups) plain (all purpose) flour
pinch of salt
1¾ teaspoons (2¼) baking powder
½ cup (⅔) milk
1 small apple, grated

Melt the first quantity of butter in a round cake pan, add the syrup and take from the heat. Wash and core the red apples (do not peel) and cut into half-inch slices. Cut all but one slice into halves

UGLI

and arrange these round the bottom of the pan in a circle. Put the whole slice in the centre. Cream the remaining butter or shortening with just over half the sugar, add the egg yolks and continue beating until the mixture is fluffy. Sift in the flour, salt and baking powder in three portions, alternately adding the milk and beating well after each addition. Add the grated apple. Beat the egg whites until stiff but not dry, add the remaining sugar to the whites and fold into the batter. Pour this mixture over the apple and bake in a moderate oven for 40 to 50 minutes. While still hot, turn the cake upside-down on to a serving dish and serve immediately with whipped cream.

URUGUAY. A wine-drinking country producing nearly 20 million gallons of wine annually, practically all home-consumed. The red, white and *rosé* wines are of fair quality. There are also some rather sweet sparkling wines.

V

VACHERIN. A cake made of large rounds of an almost meringue mixture. It is layered with a chantilly cream (which see) and sometimes with cream and fresh fruit.

   4 egg whites
   7 oz. (1 cup) castor (superfine) sugar
   3 oz. (¾ cup) plain or all purpose flour
   2 oz. (⅓ cup) crushed hazel-nuts
   2 oz. (¼ cup) unsalted butter, melted
   ½ pint (⅔) double (heavy) cream
   1 lb. fresh or frozen raspberries
Whisk the egg whites until stiff, fold in the sugar, then the flour, nuts and butter – which should be cooled. Grease and sprinkle lightly with flour three shallow sandwich pans (with removable bottoms). Spread the meringue mixture evenly and thinly in the pans. Bake in a moderate oven until pale gold and firm. Take from the oven, turn out at once and leave until cool. Whip the cream

until thick and mix with the raspberries. Spread half of this on one layer of the meringue, cover with a second layer and spread this with the remaining cream. Cover with the last meringue layer. The top can be garnished with piped whipped cream.

VACHERIN CHEESE. A French alpine cheese, like the Swiss Vacherin, soft and runny, with a firm rind. It can be eaten with a spoon. It is made with cows' milk only from October to December. Vacherins are small and round and are in season from November to May.

VACHERIN MONT D'OR. A soft, creamy-white cheese produced in several dairies in the Vaud Canton of Switzerland. It is runny, rather like a brie, with a thick rind. It is often eaten with a spoon, or if less runny with a fork, or spread on bread, and served with kümmel.

VAILLONS. See BURGUNDY WINES.

VALDEPEÑAS. See SPANISH WINES.

VALMUR. See BURGUNDY WINES.

VALPOLICELLA. See ITALIAN WINES.

VAN DER HUM. A South African liqueur made from Cape brandy, cane sugar and the *naartje* or South African tangerine.

VANDYCK. This means to accentuate the tail of a fish by cutting an acute V-shape and making two distinct points. This style is named after the small pointed beard made famous by Sir Anthony Van Dyck, court painter to Charles I of England.

VANILLA. One of the best-known flavourings. It is thought that vanilla was brought to Europe by the Spaniards from Mexico. Certainly a physician of King Philip II of Spain described the use of the vanilla fruit in spicing drinks, and wrote of the vanilla pod as 'that smell of musk and balsam from New Spain'. He believed vanilla was useful in

381

certain ailments, as a brain tonic and an antidote against poisonous bites.

The flowers of the vanilla are followed by 6-in. long flat pods and when dried for culinary purposes are black and shiny, rather like liquorice. The aroma is sweet, permeating and unique. A piece of vanilla pod about 2 in. long can be used several times in milk if rinsed after each using.

VANILLA SUGAR. Sugar flavoured with vanilla is a familiar item in the kitchen of the average Continental housewife. It is simple to prepare. Fill a large glass jar with fine sugar. Break a vanilla pod into three pieces and stick these into the sugar. Close the jar tightly and leave for several weeks before using. As the sugar is used, replenish as long as the flavour of the bean lasts.

VARIETY MEATS. See OFFAL.

VAUCOUPIN. See BURGUNDY WINES.

VAUDÉSIR. See BURGUNDY WINES.

VEAL. The meat of the calf when killed at two or three months old. The best veal sold in Britain comes from the Continent, particularly Holland. Veal calls for special preparation when the animal is slaughtered and Continental butchers understand this to perfection. The meat should be quite white, not even pink, and with little or no fat. Veal offal is of the best quality. See page 352.

VEAL FILLETS (*Médaillons de Veau*)

6 veal fillets
6 slices fat bacon
3 oz. (6 tablespoons) butter
½ lb. button mushrooms
a little vinegar
½ pint (1¼ cups) cream

Lightly pound the veal and wrap each piece in a slice of bacon. Heat the butter in a casserole and brown the meat on both sides. Cover the casserole and simmer for 30 minutes, without adding any more butter or liquid.

Clean the mushrooms and cook them until tender in boiling water to which a little vinegar is added. Drain. Add the mushrooms to the meat and continue simmering for another 10 minutes. Take out both the mushrooms and the meat, put aside but keep hot. Stir the cream into the butter in the casserole and very gently indeed heat the cream until very hot, but without letting it boil. Return the meat and mushrooms to the pan, stir and re-heat.

VEGETABLES. This term covers a wide range of edible plants, roots and even herbs. Some are cooked, others eaten raw; some can be eaten either way. The distinction between what is fruit and what is vegetable is sometimes difficult for the untutored layman to recognize. Tomatoes, vegetable marrows, beans, peas and aubergines are all vegetables to the cook, but fruits to the botanist. As far as the kitchen is concerned, those fruits which are cooked in a savoury manner are vegetables, and those which are cooked for puddings, or with plenty of sugar, are fruits.

VEGETABLE SPAGHETTI. This is not an April Fool's joke, but an unusual form of squash or marrow. To cook, wash it and cook in fast-boiling water for 25 minutes, making sure that the squash is well covered. Drain and halve, discard the seeds, then scoop out the flesh. It comes out in threads, looking like spaghetti and can be served hot with a butter sauce or cold with French dressing. It is not watery and has a delicate, but distinctive and pleasing flavour. Cold, it makes an excellent basis for a prawn cocktail as a change from the customary lettuce.

VEGETARIANISM. The theory and practice of eating only fruit and vegetables, but no animal flesh, fish or eggs. This has often been acclaimed as part of the wisdom of the East, and considering how great a proportion of the world's population have always been practically vegetarian, the importance of the subject cannot easily be overlooked.

The Mosaic Law might be taken to imply that for more than 16 centuries man lived on a vegetable diet alone. The ancient Greeks till the days of Draco in the 7th century B.C. lived entirely on the fruits of the earth, while the early fighting Romans made a meal of baked turnips or a dish of beans.

In the earliest ages of man food varied with the climate in which he lived. In the tropics a purely vegetarian diet of fruit, seeds and roots was sufficient, while in the more temperate and colder climes man developed a taste for fresh meat.

There is much written for and against vegetarianism, usually partisan. One culinary writer in the last century wrote: 'Vegetarianism in itself has much to recommend it, but the cult fails to make wholesale conversion of the generous feeder because it too often is associated with the eccentricities of food faddists, or of those barbarians who try to eat grass.'

VELOUTÉ. See SAUCES.

VENISON. The word is derived from the Latin *venari*, to hunt, and formerly applied to the flesh of any sort of game or wild beast hunted and used for food. Today the word is almost entirely restricted to the flesh of various types of deer.

VANILLA PLANT

VANILLA POD

VERBENA. See LEMON VERBENA.

VERJUICE. The acid juice of green grapes or sour fruit which is made into a green sauce called *verjus* in France. It was once sold 'with a song' in Paris streets by authorized vendors in the old days. When there was no refrigeration this king of acid condiment had its value and made it possible to eat stale meats. It can replace vinegar but nowadays it is used only in the making of mustard.

VERMICELLI. An Italian *pasta* called 'angel's hair', or a very fine spaghetti. It is usually dried separately, like spaghetti, but sometimes 20 strands or so are twisted together to resemble a bow.

VERMOUTH. A white wine which has been cooked with a number of different herbs and flavouring matters, sweetened or not, but with a mildly bitter aftertaste which is supposed to promote the flow of saliva and thus prepare the diner to enjoy and digest the meal that is to follow. Hence its place among the aperitifs, or prepandial and appetite-provoking drinks. For many years the two main types of vermouth were the French, the lighter and drier of the two, and the Italian, sweeter and darker; they were made almost exclusively in France, and in Italy immediately north and south of the Alps. Now, however, vermouths are produced in all wine-making lands. Once opened, vermouth does not keep indefinitely.

VÉRONIQUE. This usually denotes a garnish of white grapes. Sole véronique (see SOLE) is the classic example.

VERT-PRÉ. The French name of a green herb sauce or garnish. It also means grilled meats garnished with straw potatoes and watercress and a *maître d'hôtel* sauce. White meats and duckling *vert-pré* are served with green peas and beans, and asparagus heads in a butter sauce.

VICHYSSOISE SOUP. An iced leek and potato soup generally considered to be of American origin, but in fact a refinement of a French country soup. It was introduced into America in 1941 by the late Louis Diat.

VICHY WATER. A mineral water from the springs of Vichy, a French watering place. Vichy also is the name given to a garnish which includes sliced carrots cooked in cream.

VICTORIA SPONGE. A sponge mixture made with equal quantities of butter and sugar and their weight in eggs and flour. It is the English version of the French *quatre-quatre* (which see). This mixture is used for a jam sandwich, queen cakes, etc.

VIENNA BREAD or **LOAF.** A crusty bread to which milk is added while kneading.

VIENNESE PASTRIES. Pastries in Vienna are made by craftsmen, men who are certified as such after serving a seven-year apprenticeship. They put all their skill into those pastries for which Vienna has been justly famous for centuries. At the end of the 17th century the Vienna coffee house was opened and soon after the cult of the pastry began. Viennese pastries are often lovely flights of fancy.

VIENNOISE, À LA. Poultry or small cuts of meat garnished with anchovy fillets, olives, capers, and chopped hard-boiled eggs, served with a hot butter sauce. Also crustades of fried noodles filled with spinach, braised celery and plain boiled potatoes.

VIEUX, CERTAN, CH. See BORDEAUX WINES.

VILLAFRANCA DEL PANADÉS. See SPANISH WINES.

VILLEFROI or **VILLEROY.** Meat, fish or vegetables coated with a mushroom or truffle sauce, breadcrumbed and fried in deep fat.

VILLENAVE D'ORNON. See BORDEAUX WINES.

VINAIGRETTE. Basic French dressing of good wine vinegar, oil, salt, pepper, fresh herbs to taste – and garlic, if in the south of France.

VINEGAR. An acid liquid prepared from various substances by acetous fermentation of the alcohol present in all alcoholic beverages which, in the presence of oxygen, becomes ascetic acid.

The word vinegar means *vin aigre*, and has been known as long as wine itself. Originally vinegar was prepared from grapes, and still today the best and mildest vinegars are those made from grapes, by old traditional methods. However, vinegar is also made from cider and, to a much lesser extent, from perry, honey, rice, maize and all manner of vegetable substances which produce alcohol by fermentation.

Vinegar has been known for many ages, long before any other acid. It was mentioned by Moses and would seem to have been in general use amongst the Israelites and the Egyptians. It was used by the Greeks and the Romans, both in cooking and as a refreshing drink, diluted of course. Cleopatra, we read, dissolved her pearls in vinegar. Soldiers of the Roman armies always carried vinegar for mixing with water – a practise followed until recently in some of the warmer parts of Europe, particularly in Spain.

In Britain during the 17th and 18th centuries, when cities smelled offensively, people carried sponges soaked in vinegar, containing them in little silver boxes. Victorian ladies, noted for their 'vapours' were restored with cooling vinegar-soaked cloths placed gently across their foreheads.

Apart from its more general use in salad dressings and marinades, vinegar can be used in several savoury dishes and at one time vinegar cakes were popular, vinegar taking the place of eggs.

VINE LEAVES. In countries such as Turkey and Greece where stuffed vine leaves are eaten throughout the year, fresh leaves are available from spring to autumn. After that they are kept pliable and ready for use preserved in brine in large tubs. They are also exported in cans. Vine leaves are usually stuffed with a rice filling and can be eaten either hot or cold. See DOLMAS.

VINEYARD. A plantation of grape vines.

VINICULTURE. The art and science of wine production.

VINOSITY. See WINE TERMS.

VINTAGE. The gathering of the grapes; also the particular year when the grapes were gathered and the wine made. There is a vintage every year, but the quality of the grapes vintaged varies from year to year. There are wines shipped under the date of their vintage and others shipped without a date; all were made alike from grapes gathered in one or more years. The chief difference between dated (vintage) and undated (non-vintage) wines is that the first show greater promise of improving with age and should be kept, whilst the other are ready for immediate consumption and may – but need not – be kept.

There is some poor wine made even in the best of vintages, and there is also some good wine made even when the vintage is, generally speaking, a failure. Therefore one should pay more attention to the quality of the wine in one's glass than to the label on the bottle.

VINTNER. A dealer in wines, also a grower.

VIOLET. This pretty plant once had a place of honour among medicinal herbalists. Its culinary uses today are few. The petals are crystallized for cake or pudding decoration, used in a salad, also to make a liqueur, Crème de Violettes. The leaves, when tender, can also be used in salads and to flavour soups.

VIOLET TEA. Herbalists consider this a soothing beverage for people suffering from bronchitis and similar affections. Put a teaspoonful of dried violets in a jar and pour over half a pint of boiling water. Infuse for 5 minutes, strain, sweeten with honey.

VIRGINIA HAM. See HAM.

VITAMIN. Substance contained in particular foodstuffs in certain conditions and regarded as essential to nutrition. When vitamins were first discovered they were identified by the letters of the alphabet, but now that their structure is known the alternative chemical term is frequently used instead. The vitamins important to humans are A, B, C, D, E and K.

VITICULTURE. A branch of agriculture which deals with the science and art of grape growing.

VODKA. Considered by many to be the Russian national drink, but by others to be of Polish origin. Certainly the Poles make some of the best vodka; in the past, as pure alcohol was generally for sale, almost every household had old and cherished recipes for making special vodkas. Today vodka is usually distilled from potatoes, but old-type vodka was grain distilled. However, vodka has been and still is distilled from any material at hand, the cheapest at the time, and is neither coloured nor flavoured nor matured. It is served very cold, in

STUFFED VINE LEAVES (before and after wrapping)

VOL-AU-VONT

small glasses and swallowed at one gulp, neither nose nor palate wasting any time on vodka.

Vodka means 'little water' and it seems to have been drunk for centuries. However, vodka has become fashionable and there are now Dutch and American vodkas as well as the Russian and Polish. It is often used as a base for mixed drinks combined with vermouth, tonic and tomato juice.

VOL-AU-VENT. Large or small cases of puff pastry baked and then filled with creamed chicken, mushrooms or shellfish, or fricassees of any of these.

VOLNAY. See BURGUNDY WINES.

VOSNE-ROMANÉE. See BURGUNDY WINES.

VOUVRAY. See LOIRE WINES.

V.S.O.P. See COGNAC.

W

WAFER. Today this means the thinnest and lightest form of biscuit served with ice-cream or somewhat creamy puddings. Wafers, however, have been mentioned in literature for centuries; Chaucer talks of them in his *Canterbury Tales*, as does Piers Plowman. Probably these early wafers were not as thin as the present kind, but more akin to the waffle of today. They were a popular treat and were hawked throughout England. We even find them in the list of items for an archbishop's feast in 1295; and at one time it appears to have been the custom to begin a royal banquet by presenting the royal couple with hippocras, a medieval drink of sweetened and spiced wine, and wafers.

England was not alone in her love for wafers; they were similarly hawked throughout Europe.

Early wafer irons, which are today museum pieces, were used to stamp the discs of unleavened

bread used in the Mass. Such irons were stamped with various religious symbols, a cross or the letters IHS. Even those irons from which the layman's wafer was made could be similarly stamped, but more often they showed designs of flowers, landscapes, hunting scenes, or pictures of vinous merriment, appropriate for those wafers to be served with the hippocras or the punch bowl.

Wafer irons were made with long handles in two halves which fitted but were not always identical, and with space between the two to allow the spongy batter to rise and produce a 'cake'.

Wafers of all kinds were still made at home in England until the beginning of this century, but either they fell out of favour or the commercially prepared wafer took over.

WAFFLE. French *gaufre*. Waffles are made from a light spongy batter, either with eggs, as in France, or with yeast, as in Germany and parts of Belgium, or as in the United States often with rice and corn. The batter must be thin and very smooth. When it is baked (in a waffle iron) it should puff up and become crisp and a golden brown. Waffles are served both sweet and savoury: with eggs, sausages and ham for breakfast or a light meal; or sweet with butter and syrup, honey, or as in North America with maple syrup.

France has a long history of waffle making and as far back as 1433 their word for waffle iron was in use, listed in a French book as *fer à gaufres*. The following quotation from an article on waffles and wafers may be of some help: '. . . a wafer is a waffle is a (French) gaufre or gaufrette, is a (German) waffel, is a (Dutch) wafel. Waffel comes from another German word *wabe*, meaning honeycomb, which bears a resemblance to our present day waffle iron.'

As will be seen it is therefore not easy to decide whether those *gaufres* mentioned in 12th-century French ballads were wafers or waffles. But we do know that in France as in England waffles or wafers were made and sold in the streets and the *gaufre* maker would set up his stall near the church doors when there were big religious festivals.

WAFFLE IRON. Today this gadget is usually designed to cook by electricity and is thermostatically controlled. It is a hinged metal appliance with two honeycombed plates into which the batter is poured; then the iron is closed and the waffles cooked.

There are still old-fashioned waffle irons to be found, made of iron, in which the batter was cooked over a low heat, first on one side and then on the other. Truly antique irons have become museum pieces, and these show the amusing shapes and sizes the waffles used to have. Apart from those with religious motives and other scenes, some were stamped with family coats of arms.

WALNUT. The so-called European walnut, one of half a dozen species, is indigenous to Persia and is mentioned in the earliest records of civilization. The Phoenicians traded in walnuts, the Romans sanctified them, considering them food for the gods – 'the nuts of Jupiter' they called them. Ovid relates that walnuts were thrown to children during Roman weddings by the bride and groom to symbolize their taking leave of childish amusements. Magic healing powers were attributed to them and oils and elixirs were made from the leaves of the trees, and from the shells as well as the kernels.

Eventually these large nuts were carried throughout the world, mainly on English trading ships, thus becoming known as English nuts, a misnomer. Excellent walnuts do grow in Britain but they were introduced by Roman legionaries. Walnuts sold in Britain today usually come from France or Spain.

The walnut tree is a lovely thing, with flowers which are in full bloom in May. The small green fruits appear in July. At this stage, and before the inner shell has formed and become hard, many nuts are gathered to be made into pickled walnuts. In the Slav countries green walnuts are preserved in a sweet syrup. Those walnuts left on the tree turn brown and split, disclosing the nut with its hard outer covering, easily cracked to reveal the brown-skinned kernel within. When the nut is fresh this skin peels off easily. At this stage the thin skin is bitter but the nut crisp and better flavoured. Most nuts which reach the market have been dried either in the sun or in large ovens where warm circulated air blows on them.

Walnuts can be used in many dishes, both sweet and savoury, as well as being served as a dessert nut. They are sold in the shell, shelled whole and shelled and broken. In the shell the actual price per pound seems the cheapest but by the time they have been shelled the buyer has paid sometimes for more than half the weight in shells. How to buy walnuts depends on how they are to be used. Sometimes shelled nuts are better, sometimes not. Walnuts served with a glass of wine must be whole.

The American black walnut is one of the best known and the most widely distributed tree in North American forests. The nuts vary greatly in size and shape and are generally larger that the usual European varieties. They have a thick, hard shell not to be cracked with ordinary crackers, but with special nut-crackers now made in the United States. The kernels are used for confectionery, ice-cream and baked foods. The nuts have a strong, haunting flavour impossible to described and not adversely affected by cooking.

There is also the American white walnut or butternut (which see), a nut of agreeable flavour and useful in cooking and confectionery. Young butternuts after being rubbed smooth are sometimes pickled, like green walnuts. Then there are numerous wild American walnuts and research among these has revealed many types which will undoubtedly one day be cultivated.

The Japanese walnut, native to Japan, is smaller than the Persian nut and something like a butternut in appearance. Although not greatly esteemed as an eating nut, it has proved a valuable species in countries where it has been introduced.

WALNUT LIQUEUR. A speciality of the Périgord region and Corrèze where walnut husks are macerated in brandy with herbs and sugar syrup. It is called *brou*, ratafia or *eau-de-noix* in France.

WASABI. Japanese horse-radish, a pungent root much appreciated in Japanese cooking as a condiment. It is usually grated and served in a small bowl with sauces, and in particular with *sashimi* (which see).

WASSAIL BOWL. An older name for loving cup, a drink served on festive occasions in olden times in England. The tradition goes back to Anglo-Saxon days (the word wassail derives from an Old English and Old Norse salutation that meant literally 'be hale', i.e. 'be in good health') and symbolizes good cheer, health and happiness, particularly at Christmas time, New Year's Eve and other festivals. There are many recipes but the basic ingredient is heated spiced ale or beer.

WATER BISCUIT. A thin, crisp plain biscuit served with butter and cheese, also called a cracker.

WATER CHESTNUT. A fruit extensively grown in China, Japan and Thailand, also found in some parts of Europe and Africa. It grows in lowlands, especially sluggish river tributaries, lakes and ponds. Water chestnut is eaten roasted, boiled or mashed, and is an important item in Japanese, Chinese and Thai cuisines. It is also canned. Another variety, the young or ripe water caltrop,

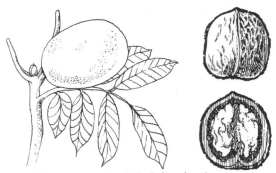

WALNUT (green nut, ripe shell, shell and nut)

WATER CHESTNUT

is also loosely known as water chestnut. This water plant is particularly valuable for its starch which is used as a binder in Eastern cookery, in much the same way as cornflour (cornstarch) is used in the West.

WATERCRESS. An aquatic plant which grows freely in most meadows or slow-running shallow streams, or in prepared beds. It is in season from late spring to the end of November. Good watercress is a deep green colour and crisp. It is used alone as a salad, to garnish other salads, to make a soup, biscuits, dumplings, or as a garnish. Its flavour is mild but slightly peppery. If the cress is fresh the stalks can be snipped off and finely chopped to be used as a flavouring in stuffings in an omelette or mashed potatoes.

Ancient recipes make frequent reference to this green herb which, it was believed, would cure a deranged mind. There is a Greek proverb which says: 'Eat cress and get more wit.' Munching fresh watercress when drinking alcohol is said to keep one sober.

WATER ICE. See SHERBET.

WATER MELON. See MELON.

WATERZOOÏ. A Flemish dish and a type of rich hearty soup characteristic of Belgian cooking. There are two kinds, one prepared with chicken and vegetables, and the other with a fish base, both served on a bed of cooked rice. The *bouillon* in which they were cooked is poured over the top, or served separately.

WEAKFISH. An excellent fish caught in large numbers off the Atlantic coasts of the United States from Cape Cod to the Gulf of Florida. It is represented in the Gulf of Mexico by a closely allied species called the sand trout. Weakfish is also called gray trout and sea trout and it may be prepared for the table like the true trout.

WEDDING CAKE. A rich almost black fruit cake heavily iced and decorated.

The wedding cake or bridecake had its origin in the Roman *confarreatio* a form of marriage in which the couple ate salt and flour cake. The bride held three ears of wheat, symbolic of plenty. In the Middle Ages wheat ears were worn or carried by a bride at her wedding and it became the custom for girls to assemble outside the church to throw grains of wheat over the bride. Later the grains were cooked into thin dry biscuits which were held over the head of the bride. In the 16th century, the biscuits were changed into small rectangular cakes, made of eggs, milk, currants and spices. Every guest had at least one and the cakes were thrown at the bride as she crossed the threshold.

With the Restoration of Charles II there arrived in England French cooks who speedily converted the small cakes into a confectionery iced with sugar, which as time went on grew into fantastic white productions of several tiers.

It is usual when cutting the wedding cake for the top one or two layers to be removed. One of these is reserved for the christening of the first child and one often for cutting into tiny portions, for sending to absent friends. The first slice of the cake is cut by the bride and groom together. Then the cake is cut and distributed among the guests. Up to recent years girls, and not only bridesmaids, have taken home their wedding cake to put under their pillows, perchance to dream of a future husband.

WELSH ONION. See ONION.

WELSH RAREBIT. See RAREBIT.

WENSLEYDALE CHEESE. A fine cheese once described by a writer on cheese as 'the superlative Yorkshire cheese, which is a rival to Stilton in the friendly sense that Bordeaux and Burgundy are sometimes said to be rivals. It would not', the writer continued, 'be possible to savour Wensleydale after Stilton, but it could perhaps be eaten before'. P. Morton Shand, who was always categorical, decided that Stilton should not be mentioned in the same breath as Wensleydale which he classed as one of the world's classic cheeses.

Most of the Wensleydale which reaches the markets today is the creamy white variety, but from time to time it is possible to find one of those rare rich blue Wensleydale cheeses which proves that Morton Shand knew what he was talking about.

Originally made in monasteries and farmhouses, it is today factory-made from the Yorkshire dales to Derbyshire, Somerset and the Welsh border.

Blue Wensleydale is a rich, double-cream cheese which will spread like butter – something like Stilton, but more delicate in flavour, neither acid nor bitter and especially rated for its aftertaste.

WEST INDIAN CHERRY. A yellowish-orange to deep crimson fruit also known as Barbados cherry, Puerto Rican cherry, or Surinam cherry, which must not be confused with *Eugenia uniflora*, the real Surinam cherry (which see). The botanical name for the West Indian cherry is *Malpighia punicifolia*, but some experts say it should more correctly be called *Malpighia glabra*.

When ripe, the fruit is soft and juicy and has a pleasant tart flavour, and when cooked resembles more an apple or crab-apple than a cherry. Each fruit usually has three small seeds enclosed separately in a yellow-pitted 'stone'. Along with rose hip it probably has the highest vitamin C content of all fruits.

It may be eaten fresh or made into juice, sherbet, ice-cream, jelly or preserve and may be used as a syrup in rum and gin drinks. Its juice can also be used to enrich numerous fruit juices and fruit nectars. It can also be fermented to make a wine.

It is believed the West Indian cherry was introduced to Florida from Cuba in the late 19th century. There is a reference to it in a nursery catalogue dated 1887–8, but it was not until 1903 that it was recognized as an edible fruit in America. Today it is as popular a fruit in Florida as it is in Puerto Rica.

WHALE. A large sea mammal whose red meat is something like beef. It has a slightly sour and tangy taste, appreciated by some. Whalemeat may be grilled or seared in hot fat, then cooked on a lower flame. It may be used for steaks or as a roast and can in fact be cooked in the same way as any red meat. If tough, the best way of cooking it is to make a stew or pot roast.

WHEAT. Man's most important food grain, grown in almost all parts of the world. Archaeologists digging in Egypt, Turkey and elsewhere have found that wheat has been used as human food for at least 6,000 years. Some authorities claim that wheat dates back 10,000 years and that the first seeds of wild barley and wheat were sown by man in western Asia where farming began. Wheat probably was the first grain which made man's wanderings in search of food unnecessary.

Wheat grew in the south of Britain in ancient times and the Romans used this part of their empire as a granary. In later times wheat exports were of some importance. By the 17th century the affluent would eschew bread not made of wheat flour. In North America wheat is an important food crop and second only to corn (maize).

Wheat is adaptable to a wide range of climates and soils. It can withstand occasional moderate flooding, and is also more drought resistant than most other crops. There are about a thousand varieties of wheat and wheat-like grasses known throughout the world.

WHELK. A shellfish which may be steamed or crisply fried in batter. In British seaside towns, the roadside stalls that sell whelks serve them on small saucers with a vinegar sauce and pepper, to be swallowed like oysters. At one time British potteries were kept busy making saucers for whelks.

WHEY. The liquid which is drained out of the curd when making cheese.

WHIP or **WHISK.** The process of beating cream or egg whites until thick and stiff. A whisk is usually employed although many people today use an electric mixer.

WHISKEY. The Irish and American type of whisky, made from a mash of barley malt and unmalted grains such as wheat, rye or oats. Usually it is not blended with grain spirits and is bottled 'straight'. It is made with three distillations instead of the usual two as in Scotland. Irish whiskey is matured in wood for at least seven years before bottling while the better types of whiskeys are matured for 12 years. It has its distinctive flavour and has its partisans. The Irish dilute their whiskey with only plain water, never soda water.

Bourbon and rye are the two main whiskeys of America.

WHISKEY, BOURBON. This is one of the best-known American whiskeys. Bourbon (pronounced burr'-bun) has a mahogany colour and a rich, clear bouquet. The method for distilling bourbon was first developed in Kentucky by the Reverend Elijah Craig in the early 19th century, and his method has scarcely been altered since. Bourbon was then, and still is, best taken with an equal part of soft limestone spring water and, in summer, a cube of ice, a mixture known as bourbon and branch water.

Although the most sought-after bourbons are

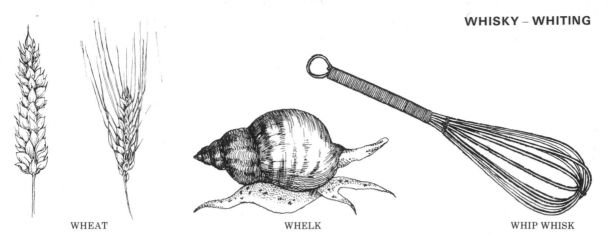

WHEAT WHELK WHIP WHISK

Kentucky bourbons, due to the suitability of the limestone spring water in the central part of the state, they are made elsewhere, and Canada, for example, makes some very fine light bourbons.

MINT JULEP

Bruise 2 stems of mint and place in a glass. Fill the glass with crushed ice and over this pour bourbon to within an inch of the top of the glass. Top the drink with as much of a mixture of 4 tablespoons of fine sugar and 4 ounces of water as is needed. Finally push a sprig of mint down into the ice.

WHISKY. A spirit distilled from malted barley in Scotland, the pride of Scotland for many years and a favourite drink throughout the world since the latter part of the 19th century. The four main producing regions each distil a whisky that is distinctive in character.

Malt whisky is distilled in a simple pot-still from a mash consisting entirely of malted barley, which gives it its flavour. This is allowed to mature in oak casks and the end product is a straight malt whisky. By law it must be allowed to mature for at least three years before it is sold for consumption. In practice some good whiskies are much older than three years.

About a hundred years ago it became the custom to blend straight malt whisky with neutral grain whisky distilled in a patent or continuous still from a mixed mash of cereal grain, preferably maize. Most of the Scotch whisky usually drunk is blended, although single pot-still straight whisky is also available. Blending whisky is an art and sometimes the blender may have to harmonize as many as 40 different whiskies to obtain a standard product.

The waters of Scotland, the superior quality of the barley grown there, and the nature of the soil all combine to produce whisky of the finest quality which cannot be imitated anywhere else in the world. Scotch whisky should be drunk neat.

WHITEBAIT. A small silvery-white fish, the fry or young of the herring in summer, and mostly baby sprats in winter. Whitebait, so called from its former use as bait, may be devilled, made into pancakes Italian-style, or simply fried; it is also fried in batter.

When whitebait used to swarm the Thames it was the custom for many years until 1895 for the Ministers of the Crown to have a whitebait dinner at the Trafalgar in Greenwich just before the close of a parliamentary session. Not to be outdone, the Shadow Cabinet of the Opposition ate a similar dinner at the Old Ship's Tavern nearby.

Whitebait is said to have been a particular favourite of Edward VII, the king insisting on uniformity, and a man was detailed to see each fish was exactly the same size.

WHITEFISH. The largest and the most important gastronomically speaking of the large family of freshwater fish which make their home mostly in the Great Lakes. Its flesh is sweet and white; it is a compressed oblong fish with a white skin, hence its name. There is also the round whitefish similar to the common species with a broad back and dark bluish skin, and the rock mountain whitefish, a fish with trout-like habits which lives in the western mountain lakes and streams from the Rockies to the Pacific and from Utah to British Columbia.

In Britain, white fish is a comprehensive term sometimes used for all white-fleshed sea fish.

WHITE SAUCE. See SAUCES.

WHITE SAUSAGE. White sausages are made in the same way as black sausages (which see) but with oatmeal, fat and seasonings. They are also cooked and eaten in the same manner.

WHITING. One of the commonest European sea fish, related to the cod family. It is gastronomically important, for although its flesh is tasteless, it is light and easily digested. Whiting are small, round, fragile fish, but do not travel and therefore should be eaten as fresh as possible. When fresh the eyes are very clear, the fish fairly rigid and the colour a lovely silver. Their sides are yellow-striped. With an average length of 16 in., they are at their best from November to March.

Whiting can be cooked in a number of ways, but for some curious reason they are most often poached and served with the tail in the mouth. Since they are voracious eaters and cannabalistic, this is appropriate, if nothing else. They can be cooked whole or filleted, made into a soufflé, served *au gratin* or braised. Their flesh is rather dry so that grilling is not recommended, and they need plenty of butter.

The name whiting is given in the United States to a number of other species, such as the sand or Carolina whiting, the silver hake and the so-called American whiting, which is a different fish. These are delicate and can be prepared in almost any manner.

WHITSTABLE OYSTERS. Considered (with the Pyefleet natives) by many connoisseurs to be the finest oysters in the world. See OYSTER.

WHOLEMEAL. See FLOUR.

WHORTLEBERRY. See BILBERRY.

WIDGEON. See DUCK, WILD.

WIENER BACKHENDL. Viennese fried spring chicken. The chicken, not a *poussin* but a true spring chicken, is cut into four, coated with flour, egg and breadcrumbs and fried in an inch of hot lard or oil until a golden colour all over. It is served with the liver and stomach of the chicken, also coated and fried, fried parsley, green salad and wedges of lemon.

WIENER SCHNITZEL. See SCHNITZEL.

WILD RICE. Some authorities say technically this is not a rice but a grain. Most gourmets agree its delicious and distinctive flavour does not need much enhancing. It is a native of America and was known to the American Indians before the European settlers arrived there. The colonists discovered wild rice and declared it a delicacy. It is cooked like brown or white rice but for a longer time. A little butter can be added to the cooked rice and it can be seasoned with sautéed mushrooms or slivers of toasted almonds. It is particularly good served with wild duck but may also be served with a variety of meats, poultry, game and game birds. Wild rice also makes a delicious stuffing.

Over-harvesting in America nearly brought extinction and legislation was passed to regulate harvestings.

Wild rice is found in freshwater and brackish swamps in many parts of America, particularly in Minnesota and Wisconsin. It is known by some 60 local names, many of American Indian origin. At least one tribe, the Menominee, got their name from an Indian word for wild rice, *menomin*. Wild rice was taken to China and Japan where it now grows.

WINE. The word more usually applied to the fermented juice of the grape. However, it also is used to denote the expressed and fermented juice of any sub-acid fruit. The presence of tartar in the grape which plays its part in wine-making, distinguishes the grape from the other fruits' Also the juice of the grape by itself will undergo a regular and complete fermentation, while the juices of other fruits need artificial additions.

Country wines are made from fruits, vegetables and flowers, such as apricots, blackberries, cherries, redcurrants etc. among the fruits; beetroots and cowslips from many vegetables and flowers. The bruised ginger root is also used to make ginger wine.

WINE, SACRAMENTAL. Wine has played an important part in religious ceremonies through the ages. Today both the Christian and Jewish faiths use wine in their religious observances. In the Christian Church wine is part of the Eucharist, Holy Communion or Mass. The Communion service commemorates the Last Supper which Christ and his disciples ate before His arrest. As they broke bread and sipped wine together, so Christians today break bread and sip wine during the Communion service as an act of worship, dedication and fellowship.

The Catholic Church rules that all wine used in the Mass must be either red or white and must be fully fermented grape juice with an alcoholic content not exceeding 12 per cent. Partially fermented or sour wine is not permitted and no chemical processing is allowed.

There is no such thing as consecrated wine in the Jewish faith but it must be prepared according to Rabbinical law and must not be sour or contain impurities. It may be red or white. Wine is used in the synagogue on Friday and Saturday evenings, also in other rituals. Pious Jews are required to drink four glasses on the two Seder nights of the Passover. The same type of wine is used in the home as in the synagogue.

WINE AND SODA. Also known as a *Spritzer*. This is a pleasant summer drink consisting of ice, wine and soda. The slightly tart German wines are the best served in this way. However, other wines can be and are used in the same manner, but naturally not wines of merit.

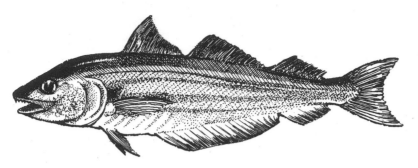

WHITING

WINE CONTAINERS.

Barrel. This can be any size container made of wood, preferably oak, in which wine is stored, aged, and often shipped.

Barrique. More commonly used in Bordeaux than elsewhere in France. It is an oak cask containing 225 litres (about 50 gallons), sometimes used to ship wine. It should produce 24 cases of wine.

Butt. A barrel or cask holding 108 gallons of sherry which ages in it before being shipped.

Cask. The best casks are made of oak but other woods are used, such as chestnut in Europe and redwood in California. They can be of various shapes and sizes depending rather on the district where the wine is produced, and vary from small ones like the *feuillette*, which holds 29 gallons, to the *foudre* which holds 220 gallons.

Feuillette. One of the smaller oak barrels, used for storing Chablis. It is going out of use and is being replaced by the *pièce*, holding 228 litres. In Burgundy *feuillette* refers to a half *pièce* barrel.

Foudre. One of the larger casks: 220 gallons in Alsace, but it varies.

Fuder. An oak cask used for storing Moselle wines, the standard size being 220 gallons (see page 118).

Gönez. An oak cask used in the Tokay region, holding 144 litres.

Halbstück. This is a cask which holds 132 gallons, used in the Rhineland. Rheingau wines are both stored and aged in *Halbstücke*.

Hogshead. A cask which varies in size according to the wine it holds, which can be 63 gallons (52½ Imperial gallons) wine; 60 gallons brandy; 57 gallons of port; 46–48 gallons of claret, and 54 gallons of cider, etc.

Pièce. The Burgundian equivalent of the Bordeaux *barrique*. Burgundian wines are stored and aged in *pièces*, which vary slightly in size: 50 gallons in the Côte d'Or and just under 47 gallons in the Beaujolais.

Pipe. A Portuguese oak barrel holding 115 gallons of port. It can vary in size and the standard Madeira pipe holds only about 92 gallons.

Puncheon. A Californian cask to hold 133 gallons of Californian wines. Originally it was a large cask for brandy holding 120 gallons, or 114 gallons of rum.

Solera. Double butts of stock wines used for maintaining the standard of shipped sherries.

Stück. Literally translated from the German this means piece, but it must not be confused with the French *pièce*. It is a cask of twice the capacity of the *Halbstück*, i.e. 264 gallons, but it is not used nowadays.

WINE IN COOKING.

Wine is used in cooking to add richness and flavour and, when using meat, succulence. It does not give a flavour of wine, but instead brings out the flavour of the food with which it is cooked. It is there to add balance and create a harmony pleasing to the palate. Wine adds flavour to bland foods and when used as a marinade tenderizes as well. It also supplies extra vitamins, salt and minerals and other food values.

Wherever wine is produced cooks have utilized it in their work, for it will transform a simple dish into a gastronomic triumph.

Cooking with wine is not expensive, even in those countries where wine is imported. No one cooks with fine wine, since the very qualities that make a vintage are lost immediately when applied to heat. On the other hand, really bad or vinegary wines are not to be 'used up' in the cooking. A wine for cooking must be definitely drinkable. If buying wine exclusively for cooking, buy in small bottles; but if opening a larger bottle and using only a little of it, either cork it tightly or better still decant it into a small bottle so that there is no air space between the level of the wine and the cork.

As certain wines go with certain dishes for the table, so they do for cooking. Keep the same pattern – but in type not in quality.

Both red and white wines are used in cooking. It is usual to reduce both before being added to the dish – this reduction is to mellow the wine, also to take away its alcohol. White wine when used to poach fish is not reduced, simply diluted with water.

WINE LABELS. These are removable plaques, originally called bottle tickets, once made of silver, although enamel or china ones are also to be found. Small, often highly decorative and nearly always charming examples of the silversmith's art, they carried the name of the wine and were laid round the neck of wine decanters.

We owe the wine label to the Methuen Treaty with Portugal, and with it the gradual appreciation of port wine and the knowledge that some wines, particularly port, improved with keeping. As bottles were not in those days labelled it was usual to write the name of the wine on a piece of parchment and stick it on to the bottle with gum. With the appearance of glass decanters something more elegant was required, and the silver bottle ticket made its appearance. This in turn went out of fashion with the coming of the stick-on wine labels on bottles. The silver labels are seldom seen today. Apart from wine labels, there were also whisky, gin, sherry, rye and bourbon labels. The full history of wine labels is fascinating.

WINE-MAKING. Wine is 'the fermented juice of freshly-gathered grapes'. How the juice is converted into wine can best be explained by following the processes for red table wine, with notes later, on differences for other principal kinds of wine. There are, of course, special procedures in various fields, but the general methods are broadly similar. Only an outline can be given in an entry of this scope.

Red table wine. The gathered grapes are taken to the winery and loaded into receptacles whence, either by mechanical crushing or from the grapes' own weight, the juice is run off, with the skins and pips (which latter must never be broken) into the fermenting vats. (The historic treading by foot is almost obsolete.) Vats are traditionally of oak, but glass, stainless steel and concrete ones are increasingly being introduced.

The bunches may have been partially or totally de-stemmed by machine, according to the tannin content of the grapes, the type of wine to be made and the various techniques of the vintners.

In the vats, under suitable temperature, fermentation begins spontaneously by the action on the juice of the yeasts carried by the skins. This may be aided, by the addition of cultured yeasts.

Fermentation converts the natural sugar of the grapes into alcohol and carbonic gas. It produces a bubbling activity in the must, and a rise in temperature. The skins, pips and stalks (to the extent to which these last have been retained) are forced up by the gas to form a floating cap, though in some fields the cap is kept partially submerged by means of a grill.

Under or around the cap the fermenting grape-juice develops a number of subtle chemical constituents, including glycerine, that give the wine its taste and bouquet. The colour comes from the contact, more or less prolonged, with the skins – for grape-juice is naturally almost colourless. Sulphating is now carried out, to neutralize bacteria, assist certain desirable chemical processes and intensify colouration. In unfavourable years, in certain fields, the addition of sugar, called *chaptalisation*, is necessary. The degree to which it is permitted is strictly controlled for fine wines.

When, in the judgment of the vintner, fermentation has reached its desired point, the freely-running juice is carried off into a large vat, where it is blended with wine extracted by pressure from the remaining must. Such *vin de presse* should not exceed 20 per cent of the entire volume.

Modern systems of temperature regulation in the vatting-rooms have greatly facilitated the control of fermentation. It is impossible to give an average time for this process; in some areas it is done in three days, in others – according to local techniques – it goes on for weeks and even months.

The blend is next run into smaller casks, usually of oak, to finish fermentation and begin maturing. Here air, penetrating the bungs and staves of the casks, temporarily excercises a beneficial effect, but excessive oxygen would turn the wine to vinegar, and before this can begin the wine is bottled.

Before this, however, the wine may have needed chemical treatment, but this is strictly controlled. It will certainly also have been topped up, to replace ullage (evaporation) and will have been racked, by siphonage, to clear away sediments; fined (by albumen, casein or gelatine) to make it bright; and finally filtered through porous pads, to render it stable.

White table wine. Because no colouration is required for this, fermentation cannot proceed in the vat with the skins. So after the grapes have been crushed and skinned, but usually with their stems left with them, their juice is run straight to un-bunged casks, where the fermentation slowly takes place. Thereafter the procedures are essentially the same as with red wine, except that treatment by blue fining is sometimes necessary to eliminate tiny metallic impurities.

Vin rosé. This is either made as red wine is, but with only slight maceration permitted between juice and skins, to minimize colouration; or by mixtures of blue and white grapes in the fermenting; or (though this is frowned on by purists) by adding tasteless cochineal to white wine.

Fortified wine. This is so-called because spirit is added to it, and consists of three main types: port, madeira and sherry. Fermentation for port starts approximately as with red table wine. But fer-

WINE LABELS

mentation removes the natural sugars from grape-juice, as these are converted into alcohol. If it is permitted to reach its natural end the wine will be dry. So for port, fermentation is stopped at the half-way stage, and the juice then poured into casks containing grape brandy. The action of the yeast ceases, the sugar is retained and the alcoholic strength increased by the spirit. Hence a strong, sweet wine.

Madeira is made similarly to port, except that the spirit is made from sugar-cane; but this is added at different junctures in the fermentation, according as an aperitif or dessert wine is desired. However, madeira then receives a unique treatment. It is stored in an *estufa* under heat, gradually brought up and then diminished, for a year more or less. This provides its slightly burnt flavour, and enables a naturally strong wine to last indefinitely without loss of quality.

Sherry on the other hand is naturally a dry wine. Any sweetening desired is effected after fermentation by blending with wine made from exceptionally sweet grapes, whose sugar is sufficient to resist the effect of fermentation (as is true with sweet white table wines such as Sauternes or Barsac). So the fermentation of sherry is allowed to proceed to its end, and the brandy added afterwards, to act as a strengthener and preservative.

Sparkling wine. Champagne grapes are forked into huge presses, with the skins quickly ejected. The must is then run off, mostly into vats, but in the case of a few fine brands into barrels. It is next pressed; the first pressing produces the *tête de cuvée*, for the *grandes marques*, the second and third for increasingly commercial wine. The cold winter air is allowed to circulate round the vats and the fermentation thus gradually arrested, to promote the secondary fermentation (which creates the fizz) in the bottles, into which the wine is placed early.

This system involves the retention of many impurities in the wine. These are gradually settled by the bottles being stood in racks inclining towards their heads, where they are daily twisted and tilted (*remuage*) till they are vertical, and the lees completely settled in the necks. Then the cork is pulled out by a swift movement (*dégorgement*) – the process is now generally assisted by the freezing of the necks – the wine containing the impurities spurts out, and the clear bottle is then topped up with similar clarified wine plus as much sugar as is desired, from a very little for *brut* to a good deal for *riche*.

Pink champagne is generally made in the same way, except that a slight contact of the juice with the skins is permitted. Sometimes, however, it is white champagne with a little still red Bouzy added.

Other good sparkling wines are generally made by the champagne method, but there is a new and cheaper system called *cuve close*. In this the secondary fermentation takes place not in bottles but in large pressurized vats. The sediment can then be filtered out as the wine is bottled, and the expensive processes of *remuage* and *dégorgement* are eliminated. Very cheap sparkling wines are made simply by pumping still wine full of gas, but the product is not to be recommended.

WINE MEASURES. See WINE CONTAINERS.

WINE TERMS.

Ageing. The life span of a wine depends on the type and varies accordingly. Wines begin the process in cask and finish it in bottle. Many wines are at their best when young. Old age does not necessarily make a wine superb; it could have passed its prime before its cork was pulled. Ageing means wine living its correct span and being drunk at the right time. It has been estimated that three-quarters of the wine produced in the world is 'aged' when a year old, and will pass its best at three years and deteriorate.

Amabile. An Italian word describing a usually dry wine that is specially (and correctly) sweet.

Apagado. This is the fresh grape juice to which 16–18 per cent of alcohol has been added to stop fermentation. This raw alcoholic product is used in Spain to sweeten cheaper grades of sherry.

Aroma. There is a distinction between aroma and bouquet. Aroma refers to the distinct taste of grapes and even soil which is noticeable in young wines but disappears with age. The word aroma describes a fruity taste which some wines have.

Asciutto. An Italian word to describe dry wine.

Austere. An undeveloped wine which can become big or full-bodied.

Balance. A term used by professional wine-tasters to describe a well-balanced wine in its own class.

Barro. A Spanish word for clay soil on which the lesser vineyards produce a heavier and coarser wine.

Beeswing. A light, filmy, floating 'crust' in some old ports, supposed to be something like an insect's wing in appearance.

Beverage wines. The opposite of vintage wines, those of average quality and strength and price and suitable for everyday drinking.

Bite. A taste expected in younger wines, a combination of tannin and acid.

Body. The quality in a wine which gives it the appearance of consistency. A full wine is a wine with body, as opposed to a light, cold or thin wine.

Bond. Wines or spirits kept in bond, that is in State-controlled warehouses until duty on them is paid.

Bouquet. The perfume of fine wine obtained by the sense of smell, as distinct from aroma, the sense of taste.

Browning. In French *tuilé*, a red wine which changes its colour to brown with old age. It is noticeable round the edges of the glass.

Brut. Champagne to which little or no sugar has been added. Another way of saying *nature*.

Character. A wine displays its character by reproducing the natural characteristics of the region in which it is grown.

Classic. This refers to the exceptionally fine wines from the classic regions, a classic Médoc for example.

Clean. As would be expected, a wine clean of defects, such as woodiness or mustiness.

Concentrated. A wine with a strong bouquet or aroma.

Départ. The final taste of wine in the mouth.

Depth. A quality in wine that has depth to its desired flavours.

Dry. No excess of sugar, i.e. opposed to sweet.

Drying. The state when a young wine dispenses with its fruit and sugar and when tannin becomes dominant to such an extent it grates on the tongue.

Earthiness. A dusty or 'earthy' taste more often found in southern wines, distinctive and sometimes not unpleasant.

Epluchage. The sorting of the grapes after they picked; unripe or bad grapes are removed in this process. See page 96.

Ethers. Components found in old wines, whiskies etc. which give character to the bouquet. When found in still or sparkling wines or spirits it shows maturity.

Fining. The clarification of wine.

Fliers. These are whitish, fluffy particles that float in white wines, generally when transported from a warm to a colder climate, but do not affect the taste of the wine. To cure, rest the bottles in a warm temperature.

Flor. A natural yeast that grows on unfortified wine, but only in Jerez and the Arbois, which makes sherry what it is. It can be artificially cultured.

Fortifying. The addition of wine-spirit to port and sherry. Nowadays it also refers to the addition of sugar to wines.

Full. This describes a wine rich in alcohol and mineral salts.

Green. This describes young, immature wine.

Hard, Harsh. An obvious expression applied to wines with an excess of tannin.

Hot. Describes wine with a peppery taste due to being grown in countries where the sun reaches high temperatures.

Length. This refers to wine with a lingering taste.

Nature. Same as *brut*, dry.

Oïdium. A mildew disease of the vine.

Oxidized. Said of wine that has been subjected to too much air, and has deteriorated.

Proof. A standard to estimate the alcoholic strength of a spirit. Different countries have different standards.

Race. A French expression to describe the top class of wine.

Racking. Separating the bright wine from the deposit, as claret from its lees.

Re-corking. The replacement of rotten corks after many years in bottle, usually notified on a label. Madeira, for example, is re-corked after 20 to 25 years.

Roundness. Terms describing a wine rich in alcohol with no acidity.

Ruby. A port midway between tawny and full, and of a reddish tinge. See PORT.

Sève. A word generally employed to indicate the vinous strength and aromatic savour which develops at the time of tasting, embalming the mouth and continuing to make itself felt after the passage of the wine through the mouth.

Stalky. A harshness due to the final pressure of the pulp.

Subtle. Where no particular flavour is pronounced but there is a delicate blend of flavours.

Sulphur. This is a necessary preservative added to wines which leaves its flavour if over-used.

Tannin. This is the element which provides long life in a wine by slowing maturation. It is extracted from the grape skin during fermentation.

Tawny. This refers to the colour and character

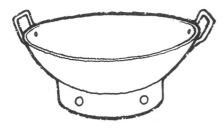

WOK ON RING

of port, also of wines that have matured in wood. See PORT.

Ullage. When a bottle or cask has leaked or its contents evaporated or extracted they are ullaged, filled up.

Vinosity. This denotes a wine with a strong, grapy bouquet.

Woody. A wine that has become tainted from a defective or rotten stave in the cask, or kept too long in the cask.

Worn. This means 'tired' and refers to brandy kept too long in cask, or clarets kept too long in bottle.

See also BIN, BREED, CHAPTALISATION, CORKED, CRUST, DEPOSIT, MUST, DÉTIL-LANT, PHYLLOXERA.

WINE VINEGAR. See VINEGAR.

WINKLE. See PERIWINKLE.

WINTER CRESS. A member of the mustard family, its dark green and shiny leaves are eaten as a salad. Also known as rocket in America.

WINTERGREEN. An aromatic wild plant of North America which grows in dry woods and bears red berries. Its leaves have a sharp pungent taste and are often used to flavour candies and chewing gums. A variety also grows in England but is very different in appearance. Also used for medicinal purposes.

WITCH SOLE. A flat-fish also called the pole dab. Its general appearance is something like the true sole and in Britain it is sometimes sold by unscrupulous fish retailers as white sole or Yarmouth sole, or even simply as sole.

WOK. Described as the jack-of-all-trades in Chinese cooking. Shaped like a coolie hat, it is a cooking pan which is round at the bottom and used for all kinds of cooking. *Woks* were designed to fit Chinese stoves which burnt wood or charcoal. It sat uneasily on modern stoves until some-

one invented a metal ring, its sides perforated with holes. This holds the *wok* steadily on top of any type of modern stove.

WOODCOCK. A game bird prized for its unusually good flavour. One of the waders, it is about the size of a grouse and is in season from September 1 to February 28. It is partially migratory; numbers of Continental woodcock join the British population in the winter months. Its diet is a mixed one of heather shoots, worms, insects and all forms of life hiding in the mud. As a result of its omnivorous habits, the woodcock carries much meat in proportion to its size, a 12-oz. bird being enough for one person of normal appetite.

Traditionally woodcock are plucked head and all, but it is not drawn as there is almost nothing to draw. The neck is twisted round the wing and the bill put through the wing and body, being used instead of a skewer. The eyes are removed.

WOOD DUCK. See DUCK, WILD.

WOODRUFF. A fragrant little plant found in woods and shady places. It is used to flavour a hock punch, usually called May wine (*Maiwein:* see GERMAN WINES).

WORCESTERSHIRE SAUCE. This commercially bottled sauce is often incorrectly called Worcester Sauce. It is made from an old recipe and comprises soy sauce, vinegar, molasses, red chilli, salted anchovies, garlic and shallots, and a number of tropical fruits and spices.

The origin of the sauce is Indian. The story is that about 1837 an ex-governor of Bengal went into one of the several shops in Worcester belonging to Mr Lea and Mr Perrins with a recipe for a sauce which he asked them to make up for him. This they did, but the result was not to his satisfaction and he refused to accept it. Several years later Mr Lea and Mr Perrins, when cleaning out the cellar, came upon a barrel containing the rejected sauce and tasted it. It was excellent. As they still had the recipe they made more and began to produce it for local consumption. Soon it was popular and found its way into the kitchens of many noble families. The fame of the sauce spread, mainly by word of mouth and through the pursers of the old passenger steamships. They discovered it was adapted 'for every variety of dish – from turtle to beef, from salmon to steaks, to all of which it gives great relish'.

Today Worcestershire Sauce is manufactured in many countries, all said to be using the same old recipe. It is a curious twist of fate that the sauce which came from Bengal has returned to India and is there manufactured as Worcestershire Sauce. The original firm continues to manufacture the sauce and even uses some of the old Victorian cast-iron and wood machinery which together with vaults full of barrels of maturing sauce have something of the atmosphere of a vineyard, but with an Eastern aroma of spices.

Apart from the uses already mentioned, Worcestershire Sauce has taken the place of vinegar in prairie oysters (which see), and is added to tomato juice, whether served neat or with a spirit.

WORMWOOD. A herb with the flavour of anisette or absinthe used in the production of vermouth. It is a native of Europe and grows wild in Britain, but is also cultivated for its medicinal qualities. There is a legend that it sprang up in the track of the Serpent as it writhed its way out of Paradise. It is good as a flavouring for fish and is regarded as a stimulating and tonic herb.

WORN. See WINE TERMS.

X Y Z

XÉRÈS. An Andalusian town famous for its wine and sherry. See SPANISH WINES.

YAM. A root vegetable of the genus *Diascorea* which varies in size from very small to enormous; the skins vary from brownish to reddish, and the flesh from white to a dirty orange colour. The texture is moist with a high sugar content. Yams take the place of potatoes in the tropical countries where they grow and are cooked in many of the ways in which potatoes are cooked. The name is sometimes mistakenly applied to the sweet potato.

YARROW. An aromatic herb, one of the oldest and most common, almost a weed. It has figured in folklore, mythology and literature in all parts of the world. Its lace-like foliage can be used instead of chervil in omelettes, salads and stews.

YEAST. The earliest form of raising agent, which was universally used until baking powder was invented. Yeasts are found growing wild in the soil, on the skins of fruit and in dust. Wild yeasts have been cultivated and their properties have been used in both brewing and baking. Yeasts for baking can vary in the speed with which they grow and produce the gas, i.e. the rise. Some bakers' yeasts are faster than others.

Both fresh and dried yeasts are generally available. Fresh is quicker to use and slightly better. It will keep for 3–4 days in a screw-top jar stored in a cool place. Dried yeast will keep for 6 months in a sealed tin. Fresh yeast is also available frozen.

YOGHOURT. Yoghourt and sour milk (clabber) are basically the same inasmuch as the principle of souring is the same. The patriarch Abraham is credited for its introduction on the strength of an ancient Eastern legend that an angel whispered the secret of souring milk to him.

Everyone knows what sour milk is; most people nowadays also know yoghourt, a semi-solid creamy curd which does not readily separate into curds and whey. It has a pleasant, acid rather than sour flavour and is made from milk to which a starter has been added. In the Balkans it is credited with properties for longevity. It is here that it is used extensively in cooking, in sauces, salads, and many meat and vegetable dishes as well as a cooling drink. See LASSI.

Most yoghourt in Britain and America is factory-produced, much of it deprived of its acid flavour and is flavoured with various fruits. It is best home-made and once successful a little can be taken from the first batch and used to start another. Starters are easily obtainable.

YORK HAMS. See HAMS.

YORKSHIRE PUDDING. A light batter which traditionally should be baked under the meat which is on the trivet in the roasting pan, but served before the meat. This custom is still followed in the North of England, but elsewhere it is usually baked separately and served with the meat.

YQUEM, CH. See BORDEAUX WINES.

YUGOSLAV WINES. Wine has been produced in this Balkan country, it is said, for 4,000 years. The first introduction to viniculture came from Thrace. Through the turbulent centuries of Balkan history wine-making had its ups and downs. The Turkish occupation of part of what is present-day Yugoslavia caused the usual hiatus in wine production, and other parts of the country were influenced by

ZUCCHINI

YULE LOG

Austria. Today wine-making is an important part of the country's economy. Vintage for Yugoslav wines is not of great importance as much of the wine is blended. Also most Yugoslav wine is best drunk on its own ground; it blends with the attractive scenery and the hospitality of its people. However, exports are increasing.

Maraschino (which see) is a well-known cherry brandy once made only in Dalmatia. And *slivovitz* (or *šljivovica*) a plum brandy, known as *rakija* in Serbia, is becoming known outside Yugoslavia, although it too seems to taste better on its home ground.

YULE LOG. English name for the *bûche de Noel*, the traditional French Christmas cake, log-shaped and coated with chocolate.

ZABAIONE or **ZABAGLIONE.** A rich Italian custard made with egg yolks, sugar and Marsala wine. It is served in small glasses, but can be frozen to make *zabaione* ice-cream.

ZABAIONE
4 egg yolks
4 tablespoons (5) fine sugar
8 tablespoons (10) Marsala wine

Beat the egg yolks until they are a pale lemon colour. Add the sugar and Marsala and whisk again until these ingredients are well blended. Pour the mixture into the top of a double boiler and cook over hot water until it thickens. Stir constantly while the mixture is cooking, and do not on any account allow it to boil or it will curdle. Serve it hot, warm or cold in a glass and eat with a spoon.

ZAKUSKI. The parent form of all hors d'oeuvre, and of Russian origin. *Zakuski* in Tzarist days must have been fabulous. Countless bowls and dishes of myriad varieties of food were all washed down by equally countless glasses of vodka, for vodka and *zakuski* went together and still do.

ZAMPONE. An Italian speciality from Modena. It is boned pigs' trotter stuffed with ground spiced pork and cooked slowly for hours. It is served with other boiled meats, vegetables or mashed potatoes and puréed lentils, and is then called *Zampone con Tenticche.*

ZEPPOLE. Sweet pastry rings sprinkled with icing (confectioners') sugar; a speciality of Naples.

ZEST. The outside rind of any citrus fruit which contains the essential oils. It is scraped off the fruit with a fine grater or by rubbing with lump sugar.

ZOMBIE. A powerful American drink basically a mixture of several types of rum. Named after the so-called walking dead of African and West Indian voodoo.

ZUCCHINI. Called *zucchine* in Italy and courgette in France and Britain, this variety of small marrow is about four to six in. long. They are usually cooked whole and unpeeled and have a fresh, delicate flavour.

ZUPPA INGLESE. Literally translated this means 'English soup', but the Italian pudding of this name is anything but a soup. Similar to the English trifle, it consists of layers of rum-soaked sponge cake and *zabaione* cream, chilled and, immediately before serving, spread thickly with whipped cream and garnished with chopped glazed fruit.

ZWIEBACK. Literally the word means twice baked, and are German rusks.

397

Selected Bibliography

Abbey, P. M., and Macdonald, G., *'O' Level Cookery*, Methuen & Co., London, 1968.

Acton, Eliza, *The People's Book of Modern Cookery*, 41st edition, Simpkin Marshall, London.
Modern Cookery for Private Families, Elek Books, London, 1966.

Adam, Hans Karl, *The International Wine and Food Society's Guide to German Cookery*, David & Charles, Newton Abbot, 1970.

Ali, Sálim, *The Book of Indian Birds*, Bombay Natural History Society, Bombay, 1946.

Apicius, *The Roman Cookery Book*, George G. Harrap & Co., London, 1958

Athenaeus, *The Deipnosophists*, William Heinemann, London, 1941.

Aylett, Mary, *Country Fare*, Odhams Press, London, 1956.

Bar-David, Molly Lyons, *Jewish Cooking for Pleasure*, Paul Hamlyn Books, London, 1965.

Barberousse, Michel, *Cuisine Normande*, Editions Barberousse, Paris.

Bazore, Katherine, *Hawaiian and Pacific Foods*, M. Barrows and Co., New York, 1949.

Beck, Simone, and Louisette Bertholle, and Julia Child, *Mastering the Art of French Cooking*, Cassell & Co., London, 1963.

Beer, Gretel, *Austrian Cooking*, André Deutsch, London, 1954.

Beeton, Mrs Isabella, *The Book of Household Management*, (facsimile of 1st edition) Jonathan Cape, London, 1968.

Blacke, Alec, *My Greengrocer Says*, Faber and Faber, London, 1958.

Blanquet, Mme Rosalie, *La Cuisinière des Ménages*, Paul Sevin, Paris.

Blochman, Lawrence (Editor), *A Round-the-World Bar Guide 'Here's How'*, The New American Library, New York, 1957.

Botafogo, Dolores, *The Art of Brazilian Cookery*, Doubleday & Co., New York, 1960.

Boulenger, E. G., *A Naturalist at the Dinner Table*, Gerald Duckworth & Co., London, 1927.

Bravery, H. E., *Home Wine-Making*, Arco Publications, London, 1966.

Brown, R. H. W., *Gardening Complete*, Faber and Faber, London, 1968.

Brownslow, M., *Herbs and Fragrant Garden*, Darton, Longman & Todd, London, 1957

Burke, Helen, *Good Fish from the Sea*, André Deutsch, London, 1965.

Campbell, Elizabeth, *Encyclopedia of World Cookery*, Paul Hamlyn Books, London, 1958.

Carrier, Robert, *Great Dishes of the World*, Thomas Nelson & Sons, London, 1963.

Cassell's Dictionary of Cookery, Cassell, Petter, Galpin & Co., London, 1904.

Cayley, Neville W., *What Bird Is That?*, Angus & Robertson, Sydney, 1963.

Chamberlain, Samuel, *Bouquet de France*, Hamish Hamilton, London, 1960.
British Bouquet, Hamish Hamilton, London, 1963.

Chao, B. Y., *How to Cook and Eat in Chinese*, Faber and Faber, London, 1956.

Chu, Grace Zia, *The Pleasures of Chinese Cooking*, Faber and Faber, London, 1962.

Chung, Su, *Court Dishes of China*, Charles Tuttle Co., Tokyo, 1965.

Claiborne, Craig, *A Herb and Spice Cookbook*, Faber and Faber, London, 1963.

Clair, Colin, *Of Herbs and Spices*, Abelard-Schuman, London, 1961.
Kitchen and Table, Abelard-Schuman, London, 1964.

Clusells, Sylvain, *Cooking on Turning Spit and Grill*, Arthur Barker, London, 1966.

Conil, Jean, *The Epicurean Book*, George Allen & Unwin, London, 1962.
Haute Cuisine, Faber and Faber, London, 1961.

Coombs James H., *Bar Service Vol. I – Careers Behind the Bar*, Barrie & Rockliff, London, 1965.

Cowan, Lore, *Let's Love Fish*, Macdonald & Co., London, 1966.

Cowen, D. V., *Flowering Trees and Shrubs in India*, Thacker & Co., Bombay, 1952.

Cox, Helen, *Traditional English Cooking*, Angus & Robertson, London, 1961.

Craig, Elizabeth, *The Scottish Cookery Book*, André Deutsch, London, 1967.

Croft-Cooke, Rupert, *English Cooking*, W. H. Allen & Co., London, 1960.
Cooking for Pleasure, William Collins Sons & Co., London & Glasgow, 1963.
Wine and Other Drinks, William Collins Sons & Co., London & Glasgow, 1966.

Cross, Kate, *Cooking Round the World*, Blandford Press, London, 1964.

Dallas, E. S., *Kettner's Book of the Table*, Centaur Press, Arundel, 1968,

David, Elizabeth, *French Provincial Cooking*, Michael Joseph, London, 1965.
Italian Food, Macdonald & Co., London, 1955.

David-Perez, Enriqueta, *Recipes of the Philippines*, E. D. Perez, Manila, 1955.

Davis, J. Charles, *Fish Cookery*, Thomas Yoseloff, London, 1967.

Day, Harvey, *The Complete Book of Curries*, Nicholas Kaye, London, 1966.

Deeley, Lilla, *Hungarian Cookery*, The Medici Society Ltd., London, 1938.

Diat, Louis, *Louis Diat's French Cooking for Americans*, J. B. Lippincott Co., New York, 1946.

Dictionnaire de l'Academie des Gastronomes, Aux Editions Prisma, Paris, 1962.

Dictionary of Foods and Culinary Encyclopedia, Ward Lock, London.

Donon, Joseph, *The Classic French Cuisine*, Cassell & Co., London, 1960.

Douglas, Norman, *Venus in the Kitchen*, William Heinemann, London, 1952.

Doxat, John, *Booth's Handbook of Cocktails and Mixed Drinks*, Arthur Barker, 1966.

Drummond, J. C., *The Englishman's Food*, Jonathan Cape, London, 1957.

Dutrey, Marius, *Calendrier Gastronomique*, Frederick Books, London, 1960.

Ellinson, J. Audrey, *The Great Scandinavian Cook Book*, George Allen & Unwin, London, 1966.

Encyclopaedia of Practical Cookery – Paul Hamlyn Books, London, 1960.

Escoffier, A., *The Escoffier Cook Book*, Crown Publishers, New York, 1945.

Fawcett, W., *The Banana*, Gerald Duckworth & Co., London, 1921.

Fisher, M. F. K., *The Art of Eating*, Faber and Faber, London, 1943.

FitzGibbon, Theodora, *The Art of British Cooking*, Phoenix House, London, 1965.

Fry, Pamela, *Cooking the American Way*, Paul Hamlyn Books, London, 1963.

Frazer, J. G., *The Golden Bough*, Macmillan & Co., London, 1911.

Frazer, Mrs., *Practice of Cookery*, Peter Hill, Edinburgh, 1804.

Fuller, John, *Restaurateur's Guide to Guéridon and Lamp Cookery*, Barrie & Rockliff, London, 1964.
Hotel Keeping and Catering as a Career, B. T. Batsford, London, 1965.
(and E. Renold), *Chef's Compendium of Professional Recipes*, William Heinemann, London, 1963.

Gerber, Hilda, *Cape Cookery Old and New*, H. B. Timms: Bailey Brothers, London, 1955.

Gerrits, H. A., *Pheasants Including Their Care in the Aviary*, Blandford Press, London, 1961.

Glasse, Hannah, *The Art of Cookery Made Plain and Easy*, Rivingtons, London, 1796.

Good Housekeeping Cookery Book, Sphere Books, London, 1966.

Good Housekeeping's Cookery Encyclopaedia, Ebury Press, London, 1964.

Gould-Marks, Beryl, *Eating the Russian Way*, George G. Harrap & Co., London, 1963.

Gouy, Louis P. de, *Gold Cook Book*, Greenberg, New York, 1948.

Grossinger, Jennie, *The Art of Jewish Cooking*, Bantam Books, New York, 1965.

Grossman, Harold J., *Guide to Wines, Spirits and Beers*, Frederick Muller, London, 1964.

Hackwood, Frederick W., *Good Cheer*, T. Fisher Unwin, London, 1911.

Hallgarten, Peter, *Liqueurs*, Wine and Spirit Publications, London, 1967.

Harrison, Michael, *Beer Cookery*, Neville Spearman and John Calder, London, 1953.

Harrison, William, A., *A Description of England*, London, 1577.

Hartley, Dorothy, *Food in England*, Macdonald & Co., London, 1962.

Haselgrove, N. M. and K. A. Scallon, *The How and Why of Cookery*, Arco Publications, London, 1963.

Hayes, Elizabeth S., *Herbs, Flavours and Spices*, Faber and Faber, London, 1963.

Heath, Ambrose, *The International Wine and Food Society's Guide to Meat*, London, 1968.

Heaton, Nell, *Seafood*, Arco Publications, London, 1963.
Traditional Recipes of the British Isles, Faber and Faber, London, 1951.

Hemphill, Rosemary, *Fragrance and Flavour*, Angus and Robertson, London, 1959.
Spice and Savour, Angus and Robertson, London, 1965.

Herbert, D. A., *Gardening in Warm Climates*, Angus and Robertson, London, 1953.

Hering's Dictionary of Classical and Modern Cookery (11th edition), Dr. Ptanneberg & Co., Giessen, 1958.

Howe, Robin, *Sultan's Pleasure*, Peter Garnett, 1952.
German Cooking, André Deutsch, London, 1953
Italian Cooking, André Deutsch, London, 1953.
Cooking from the Commonwealth, André Deutsch, London, 1958.
A Cook's Tour, J. M. Dent & Sons, London, 1958.
Rice Cooking, André Deutsch, London, 1959.
Greek Cooking, André Deutsch, London, 1960.
Making Your Own Preserves, Foyle, London, 1963.
Russian Cooking, André Deutsch, London, 1964.
French Cooking, Foyle, London, 1964.
Balkan Cooking, André Deutsch, London, 1965.
The International Wine and Food Society's Guide to Soups, London, 1967.
The International Wine and Food Society's Guide to Far Eastern Cookery, London, 1969.

Howes, F. N., *Nuts*, Faber and Faber, London, 1948.

Hume, Rosemary and Muriel Downes, *The Penguin Dictionary of Cookery*, Penguin Books, London, 1966

Hutchins, Sheila, *English Recipes and Others*, Methuen & Co., London, 1967.

Hvass, Else, *Plants That Feed Us*, Blandford Press, London, 1966.
Plants That Serve Us, Blandford Press, London, 1966.

Hyams, Edward, *Odhams Fruit Growers Encyclopaedia*, Odhams Press, London, 1960.

Johnson, Ronald James, *Food and Cookery: A Practical Guide to Culinary Art*, J. M. Dent & Sons, London, 1965.

Joya, Mock, *Things Japanese*, Tokyo News Services, Tokyo, 1958.

Keys, John D., *Japanese Cuisine*, Prentice-Hall International, Hemel Hempstead, 1966.

King, Aileen, *Uncommon Preserves* – No. 1, Mills & Boon, London, 1960

King and Dunnett, *The Home Book of Scottish Cookery*, Faber and Faber, London, 1967.

Lady's Companion, The, J. Hodges and R. Baldwin, London, 1733.

Lapolla, Garibaldi M., *Good Food From Italy*, Frederick Muller, London, 1964.

Layton, T. A., *Choose Your Vegetables*, G. Duckworth & Co., London, 1963.
The International Wine and Food Society's Guide to Cheese, London, 1967.

Lee, Beverly, *The Easy Way to Chinese Cooking*, Oldbourne Press, London, 1964.

Levinson, Leonard Louis, *The Complete Book of Pickles and Relishes*, Hawthorn Books, New York, 1965.

Lichine, Alexis, *Wines of France*, Cassell & Co., London, 1964.

Lyon, Ninette, and Peggie Benton, *Fish for All Seasons*, Faber and Faber, London, 1966.

Lyon, Ninette, *Chicken and Game*, Faber and Faber, London, 1964.

Mackenzie, David, *Goat Husbandry*, Faber and Faber, London, 1957.

Mann, Gladys, *Traditional British Cooking for Pleasure*, Paul Hamlyn Books, London, 1967.

Marquis, Vivienne and Patricia Haskell, *The Cheese Book*, Simon & Schuster, New York, 1964.

Mason, Anne, *Swiss Cooking*, André Deutsch, London, 1964.

Mayer-Browne, Elizabeth, *Home Book of Austrian Cooking*, Faber and Faber, London, 1965.

Mazda, Maideh, *In a Persian Kitchen*, C. E. Tuttle Co., Tokyo, 1960.

McCully, Helen, *Nobody Ever Tells You These Things About Food and Drink*, Angus & Robertson, London, 1968.

McNeill, F. Marian, *The Scots Kitchen*, Blackie & Son London, 1957.

McWilliams, Margaret, *Food Fundamentals*, J. Wiley & Sons, Chichester, 1966.

Menage, R. H., *Gardening for Adventure*, Phoenix House, London, 1966.

Merory, Joseph, *Food Flavouring*, The Avi Publishing Co., Connecticut, 1960.

Miller, Carey D. and Katherine Bazore, and Mary Bartow, *Fruits of Hawaii*, University of Hawaii Press, Honolulu, 1965.

Monckton, H. A., *A History of English Ale and Beer*, Bodley Head, London, 1966.

Montagné, Prosper, *Larousse Gastronomique*, Paul Hamlyn Books, London, 1961.

Nash, S. Elizabeth, *Cooking Craft*, Sir Issac Pitman & Sons, London, 1950.

Nilson, Bee, *Pears Family Cookbook*, Pelham, Books, London, 1964.

Ochorowicz-Monatowa, Marja, *Polish Cooking*, André Deutsch, London, 1960.

Ogrizek, Doré, *Le Monde a Table*, Odé, Paris, 1952.

Oliver, Raymond, *The International Wine and Food Society's Guide to Classic Sauces and Their Preparation*, London, 1967.

Ouei, Minnie, *The Art of Chinese Cooking*, W. H. Allen, London, 1961.

Parker, Netta, *The Home Book of Oriental Cookery*, Faber and Faber, London, 1966.

Parloa, Maria, *Kitchen Companion*, Estes and Lauriat, Boston, 1887.

Pearson, Lorentz, *Principles of Agronomy*, Reinhold Publishing Corp., New York, 1966.

Pellaprat, H. P., *Good Food From France*, Frederick Muller, London, 1965.

Penzer, N. M., *The Book of the Wine Label*, Home & Van Thal, London, 1947.

Peterson, Roger, and Guy Mountfort, and P. A. D. Hollom, *A Field Guide to the Birds of Britain and Europe*, William Collins Sons & Co., London, 1954.

Price, Pamela Vandyke, *France: A Food and Wine Guide*, B. T. Batsford, London, 1966.
Art of the Table, B. T. Batsford, London, 1962.

Prunier, S. B., *Madame Prunier's Fish Cook Book*, Penguin, London, 1963.

Pyke, Magnus, *Food Science and Technology*, John Murray, London, 1964.

Rainbird, George, *Pocket Book of Wine*, Evans Brothers, London, 1963.

Rankin and Hildreth, *Food and Nutrition*, Allman & Son, London, 1966.

Ray, Cyril, *Wines of Italy*, McGraw-Hill, New York, 1966.
Receipts and Relishes, Whitbread & Co., London, 1950.

Renner, H. D., *The Origin of Food Habits*, Faber and Faber, London, 1944.

Richter, Walter, *The Orchid World*, Studio Vista, London, 1965.

Roberts, Patricia Easterbrook, *Table Settings, Entertainment and Etiquette*, Thames and Hudson, London, 1967.

Robertson, J. and A., *Food and Wine of the French Provinces*, William Collins Sons & Co., London, 1968.

Robertson, J. and M., *Famous American Recipes Cookbook*, Collier-Macmillan, London, 1957.

Roden, Claudia, *A Book of Middle Eastern Food*, Thomas Nelson and Sons, London, 1968.

Rohde, Eleanour Sinclair, *Vegetable Cultivation and Cookery*, Medici Society, London, 1938.

Rombauer, Irma S., *The Joy of Cooking*, The Bobb-Merrill Co., Indianapolis, 1946.

Rösch, Rudolf, *So Kocht Man in Wien*, Gerlag & Diedling, Vienna, 1956.

Roux, Willan C., *What's Cooking Down in Maine*, Barre, Massachusetts, 1968.

Samuelson, M. K., *Sussex Recipe Book*, Country Life, London, 1937.

Saulnier, L., *Le Répertoire de la Cuisine*, Dupont & Malgat, 1947.

Schoonmaker, Frank, *Encyclopaedia of Wine*, Thomas Nelson & Sons, London, 1967.

Scott, J. M., *The Tea Story*, William Heinemann, London, 1964.

Senn, C. H., *Practical Gastronomy*, Spottiswoode & Co., London, 1892.
Dictionary of Foods and Culinary Encyclopaedia (7th edition), Ward Lock & Co., 1908.

Shand, P. Morton, *A Book of Food*, Jonathan Cape, London, 1927.
A Book of Other Wines – Than French, Alfred A. Knopf, London, 1929.

Sherman, Margaret, *The International Wine and Food Society's Guide to Eggs*, London, 1968.

Sherson, Erroll, *The Book of Vegetable Cookery*, Frederick Warne & Co., ca. 1931.

Sichel, Allan, *Penguin Book of Wines*, Penguin Books, London, 1965.

Simmonds, N. W., *Bananas* (2nd edition), Longmans, Green & Co., Harlow, 1966.

Simon, André L., *Cheeses of the World*, Faber and Faber, London, 1956.
Guide to Good Food and Wine, William Collins Sons & Co., London, 1963.
Wines of the World, McGraw-Hill, London, 1967.
Gourmet's Weekend Book, Seeley, Service & Co., London, 1952.

Slater, Mary, *Cooking the Caribbean Way*, Spring Books, London, 1965.

Smith, Henry, *The Master Dictionary of Food and Cookery and Menu Translator* (2nd edition), Practical Press Ltd., 1954.
Classical Recipes of the World and Master Culinary Guide, Barrie & Rockliff, London, 1954.

Soyer, Alexis, *The Modern Housewife or Ménagère*, G. Routledge & Co., London, 1850.
The Pantropheon, G. Routledge & Co., London, 1853.
Soyer's Culinary Campaign, G. Routledge & Co., London, 1857.

Squire, John, *Cheddar Gorge*, William Collins Sons & Co., London, 1937.

Standish, Robert, *The First of Trees*, Phoenix House, London, 1960.

Stevenson and Miller, *Introduction to Foods and Nutrition*, John Wiley & Sons, London, ca. 1960.

Stevenson, Violet, *Your Vegetable Garden*, Harvill Press, London, 1951.

Stewart, Gertrude, *Manila Cook Book*, The Evening News, Manila, 1958.

Stobart, Tom, *The International Wine and Food Society's Guide to Herbs, Spices and Flavourings*, London, 1970.

Stodala, Dr Jiri, *Encyclopaedia of Water Plants*, T. F. H. Publications, Surrey, ca. 1967.

Suzanne, *Danish Cookery*, Andr. Fred. Høst & Søn, Copenhagen, 1950.

Tante, Marie, *La Véritable Cuisine de Familie*, A. Taride, Paris.

Thomas, Arthur, *Farming in Hot Countries*, Faber and Faber, London, 1967.

Toulouse-Lautrec, Henri de, *The Art of Cuisine*, Michael Joseph, London, 1966.

Toulouse-Lautrec, Mapie, Contesse Guy de, *Good French Cooking*, Paul Hamlyn Books, London, 1956.

Trevisick, Charles H., *Fancy Pheasants, Peafowl and Jungle Fowl for Beginners*, Iliffe Books, London, 1958.

Truax, Carol, *The Art of Salad Making*, W. H. Allen, London, 1968.

Urban, Dr Erich, *Das Alphabet der Küche*, Ullstein, Berlin, 1929.

Uttley, Alison, *Recipes From An Old Farmhouse*, Faber and Faber, London, 1966.

Waldo, Myra, *The International Encyclopaedia of Cooking*, Collier-Macmillan, London, 1967.

Wales Gas Board, *A Welsh Welcome*, Her Majesty's Stationery Office, London, 1965.

Wells, A. Laurence, *The Observer's Book of Freshwater Fishes of the British Isles*, Frederick Warne & Co., London.

Whistler, Hugh, *Popular Handbook of Indian Birds*, Oliver and Boyd, Edinburgh, 1949.

White, Florence, *Good Things in England*, Jonathan Cape, London, 1932.

Whitehead, Stanley B., *Everyman's Encyclopaedia of Gardening*, J. M. Dent & Sons, London, 1966.

Whitfield, Nella, *Kitchen Encyclopaedia*, Spring Books, London.

Whitlock, Ralph, *Farming From the Road*, John Baker, London, 1967.

Widenfelt, Sam, (Editor), *Swedish Food*, Esselte, Gothenburg, 1950.

Wise Encyclopaedia of Cookery, W. H. Wise & Co., New York, 1951.

Women's Institute, *Good Food From Gloucestershire*, Glos. Fed. of W.I., Gloucester, 1966.

Wulff, Lee, *The Sportsman's Companion*, Harper & Row, New York, 1968.

Valldejuli, Carmen Aboy, *The Art of Caribbean Cookery*, Doubleday & Co., New York, 1957.

Younger, William, *Gods, Men and Wine*, London, 1966.

Yule, Henry, *A Glossary of Anglo-Indian Colloquial Words and Phrases*, John Murray, London, 1886.